FINANCIAL TIMES HANDBOOK
OF FINANCIAL ENGINEERING

D1561225

FINANCIAL TIMES HANDBOOK OF FINANCIAL ENGINEERING

Using Derivatives to Manage Risk

3rd edition

Lawrence Galitz

PEARSON

Harlow, England • London • New York • Boston • San Francisco • Toronto • Sydney
Auckland • Singapore • Hong Kong • Tokyo • Seoul • Taipei • New Delhi
Cape Town • São Paulo • Mexico City • Madrid • Amsterdam • Munich • Paris • Milan

PEARSON EDUCATION LIMITED
Edinburgh Gate
Harlow CM20 2JE
United Kingdom
Tel: +44 (0)1279 623623
Web: www.pearson.com/uk

First published 1993 (print)
Second edition published 1994 (print)
Third edition published (print and electronic)

© Lawrence Galitz 1993, 1994, 2013 (print and electronic)

The right of Lawrence Galitz to be identified as author of this work has been asserted by him in accordance with the Copyright, Designs and Patents Act 1988.

Pearson Education is not responsible for the content of third-party internet sites.

ISBN: 978-0-273-74240-1   (print)
      978-0-273-74241-8   (PDF)
      978-0-273-74242-5   (ePub)

British Library Cataloguing-in-Publication Data
A catalogue record for the print edition is available from the British Library

Library of Congress Cataloging-in-Publication Data
A catalog record for the print edition is available from the Library of Congress

The screenshots in this book are reprinted by permission of Microsoft Corporation.

Contains public sector information licensed under the Open Government Licence (OGL) v1.0. www.nationalarchives.gov.uk/doc/open-government-licence.

The Financial Times. With a worldwide network of highly respected journalists, *The Financial Times* provides global business news, insightful opinion and expert analysis of business, finance and politics. With over 500 journalists reporting from 50 countries worldwide, our in-depth coverage of international news is objectively reported and analysed from an independent, global perspective. To find out more, visit www.ft.com/pearsonoffer.

10 9 8 7 6 5 4 3 2 1
16 15 14 13 12

Print edition typeset in 10/13pt ITC Century Light by 30
Print edition printed and bound by Ashford Colour Press Ltd, Gosport

NOTE THAT ANY PAGE CROSS-REFERENCES REFER TO THE PRINT EDITION

To Valerie

CONTENTS

PART II: TECHNIQUES

ABOUT THE AUTHOR

Lawrence Galitz is a director and founder of ACF Consultants, a leading provider of financial markets training to major investment banks, central banks, investment institutions and corporations around the world. He is also a director of Acumen Technologies, which produces eLearning and learning management solutions. In these roles he has developed an international reputation both as a dynamic and exceptionally gifted instructor, and also as a writer of great clarity. His innovative blended learning techniques, integrating eLearning and simulation with instructor-led training, create a highly motivating, multi-faceted learning experience.

Lawrence Galitz has a PhD in banking and finance and has extensive experience of consulting for a wide range of clients in the global financial markets.

ACKNOWLEDGEMENTS

First I must thank Christopher Cudmore and his team at Pearson for their encouragement, support and limitless patience over the two-year period while the book was being re-written.

I am grateful to Ariel Amdur who went to considerable effort to read through the three new chapters on credit derivatives, and who made many helpful comments and suggestions. Thanks are also due to Mandy Parke and Jodie Gray who arranged for me to have access to the *Barclays Live* information system, which proved invaluable for preparing the majority of the charts in Chapter 22.

I am also indebted to the late Professor John Welch SJ, who read the first edition of the book and made innumerable helpful suggestions on improving the clarity of the text, style and grammar. The many lessons I learned from him have hopefully not been forgotten.

Of course, any mistakes remaining are my own.

On a lighter note, I must thank the baristas and owners of a considerable number of coffee bars and cafés around the world – not least Books and Books (Coral Gables), the NYU Bookstore (New York) and Baruffa Cafè (Castel Gandolfo) – for providing copious quantities of coffee, a quiet table and WiFi access. Many of these are situated within bookstores and it seemed somehow appropriate to write a book surrounded by the works of others.

Lawrence Galitz

PUBLISHER'S ACKNOWLEDGEMENTS

We are grateful to the following for permission to reproduce copyright material:

Table 2.1 courtesy of World Federation of Exchanges (WFE); Figures 2.2 and 2.3 from Damodaran, Aswath, *Equity Risk Premium, (ERP) Determinants, Estimation and Implications-The 2010 edition* (Leonard N. Stern School of Business, 2012); Figures 2.1, 8.1 and 8.2 from http://www.bis.org, courtesy of the Bank For International Settlements (BIS); Figure 5.3 from *Futures Industry Magazine*, November 2010; Figures 6.4, 8.6, 22.1, 22.2, 22.8, 22.9, 22.10, 22.12, 22.13, 22.14, 22.16, 22.17, 22.19, 22.20, 22.21, 22.22, 22.23 and Table 22.7 courtesy of Barclays Bank; Figures 7.6 and 7.7 reprinted with permission from Yahoo! Inc. YAHOO! and the YAHOO! logo are trademarks of Yahoo! Inc.; Table 14.2 from Fitch US High Yield Default Insight, Fitch Ratings, March, 2011, courtesy of Fitch Ratings; Tables 14.4, 14.5, 14.6, 14.7 and 14.8 from creditfixings.com, courtesy of Creditex; Table 20.7 courtesy of Bank Vontobel AG; Figures 20.12 and 20.13 courtesy of iVolatility.com; Figure 22.7 from Standard & Poor's Global Fixed Income Research and Standard's & Poor's CreditPro®, reproduced with permission of Standard's & Poor's Financial Services LLC; Figure 23.2 courtesy of HSBC Holdings plc.

In some instances we have been unable to trace the owners of copyright material, and we would appreciate any information that would enable us to do so.

PREFACE TO THE SECOND EDITION

There are many books which concentrate on specific financial products like options or swaps, but there are very few which deal with the entire range of products. Again, there are a number of books which examine particular applications, like the management of interest rate risk, but few which deal with all manner of financial risks.

This book attempts to fill this gap, by providing a comprehensive and integrated treatment of a wide spectrum of financial engineering products and applications.

The first part of the book explains each of the important financial engineering tools: FRAs, futures, swaps and options. The second part shows how the various tools can be used, either singly or in combination, to manage and structure currency risk, interest rate risk, equity risk, commodity risk and credit risk.

The topics covered are important for a wide readership, and I have therefore tried to write the book so that there is something for everyone.

Beginners will find that each new topic starts with a gradual introduction, defining each financial product, and explaining the terminology involved. The coverage then develops so that advanced users will be able to enhance their understanding of the finer nuances of each tool, and learn about the latest ideas and techniques. Theoreticians will discover that virtually every formula and relationship is explained and justified, sometimes in a novel way. Practitioners, on the other hand, can skip the detailed mathematics and look at a wide variety of real-life applications, complete with numerous worked examples.

In a subject like financial engineering, it is difficult to avoid some mathematics and formulae. For those who take fright when they see an equation, please don't be discouraged! It is not strictly necessary for everyone to understand the minutiae of derivatives pricing, just as it is not necessary to understand the detailed workings of the internal combustion engine in order to drive a car. The detailed sections on swap pricing (chapter nine) and on option pricing (sections 10.5 to 10.10) can be omitted by those readers who just want to get on and use the products. However, these sections are included in the main body of the text, rather than relegated to an appendix, so that the interested reader can follow the conceptual flow without interruption.

Practitioners mainly interested in applications can concentrate on Part Two, where a myriad of examples and comparisons demonstrate how the financial tools available can successfully be used to manage risk. Each practical use is fully illustrated with a worked example, so that readers can see exactly how to apply the techniques for themselves.

PREFACE TO THE THIRD EDITION

When I first discussed the idea of updating *Financial Engineering* with Christopher Cudmore – my editor at Pearson – I didn't anticipate that it would take much time to complete. I imagined that all I needed to do was to update the numerical examples, add a few paragraphs here and there, and I'd be done by tea-time. To allow some margin, however, we agreed that six months should be more than enough.

It actually took two years, and the result is a book that is 50% longer than the previous edition. There are five totally new chapters, and four more chapters where the content has been completely re-written. Everywhere else the text has been completely revised and brought up-to-date.

Why all these changes? The financial markets are constantly in flux, witnessing in recent years the creation of credit derivatives, new swap instruments including the now-important OIS, and ever more colourful exotics. There has also been a proliferation in the range of structured products available. Importantly, the credit crisis of 2007–08 has brought about a sea-change in the way that the derivatives markets work. All of these have led to the inclusion of totally new content in the book. In addition, the sections dealing with swap pricing, collateral, credit risk, option pricing, volatility, delta hedging and exotics have all been considerably expanded.

I hope that the wait has been worthwhile.

PART I

TOOLS

1

INTRODUCTION

1.1 Forty years of evolution

As we look around us, it is easy to think that the world has always been just as we see it today.

We take for granted smart phones, laptop PCs, satellite TV and instant global communications. We don't marvel that we can sit in an office in London and use our PC to set up an instant three-way video conference call with Japan and San Francisco. Need to send an urgent document to Tokyo? We simply scan and email it, knowing that our document will arrive just seconds after we send it.

The media bombard us daily with world news, economic figures and analysis, and we know that the financial markets will respond without delay. Stock markets will rally or collapse, interest rates will tighten or ease, and new exchange rates will alter the relative value of currencies and even the prestige and wealth of whole countries.

It wasn't always like this.

In 1970, a four-function pocket calculator was an expensive novelty, and financial calculators were unknown. Computers really did sit in big air-conditioned rooms, and were the preserve of scientists and mathematicians, or were used for the routine bulk processing of commercial accounts.

In 1970, exchange rates were fixed and the euro hadn't been invented. The dollar would be worth four Deutschmarks today, four Deutschmarks tomorrow and four Deutschmarks next month. Interest rates were stable, and the price of a barrel of oil rarely changed.

The last 40 years have seen enormous changes in both the financial and technological environments, but the revolution in finance would not have been possible without parallel advances in technology. Today's markets rely on the global dissemination of price-sensitive information, traders' ability to communicate instantly, and the availability of powerful computers and sophisticated analytical software at dealers' fingertips.

Some of the financial changes would have taken place anyway. For example, the switch from fixed to floating exchange rates in the early 1970s was precipitated by irreconcilable differences in growth rates between different economies, principally those of Germany and the United States. We would have had floating exchange rates even if satellites had not been available to carry the news. However, many would argue that the volatility of financial markets is a product of the speed with which new information reaches traders, and the swiftness with which traders and their computer systems can respond.

In other cases, one can argue that financial innovation was made possible only through technology. For example, the seminal paper which made modern option pricing viable was published in 1973 by Professors Black and Scholes. Although trading in individual stock options started in the same year with the opening of the Chicago Board Options Exchange, it was at least ten years before currency options and interest rate products such as caps and floors became readily available. Could it be that these products had to await the arrival of desktop PCs before traders were able to price and hedge them effectively?

Regardless of how today's environment came about, two things are certain. First, the volatility of market rates has created an ever-increasing demand for clever financial products to manage financial risk. Second, current technology has made it possible for financial institutions to create, price and hedge products specifically designed to neutralise these financial risks. From these foundations, financial engineering was born.

1.2 What is financial engineering?

The term *engineering* has many connotations. It may suggest the honing of precision components which form part of a complex system, working with special tools or instruments, or tinkering with adjustments to achieve mechanical perfection. Financial engineering has many associations with its mechanical cousin.

The tools used by financial engineers comprise the new financial instruments created over the past four decades: forwards, futures, options and swaps, to name but a few. These instruments are both the tools of the trade and the components used to build more complex systems. Like mechanical components, these financial instruments can be used in standard form 'off the shelf', or may be individually tailored to meet a particular requirement. Like mechanical components, they can also be combined in many different ways. For example, currency options can be combined in one way to create a *zero-cost collar*, or in another way to create a *participating forward*. If one configuration is not quite right, financial instruments can be tinkered with or adjusted to behave in exactly the way desired.

Mechanical perfection for the financial engineer is the achievement of a particular financial goal. For the investor, it may be the superior expected returns available from a foreign stock market, but without the currency risk. For a financier, it may be the funding of a large construction project at rates below the current market norm, coupled with a guarantee that rates will never be more than $x\%$. For the company treasurer, perfection may be the elimination of currency exposure on a project that has reached only the tendering stage. There are limitless examples, but there is a unifying theme which provides a useful definition of the concept of *financial engineering*:

Financial engineering is the use of financial instruments to restructure an existing financial profile into one having more desirable properties.

Of course, what is desirable for one party may be undesirable for another, but that should not cause any problems. After all, an investor choosing to buy a share costing $10 may think it desirable to buy at that price, while the trader selling it may think it undesirable to hold at that price. Both may be happy to execute the deal despite having differences of opinion.

Financial engineering can help achieve excellence, but not the impossible. The cleverest financier will not be able consistently to raise funds at a negative interest rate, and it is unthinkable that someone nowadays could steadily sell the pound sterling at £1=$2.80 (the rate prevailing in the early 1960s). These are the same kinds of limitations that prevent the mechanical engineer from building a car capable of 100 miles per gallon and 200 miles per hour.[1] Financial engineering is nevertheless capable of achieving striking and valuable results, as the remainder of this book will illustrate.

1.3 The nature of risk

Even if there were no uncertainty, financial engineering would provide users with valuable alternatives. For example, the treasurer borrowing for five years at a floating rate may prefer to use an interest rate swap to create a level cost of funds in order to simplify budgeting decisions. However, in the presence of risk, financial engineering techniques come into their own.

But what is risk? Intuitively, we all have a feel for what risk is, and normally associate risk with the unexpected and the undesirable. However, we really need a more reliable definition, both qualitatively and quantitatively:

Risk is *any* variation in an outcome.

This definition is useful because it includes both undesirable and desirable outcomes. This may seem strange in the everyday world – we would not normally think of winning the jackpot at Las Vegas as a risk – but it makes sense in the financial world where there are always two easily identified parties to every deal, and these parties have diametrically opposed viewpoints. Consider, for example, a bank lending floating-rate funds to a company. A sudden rise in interest rates would be undesirable for the borrower, but an attractive outcome for the lender. Similarly, a fall in interest rates would be an adverse risk to the lender, but a beneficial risk to the borrower. In either case, the risk exposure to both these parties arises from the same event – a change in interest rates. It therefore makes sense to think of any change in interest rates, up or down, beneficial or adverse, as being a risk.

The above definition gives us a good qualitative definition of risk. If the outcome to a situation or event is absolutely fixed and determined, there is no risk; if some variation in outcomes is possible, the situation involves risk. In using the term *variation*, the definition also provides a clue as to how we can calculate risk quantitatively. If we can find a precise mathematical way to measure the degree of variation, then we have a numerical indicator for the degree of risk. Fortunately, such a method has existed since the eighteenth century, and statisticians have been using the *standard deviation* as a precise way to measure variation. Chapter 11 (section 11.1) will demonstrate how the standard deviation can be calculated and how this has important implications for options pricing.

Even without a quantitative measure of risk, one can see just by looking at Figures 1.1 and 1.2 that the financial world has been a risky place over the past 20 or so years. As the charts show, the 1980s started with US interest rates at almost 20% and the 1990s started with rates of almost 10%, but by 2009–2010 rates had fallen to almost zero. In a similar way, the euro started the millennium more or less at parity with the US dollar. A year later it had slipped in value by almost 20% to around €1=$0.80, but then doubled in value to €1=$1.60 by early 2008, before falling 25% to below €1=$1.20 by the middle of 2010.

With the collapse of fixed parities in the early 1970s, exchange rates were free to fluctuate according to the supply and demand for different currencies. Some of the currency flows were long term and strategic, giving rise to secular movements and trends in rates. Other flows arose from the short-term decisions of currency speculators, and led to brief bouts of extreme volatility. Both combined to create a far greater instability than had previously been known.

Once exchange rates were free to float, interest rates became one of the weapons of exchange rate policy, and a victim of the same forces. An extreme example arose shortly after the 1991 Maastricht Treaty was signed – a treaty which created the framework for the single European currency. In September 1992, amidst a period of considerable turmoil in the financial markets, the Swedish authorities, in their attempt to keep the Swedish kroner shadowing the Deutschmark, raised money market rates from 20% to 75%, and eventually to 500%. More recently, interest rates in Iceland went from 16% to 12% to 18% to 8% all in the space of one year, from September 2008 to September 2009, while the Icelandic kroner weakened from 120 to 300 against the euro in late 2008. By

FIGURE 1.1
€/$ exchange rate 2000–2010

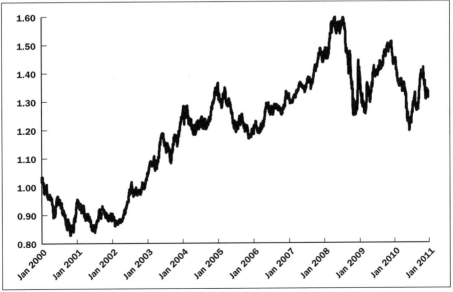

Source: www.oanda.com

FIGURE 1.2

US dollar interest rates 1970–2010

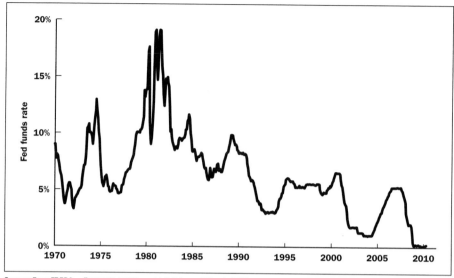

Source: From FRED® – Economic and Financial Database (St Louis FRB).

the end of 2010, Icelandic interest rates were down to 4%, while the exchange rate has recovered to 150 against the euro.

Interest rates are also the victim of economic and monetary policy. As Figure 1.2 shows, there were major reductions in US interest rates in 2001–2002 and again in 2008, both arising from the Federal Reserve's desire to stimulate the economy after severe downturns in the US economy.

1.4 Financial engineering and risk

In the face of risk, financial engineering can offer two broad alternatives. In the first instance, risk can be replaced with certainty. The second alternative is to replace only the adverse risk, leaving the beneficial risk alone. We shall examine each alternative in turn.

Forwards, FRAs, futures and swaps are all examples of financial engineering tools which can offer the comfort of certainty to anyone exposed to financial risk. For example, a US company with a euro payable in three months can buy euros today for delivery three months in the future, *at a fixed price*. This forward deal completely eliminates the currency risk. No matter what the exchange rate turns out to be in three months' time, the company has purchased its euros at a known and fixed price, and will not be affected by the then prevailing rate.

Figure 1.3 contrasts the risk profile for the company by plotting the effective €/$ exchange rate against the spot rate prevailing in three months. The diagonal dashed line shows the position before the company hedges by buying euros forward. The company must pay whatever spot prevails at the time, which might

FIGURE 1.3
Hedging currency risk using a forward deal

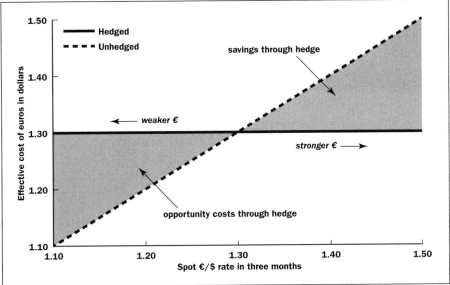

be only $1.10 to buy €1 if the euro weakens, or as much as $1.50 to buy €1 if the euro strengthens. The horizontal solid line shows the position if the company buys its euros forward at the fixed rate of €1=$1.30. In that case it does not matter what spot exchange rate prevails at the time; the company will pay exactly $1.30 to buy each euro regardless.

In this example, if the euro strengthens during the three-month exposure period the company is certainly delighted that it chose to hedge, because it still buys its euros at the original fixed price of €1=$1.30. The shaded area on the upper-right of the diagram shows the savings provided by the hedge. But what if the euro were to weaken? The company must originally have been prepared to buy its euros at €1=$1.30, otherwise it would not have entered into the forward deal in the first place. So even if the euro turns out to be weaker in three months, the company should still be happy!

Of course, everyone understands the discomfort that the company treasurer may feel, thinking that the company would have been better off had it not hedged but simply bought its euros at the prevailing rate when they were needed. The shaded area on the bottom-left of Figure 1.3 shows the opportunity costs incurred by the existence of the hedge. While understandable, it would be quite wrong for the treasurer to think in this way. His original decision was based on the desire to avoid risk and create certainty; his later regret was based on hindsight, once he knew which way rates eventually turned out.

The first alternative offered by financial engineering replaces risk with certainty, but in eliminating the adverse risks it also eliminates the beneficial risks. Chapter 16 discusses risk assessment, attitudes to risk, and setting hedging objectives (see sections 16.2–16.4). In many cases, eradicating all risk is just what is wanted, but it is easy to imagine the desire to eliminate only the adverse risk, leaving the beneficial risks in place. Fortunately, financial engineering can also offer something approaching this as a second alternative.

Figure 1.4 illustrates a perfect hedge, providing all the benefits of the forward deal if the euro eventually becomes stronger than €1=$1.30, but all the benefits of no hedge if the euro were to weaken. Unfortunately, such a hedge is impossible to achieve in practice, because no bank would be willing to take the opposing position, where it could only lose and never gain! Nevertheless, while the perfect hedge is unachievable, financial engineering allows something very close.

Instead of buying euros forward at €1=$1.30, the treasurer could instead buy a currency option granting the right to buy euros in three months at €1=$1.30, *but not the obligation to do so*. Such an option might cost 3 US cents per euro. If the euro were stronger than €1=$1.30 in three months, the treasurer would exercise his right under the option and buy euros at €1=$1.30, just as if a forward deal had been executed. However, if the euro were weaker than €1=$1.30, he would buy euros in the market, taking advantage of the cheaper prevailing rate, and simply allow the option to expire worthless. In this way, the treasurer would obtain the best of both worlds – the protection of a fixed rate if required but the flexibility of an open commitment if that turned out to be the best choice. Figure 1.5 shows the new risk profile under this second alternative.

Later chapters will illustrate how the treasurer could choose from an almost unlimited number of permutations. The degree of protection against an adverse move in market rates, the level of gains realised for a beneficial move, the range

FIGURE 1.4
The perfect hedge

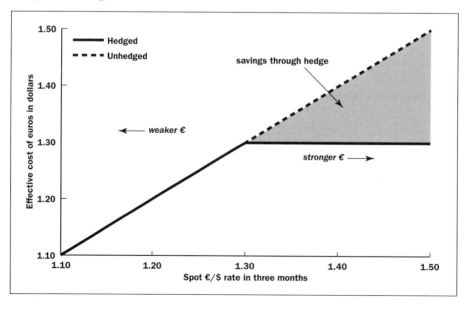

FIGURE 1.5

Hedging currency risk using a currency option

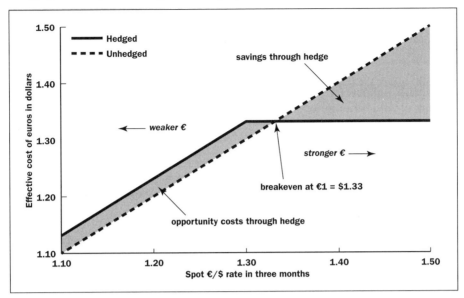

over which protection was granted, the range over which gains were possible, the cost of protection – all of these could be varied to suit the hedger's objectives. Want to obtain protection but pay nothing for it? No problem, but the bank will want to share some of your profit opportunities. The beauty of financial engineering is that it offers an almost unlimited range of possibilities, allowing deals and hedges to be tailored precisely to match individual requirements.

Financial engineering thus offers the user two broad alternatives. One choice is for risk to be eliminated completely, while the other approach gives those affected by financial risk the means to adjust their exposure profile according to their preferences.

1.5 Layout of this book

This book is divided into two main sections. Part I covers the *tools* of financial engineering, dealing with:

- FRAs
- financial futures
- currency and interest-rate swaps
- equity and commodity swaps
- volatility and variance swaps
- equity, currency, and other options

- interest rate options and IRGs
- caps, floors and collars
- swaptions
- exotic options (like barriers and digitals)
- credit default swaps
- credit index swaps.

Various chapters define every instrument carefully, describe the markets on which they are traded, and explain in considerable detail how each product is priced and hedged.

Part II then goes on to consider the *applications* in which financial engineering techniques may be applied. Here we are concerned with the practical use of financial instruments in handling interest rate, currency, credit, equity and commodity risk. Questions addressed will include:

- Should we buy a cap, buy a collar, or pay the fixed rate on an interest-rate swap?
- Are futures better than forwards?
- Is 11.5¢ a fair price for this option, or are we paying over the odds?
- How can we obtain protection against credit and counterparty risk?

To discover more about the tools of financial engineering, and exactly how they are used in practice, read on.

Note

1   About 3 litres per 100km and 300km/h.

2

THE CASH MARKETS

This chapter provides a brief description of the *cash markets*, describing traditional financial markets such as the foreign exchange and money markets. This will provide the necessary foundation for studying the derivatives markets, the important markets within which the instruments of financial engineering are created and traded.

2.1 Overview of financial markets

With the developments in finance over the past 40 years, there may seem to be a bewildering array of financial products. To bring order to this confusion, we can organise markets under a number of clear headings:

- the foreign exchange market
- the money market
- the bond market
- the equities market
- the credit market
- the commodities market

while instruments can be categorised under:

- cash instruments
- derivatives.

Later sections in this chapter will introduce these markets in a little more detail and explain the key differences between cash instruments and derivatives. First, however, we should consider why these markets exist in the first place and what purposes they serve.

The money, bond and equities markets are often grouped together under the term *capital markets*.[1] Their principal purpose, as the generic heading suggests, is for the raising of capital by companies, financial institutions and even whole countries. These markets bring together on the one hand those who wish to raise funds and who are willing to pay for the use of those funds, and on the other hand investors who seek a return on the capital they have available to invest, and financial institutions which intermediate between the two.

In a world increasingly dominated by international trade, the foreign exchange market provides the means by which exporters in one country can receive payment in their domestic currency, while importers in another country can make payment in their currency. The FX market is therefore instrumental in facilitating international commercial trade, and for centuries has fulfilled this role. More recently, the FX market has become an important adjunct to the international capital markets, allowing borrowers to meet their financing requirements in whichever currency is most conducive to their needs. This is especially relevant to multinational corporations, which buy materials, manufacture and sell their goods in a number of countries and therefore have complex FX exposure in a range of currencies.

We have so far seen that two of the reasons why these markets exist are to enable financing and investing, and to facilitate commercial trade. A third important reason is to allow hedging and speculation. It may seem strange to group both these activities together, but the trades executed by hedgers and speculators may be identical even though their motivations may be different. A hedger may buy euros because they are needed for the purchase of goods from Germany. A speculator may buy euros because he thinks that the euro will strengthen against other currencies.

Now that we have a better idea of why the financial markets exist, we can take a very brief look at each one. At the end of this chapter there are suggestions for further reading for the reader who wishes to study particular markets in greater depth.

2.2 The foreign exchange market

The foreign exchange market is the international forum for the exchange of currencies. Until the early 1970s, major currencies like the Japanese yen and the Deutschmark (the German national currency prior to the introduction of the euro) were linked to the US dollar through a system of fixed parities. This system was established by the Bretton Woods agreement in 1944 and, despite occasional adjustments to the scheme, worked well for a quarter of a century. By the 1960s, however, differences in economic growth between countries became more prominent, and there was a series of currency realignments, which became more and more frequent. Eventually the system of fixed exchange rate parities broke down completely in the early 1970s, and a system of floating exchange rates took its place.

This change revolutionised the foreign exchange market. Instead of steady exchange rates, punctuated by the occasional parity change, FX rates were free to fluctuate continuously, and without bounds. Governments would intervene from time to time, usually to support their currency, but for the most part exchange rates were free to follow supply and demand.

This new environment of floating exchange rates created a need for banks and their clients to manage their currency exposure on an active and continual basis. At the same time, it provided an opportunity for speculators to bet on which major currencies would strengthen and which would weaken. Coincidentally, developments in computers and telecommunications made possible the instant global dissemination of news and comment, and the instant trading facilities that characterise the foreign exchange market as we know it today.

Unlike traditional stock exchanges, the FX market is not to be found in any one place but is spread throughout the world in trading rooms linked to each other through a web of computer networks. As Figure 2.1 illustrates, although trading takes place in each of the world's financial capitals, three centres are dominant: London, New York and Tokyo. The figures show the estimated daily volume of transactions in dollar equivalents but are only approximate, for in the absence of any central clearing agency, no one knows for sure the actual amounts traded.

According to the April 2010 BIS Triennial FX Survey, the daily volume of transactions worldwide has grown to $4tn, but this is more than just a 'telephone number' magnitude. To try to comprehend a number on this scale, imagine that you were charged with the task of counting out this sum of money in cash, and you were able to count out two notes every second and could work non-stop without taking a break. To be reasonable, suppose that the $4tn was paid not in dollar bills but in $100 bills. You could therefore count as much as $12,000 per minute, $720,000 per hour and $17,280,000 per day. Yet it would still take you more than 600 years to complete the task! (Remember, this was the trading volume arising from just *one day*.)

It is difficult to know exactly what proportion of this trading volume arises from commercial transactions. The April 2010 BIS Survey reports just 13% of the FX trades executed by the dealers surveyed were with non-financial custom-ers, but this does not mean that the remaining 87% of trades were speculative. Many of these latter trades were interbank transactions executed as one bank laid off its position with another. A single commercial transaction may set off a dozen interbank trades as the component currencies are broken up and spread between banks operating around the globe.

Of FX trades, 37% of the volume is for *spot* delivery. This is normally two working days after the trading date to allow for settlement instructions to be processed in different time zones. Most of the remainder of trades are *forward* deals, the majority of which are short-term but some may be up to one year after the spot date. Forward deals are either *outright forwards*, where there

FIGURE 2.1
Daily FX trading volumes

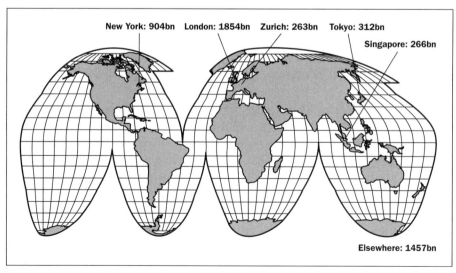

Source: BIS Triennial Central Bank Survey 2010 (published September 2010).

is a single exchange of currencies on some future date, or *FX swaps*, where there is an exchange of currencies on one date and a re-exchange in the opposite direction on another date. The concept of quoting forward exchange rates will be discussed later (in section 3.1 of Chapter 3).

2.3 The money markets

The money market is an electronic marketplace for the trading of short-term debt. Maturities range from as short as overnight (i.e. literally from one day to the next) to as long as one year, and the size of a typical trade can range from the equivalent of $500,000 up to $100m or even more.

Some of this debt is based on negotiable paper, and instruments traded include:

- Treasury bills
- bank certificates of deposit (CDs)
- trade bills
- commercial paper (CP)
- euro-commercial paper (ECP)
- euronotes.

For most of these negotiable instruments, secondary markets exist which allow buyers and sellers to trade debt prior to maturity. This means that an investor who buys a negotiable six-month CD, and who then needs access to his funds after just one month, can sell the CD to another investor for cash. The price at which an instrument is issued or traded depends upon a number of factors, including its time to maturity, credit quality, prevailing rates of interest and any interest accrued. Some instruments, like CDs, carry a specific rate of interest and are issued at a price near or at par. Other instruments, like bills and CP, pay no interest at all and are always issued at a discount relative to their face value. The investor's return on these *discount instruments* is based on the difference between the price originally paid and the face value at maturity.

In contrast to paper-based debt, a substantial section of the money markets revolves around non-negotiable debt, including:

- interbank deposits
- repos and reverses
- local authority deposits (in the UK)
- Federal funds (in the US).

Although an active primary market exists in all these instruments, there is no secondary market upon which a depositor or investor can trade these assets. Once Bank A has lent Bank B €10m for three months, there is no recognised way in which Bank A can gain access to these funds before the deposit is repaid. Much of this market is therefore very short term, like the US Federal funds market which is predominantly a market in overnight funds. Yields for non-negotiable instruments tend to be a little higher than yields for the corresponding paper-based instruments. For example, a bank bidding for three-month interbank deposits may have to offer a rate 10bp or 20bp more than for its three-month CDs.

Interest rates for most discount instruments are normally quoted on a *discount yield* basis, which is the discount expressed as a percentage of the face value and then converted to an annual basis. For example, a T-Bill priced at 99 and redeemed at par in three months might be quoted as a discount yield of 4%. Other money market instruments are normally quoted on a *money market yield* basis, which expresses the interest as a percentage of the current price rather than the face value. To complicate things further, both these bases can be quoted using either a 360-day or a 365-day year. This means that yield comparisons among different money market instruments must be undertaken with the utmost care.

2.4 The bond markets

The segregation between money markets and bond markets is mainly on the basis of maturity. While most money market instruments have an original maturity of one year or less, notes and bonds are issued with a maturity greater than one year. The majority of these instruments have original maturities in the range from 2–30 years, but maturities of up to 100 years are not unknown, and some bonds are perpetual, having no fixed maturity date.

The biggest issuers of notes and bonds in most countries are central government and local government agencies, while most of the remainder are issued by financial institutions and other large corporations. This leads to the following convenient classification:

- government bonds
- corporate bonds
- floating-rate notes (FRNs)
- eurobonds
- medium-term notes (MTNs) and euro-MTNs.

Most bonds pay a regular interest payment called the *coupon*, although there are some zero-coupon bonds which are, to all intents and purposes, long-term bills. The coupon for most bonds is fixed in advance, giving rise to the term *fixed-income securities*, but a number of issues have coupons which are reset on a regular basis and therefore float, hence the term *floating-rate note*. With the growth in international finance, prime borrowers can issue securities in a range of currencies or countries, and a bond issued outside the country and currency of the borrower is a *eurobond*. Finally, the range of debt instruments open to large corporate borrowers has expanded to encompass bills and commercial paper at the short end of the maturity spectrum, corporate and eurobonds at the longer end, and *medium-term notes* in between.

The yield, and hence the price, at which bonds trade depends upon the level of interest rates generally prevailing in a particular currency. Yields will usually differ for different maturities, giving rise to the *yield curve*, which defines the current yield for each possible maturity. It is usually the case that yields increase for longer maturities, rewarding the investor for the additional risk involved in holding bonds with longer maturities. One component of this risk is the chance that the bond issuer will default. Bonds issued by most major governments normally are considered riskless, and set the base level for bond yields in a particular currency. Bonds issued by other borrowers are considered to have a finite risk of default.

The level of this default risk has traditionally been assessed by bond rating agencies, which assign ratings to issuers and particular instruments. The lower the rating for a particular bond, the higher will be its yield in comparison with government bonds of the same maturity. More recently, credit derivatives (see Chapters 14 and 15) have become more and more important as a means of pricing and trading credit risk, especially as credit derivative prices change from moment to moment, reflecting current sentiment much more quickly than credit ratings, which may take weeks or months to revise.

The largest bond markets are those denominated in US dollars, euros and Japanese yen, which together account for more than 80% of the world market in bonds.[2] The huge size of these markets reflects the large amount of government debt issued in these countries. The bond markets in the British pound, Chinese yuan and Canadian dollar come next in size, and are also driven largely by the size of government debt.

2.5 The equities markets

The money markets and bond markets both involve debt instruments. With a debt instrument, there is a great deal of certainty regarding the cash flows which an investor will receive. Either the value at maturity will be defined, as with all discount instruments, or the stream of regular coupons will be known in advance, as with all fixed-income securities, or both.

Equities are quite different. An equity or common share is a participation in the ownership of a company. Although a share certificate may have some face value, this is purely nominal, as there is no promise to repay that face value at any time. Nor is there any certainty as to the stream of dividends that will be paid. A company issuing shares has sole discretion each year as to the size of the dividend paid, or even whether a dividend will be paid at all. In the event that the company goes into liquidation, the shareholders are the last to receive any benefit from the sale of assets, as all other liabilities must be discharged first.

Equities are therefore much more risky, both in the expectation of future income and in the event of the company going bankrupt. In the light of their seemingly unattractive position, the reason why any investor should wish to hold shares is the hope of better returns than those available from debt instruments. Over the long term, equities normally outperform debt securities, although this will not necessarily happen every year or over the shorter term. This additional return is necessary to compensate investors for the additional risk they face with equities, and an important theory in finance, the Capital Asset Pricing Model (CAPM), seeks to relate the risk and return available from different investments.

Figures 2.2 and 2.3 illustrate the relative performance of equities vs. ten-year US Treasury Notes over two recent periods, 1988–2009 and 1998–2009.[3]

Figure 2.2 vividly shows both the cumulative outperformance of equities and their relative risk over the 21-year period. $100 invested in the stocks comprising the S&P 500 index at the end of 1988 would have grown to $627 by the end of 2009, an annualised return of 9.1%, while a similar amount invested in ten-year US Treasury Notes would have grown to just $440, equivalent to 7.3% p.a. Although equities outperformed the bonds by more than 40%, they were much more risky. The standard deviation of annual equity returns was 19.6%, more than double that of the bonds, which was 9.5%.

However, if we look instead at the 11-year period from 1998 to 2009, an altogether different picture emerges. As Figure 2.3 shows, this time bonds out-

FIGURE 2.2
Stock vs. bond performance 1988–2009

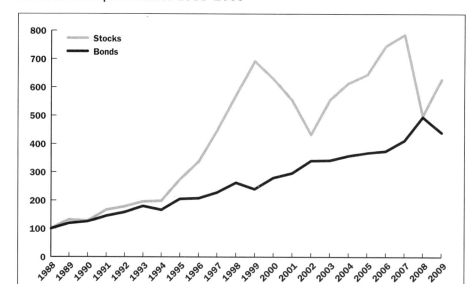

Source: Aswath Damodaran, Equity, Risk Premiums (ERP) Determinants, Estimation and Implications – The 2010 Edition (Stern School of Business), Feb 2012

performed equities, with annualised bond returns averaging 4.8% compared with equities which realised only 0.9% p.a., having been hit by the bursting of the dot-com bubble in 2000–2002 and by the collapse in equity markets following the 2007–2008 credit crisis. Risk, as measured by the standard deviations of returns, was virtually the same as for the longer 1988–2009 period.

The two largest equity markets in the world are both in the United States, with the New York Stock Exchange (NYSE) and the National Association of Securities Dealers' Automated Quotation stock exchange (NASDAQ) both being based in New York. Next in size comes the Tokyo Stock Exchange and the London Stock Exchange. Table 2.1 shows the world's top ten exchanges in November 2010, as measured by market capitalisation.

FIGURE 2.3
Stock vs. bond performance 1998–2009

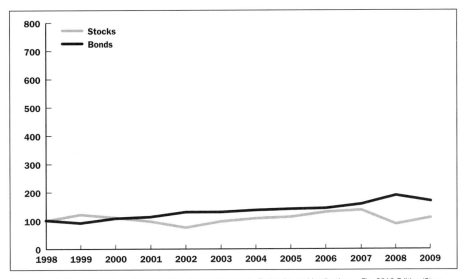

Source: Aswath Damodaran, Equity, Risk Premiums (ERP) Determinants, Estimation and Implications – The 2010 Edition (Stern School of Business), Feb 2012.

TABLE 2.1
Top ten stock exchanges in November 2010

Exchange	Domestic market capitalisation ($bn)
NYSE Euronext (US)	13.0
NASDAQ OMX	3.6
Tokyo SE	3.5
London SE Group	3.4
Hong Kong Exchanges	2.7
NYSE Euronext (Europe)	2.7
Shanghai SE	2.7
TSX Group	2.0
Bombay SE	1.5
National Stock Exchange India	1.5

Source: World Federation of Exchanges

Although we have drawn a sharp distinction between debt and equity markets, there are some financial instruments which straddle the divide. Preferred shares are like bonds, in that their dividends are a pre-specified percentage of their face value, but unlike bonds, in that failure to pay a dividend does not constitute a default. Likewise, in the event of the issuer entering into liquidation, preferred shares usually rank between bonds and equity in terms of any claim to the issuer's assets. A convertible bond is another hybrid instrument that starts life as a bond, but gives the holder the right to convert the bond into a certain number of shares of the issuing company at certain times or periods.

2.6 The commodities markets

Commodities have been traded for centuries and are a vital part of the global economy. The commodity markets can be split into three main parts:

- agricultural commodities – grains (corn, wheat, etc.), meats (e.g. cattle, pigs) and softs (coffee, cocoa, sugar, cotton, orange juice, lumber, etc.)
- metals – base (e.g. copper, aluminium, etc.) and precious (e.g. gold, platinum, etc.)
- energy – crude oil, natural gas, heating oil, coal, electricity, etc.

There has been an increasing focus on commodities in recent years, largely fuelled by two main factors. First, commodity prices have become much more volatile, leading producers and consumers to use the commodity markets to manage their price risk more effectively. Second, investors seeking higher potential returns and diversification are using commodities as an alternative asset class. To these we can add a third influence – China. The rapid economic development of China, particularly over the past ten years, has seen China become both a major consumer and producer in a number of commodities, such as steel, copper and oil.

Commodities trade in a number of ways. First, there is the *spot market*, where commodities trade for immediate delivery. Next, there are *futures markets*, which establish the price today for delivery that will take place during a specified month in the future. The world's largest commodities exchanges are the CME Group (which includes the CBOT, NYMEX and COMEX), Intercontinental Exchange (ICE) and the London Metal Exchange (LME).

2.7 Cash instruments versus derivatives

In the case of all the markets discussed so far, trades executed result in flows of cash – or flows of principal to be more precise – at some time or other. For example, if IBM Corporation issues a $130m bond paying a 5% coupon, it will receive $130m (less fees) when the bond is actually issued, pay out around $6.5m a year in coupons, and eventually repay $130m when the bond matures. If the Ford Motor Corporation sells €100m spot against US dollars at €1=$1.30, it will pay €100m and receive $130m in cash in two working days' time.

For this reason, the foreign exchange, money, bond, equities and spot commodity markets are all considered *cash* markets. However, one of the consequences of there being actual cash flows is that parties are exposed to considerable risk if something goes wrong. Probably unthinkable, but what if IBM were unable or unwilling to repay its borrowing of $130m when the bond matured? What if Ford had paid away its €100m in Frankfurt and then found that the dollars it expected to receive in New York later that day were not there? In both cases there is a potential loss to one party of $130m.

In many cases, the flow of cash is essential to the trade. For example, if a borrower requires finance, nothing else but cash will do. However, when it comes to hedging or speculation, the actual flow of cash is often not only unnecessary but even undesirable. This is not to say that cash markets are not used for these purposes. On the contrary, a good deal of the trading volume within the cash markets arises from hedging and speculation. Since the 1970s, however, the evolution of derivative markets and instruments has provided a far more efficient way of managing risk. Derivatives are usually linked to the corresponding instruments in the cash markets. For example, a currency option is linked to particular currency pairs in the FX market, a bond future to certain bonds in the bond market, and stock-index futures to the performance of a specified stock market. Derivatives provide holders with similar exposure to currency fluctuations, interest rates, or stock market swings, as their parallels in the cash markets, *but without the exposure to loss of principal.*

For example, if you held an option to buy $1bn against sterling, you would be exposed to similar profits or losses to those experienced by someone who actually had bought $1bn spot against a sale of sterling.[4] However, if the bank which sold you the option collapsed, the most you could lose would be the value of the option today, which would be just a few percent of the $1bn underlying value. Someone who executed the spot trade in the cash market could conceivably lose the full $1bn.

Since the risk from derivatives is smaller than that of the underlying instruments, commercial banks are required to set aside less capital for their use, as we shall see in the next section.

2.8 Capital adequacy requirements

Commercial banks, over the decades, have been subject to various regulations and controls. One of the most important demands within the system of supervision is the requirement for banks to have sufficient capital. Although banks, like other corporate entities, use capital to support their infrastructure and general operations, banks need capital as a cushion against the risks they face in their everyday operations.

Starting in the late 1980s, the Basel Committee on Banking Supervision has laid down a series of rules to determine how much capital a bank requires. The first standard, now called Basel I, came into force at the end of 1992. It was superseded at the end of 2006 by Basel II, and now Basel III is being implemented over a five-year period from 2013 to 2018.

Although each new standard from Basel adds increased sophistication, there has always been a common theme – a minimum ratio of capital to *weighted risk assets*. To arrive at weighted risk assets, each asset on the bank's balance sheet is assigned a weighting, which can range from 0% for assets considered riskless to 150% or more for the most risky assets. Basel I and II then defined the minimum level of capital to these weighted risk assets to be 8%, while Basel III has effectively raised this to 10.5%.

Capital for banks is a scarce and expensive commodity, and some fairly simple calculations can demonstrate that the cost of the capital required to support an asset with a 100% risk weighting can easily reduce the *net interest margin* (the difference between the interest rate charged on a loan less the interest paid on deposits) by as much as 200bp.[5] This means that a bank borrowing funds at LIBOR –50bp, and lending to a prime corporate customer at LIBOR +150bp, is just breaking even when the cost of capital is taken into account, and banks face a host of other costs as well.

The capital requirements for derivative products are far less because the principal is rarely at risk. Under the Basel III framework, capital is not required against the principal underlying the transaction, but only against counterparty risk. If the counterparty to a derivative transaction were to default, the potential loss incurred by the surviving counterparty is essentially the *replacement cost* – the cost incurred in replacing the defaulted transaction with a new one at current market rates. This is invariably a fraction of the principal amount. Moreover, market practice usually involves each party depositing collateral with the other party, an amount equal to the current replacement cost of the transaction, plus an add-on to allow for potential future exposure. That way, if one party defaults, the other party should already hold collateral equal to or greater than the replacement cost. Under these circumstances, and also if the derivative is exchange-traded or cleared using a central counterparty, the capital requirement could even be zero.

That the capital requirements are but a fraction of those for any equivalent on-balance sheet product is one reason why derivatives are such attractive tools for banks to use in the management of their own risk and that of their clients. Another reason is their flexibility and versatility. It is therefore no surprise to find that derivative products have become the essential tools of financial engineering, and the remaining chapters in this book are devoted to explaining how derivatives work, and how they are used in practice to create efficient and effective risk management solutions.

Further reading

Foreign exchange
Shamah, Shani (2008) *A Foreign Exchange Primer*, Wiley.
Weithers, Tim (2006) *Foreign Exchange: A Practical Guide to the FX Markets*, Wiley.

Money markets
Choudhry, Moorad (2005) *The Money Markets Handbook*, Wiley.
Stigum, Marcia (2007) *Stigum's Money Market*, McGraw-Hill, 4th edition.

Bond markets
Fabozzi, Frank (2010) *Bond Markets, Analysis and Strategies*, Pearson, 7th edition.
Fabozzi, Frank J (2006) *Fixed Income Mathematics*, McGraw-Hill, 4th edition.

Equities markets
Tagliani, Matthew (2009) *The Practical Guide to Wall Street*, Wiley.

Commodities markets
Geman, Hélyette (2005) *Commodities and Commodity Derivatives*, Wiley.
Schofield, Neil (2007) *Commodity Derivatives: Markets and Applications*, Wiley.

General
Valdez, Stephen and Molyneux, Philip (2010) *An Introduction to Global Financial Markets*, Palgrave Macmillan.

Notes

1 Some use the term *capital markets* to take in virtually all the financial markets, including FX and all derivatives. I prefer to restrict the term to those markets directly involved in the raising of capital. Others limit the definition even further and include only markets dealing in instruments having an original maturity greater than one year.

2 Source: *BIS Quarterly Review*, December 2010.

3 Data extracted from: Aswath Damodaran, *Equity Risk Premiums (ERP): Determinants, Estimation and Implications – The 2010 Edition* (Stern School of Business, Feb 2010).

4 The precise exposure from holding an option will actually depend on the option's delta (a concept explored in section 11.5 of Chapter 11).

5 If the weighted average cost of capital is 20%, and a bank needs to have capital at around 10%, the effective cost of capital against the margin is 10% × 20% = 2% or 200bp.

3

FORWARD RATES

Before looking at financial engineering products such as FRAs and futures, it is necessary to introduce the important concept of the *forward rate*. The forward rate is the price the market sets for an instrument traded today, but where the resulting transaction is executed on some date in the future, sometimes the far distant future. The most common forward rates are those quoted for forward FX deals and forward interest rates. These are now discussed in turn.

3.1 Forward exchange rates

At first sight, it may seem highly risky for a bank to quote the rate for a foreign exchange deal set in the future, when it is difficult enough to estimate where the exchange rate will be in just a few hours' time. Fortunately, it is not necessary for bank traders to look into a crystal ball to predict the future. Instead, they can price a forward FX deal using the principle of *risk-free arbitrage*.

The concept of risk-free arbitrage is an important one, and is used for pricing a wide range of derivative products, as well as forward foreign exchange. To price an instrument using this technique, a trader will consider how to hedge the resulting position using other transactions whose price is known.

Consider a forward foreign exchange trader working for a UK bank, who is asked by a German client to quote a rate for US dollars against the euro, for delivery one year after spot. The customer wants to buy exactly $1,313,000 from the bank in order to settle an account that will be payable at that time, and so the bank will be selling $1,313,000 and receiving euros. The questions to be resolved are:

i)   How many euros should the bank receive in exchange for the US dollars?

ii) What is the fair exchange rate for €/$ one year forward?

Of course, the answer to the first question implies the answer to the second.

Suppose that our trader knows that the spot rate is €1 = $1.3000, that the one-year dollar interest rate is 1%, and the one-year euro interest rate is 2%. Figure 3.1 shows the sequence of transactions that would allow the trader to hedge the forward €/$ transaction with other deals, all at known rates. (The figure shows all cash flows from the trader's viewpoint.) Figure 3.1a shows the bank's exposure after agreeing to sell $1,313,000 to its client in one year. In order to have this sum of dollars, the bank could lend a sum of dollars now, such that the dollars repayable in one year together with interest would be exactly $1,313,000. With US one-year interest rates at 1%, the bank should therefore lend exactly $1,300,000. The interest on this sum would be $13,000, giving the total of $1,313,000 repayable in one year, just what is required.

Figure 3.1b shows the cash flows after the bank lends the $1,300,000, showing that the forward outflow of $1,313,000 has been completely hedged. But where does the bank get the $1,300,000 to lend? How does the bank hedge its exposure to dollars, as it is still short of dollars? The answer: the bank simply buys $1,300,000 spot in exchange for euros, as shown in Figure 3.1c. With the spot exchange rate at

FIGURE 3.1
Pricing forward foreign exchange

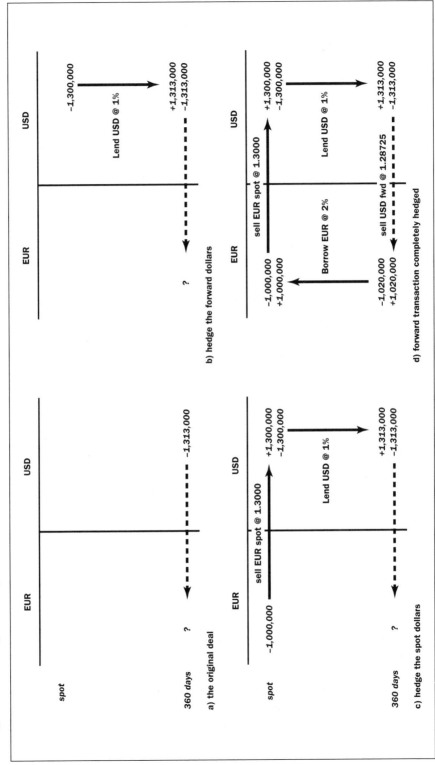

€1 = \$1.3000, the bank sells exactly €1m to receive \$1,300,000 spot, and has now completely hedged all the cash flows in dollars, both spot and forward.

Unfortunately, this still leaves an outflow of €1m spot, but this can easily be financed by borrowing euros. If the bank borrows the €1m required right now, this will eliminate the spot deficit, but will require the repayment of €1,020,000 in one year, including the 2% interest.

We have now come almost full circle. The bank has transformed the original \$1,313,000 liability one year forward into a €1,020,000 liability, also in one year. However, if the bank demands this sum of euros from its client in exchange for the dollars being sold, the bank will have hedged every cash flow from the original transaction. In the process, we have determined the amount of dollars the bank should receive, and the correct exchange rate of 1,313,000 ÷ 1,020,000 = 1.28725.

Figure 3.1d shows the bank's position after quoting €1 = \$1.28725 as the forward rate for the client transaction.[1] By executing a spot deal, lending dollars and borrowing euros, the trader has hedged the complete exposure arising from the forward foreign exchange transaction, and has eliminated the bank's exposure to market rate risk. The trader is not concerned how the spot €/\$ rate will evolve over the next year, nor does he worry what the spot rate will be on the settlement date in one year. Whether the exchange rate for euros against dollars is above or below 1.28725 will not affect the cash flows arising from the original lending and borrowing, and it is these cash flows which are hedging the client's forward transaction.

Since all rates for the hedging deals are known in the market today, the trader has successfully priced a forward FX deal, without necessarily having any opinion on where the spot rate will be in the future. This is the essence of risk-free arbitrage pricing. A spot rate of €1 = \$1.3000, and 12-month rates in euros and dollars of 2% and 1% respectively, imply a 12-month forward FX rate of €1 = \$1.28725.

From the above relationships, we can derive a simple formula[2] to price a forward exchange rate:

$$ F = S \times \frac{\left[1 + \left(i_p \times \dfrac{DAYS}{BASIS_p} \right) \right]}{\left[1 + \left(i_b \times \dfrac{DAYS}{BASIS_b} \right) \right]} \tag{3.1} $$

where:

F	is the outright forward exchange rate
S	is the current spot exchange rate
i_p	is the interest rate in the pricing currency (e.g. dollars)
i_b	is the interest rate in the base currency (e.g. euros)
$DAYS$	is the number of days from spot to the forward date
$BASIS_p$	is the day count convention in the pricing currency (360 for dollars)
$BASIS_b$	is the day count convention in the base currency (also 360 for euros)

and all interest rates are quoted as decimal fractions (e.g. 1% would be 0.01).

In practice, the foreign exchange market does not quote forward exchange rates as an absolute figure – the outright forward rate – but rather as the difference between the spot and forward rate – the forward or *swap points*.[3] This is because the outright forward rate is sensitive to movements in the spot rate, and moves almost exactly one-for-one with the spot rate. The forward FX trader would have to adjust his quote with every slight movement in the spot rate. The swap points, on the other hand, are hardly affected by the spot rate and quotations are therefore much more stable. Equation 3.2 shows the formula for swap points:

$$W = S \times \left[\frac{1 + \left(i_p \times \frac{DAYS}{BASIS_p} \right)}{1 + \left(i_b \times \frac{DAYS}{BASIS_b} \right)} - 1 \right] = F - S \qquad (3.2)$$

where:

  W is the forward or *swap points*

and all the other symbols are as before.

As an example, if the spot rate in the previous example were to move 100 points from 1.3000 to 1.2900, the outright rate would decrease from 1.28725 to 1.27735 – a fall of 99 points, but the swap rate would only move from 127.5 points to 126.5 points – just a one-point move. The change in swap points for a forward deal of shorter maturity would be even less.[4]

3.2 Forward interest rates

As finance developed in the latter part of the 20th century, banks were able to offer their customers an increasing range of borrowing facilities. In particular, the medium-term loan became a popular financing vehicle, allowing customers to borrow for up to seven or ten years, instead of having to rely on the frequent renewal of short-term facilities. Banks in turn, however, were compelled to finance themselves short term from retail or money market deposits. This was no great problem, for one of the roles traditionally ascribed to banks is to borrow short and lend long, the so-called *maturity transformation* function.

Banks were not terribly worried about their ability to roll over their funding requirements as, short of a full-blown banking crisis,[5] they had confidence in their ability to raise funds from the market if necessary. Banks may have had to bid an additional 10 or 20 basis points[6] to obtain the funds they needed, but raise the funds they did.

What banks were unable to do was to fix in advance the interest rate for the funds thus raised. Banks were forced to pay the going rate at the time, and then had to pass on that rate to their borrowers. Medium-term loans could therefore guarantee the availability of funds for a company, but not the rate at which those funds were provided. As interest rates became more volatile, corporate treasurers sought from their banks a means to protect their exposure to higher borrowing costs. To an extent, banks were able to offer a limited solution in the form of the *forward-forward* loan, so-called because both the draw-down and repayment dates were in the future.

Let's say that on 30 September 2010 a bank is asked to quote a fixed rate for a six-month loan of €1m, to start six months from now. The bank wishes to take no risks, and therefore needs to fix its own financing costs for the six-month period starting in six months. The bank might find that prevailing six-month cash rates were 1.13%, while 12-month cash rates were 1.42%, but these were rates for funds drawn down right now, not in six months from now.

Once again, however, the principle of risk-free arbitrage can be applied to determine the fair rate to be quoted. To fix the costs for the six-month period starting in six months, the bank borrows now for 12 months at 1.42%. Unfortunately, this not only covers the forward period, but also the first six months when finance is not required. To cope with these unwanted funds, the bank lends them for the first six months at 1.13%. The proceeds of this six-month loan are then available to the client in six months' time, and the repayment from the client 12 months from now should, if our arithmetic is correct, be just enough to repay the bank's original 12-month borrowing.

Figure 3.2 demonstrates the cash flows arising from these transactions. The bank borrows €994,382 for 12 months at 1.42%, and immediately lends it for six months at 1.13%. The maturing proceeds from the six-month loan come to exactly €1m with interest, and provide the funds to lend to its client. If the bank quotes at least 1.7004% for this forward-forward loan, the proceeds will be enough to repay the principal and interest on the original 12-month borrowing, namely €1,008,502.

By borrowing long term and lending short term, the bank has created a *synthetic* forward borrowing, which enables it to quote a rate for forward-forward lending, and then to finance such lending without suffering interest rate risk. As we saw in the previous chapter with forward exchange deals, the bank need not be concerned with the level of interest rates which eventually prevail; the combination of 12-month borrowing at 1.42% and six-month lending at 1.13% guarantees a source of finance at 1.7004% regardless of market rates at the time.

As before, the principle of risk-free arbitrage pricing has enabled us to derive a forward rate – this time a forward interest rate – without having any opinion on where interest rates in the future will be. Six-month rates of 1.13% and 12-month rates of 1.42% imply a six-month forward rate in six months' time of 1.7004%.

Forward-forward loans were in demand in the late 1970s, but were not popular from the banks' viewpoint. What made these loans unattractive was the need for banks to borrow money the entire time from the dealing date until the final

FIGURE 3.2

Forward-forward loan

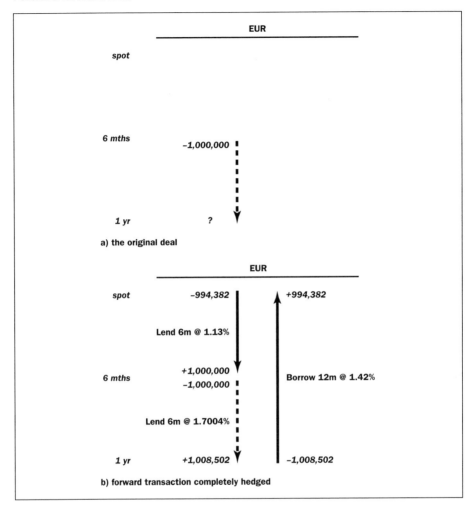

b) forward transaction completely hedged

maturity of the forward-forward loan. In the above example, the bank would need to borrow for 12 months even though the client required finance for just six months. When a bank borrows, it consumes both lines of credit and capital, both of which are limited and expensive resources.

To illustrate the problem, suppose that a bank can borrow from and lend to the interbank markets at 2%, can lend to corporate clients at 4%, and pays 15% for its capital. Assume also that the bank is required to hold capital amounting to 8% of the value of its lending, corresponding to the BIS capital adequacy requirement for 100% risk-weighted loans. We can draw up a simple balance sheet and profit and loss account for a six-month client loan of €1m financed by an interbank deposit.

Balance sheet

Assets		Liabilities and capital	
Customer loan (6mth)	1,000,000	Interbank deposit (6mth)	920,000
		Capital	80,000
Total assets	1,000,000	Total funds	1,000,000

Profit and loss account (six months)

Income		Expense	
Customer loan	20,000	Interbank deposit	9,200
		Capital	6,000
Total income	20,000	Total expense	15,200

This leaves a net profit of €4,800, corresponding to an additional annualised return on capital of 12%. But what if the bank were to extend the same facilities as a six-month forward-forward loan? During the first six months, the balance sheet would look like this:

Balance sheet (first six months)

Assets		Liabilities and capital	
Interbank loan (6mth)	1,000,000	Interbank deposit (12mth)	920,000
		Capital	80,000
Total assets	1,000,000	Total funds	1,000,000

and for the last six months:

Balance sheet (last six months)

Assets		Liabilities and capital	
Customer loan (6mth)	1,000,000	Interbank deposit (12mth)	920,000
		Capital	80,000
Total assets	1,000,000	Total funds	1,000,000

The resulting profit and loss account would therefore show a much reduced profit:

Profit and loss account (12 months)

Income		Expense	
Interbank loan	10,000	Interbank deposit (12mth)	18,400
Customer loan	20,000	Capital	12,000
Total income	30,000	Total expense	30,400

The result is now a loss of €400 for a full year, a negative 0.50% return on capital. It is no wonder that banks disliked forward-forward lending!

The greatest damage to the bank's profits in this example arises from the bank's need for capital to support the balance sheet for the extended period involved. There is a sound reason why central banks insist on this capital requirement; it is to protect banks' depositors in the event of excessive losses on their loans. With an 8% capital requirement, it is theoretically possible for 8% of a bank's loans to go bad without prejudicing the bank's depositors. If a way could be found to remove forward-forward loans from the balance sheet, this would eliminate the need for capital, and restore profitability to the banks. As we will see in the next chapter, this is where the FRA comes in.

3.3 Do forward rates predict future spot rates?

Expectations are *subjective* estimates of where prices will be in the future. In contrast, this chapter has thus far presented forward prices as being *objectively* derived from current market rates using risk-free arbitrage calculations. Inasmuch as these forward prices are mathematically derived from prevailing market rates, there is no need to refer to subjective expectations in order to derive objective forward prices.

Nevertheless, we can prove that objective forward prices must necessarily match subjective expectations. If they did not, market forces would drive current prices so as to achieve equality. This is an important point. For example, suppose that the spot €/$ exchange rate was €1 = $1.3000, and using current market interest rates the one-month outright forward rate was calculated objectively to be €1 = $1.2989. One can therefore say that market expectations for the spot rate in one month must also be €1 = $1.2989. Why?

Imagine for one moment that the market really expected the spot rate in one month to be higher, say €1 = $1.3200. In that case, traders would execute deals today to buy euros outright for delivery one month later at the current one-month forward rate of €1 = $1.2989, and then just wait for one month. Two days before the value date for these deals, they would sell the dollars at the then prevailing spot rate. If they had been right in their original expectations, that spot rate would be €1 = $1.3200, realising a 211-point profit, equivalent to $21,100 per €1m traded. A €100m position would realise over $2m profit.

With such an incentive, everyone would buy euros forward, to profit from their expectations. Of course, the demand for forward euros would force the price up, but traders would still keep buying and buying. They would only stop buying when the forward price equalled the expectation of €1 = $1.3200. A similar argument in the opposite direction would apply if traders had thought that the forward price was overvalued.

In other words, market forces will always drive forward rates (and spot rates with them) until forward rates equal market expectations for the spot rate on that date. Therefore the forward rate one actually observes in the market must be equal to market expectations for the spot rate on that date.

Although this argument has been developed in the context of exchange rates, the same applies to interest rates. The forward interest rate is not only determined objectively by manipulating cash market rates for different maturities, it is also the subjective forecast of where the cash market rate will be in the future. For example, if six-month rates are 1.13% and 12-month rates are 1.42%, we calculated earlier that the rate for a forward-forward loan of six months starting in six months was 1.7004%. This also implies that the current market expectation for six-month interest rates is that they will rise from their present level of 1.13%, and will reach 1.7004% six months from now[7].

3.4 Spot and forward rates in practice

Many studies have been undertaken to answer the question: do spot rates in practice eventually match up to prior expectations? The answer is: no, they do not. The grey line in Figure 3.3 shows the spot exchange rate for euros against dollars from May through September 2010. The black line shows the one-month forward rate one month earlier. The two are almost never the same. Figure 3.4 shows even more clearly the gap between the spot rate and the one-month forward rate one month earlier.

But this seemingly disappointing answer has no bearing on the conclusion established in the previous section, that forward rates must match the market's expectations of future spot rates.

At any given time, the market absorbs all available information, and establishes spot and forward prices. At that moment, a one-month forward rate reflects expectations for the spot rate in one month. However, during the one-

FIGURE 3.3
Spot rates compared with forward rates one month earlier

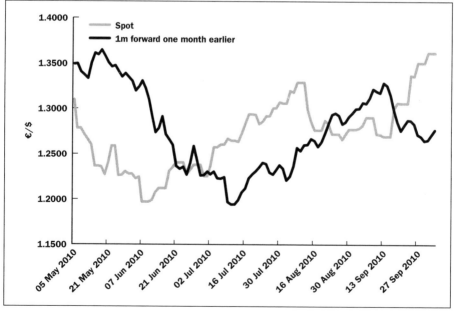

Source: FX rates from www.oanda.com, LIBOR rates from British Bankers Association.

FIGURE 3.4

Gap between spot rates and forward rates one month earlier

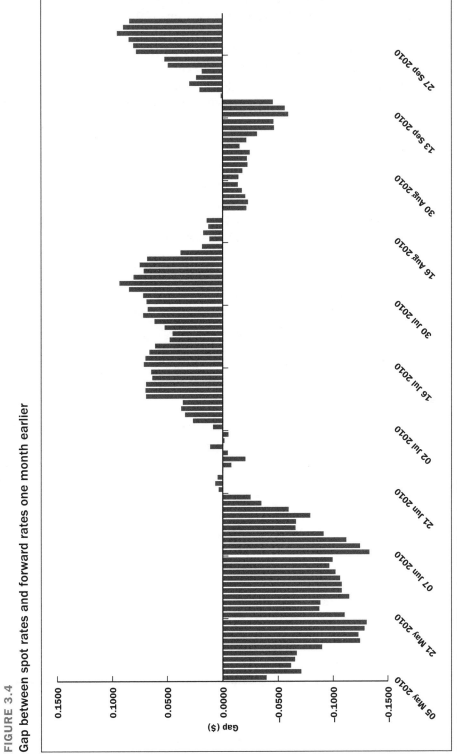

Source: FX rates from oanda.com, LIBOR rates from British Bankers Association.

month period, many things can happen. There will be economic and political developments, and dramatic events could occur. All of these alter market expectations and prices will adjust accordingly.

So when studies compare the spot rate with the one-month forward rate quoted one month earlier, they are trying to compare rates based on two sets of price-sensitive information. No wonder the rates turn out to be different *ex-post facto*. This does not negate the fact that forward rates and expectations of future spot rates were once the same.

Notes

1 In fact, the trader would have to quote a rate slightly lower than 1.28725 so that the bank received slightly more than the €1,020,000 indicated by the above trades. Otherwise there would be no profit for the bank in executing the forward deal with the client.

2 This formula applies to forward rates up to one year in the future. For long-term FX (LTFX) transactions, the formula must be modified to include compound interest.

3 For a currency quoted to four decimal places, each *point* is one ten thousandth of the pricing currency. So for euros against dollars, one point is $0.0001.

4 Using calculus it is easy to show that $\frac{\partial F}{\partial S} \approx 1$ but $\frac{\partial W}{\partial S} \approx 0$.

5 Occasionally crises do occur. Most recently, in the 2007–2008 credit crisis, the market for interbank funds dried up and central banks around the world were forced to act as lenders of last resort, one of the traditional roles of central banks.

6 A basis point is one hundredth of 1%, i.e. 0.01%.

7 Since the 2007–08 credit crisis, however, this assertion has to be modified to take into account the increased credit risk associated with longer-term interest rates. This is discussed in section 4.6 of Chapter 4.

4

FRAs

The previous chapter introduced and explained the concept of forward rates. This chapter looks at one of the earliest financial engineering instruments, the FRA. The FRA, originating from the money markets, offers a flexible tool for hedging against or speculating on the movements of a specific interest rate.

4.1 What is an FRA?

The initials FRA stand for *forward rate agreement*. In essence, an FRA is like a forward-forward loan granted at a fixed interest rate, but *without the actual lending commitment*. Removing the flows of principal from the FRA takes the instrument off the balance sheet, and removes the onerous capital requirements that made forward-forward loans so unattractive. While there is still a requirement for banks to allocate some capital to cover their FRA books, the amount is a tiny fraction of the requirement demanded for forward-forward loans.

But what exactly is an FRA? One way to answer that question is to look at FRAs from the user's viewpoint:

An FRA is an agreement between two parties motivated by the wish either to hedge against or to speculate on a movement in future interest rates.

The hedger already has interest rate exposure, but wants to obtain protection against rate movements. After taking a position in FRAs, the hedger's net risk will be reduced or eliminated. The speculator, on the other hand, starts with no exposure, but wants to profit from an anticipated movement in interest rates. Taking a position in FRAs creates for the speculator precisely the exposure desired. Since their inception in the early 1980s, FRAs have provided a very useful tool in the management of interest rate risk.

FRAs are an *over the counter*[1] (OTC) product offered by banks. Like the foreign exchange market, the market for FRAs is a global market offered by banks operating from their trading rooms, linked together by telephone and computer networks. The two parties to an FRA are usually a customer and a bank, or two banks. As with their other activities in the financial markets, banks intermediate between those who are exposed to risk. Alternatively, banks can absorb customers' risks within the totality of their trading books across all the financial markets.

The FRA market is sizeable, and has grown substantially over the decade from 2000 to 2010. According to figures published by the BIS,[2] notional amounts outstanding grew from $6.8tn in June 2000 to $56.2tn by June 2010, an eight-fold increase over the ten-year period. Daily turnover increased from $129bn in April 2001 to $601bn by April 2010, almost a five-fold increase over nine years. Over 80% of this turnover is in US dollar and euro FRAs, and a further 9% is in pound sterling FRAs.

For the major currencies banks post prices for all combinations of standard three-, six- and nine-month periods with final maturity dates up to two years

FIGURE 4.1

Example of FRA rates for the US dollar on 14 January 2011

Tenor	Bid	Ask	Tenor	Bid	Ask	Tenor	Bid	Ask
1 × 4	0.310	0.350	1 × 7	0.355	0.395	2 × 11	0.432	0.472
2 × 5	0.332	0.372	2 × 8	0.382	0.422	3 × 12	0.472	0.512
3 × 6	0.365	0.405	3 × 9	0.415	0.455	7 × 13	0.571	0.611
4 × 7	0.397	0.437	4 × 10	0.448	0.488	8 × 14	0.615	0.655
5 × 8	0.425	0.465	5 × 11	0.479	0.519	9 × 15	0.676	0.716
6 × 9	0.458	0.498	6 × 12	0.523	0.563	11 × 14	0.696	0.736
7 × 10	0.496	0.536	12 × 18	0.878	0.918	15 × 18	0.989	1.029
8 × 11	0.533	0.573	18 × 24	1.403	1.443			
9 × 12	0.587	0.627						
12 × 15	0.765	0.805						

Source: Garban ICAP.

into the future. Banks also stand ready to quote prices for odd dates and non-standard periods. Figure 4.1 illustrates a typical broker's screen carrying FRA rates for the US dollar. The meaning of each of the numbers will become clearer once all the terminology has been defined in the next two sections.

4.2 Definitions

We know so far that an FRA is an agreement between two parties wishing to modify their exposure to interest rates. Let us take a closer look at the features of that agreement.

One party to an FRA is defined to be the *buyer* of the FRA, the other party is the *seller*. The seller of an FRA agrees notionally to lend a particular sum of money to the buyer. The terms 'buyer' and 'seller' therefore have nothing to do with who is providing a service, they refer to which party is the notional borrower and which the notional lender. Banks can be buyers and sellers, as can customers.

The notional loan is of a specified size in a specified currency, will notionally be drawn down on a particular date in the future, and will last for a specified duration. Most importantly of all, the notional loan will be made at a fixed rate of interest, this rate being agreed when the FRA deal is struck.

Let's recap on these important concepts.

Under an FRA:

- the *buyer* agrees notionally to *borrow*
- the *seller* agrees notionally to *lend*
- a specified notional principal amount
- denominated in a specified currency

- at a *fixed* rate of interest
- for a specified period
- to commence on an agreed date in the future.

The *buyer* of an FRA is therefore a notional borrower, and is protected against a rise in interest rates, though he must pay if rates fall. The buyer may have a real borrowing requirement, and is using the FRA as a hedge. Alternatively, the buyer may have no underlying interest-rate exposure, but may be using the FRA simply to speculate on a rise in interest rates.

The *seller* of an FRA is a notional lender, and fixes the rate for lending or investing. The FRA seller is therefore protected against a fall in interest rates, but must pay if rates rise. A seller may be an investor who would really suffer if rates fell, but could also be someone with no underlying position who just wanted to profit from a fall in rates.

We have repeatedly emphasised the word *notional*. It is important to remember that no lending or borrowing actually takes place under the FRA itself. Although one or both parties may have borrowing or investment commitments, separate arrangements to handle these requirements must be made. What the FRA does provide is protection against a movement in interest rates. This protection manifests itself in the form of a cash payment – the *settlement sum* – which compensates each party for any difference between the rate of interest originally agreed and that prevailing when the FRA eventually matures. An example should serve to make this clearer.

Consider a company which anticipates the need to borrow $1m in three months' time for a six-month period. For simplicity, we will assume that the borrower is able to raise funds at LIBOR flat. Suppose that six-month interest rates are around 4% right now, but the borrower fears that these rates may rise over the next three months. If the borrower does nothing, he could face a much higher interest rate when the loan is drawn down in three months' time.

To protect against this interest rate risk, the borrower could today buy an FRA to cover the six-month period starting three months from now. This would be known in the market as a '3-against-9 month' FRA, or simply a 3×9 FRA. A bank might quote a rate of 4.25% for such an FRA, and this would enable the borrower to lock into a borrowing rate of 4.25%. There is no 'insurance premium' payable when buying or selling FRAs, although banks would normally charge their clients a commission on the deal.

Now suppose that the borrower's fears were realised, and six-month interest rates did indeed rise over the initial three-month period to 5%. Despite the FRA, the borrower is still forced to borrow in the market and pay the going rate, namely 5%. Over a six-month period, the borrower would therefore have to pay an extra $3,750 interest on the $1m borrowed. This is where the FRA comes in. Under the FRA, the company would receive approximately $3,750[3] to compensate for the extra 0.75% interest payable on the $1m loan over the six-month period, the settlement sum effectively offsetting the higher borrowing costs.

While the FRA has not guaranteed the interest rate on the specific financing facility used by the company, the borrower has nonetheless managed to secure its finance at the rate fixed by the FRA, which operates to bring the effective cost of the loan down to the level originally agreed.

4.3 Terminology

Nearly all FRAs dealt in practice fall under standard market documentation drawn up by the British Bankers' Association, the so-called 'FRABBA terms'. In addition to establishing the proper legal arrangements, the documentation defines a number of important terms:

- *contract amount* – the principal sum notionally lent or borrowed
- *contract currency* – the currency in which the contract amount is denominated
- *dealing date* – the date when the FRA deal is struck
- *settlement date* – the date when the notional loan or deposit commences
- *fixing date* – the date when the reference rate is determined
- *maturity date* – the date when the notional loan or deposit matures
- *contract period* – the number of days between settlement and maturity dates
- *contract rate* – the fixed interest rate agreed under the FRA
- *reference rate* – the market-based rate used on the fixing date to determine the settlement sum
- *settlement sum* – the amount paid by one party to the other on the settlement date, based on the difference between the contract and reference rates.

Figure 4.2 illustrates many of these key concepts, and may make the terms more readily understood.

We start on the dealing date, when the two parties to the FRA agree all the terms. Let's suppose that the *dealing date* is Monday 9th April 2012, and the two parties agree to trade a 1 × 4 FRA in $1m at 4.25%. The *contract currency*

FIGURE 4.2
Timing diagram for FRAs

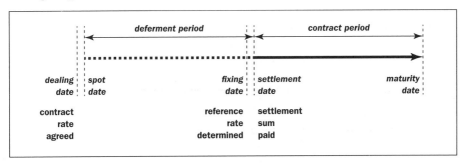

is therefore the US dollar, the *contract amount* is one million, and the contract rate is 4.25%.

The '1 × 4' refers to a one-month period between the normal spot date and the settlement date, and a four-month period between the spot date and the final maturity date of the notional loan. Spot date is normally two days after the dealing date, making it Wednesday 11th April 2012 in this case. This means that the notional loan or deposit would start on Friday 11th May, exactly one month after spot, and would mature on Monday 13th August, just over three months later.[4] The *settlement date* is therefore 11th May, the *maturity date* 13th August, and the *contract period* is 94 days.

For a regular Eurocurrency loan or deposit, the rate is fixed on the dealing date, but the principal does not change hands until the value date, normally two working days later. This pattern is repeated with FRAs. The notional loan or deposit would theoretically be drawn down on the settlement date, Friday 11th May in the above example, but the rate would be determined two days earlier on the *fixing date*, Wednesday 9th May here.

Under most FRAs, the *reference rate* is the LIBOR fixing on the fixing date. LIBOR in its turn is determined by seeking quotes for interbank borrowing rates from a number of designated banks at the appointed time, ranking the quotes in order from lowest to highest, striking out the lowest and highest quartiles, and then taking the simple arithmetic average of the remaining figures.[5] Let's suppose that the reference rate on the fixing date, 9th May, turns out to be 5.00%.

The final step is to calculate the *settlement sum*. We have all the information we need to do this, and the next section explains exactly how.

4.4 The settlement process

In the above example, the buyer of the FRA has theoretically locked into a borrowing rate of 4.25%, but now faces a market rate of 5.00% on the fixing date. The extra interest payable on a $1m facility for 94 days can easily be calculated:

$$extra\ interest = \frac{(5.00 - 4.25)}{100} \times \$1,000,000 \times \frac{94}{360} = \$1,958.33 \quad (4.1)$$

This extra interest cost would be suffered when the interest payment for the borrowing was made, which is on the final maturity date of the underlying loan. If the settlement sum under the FRA were paid on the same date, then it should also be $1,958.33 so as to compensate exactly for the higher interest rate on the borrowing.

In practice, however, FRAs usually pay the settlement sum on the settlement date, which is at the *beginning* of the underlying loan or deposit. As this sum is paid earlier than it is needed, it could be invested to earn interest. To adjust for this timing, the settlement sum is reduced by exactly the interest that could be earned on the settlement sum from the settlement date to the maturity date.

The standard formula for calculating the settlement sum is thus:

$$settlement\ sum = \frac{(i_r - i_c) \times A \times \dfrac{DAYS}{BASIS}}{1 + \left(i_r \times \dfrac{DAYS}{BASIS}\right)} \tag{4.2}$$

where:

i_r	is the reference interest rate
i_c	is the contract interest rate
A	is the contract amount
$DAYS$	is the number of days in the contract period
$BASIS$	is the day count convention (e.g. 360 for dollars, 365 for sterling)

and all interest rates are quoted as decimal fractions (e.g. 4.25% would be 0.0425).

Showing the formula in this way shows directly how it is derived. The numerator is simply the extra interest cost caused by the change in interest rates from the original rate agreed i_c to the rate eventually prevailing i_r. In the example of equation 4.1, this would be $1,958.33. The denominator then discounts this to allow for the fact that the settlement sum is paid at the beginning rather than at the end of the contract period. If we insert the values of the previous example, we will get a settlement sum of $1,933.10 due to the FRA buyer on the settlement date.

It is important to remember that FRAs are a class of financial engineering instrument which replaces risk with certainty. In this example, as rates have turned out higher than the contract rate of 4.25%, the buyer of the FRA receives the settlement sum from the seller to compensate for higher borrowing costs. If rates had turned out to be lower, however, the buyer would have to pay the seller to compensate the notional lender for lower than expected investment rates. In either case, both buyer and seller end up with an effective LIBOR of 4.25%, whatever LIBOR actually turns out to be.

Equation 4.2 is defined in such a way that a positive settlement sum implies a payment from seller to buyer, while a negative settlement sum implies a payment from buyer to seller. Another way to think of this is to consider the settlement sum as being the value of the FRA to the buyer, the party who is 'long' the FRA. If $i_r > i_c$ the settlement sum will be positive. The buyer has purchased an FRA when rates were lower, rates have subsequently risen, and a positive value will be realised. This is nothing other than a trader's 'buy low sell high' mentality. If $i_r < i_c$ the settlement sum will be negative, and it will now be the seller, who is 'short' the FRA, that will realise again.

It is possible to rearrange equation 4.2 in order to get a slightly simpler formulation:

$$settlement\ sum = \frac{(i_r - i_c) \times A}{\dfrac{BASIS}{DAYS} + i_r} = 1,933.10 \tag{4.3}$$

4.5 Hedging with FRAs

In the previous example, the FRA buyer would receive $1,933.10 as the settlement sum, but would pay a higher interest rate at the maturity of the three-month loan. Let's check to make sure that the arithmetic of the FRA really works.

On the fixing date, Wednesday 9th May, the settlement sum will be known, and the borrower should make arrangements to invest it for exactly three months. The settlement sum received on Friday 11th May, the settlement date, is thus invested to earn 5.00%, the prevailing LIBOR. After 94 days, the interest earned will be $25.24, bringing the value of the settlement sum with interest up to $1,958.33.

Wednesday 9th May will also be the date when the rate for the three-month borrowing facility will be fixed at 5.00%. The funds would be drawn down on Friday 11th May, and repaid on Monday 13th August together with interest of $13,055.56. The invested settlement sum will, however, reduce the effective interest cost to $11,097.22. What interest rate does this sum represent?

$$effective\ interest\ cost = \frac{11,097.22}{1,000,000} \times \frac{360}{94} = 4.25\% \qquad (4.4)$$

In this example, the FRA has indeed lowered the borrower's effective cost to the contract rate agreed when the FRA was bought.

In practice, there are two minor departures from this simple illustration. First, most borrowers are compelled to pay some margin above LIBOR, say 1.00% above LIBOR. This means that the effective borrowing will be effected at the same margin above the contract rate. For example, a borrower used to paying 1.00% above LIBOR who buys an FRA at 4.25% will be locking his borrowing cost at 5.25%, regardless of the eventual outcome for LIBOR. Second, the discounting implicit in determining the settlement sum assumes that parties to the FRA can invest or borrow the settlement sum at LIBOR. In practice, only banks may be able to do this; commercial customers would normally only achieve a margin underneath LIBOR.

Let's rework the above example assuming that the borrower must pay LIBOR plus 1.00% for his funds, but can only earn LIBOR minus 1.00% on funds invested. The borrower buys an FRA at 4.25%, the reference rate turns out to be 5.00%, leading to the same settlement sum being paid as before.

	$
Settlement sum	1,933.10
Interest earned on settlement sum invested for 94 days at 4.00%	20.19
Total proceeds from FRA	1,953.29
Interest payable on $1m borrowed for 94 days at 6.00%	15,666.67
Net borrowing costs after deduction of FRA proceeds	13,713.38

The effective interest rate implied by net borrowing costs of $13,713.38 is 5.25%, still 1.00% above the contract rate originally agreed. The lower interest earned on the settlement sum only costs the borrower $5.05, equivalent to just 0.002% on borrowings of $1m for 94 days, a negligible amount.

4.6 Pricing FRAs

The simplest way to think about FRA pricing is to think about an FRA as 'filling the gap' between different maturities in the cash market. Consider someone with funds available right now to invest for one year. Suppose that six-month rates are at 3%, but 12-month rates are at 4%. The investor has many choices, including these two alternatives:

i) Invest for one year and earn 4%.

ii) Invest for six months and earn 3%. At the same time, sell a 6 × 12 FRA to lock in a guaranteed return for the second six-month period.

These two possibilities are pictured in Figure 4.3.

In the diagram, there are two ways of getting from A to B, as is often the case in financial markets. When this happens, the efficiency of the financial markets will ensure that, whichever path is chosen, the end result should be the same. In this example, the investor placing his money for a year under alternative (i) will earn an additional 1% for the first six months when compared with alternative (ii). For both these alternatives eventually to come out the same, the return over the second six months must gain 1% for the investor who chooses alternative (ii). To a first approximation, the 6 × 12 FRA must be priced at 5%, as pictured in Figure 4.4.

FIGURE 4.3
FRA pricing: 'filling the gap'

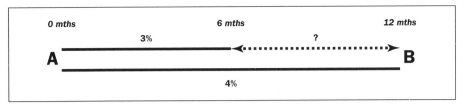

FIGURE 4.4
Determining the rate for a 6 × 12 FRA

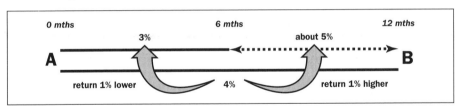

This technique gives us an intuitive insight into the pricing of FRAs, and also provides a 'quick and dirty' way of estimating the price for any given FRA, if we know the appropriate rates in the cash markets. Figure 4.5 extends the technique and shows how to price 6 × 9 and 9 × 12 FRAs.

In Figure 4.5c, the investor placing funds for nine months receives 1% less return than the investor placing money for one year. This 1% gap must be made up in the remaining three months, just one-third of the time over which this difference can be recouped. The gain must therefore be three times as great, implying that the 9 × 12 FRA must be 3% higher than the 12-month rate, or around 7%.

In all these cases, this 'quick and dirty' technique has been able to give only a rough estimate for the FRA rate. This is because an investor choosing the shorter-term investment followed by another short-term investment protected by an FRA has the opportunity to earn interest-on-interest. Not only can the principal be reinvested over the second term, but the interest on that principal as well. This means that in all these examples, the actual FRA rate would be somewhat lower than the rough estimates. In the case of the 6 × 12 FRA, the true FRA rate should be 4.93%, a little bit less than the 5% previously estimated.

While thinking about FRAs as 'filling the gap' provides a useful introduction to the concept of FRA pricing, there is a need for a more accurate formula for use in practice. Figure 4.6 generalises the risk-free arbitrage process using algebraic symbols, and derives the desired formula including consideration of the interest-on-interest.

FIGURE 4.5
Further examples of FRA pricing

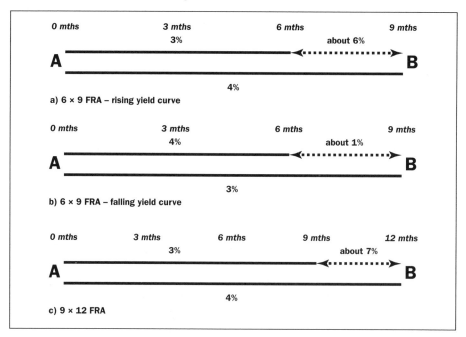

a) 6 × 9 FRA – rising yield curve

b) 6 × 9 FRA – falling yield curve

c) 9 × 12 FRA

FIGURE 4.6

Algebraic terms used for FRA pricing

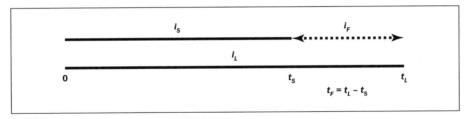

If we equate the returns through both investment paths in the diagram, we obtain this equality for periods of time up to one year:

$$(1 + i_s t_s)(1 + i_F t_F) = (1 + i_L t_L) \tag{4.5}$$

where:

i_S is the cash market interest rate to the settlement date
i_L is the cash market interest rate to the maturity date
i_F is the FRA rate
t_S is the time from spot date to the settlement date
t_L is the time from spot date to the maturity date
t_F is the length of the contract period

and all interest rates are quoted as decimal fractions; all times as fractions of a year.

Substituting day counts instead of time fractions, equation 4.5 can be rearranged to solve for i_F:

$$i_F = \frac{i_L D_L - i_S D_S}{D_F \left(1 + i_S \dfrac{D_S}{B} \right)} \tag{4.6}$$

where:

D_S is the number of days from spot date to the settlement date
D_L is the number of days from spot date to the maturity date
D_F is the number of days in the contract period
B is the day count convention (e.g. 360 for dollars, 365 for sterling)

and the other symbols are as in equation 4.5.

For example, if we take the dates given earlier in this chapter for the 1 × 4 FRA, we get $D_S = 30$, $D_L = 124$ and $D_F = 94$. If $i_S = 4\%$ and $i_L = 4.20\%$, we can solve for i_F as follows:

$$i_F = \frac{0.0420 \times 124 - 0.04 \times 30}{94 \times \left(1 + 0.04 \times \dfrac{30}{360} \right)} = 0.042497 \approx 4.25\% \tag{4.7}$$

Now let's look at some actual cash market rates and FRA quotations, to see how they compare in practice with the formula above. On Friday 14th January 2011, US dollar LIBOR for different maturities were as shown in Table 4.1.

TABLE 4.1
US dollar LIBOR rates on 14th January 2011

Maturity	$ LIBOR
1 mth	0.26125%
3 mth	0.30313%
4 mth	0.34500%
6 mth	0.45469%
9 mth	0.61313%
12 mth	0.77969%

From these rates, we can first construct the dollar yield curve, which is pictured in Figure 4.7.

We can use these figures in conjunction with equation 4.6 to calculate the theoretical FRA rates for US dollars, and Table 4.2 compares these with the actual FRA offer rates quoted that day.

Although the calculated 1 × 4 rate is within a few basis points of the actual FRA rates quoted in the market, there are considerable discrepancies between calculated and actual rates for the other FRA periods.

FIGURE 4.7
US dollar LIBOR yield curve on 14 January 2011

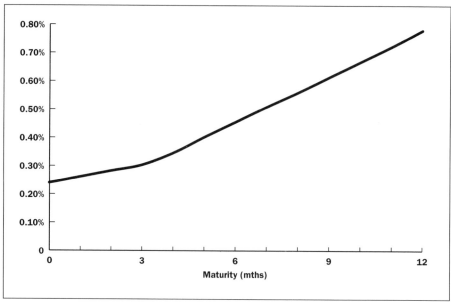

Source: LIBOR rates from British Bankers Association.

TABLE 4.2
Comparison of actual and theoretical US dollar FRA rates

FRA period	Calculated rate	Market rates	Difference (bp)
1 × 4	0.38%	0.35%	+3
3 × 6	0.60%	0.41%	+19
6 × 9	0.92%	0.50%	+42
9 × 12	1.27%	0.63%	+64
6 × 12	1.10%	0.56%	+54

In the past there used to be a much closer agreement between the two sets of rates. In the aftermath of the credit crisis of 2007–2008, however, a gap has opened up between actual LIBOR rates and the prices of derivatives derived from them. The reason for this is credit risk. Someone selling an FRA on $1m is *notionally* making a deposit, and if the counterparty were to default the loss is limited to the potential settlement sum to be received, a tiny fraction of the $1m notional. Someone depositing $1m would stand to lose everything if the counterparty were to default, a much bigger credit risk. As a result, LIBOR rates embed a premium for credit risk which is greater the longer the tenor, whereas FRA and other derivative rates have little or no such embedded premium. This is one factor explaining the widening difference seen in Table 4.2.

Another aspect of this credit risk affects the term structure of LIBOR itself. It used to be the case that an investor should be indifferent between receiving three-month LIBOR and receiving one-month LIBOR compounded over three successive months. By extension this meant that all LIBOR tenors were considered to be financially equivalent. Since 2007 credit risk has eroded this equivalence; three-month LIBOR is now greater than the compounding of the three one-month rates because of the greater credit risk involved in lending for a single three-month period compared with lending for one month at a time.

Another way to visualise this is to calculate the six-month rate by compounding the three-month LIBOR rate with the 3 × 6 FRA rate, and compare this with the six-month LIBOR rate itself. Figure 4.8 illustrates this and shows how the world changed in 2007. From January 2000 until July 2007 the two rates pictured in the upper chart are virtually identical; the average difference between them was just 2bp. From August 2007 onwards the six-month LIBOR rate averaged 21bp higher than the compounded three-month rates. Quotes simply reflected investors' fears that lending to a bank for six months was a more risky proposition than lending for three months and then reviewing the alternatives.

The fact that there is a gap between the LIBOR-implied FRA rates and actual FRA rates does not imply that there is a risk-free arbitrage opportunity. If you lent $1m for 12 months to Bank X at 0.78%, borrowed $1m for 9 months at 0.61% from Bank Y, and bought the 9 × 12 FRA for 0.63% you would not lock in a risk-free profit of 65bp p.a. for three months. If Bank X were to fail at any time over the 12-month period, you would lose your $1m – and all for a potential profit of $1,633.

FIGURE 4.8
Three-month LIBOR and 3 × 6 FRA compared with six-month LIBOR 2000–2012

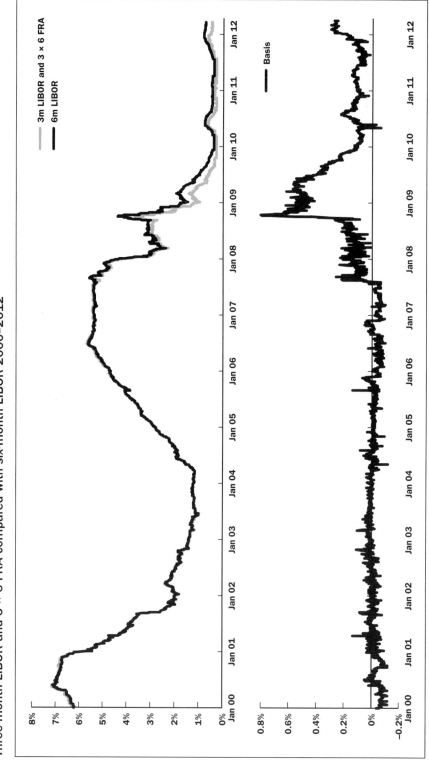

Source: LIBOR rates from FRED® – Economic and Financial Database (St Louis FRB); FRA rates from Barclays.

There is an analogous example in section 6.2 of Chapter 6, which looks at the pricing of short-term interest rate (STIR) futures contracts. Interestingly, we show at the end of that section that while there may not be a close fit between FRA rates and LIBOR rates, there is a close connection between FRA rates and STIR futures prices. This is not surprising because FRAs in practice are hedged with interest rate futures rather than Eurocurrency deposits.

4.7 Behaviour of FRA rates

We have so far determined what FRA rates should be in absolute terms. This is an important consideration for anyone buying or selling FRAs in order to hedge existing interest rate exposures, or using FRAs to speculate. A bank trading FRAs, however, will also be very concerned about the sensitivity of FRA rates to *changes* in interest rates.

To see how FRA rates move, let's go back to the 6 × 9 FRA shown in Figure 4.5a. The figures showed that if six-month rates were 3% and nine-month rates were 4%, the 6 × 9 FRA would be priced at about 6%. Now consider what would happen if these component rates were to change. Figure 4.9 analyses the effects of a 1% rise in just the six-month rate, a 1% rise in just the nine-month rate, and then a rise in both rates together.

Remember that the principle of risk-free arbitrage requires that the total return be the same, whichever way the investor gets from A to B. If the rate for the first period increases as in Figure 4.9a, the FRA rate must decrease. How much the FRA rate falls depends on the ratio of the deferment period to the contract period. In this example, the deferment period of six months is twice as long as the contract period of three months. For a 1% rise in the six-month rate, the FRA rate therefore should fall by about 2%.

Similarly, if the rate for the total period increases, the FRA rate must now increase, this time depending on the ratio of the total period to the contract period. For a 6 × 9 FRA, we would therefore expect the FRA rate to increase by 3% for a 1% rise in the nine-month rate. This is illustrated in Figure 4.9b.

FIGURE 4.9a
Sensitivity of FRA rates to changes in interest rates

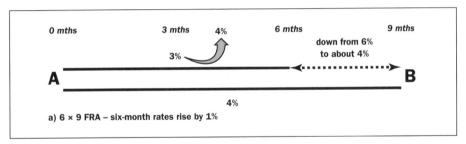

a) 6 × 9 FRA – six-month rates rise by 1%

FIGURE 4.9b–c

Sensitivity of FRA rates to changes in interest rates

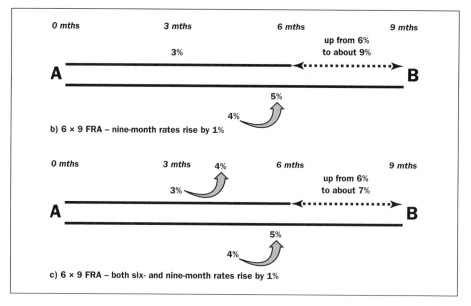

Finally, common sense tells us that FRA rates should follow interest rates generally. For a general rise in interest rates of 1%, as pictured in Figure 4.9c, we would expect FRA rates also to increase by about 1%, and this is what we find. If the two previous scenarios are combined, the same result follows. A 1% rise in both the six- and nine-month rates should drop the FRA rate by 2% and then immediately raise it by 3%, a net increase of 1%.

We could obtain the same result mathematically by applying calculus to equation 4.6. If we take the partial derivatives of i_F with respect to i_S and to i_L, we obtain to a first approximation:

$$\frac{\partial i_F}{\partial i_S} \approx -\frac{D_S}{D_F} \tag{4.8}$$

$$\frac{\partial i_F}{\partial i_L} \approx \frac{D_L}{D_F} \tag{4.9}$$

$$\frac{\partial i_F}{\partial i_{ALL}} \approx 1 \tag{4.10}$$

Equation 4.10 showing the sensitivity of FRA rates to a general movement in interest rates follows from equations 4.8 and 4.9 because $D_F = D_L - D_S$.

A useful way to summarise these findings is to construct a 'behaviour profile' for some of the standard FRAs. Figure 4.10 demonstrates how many basis points each FRA moves if:

FIGURE 4.10
FRA behaviour profiles

	$i_S \nearrow$ 1bp	$i_L \nearrow$ 1bp	i_S & $i_L \nearrow$ 1bp
3–6mth FRA	–1	+2	+1
6–9mth FRA	–2	+3	+1
9–12mth FRA	–3	+4	+1
6–12mth FRA	–1	+2	+1

i) the short-term interest rate i_S increases by one basis point

ii) the long-term interest rate i_L increases by one basis point

iii) both rates increase by one basis point.

We now have a good idea of what FRAs are, how FRA rates are derived, and how these prices change when interest rates move. This chapter has also provided some basic examples illustrating the use of FRAs in practice. Chapter 18 provides a deeper appraisal of FRA applications, and compares FRAs with other interest rate risk-management tools.

Notes

1 The term *over the counter* describes transactions undertaken directly between two parties – typically between a bank and a customer, or between two banks. This is in contrast to exchange-traded products such as futures, where transactions take place on an organised exchange, and where prices are widely disseminated.

2 Notionals outstanding come from the *BIS Quarterly Review* (December 2010 and June 2002), while turnover figures come from the *Triennial Central Bank Survey* (September 2010 and March 2005).

3 As section 4.4 explains, the exact sum depends upon the number of days in the period covered, and is then discounted to adjust for the timing of the payment.

4 As 11th August 2012 is a Saturday, the maturity date of the three-month period starting on 11th May rolls forward from 11th August to 13th August, the following business day.

5 The full details of the LIBOR methodology are set out on the British Bankers' Association website: www.bbalibor.com. However, the Wheatley Review of LIBOR published in September 2012 made a number of recommendations for changes to the LIBOR rate determination mechanism. At the time of writing, the final details of the resulting changes are being discussed.

5

FINANCIAL FUTURES

Futures contracts and futures exchanges have been in operation since the middle of the nineteenth century, when the Chicago Board of Trade first started to offer 'to arrive' and 'time' contracts on agricultural products. Surprisingly, more than 100 years were to pass before *financial futures* contracts were conceived in the early 1970s. Since then, financial futures have become a vital mainstay for the other financial markets.

Financial futures contracts are used directly by those exposed to risk and, more significantly, by financial institutions needing to hedge their books of OTC products. Trading in financial futures has become so significant that in a number of important markets the volume of futures traded exceeds that in the original market upon which the contract was based. For example, the value of the shares represented by trading in S&P stock-index futures each day normally exceeds that of the actual shares traded on the New York Stock Exchange.[1]

This chapter introduces financial futures, and explains some of the terminology and procedures unique to the futures markets. Chapters 6 and 7 then go on to explore specific types of futures contract in more detail.

5.1 A brief history of futures markets

It was the collapse of the fixed exchange rate regime in the early 1970s that provided the initial impetus for financial futures. Figure 5.1 shows the €/$ exchange rate in the period 1963–2010, compiled from $/DEM figures from 1963–1998 and €/$ figures from 1999–2010. The chart clearly shows the transition from fixed exchange rates in the 1960s to floating exchange rates in the 1970s and beyond.

FIGURE 5.1
€/$ exchange rate 1963–2010

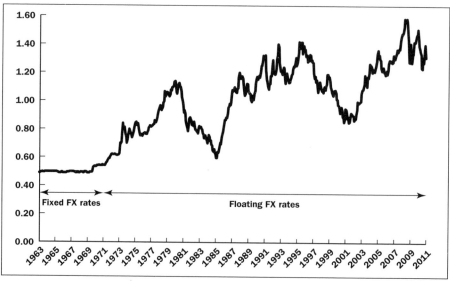

Source: FX rates from www.oanda.com

The resultant impact on volatility[2] over the same period is pictured in Figure 5.2. Annual volatility averaged only 0.4% over the five-year period from 1963 to 1967, but increased sevenfold to 2.9% over the next five years, 1968 to 1972. Then, over the next four decades annual volatility averaged around 9%, a further increase of between three and four times.

Officials at the Chicago Mercantile Exchange – then and now one of the largest futures exchanges in the world – correctly anticipated that demand for an efficient way to hedge financial risk would grow. Research was undertaken to determine the viability of trading contracts based on financial instruments rather than on physical commodities. This project culminated in the establishment of the International Monetary Market (IMM) of the CME, and the launch in 1972 of futures contracts based on foreign currencies.

The new regime of floating exchange rates was to lead to increased volatility in interest rates, both short-term and long-term. In 1975, the first interest-rate futures contract – based on the US Government National Mortgage Association (GNMA) securities – was launched by the 'other' Chicago futures exchange, the Chicago Board of Trade.

The 1980s and 1990s saw the expansion of futures trading to other countries. In the UK, the London International Financial Futures Exchange (LIFFE) opened its doors in 1982 with a range of contracts, some based on the dollar, some on the pound sterling. In France, the Marché A Terme d'Instruments

FIGURE 5.2
Annual volatility of $/DEM and €/$ exchange rates 1963–1998 and 1999–2010

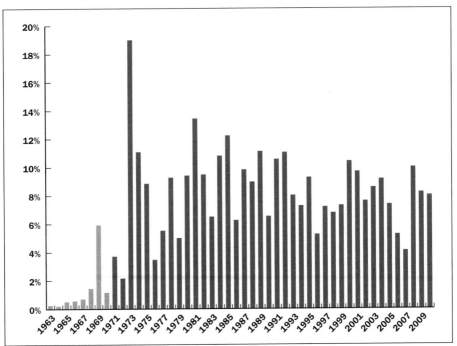

Source: FX rates from www.oanda.com and author's calculations.

Financiers (MATIF) started futures trading in Paris in 1986. SOFFEX opened in Switzerland (1988), the DTB in Germany (1990), the ÖTOB in Austria (1991) and the MIF in Italy (1992).

In the 2000s, there was massive consolidation between futures exchanges. LIFFE was acquired by Euronext in 2002, which in turn was acquired by the NYSE in 2007. It is now known as NYSE Liffe. The MATIF merged with the Paris Bourse in 1999, which then became Euronext, and its surviving contracts now trade on NYSE Liffe. In 1998 SOFFEX merged with the DTB (by then already part of the Deutsche Börse Group) to form Eurex. ÖTOB was merged with the Vienna Stock Exchange in 1997, and MIF was acquired by the Borsa Italiana in 1998, which in turn was acquired by the London Stock Exchange in 2007. Finally, and perhaps most importantly, in 2007 the CME and CBOT merged to form the CME Group.

As a result of this consolidation, there are now just three futures exchanges of global importance: the CME Group in Chicago, Eurex in Frankfurt and NYSE Liffe in London.

Table 5.1 lists those futures contracts in which the heaviest trading currently takes place, and provides some indication of the relative trading volumes in US dollar equivalents. The contracts listed fall into four categories:

- short-term interest rate futures – like the Eurodollar, Euribor and three-month sterling

- stock-index futures – like the S&P 500, Euro STOXX 50, FTSE 100 and Nikkei 225

- bond futures – like the US T-Note and the Euro-Bund

- currency futures – like the euro against the US dollar.

TABLE 5.1

Top futures contracts

Contract	Exchange	Monthly volume[1] (contracts)	Monthly volume[2] ($bn equivalent)	Open interest[3] (contracts)
Eurodollar	CME	55,512,933	$55,513bn	8,100,388
E-mini S&P 500	CME	45,467,901	$2,684bn	2,870,309
Euro STOXX 50	Eurex	30,671,840	$1,131bn	2,787,734
10yr US T-Note	CME	29,360,310	$2,936bn	1,360,397
Euro-Bund	Eurex	21,850,173	$3,717bn	974,038
Euribor	NYSE Liffe	19,446,398	$25,656bn	2,938,430
3-mth sterling	NYSE Liffe	10,596,045	$8,191bn	2,142,565
Euro	CME	8,241,782	$1,359bn	203,940
FTSE 100	NYSE Liffe	2,467,092	$218bn	623,146
Nikkei 225	Osaka	1,493,540	$174bn	416,375

Source: Author's calculations based on published exchange statistics.

[1]November 2010.

[2]Based on market rates 30th November 2010 (€1=$1.3193).

[3]At end of November 2010.

Although some of the earliest contracts – like that on the GNMA – have since diminished in importance or been withdrawn, the growth in financial futures has continued unabated, to the extent that financial futures nowadays completely dominate the activity of futures markets around the world. In 1971, futures exchanges traded only commodities contracts – agricultural, energy and metals. By the end of 2010, financial futures had grown to take up 87% of total futures exchange trading volume, squeezing traditional contracts to less than 13%. Figure 5.3 highlights this by showing the breakdown of trading volume by category, and demonstrating the total dominance of financial futures.

Competition between exchanges has ensured progression and innovation, in both the variety of contracts offered and the systems used for futures trading. In particular, electronic trading has now replaced the traditional trading pits where face-to-face trading used to take place (this development is discussed in section 5.3).

5.2 What is a financial future?

The standard textbook definition of a futures contract goes something like this:

- a legally binding agreement
- to take or make delivery
- of a given quantity and quality of a commodity
- at an agreed price
- on a specific date or dates in the future.

However, there is a much simpler way to define the essence of a futures contract:

A futures contract fixes the price and conditions

NOW

for a transaction that will take place in the

FUTURE.

Before the advent of financial futures, the commodities that were the subjects of futures contracts included agricultural products such as sugar, soybeans or live cattle, and physical commodities such as crude oil, aluminium or gold. A financial future is just like any other futures contract, except that the 'commodity' is a financial instrument. In some cases the instrument is tangible, like a treasury bond or foreign currency. In other cases the instrument is intangible, like a stock index or an interest rate. Section 5.7 explains what happens on the expiry date of a futures contract when the underlying instrument is intangible and cannot actually be delivered.

In the jargon of futures trading, the markets in which the underlying commodities are traded are called the *cash markets*, because cash normally changes hands when the commodities are bought and sold. In the wider context, the term 'cash markets' includes all the markets other than the derivatives markets.

FIGURE 5.3

Breakdown of futures exchange contracts by category

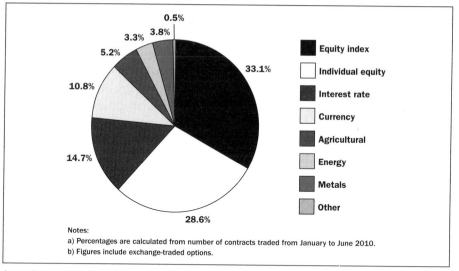

Notes:
a) Percentages are calculated from number of contracts traded from January to June 2010.
b) Figures include exchange-traded options.

Source: Futures Industry Association
* The breakdown of futures exchange contracts by category is based on the number of futures and options contracts traded from January to June of 2010.

5.3 Futures trading – from pits to screens

In its day, the 1983 film *Trading Places* probably did much to create the image of futures markets in the popular mind. While life on the floor of a futures exchange may not always have been as frenzied as Eddie Murphy and Dan Aykroyd portrayed, the film focused attention on the *futures pit* where futures trading once took place.

Until the late 1980s, futures exchanges were similar to traditional stock exchanges. Orders to buy and sell futures contracts may have come from any-where in the world, but they all converged on one small and crowded spot located on the floor of the futures exchange, the futures pit. It was there that all trades actually took place. Brokers representing the interests of buyers and sellers would shout or quickly flash hand signals to each other to execute the trades. The motivation for executing all trades in one physical location was *transparency*. Everything was done in full public view and was subject to care-ful scrutiny by the exchange authorities. Traders signalled the prices at which they were prepared to deal. Only the highest bids and lowest offers prevailed; traders with other prices remained silent. All trades had to be executed within the pit, in public, out loud. The market forces of supply and demand – the rela-tive volume of buyers and sellers – were there for all to see.

More recently, however, technology has provided the futures markets with a modern alternative – screen trading and high-speed electronic execution. It started in 1988 with SOFFEX (the Swiss Options and Financial Futures

Exchange), which was the first fully automated futures exchange. The DTB (the Deutsche Terminbörse) followed suit in 1990, licensing SOFFEX's proprietary system. Both SOFFEX and DTB started as 100% electronic exchanges.

At first it was thought that an electronic trading system located in cyber-space could not replicate the perceived efficiency and flexibility of face-to-face trading on the floor of a physical exchange, especially in times of high volatility. However, advances in communications and systems have since turned the tables. Within two years of its opening, the DTB became the third-largest derivatives exchange in Europe. By 1996 it had overtaken the MATIF, and by mid-1997 the DTB had captured more than 50% of the lucrative Bund contract previously dominated by LIFFE. A year later, the DTB – which had by then evolved into Eurex – took the remaining 50% market share from LIFFE.

It was this sudden and dramatic loss of market share of a product that had once been a third of its total business that prompted LIFFE to change track completely. In 1998, it started developing the LIFFE CONNECT electronic trading system, and by the end of 1999 all of LIFFE's pit trading was successfully transferred to the new system and its trading floors were closed down. This move was the right strategic choice, and LIFFE has since licensed its system to a number of futures exchanges around the world. Even the original home of futures, Chicago, has gone the same way. In 2010, 98% of futures trades across all types – including traditional commodity futures – were executed electronically. Trading pits have gone the way of the dinosaur.

The efficiency of electronic trading, coupled with execution speeds measured in milliseconds, guarantees that the price obtained is the very best available at the very moment the trade is executed. High volumes in important contracts like the Eurodollar, E-mini S&P 500, Euro STOXX 50, 10yr T-Note and Euro-Bund futures, ensure that the spread between bid and offer is usually just one *tick*.[3]

One of the factors which contributes to volume is *standardisation*. Matters such as the underlying financial instrument, the amount of the underlier traded, delivery dates and other technical specifications are all pre-defined. This leaves only two details to be settled when a futures trade takes place: the number of contracts bought or sold, and the price.

This standardisation within the futures market means that users of futures contracts may sometimes have to accept a compromise: the futures contract they buy or sell may not match their precise needs. However, funnelling trades from a broad cross-section of users down to a small number of futures contracts creates tremendous liquidity. Futures like the ones just mentioned each trade more than 1 million contracts each day. Moreover, simplifying the negotiations to the fixing just of size and price makes for speed. The resultant volume of trading, speed of execution and transparency of prices are all fundamental to the success of futures markets.

What the OTC market can offer instead is flexibility. Almost every aspect of an OTC deal can be negotiated and the terms varied to suit the parties' particular needs.

5.4 Buying and selling

In the cash markets, there is sometimes a procedural distinction between the act of buying and the act of selling. This is particularly true when the commodity is a security, such as a bond or a share, where market rules sometimes impose restrictions on selling short, i.e. selling something that one does not currently own.

In the futures markets there is no such distinction. Buying and selling contracts are completely symmetrical transactions, and the conditions imposed on holders of long and short positions are identical. This is entirely appropriate, because a futures contract binds the parties to a transaction which will take place on a future date, not now. It is true that the party who is short futures is obligated to deliver the underlying commodity on the maturity date of the contract. However, while the short may not be in possession of the underlying asset right now, there is nothing preventing him from purchasing the commodity in the meantime, or from reversing the futures contract before maturity.

5.5 The clearing mechanism

An important aspect of futures markets is the clearing mechanism. This mechanism simplifies trading, increases liquidity, and effectively eliminates counterparty risk. The last feature has proven particularly attractive following the 2007–2008 credit crisis, and has since been adapted for use in some of the OTC derivatives markets.

For any trade to take place there must first be a buyer and a seller, who come together in order to consummate the deal. Their relationship is but a fleeting one, however, because the clearing mechanism interposes a third party – the *clearing house* – between buyer and seller. Figure 5.4 illustrates how the clearing house fits in. As we will see, this intervention provides a number of significant benefits.

The clearing house is the organisation responsible for all the settlement procedures arising from futures trading at a particular exchange. It may be owned by the futures exchange itself, like CME Clearing, or may be independent, like LCH.Clearnet in London.

Only members of the futures exchange are allowed to execute futures trades, acting either for themselves or on behalf of customers who wish to trade futures. After every trade is executed, however, the clearing house interposes itself between buyer and seller, as Figure 5.4b illustrates. This is a very important feature of futures trading because it effectively removes counterparty risk. Although the clearing house never initiates any transaction, after every trade it becomes the buyer to every seller, and the seller to every buyer.

In the OTC market, customers and banks are justifiably concerned about the integrity of the counterparties with whom they are dealing, and potential trades may be called off if the counterparty risk is considered too high.

By contrast, there is little need to fear counterparty risk when dealing in the futures markets. The identity of the counterparty when a deal is struck is of no

FIGURE 5.4
The clearing mechanism

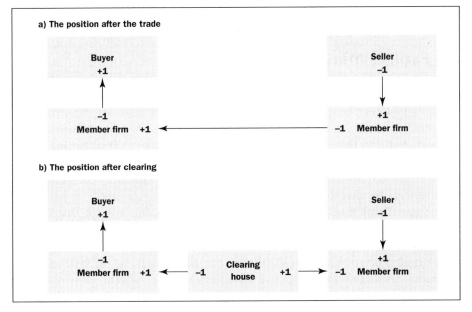

concern at all; whoever one buys from or sells to will immediately be replaced by the clearing house. Of course, this is not a complete elimination of risk, but a transfer of risk from the multitude of potential counterparties to one specific one, the clearing house itself. However, clearing houses are invariably well capitalised, and owned either by one or more exchanges or by a broad consortium of major financial institutions. No futures clearing house has ever failed, since the bankruptcy of a clearing house would probably imply the collapse of the entire financial system, an event that hopefully is only a very remote possibility.

Removing specific counterparty risk means that trading can proceed swiftly, without pausing to check credit risk. Once again, there are only two variables which need to be agreed when trading in futures: size and price.

The clearing mechanism has a further important advantage. No matter how many times one enters the market to buy or sell, and no matter when the deals are struck, there will always be one ultimate counterparty, the clearing house. If a customer buys ten contracts one day and sells these contracts one week later, the customer will end up with no position. This is not the same as having two offsetting positions which remain on the books. Once a futures position is closed out, all profits or losses to date are realised, and nothing whatsoever remains on the customer's books. This feature enhances liquidity and makes it very easy to reverse any position in futures.

This is in sharp contrast to the OTC market. If a customer buys an FRA from one bank and then sells an identical FRA to another bank, there are two FRAs on the customer's books. This will utilise two credit lines, and result in two settlement sums, even if the FRAs cover the same period. Of course, most banks stand ready to quote a price to a customer for cancelling an FRA or other OTC derivative, but the customer must accept this price if he wants to liquidate the position completely.

5.6 Futures margins

An important benefit of the clearing mechanism is the transfer of counterparty risk from members of the futures exchange to the clearing house. However, the potential for loss is enormous when one considers the volume of futures contracts traded, and the underlying positions these represent. The clearing house could not contemplate taking on such a risk without some means of protecting its own financial position in the event of default by a member. The protection necessary is provided through the *margining system*.

The specification of every futures contract defines the level of margin that must be deposited by members with the clearing house. For example, at the time of writing, the initial margin required for positions in the ten-year T-Note future traded on the CBOT is $2,160 per contract. If a member were long 100 contracts, he would have to deposit cash or securities with the clearing house to the value of $216,000. The margin requirement would be just the same if the position were short 100 contracts.

The margin is in no way a 'down-payment' for the underlying commodity. As we will see in the next section, futures contracts seldom result in physical delivery of the underlying, so it would be inappropriate to levy such a requirement. Futures margins are therefore quite unlike buying shares or bonds on margin, where the margin does act like a deposit. Instead, futures margins act as a 'performance bond'. They provide the clearing house with a financial guarantee against default by a member. When the member eventually closes out a position, the margin is refunded.

How large should the margin requirement be? The simple answer is that the margin per contract should exceed the maximum amount that could potentially be lost while running a position. Unfortunately, some contracts have maturity dates stretching years into the future. If the margin were deposited just once, when the position was initially established, and then refunded when the position was finally liquidated, the potential losses could be sizeable over a long holding period. Such a simple margining system would not function effectively.

To make the system work, an integral part of the margining process is a daily marking-to-market. At the close of trading, the futures exchange publishes the *settlement price*, the official closing price that day. Every outstanding position is then marked to this closing price. Any losses incurred since the previous settlement price, or the trading price for new positions established that day, are debited to the member's margin account and must be made good the following morning. Any profits are credited to the account and may be withdrawn the next day. This creates a distinction between the *initial margin* paid in when a position is first established, and the *variation margin*, which may be positive or negative, which are the daily cash flows arising from the regular marking-to-market procedure.

A number of exchanges, particularly those in the United States, adopt a two-tier margining system. A lower margin level, called the *maintenance margin*, is set usually at between 74% and 80% of the initial margin level. When a futures position is first established, the member must deposit the initial margin in the usual way. However, margin calls then occur only when the margin account falls below the maintenance level, at which juncture the member is required to restore the balance once again to the level of the initial margin.

With the daily marking-to-market process, the margin accounts are replenished every working day. The potential loss is then limited to the maximum amount the market price can move in a single day, rather than over the entire life of the contract.

An illustration of the daily workings of the margining system may help to clarify the process. Let us suppose a member is long one contract in the E-mini S&P 500 stock-index future traded on the CME. The value per full point is defined as $50 and, at the time of writing, the initial margin is $5,625 per contract, while the maintenance level is $4,500. Let us further suppose that the contract was purchased on Monday at a price of 1275, the daily settlement prices from Monday to Thursday were 1280, 1260, 1250 and 1255, and that the position was liquidated on Friday at a price of 1265. The resulting margin flows are illustrated in Table 5.2.

TABLE 5.2
Illustration of margin flows

Day	Closing price	Change in price	Margin account ($)	Margin flow[1] ($)	Explanation
Monday	1280	+5	5,625	−5,375	Initial margin of $5,625 *less* profit of $250
Tuesday	1260	−20	4,625	0	Although the position has lost $1,000, the margin account is still above the maintenance level
Wednesday	1250	−10	5,625	−1,500	A further loss of $500 depletes the margin account to $4,125. The margin call restores the account to the initial margin level
Thursday	1255	+5	5,875	0	Member opts to leave $250 profit in margin account
Friday	n/a	+10	0	+6,375	Previous day's margin account of $5,875 plus today's profit of $500

[1]These flows all take place the following morning.

The member need only pay $5,375 into the margin account on Monday, because the $250 profit earned will be credited to the margin account, bringing the total balance to the $5,625 required. Losses on Tuesday reduce the margin account to $4,625 but, as this is still above the maintenance level of $4,500, there is no margin call. Unfortunately, a further loss of $500 on Wednesday leads to the margin account falling to $4,125. This is now too low, and the margin call of $1,500, which must be paid in the following morning, restores the margin account back to the initial level of $5,625. On Thursday, a profit of $250 is earned, which could be withdrawn in cash on Friday morning. Instead, the member elects to have the balance credited to the margin account, bringing the balance to $5,875. Friday's profit of ten points – the difference between Thursday's settlement price and the selling price of 1265 – is also credited to the margin account, which can finally be liquidated on Monday.

Adding up the total margin flows, the member pays in $6,875 and is refunded $6,375. The net loss of $500 represents the ten-point difference between the original purchase price of 1275 and the final selling price of 1265.

While margin can certainly be posted as cash, sometimes in a range of currencies, most futures exchanges will also accept a wide range of securities including national and international sovereign debt, gold, shares, and other securities, although most of these will be subject to a *haircut*.[4] By depositing interest-bearing securities, members can effectively earn interest on their margin accounts. In addition, exchanges like the CME Group have also set up Collateral Management Programs, also known as Interest Earning Facilities (IEFs), which allow members to deposit margin in selected interest-bearing money market mutual funds administered by banks like JP Morgan, but controlled by the exchange.

The operation of the margining system leads to a useful side effect. All profits and losses are realised on a daily basis *in cash*. This differs from the so-called cash markets where mark-to-market losses, while real enough, are only on paper. A losing position in the cash markets can accumulate paper losses, but these may not be heeded until the position is closed out, by which time it is too late. By contrast, a losing position in the futures markets results in a steady stream of margin calls, and the resulting cash drain enforces a financial discipline on everyone using futures.

Variation margins are calculated at the end of the trading day by using the settlement price that evening, and are normally due for payment by a specified time the following morning. In the unusual event that a member defaults by failing to pay in sufficient variation margin, the exchange has the right to liquidate the futures position, take any losses out of the margin account, and eventually refund anything remaining. The clearing house would suffer a loss only if the price movement that day exceeded the margin account; in such a case the loss would be met from a general fund maintained by all members of the exchange. However, by setting the margin level for each contract higher than the maximum likely daily loss, the chance of such occurrences is minimised.

There are some variations on margining systems adopted by different futures exchanges around the world. Most exchanges recognise that a member who is long a futures contract for one delivery date, and short *the same contract* for another delivery date, is exposed to far less risk than an outright position in either date. Rather than exacting a separate margin for each contract, exchanges usually specify a reduced margin for the combined position. This reduced margin is called a *spread margin* or *intra-commodity margin*. For example, recall that the E-mini S&P 500 stock-index contract introduced earlier had an initial margin of $5,625 and a maintenance margin of $4,500 at the time of writing. However, the spread margins were respectively just $38 and $30 for the pair of offsetting contracts, less than 1% of the corresponding outright margins. These intra-commodity spread margins – applying to offsetting positions in different dates for the same contract – are quite common. Some exchanges also allow inter-commodity spreads, offering a reduced margin requirement for offsetting positions in related contracts, for example, E-mini S&P 500 against E-mini NASDAQ Composite.

Earlier we mentioned that some futures exchanges define both an initial margin and a lower maintenance margin level. Rather than insisting that the margin account always be maintained at the level of the initial margin, the futures exchange tolerates the balance in the margin account lying between the levels defined by the initial and maintenance levels. This can drastically reduce the frequency of margin calls, particularly when the futures price is fluctuating up and down, because such calls will occur only if and when the margin account falls below the maintenance level. This system therefore reduces the cost and administrative burden associated with running a futures account.

This is illustrated in Figure 5.5, which contrasts the margin payments under a scheme having just one margin level, with a scheme having a maintenance margin level as well. In this example, the maintenance level is set at five ticks below the initial margin level, and the settlement price movements in both cases follow the sequence: –3, +2, –3, –5, +2, +3, –2, –4, –3.

Figure 5.5a shows that nine separate flows of variation margin occur, one following every change in the settlement price. Compare this with Figure 5.5b, where there is only one margin call after the fourth day when the balance in the margin account fell below the maintenance margin level.

FIGURE 5.5
Comparison of margining systems

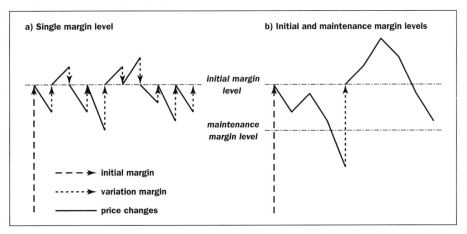

Finally, in this chapter we have discussed margin requirements only for members of the futures exchange. Non-members – many banks, and most corporate customers and private individuals – are also subject to margin requirements, but these are set at the discretion of the member firm through which they are dealing. The largest corporate customers, ones who can offer adequate security and have access to same-day payments systems, may be offered the same terms as the member firm itself. Other customers would be expected to lodge additional security and maintain margin levels at some multiple of those set by the exchange. Even so, the tremendous leverage and opportunities offered through futures markets still make them a highly attractive tool in financial engineering applications. Remember also that the amount of margin deposited is not a cost but a temporary transfer of assets. It is only interest forgone on the margin that constitutes a cost. If interest-bearing securities are lodged, or an IEF is used, the margin account is effectively costless.

5.7 Physical delivery versus cash settlement

The definitions of futures contracts have traditionally been based upon the physical delivery of some underlying commodity. For example, the crude oil contract traded on the New York Mercantile Exchange (part of the CME Group) calls for the delivery of 1,000 barrels (42,000 US gallons) of West Texas Intermediate crude oil. Although speculators undoubtedly form a significant proportion of the oil futures market, many of those using this contract will be oil producers or consumers. It may therefore come as a surprise to learn that only a tiny fraction of these contracts results in the physical delivery of oil. The remainder are reversed prior to the expiry of the contract and any profits or losses realised in cash. This feature is not unique to the oil futures market; few futures contracts of any kind result in physical delivery of the underlying commodity.

To understand why most holders of futures contracts choose to close out their position prior to maturity, one must look at the reasons for using futures contracts. Here one must consider separately the motives of the two principal classes of user.

Speculators intend to benefit from an anticipated movement in market prices; they are just seeking profits and certainly have no wish to get involved with the underlying commodity. Speculators will normally reverse their positions well before the maturity date of the contract.

Hedgers seek protection against adverse price movements in the underlying commodity, and futures provide an efficient means to manage this price risk. In this light, futures should be considered as a means to reduce or eliminate price risk, rather than as a source of supply for the underlying commodity. Those whose business involves handling the commodity will have long-standing arrangements for buying and selling the commodity, and well-established links with suppliers, shippers and agents. Therefore, even when hedgers may need to execute the underlying transaction, they will normally find it more convenient to use their existing channels to execute the physical transaction, and use futures as the means to reduce the price risk arising from these transactions. So hedgers will normally also close out their positions before the futures contracts mature.

Given that physical delivery of the underlying commodity seldom occurs, it became apparent that having to design futures contracts to include the provision for physical delivery imposed unnecessary restrictions and complexities. This paved the way for the concept of futures contracts based on intangible commodities like the level of a stock-index, or the rate of interest.

A good example of such a contract is the E-mini S&P 500 contract introduced earlier. In this contract, the index is given a financial value of $50 per full point. If the index were at 1500, it would be deemed to be 'worth' $75,000. If the index rose to 1510, it would then be 'worth' $75,500. Someone who bought an E-mini S&P 500 contract at 1500, and sold it at 1510 would make $500 profit. This profit would be realised in cash through the margining process. Even if the position were held until maturity, the value of the contract would be determined in just the same way, and *cash-settled*. With these contracts, physical delivery is never a consideration; all positions will be rewarded or penalised by a cash payment from one party to the other through their respective margin accounts.

Although many financial futures contracts allow for physical delivery, the most notable examples being contracts on government bonds, many of the newest contracts usually specify cash settlement, and preclude physical delivery. This simplifies the management of a futures book, and avoids a particular problem faced by those holding long futures positions. This problem arises when someone holding a short position in futures notifies their intention to make physical delivery. The futures exchange nominates someone who is long the futures, and calls on that person to receive the physical commodity. The nominee suddenly finds that, not only is their position closed out unexpectedly, but they must also go to the trouble of receiving and paying for the underlying, which may be inconvenient or costly.

Although the concept of cash settlement allows a much wider scope for the design of new futures contracts, it must still be possible for someone physically to create a matching position from other instruments, if they want to replicate the new futures contract. Were this not the case, it would be impossible to determine a fair price for the future, and would leave the new contract open to price manipulation. As the next two chapters will show, the design of interest-rate and stock-index contracts – two of the most heavily traded contracts involving cash settlement – allows these contracts to be synthesised from instruments readily traded in the cash markets. This guarantees that the cash and futures markets move closely in line with each other.

5.8 Futures and cash markets compared

We have examined the operation of futures markets and, where appropriate, contrasted futures with the cash and OTC markets. Table 5.3 summarises these differences.

TABLE 5.3

Futures markets and cash markets compared

Futures market	Cash or OTC market
■ Contract specifications are standardised	■ Every aspect of deal is negotiable
■ Clearing house guarantees against default of any specific counterparty	■ For standardised derivatives cleared with a central counterparty (CCP), the CCP guarantees performance; for other transactions there is counterparty risk
■ Positions easily reversed with anyone at any time	■ Positions can only be offset at discretion of deal counterparty
■ Requirement to meet daily margin requirements	■ No mandatory requirement for margin on non-CCP trades (although, in practice, most banks will require collateral)
■ Profits and losses realised in cash daily	■ Mark-to-market profits realisable only on paper
■ Most contracts are reversed or cash-settled; delivery of underlying is rare	■ Physical delivery is usual (except for certain derivatives)

5.9 The advantages of futures

We can summarise the advantages of the futures markets under a number of headings:

■ **Liquidity** – the standardisation of contracts and the efficiency of trading serve to encourage tremendous liquidity. In a number of cases, liquidity in the futures market exceeds that in the underlying cash market.

■ **Clearing** – the clearing mechanism removes individual counterparty risk and allows for the easy reversal of existing futures positions.

■ **Margining** – the margining system offers holders of futures contracts the ability to control large positions in the underlying financial commodity with the minimum of capital. Hedgers can reduce their risk exposure cheaply, and without the physical purchase or sale of underlying instruments. Speculators can exploit their views of market movements without committing vast cash resources or tying up credit lines.

- **Transaction costs** – futures exchanges aim to keep trading costs as low as possible. Normally, the cost of executing a futures contract is a fraction of the equivalent transaction in the OTC market.

These advantages must also be set against some of the limitations of futures markets:

- **Inflexibility** – futures markets require that the specification of each futures contract be rigidly standardised. OTC markets allow every aspect of a transaction to be individually negotiated.
- **Liquidity** – while liquidity may be very high for the futures contract with the nearest delivery date (the 'front contract'), for many futures there is limited or no liquidity in the 'back contracts'.
- **Margining** – some find that managing the margin account, and the resultant daily cash flows, is a considerable administrative burden.

These advantages and limitations must be weighed against each other before deciding which is more suitable for a given need: a futures contract or the corresponding OTC product. Chapter 18 provides a number of examples illustrating where and when futures can be used to achieve a particular hedging objective.

Notes

1   In November 2010, the value of shares traded on NYSE Euronext in New York was $1.4tn, but the dollar value of the 45m E-mini S&P 500 and S&P 500 contracts traded at the CME in Chicago was more than $2.8tn, twice as much.
2   The concept of volatility is explained in section 11.1 of Chapter 11.
3   A tick is the smallest difference between two adjacent prices.
4   A haircut is like a discount applied to the market value of the securities lodged. For example, a ten-year US Treasury Note might be subject to a 5% haircut, gold to 15% and S&P 500 stocks to 30%. This means that a member depositing shares currently valued at $1m would find that only $700,000 was counted as contributing to the margin requirement.

6

SHORT-TERM INTEREST
RATE FUTURES

The previous chapter introduced financial futures, and explained the terminology and procedures common to all contracts. In this chapter we will explore in detail one of the most heavily traded contracts – the short-term interest rate (STIR) future. Nearly all major exchanges offering financial futures contracts provide a market in these instruments, sometimes in more than one currency. NYSE Liffe, for example, lists three-month contracts in sterling, dollars, euros, Swiss francs and the Japanese yen. The CME in Chicago and SGX in Singapore both offer contracts in dollars and the yen. Sections in this chapter will explain how these contracts are priced, how they respond to shifts in market rates, their basic use in hedging, the link between these interest rate contracts and OTC products like FRAs, and the concept of spread positions. First, however, we need to define exactly what a short-term interest rate future is.

6.1 Definitions

Chapter 5 provided a simple but clear definition of any futures contract: a futures contract fixes the *price* and conditions now for a *transaction* that will take place in the future. In the case of a STIR future, the transaction is a notional fixed-term deposit, and the 'price' is the fixed rate of interest that will apply during the term of that deposit, which covers a particular period in the future. Buying a STIR contract is equivalent to making a deposit, while selling a STIR contract is equivalent to taking a deposit, or borrowing. However, it is important to note that, with a STIR contract, no actual depositing of cash or borrowing takes place. The purpose of the future, like an FRA, is to secure the interest rate for the future period in question, rather than to obtain a deposit facility or a credit line.

The three-month Eurodollar contract traded on the CME provides a typical example, and this contract is defined in Table 6.1. There are many similarities with the definition of an FRA, as the two products have much in common. Nonetheless, there are some important differences, as will be evident when we study each of the above terms in more detail. Each Eurodollar contract covers a notional dollar deposit having a fixed size of $1,000,000, and this defines the unit of trading. It is possible to buy or sell any whole number of contracts, but this restricts the size of deals to a multiple of $1,000,000 as contracts are not divisible. An FRA, by contrast, can be negotiated in any marketable amount, not necessarily an exact multiple of $1m.

Futures contracts originally involved the physical delivery of the underlying asset but, as we saw in Chapter 5 (section 5.7), cash settlement is normally the rule with financial futures contracts. Nonetheless, the term 'delivery' is still used to denote the date and time when contracts expire. All futures contracts follow a rigid calendar with pre-defined delivery dates, usually four per year, and nearly all financial futures are designed to have these dates falling in March, June, September and December. The *delivery months*, *delivery date* and *last trading day* together define exactly when these delivery dates occur.

TABLE 6.1

Definition of Eurodollar contract at the CME

Unit of trading	$1,000,000
Delivery months	March, June, September and December, plus the next four serial months not in the normal quarterly cycle
Delivery date	Third Wednesday of delivery month
Last trading day	11.00am two London business days prior to delivery date
Quotation	100.00 minus rate of interest
Tick size (minimum price movement)	0.0025% (nearest expiring contract) 0.0050% (all other contracts)
Tick value	0.0025% = $6.25 0.0050% = $12.50
Final settlement price	100 minus the BBA settlement rate for three-month US dollar deposits at 11:00am on the last trading day
Trading hours (open outcry)	07:20–14:00 CT
Trading hours (Globex electronic market)	17:00–16:00 CT (Sunday through Friday)

Source: Taken from the correct definition published by the CME in its website www.cmegroup.com

As an example, the March 2011 Eurodollar contract ceased trading at 11am on Monday 14th March 2011, and final cash settlement took place the following day. The notional deposit underlying this contract is one that would start on Wednesday 16th March and mature three months later. The two-day gap between the last trading date and the start of the underlying deposit arises from the definition of BBA LIBOR, which is the interbank deposit rate underlying the futures contract. For all currencies other than sterling, the LIBOR value date (i.e. the date when the deposit is actually made) is two days after the fixing date (the date when the rate is set). So the three-month dollar rate set at 11am on Monday 14th March 2011 applies to a three-month deposit placed on Wednesday 16th March and maturing on 16th June.

Recall that, by definition, buying a futures contract is equivalent to making a fixed-rate *deposit*. Someone who wanted to speculate using futures would wish to deposit funds (buy futures) at a high interest rate, and borrow funds (sell futures) at a low interest rate. Unfortunately, this implies a 'buy high, sell low' strategy, which is unnatural. For this reason, the original designers of interest rate futures decided that these contracts would be traded on an indexed 'price' rather than the interest rate itself, where the price is defined as:

$$P = 100 - i \tag{6.1}$$

where:

P is the price index

i is the futures-implied interest rate in percent

This system of *quotation* simply reverses the behaviour of futures prices when interest rates change. If interest rates rise, then the price falls; when rates fall, the price rises. Now traders can follow a 'buy low, sell high' strategy with success, so long as they follow the quoted price, rather than the rate.

As an example, suppose that futures were trading at exactly 96.00, corresponding to a futures-implied interest rate of 4.00%. A trader anticipates that rates will fall, and the price will rise. He buys ten contracts and waits. Within a few minutes, futures-implied interest rates have edged down to 3.95%, so that the futures price rises to 96.05. The trader closes out his position and makes five basis points of profit, having bought at 96.00 and sold at 96.05.

It is important to note that the futures price for these short-term contracts is not a price in the usual sense. A price of 96.00 does not mean $96, £96, or any other monetary amount. Rather, the futures price is just an alternative representation for the interest rate at which the underlying notional deposit or loan could be executed; it is a token for the general level of interest rates. The futures price is therefore more similar to a stock index, which indicates the general level of the stock market rather than the actual price of any particular share or group of shares.

Note that there is no need for these contortions when working with FRAs, because they were defined so that the buyer of an FRA is the notional borrower, not the depositor. If short-term interest futures had originally been defined in the same way, they could be traded by quoting the interest rate directly, just like FRAs.

All contracts specify the *minimum price movement* or *tick*, the smallest difference between two consecutive price quotations. This, along with the other definitions, enables the *tick value* to be calculated. With a minimum price movement of 0.005% for all but the front Eurodollar contract, a trading unit of $1,000,000, and a three-month contract period, the tick value is:

$$0.005\% \times \$1,000,000 \times \frac{3}{12} = \$12.50 \qquad (6.2)$$

Equation 6.2 is similar to equation 4.2, which defined the settlement sum for an FRA, but there are two notable differences.

As we have just seen, Eurodollar contracts currently use tick sizes of 0.005% and 0.0025%. Originally, however, these contracts were quoted to the nearest whole basis point, making the tick size 0.01% and the tick value $25. For this reason, you will sometimes still see references to the *full tick*, meaning the original tick size of 0.01%.

First, the futures contract is for a three-month deposit, and it therefore seems natural to use $\frac{3}{12}$ as the appropriate fraction of a year. However, nearly every other financial market uses a day-count fraction divided by 360 or 365. A three-month contract in the normal deposit and FRA markets would involve three calendar months, the period of which could vary between 87 and 94 days.[1] For example, the three-month period from Wednesday 16th March to Thursday

16th June is 92 days long. If the tick value for a 0.005% tick size were calculated using the exact number of days in the period and a divisor of 360, it would be $12.78 in this specific case, and in general could lie between $12.08 and $13.06. Furthermore, although the actual period between futures contracts is normally 91 days (i.e. from the third Wednesday in one delivery month to the third Wednesday in the delivery month three months later), it can occasionally be 84 or 98 days (e.g. Jun 2011 to Sep 2011). If the tick value were calculated using these day counts, it could fall between $11.67 and $13.61, a considerable range.

Second, the final cash settlement for a future takes place on the expiry date of the contract, which is at the *beginning* of the period covered by the underlying deposit.[2] Yet interest in the normal deposit markets is paid at the *end* of this period. FRAs allow for this by discounting the settlement sum, as explained in Chapter 4 (section 4.4). If the tick value for futures allowed for this, it could be as low as $11.53 for an 84-day period, if interest rates were at 5%.

Yet despite all this, the tick value for these particular futures contracts is always defined to be $12.50 for a 0.005% tick size. While this simplicity makes trading and settlement that much more straightforward, it can create extra work for those wishing to hedge the interest rate risk on an underlying exposure for which the interest is calculated using actual day counts. Adjustments can be made to account for the tick value always being $12.50, and these are explained in Chapter 18 (section 18.3).

The short-term interest rate contracts in other currencies are all defined in exactly the same manner, differing only in the unit of trading, the tick size, and in technical details like trading hours. For example, for the three-month sterling contract traded on NYSE Liffe the unit of trading is £500,000, the tick size is 0.01%, the tick value is £12.50, and the last trading date is the third Wednesday of the delivery month (not two days earlier, as with the Eurodollar contract).

6.2 STIR contracts pricing

Interest rate futures are invariably cash-settled, and the transaction that takes place on the delivery date is therefore only a notional depositor loan, not an actual one. Nonetheless, futures prices must still be closely related to rates in the cash markets just as FRA rates are.

What guarantees this relationship is the procedure on the last trading date, where the final settlement price for contracts is not determined by prices in the futures market, but rather by reference to the prevailing rates in the cash market itself. For example, the Exchange Delivery Settlement Price (EDSP) for the Eurodollar contract at the CME is defined as 100 minus the British Bankers' Association LIBOR rate for three-month dollar deposits at 11am that day, rounded to four decimal places (i.e. to the nearest 0.0001%). That for the sterling contract on NYSE Liffe is 100 minus the BBA LIBOR rate for three-month sterling deposits at 11am, this time rounded to three decimal places.

When a short-term interest rate futures contract expires, the futures price will be exactly equal to 100 minus the cash market interest rate, by definition.

In algebraic terms, we can say:

$$P_{EDSP} = 100 - i_{REF} \qquad (6.3)$$

where:

P_{EDSP} is the exchange delivery settlement price
i_{REF} is the reference market interest rate in percent

This definition ensures that, no matter what occurs during the life of a futures contract, the very final price will always match that in the cash markets.

Knowing this gives us the insight necessary to understand how futures prices should behave during the lifetime of the contract. The three-month cash market rate will act like a magnet, drawing the futures price ever closer. Prior to maturity, however, the futures price will not depend on where the cash market rate is right now, but where that rate is expected to be when the contract expires. Under normal market conditions, this will be the forward rate.

Chapter 4 (section 4.6) developed a formula for calculating the forward rate, and hence for pricing FRAs. Equation 4.6 can be used almost as it stands, except that we must first define some additional terms.

Let:

T_0 be the dealing date when the future is originally bought or sold
T_D be the last trading (or expiry) date for the futures contract
T_{SPOT} be the normal value date for cash market deposits traded on T_0
T_S be the normal value date for cash market deposits traded on T_D
T_L be the maturity date for a three-month cash market deposit traded on T_D

Equation 4.6 can then be modified to obtain P, the futures price prior to expiry:

$$P = 100 - \left[\frac{i_L D_L - i_S D_S}{D_F \left(1 + i_S \dfrac{D_S}{B}\right)} \right] \qquad (6.4)$$

where:

P is the futures price
i_S is the cash market interest rate to T_S
i_L is the cash market interest rate to T_L
D_S is the number of days from T_{SPOT} to T_S
D_L is the number of days from T_{SPOT} to T_L
D_F is the number of days from T_S to T_L
B is the day count convention (e.g. 360 for most currencies, 365 for sterling)

Suppose that today is Monday 19th July 2010, so that T_{SPOT} will be Wednesday 21st July. The last trading date T_D of the September 2010 contract is Monday 13th September, making T_S Wednesday 15th September, and T_L Wednesday 15th December. This makes D_S = 56 days, D_L = 147 days and D_F = 91 days. Suppose also that cash market rates are 0.33688%, 0.42188%, 0.58313% and 0.64463% for one-, two-, four- and five-month dollar LIBORs respectively. From these figures, we can interpolate the 56-day rate to be 0.40429%, and the 147-day rate as 0.63191%. Inserting these values in equation 6.4 gives the three-month forward rate for value date 15th September to be 0.771%, and hence the theoretical futures price should be 99.229.

Let's compare some actual cash market rates with futures prices, to see how they relate in practice. Table 6.2 shows the actual US dollar LIBOR fixings on Monday 19th July 2010.

TABLE 6.2

US dollar LIBOR rates on 19th July 2010

Tenor	Rate	Tenor	Rate	Tenor	Rate
s/n-o/n	0.26375%	3m	0.51781%	8m	0.84313%
1w	0.31313%	4m	0.58313%	9m	0.90625%
2w	0.32113%	5m	0.64463%	10m	0.97250%
1m	0.33688%	6m	0.71813%	11m	1.04750%
2m	0.42188%	7m	0.78250%	12m	1.11656%

Interpolating these rates enables us to calculate theoretical values for the September, December and March STIR contract prices. Table 6.3 compares these theoretical values with the actual futures prices that day.

TABLE 6.3

Comparison of actual with calculated STIR futures prices

Contract	Actual price	Calculated price	Difference (bp)
SEP 2010	99.485	99.229	25.6
DEC 2010	99.440	98.849	59.1
MAR 2011	99.385	98.451	93.4

Disappointingly, there are considerable differences between the theoretical figures calculated from the interpolated LIBOR rates, and the actual futures prices. It wasn't always thus. Prior to the credit crisis in 2007–2008, an exercise like that carried out in Table 6.3 would usually lead to a near-perfect match between the two sets of figures.

Since the credit crisis, however, there can be discrepancies between STIR futures prices and forward rates calculated from LIBORs. These occur because of the different credit risks arising from deposit market transactions compared with futures market transactions, and because of credit risk nowadays implicit within the LIBOR curve itself.[3] If a bank or corporation deposits $1m at Bank X, and Bank X files for bankruptcy before repaying the money, the depositor can potentially lose $1m. By contrast, if a bank or corporation buys a STIR contract with a notional size of $1m, which creates a synthetic deposit, the credit risk is virtually zero.

Credit risk has a cost (as we will see when we explore credit derivatives in Chapters 14 and 15). This means that forward rates calculated from LIBORs embed a premium reflecting the future potential credit risk, whereas the forward rates implied by STIR contracts do not. In July 2010, the three-month rate from March 2011 implied by the futures contract was 0.615%, while that implied by the LIBOR curve was 1.549%. From these figures we can say that in July 2010 the financial markets expected three-month rates in March 2011 to be 0.615%, not 1.549%, and that's why the March 2011 STIR contract was priced at 99.385.

Note that the fact that there is a difference between the LIBOR-implied and futures-implied forward rates does not present a risk-free arbitrage opportunity like the ones presented in Chapter 3. Let's suppose that you are a bank able to access interpolated LIBOR rates and, back in July 2010, you sell one Mar 2011 Eurodollar future at 99.385, borrow $994,528 for just under eight months at 0.83230%, and lend the same amount for just under 11 months at 1.0346%. Lending the 11s and borrowing the 8s is effectively lending forward at 1.549%, while selling the futures contract is effectively borrowing forward at 0.615%. This sounds like you should make some money...

Continuing the example, eight months later, the original borrowing matures and you repay the principal plus interest, which comes to exactly $1m. You then have to refinance the borrowing for a further three months. As we will see in section 6.5 later in this chapter, it doesn't matter what three-month LIBOR rates in March 2011 turn out to be; you will always be able to borrow for a further three months at an effective rate of 0.615%,[4] repaying $1,001,572 in June 2011. The maturing 11-month deposit delivers proceeds of $1,003,959, making an apparent profit of $2,388. This is equivalent to 0.934% p.a. over the 92-day period, equal to the difference between the LIBOR-implied three-month forward rate of 1.549% and the futures-implied rate of 0.615%.

This is not a risk-free profit, though. At any time over the 11-month period, the bank which had taken your deposit could go bankrupt, leaving you nursing potential losses of around $1m. Of course, you could buy protection against such a credit event, but this would probably cost you around 1% p.a. for 11 months – more than $9,000. The apparent profit of $2,388 would be completely swallowed up by the cost of eliminating the credit risk. That's why there can be a gap between two apparently equivalent rates – the LIBOR implied 8 × 11 rate of 1.549% and the futures-implied rate of 0.615% for the same period. The difference arises because of credit risk.

Before 2007–2008 it was believed that big banks couldn't go bust, either because the probability of such an event was negligible or because they were simply too big to fail. Credit risk was ignored and STIR futures prices were close to the LIBOR-implied forward rates. The world is more complicated now.

Interestingly enough, if one compares futures prices with FRA rates, there is an almost perfect fit. That's because both FRAs and STIR futures are derivatives rather than cash market instruments, and counterparty risk is very small (with FRAs) or non-existent (with futures). Table 6.4 extracts actual FRA rates from Figure 4.1 in Chapter 4 and actual STIR prices from Table 6.9 later in this chapter, both of which refer to the same date – Friday 14th January 2011. By comparing the mid-rate of each FRA with the futures-implied rate for the contract having almost identical dates we can see that these match within a basis point. Banks make extensive use of futures contracts in order to hedge their FRA books, so the prices of the two instruments track each other very closely, even more closely than either of them tracks the cash market prior to expiry.

TABLE 6.4
Comparison of actual FRA rates and STIR futures prices

FRA-tenor	Bid	Ask	Mid	Futures contract	Futures-implied rate	Difference
1 × 4	0.310%	0.350%	0.330%	Feb-11	0.3250%	0.005%
2 × 5	0.332%	0.372%	0.352%	Mar-11	0.3550%	–0.003%
3 × 6	0.365%	0.405%	0.385%	Apr-11	0.3850%	0.000%
5 × 8	0.425%	0.465%	0.445%	Jun-11	0.4450%	0.000%
8 × 11	0.533%	0.573%	0.553%	Sep-11	0.5600%	–0.007%

Source: Barclays.

6.3 Basis

Prior to expiry, there will usually be a gap between the futures-implied rate and the cash market rate right now. This is nothing to do with the credit risk discussed in the previous section – it simply reflects that the two rates cover different three-month periods. The gap between cash prices and prices in the futures market is given a special name in futures terminology – the *basis*. Basis is formally defined as:

$$BASIS = CASH\ PRICE - FUTURES\ PRICE \qquad (6.5)$$

Note that this definition is couched in terms of prices rather than rates, with the simple equation 6.1 linking the two.

One of the factors influencing basis for STIR contracts is the slope of the yield curve. Recall the idea introduced in Chapter 4 (section 4.6) where the FRA was said to 'fill the gap' between different maturities in the cash market. The same idea should apply to interest rate futures. Consider the two situations depicted in Figure 6.1.

In Figure 6.1a, three-month rates are 3% while six-month rates are 4%. This is a steeply positive, or upward-sloping, yield curve. Under these circumstances, the 3 × 6 forward interest rate of around 5% lies well above the cash market rate of 3%. In Figure 6.1b, the opposite is true. Three-month rates of 4% and six-month rates of 3% create a negative yield curve sloping steeply downwards.

FIGURE 6.1

Rising and falling yield curves

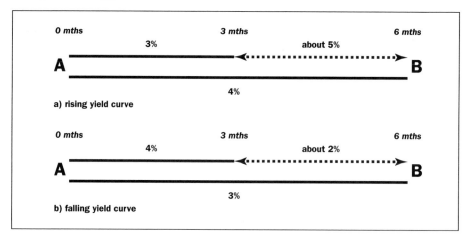

The 3–6 forward interest rate of around 2% in this case lies well below the cash market rate of 4%.

This example illustrates a general rule:[5]

Positive yield curve: forward rates are higher than cash rates

Negative yield curve: forward rates are lower than cash rates

If we convert this rule into futures terminology by transforming rates into prices, we obtain:

Positive yield curve: cash prices are higher than futures prices

Negative yield curve: cash prices are lower than futures prices

Applying the definition of basis given in equation 6.5, we can see that basis and the yield curve are closely related. A positive basis should arise when the yield curve is positive, and a negative basis should arise when the yield curve has a negative slope. This is pictured in Figure 6.2.

If we apply this reasoning to the dollar yield curve depicted in Table 6.2, the positive yield curve should imply that cash prices are higher than futures prices. However, if we compare the three-month cash price of 99.482 (from the 3m rate of 0.518%) with the September 2010 futures price of 99.485, the cash price was, in fact, lower than the futures price.

Once again, the spectre of credit risk rears its ugly head. A second factor influencing basis for STIR futures is the additional risk arising from LIBOR market transactions. This makes LIBOR-implied forward rates higher than they otherwise should be, and therefore cash prices lower. In 2010, interest rates and the slope of the short-term yield curve were both relatively low, whereas credit risk was still relatively high. The net result is that basis was negative, with the effect of credit risk (leading to a negative basis) dominating the effect of yield curve slope (leading to a positive basis).

FIGURE 6.2

Basis and the yield curve

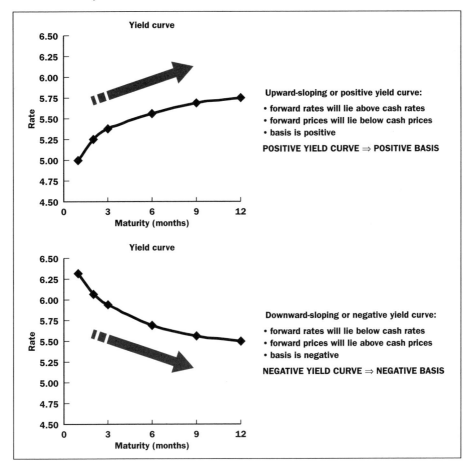

6.4 Convergence

Some hedgers believe that futures contracts provide a way of locking into today's cash market rates for a future transaction. Such a possibility would often be very useful, but that is not what futures provide. Futures allow a user to lock into a rate for a future transaction, but that rate is the forward rate. The basis is the gap between today's cash market rate, and the forward rate on a particular date in the future.

As the last trading date of a futures contract approaches, cash and futures prices will always move closer together. This process is known as *convergence*, and it can best be understood by comparing the periods covered by a three-month cash-market deposit, and a three-month futures contract. Figure 6.3 illustrates this using the June 2010 Eurodollar contract as an example.

FIGURE 6.3

Comparison of periods covered by cash and futures

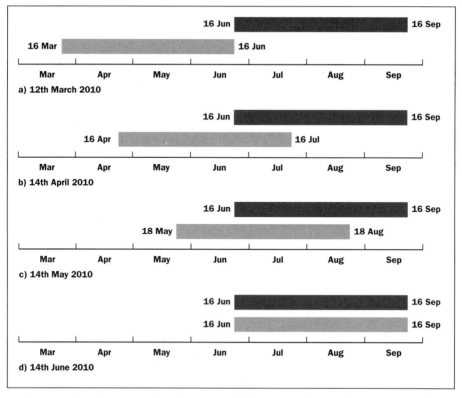

a) 12th March 2010

b) 14th April 2010

c) 14th May 2010

d) 14th June 2010

The last trading date for the June 2010 contract was Monday 14th June 2010, and the three-month period covered by the underlying deposit started on Wednesday 16th June and finished on Thursday 16th September. This period is fixed, and never changes.

Figure 6.3a starts by examining the period covered by a three-month deposit traded on 12th March 2010, which would have had a value date of 16th March and a maturity date of 16th June. As is evident, there is no overlap whatsoever between the period covered by the cash-market deposit, and the period covered by the futures contract. As they relate to two different periods of time, cash and futures rates might be quite different.

One month later, cash market rates on 14th April 2010 related to the period from 16th April to 16th July. Now there are 30 days of overlap between the period covered by the cash market, and the period covered by the future, as Figure 6.3b illustrates. On 14th May, one month later still, there are now two months (63 days) of overlap between the period covered by the cash-market deposit, and the futures contract period. There is now much more in common between these two periods, and we would expect the rates to be closer. Finally, on the last trading date of the futures contract, the period covered by cash and futures are one and the same, as Figure 6.3d demonstrates. On this day, cash and futures prices must also be the same, and convergence is complete.

FIGURE 6.4

Illustration of convergence – June 2010 Eurodollar contract

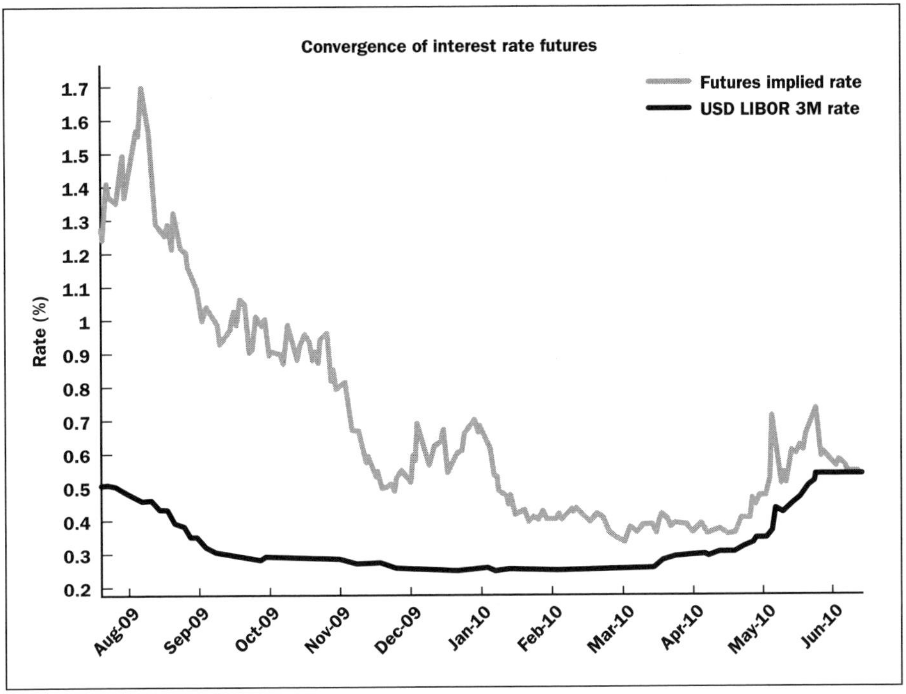

Source: Barclays.

Any influence that credit risk may have had on the basis disappears by the time the Eurodollar contract expires. Were there any gap between the futures-implied rate on the last trading day and the LIBOR fixing for three-month rates, this would allow a risk-free profit through arbitrage simply because the final futures price is 100 minus the LIBOR rate, by definition.

Figure 6.4 provides an actual illustration of the convergence between three-month dollar LIBOR and the June 2010 Eurodollar contract. A year before expiry, the futures market expected that three-month dollar rates in June 2010 would rise from the prevailing level of 0.5% to 1.25%, a basis of +75bp. Over the next six months, three-month LIBOR fell to 0.25% and the futures-implied rate fell to 0.5%, a narrower basis of +25bp. Finally, three-month LIBOR rose to 0.54% and the futures-implied rate rose to the same level, so that the basis became zero on the last trading date of the contract. At this point convergence was complete.

6.5 Behaviour of futures prices

Equation 6.4 defines the theoretical relationship between futures prices and rates in the cash markets, and this equation is almost identical to equation 4.6 which was used to price FRAs from cash-market rates. These formulae tell us how to calculate what the implied forward rates are if we know the interest rates for the relevant maturities.

Chapter 4 (section 4.7) then went on to examine how FRA prices should respond when market rates move, and we can employ the same techniques to determine how STIR futures prices should be affected in similar circumstances. Even if credit risk considerations mean that the *levels* of futures prices are different from the LIBOR-implied forwards, the *sensitivity* of those futures prices to changes in LIBOR rates should be unaffected by credit risk.

If interest rates generally rise, then futures prices will generally fall, and by the same amount. This follows from the basic definition of futures price quotations given in equation 6.1. If, however, the yield curve changes shape – if interest rates of different maturities move by different amounts – then futures will move by a lesser or greater amount.

Applying calculus to equation 6.4, we can see how the futures price P will react to changes in i_S and i_L. To a first approximation, we obtain:

$$\frac{\partial P}{\partial i_S} \approx \frac{D_S}{D_F} \tag{6.6}$$

$$\frac{\partial P}{\partial i_L} \approx -\frac{D_L}{D_F} \tag{6.7}$$

$$\frac{\partial P}{\partial i_{ALL}} \approx -1 \tag{6.8}$$

Equation 6.8 confirms the inverse relationship between interest rates and futures prices, while equation 6.7 demonstrates a similar effect if just long-term rates move. Equation 6.6, however, implies that rises in short-term rates will be accompanied by a *rise* in futures prices, if long-term rates do not move. This can be understood if we return to the analogy of futures contracts 'filling the gap' between short-term and long-term rates.

Let's suppose that there is a STIR futures contract which matures in exactly three months' time. By buying such a contract, an investor can effectively lock into a fixed-rate deposit for the three-month period starting in three months. The futures price will fix the rate such that the two strategies:

a) invest for six months

b) invest for three months and buy a future to lock in the rate for the second three months

will achieve the same end result. If three-month interest rates then rose, while six-month interest rates stayed the same, the return from strategy (a) would be unchanged. In order for the return under strategy (b) also to remain the same, the interest guaranteed by the futures contract would have to fall, meaning that futures prices would have to rise.

Figure 6.5 summarises the way in which different futures contracts would react if short-term rates i_s increase by one basis point, long-term rates i_L increase by one basis point, and interest rates generally rise by one basis point. This is very similar to the FRA 'behaviour profile' described in Chapter 4 (section 4.7).

FIGURE 6.5
Behaviour profile for interest rate futures

Contract maturing in...	$i_s \nearrow$ 1bp	$i_L \nearrow$ 1bp	$i_s \,\&\, i_L \nearrow$ 1bp
1 month	+0.33	−1.33	−1
3 months	+1	−2	−1
6 months	+2	−3	−1
9 months	+3	−4	−1

This is the theory. As an example of what happens in practice, we can study what happened between 19th July and 19th August 2010, when dollar rates eased by up to 20bp. Specifically, one-month and three-month rates fell by 7bp and 18bp respectively, six-month rates dropped by 16bp, and 12-month rates by 20bp. Figure 6.6 shows the cash-market yield curve and the interest rates implied by the Eurodollar futures prices, both before and after the change in rates.

The effect on the series of Eurodollar futures varied from contract to contract. As interest rates fell for all maturities, futures prices rose. The contract expiring on 15th September 2010 rose by 17bp, the Dec 2010 and March 2011 contracts rose by 16bp, and the June 2011 contract by 18bp.

We can calculate what effect the change in interest rates should have had on the September future by using equations 6.6 and 6.7. The 'behaviour profile' for this contract, maturing in a month, should be (+0.3 −1.3). One-month rates fell around 7bp which, by itself, should have dropped the future by 2bp. The fall in four-month rates of 17bp should, however, have raised the futures price by 22bp. Together this gives an expected net rise of 20bp in the futures price, compared with the 17bp rise which actually occurred.

A similar analysis predicts a rise in the December 2010 contract of 16bp, which is exactly what happened, and a rise in the March 2011 contract of 22bp, against an actual rise of 16bp. Table 6.5 presents a summary of these figures. Apart from some small differences, these results demonstrate that changes in futures prices and changes in LIBOR rates go hand in hand.

TABLE 6.5
Analysis of changes to LIBOR rates and Eurodollar futures prices

Contract	'Profile'	Change in LIBOR		Expected change in future	Actual change in future	Difference
		Short	Long			
SEP 2010	(+0.3 −1.3)	−0.072%	−0.174%	+20	+17	3
DEC 2010	(+1.3 −2.3)	−0.174%	−0.168%	+16	+16	0
MAR 2010	(+2.3 −3.3)	−0.168%	−0.184%	+22	+16	6

Source: Taken from the settlement prices published by the CME on its website, www.cmegroup.com

FIGURE 6.6
Dollar LIBOR rates and Eurodollar futures prices on 19 July and 19 August 2010

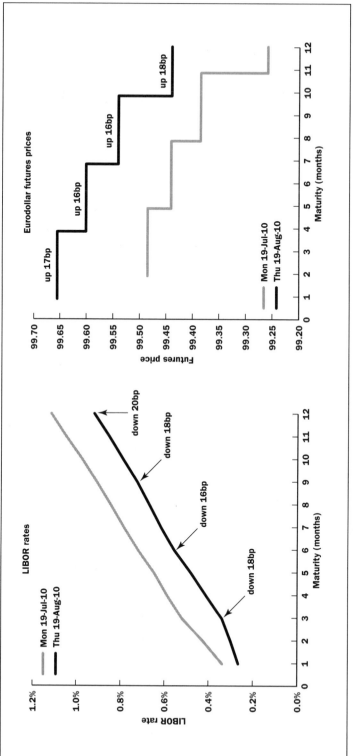

Source: LIBOR rates from British Bankers Association; Futures prices from CME.

6.6 Basic hedging example

Jim Baker is an investment manager who makes regular use of the euromarkets for placing short-term funds in dollars until strategic long-term investment opportunities are identified. Today is Friday 10th July 2009 and three-month dollar LIBOR is as low as 0.50% because governments and central banks around the world have slashed rates over the past year in an attempt to stimulate the global economy. The STIR futures market believes that these efforts will be successful, and that interest rates will rise steadily over the next two years. This is clear from Table 6.6 which shows the market prices for Eurodollar contracts maturing over the next two years.

TABLE 6.6
Eurodollar prices on 10th July 2009

Contract expiry	Price	Implied interest rate
Sep-09	99.4550	0.5450%
Dec-09	99.2500	0.7500%
Mar-10	99.0650	0.9350%
Jun-10	98.7800	1.2200%
Sep-10	98.4650	1.5350%
Dec-10	98.0950	1.9050%
Mar-11	97.7600	2.2400%
Jun-11	97.4250	2.5750%

Source: Taken from the settlement prices published by the CME on its website www.cmegroup.com

Jim, however, has the opposite view. Although he believes that the global economy will recover eventually, Jim thinks that recovery will be much slower, and that interest rates will therefore rise more slowly than those implied by Eurodollar futures, if they rise at all.

Jim knows that the fund that he manages will be receiving a $100m inflow at the beginning of September next year, and wants to hedge against the risk that interest rates will still be low at that time. On 10th July 2009, the September 2010 Eurodollar contract was trading at 98.4650, implying a three-month interest rate of 1.5350%. Jim buys 100 contracts at that price and waits.

Just over a year later, it looks as if Jim's view was correct. On Wednesday 1st September 2010, three-month dollar LIBOR fixes at 0.295625%, even lower than it was a year earlier. Futures prices that day are correspondingly higher, as shown in Table 6.7.

TABLE 6.7
Eurodollar prices on 1st September 2010

Contract expiry	Price	Implied interest rate
Sep-10	99.6875	0.3125%
Dec-10	99.5800	0.4200%
Mar-11	99.5150	0.4850%
Jun-11	99.4200	0.5800%

Source: Taken from the settlement prices published by the OME on its website www.cmegroup.com

That day, Jim commits to lend the $100m for three months, obtaining a rate of only 0.28%, a fraction below the prevailing three-month dollar LIBOR rate. He lifts the futures hedge at the same time, selling the Sep-10 futures at the prevailing price of 99.6875, making a 122.25-full-tick profit (the difference between the original buying price of 98.4650 and the selling price of 99.6875) on the 100-contract futures hedge. When everything is taken into account, the all-in effective deposit rate turns out to be 1.49%, just $4\frac{1}{2}$ basis points lower than the original implied futures rate of 1.5350%. Table 6.8 sets out the calculations to arrive at this figure.

TABLE 6.8

Calculating the effective profits from a futures hedge

Description	Calculation	Result
Futures profit	$122.25 \times \$25 \times 100$	$305,625.00
Add 91 days of interest on futures profit	$\$305,625 \times 0.28\% \times \frac{91}{360}$	$216.31
Lend $100m for 91 days at 0.28% p.a.	$\$100m \times 0.28\% \times \frac{91}{360}$	$70,777.78
Total proceeds		$376,619.09
Effective rate	$(\$376{,}619.09/\$100m) \times \frac{360}{91}$	1.4899%
Original implied rate	$100 - 98.4650$	1.5350%

If the futures hedge had been perfect, it would have generated an additional $125\frac{1}{2}$ basis points of profit. Measuring the actual profits of 121 basis points (1.49% *less* 0.28%) against the target profits of $125\frac{1}{2}$ basis points means that the futures hedge was more than 96% efficient in this case. Not bad!

The reasons why the futures hedge was almost, but not quite perfect, can be summarised under three headings:

■ The investor could not invest at LIBOR – the underlier for the STIR contract – but at a deposit rate slightly lower. This explains 1.6bp of the shortfall.

■ The hedge was lifted on 1st September, but the contract did not expire until 15th September, two weeks later. Convergence between STIR futures prices and three-month LIBOR rates is only complete when the contracts expire. Prior to this, as we saw earlier in this chapter, there is a basis between cash and futures prices. In this example, the cash market rates were 0.295625%, whereas the Sep-2010 Eurodollar futures were implying a rate of 0.3125%. This difference explains another 1.7bp of the shortfall.

■ The deposit was for 91 days, but the $25 full tick value implies a notional 90-day period. If the cash market deposit had been for only 90 days, the effective rate would have been 1.5034%, not 1.4899%. This explains a further 1.3bp of the shortfall.

Adding these three factors gives 4.6bp, fully explaining the $4\frac{1}{2}$bp difference between the 1.5350% rate anticipated by the hedge, and the 1.4899% achieved.

If the investment manager had wanted to avoid even this small difference, Chapter 18 (sections 18.3 to 18.8) explains how to calculate more accurate futures hedge ratios, and how to use more complex techniques to manage the basis risk.

6.7 Short-term futures contracts compared

The three-month Eurodollar future illustrated so far in this chapter is by far the most heavily used contract for hedging short-term interest rate risk, and is available in a range of major currencies including the US dollar, the euro, the pound sterling, the Swiss franc, and the Japanese yen. Some of these contracts are offered by more than one futures exchange around the globe, giving users access to particular contracts 24 hours a day. In certain cases, exchanges have linked their margining and clearing procedures so that contracts opened on one exchange may be closed on another. An example of this is the Mutual Offset System Agreement (MOSA) link between SGX in Singapore and the CME in Chicago.

In addition to the three-month future, there are a number of other short-term contracts available, and these fall into two groups:

a) contracts based on a notional deposit, but for a different maturity

b) contracts based on other short-term securities.

The only active[6] contracts in the first group are the 30-day Federal Funds contract traded on the CBOT, and the one-month Eurodollar contract traded on the CME.

The 30-day Federal Funds contract trades in modest volumes compared to the Eurodollar contract – only around 40,000 contracts per day in 2010 compared to the 2m daily volume for the three-month Eurodollar contract. It is an interesting contract, nonetheless, because of the way in which the final settlement price is established on the last trading date, which is always the last business day in the month. The final settlement price for most other futures contracts is determined by the price of the underlier only on the final trading day. In contrast, the final settlement price for the Fed Funds contract is the *average* of the overnight Fed Funds rates throughout that month, as reported by the Federal Reserve Bank of New York.

The contract specification for the one-month LIBOR contract is identical to that for the three-month contract, including the same full-tick value of $25 per contract. This is accomplished by increasing the size of the notional underlying deposit from $1m for the three-month contract to $3m for the one-month contract:

$$\$1,000,000 \times 0.01\% \times \tfrac{3}{12} = \$25$$
$$\$3,000,000 \times 0.01\% \times \tfrac{1}{12} = \$25$$

Tables 6.9 and 6.10 illustrate some trading statistics for these two contracts. The columns show:

i)   the opening, highest, lowest and settlement futures prices that day
ii) the change in settlement price between yesterday and today
iii) the yield implied by the futures price (i.e. 100 less the futures price)
iv) the estimated trading volume that day
v)   the open interest – the total number of long (or short) contracts outstanding at the end of the day (i.e. the aggregate number of positions carried forward from day to day rather than being closed out during the day).

TABLE 6.9

Three-month Eurodollar contract: trading statistics for 14th January 2011

	Open	High	Low	Change	Settle	Yield	Volume	Open interest
Jan-11	99.6975	99.6975	99.695		99.695	0.3050%	11,816	74,752
Feb-11	99.680	99.680	99.670	–0.005	99.675	0.3250%	13,390	30,417
Mar-11	99.645	99.650	99.640		99.645	0.3550%	146,470	1,183,975
Apr-11	–	–	–		99.615	0.3850%	–	905
May-11	–	–	–	–0.005	99.585	0.4150%	–	278
Jun-11	99.555	99.565	99.540		99.555	0.4450%	168,115	1,133,992
Jul-11	–	–	–		99.440	0.5600%	–	–
Sep-11	99.445	99.455	99.410	–0.005	99.440	0.5600%	187,392	980,921
Dec-11	99.280	99.300	99.235	–0.005	99.275	0.7250%	206,320	796,043
Mar-12	99.075	99.100	99.015	–0.010	99.060	0.9400%	307,525	862,123
Jun-12	98.825	98.855	98.750	–0.010	98.800	1.2000%	243,058	544,421
Sep-12	98.560	98.605	98.480	–0.015	98.530	1.4700%	188,969	445,869
Dec-12	98.295	98.350	98.210	–0.020	98.260	1.7400%	183,560	301,959
Mar-13	98.030	98.095	97.950	–0.025	98.000	2.0000%	130,797	199,029
Jun-13	97.765	97.840	97.695	–0.025	97.735	2.2650%	78,891	157,872
Sep-13	97.520	97.590	97.450	–0.030	97.480	2.5200%	71,400	180,614
Dec-13	97.260	97.340	97.200	–0.030	97.225	2.7750%	57,506	142,608
Mar-14	97.040	97.120	96.980	–0.035	97.000	3.0000%	24,979	109,274
Jun-14	96.810	96.890	96.750	–0.035	96.770	3.2300%	20,306	104,294
Sep-14	96.585	96.665	96.520	–0.035	96.545	3.4550%	16,264	62,143
Dec-14	96.355	96.440	96.300	–0.035	96.320	3.6800%	17,493	71,633
Mar-15	96.180	96.250	96.110	–0.035	96.135	3.8650%	11,512	52,062
Jun-15	95.995	96.070	95.935	–0.035	95.955	4.0450%	11,424	35,729
Sep-15	95.840	95.905	95.770	–0.040	95.790	4.2100%	9,875	29,531
Dec-15	95.675	95.75	95.615	–0.040	95.635	4.3650%	10,128	20,977
Mar-16	95.545	95.605	95.485	–0.040	95.505	4.4950%	1,482	15,185
Jun-16	95.420	95.485	95.36	–0.040	95.385	4.6150%	2,216	12,777
Sep-16	95.310	95.37	95.250	–0.045	95.275	4.7250%	918	9,064
Dec-16	95.200	95.265	95.145	–0.045	95.175	4.8250%	1,382	11,350
Mar-17	95.135	95.19	95.085	–0.045	95.115	4.8850%	348	6,890
Jun-17	95.070	95.13	95.065	–0.050	95.050	4.9500%	245	4,726
Sep-17	95.045	95.08	94.980	–0.050	95.000	5.0000%	313	7,326
Dec-17	94.980	95.02	94.930	–0.050	94.940	5.0600%	281	4,660
Mar-18	–	95.00	94.91	–0.050	94.920	5.0800%	–	1,728
Jun-18	–	94.965	94.875	–0.050	94.885	5.1150%	–	1,801
Sep-18	–	94.93	94.84	–0.050	94.850	5.1500%	–	2,244

	Open	High	Low	Change	Settle	Yield	Volume	Open interest
Dec-18	–	94.89	94.80	–0.050	94.810	5.1900%	–	1,559
Mar-19	–	94.855	94.745	–0.050	94.775	5.2250%	–	1,203
Jun-19	–	94.82	94.71	–0.050	94.740	5.2600%	–	904
Sep-19	–	94.785	94.675	–0.050	94.705	5.2950%	–	1,249
Dec-19	–	94.74	94.63	–0.050	94.660	5.3400%	–	1,638
Mar-20	–	94.705	94.585	–0.050	94.625	5.3750%	–	675
Jun-20	–	94.655	94.535	–0.050	94.575	5.4250%	–	423
Sep-20	94.550	94.60	94.48	–0.050	94.520	5.4800%	30	484
Dec-20	94.480	94.545	94.425	–0.055	94.460	5.5400%	30	169
Total							2,124,435	7,607,476

Source: Taken from the end of day data published by the CME on its website www.cmegroup.com

TABLE 6.10

One-month Eurodollar contract: trading statistics for 14th January 2011

	Open	High	Low	Change	Settle	Yield	Volume	Open interest
Jan-11	99.7375	99.7400	99.7375		99.7375	0.2625%	23	13,651
Feb-11	99.7300	99.7325	99.7300		99.7300	0.2700%	328	8,248
Mar-11	99.7150	99.7150	99.7150		99.7150	0.2850%	315	4,504
Apr-11	99.6925	99.6925	99.6925		99.6925	0.3075%	1	4,308
May-11	–	–	–		99.6775	0.3225%	–	1,434
Jun-11	–	–	–	–0.0075	99.6425	0.3575%	–	443
Jul-11	–	–	–	–0.0100	99.6150	0.3850%	–	921
Aug-11	–	–	–	–0.0100	99.5875	0.4125%	–	1,301
Sep-11	–	–	–	–0.0025	99.5450	0.4550%	–	1,111
Oct-11	–	–	99.5175	–0.0050	99.5150	0.4850%	–	116
Nov-11	–	–	99.4975	–0.0050	99.4950	0.5050%	–	57
Dec-11	–	–	–	–0.0075	99.3950	0.6050%	–	–
Jan-12	–	–	–		99.2950	0.7050%	–	–
Total							667	36,094

Source: Taken from the end of day data published by the CME on its website, www.cmegroup.com

From these two tables, there are a number of interesting features to note:

■ Both contracts clearly show market expectations. For example, the three-month contract demonstrates the market's view that three-month dollar rates will rise from around 0.3% at the beginning of 2011 to around 5% by 2017.

■ Liquidity in the three-month contract extends to contracts maturing in five years' time, while liquidity in the one-month contract tails off rapidly after the first few contracts.

■ Trading volume in the three-month contract is thousands of times that of the one-month contract, while open interest is some 200 times larger.

Despite the much-attenuated liquidity of the one-month contract, it may prove more suitable when trying to hedge an exposure whose interest rate risk is linked to one-month rather than three-month rates. For example, a company issuing 30-day commercial paper may find that the one-month futures contract provides a more accurate hedge than the three-month contract.

The second group of short-term futures contracts are based on securities like Treasury Bills. In fact, the first short-term interest rate contract ever traded was the 13-week T-Bill contract at the CME, introduced in 1976. Despite its history, T-Bill futures, while still listed on the CME, no longer trade. Hedging of short-term interest rate risk is the purview of the ubiquitous three-month contract.

6.8 Comparison of futures and FRAs

Table 5.3 in Chapter 5 summarised the principal institutional and operational differences between the futures and cash markets. Here we discuss some additional technical distinctions between Eurocurrency futures and FRAs.

The definition of the futures contract implies that someone who buys one futures contract and holds it until maturity will receive a payoff defined by:

$$PAYOFF = (P_{EDSP} - P_0) \times 100 \times TV = (i_0 - i_{EDSP}) \times 100 \times TV \quad (6.9)$$

where:

P_{EDSP} is the exchange delivery settlement price
P_0 is the original purchase price
i_{EDSP} is the reference interest rate used to determine P_{EDSP} (in percent)
i_0 is the original interest rate implied by the futures contract $(100 - P_0)$
TV is the full tick value of the contract

Equation 6.9 is very similar to equation 4.2, which defined the settlement sum for an FRA. The reference rate i_{EDSP} in (6.9) corresponds to i_r in (4.2), while the original rate i_0 in (6.9) matches i_c in (4.2). There are two differences, however:

i) Equation 6.9 features $(i_0 - i_{EDSP})$, while equation 4.2 uses $(i_r - i_c)$. The order of the corresponding terms is reversed, because buying futures is defined as making a deposit, while buying FRAs is equivalent to taking a loan.

ii) Equation 6.9 uses a constant tick value, while equation 4.2 calculates the tick value according to the period of time covered by the FRA, and then discounts this to allow for the settlement sum being paid at the beginning rather than at the end of the FRA contract period.

Depending upon the day count and the level of interest, the payoff from a futures contract and an FRA maturing on the same day could differ by up to 10% in extreme cases. For banks hedging large FRA books with futures, this can be accommodated by adjusting the number of futures contracts purchased, as explained in Chapter 18 (section 18.3).

A further distinction arises through the operation of the margin account. As Chapter 5 (section 5.6) explained, the flows of variation margin compel holders of futures to realise their profits and losses on a daily basis, in cash. Holders of positions in FRAs may also mark their positions to market on a daily basis, but there is only one occasion when the profit or loss is paid in cash, and that is on the settlement date. This makes a difference when one accounts for the interest earned or forgone through the flows of variation margin.

As an example, consider a bank which anticipates a fall in forward interest rates over the next three months, and simultaneously buys futures and sells FRAs, both maturing on the same date.[7] If the bank is correct, as time passes, profits will be earned both on the long futures position and on the short FRA position. The futures profit, however, will be credited to the margin account as variation margin, can be drawn off as cash, and can be invested to earn interest. The FRA profits are only mark-to-market profits, and these can only be realised in cash when the position is closed out, or the FRA matures.

The effect of interest on variation margin flows can be taken into account when designing more advanced hedging strategies, and the method is also explained in Chapter 18 (section 18.3).

Finally, the vast majority of FRAs are quoted with fixed periods. A 3×6 FRA, for example, covers a moving three-month period always commencing three months after the spot value date. The period covered by a 3×6 FRA traded today will therefore be different from the period covered by a 3×6 FRA traded tomorrow. Futures are based on fixed dates rather than fixed periods. As the last trading date approaches, the price of a specific futures contract and three-month cash rates will move ever closer together. No such convergence between 3×6 FRA prices and cash rates takes place.

6.9 Spread positions

The concept of a spread of futures contracts was first introduced in the previous chapter in the context of spread margins. It was explained that offsetting positions for different dates in the same contract, an intra-commodity spread, attracted a substantially smaller margin than was normally levied for the positions separately. At the time of writing, Eurodollar contracts at the CME expiring within one year attract a normal full margin of $878 per contract, corresponding to a 35bp move in interest rates, but the spread margin for a pair of such contracts was just $135.

It is clear that someone who is long futures for one date, and short the same number of contracts for another date, has an offsetting position that is much less exposed to movements in interest rates. This raises the question: what exactly is the residual exposure?

To understand the exposure of a spread position to changes in interest rates, we need to refer back to the futures 'behaviour profile' illustrated in Figure 6.5. This quantified how any futures contract would respond to movements in i_S and i_L. For a contract maturing in three months' time, the profile (+1 –2) means that the future will rise one tick for a 1bp rise in the three-month rate, and will fall two ticks for a 1bp rise in the six-month rate. For another futures contract maturing in six months' time, the profile (+2 –3) means that this future will rise two ticks for a 1bp rise in the six-month rate, and will fall 3bp for a rise of 1bp in the nine-month rate.

Now consider a spread position, which is:

- long one contract which matures in three months' time
- short one contract which matures in six months' time.

Being long the near-dated contract and short the far-dated contract is known as being *long the spread*.

The combined profile will now comprise three numbers, showing the separate exposure to three-, six- and nine-month rates. It can be obtained by combining the (+1 –2) profile for the long contract, and minus (+2 –3) for the short contract:

$$
\begin{array}{llll}
(& +1 & -2 &) \\
(& & -2 & +3 &) \\
\hline
(& +1 & -4 & +3 &)
\end{array}
$$

The resulting profile (+1 –4 +3) means that the spread position will:

- increase in value by one tick for a 1bp rise in three-month rates
- decrease in value by four ticks for a 1bp rise in six-month rates
- increase in value by three ticks for a 1bp rise in nine-month rates.

This composite behaviour profile gives us a very powerful way of quickly evaluating the effect on a spread position of any possible movement in the yield curve. Of course, there are an infinite number of ways in which interest rates could change, but it is interesting to consider three specific types of move:

a) a parallel shift in the yield curve, where rates for all maturities move up or down by the same amount

b) a non-parallel shift in the yield curve, where the slope of the yield curve becomes more positive

c) a non-parallel shift in the yield curve, where the slope of the yield curve becomes more negative.

The case of the parallel shift is easy to evaluate. Let's suppose that all rates go up by exactly 1bp. The effect on the spread will then be:

$$(+1 \times +1) + (-4 \times +1) + (+3 \times +1) = 0$$

In other words, the spread is *totally unaffected* by a parallel shift in the yield curve. Under such circumstances, the long and the short positions offset each other perfectly.

Now consider the general situation where the slope of the yield curve becomes more positive. For this to happen, the six-month rate must increase by more than the three-month rate, and the nine-month rate must increase by more again. If d_3, d_6 and d_9 are defined as the respective increases in these three rates, we can say that:

$$d_9 > d_6 > d_3$$

and that:

$$(d_9 - d_6) \geq (d_6 - d_3)$$

From the spread behaviour profile, the change in value of the spread position will be:

$$d_3 - 4d_6 + 3d_9$$
$$= 3(d_9 - d_6) - (d_6 - d_3)$$
$$> 0$$

since $(d_9 - d_6) \geq (d_6 - d_3)$. This means that someone who is long the spread will always profit if the yield curve becomes more positive, regardless of what happens to the general level of rates. The above proof will also hold true if all the d's are negative, i.e. if rates generally decline, so long as the slope of the yield curve becomes more positive.

In the last situation where the slope of the yield curve becomes more negative, we can reverse the inequalities in the preceding proof to demonstrate that someone who is long the spread will always lose money, no matter what happens to the general level of interest rates.

Table 6.11 summarises the effect of movements in interest rates on outright and spread positions.

TABLE 6.11
Effect of yield curve on futures position

	Long futures	Short futures	Long spread	Short spread
Interest rates higher	−	+	0	0
Interest rates lower	+	−	0	0
Yield curve slope more +ve	depends	depends	+	−
Yield curve slope more −ve	depends	depends	−	+

As an illustration of the effect of changing interest rates on a spread position, consider the family of yield curves illustrated in Figure 6.7.

The initial yield curve in all cases has three-, six- and nine-month yields at 5%, $5\frac{1}{2}$% and $5\frac{3}{4}$%, respectively. In the two scenarios illustrated in the first graph, the yield curve first rises by $\frac{3}{4}$% ('up' scenario), and then falls by $\frac{3}{4}$% ('down' scenario), both movements being parallel shifts. In the three scenarios illustrated in the second graph, the slope of the yield curve always becomes $\frac{1}{2}$% more positive, but rates either rise $\frac{3}{4}$% ('up' scenario), fall $\frac{3}{4}$% ('down' scenario), or remain at the same general level ('pivot' scenario).

FIGURE 6.7

Parallel and non-parallel yield curve shift scenarios

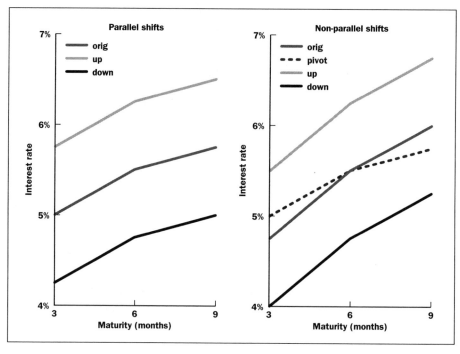

We can now analyse the effect of these various scenarios on a June/September spread, purchased immediately after the expiry of the March contract. The set of fair futures prices for the June and September contracts can be calculated using equation 6.4. These prices, along with the resultant profits and losses, are presented in Table 6.12.

TABLE 6.12

Evaluation of rate scenarios on futures spread

		Fair prices		Profits (bp)		
		JUN	SEP	JUN	SEP	Net
	Original	94.07	93.92			
Parallel shift	up	93.35	93.21	−72	+71	−1
	down	94.81	94.63	+74	−71	+3
	pivot	93.82	93.19	−25	+73	+48
Non-parallel shift	up	93.09	92.48	−98	+144	+46
	down	94.55	93.89	+48	+3	+51

As expected from the preceding analysis, the spread is virtually unaffected by a parallel shift in the yield curve, but produces an almost consistent 50bp of profit when the slope of the yield curve increases by 50bp. Although not evaluated here, the spread would consistently lose 50bp if the slope of the yield curve were to decrease by 50bp.

We will demonstrate later (Chapter 18) how interest rate futures, FRAs and interest rate swaps may be used to manage interest rate risk in both simple and more complex situations. In the meantime, the next chapter reviews the other major types of futures contracts: bond futures and stock index futures.

Notes

1 Taking into account adjustment for weekends, holidays and the so-called end-month rule.

2 In fact, the flows of variation margin mean that the settlement sum is actually paid or received *continuously* while the contract is being held.

3 This point was first raised in Chapter 4 and will surface again in Chapters 8 and 9. Investors (including other banks) used to believe that lending to a major bank was essentially riskless. Since 2007–2008, and especially since the collapse of Lehman Brothers, investing for a single six-month period is now considered to be more risky than lending for three months and then rolling the deposit for a further three months.

4 Let's suppose three-month LIBOR rates in March 2011 turn out 10bp higher at 0.625%. The March 2011 Eurodollar future will then fall to 99.375, and you will be able to buy back the contract at this price. Having originally sold the contract at 99.385, you make 10bp profit, which exactly compensates you for the 10bp higher refinancing costs. Your effective borrowing cost is therefore still 0.615%.

5 Strictly speaking, $i_F > i_S$ only when $i_L > i_S\left(1 + i_S \frac{t_S t_F}{t_L}\right)$. This means that forward rates will also be lower than cash rates when the yield curve is flat (i.e. when $i_S = i_L$).

6 Other contracts, such as the three-month Overnight Index Swaps (OIS) contract at the CME or the one-month EONIA contract at NYSE Liffe, may be listed but had little or no liquidity at the time of writing.

7 This is possible because banks make an active market in FRAs for which the dates match those of the futures contracts, the so-called IMM dates.

7

BOND AND STOCK INDEX FUTURES

As Table 5.1 showed, while short-term interest rate futures are the most important futures contracts when ranked by trading volume, stock index futures – like the E-mini S&P 500 – and bond futures – like the 10yr T-Note contract – are also very important, with contracts representing trillions of dollars of assets being traded every month.

Although bond futures are based on a tangible asset, while stock index contracts are based on an abstract number, both are contracts on capital market instruments and there are great similarities in the way they are priced.

This chapter starts by explaining exactly what bond futures are, then moves on to deal with pricing, the delivery mechanism and simple hedging applications. Later sections discuss the pricing and application of stock index futures.

7.1 Definition of bond futures contracts

It is easier to understand the concept of a bond future than it is to understand the short-term interest rate contracts discussed in the previous chapter. This is because bond futures, like most commodity futures, are based on the delivery of a tangible asset – a particular bond – at some date in the future. As an example, the CBOT 10yr T-Note contract, the most active of this kind of financial futures contracts, is defined in Table 7.1.

TABLE 7.1

Definition of 10yr T-Note contract at the CBOT

Unit of trading	US Treasury Note having a face value of $100,000 and a coupon of 6%
Deliverable grades	US T-Notes with a time to maturity between $6\frac{1}{2}$ and 10 years from the first day of delivery month
Delivery months	The first five consecutive contracts in the usual March, June, September and December quarterly cycle
Delivery date	Any business day during delivery month
Last trading day	Seventh business day before last business day of delivery month at 12:00 noon
Price quotation	Percentage points and half $\frac{1}{32}$nds of a percentage point. For example, 110'16 means $110\frac{16}{32}$ percent, while 110'165 means $110\frac{16.5}{32}$ percent
Minimum price movement	One half of $\frac{1}{32}$nd of a percent
Tick value	$100,000 \times \frac{1}{64}\% = \$15.625$
Trading hours	Open outcry: 07:20–14:00 (Mon–Fri)
	Globex: 17:30–16:00 (Sun–Fri)

Source: Taken from the contract definition published by the CBOT on its website www.cmegroup.com

The definition of this contract calls for the delivery of a US Treasury Note with a maturity of between $6\frac{1}{2}$ and 10 years, and a 6% coupon. We could envisage the holder of a long position in T-Note futures paying the futures price in dollars on the delivery date, and receiving such a bond.

However, there would be problems if the definition of deliverable bonds were restricted solely to those with a coupon of exactly 6%. Sometimes there may simply be no bonds having this precise coupon. Even if there were one or two such bonds, the size of the futures market in relation to the size of the bond issue could expose the bond futures market to price manipulation. It would not be difficult for a group of investors to buy T-Note futures contracts *and* a major portion of the underlying bonds. When the delivery month came, those who were short the futures contracts would either have to close out their positions or buy up the underlying bonds. Futures prices and bond prices would both be driven up while this *short squeeze* was on, resulting in a handsome profit for the original investors.

To avoid this, futures exchanges design contracts in such a way as to prevent anyone cornering the market. In the case of the T-Note and most similar contracts, this is achieved by allowing delivery of *any* bond with the requisite maturity. Of course, the holder of a long position in futures would prefer to receive a high-coupon bond with significant accrued interest, while those who were short futures would favour delivering a cheaper low-coupon bond shortly after the coupon date. This apparent conflict of interests is resolved by adjusting the *invoicing amount* – the amount paid in exchange for the bond – to account for coupon rate and timing of the bond actually delivered. Equation 7.1 defines the invoice amount.

$$INVAMT = FP \times CF + ACC \qquad (7.1)$$

where:

INVAMT	is the invoice amount
FP	is the futures price
CF	is the conversion factor
ACC	is the accrued interest

Every bond deliverable under a particular futures contract will have its own conversion factor, which is intended to compensate for the coupon and timing differences of deliverable bonds. The futures exchange publishes tables of conversion factors well in advance of each delivery date. These numbers will be smaller than 1.0 for bonds having coupons less than 6%, and greater than 1.0 otherwise. As an example, Table 7.2 lists the set of conversion factors calculated by the CBOT for bonds deliverable into the March 2011 10yr T-Note futures contract.

TABLE 7.2

Conversion factors for 10yr T-Note futures deliverable into the March 2011 contract

Coupon (%)	Maturity	Amount ($bn)	Conversion factor
$1\frac{7}{8}$	30 Sep 17	$29.0	0.7807
$1\frac{7}{8}$	31 Oct 17	$29.0	0.7807
$4\frac{1}{4}$	15 Nov 17	$21.0	0.9069
$2\frac{1}{4}$	30 Nov 17	$29.0	0.8006
$2\frac{3}{4}$	31 Dec 17	$29.0	0.8217
$3\frac{1}{2}$	15 Feb 18	$33.0	0.8628
$3\frac{7}{8}$	15 May 18	$26.0	0.8800
4	15 Aug 18	$29.0	0.8837
$3\frac{3}{4}$	15 Nov 18	$52.0	0.8657
$2\frac{3}{4}$	15 Feb 19	$57.0	0.8009
$3\frac{1}{8}$	15 May 19	$60.0	0.8194
$3\frac{5}{8}$	15 Aug 19	$63.0	0.8472
$3\frac{3}{8}$	15 Nov 19	$67.0	0.8272
$3\frac{5}{8}$	15 Feb 20	$67.0	0.8401
$3\frac{1}{2}$	15 May 20	$66.0	0.8281
$2\frac{5}{8}$	15 Aug 20	$66.0	0.7630
$2\frac{5}{8}$	15 Nov 20	$66.0	0.7583

Source: Taken from data published by the CBOT on its website www.cmegroup.com

A particular bond deliverable on several dates will have similar, but not identical, conversion factors. For example, the 4% bond maturing on 15th August 2018 has conversion factors of 0.8837, 0.8870, 0.8902 and 0.8937, for the contracts maturing in March, June, September and December 2011, respectively.

In the bond market, bonds with a high coupon tend to trade at a higher price than those with a low coupon. An investor choosing between two bonds with similar maturities but different coupons would have to weigh up the advantage of receiving a higher coupon against the disadvantage of paying a higher price. In a perfect market, the prices would adjust so that the effective return to the investor was identical for both bonds.

To take a simple example, consider two bonds with just one year to mature. One pays an annual 2% coupon, while the other pays an annual 6% coupon. If the price of the low-coupon bond were 98.08, and the price of the high-coupon bond were 101.92, the investor should be indifferent between the two as both would offer a return of 4% on the money invested.

In the first case, the investor would invest 98.08, and would receive the face value of 100 at maturity plus the coupon payment of 2, a total of 102. The effective annual return is then 4%:

$$\frac{102 - 98.08}{98.08} = 4\%$$

In the case of the high-coupon bond, the investor would receive at maturity the face value of 100 plus a coupon of 6, 106 in total, for an original investment of 101.92. The effective annual return here is also 4%:

$$\frac{106 - 101.92}{101.92} = 4\%$$

In other words, by adjusting the price, the market can provide investors with the same return from two bonds with completely different coupon rates.

Exactly the same principle is used to calculate the conversion factors for different bonds. The conversion factor for each bond is simply the price per $1 (or per £1, €1, etc.) such that every bond would provide an investor with the same yield if purchased. The yield selected for the calculations is the same as the notional coupon rate in the definition of the futures contract, 6% in the case of the US Treasury futures contracts at the CBOT.

Other things being equal, bonds with a higher coupon will have larger conversion factors than those with lower coupons. As an example, compare the $1\frac{7}{8}\%$ of Oct 2017 whose conversion factor is 0.7807 with the $4\frac{1}{4}\%$ of Nov 2017 which has a conversion factor of 0.9069. Both bonds mature at almost the same time, but the bond carrying the $4\frac{1}{4}\%$ coupon has the higher conversion factor. This follows directly from the simple example given above, which demonstrated that bonds bearing a higher coupon trade at higher prices.

For bonds with the same coupon, maturity has an influence, though this is slightly less obvious. For bonds with coupons below the nominal coupon rate defined in the contract specification, the conversion factor is smaller for bonds with a longer maturity. Compare the conversion factor of 0.8628 for the $3\frac{1}{2}\%$ of Feb 2018 with 0.8281 for the $3\frac{1}{2}\%$ of May 2020. The opposite is true for bonds carrying coupons in excess of the nominal coupon rate, for which the conversion factor will be larger the longer the maturity.

This latter effect stems from the mathematics of fixed-interest securities. Bonds whose coupon lies below current market yields will trade at a discount. This discount is larger the longer the maturity, because it is a disadvantage to hold a bond paying a coupon lower than current market rates, and this disadvantage is greater the longer the period until the bond matures. Conversely, bonds with coupons above current market yields trade at a premium, which will be greater the longer the maturity.

Most futures exchanges calculate conversion factors effective on the exact delivery date if a single date is defined, or on the first day of the delivery month if delivery can take place at any time during that month. The CBOT, however, rounds the maturity of the bond down to the nearest quarter of a year before performing the calculation. For example, on 1st March 2011 the $3\frac{1}{2}$% bond of May 2020 has a maturity of just under $9\frac{1}{4}$ years until its maturity date on 15th May 2020. The CBOT would therefore use an effective maturity of 9 years. With a bond calculator, it is possible to verify that the price at which the above bond would yield 6% with exactly 9 years to mature is indeed 0.8281.[1]

This chapter has so far concentrated on the 10yr T-Note contract traded at the CBOT, the most liquid of all bond futures contracts. Table 7.3 summarises some of the other major bond futures contracts traded. As the table demonstrates, the different futures contracts differ only in some of the finer details. The principles underlying their pricing, behaviour and applications are all identical.

7.2 The cheapest-to-deliver bond

The system of conversion factors provides a good but not a perfect system for making all deliverable bonds perfect substitutes for one another.

For a start, we have already seen how the CBOT rounds the bond maturity to the next lowest quarter before calculating the conversion factor. Even if it did not, bonds can be delivered any day during the delivery month against the CBOT contract, while the conversion factor remains constant throughout. Some other exchanges avoid this particular problem by defining a single day as the delivery date and calculating the conversion factor as of that date.

Nonetheless, there is still a fundamental flaw. Conversion factors are calculated to equalise returns at a single uniform yield, the coupon rate specified in the contract definition. In practice, however, different bonds trade at different yields (giving rise to the concept of a yield curve first discussed in Chapter 2, section 2.4). Even if all bonds traded at the same yield, it is unlikely that this would be exactly the same as the coupon rate specified in the definition of the bond futures contract.

To see why the system of conversion factors is less than perfect, let's first review what would happen if bonds all traded at the same yield as the notional coupon rate specified in the futures contract. Table 7.4 examines three of the bonds deliverable into the March 2011 10yr T-Note contract when all bond yields on 1st March 2011 are 6%.

TABLE 7.3

Definitions of major bond futures contracts

Contract	2yr US T-Note	3yr US T-Note	5yr US T-Note	10yr US T-Note	T-Bond	Ultra T-Bond	Long Gilt	Bund	JGB
Exchange	CBOT	CBOT	CBOT	CBOT	CBOT	CBOT	NYSE Liffe	Eurex	TSE
Unit of trading	US Treasury Note	US Treasury Note	US Treasury Note	US Treasury Note	US Treasury Bond	US Treasury Bond	UK Government Bond (Gilt)	German Government Bond	Japanese Government Bond
Face value	$200,000	$200,000	$100,000	$100,000	$100,000	$100,000	£100,000	€100,000	¥100m
Notional coupon	6%	6%	6%	6%	6%	6%	4%	6%	6%
Deliverable grades	US T-Notes with $1\frac{3}{4}$–$5\frac{1}{4}$ yrs to mature	US T-Notes with $2\frac{3}{4}$–$5\frac{1}{4}$ yrs to mature	US T-Notes with $4\frac{1}{4}$–$5\frac{1}{4}$ yrs to mature	US T-Notes with $6\frac{1}{2}$–10yrs to mature	US T-Bonds with 15–25yrs to mature	US T-Bonds with >25yrs to mature	UK Gilts with $8\frac{3}{4}$–13yrs to mature and cpn 1%–7%	Federal debt with $8\frac{1}{2}$–$10\frac{1}{2}$ yrs to mature	JGBs with 7–11 years to mature
Delivery months	Mar, Jun, Sep, Dec	Mar, Jun, Sep, Dec	Mar, Jun, Sep, Dec	Mar, Jun, Sep, Dec	Mar, Jun, Sep, Dec	Mar, Jun, Sep, Dec	Mar, Jun, Sep, Dec	Mar, Jun, Sep, Dec	Mar, Jun, Sep, Dec
Delivery dates	Three days after the last trading date	Three days after the last trading date	Three days after the last trading date	Any business day during delivery month	Any business day during delivery month	Any business day during delivery month	Any business day during delivery month	10th calendar day of delivery month	20th calendar day of delivery month
Last trading day	12:00 noon last business day of delivery month	12:00 noon last business day of delivery month	12:00 noon last business day of delivery month	12:00 noon seven business days before last business day of delivery month	12:00 noon seven business days before last business day of delivery month	12:00 noon seven business days before last business day of delivery month	11:00 two business days before last business day of delivery month	12:30 two business days before delivery date	11:00 seven business days before delivery date
Quotation	Points and one quarter of a $\frac{1}{32}$ nd of a point	Points and one quarter of a $\frac{1}{32}$ nd of a point	Points and one quarter of a $\frac{1}{32}$ nd of a point	Points and one half of a $\frac{1}{32}$ nd of a point	Points and $\frac{1}{32}$ nds of a point	Points and $\frac{1}{32}$ nds of a point	Points and 0.01 of a point	Points and 0.01 of a point	Points and 0.01 of a point
Tick value	$15.625	$15.625	$7.8125	$15.625	$31.25	$31.25	£10	€10	¥10,000
Open-outcry	07:20–14:00 M–F	07:20–14:00 M–F	07:20–14:00 M–F	07:20–14:00 M–F	07:20–14:00 M–F	07:20–14:00 M–F			
Electronic trading	17:30–16:00 S–F	17:30–16:00 S–F	17:30–16:00 S–F	17:30–16:00 S–F	17:30–16:00 S–F	17:30–16:00 S–F	08:00–18:00	08:00–22:00	09:00–11:00 12:30–15:00 15:30–18:00

Source: Compiled from the contract definitions published by the various futures exchanges on their websites

TABLE 7.4

Effectiveness of conversion factors – all yields at 6%

Coupon	Maturity	Conversion factor (CF)	Relative value (using CF)	Bond price	Relative value (using price)	Difference in relative values
1.875%	30 Sep 17	0.7807	0.9501	77.84	0.9494	–0.07%
2.750%	31 Dec 17	0.8217	1.0000	81.99	1.0000	
4.000%	15 Aug 18	0.8837	1.0755	88.11	1.0746	–0.08%

The relative values in the fourth column are calculated simply by dividing each conversion factor in turn by the conversion factor of the 2.75% bond, which we will use as the benchmark for comparisons. The bond prices in the fifth column are calculated using the standard bond pricing formula for Treasury Notes, assuming settlement on 1st March 2011 and that yields on that day are 6% for all bonds. The relative values in the sixth column are then calculated by comparing these bond prices, again using the 2.75% bond as the benchmark.

Note that the final column shows that there is virtually no difference between the two sets of relative values. If the holder of a long position in these T-Note futures were delivered the 4% note instead of the 2.75% note, they would pay 107.55% as much to receive a bond worth 107.46% as much; the discrepancy of –0.08% is tiny. This means that conversion factors do a very good job of adjusting for different deliverable bonds when prevailing yields match the notional coupon defined in the futures contract.[2]

But what if the prevailing yields are different from 6%? Table 7.5 repeats the analysis, but in a world where all yields are 3% in the delivery month.

TABLE 7.5

Effectiveness of conversion factors – all yields at 3%

Coupon	Maturity	Conversion factor (CF)	Relative value (using CF)	Bond price	Relative value (using price)	Difference in relative values
1.875%	30 Sep 17	0.7807	0.9501	93.32	0.9478	–0.23%
2.750%	31 Dec 17	0.8217	1.0000	98.46	1.0000	
4.000%	15 Aug 18	0.8837	1.0755	106.64	1.0831	+0.76%

Now the differences between the two sets of relative values are significant. This time, if the holder of a long position in the March 2011 T-Note futures were delivered the 4% note instead of the 2.75% note, they would pay 107.55% as much to receive a bond worth 108.31% as much; this discrepancy of +0.76% would be equivalent to $76,000 on $10m face value of bonds, and would be even more if yields were lower. However, such good fortune would be unlikely to occur. When bond futures contracts end in physical delivery, it is the party who is short futures who chooses which bond to deliver, and they would clearly prefer to deliver the 1.875% of Sep 2017 instead, saving 0.23% rather than wasting 0.76%.

This demonstrates that, despite using conversion factors, not all bonds are equal when it comes to delivery. Some bonds will be relatively more expensive, some will be cheaper, and one in particular will be the *cheapest-to-deliver bond* – an important concept when it comes to the pricing of bond futures contracts.

To determine which bond is the cheapest-to-deliver (CTD) in the delivery month itself, consider someone who executes the following strategy:

a) Buy $100,000 face value of a deliverable bond.

b) Sell one futures contract.

c) Immediately initiate the delivery process.

The amount paid out for the bond will simply be the prevailing market price plus any accrued interest:

$$BNDAMT = P + ACC \qquad (7.2)$$

where:

BNDAMT	is the amount paid to purchase the bond
P	is the prevailing market price of the bond
ACC	is the accrued interest

The invoice amount *INVAMT* received when delivering the bond against the short futures position has already been defined in equation 7.1. The resultant profit from the complete strategy is then:

$$
\begin{aligned}
PROFIT &= INVAMT - BNDAMT \\
&= (FP \times CF + ACC) - (P + ACC) \qquad (7.3) \\
&= (FP \times CF - P)
\end{aligned}
$$

The bond for which this expression is maximised will be the CTD bond during the delivery month. A slightly more complex formula taking into account carrying costs can be derived to determine which bond is the cheapest-to-deliver prior to the delivery month (see section 7.4).

As an example, on 1st December 2010 the bonds deliverable into the December 2010 10yr T-Note contract were available at the prices summarised in Table 7.6. On the same date, the December contract was trading in the range 123'27 to 124'025, and settled at 123'275. Table 7.6 demonstrates for each deliverable bond the profit that would be available from buying the bond, selling the futures contract at 123'275 and then immediately delivering the bond against receipt of the invoice amount. As the table illustrates, the results span the range from –0.38 down to –3.78, the figures representing the dollar losses per $100 of bonds traded. The best (or least bad) result arises from using the $4\frac{3}{4}$% of Aug 2017, which is therefore the CTD bond in this example. The figure of –0.38 therefore implies a loss of $380 if the strategy were executed for $100,000 face value of bonds.

It is interesting to note that all the bonds produce a small negative result for the strategy of buying the bond, selling the futures and initiating the delivery process. This might suggest that the opposite strategy, buying the futures and

TABLE 7.6

Determining the cheapest-to-deliver T-Note on 1st December 2010

Cpn (%)	Maturity	Bond price	Conversion factor	FP×CF–P	Modified duration (yrs)
4.750%	15 Aug 17	116.00	0.9335	–0.38	5.77
4.250%	15 Nov 17	112.77	0.9040	–0.80	6.08
1.875%	31 Aug 17	97.69	0.7807	–0.99	6.26
2.375%	31 Jul 17	100.99	0.8072	–1.01	6.09
2.500%	30 Jun 17	101.91	0.8139	–1.10	5.99
2.250%	30 Nov 17	99.58	0.7943	–1.20	6.44
3.500%	15 Feb 18	107.72	0.8588	–1.35	6.33
1.875%	31 Oct 17	97.33	0.7738	–1.49	6.43
1.875%	30 Sep 17	97.49	0.7738	–1.65	6.34
3.875%	15 May 18	110.25	0.8765	–1.68	6.51
4.000%	15 Aug 18	110.98	0.8806	–1.91	6.62
3.750%	15 Nov 18	109.03	0.8621	–2.25	6.91
2.750%	15 Feb 19	101.13	0.7959	–2.55	7.26
3.125%	15 May 19	103.54	0.8150	–2.59	7.41
3.625%	15 Aug 19	107.12	0.8437	–2.62	7.42
3.375%	15 Nov 19	104.85	0.8232	–2.88	7.72
3.625%	15 Feb 20	106.60	0.8367	–2.96	7.77
3.500%	15 May 20	105.27	0.8244	–3.16	8.05
2.625%	15 Aug 20	97.46	0.7583	–3.54	8.42
2.625%	15 Nov 20	97.11	0.7535	–3.78	8.67

selling the bond short (known as a reverse cash-and-carry), would lead to a profit. Remember that it is the party who is short futures who initiates the delivery process and can, among other things, choose which bond to deliver. Anyone tempted to execute a reverse cash-and-carry by shorting the 2.625% of Nov 2020, in a bid to secure a 3.78% riskless profit, should therefore note that the seller would be most unlikely to deliver that particular bond. In addition to choosing which bond to deliver, the futures seller can exploit a number of features inherent in the delivery process to gain a slight advantage over the party who is long futures. These features (which will be explained in section 7.5) are called *seller's options* and have a positive value to the holder of a short futures position, offsetting the small losses revealed in Table 7.6.

Table 7.6 also shows the modified duration for each of the deliverable bonds and you can see that, with few exceptions, the shorter the modified duration, the more favourable the result. In particular, the bond with the shortest modified duration is also the cheapest-to-deliver. This is generally the case in an environment where yields are lower than the nominal coupon rate defined in the bond futures contract, which was very much the case in December 2010 when the yields for deliverable bonds ranged from 2.17% to 2.96% compared with the nominal coupon rate of 6%.

To understand why the CTD bond in a low-yield environment is most likely to be the bond with the shortest modified duration, let's analyse what happens as yields fall from the 6% level defined in the contract. As yields fall, all bond prices will rise, but the bonds that will rise the most are those with the longest modified durations, making them relatively expensive to deliver. In contrast, the bond that will rise the least will be the one with the shortest modified duration, making it the cheapest to deliver.

In the earlier example given in Tables 7.4 and 7.5, the modified duration of the 1.875% bond maturing Sep 2017 starts at 5.92 years compared with 6.25 years for the 4% bond maturing Aug 2018. When yields fall, it is the shorter-maturity bond that rises the least, 19.9% instead of 21.0%, making it the cheapest of the three to deliver.

7.3 Cash-and-carry pricing for bond futures

The previous section discussed the strategy of buying a deliverable bond and selling the futures contract, and demonstrated how this can provide a method for determining which bond is the cheapest-to-deliver during the delivery month. Among all the deliverable bonds, the one which maximises the expression in equation 7.3 is the cheapest-to-deliver. Table 7.6 demonstrated that the result from executing this strategy was almost zero, and would be zero if the value of the seller's options is taken into account.

This near-zero result is to be expected, of course. If the strategy created a significant profit for any bond, arbitrageurs would intervene immediately to exploit the opportunity. Their action would drive up the price of the CTD bond and drive down futures prices, thereby eliminating the profit potential.

So far, the strategy of buying a bond and selling the futures contract has been applied only to the delivery month, and only as a means of determining which bond is the cheapest-to-deliver against a short position in the futures. However, the idea can be extended to yield two very important benefits. First and foremost, the strategy can be exploited in order to determine what the fair price is at which bond futures contracts should trade. Second, this technique can be applied not only in the delivery month but at any time prior to the contract's maturity.

Consider the following strategy executed by an arbitrageur some time before the delivery month:

a) Buy $100,000 face value of a deliverable bond.

b) Finance the bond through a repo (sale and repurchase agreement – a form of secured borrowing).

c) Sell one futures contract.

d) Hold the bond until the last day of the delivery month.[3]

e) Deliver the bond against the short futures position.

As this involves buying a bond for cash, and carrying it for a period of time, the strategy is known as a *cash-and-carry*. It is easier to understand the underlying principles if the transactions are summarised pictorially, as in Figure 7.1. This starts at the top-left with the arbitrageur borrowing a sum of money. The top leg of the figure represents the *cash* part of the cash-and-carry operation. This money is used to finance the purchase of a deliverable bond, which is held or carried until the end of the delivery month. The bottom leg illustrates the *carry* part of the cash-and-carry operation. Finally, on the last day of the delivery month the bond is delivered to extinguish the short futures position, and the proceeds are used to repay the original borrowing.

FIGURE 7.1

Pictorial representation of cash-and-carry

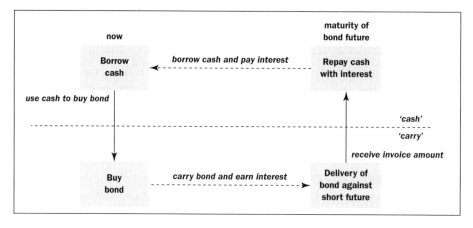

Worked example 7.1

Suppose that on 30th September 2010 an arbitrageur decides to undertake a cash-and-carry using the $4\frac{3}{4}$% of 15th August 2017, the bond that turned out to be cheapest-to-deliver against the December contract in the delivery month. The arbitrageur therefore buys this bond and sells the Dec 2010 contract, with the intention to deliver the bond at the end of December. The rates prevailing for the various transactions would be as follows:

a) Trading date: 30th September 2010
    Value date: 1st October 2010
b) Bond: $4\frac{3}{4}$% maturing 15th August 2017
    Bond price: 118'24
    Conversion factor: 0.9335
c) Repo rate: 0.52%
d) Future: Dec 2010 T-Note future
    Futures price: 126'03
e) Holding period: 91 days
f) Final delivery date: 30th December 2010

Figure 7.2 shows the detailed cash flows arising from these transactions.[4]

FIGURE 7.2

Detailed cash flows for T-Note futures cash-and-carry strategy

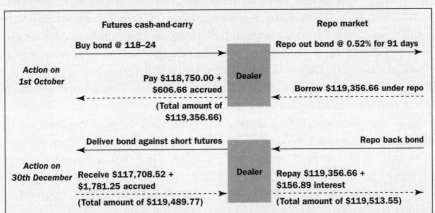

At the inception of the strategy, the bond is purchased for a total consideration of $119,356.66. This comprises the $118,750.00 quoted price of the bond plus 47 days' accrued interest of $606.66. The bond is immediately repo'd out in order to obtain the funds required to finance the purchase of the bond in the first place.

The strategy terminates at the end of the delivery month, when the bond is delivered against the short futures position. Remembering that the idea of a futures contract is to fix the price at the outset at which a transaction will be executed in the future, the invoice amount should be the futures price at the outset multiplied by the conversion factor of the delivered bond, plus the accrued interest on the delivery date. This sum can be calculated by inserting the appropriate values into equation 7.1:

$$INVAMT = \frac{126.09375 \times 0.9335 + 1.78125}{100} \times \$100,000 = \$119,489.77$$

The amount repaid under the repurchase agreement is the principal of $119,356.66 plus interest at 0.52% for 91 days:

$$REPAMT = 119,356.66 \times \left(1 + 0.0052 \times \frac{91}{360}\right) = \$119,513.55$$

These two sums are virtually identical, being within 0.02% of each other. The small shortfall in the invoicing amount arises once again from the seller's options (to be discussed more fully in section 7.5).

With these rates, an arbitrageur executing a cash-and-carry operation would obtain neither a profit nor a loss. The same would be true, of course, if the opposite strategy – a reverse cash-and-carry – had been executed. This implies that the futures price of 126'03 must have been fair. If the price had been any different, the arbitrageur would have been able to exploit the opportunity and profit as a result.

In the preceding analysis, we based the invoice amount on the futures price at the outset, on the basis that a futures contract fixes the price at the outset at which a future transaction will take place. In principle this is correct. In practice, however, the daily margining process adds a small complication. All futures positions are marked to market on a daily basis, and any profits or losses generated are added to or subtracted from the margin account. To compensate for this, the invoice amount is determined by the futures settlement price just before delivery, rather than on the initial futures price. These two components more or less cancel out, as we shall see.

In the preceding example, we calculated the final cash flows based on the initial futures price of 126'03. In practice, the final settlement price achieved by the Dec 2010 contract was actually 121'08. This means that the arbitrageur would have made an extra $4,843.75 profit over the course of the carry period, being the difference of 4'27 between the initial and final futures prices. However, the invoicing amount would have been different:

$$INVAMT = \frac{121.25 \times 0.9335 + 1.78125}{100} \times \$100,000 = \$114,968.13$$

This is $4,521.64 less than before, wiping out all but $322.11 of the futures profit.[5] As this difference between futures profit and the adjustment to the invoice amount is small, we will ignore these offsetting factors in the ensuing analysis and assume, as we did initially, that the initial futures price determines the invoice amount.

Worked example 7.2

We can now use the findings from the cash-and-carry strategy to determine what a fair futures price should be. An important feature of the strategy is that all rates are known in advance. The purchase price of the bond, the conversion factor, the repo rate and the selling price of the future are all fixed at the inception of the strategy. Nothing remains to be negotiated or determined thereafter. The profit or loss through entering into the cash-and-carry can therefore be determined in advance, and has three components.

First, the invoice amount from equation 7.1 is:

$$INVAMT = FP \times CF + ACC_D \tag{7.4}$$

where:

$INVAMT$	is the invoice amount
FP	is the futures price
CF	is the conversion factor
ACC_D	is the accrued interest when the bond is delivered

Second, the amount repaid under the repurchase agreement is:

$$REPAMT = (P + ACC_0) \times (1 + rt) \tag{7.5}$$

where:

$REPAMT$	is the amount repaid to repurchase the bond
P	is the quoted (clean) price of the bond
ACC_0	is the accrued interest when the bond is purchased
r	is the repo rate (expressed as a decimal fraction)
t	is the fraction of a year over which the bond is repo'd

Finally, we must take into account any coupons paid while the bond is being carried, which belong to the owner of the bond even though it has been repo'd out. We can assume that the coupons can also earn the repo rate, so that the total value of coupons plus interest earned is:

$$CPNINT = \sum_{i=1}^{N} CPN_i \, (1 + rt_{i,D}) \tag{7.6}$$

where:

$CPNINT$	is the value of coupons received plus interest earned thereon
N	is the total number of coupons received during the carrying period
CPN_i	is the i'th coupon
r	is the repo rate (expressed as a decimal fraction)
$t_{i,D}$	is the fraction of a year from receipt of the i'th coupon until the delivery date

The net profit from the cash-and-carry strategy is therefore:

$$
\begin{aligned}
PROFIT &= INVAMT + CPNINT - REPAMT \\
&= FP \times CF + ACC_D + \sum_{i=1}^{N} CPN_i \, (1 + rt_{i,D}) - (P + ACC_0) \times (1 + rt)
\end{aligned}
\tag{7.7}
$$

If we set the net profit to be zero, so that arbitrageurs cannot gain from either the forward or reverse cash-and-carry strategy, we can rearrange equation 7.7 to obtain an expression for the fair futures price:

$$FP = \frac{(P + ACC_0) \times (1 + rt) - \sum_{i=1}^{N} CPN_i \, (1 + rt_{i,D}) - ACC_D}{CF} \tag{7.8}$$

If we insert the values used in the previous illustration, we obtain:

$$FP = \frac{(118.75 + 0.60666) \times \left(1 + 0.0052 \times \frac{91}{360}\right) - 0 - 1.78125}{0.9335}$$

$$= 126.119 \approx 126\text{-}04$$

This is within $\frac{1}{32}$nd of the futures price actually observed.

All the prices used in this illustration were actual market rates on 30th September 2010. The difference between the actual price of 126'03 and the theoretical price of 126'04 probably represents the value of the seller's options previously referred to and discussed more fully in section 7.5. The fact that these contracts in practice trade at two ticks below their theoretical price is another way of measuring the value of the seller's options.

Let's summarise the key points behind cash-and-carry pricing:

- A cash-and-carry strategy comprises borrowing money, buying a deliverable bond and selling the future.

- The prices, rates and final outcome are all known at the outset when the cash-and-carry is executed.

- The cash-and-carry strategy is virtually riskless[6] if the bond is delivered against the short futures position.

- The net profit must be zero when the seller's options are taken into account given that:
    - all prices are known at the outset.
    - the strategy is a riskless one.

- The fair price for a futures contract can therefore be derived by applying the zero profit constraint to the cash-and-carry strategy.

There is therefore no need to forecast future bond prices in order to price a bond futures contract. Just as with short-term interest rate contracts, it is possible to construct a set of trades at known rates to hedge completely a bond futures position. With short-term futures contracts, the hedge comprised borrowing at one maturity and lending at another maturity, to create a synthetic forward-forward position. With bond futures contracts, the hedge comprises borrowing money and buying the cheapest-to-deliver bond.

Running a cash-and-carry position involves paying out interest at the repo rate, and earning interest at the coupon rate on the cheapest-to-deliver bond. When repo rates are higher than the coupon rate, it will cost money to carry the bond. This is called *negative carry*, and bond futures prices will be higher the longer the carry period. On the other hand, if repo rates are lower than the coupon rate, someone running the cash-and-carry will benefit. In this *positive carry* environment, futures prices will be lower for later delivery months. This compensates the party that is long futures who must wait longer for delivery, and who therefore forgoes the opportunity to earn the attractive coupon interest while they are waiting.

As an example, consider the set of T-Note futures prices at the close of business on 14th January 2011 shown in Table 7.7.

TABLE 7.7
Closing prices on 14th January 2011 for 10yr T-Note futures

Contract	Closing price
Mar 11	120'275
Jun 11	119'220
Sep 11	118'195
Dec 11	117'170
Mar 12	116'145

Source: Taken from the US settlement prices published by the CBOT on its website www.cmegroup.com

The futures prices decline by about one full point between successive delivery months, which is equivalent to around 4% per annum. This reflects the positive carry caused by repo rates of about 0.7% and the coupon rate of 4.75%. The gap between Dec 11 and Mar 12 contracts of 69 ticks is slightly less than that between March 11 and June 11 contracts of 75 ticks, reflecting market expectations that repo rates will rise gently in the future.

7.4 The implied repo rate

In the worked examples discussed in the previous section, the $4\frac{3}{4}$% of August 2017 was used to illustrate cash-and-carry pricing, but why choose this particular bond? For anyone contemplating executing a cash-and-carry strategy, the correct bond to choose is the one which maximises the net profit when delivered against the short futures position, in other words, the cheapest-to-deliver bond. During the delivery month, this is the one which maximises equation 7.3. Before the delivery month, the cheapest-to-deliver bond is the one which maximises the net profit defined in equation 7.7.[7] We can write this latter condition as follows:

$$\max\left(PROFIT\right) \Rightarrow \max$$

$$\left(FP \times CF + ACC_D + \sum_i^N CPN_i\left(1 + rt_{i,D}\right) - \left(P + ACC_0\right) \times \left(1 + rt\right)\right) \quad (7.9)$$

There are a number of ways of solving this problem, all of which are equivalent and will lead to the same choice of CTD bond. The most obvious method is simply to calculate the net profit for each deliverable bond and find which bond gives the largest profit. Alternatively, we could use the device of setting the net profit to zero and rearrange the equation to solve for the bond giving the lowest fair futures price, as in equation 7.8. As a final alternative, we could once again set the net profit to zero and search for the bond giving the highest repo rate. The last method has the attraction that the futures price is more readily observable and therefore easier to insert into an equation than the repo rate.

By setting the net profit to zero, and rearranging equation 7.9, we can obtain an expression for the *implied repo rate*.

$$
r = \frac{(FP \times CF + ACC_D) - (P + ACC_0) + \sum_i^N CPN_i}{t(P + ACC_0) - \sum_i^N (CPN_i t_{i,D})}
\tag{7.10}
$$

where:

r is the implied repo rate

The implied repo rate is the repo rate at which a cash-and-carry strategy would produce a zero profit. If the cash-and-carry could be executed at a repo rate lower than the implied repo rate, the strategy would result in a profit. If the actual repo rate were higher than the implied repo rate, the cash-and-carry would make a loss. The implied repo rate is therefore a break-even interest rate – the higher the rate, the better.

An alternative way to look at the implied repo rate is to liken the cash-and-carry strategy to an ordinary investment. The cash-and-carry involves a cash outflow at the beginning, arising from buying the bond at the outset. When the bond is eventually delivered against the short futures position, there is a cash inflow. With an ordinary investment, there is a cash outflow at the outset when the investment is made, and a cash inflow at the end when the investment is liquidated. In both cases, the rate of return can be measured by comparing the cash inflow at the end with the cash outflow at the beginning. Looked at this way, the implied repo rate is simply the rate of return earned by investing in a bond and selling it at the price originally fixed by the futures contract.

Table 7.8 shows the implied repo rates on 30th September 2010 (value date 1st October) for the set of bonds then deliverable into the December 2010 T-Note futures contract, assuming that delivery would take place on 31st December. In each case, the implied repo rate is calculated according to equation 7.10. For example, using the $4\frac{3}{4}\%$ of August 2017 as the deliverable bond gives an implied repo rate of 0.44%.

$$
r = \frac{(126.09375 \times 0.9335 + 1.78125) - (118.75 + 0.60666) + 0}{\frac{91}{360} \times (118.75 + 0.60666) - 0} = 0.44\%
$$

TABLE 7.8

Implied repo rates on 30th September 2010 for T-Notes deliverable into the December 2010 contract

Coupon (%)	Maturity	Implied repo rate (%)
4.750%	15 Aug 17	0.44%
2.500%	30 Jun 17	–3.47%
2.375%	31 Jul 17	–3.48%
1.875%	31 Aug 17	–3.96%
3.500%	15 Feb 18	–4.69%
4.000%	15 Aug 18	–5.94%
1.875%	30 Sep 17	–6.78%
4.250%	15 Nov 17	–9.43%
3.625%	15 Aug 19	–9.68%
2.750%	15 Feb 19	–10.30%
3.875%	15 May 18	–11.62%
3.625%	15 Feb 20	–11.81%
3.750%	15 Nov 18	–13.87%
3.125%	15 May 19	–15.82%
3.375%	15 Nov 19	–17.31%
2.625%	15 Aug 20	–18.25%
3.500%	15 May 20	–19.70%

As the figures in Table 7.8 demonstrate, the implied repo rate varies from –19.70% to +0.44%, being highest for the $4\frac{3}{4}$% of August 2017. Using the criterion of highest implied repo rate, this bond is therefore the cheapest-to-deliver, and explains why this particular bond was chosen to illustrate all the examples in this section. It is also the bond with the shortest modified duration, as discussed earlier in section 7.2.

7.5 The delivery mechanism

The vast majority of futures positions are closed-out, reversed or liquidated prior to maturity. As a clear example of this, consider the statistics illustrated in Figures 7.3 and 7.4. These show respectively the open interest and trading volume figures for the December 2010 and March 2011 CBOT T-Note contracts during November and December 2010.

From an average of over 1,250,000 contracts traded each day from 1st to 29th November, trading volume in the December 2010 contract drops immediately to 493,665 contracts on the last day in November, and down to 56,373 by 6th December, one-tenth the volume of the previous week. At the same time, volume in the March 2011 contract increases ten-fold, from around 30,000 contracts per day in the third week of November to an average of over 1,100,000 contracts in December, including over 1,500,000 contracts on 1st December alone.

FIGURE 7.3

Open interest for CBOT 10yr T-Note futures November–December 2010

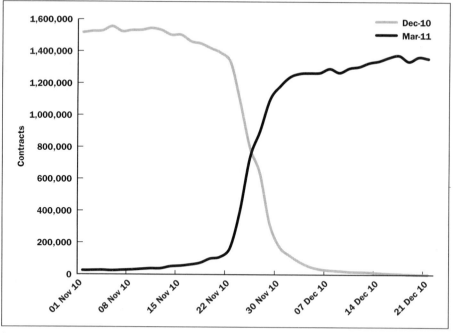

Source: CBOT (part of CME Group).

Open interest in the December 2010 contract declines in a similarly spectacular fashion, from a steady figure of over 1,500,000 contracts throughout the first three weeks of November, down to half this figure in the last week of that month, down to 51,168 at the end of the first week of December, and finally petering out to just 841 contracts after the last trading day. The declining interest in December contracts is mirrored by an increase in the March 2011 contract, up from around 25,000 contracts at the start of November to a steady 1,350,000 contracts by the end of December.

Although these figures demonstrate that positions in the vast majority of expiring T-Note contracts are rolled into the next liquid contract as the delivery month approaches, the 841 December 2010 contracts remaining after the last trading day on 21st December 2010 represent the small percentage of contracts, less than 0.1% in this case, which result in physical delivery. All 841 of these contracts resulted in delivery of the 4.75% of 15 August 2017 note – identified in Tables 7.6 and 7.8 as the CTD bond – on 31st December 2010, the last possible delivery date for this contract.

Table 7.9 analyses which bonds were actually delivered against all the expiring T-Note futures contracts in 2010. An average of just under 10,000 contracts went to physical delivery, representing around 0.6% of the open interest one month earlier. In nearly every case, just one bond – the CTD bond – was the one chosen for actual delivery. When a bond different from the CTD was delivered, as in March or June 2010, it was the second cheapest to deliver, and very similar in characteristics to the CTD itself.

FIGURE 7.4
Trading volume for CBOT T-Note futures November–December 2010

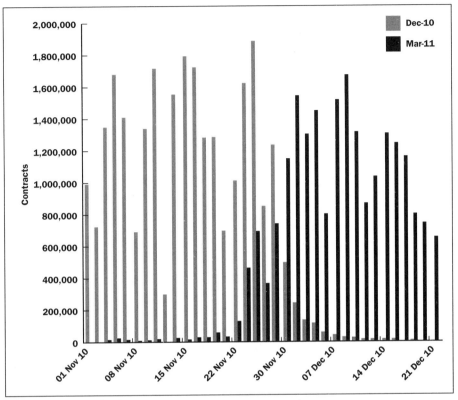

Source: CBOT (part of CME Group).

TABLE 7.9
Physical deliveries against T-Note futures contracts in 2010

Contract	Cpn (%)	Maturity	Contracts delivered	Date delivered
Mar-10	4.625%	15 Nov 2016	7,552	31 Mar 2010
Mar-10	2.750%	30 Nov 2016	3,663	31 Mar 2010
Jun-10	4.625%	15 Feb 2017	6	28 Jun 2010
Jun-10	4.625%	15 Feb 2017	7,582	30 Jun 2010
Jun-10	3.125%	31 Jan 2017	100	30 Jun 2010
Sep-10	4.500%	15 May 2017	1	01 Sep 2010
Sep-10	4.500%	15 May 2017	1	02 Sep 2010
Sep-10	4.500%	15 May 2017	1	22 Sep 2010
Sep-10	4.500%	15 May 2017	1	23 Sep 2010
Sep-10	4.500%	15 May 2017	500	27 Sep 2010
Sep-10	4.500%	15 May 2017	6,000	29 Sep 2010
Sep-10	4.500%	15 May 2017	13,535	30 Sep 2010
Dec-10	4.750%	15 Aug 2017	841	31 Dec 2010

Source: Chicago Board of Trade (CME Group).

When physical delivery takes place, it is always the party who is short futures who initiates the delivery process. Most exchanges require shorts to declare their intention to deliver two days before the required delivery date. If the *delivery day* is called D, the *intention day* is then D-2. On the intention day, D-2, the exchange assigns a party who is long futures to receive delivery. Some exchanges select a long systematically: the oldest long position, the largest long position, or pro rata amongst the largest long positions. Other exchanges may simply select a long at random. Also on D-2, the short names the particular bond that is to be delivered. On the *notice day*, D-1, the short invoices the long for the note or bond to be delivered according to equation 7.1, using the previous day's settlement price. In turn, the long provides details of their bank to the short. Finally, on D-day itself, the short delivers the bond, usually by electronic transfer, and the long makes payment for value that day.

Although this scheme may seem perfectly straightforward, the delivery sequence operating in conjunction with the definition of the bond futures contract gives rise to a number of advantages for the holder of a short position in futures. These advantages, collectively called the *seller's options*, are now explained in more depth.

The timing option

Some exchanges specify a range of dates when delivery may take place, often allowing delivery on any date in the delivery month. This gives the short the right to choose when during the delivery month to effect delivery. If repo rates are lower than the nominal coupon rate, the short would usually choose to defer delivery until late in the month, and benefit from positive carry; the opposite would be true if repo rates were higher. All the examples in this chapter involve delivery on the last possible date because of the very low repo rates prevailing.

If repo rates are quite different from the nominal coupon rate, everyone involved can anticipate when delivery will take place, and the futures pricing will reflect this. If repo rates are close to the nominal coupon rate, there is greater uncertainty as to when delivery will take place. Suppose interest rates start a little lower than the nominal coupon rate, so that the market anticipates delivery at the end of the delivery month and prices accordingly. If rates then rise, the seller can opt to switch delivery to the beginning of the delivery month, forcing the long to take delivery in what would then be a negative carry environment. The timing option therefore has value for the seller only when repo rates are close to the nominal coupon rate defined in the futures contract.

The wildcard option

On some exchanges, the futures settlement price for invoicing purposes, normally the closing futures price, may be fixed before the last possible time when a short may notify his intention to deliver. For example, the CBOT publishes daily settlement prices at 2pm Chicago time each day, but shorts can declare their intention to deliver at any time until 6pm. If bond prices decline after the futures settlement price is established, the short may elect to start the delivery process and profit from delivering a bond bought at 5pm prices but invoiced at a price linked to 2pm prices.

The quality option

The short can choose which of the deliverable bonds will actually be delivered. As bond prices fluctuate over time, the CTD bond can change and the seller can take advantage by buying a more attractive bond than the one originally used to price the futures contract.

The end-of-month option

Once again, for those exchanges which allow delivery to take place at any time during the delivery month, trading in the futures contracts ceases several days beforehand. Bond prices may therefore move after the final futures settlement price is determined, but before the final delivery date.

In each case, these features operate in favour of the short, who can act on favourable movements in bond prices, but can wait out unfavourable ones. For this reason, bond futures will normally trade a few ticks below the theoretical futures price given by equation 7.8. In the second worked example given in section 7.3, the December 2010 future should trade at 126'04, but the actual price observed was 126'03, valuing the seller's options at $\frac{1}{32}$nd of a point.[8]

7.6 Basic hedging with bond futures

One of the principal uses for bond futures is to hedge existing bond portfolios. A full discussion of the technique appears in Chapter 18 (section 18.12), but we can illustrate here an example of hedging a simple portfolio, one containing just the cheapest-to-deliver bond.

At first sight, it would seem sensible to hold futures contracts so that the notional value of the contracts matched that of the bonds held. For a $10m bond portfolio, 100 T-Note contracts, each with a notional underlying amount of $100,000, would seem to be the right number. However, this does not take into account the difference between the notional bond underlying the futures contract and the actual bonds held in the portfolio.

From equation 7.8, which provides an expression for the fair futures price, we can derive an equation which shows how the futures price will move for small changes in the price of the cheapest-to-deliver bond:

$$\frac{\partial FP}{\partial P} = \frac{1 + rt}{CF} \qquad (7.11)$$

therefore,

$$\Delta FP \approx \frac{\Delta P}{CF} \qquad (7.12)$$

where:

    FP is the futures price
    P is the bond price
    CF is the conversion factor

Equation 7.12 means that, for small changes in the bond price ΔP, the futures price will move a small amount $\Delta P/CF$. The futures price follows price movements of the CTD bond, not one-for-one but divided by the conversion factor (CF). If the conversion factor were 1.3333, for example, a four-point movement in the bond price would be followed by just a three-point movement in the futures price.[9]

Thus, in order to hedge the CTD bond, it is necessary to hold futures contracts equivalent to CF times the value of the bonds held. If the conversion factor of the CTD bond were greater than one, more futures contracts would need to be held, to adjust for the fact that movements in the futures price would be less than movements in the bond price, as illustrated in the previous paragraph. The opposite would be true if the conversion factor were less than one.

Suppose that an investor holding $10m face value of the $4\frac{3}{4}$% of August 2017 on 30th September 2010, seeing that yields had fallen almost 150bp over the previous six months, was now concerned to protect the value of the investment against an anticipated rise in yields. The investor could sell T-Note futures to hedge the portfolio against any further movements in bond prices.

On 30th September 2010, the relevant details were:

a) Trading date: 30th September 2010
b) Bond: $4\frac{3}{4}$% maturing 15th August 2017
      Bond price: 118'24
      Bond yield: 1.8334%
      Face value held: $10m
      Conversion factor: 0.9335
c) Future: December 2010 T-Note future
      Futures price: 126'03
      Underlying amount: $100,000 per contract

With the conversion factor in this case being 0.9335, the investor would need to sell 93 contracts in order to hedge the $10m bond portfolio.

Over the next couple of months, yields did indeed rise by more than 80bp, but by mid-December the investor thought that yields were at their peak. He therefore decided to lift the hedge and issued an instruction to his futures broker to buy back the 93 contracts at the opening of the market on 16th December. That morning, prices were:

a) Trading date: 16th December 2010

b) Bond price: 112'18

c) Opening futures price: 120'145

We can now evaluate the effectiveness of this hedge. Over the 77-day period, the bond price fell 6'06, resulting in a decrease in the value of the holding of exactly $618,750. Over the same period, the futures hedge made 361 ticks, because the investor sold initially at 126'03 and bought back at 120'145. Recalling that the tick value for T-Note contracts is $15.625, the magnitude of this profit on the 93 contracts can be calculated as:

$$361 \times \$15.625 \times 93 = \$524,578$$

While the bonds lost money, the futures made money, although at first sight it may appear that the hedge was less than perfect because the profit from the futures was less than the loss on the bonds. To understand why the financial result was nonetheless a good one, we need to understand conceptually what the bond futures hedge actually achieves. Combining a long position in bonds with a short position in bond futures creates a synthetic money-market investment. We can write this symbolically like this:

$$+\text{BONDS} - \text{BOND FUTURES} \equiv +\text{MONEY MARKET}$$

The plus and minus signs in this equation represent 'long' and 'short' respectively.

A money-market investment should generate money-market rates, around 50bp in this example. However, the investor still accrues coupon income from the bonds at the rate of 4.75% per annum. If we calculate the difference between 4.75% and 0.50% for the 77-day hedging period on the $10m bond holding, the additional coupon income reduces the bond loss by $90,903 to $527,847. Comparing this net loss to the futures profit of $524,578 shows that the hedge has been almost perfect after all.

To measure the success of the hedge, it is not enough simply to see whether the futures position made or lost money. Instead, it is necessary to compare the futures result with that of the underlying position, to see to what extent the futures and underlying positions mirrored each other. Equation 7.13 provides a simple measure of hedge efficiency:

$$Hedge\ efficiency = -\left[\frac{Futures\ result}{Bond\ result}\right] = -\left[\frac{524,578}{-527,847}\right] = 99.4\% \quad (7.13)$$

The total result for the investor is that the value of the portfolio has indeed been protected against any developments in bond prices after 30th September, when the hedge was established. The investor has effectively converted the bond portfolio into a synthetic money-market investment for the duration of the hedge, earning just a money-market rate of return, but rendering it almost completely immune from fluctuations in bond prices.

7.7 Stock indices and stock index futures

Short-term interest rate futures and bond futures are among the most heavily traded futures contracts. In addition, however, there is a highly active market in futures based on stock market indices, in which the two most active stock index futures accounted for trading volume of almost 1 billion contracts during 2010.

Most people are familiar with the basic concept of a stock index as being a mathematically derived number representing the relative level of the stock market at any moment in time. The best known indices are probably the Dow-Jones Industrial Average (DJIA), the S&P 500, the Nikkei 225 and the FTSE 100.

From the entire population of companies quoted on the particular stock exchange a subset is selected which attempts to reflect the market as a whole. This subset usually comprises the largest companies, or the most representative companies from each of the major industry classifications. In the most basic case, an index can be calculated by adding the prices of the companies and taking a simple average. The DJIA is the best example of such a *price-weighted* index. This technique benefits from simplicity, but unfortunately gives undue weight to those companies with relatively few high-priced shares, while diminishing the importance of those with a larger number of low-priced shares.

A better scheme is one adopted by most other indices which sum not the share prices themselves but the market capitalisations of each company in the subset. If share prices rise, then the market capitalisations will also rise. However, the index will respond in proportion both to the percentage rise in the share prices and to the relative size of companies. Such a construction leads to a *market-weighted* index.

Although the DJIA average is the best-known US stock index, the major US stock index futures are based on the S&P 500 index. The S&P possesses the twin advantages of being a market-weighted index and being based on a broader set of 500 quoted companies accounting for about 75% of the capitalisation of US stocks. This is much broader and more reliable than the limited set of 30 companies whose prices comprise the DJIA. In a similar fashion the FTSE 100 index, representing approximately 80% of London's stock market capitalisation, has taken over from the older FT Ordinary share index which was also based on just 30 shares. In addition to being as broadly based as possible, an index suitable as the basis for a stock index future must be calculated continuously and be available in real time.

7.8 Definition of stock index futures contracts

Although stock indices are mathematically derived from the share prices and capitalisations of quoted companies, they only convey information about relative movements in share prices over time, but say nothing about the absolute level of the market. This is because the initial value for the index is an arbitrary number chosen when the index is first established or rebased.

For example, the S&P 500 is quoted relative to the average price of shares in the years 1941–1943, which were arbitrarily assigned the index value 10. If the S&P 500 index has a value of 1293.24 on 14th January 2010, one can say that the shares within the index on that date are worth 129 times their value in 1941–1943. One could not, however, compare the S&P 500 index with the value of the FTSE 100, which was 6002.07 on that date, and say that UK stocks are worth five times those of US stocks! The reason why the FTSE 100 index is so much larger is simply because the total market capitalisation of the component shares was assigned the arbitrary value of 1000 when the FTSE 100 was initiated.

Although the absolute level of a stock index is therefore arbitrary, it can be turned into something more meaningful by assigning a monetary value for each level of the index. For example, each full point of the FTSE 100 could be arbitrarily assigned £10 in value, so that an index level of 6002 would be 'worth' £60,020. It may seem that we are getting further and further from reality by assigning an arbitrary monetary value to an index whose absolute level is also arbitrary. However, this device makes it possible to equate the 'value' of a stock index with that of a specific basket of shares having the following specification:

- The total value of the shares must match the monetary value of the index.
- The shares selected must correspond to the set of shares used to create the index.
- The amount of each holding must be in proportion to the market capitalisation of each of the companies.

If the FTSE 100 stood at 6002, the specific basket could be created by buying a portfolio of shares worth £60,020. The shares selected would be those of the 100 companies comprising the FTSE 100 index, and the relative value of each individual holding would correspond to the relative market capitalisations of each company within the index. The behaviour of this basket would then replicate the index exactly.[10] If the index went from 6002 to 6052, the arbitrary value of the index would increase from £60,020 to £60,520, and the value of the basket of shares would also increase to £60,520.

The definition of stock index futures takes advantage of this feature. A stock index future is a contract to buy or sell the face value of the underlying stock index, where the face value is defined as being the value of the index multiplied by a specified monetary amount. Table 7.10 illustrates the face values of the major stock index futures contracts on 14th January 2010. As the figures demonstrate, there is a wide disparity between the index numbers and the multipliers, with the largest numbers being some ten times as big as the smallest ones. Nevertheless, the contracts have been designed so that the face values fall within a much narrower range, mostly between $40,000 and $130,000 equivalent.

Table 7.11 provides a fuller specification of one typical contract, the E-mini S&P 500 stock index future.

As stock index futures do not involve physical delivery, there has to be a mechanism that ensures that these futures contracts converge to the underlying stock index on the last trading day. To ensure that the final settlement price

TABLE 7.10

Stock index futures face values on 14th January 2011

Index	Value	Futures exchange	Multiplier	Face value	Dollar equivalent
S&P 500	1,293.24	CME	$250	$323,310	$323,310
E-mini S&P 500	1,293.24	CME	$50	$64,662	$64,662
Nikkei 225	10,499.00	OSE	¥1,000	¥10,499,000	$126,697
FTSE 100	6,002.07	NYSE Liffe	£10	£60,021	$95,250
Euro STOXX 50	2,920.40	Eurex	€10	€29,204	$39,098
CAC 40	3,983.28	NYSE Liffe	€10	€39,833	$53,328
DAX	7,075.70	Eurex	€10	€70,757	$94,729

Source: Compiled from the settlement prices published by the various futures exchanges on their websites, and authors calculations.

TABLE 7.11

Definition of E-mini S&P 500 contract on the CME

Unit of trading	$50 per index point of S&P 500 index
Tick size	0.25 index point
Tick value	0.25 × $50 = $12.50
Delivery months	March, June, September, December (5 contracts listed)
Last trading day	08:30
	Third Friday in delivery month
Final settlement	Cash settlement based on Special Opening Quotation of the S&P 500 stock price index
Trading hours	3:30pm–4:30pm; 5:00pm–3:15pm (Mon–Thurs) 5:00pm–3:15pm (Sunday)

Source: Taken from the contract definition published by the CME on its website www.cmegroup.com

reflects the price at which share trades could actually be executed, the futures exchange itself calculates the value of the underlying index from the constituent stock prices rather than simply using the published value for the index, which might be a blend of current and stale prices. To do this calculation, the futures exchange uses the opening price for each stock on the last trading date, called the *Special Opening Quotation* (SOQ).

As not all stocks within the index will start trading the moment the stock exchange opens, the SOQ may not be known immediately. The CME reports that 95% of S&P 500 stocks open within 15 minutes of the start of trading, and 98% within 30 minutes. In the unlikely event that one or more stocks fail to trade at all on the last trading day, the last sale price on the previous day is used. When all the constituent stock prices are known, the futures exchange calculates the index value, and this is used as the final settlement price for the expiring futures contract.

7.9 Advantages of using stock index futures

Created in 1982, stock index futures provide investors and portfolio managers with an important tool, having a number of significant advantages:

a) Stock index futures permit investment in the stock market without the trouble and expense involved in buying the shares themselves. Section 7.12 provides an example of such a transaction.

b) Operating under a margining system, like all other futures, stock index contracts allow full participation in market moves without significant commitment of capital. Margin levels allow leverage typically between ten and twenty times.

c) Transaction costs are usually many times lower than those for share transactions. The fees for a 'round trip' – the creation and subsequent liquidation of a futures position – are often around $5 to $10 per contract, sometimes less. The costs involved in buying or selling an equivalent volume of shares would be a significant multiple of this.

d) It is much easier to take a short position. When selling securities short it is often necessary to enter into a share-borrowing arrangement so that the shares sold can be delivered. In addition, some stock markets impose an 'up-tick' rule permitting short sales only after the market has moved up. No such hindrances operate in the futures market.

e) Portfolio managers responsible for large share portfolios can hedge the value of their investment against bear moves without having to sell the shares themselves. This is also illustrated in section 7.12.

These advantages provide valuable opportunities for investment managers and speculators alike.

7.10 Cash-and-carry pricing for stock index futures

Although bond futures specifically permit physical delivery of a bond, whereas stock index contracts are invariably cash settled, there are many parallels between the two contracts. Both are capital markets instruments: the bond future works in conjunction with treasury and other bonds, while the stock index future works with equities. Furthermore, despite the fact that there is no deliverable instrument in the case of a stock index future, the contracts can be priced using the same cash-and-carry principles as were used to determine a fair price for bond futures.

Consider the following strategy executed before the delivery day:

a) Buy a portfolio of shares which replicates the stock index (with proportions matching construction of index, and total value equal to face value of index).

b) Finance the portfolio by secured borrowing.

c) Sell one stock index futures contract.

d) Hold the portfolio until the last trading day, collecting and investing any dividends received.

e) Liquidate the shares immediately when trading in the future ceases.

f) Cash-settle the futures contract.

g) Use the proceeds of the share sale and futures settlement to repay the borrowing.

As with the bond future arbitrage, this is also a cash-and-carry operation because the portfolio of shares is bought with cash and carried until the maturity of the futures contract. Figure 7.5 pictures this sequence of transactions, which is similar to Figure 7.1 but with some subtle differences.

The middle and lower parts of Figure 7.5 represent the cash-and-carry: borrowing money to buy the portfolio of shares and repaying the loan with the proceeds of the portfolio liquidation. The top part of the figure shows the parallel transactions in the futures market, which hedge the portfolio against movements in the market. For example, if the stock market dropped while the cash-and-carry was in progress, the proceeds from selling the shares may not be enough to repay the borrowing. However, the futures contracts would make a profit under these circumstances.

If the selection and amounts of the share deals are chosen carefully, the cash-and-carry operation together with the futures contracts form a riskless combination and can be used to determine a fair price for the futures contracts themselves.

FIGURE 7.5

Cash-and-carry for stock index futures

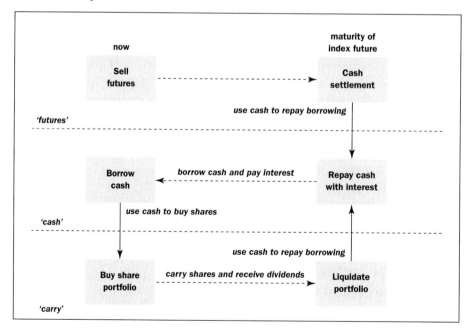

Worked example 7.3

Suppose that on 30th September 2010 market rates were:

a) S&P 500 index: 1,141.20
b) Face value of index: $57,060
c) Dividend yield: 1.96%
d) Future: Dec 2010 E-mini S&P 500 future
   Futures price: 1,136.75
   Last trading day: Friday 17th December 2010
e) Holding period: 74 days
f) Interest rate: 0.2795%

On that date an investor borrows $57,060, buys the constituent shares of the S&P 500 index in the correct proportions, and sells one Dec 2010 E-mini S&P 500 futures contract.

On 17th December 2010 – the last trading day of the futures contract – the investor sells the shares first thing in the morning at the market's open and closes out the futures position by buying back one contract also at the prevailing price. On that date the S&P 500 index opened at 1243.63, which represented a rise of 102.43 points or 8.98%. As the shares purchased matched exactly those in the index, they would rise by a similar amount and be worth $62,181.50 at the end of the holding period. That same morning, the futures were trading in the range 1240.75–1245.00 and the investor was able to close out at 1242.50. With the parallel rise in the futures price over the period of 105.75 full points, the futures position would lose:

$$105.75 \times \$50 = \$5,287.50$$

Summarising the resulting cash flows at the beginning and end of the cash-and-carry operation:[11]

30th September 2010	
Purchase of shares to match index	–57,060.00
Borrowing	+57,060.00
Sale of future	0.00
Net cash flow	0.00
17th December 2010	
Sale of shares	+62,181.50
Dividends received during period	+229.89
Loss on futures	–5,287.50
Repayment of borrowing plus interest	–57,092.78
Net cash flow	+31.11

Apart from the small residual of $31.11, equivalent to just 0.05% of the value of the shares purchased, the end result of the cash-and-carry is effectively zero, showing that the future was appropriately priced on 30th September 2010.[12] Had the futures price been any higher or lower, an arbitrageur would have been able to make a riskless profit through executing the cash-and-carry or the reverse cash-and-carry.

In principle, therefore, the concept of the riskless cash-and-carry can be applied to price stock-index futures in exactly the same way as for bond futures. Equation 7.8 can be adapted to provide a formula for pricing these contracts:

$$FP = I_0\,(1 + rt) - \sum_{i=1}^{N} DIV_i(1 + rt_{i,D})\qquad(7.14)$$

where:

FP	is the fair stock index futures price
I_0	is the stock index when the cash-and-carry is established
r	is the borrowing rate (expressed as a decimal fraction)
t	is the fraction of a year over which the cash-and-carry operation is executed
N	is the total number of shares in the index
DIV_i	is the dividend paid on the i'th share during the cash-and-carry period
$t_{i,D}$	is the fraction of a year between receipt of the i'th dividend and the delivery date

Equation 7.14 allows for the receipt of discrete dividends during the cash-and-carry period, and should be used because the stream of dividends will be 'lumpy' rather than a smooth flow. For a very broad-based index like the S&P 500, where dividends may be more evenly spread throughout the year, it is sometimes possible to approximate the flow of discrete dividends with a dividend yield instead. This leads to a simple formulation for the fair futures price:

$$FP = I_0\,[1 + t(r - d)]\qquad(7.15)$$

where:

d is the dividend yield

Substituting the figures in the previous example into equation 7.15 gives:

$$FP = 1141.20\left[1 + \frac{74}{360} \times (0.002795 - 0.0196)\right] = 1137.26 \approx 1136.75$$

This approximation works well in this example. However, there are some practical difficulties in hedging stock index futures with shares. These problems sometimes lead to discrepancies between the calculated futures price and the actual price observed, and are discussed in the next section.

7.11 Stock index futures prices in practice

The example in the previous section demonstrated that the actual futures price was very close to the fair futures price calculated using equations 7.14 and 7.15. However, the two may not be exactly equal in practice because of several difficulties in executing the cash-and-carry trade. These include the following:

Constructing the index portfolio: stock indices used as the underlier for index futures comprise up to 500 separate shares. Buying this number of different shares is in sharp contrast to the bond future, where only a single bond needs to be held. This complexity can create difficulties and increase the costs of constructing a share portfolio designed to mimic the index.

Transactions costs: these will be much greater than for bond futures, reflecting the number of separate transactions involved. Transactions costs will also be doubled because the share portfolio must be bought initially and then liquidated at the end of the cash-and-carry operation. With a bond future, it is possible to deliver the bond and therefore avoid the final transaction cost of liquidating the hedge.

Tracking error: in practice, some market-makers hedge stock index futures by using a smaller subset of the companies within the index. The aim is to capture a significant proportion of the composition of the index with relatively few transactions. While this can reduce transactions costs, it introduces a tracking error, in that the value of the share portfolio may not correlate perfectly with movements in the index.

Changes in index composition: the index composition may change during the cash-and-carry period. This may arise from stock splits, capital restructurings, the shrinkage or disappearance of some companies, or the growth of others. If this happens, new transactions must be executed to bring the shares held in line with the new formulation of the index. (This is somewhat analogous to the situation when the cheapest-to-deliver bond changes.)

Short sales: some stock markets impose certain restrictions on short sales of shares, and this could impair the efficiency of a reverse cash-and-carry operation which involves selling shares and buying futures.

Dividends: with a bond, the coupon is constant, known in advance, and is paid on set dates. Dividends on shares can only be estimated in advance and are paid at various times during the year. Even for broad-based indices like the S&P 500, there is a strong bunching of dividends in January–February, April–May, July–August and October–November. The effective carrying cost can therefore vary substantially throughout the year, especially before the payment of a large dividend on a narrow-based stock index. This means that hedging a stock index future can at best only be an approximate rather than an exact science.

The result of all these practical difficulties is to create a band of fair prices, rather than a single price. This band will be wider when there are high transactions costs, more uncertainty regarding dividends, more volatility, and less market efficiency. It must be remembered that the force which keeps actual market prices in line with theoretical ones is the possibility for arbitrageurs to make a risk-free profit. If this possibility is reduced or eliminated through excessive transaction costs or market inefficiency, market prices can drift away from theoretical prices.

Despite being one of the broadest based of stock indices, the S&P 500 actually exhibits the closest relationship in practice between actual and theoretical futures prices, this being aided by the existence of highly efficient computerised order execution systems. These reduce transactions costs and make it much easier to execute the hundreds of transactions necessary in performing cash-and-carry arbitrage deals. The S&P 500 index future normally trades within ±0.2% of its theoretical price.

7.12 Turning cash into share portfolios and share portfolios into cash

Stock index futures mimic the behaviour of the stock market as a whole, and they are easy to trade. They therefore provide the portfolio manager with a flexible and effective tool for restructuring an investment portfolio. Combining a long position in cash (i.e. an interest-bearing deposit) with the requisite number of stock index futures will effectively convert cash into shares. Alternatively, combining a long position in shares with a short position in futures will effectively turn the share portfolio into cash. Just as we did when we looked at hedging with bond futures, we can represent this symbolically as:

+ MONEY MARKET +STOCK INDEX FUTURES ≡ +SHARES

+ SHARES –STOCK INDEX FUTURES ≡ + MONEY MARKET

Both these possibilities are illustrated with brief examples in the following paragraphs.

Cash into shares

During the summer of 2010 the S&P 500 index had fallen from the highs above 1200 reached in late April, and was trading in the 1050–1150 band with little upward momentum. As a result, in mid-June 2010 an investment manager has decided to switch to cash and has placed $10m on deposit to earn interest fixed at 0.6%. The funds were placed on 15th June for six months and will be repaid on 15th December. There is no provision for early withdrawal of these funds. Figure 7.6 shows the evolution of the S&P 500 index over this period.

By the end of August, with the index having fallen through 1050 for the fourth time, the investment manager now expects US share prices to stage a significant rally and wishes to benefit from this view. Unfortunately, the investment funds have already been committed and are no longer available to invest in shares, at least for the time being. The investment manager therefore decides to buy S&P 500 futures in order to profit from any rise in the market. On Wednesday 31st August 2011, the S&P 500 stands at 1049.33, and E-mini December 2010 contracts are quoted at 1043.25. The face value of the S&P 500 is therefore:

$$\$50 \times 1049.33 = \$52,466.50$$

FIGURE 7.6
S&P 500 index in 2010

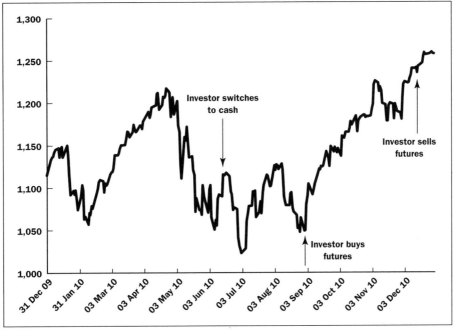

Source: Reprinted with permission from Yahoo! Inc. YAHOO! and the YAHOO! logo are trademarks of Yahoo! Inc.

The manager therefore needs to buy:

$$\frac{\$10,000,000}{52,466.50} = 191 \text{ contracts}$$

On Thursday 15th December 2010, the S&P 500 was 17.7% higher at 1235.23, while the December contract traded in the range 1234–1244.25. Let's suppose that the investment manager was able to close out the futures position at 1234. We can now compare the performance of the cash plus futures strategy with the performance of the stock market itself, had the portfolio manager been able to switch into shares on 31st August.

Cash plus futures

$10m plus 0.6% interest for 106 days	10,017,666.67
Profit on futures: 763 ticks × $12.50 × 191 contracts	1,821,662.50
TOTAL	$11,839,329.17

Shares

$10m index portfolio plus 17.7% capital appreciation	11,771,606.64
Dividends received at annual yield of 1.98% for 106 days	58,300.00
TOTAL	$11,829,906.64

These two results are within 0.1% of each other,[13] demonstrating that the combination of an interest-earning deposit plus the appropriate number of futures contracts replicates the performance of an index portfolio very well.

Shares into cash

Another investment manager is evaluating the performance of his portfolio at the end of April 2010. Although up 6.4% since the start of the year, the market as a whole has traded sideways for the past few weeks, and many are talking about a temporary downward correction in the near future. The investment manager, who is long ten different S&P stocks, decides to use stock index futures in order to hedge the portfolio against such a bear move. Table 7.12 shows the composition and valuation of the portfolio on 30th April 2010.

TABLE 7.12
Share portfolio on 30th April 2010

	No of shares	Share price ($)	Value of holding ($)
Apple Inc	3,830	251.53	999,974.70
Chevron Corp	12,279	67.86	1,000,001.76
Exxon Mobil	14,756	57.07	1,000,014.12
General Electric Co	53,022	14.42	999,994.92
IBM Corp	7,752	123.48	1,000,008.00
Johnson & Johnson	15,552	59.06	999,993.60
JP Morgan Chase & Co	23,486	36.61	1,000,033.88
Microsoft Corp	32,748	23.01	999,960.18
Procter & Gamble	16,088	59.98	1,000,030.08
Wells Fargo & Co	30,202	25.60	999,988.22
TOTAL			9,999,999.46

Source: Share prices from finance.google.com

All of these shares are included in the S&P 500 index, and in total represent approximately 20% of the weighting of the index. The investment manager decides that the portfolio is sufficiently representative of the market that using September 2010 E-mini S&P 500 contracts will provide an adequate hedge. With the S&P 500 index at 1186.69 and the full-point value of the futures contract being defined as $50, the face value of the index is $59,334.50. Having a portfolio worth $10m to hedge, it is necessary to work with:

$$\$10,000,000 / \$59,334.50 = 169 \text{ contracts}$$

This time, however, the investment manager must sell futures in order to hedge a long position in shares. He therefore sells 169 of the Sep 2010 contracts at the market price of 1178.75.

As Figure 7.7 shows, by the end of June that year, the US stock market was down 13%, so the investment manager was delighted that he had chosen to hedge his portfolio. The signs were, however, that the market was about to turn, so at this point he decided to lift the hedge. Table 7.13 summarises the performance of the share portfolio over the 61-day period.

FIGURE 7.7

S&P 500 index January–June 2010

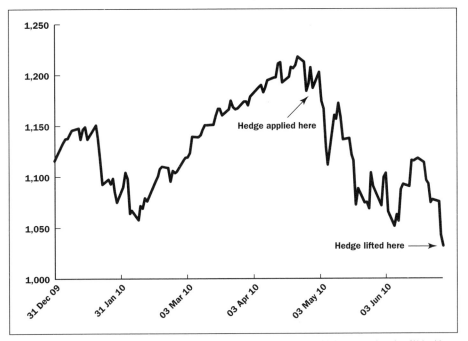

Source: Reprinted with permission from Yahoo! Inc. 2012 Yahoo! Inc. YAHOO! and the YAHOO! logo are trademarks of Yahoo! Inc.

TABLE 7.13

Share portfolio on 30th June 2010

	No of shares	Divis paid ($)	Share price ($)	Value of holding (inc. divis)	% change	Price decrease	Dividend yield
Apple Inc	3,830		251.53	$963,359.90	–3.66%	–3.66%	0.00%
Chevron Corp	12,279	0.72	67.86	$842,093.82	–15.79%	–16.67%	0.88%
Exxon Mobil	14,756	0.44	57.07	$848,617.56	–15.14%	–15.79%	0.65%
General Electric Co	53,022	0.10	14.42	$769,879.44	–23.01%	–23.54%	0.53%
IBM Corp	7,752	0.65	123.48	$962,255.76	–3.78%	–4.28%	0.50%
Johnson & Johnson	15,552	0.54	59.06	$926,899.20	–7.31%	–8.15%	0.84%
JP Morgan Chase & Co	23,486		36.61	$859,822.46	–14.02%	–14.02%	0.00%
Microsoft Corp	32,748	0.13	23.01	$757,788.72	–24.22%	–24.64%	0.43%
Procter & Gamble	16,088	0.48	59.98	$972,709.44	–2.73%	–3.51%	0.78%
Wells Fargo & Co	30,202	0.05	25.60	$774,681.30	–22.53%	–22.68%	0.15%
TOTAL				$8,678,107.60	–13.22%	–13.69%	0.48%

Source: Share prices and dividends from finance.google.com

The share portfolio has shown an overall fall in value of 13.22%, comprising an average fall in price of the shares held of 13.69% and dividends received equivalent to 0.48% of the portfolio's original value.[14] In particular, the holdings of GE, Microsoft and Wells Fargo proved to be the worst performers over the period, each losing more than 22% over the holding period.

However, with the general fall in share prices the futures made money over the period. On 30th June 2010, the investment manager was able to buy back the Sep 2010 E-mini S&P 500 contract at 1026.50, resulting in a profit of:

$$609 \text{ ticks} \times \$12.50 \times 169 \text{ contracts} = \$1,286,512.50$$

The total result was therefore $8,678,107.60 (the value of the share portfolio plus dividends received) plus the $1,286,512.50 futures profit, a net value of $9,964,620.10 corresponding to a small loss of 0.35%.

If the investment manager had instead decided to liquidate the shares and invest short term at 0.3% for 61 days, the fund including interest would have stood at $10,005,082.79. This would have been a gain of 0.05% over the period. So the hedged portfolio underperformed a money-market investment by 0.40%.

In this particular example, combining the long position in shares with a short futures position did produce a return close to that of the alternative money market position, but the results did not coincide exactly. This is because the ten shares actually held underperformed the market in price (although they outperformed in dividend yield). Let's look at the figures in detail. The market as a whole fell 13.14%, while the particular shares fell 13.69%, an additional loss of 0.55%. However, at an annual dividend yield of 1.9% for the S&P 500 the dividends should have been only 0.32% over the period, but they actually amounted to 0.48%, an additional profit of 0.15%. Combining these two gives a net shortfall of 0.40%. This explains why the hedged shares produced a return of –0.35%, 0.40% under the expected return of 0.05% from a pure money-market investment.

If the shares held had been more representative of the index portfolio, the combination of shares and short futures would have generated a return closer to the 0.05% cash return over the period, and the futures would have been more effective at turning shares into cash. Of course, a perfect result would have arisen had the investment manager held the index portfolio, just as in the previous example. Nonetheless, the stock index futures have done a pretty good job, turning an unhedged 13.22% loss into a hedged 0.35% loss, and saving the portfolio manager well over $1m.

Chapter 20 will illustrate more sophisticated hedging and trading strategies, especially those involving options. These allow investment managers to protect their portfolios against detrimental market movements, while still allowing them to gain from beneficial developments.

Notes

1 If the exact maturity were used, the conversion factor would work out at 0.8250.

2 Actually, the conversion factors would do a perfect job in a 6% yield environment if the CBOT calculated them without rounding down the bond maturities to the nearest quarter year.

3 Or until the specific delivery date in the case of contracts which define a single day on which delivery can take place.

4 For simplicity, we will initially ignore the margin flows arising from the futures position.

5 This small difference arises from the conversion factor:
$4,521.64 / 0.9335 = $4,843.75.

6 Recall that as bond prices move over the carry period, there is a small residual risk arising from the small discrepancy between futures profits and changes to the invoice amount. If bond prices drift downwards and the conversion factor is smaller than 1, this works in favour of the futures seller.

7 Equation 7.3 is actually a simplified version of equation 7.7, and can be obtained by assuming that purchase and delivery are actioned at the same time, so that $ACC_0 = ACC_D$, N = 0 and t = 0.

8 For a formal analysis of the valuation of the seller's options, see Gay, G. and Manaster, S. (1986) 'Implicit delivery options and optimal exercise strategies for financial futures contracts', *Journal of Financial Economics*, 16, pp. 41–72, or Arak, M. and Goodman, L. (1987) 'Treasury bond futures: valuing the delivery options', *Journal of Futures Markets*, 7, pp. 269–86.

9 Like the proverbial chicken and egg, it is difficult to say which comes first, movements in the bond price or movements in the futures price. Suffice it to say that they will move in tandem.

10 This is true so long as the stock index is calculated as the weighted *arithmetic* average of the market capitalisations of the component companies.

11 The simple example here ignores the small amount of interest that could be earned on reinvesting dividends, and also the non-trivial costs of executing the share transactions.

12 The residual of $31.11 is equivalent to 0.62 index points. In fact, on 30th September the futures were trading at 0.51 points lower than the fair value at the time, and at expiry the sale price achieved for the shares was 1.13 points higher than the futures final settlement price. Combining these (1.13 *less* 0.51) explains the 0.62-point discrepancy.

13 The results would have been even closer had interest rates not fallen from 0.6% to 0.3% between June and August. If the original deposit had been placed at 0.3%, the rate prevailing at the end of August when the futures contracts were bought, the two results would have been within 0.005% of each other.

14 For simplicity we assume here that the dividends received are not invested to earn interest.

8

SWAPS

Swaps are one of the outstanding success stories of the derivatives markets, and are a vivid illustration of the benefits brought about through financial innovation. From virtually nothing in 1980, the swap market had grown to around $400tn notional principal outstanding by the end of 2011. This chapter starts by summarising the development of the swap market, then goes on to explain the two principal types of swap product: interest rate and cross-currency swaps. We then look at a range of other swaps developed from these original products, including asset swaps, inflation swaps, equity swaps, commodity swaps and even volatility swaps. The next chapter explains how swaps are priced and valued, while some of the many and varied applications for swaps are dealt with in Chapter 18.

8.1 Definition of interest rate and cross-currency swaps

In order to understand how the swap market developed, we need to start with a basic definition of interest rate and cross-currency swaps. Later sections in this chapter provide more details and much more rigid and detailed definitions of the two major types of swap products.

An interest rate swap is:

- an agreement between two parties
- to exchange a stream of cash flows
- denominated in the same currency
- but calculated on different bases.

The most common type of interest rate swap is where one stream of cash flows comprises the fixed-rate coupons on a notional principal sum, while the other stream comprises floating-rate coupons. For example, one party may agree to pay fixed annual coupons of 4% on a notional principal sum of $10m, in return for receiving the prevailing US dollar LIBOR rate on the same principal. The fixed-rate payer would benefit if LIBOR were higher than 4% in a given period, but would lose if LIBOR were lower than 4%. An interest rate swap is therefore similar to an FRA, but operates over multiple periods.

A cross-currency swap is:

- an agreement between two parties
- to exchange a stream of cash flows
- denominated in different currencies
- calculated on similar or different bases.

The distinguishing feature of a cross-currency swap is that the two streams of cash flows are denominated in different currencies. For example, one party could agree to pay quarterly coupons fixed at 3% per annum on a notional principal of €10m, while receiving quarterly floating-rate coupons determined by three-month dollar LIBOR on a notional principal of $14m. In practice, both streams of coupons can be fixed-rate, both floating-rate, or one fixed and the other floating.

8.2 Development of the swap market

Swaps evolved from parallel and back-to-back loans which were once a feature of international finance. At the time, exchange controls operating in most countries limited the opportunities for companies to obtain cross-border finance or for investors to lend overseas. These inter-company loans provided an initial answer, although they were not ideal. As exchange controls were relaxed and eventually removed, parallel loans evolved into the first kind of currency swaps.

At the beginning, these were negotiated directly between interested parties, as in the famous cross-currency swap between IBM and the World Bank executed in August 1981. Banks played a very limited role, acting solely as brokers bringing interested parties together, and charging a commission. As the market evolved, however, banks started acting as principals in the transactions, thereby avoiding the need to have a pair of companies with exactly complementary financial requirements. In this mode, banks started to fulfil their true role as financial intermediaries, taking upon themselves rate and counterparty risk rather than expecting their clients to absorb these risks. The concept of a swap warehouse was introduced, whereby banks would 'warehouse' non-matching swaps until a corresponding counterparty could be found. In the meantime, residual mismatches could be hedged using STIR futures or other interest rate derivatives.

These developments increased liquidity tremendously. Figure 8.1 shows the growth of cross-currency swap transactions, while Figure 8.2 shows the even more impressive growth of interest rate swaps since the mid-1980s, making them the biggest derivatives market by far.

Swaps have now established themselves as one of the principal tools of financial engineering, helping to break down traditional national boundaries and create the global financial markets that we witness today. Swaps make it much easier for companies in one country to issue bonds in another country and currency, and likewise for investors to invest wherever they identify good opportunities. Swaps are widely understood by large companies and investment institutions, and are offered by banks of all sizes. In addition to standard swap products, some banks can tailor swaps to match the precise needs of borrowers and investors.

Banks specialising in swaps now integrate their currency and interest rate risk management across all derivative products. Swaps are no longer hedged by matching two identical but opposing swaps. Instead, swaps are hedged by combining positions in spot, forward and long-term FX, bonds, FRAs, short-term interest rate futures, bond futures, option-based products such as caps and floors, and other swaps, of course. In this way, banks can offer comprehensive risk management without the cost involved in hedging individual deals. The swap market has come a long way since the 1980s.

146 HANDBOOK OF FINANCIAL ENGINEERING

FIGURE 8.1

Growth of cross-currency swap transactions

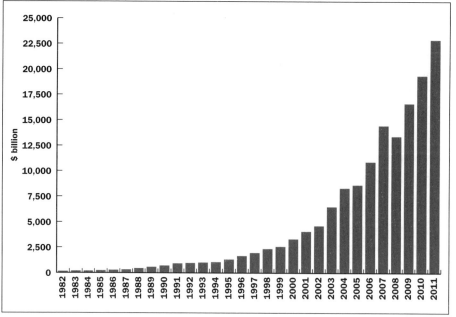

Source: BIS.

FIGURE 8.2

Growth of interest rate swap market

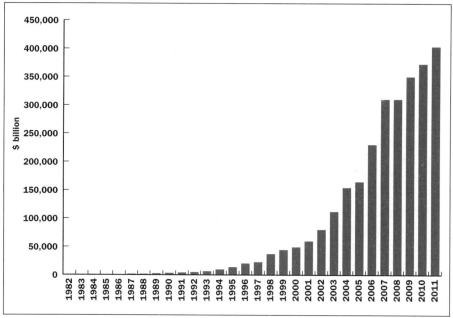

Source: BIS.

8.3 Interest rate swaps

A basic definition of interest rate swaps was provided at the beginning of this chapter; it is now appropriate to refine the definition and provide more detail.

A standard interest rate swap (IRS) is where:

- an agreement is made between two parties
- each party contracts to make periodic interest payments to the other
  - on a predetermined set of dates in the future
  - based on a notional principal amount
  - denominated in the same currency
- one party is the *fixed rate payer* – the fixed rate being agreed at the inception of the swap
- the other party is the *floating rate payer* – the floating rate being determined during the lifetime of the swap by reference to a specific market rate
- there is no exchange of principal – only exchange of interest.

The cash flows resulting from a typical interest rate swap are illustrated in the first two parts of Figure 8.3 using the normal convention where cash inflows are shown as an arrow pointing up, while cash outflows are shown as an arrow pointing down. The final part of Figure 8.3 shows an alternative representation of an interest rate swap as a 'plumbing diagram', where the arrows simply show the general direction of the cash flows rather than each individual one.

Figure 8.3 also highlights some of the key dates during the lifetime of a swap. The *trade date* – shown as t_0 in the figure – is the date on which the two parties to the swap agree to their contractual commitments. Given the volume of swaps trading that takes place, nearly all swaps conform to standard documentation prepared by the International Swaps and Derivatives Association (ISDA), and the legal arrangements are therefore usually a formality. Although the form of the contract is standard, there are a number of important items which must be agreed at the inception of the swap. The most important of these are:

- the fixed rate at which the fixed interest payments will be calculated
- the reference for determining the floating rate each period – this is usually the LIBOR rate of the appropriate tenor
- the frequency and basis for both the fixed-rate and floating-rate payments – payments are usually annual, semi-annual, or quarterly, but various day count conventions can apply (these are discussed shortly).

The trade date is usually also the first *setting date* – shown as t_{s1} in Figure 8.3 – when the floating rate for the next period is determined. Most swaps use LIBOR as the market rate for the floating leg and, just as is conventional with Eurocurrency deposits and FRAs, the rate is normally set two business days before the period commences. The second setting date t_{s2} will occur just before

FIGURE 8.3

Cash flows for typical interest rate swap

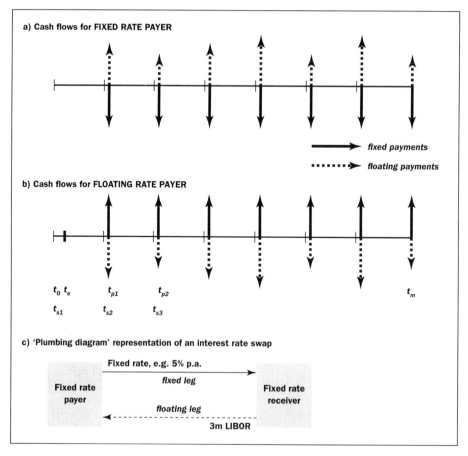

the beginning of the second swap period; again this is normally two business days beforehand. Subsequent setting dates follow the same pattern until the last setting date, just prior to the last swap period.

The *effective date* – shown as t_e in Figure 8.3 – is the date when interest starts to accrue on both the fixed and floating legs of a swap, and this is usually two business days after the trade date. The time lag is designed to correspond with the similar gap between dealing date and value date in the Eurocurrency markets. Since the floating rate for each period is always determined in advance of that period, both parties therefore know the rates at which they should be accruing interest, and thus the size of both the fixed and floating payments at the end of that period.

The first *payment date* t_{p1} comes at the end of the first swap period, when one party will be a net creditor while the other will be a net debtor. Rather than each party paying the entire interest payment to the other, the net debtor simply pays over the difference to the creditor. Most swaps involve each party being a net creditor for part of the time, and a net debtor for the remainder.

This cycle then repeats itself until the final net payment is made on the *maturity date* (or termination date) of the swap t_m.

The interest payments themselves are calculated using the standard formula:

$$INT = P \times r \times t \qquad (8.1)$$

where:

INT	is the interest payment
P	is the nominal principal
r	is the annual interest rate for the period (expressed as a fraction)
t	is the day count fraction

Although the principal is never exchanged in an interest rate swap, the parties to the swap must nonetheless agree a nominal principal amount in the agreed currency in order for the interest payments to be calculated. The day count fraction is the proportion of the year covered by the particular swap period and can be calculated in a number of ways:

- Actual/365 (Fixed): this uses the actual number of days in the particular swap period divided by 365, even in a leap year. This convention is commonly used for sterling interest rate swaps.
- Actual/360: this also uses the actual number of days in the swap period but divides by 360; this is common for the floating leg of non-sterling swaps.
- 30/360: this convention assumes that each month has exactly 30 days and uses the nominal number of days in the swap period divided by 360. For example, if the period covered 15th July to 15th October, the numerator would be 90 days, even though there are actually 92 days in that period. This convention usually applies to the fixed leg of dollar- and euro-denominated swaps.

As an example, consider a swap having the following characteristics:

Principal:	$10,000,000
Fixed rate:	2.50%
Floating rate:	LIBOR flat
First floating-rate setting:	0.80%
Day count convention (fixed):	30/360
Day count convention (floating):	Actual/360
Trade date:	1st February 2011
Effective date:	3rd February 2011
Maturity date:	3rd February 2016
Payment frequency (fixed):	Annual (every 3rd Feb or modified following business day)
Payment frequency (floating):	Annual (every 3rd Feb or modified following business day)

Let's assume that LIBOR eventually turned out to be 1.34%, 2.41%, 3.38% and 4.19%, on the four remaining setting dates. Table 8.1 illustrates the cash flows that would result on each payment date, from the viewpoint of the fixed-rate payer.

TABLE 8.1

Example of cash flows from interest rate swap

Date	Days	LIBOR fixing	Floating receipt	Fixed payment	Net cash flow
Thu 03 Feb 2011					
Fri 03 Feb 2012	365	0.80%	81,111.11	250,00.00	(168,888.89)
Mon 04 Feb 2013	367	1.34%	136,605.56	250,00.00	(113,394.44)
Mon 03 Feb 2014	364	2.41%	243,677.78	250,00.00	(6,322.22)
Tue 03 Feb 2015	365	3.38%	342,694.44	250,00.00	92,694.44
Wed 03 Feb 2016	365	4.19%	424,819.44	250,00.00	174,819.44

It is interesting to note that the fixed-rate payer is the net payer in the first three periods, but a net receiver later on. This is quite typical; it would be odd for anyone to enter into a swap transaction expecting to be a net payer (or receiver) throughout the swap's life.

The swap illustrated in Table 8.1 is an example of a *vanilla* swap, which is the most common swap encountered in practice. Vanilla swaps have the following fundamental characteristics:

- One leg of the swap is fixed while the other leg is floating.
- The fixed rate remains constant throughout the life of the swap.
- The floating rate is set in advance of each period and paid in arrears.
- Both legs have regular payments.
- The original swap maturity is 1, 2, 3, 4, 5, 6, 7, 8, 9, 10, 12, 15, 20, 25 or 30 years.
- The notional principal remains constant throughout the life of the swap.

However, interest rate swaps can be created nowadays with many variations, and the resultant flexibility of swap contracts is one of the factors which has led to their success. The next section explains some of the more common permutations.

8.4 Non-standard interest rate swaps

Virtually any of the characteristics of a swap contract can be modified to give a *non-standard* swap contract which can be tailored more closely to meet the needs of one or both the swap counterparties.

Accreting, amortising and roller-coaster swaps

Instead of remaining constant, the notional principal can vary through the life of the swap according to a pre-determined pattern. An *accreting* or *step-up* swap is where the principal starts off small, then increases over time. The converse, where the principal reduces in successive periods, is called an *amortising* swap. If the principal increases in some periods and reduces in others, the swap is described as a *roller-coaster* swap. Figure 8.4 depicts these three alternatives.

The accreting swap would be attractive in, for example, construction finance, where the amount being borrowed gradually increases during the lifetime of the project. The amortising swap, meanwhile, might be ideal for a borrower hedging a bond issue which featured sinking fund payments. For project finance, where the amount borrowed may increase initially and then reduce as stage payments are made to the contractor, a roller-coaster swap can be designed to match the outstanding principal in every period. In each case, it is not necessary for the underlying principal to follow a regular pattern; the only requirement is that the notional principal for each swap period be defined at the inception of the swap.

Basis swaps

In a vanilla swap, one leg is fixed while the other is floating. In a *basis* swap, both legs are floating but linked to different bases. One floating leg is normally linked to LIBOR of a particular period, while the other may be linked to a

FIGURE 8.4

Accreting, amortising and roller-coaster swaps

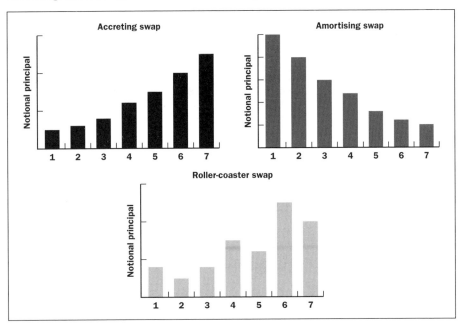

different market-determined rate, e.g. commercial paper, CD, or Federal funds rates. A company might, for example, have assets yielding LIBOR financed by a rolling commercial paper programme; a basis swap would eliminate the basis risk between income and expense streams. Alternatively, a company issuing commercial paper might wish to fix its cost of funds and combine a basis swap with a vanilla swap, thereby switching a floating CP rate first into a floating LIBOR rate, and then into a fixed rate. With a basis swap, one of the floating legs will normally involve a fixed margin added to the floating reference, for example, one-month LIBOR plus a fixed margin of 12bp.

A variation of the basis swap is where both floating rates are linked to the same type of market rate, but for different tenors, e.g. one-month LIBOR against six-month LIBOR. In such cases, not only is the basis different but the payment frequencies may also differ. The party receiving six-month LIBOR and paying one-month LIBOR would make five successive monthly interest payments before receiving the net of the six-month rate less the final one-month rate. Counterparty risk in such swaps is higher than for swaps where the payment frequencies coincide. To avoid this, an alternative is for the party paying the shorter-term LIBOR to accumulate and compound the payments and then for the two parties to make a net settlement at the frequency of the longer-term LIBOR.

Table 8.2 provides an example of maturity basis swaps for a range of maturities for the euro on 11th January 2011. As an example, the very first quotation implies that the market-maker would exchange 3m Euribor + 22.9bp against 6m Euribor flat for the next year. Note that the quotations for different bases are mostly consistent. For example the 1yr quotation for the 1m vs. 6m basis swap of 42.1bp is simply the sum of the 19.2bp for the 1m vs. 3m swap plus the 22.9bp for the 3m vs. 6m basis swaps

TABLE 8.2

Example of euro maturity basis swaps on 11th January 2011

(All quotations are in basis points and based on Euribor)

Tenor	3m vs. 6m	1m vs. 3m	1m vs. 6m	6m vs. 12m	3m vs. 12m
1yr	22.9	19.2	42.1	1.5	24.3
2yr	19.6	19.5	39.2	2.4	22.1
3yr	18.1	19.3	37.4	2.5	20.6
4yr	17.1	19.0	36.1	2.4	19.5
5yr	16.3	18.6	34.9	2.2	18.5
6yr	15.6	18.2	33.8	2.0	17.6
7yr	15.0	17.6	32.6	1.8	16.8
8yr	14.4	16.9	31.3	1.6	16.0
9yr	13.9	16.2	30.1	1.5	15.4
10yr	13.4	15.6	28.9	1.4	14.8

Source: Intercapital

Margin swaps

Another variation on the floating side is to include a margin above or below LIBOR, instead of using LIBOR flat. Not surprisingly, such swaps are called *margin* swaps. A borrower raising finance at LIBOR+50bp may prefer to enter into a swap receiving LIBOR+50bp rather than LIBOR flat, so that the floating cash flows match exactly. However, the net result is little different from adding the margin to the fixed rate on a vanilla swap. For example, if the rate for a vanilla swap were 3.00% fixed against LIBOR flat, the quote for a similar margin swap might simply be 3.50% against LIBOR+50bp. A difference would arise only if the day count conventions or payment frequencies on each side of the swap were to differ, e.g. Act/365 fixed against Act/360 floating.

Forward-start swaps

A *forward-start* swap is one where the effective date is not just one or two days after the trade date but is deferred by weeks, months or even longer. A swap counterparty may wish to fix the effective cost of borrowing for floating-rate financing to be arranged some time in the future. For example, a company may have just won a project mandate and now be committed to raise finance that will be drawn down on some future date. If the company were to wait until later before arranging the swap, it would run the risk that interest rates in the meantime may rise more than anticipated. These swaps are also known as *delayed start* swaps.

Off-market swaps

Most swaps are priced so that there is no advantage to either side at the outset and so there is no need for any payment from one counterparty to the other at inception. With an *off-market* swap, however, the fixed rate differs from the standard market rate, and one party must therefore compensate the other accordingly. One application for such a swap is when a company issues a floating-rate bond and wishes to use a swap not only to convert its floating obligations into a fixed interest stream but also to pay for the up-front costs of issuing the bond. An off-market swap can be designed so that the issuer receives an initial sum and periodic floating-rate interest payments, against paying a fixed rate slightly higher than the market rate for a vanilla swap. The extra fixed-rate margin effectively amortises the up-front issuing costs over the lifetime of the swap.

Zero-coupon and back-set swaps

There are a number of other variations. A *zero-coupon* swap replaces the stream of fixed payments with a single payment, either at the beginning or, more usually, when the swap matures. In a *back-set* swap the setting date is just before the end of the accrual period, not just before the beginning. The floating rate is therefore set in arrears rather than in advance, which is why this kind of swap is also known as a *LIBOR-in-arrears swap*. Such swaps would be attractive to a counterparty who thought that interest rates would evolve differently from market expectations. For example, in a rising yield curve environment, forward rates will be higher than current market rates, and this will be reflected in pricing the fixed rate of a swap. A back-set swap would be priced higher still. If the fixed-rate receiver believed that interest rates would rise more slowly than the forward rates suggested, a back-set swap would be more advantageous than a conventional swap.

Diff swaps

The *diff swap* (also known as a *quanto swap*) is a kind of basis swap whereby two floating-rate cash flows are exchanged. One stream comprises the floating-rate coupons in one currency. The other stream comprises coupons based on the floating-rate index in another currency, plus or minus a margin, but denominated in the first currency. Diff swaps are attractive only under specific circumstances: when one currency features low interest rates and a steeply upward sloping yield curve, the other currency has high interest rates and a downward sloping yield curve, and the investor believes that interest rates will stay fairly static. For example, if six-month US dollar rates were 1% with a positive yield curve and six-month AUD rates were 5% with a negative yield curve, an investor might pay six-month US dollar LIBOR on a notional principal of $10m, and receive six-month AUD LIBOR less 1% but also paid in US dollars on the same notional principal, thereby receiving net payments under the swap, at least initially. If interest rates followed the implied forward yields, these net receipts would turn to net payments later on. However, if the investor believed that US dollar rates would remain lower than the implied forwards, while AUD rates would remain higher, he would benefit under the swap for a much longer period, possibly even throughout.

8.5 Overnight indexed swaps

At its simplest, you can think of overnight indexed swaps (OIS) as interest rate swaps where the floating reference is an overnight interest rate rather than a term interest rate like three-month or six-month LIBOR, and the setting frequency is therefore daily. However, there is rather more to OIS than this. First, the mechanics of OIS differ from those of the vanilla interest rates swaps that we have so far discussed. Second, a comparison of OIS quotations with LIBOR, the so-called *LIBOR–OIS* spread, has become an important indicator of confidence in banks in the aftermath of the 2007–2008 credit crisis. We will look at each aspect in turn.

Instead of using term LIBOR as the floating reference, OIS use one of the following instead:

- For US dollar OIS – the daily effective Federal funds rate as published by the Federal Reserve in its daily H.15 report. This is the volume-weighted average rate for overnight Fed funds transactions arranged through the main money brokers.

- For euro-denominated OIS – the European OverNight Index Average (EONIA) calculated by the European Central Bank (ECB) and published by Reuters every evening. This is calculated as the volume-weighted average rate for all overnight unsecured loans on the interbank market initiated by the Euribor Panel Banks.[1]

- For sterling-denominated OIS – the Sterling OverNight Index Average (SONIA) rate. This is the volume-weighted average of all unsecured overnight deposits of more than £25m made through members of the Wholesale Markets Brokers' Association in London.

Although the setting frequency is daily, it would be tedious for parties to make net interest payments on a daily basis because the amounts would be quite small. For example, a 10bp interest rate differential on an OIS with a notional of $100m would amount only to a net payment of $278. Instead, parties accumulate and compound the payments, then settle at the maturity of the OIS, which are typically between one week and one year, although with a longer maturity swaps are sometimes traded.

As an example, let's suppose that on Monday morning a bank has agreed to pay the fixed rate of 1.20% for a one-week OIS on $100m notional. As the week progresses, the daily effective Federal funds rates turn out as follows:

Monday	1.10%
Tuesday	1.05%
Wednesday	1.42%
Thursday	1.25%
Friday	1.37%

The fixed payment is simply:

$$PMT_{Fixed} = 100,000,000 \times 1.20\% \times \frac{7}{360} = 23,333.33$$

The calculation for the floating payment is a little more complex because overnight rates assume daily settlement, with the ability of the recipient to invest previous payments at overnight rates and therefore earn compound interest over a period of days. If settlement is not done daily, then the receiver needs to be compensated by compounding the rates instead:

$$PMT_{Float} = 100,000,000 \times$$
$$\begin{bmatrix} \left(1 + 1.10\% \times \frac{1}{360}\right) \times \left(1 + 1.05\% \times \frac{1}{360}\right) \times \left(1 + 1.42\% \times \frac{1}{360}\right) \times \\ \left(1 + 1.25\% \times \frac{1}{360}\right) \times \left(1 + 1.37\% \times \frac{3}{360}\right) - 1 \end{bmatrix}$$
$$= 24,807.75$$

Note that the 1.37% overnight rate for Friday counts for three days, as it covers the weekend period.

The bank therefore receives a net payment of $1,474.42. This is because the compounded weighted average of the five overnight rates is 1.275827% against the fixed rate of 1.20%. The net payment represents the difference between these two rates over the seven-day period.

Banks can use OIS to secure term funding but at a rate close to overnight rates. As an example, suppose that a bank enters into a three-month OIS receiving the fixed rate of 1.40% against paying the floating overnight rate, and at the same time borrows for three months at 1.50% on the interbank markets. The bank has effectively funded itself at overnight rates plus 10bp. Although it is exposed to the fluctuations in average overnight rates, it has locked in the margin of 10bp for three months. The alternative would have been for the bank simply to borrow overnight and roll over the borrowing each day. Such a strategy would, however, have left the bank vulnerable to a widening of the credit spread it might pay for overnight funds, and even to the drying-up of the overnight market.

Liquidity in the interbank markets became a real problem during the 2007–2008 credit crisis, and the LIBOR–OIS spread became a barometer of fear vs. confidence in banks during this period. To see why, let's compare the three-month LIBOR rate with the three-month OIS rate. The LIBOR rate is the rate at which banks borrow in the interbank market and represents the rate at which actual cash transactions take place. As such, Bank A lending $100m to Bank B for three months at the three-month LIBOR rate faces the risk that Bank B may not be able to repay the borrowing at maturity. Prior to the 2007–2008 credit crisis, LIBOR rates were effectively considered to be riskless; with the weakening and failure of a number of banks around the world, the riskiness of lending at LIBOR became all too apparent. Bank A could potentially lose $100m if Bank B were to default.

In contrast, suppose Bank A enters into a three-month OIS with Bank B on a notional principal of $100m, and Bank B eventually reneged on its obligations. At worst, Bank A might lose the net payment on the swap, but this would typically amount to only a few tens of thousands of dollars, a fraction of a percent of the notional. At best, if the swap were collateralised (where each party posts collateral with the other), Bank A should lose nothing.

While it is true that the three-month OIS rate reflects the weighted average of the expected overnight rates over the lifetime of the swap,[2] and these overnight rates do reflect the credit risk involved in Bank A lending to Bank B, this is not significant under normal circumstances because it is most unlikely that a major bank would suddenly fail within a 24-hour period without any warning. So there is little credit risk in lending overnight, and virtually none in executing a three-month OIS, but there *is* potential credit risk in lending to another bank for longer periods like three months. The three-month LIBOR rate therefore includes an implicit margin reflecting the perceived credit risk of banks over this period, and the LIBOR–OIS spread expresses the magnitude of this credit risk.

FIGURE 8.5
Three-month USD LIBOR–OIS spread 2007–2011

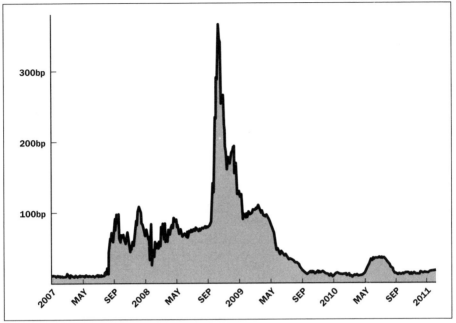

Source: Bloomberg.

Prior to 2007, the three-month US dollar LIBOR–OIS spread was around 7–8bp, reflecting the very low perceived risk of lending funds interbank for this period of time. As Figure 8.5 shows, however, this spread widened to 60–100bp from August 2007 to August 2008, then spiked to reach more than 350bp in the autumn of 2008 following the collapse of Lehman Brothers and the various bank rescue packages that were launched at the time. Finally, as 2011 dawned, and credit markets finally reached some degree of normality, the spread tightened to around 15bp, close to the pre-crisis levels. Since then, however, the Eurozone crisis has had a similar effect on the euro LIBOR–OIS spread which widened from around 20bp in July 2011 to reach a peak of 105bp in December that year. Given the potential global contagion, the US dollar LIBOR–OIS spread widened at the same time, though not so much, as Figure 8.6 shows.

8.6 Cross-currency swaps

Now that we have defined interest rate swaps more precisely, it is easier to discuss cross-currency swaps in greater depth. One way of defining a cross-currency swap is to liken it to a special kind of interest rate swap.

A standard cross-currency swap is like an interest rate swap, except:

FIGURE 8.6

Three-month LIBOR–OIS spread for EUR and USD 2010–2012

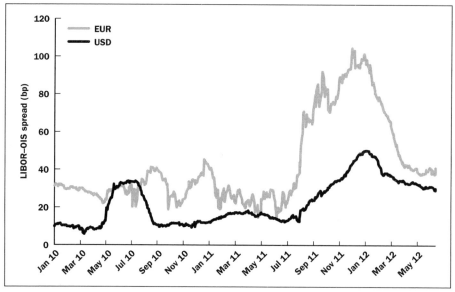

Source: Barclays.

- the currencies of the two legs are different
- there are two principals involved – one for each currency
- there is always an exchange of principal at maturity
- there is optionally an exchange of principal on the effective date
- both exchanges of principal are executed at the FX spot rate originally prevailing
- the legs may be:
  - both fixed-rate
  - both floating-rate
  - one fixed and one floating.

Alternatively, one could think of an interest rate swap as being a special kind of cross-currency swap for which both currencies were the same. In that analogy the exchange of principals is irrelevant; being in the same currency they would always net to zero.

It is important to remember that the drivers of currency swaps are *interest rates*, not FX rates; interest rates determine the size of each regular payment, not the spot FX rate. In fact, currency swaps were once referred to as 'cross-currency interest rate swaps'. Though more cumbersome, the full title more accurately reflected what a currency swap is – an interest rate swap where the interest rates and regular payments are denominated in a pair of currencies rather than a single currency.

Figure 8.7 provides two examples of the cash flow streams arising from a cross-currency swap. In the first example, the swap exchanges fixed-rate ster-

FIGURE 8.7

Examples of cash flows from cross-currency swaps

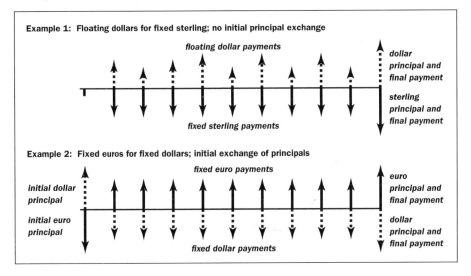

ling for floating-rate dollars, but with no initial exchange of principals. The second example illustrates the cash flows where there is an initial exchange of principals, followed by the exchange of fixed-rate dollars for fixed-rate euros. In both cases illustrated by Figure 8.7, there is the mandatory final exchange of principals that is always a feature of standard cross-currency swaps. At first sight, this may appear to create a currency risk. Paradoxically, however, it is the final exchange of principals which removes the currency risk that would otherwise be present. This point will be proved in the next chapter (in section 9.7).

In practice, it matters little whether or not there is an initial exchange of principals. A spot exchange deal can always be executed at the inception of the swap to create a desired initial exchange of principals if this is absent from the swap. Similarly, a spot deal can reverse the effect of an unwanted initial exchange of principals.

8.7 Basic applications for swaps

Interest rate and cross-currency swaps have opened up innumerable opportunities in a wide number of applications. Chapter 18 will explore these in greater depth, but the following examples illustrate the major areas in which swaps have made an impact.

Fixing financing costs

A company currently borrowing at six-month LIBOR+100bp fears that interest rates may rise in the three remaining years of its loan. It enters into a three-year semi-annual vanilla interest rate swap as the fixed-rate payer at 3.75% against receiving six-month LIBOR. This fixes the company's borrowing costs at 4.75% (4.81% effective annual rate) for the next three years, as Figure 8.8 illustrates.

Asset-linked swap

A US-based insurance company is seeking to improve the yield on its portfolio of dollar-denominated securities. Ten-year US T-Bonds are currently yielding 4.14%, while German Bunds are offering a return of 4.45% for bonds of a similar tenor. Banks are quoting ten-year fixed-fixed dollar–euro cross-currency swaps whereby the insurance company could pay euros fixed at 4.45% against receiving dollars fixed at 4.51%. If the company were to buy Bunds and enter into the swap, it would receive a dollar income stream yielding 8.51%, some 37bp higher than investing directly in US Treasuries.[3] This is illustrated in Figure 8.9.

Liability-linked swap

A British company, having already made extensive use of the domestic capital market, is now seeking to raise additional finance. However, the quotes of 6.50% fixed or LIBOR+90bp floating reflect the reluctance of the sterling market to provide further funds at this time. The company therefore decides to turn to the EUR bond market where it can raise fixed-rate funds at 4.75%. The company does not, however, wish to be exposed to the risk that sterling could weaken against the euro, and therefore enters into a fixed-floating sterling–euro cross-currency swap, where it pays sterling LIBOR+50bp against receiving euro fixed at 4.75%. The net result shown in Figure 8.10 is to secure synthetic sterling financing at LIBOR+50bp, which is 40bp cheaper than the rate available by borrowing sterling directly.

FIGURE 8.8

Fixing financing costs with interest rate swap

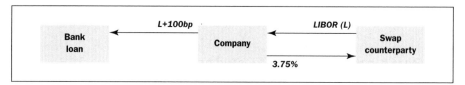

FIGURE 8.9

Asset–linked cross-currency swap

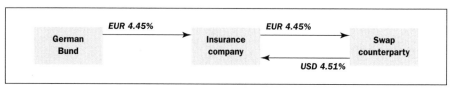

FIGURE 8.10
Liability-linked cross-currency swap

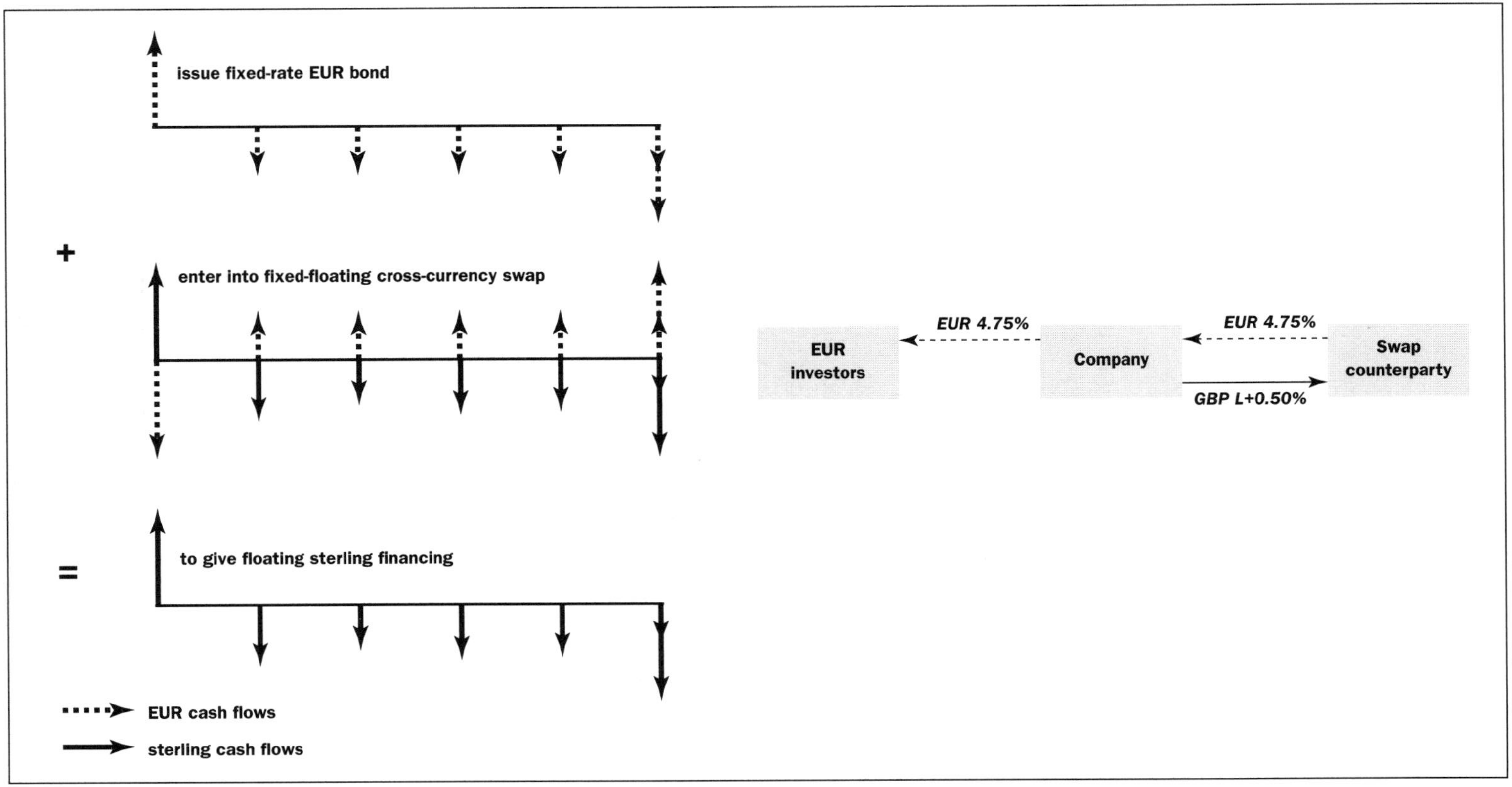

8.8 Asset swaps

An *asset swap* is an interest rate swap that has been tailored to match a specific bond. The customisation can be at two levels. For a straightforward *asset swap* the fixed payments of the swap are adjusted to coincide exactly with the coupon payments of the bond specified. For a *par asset swap* there is, in addition, an up-front payment equal to the discount or premium at which the specified bond is currently trading. The example shown in Figure 8.11 will make this clearer.

Worked example 8.1

Imagine that an investor is thinking of buying a five-year bond paying a coupon of 6.5%, and priced at 97. The only problem is that, like all fixed-income investments, this bond has interest rate risk – if yields rise, the value of the bond will fall, and our investor believes that rates might indeed rise. One solution is for the investor to use a vanilla swap, like the one pictured in Figure 8.11a. This goes some way towards removing the interest rate risk, but it is by no means perfect. The problem is that five-year swap rates will seldom match the coupon rate on a specific five-year bond, so usually there will be a mismatch. In the example illustrated, vanilla swap rates of 5% will convert most of the 6.5% coupon into a floating payment, but still leave a residual.

Suppose that the bank quoting the swap agrees to tailor the fixed rate of the swap to match the coupons of this bond. In the simple example illustrated in Figure 8.11b, adding 1.5% to the fixed rate means adding 1.5% to the floating leg. In practice, while the floating leg will be close to L+150bp, the margin may be slightly different from 150bp, because tailoring the swap involves:

- setting the final maturity of the swap to match the maturity date of the bond

- matching the payment frequency of the swap to the payment frequency of the bond

- matching the day count convention of the swap to the day count convention of the bond

- matching the payment dates of the swap to the coupon dates of the bond.

This means that the floating leg of the swap might need to be at L+147bp, or L+152bp, or something similar. We have now created an asset swap.

Now suppose that for one or more reasons (maybe tax related) the investor wants to pay par for the bond rather than pay a premium or discount price. One way to handle this is for the swap to feature an up-front payment equal to the off-par amount. In the example illustrated in Figure 8.11c the investor makes the swap counterparty a one-off payment of 3% up-front, making his total investment equal to 100. This is akin to the investor lending

FIGURE 8.11
Creating asset swaps and par asset swaps

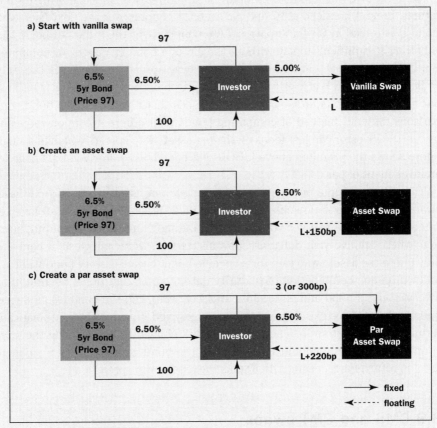

300bp to the swap counterparty. Using normal time-value-of-money calculations,[4] we can work out that spreading this up-front payment of 300bp over five years when five-year rates are 5% means regular repayments of just under 70bp. In Figure 8.11c we have added this 70bp to the existing L+150bp asset swap rate to give a *par asset swap* rate of L+220bp.

The investor who buys the bond at 97 and immediately enters into the par asset swap illustrated in Figure 8.11c ends up paying par for the investment, and then receives LIBOR plus 220bp for five years, with an eventual redemption at par. The value of the par asset swap package – the combination of bond plus swap – will never drift far from par because the investor is receiving a floating rate. If rates go up, the flow of payments goes up as well, removing the normally detrimental effect of a rise in interest rates on a fixed-income investment. Interest rate risk has therefore been virtually eliminated.

In these examples, the margin added to the floating leg is called the *asset swap spread* (or par asset swap spread for a par asset swap).

Par asset swaps can be used in exactly this way to hedge the value of a fixed income portfolio, but they can also be used simply for comparison purposes. Imagine an investor needs to compare two bonds with similar maturities and ratings. Bond A is priced at 97 and pays a 6.5% coupon over the next five years. Bond B is priced at 99.4 and pays a 7.0% coupon over the same period. Which is better? It is difficult to say without the aid of a bond calculator or computer. But if the investor is told that the par asset swap spread for Bond A is L+220bp, while that for Bond B is L+215bp, the comparison becomes easy. This is because par asset swaps standardise all the differences that normally make bond comparisons difficult. Instead of comparing bonds with different coupon rates and prices, the investor can just focus on the par asset swap spread, which in a single figure shows the premium above LIBOR that each bond will pay in exchange for an investment of par.

There are a couple of things worth noting about asset swaps and par asset swaps. First, there is no such thing as a 'vanilla' asset swap. While an investor can ask 'where are five-year dollar swaps trading?', the similar-sounding question 'where are five-year dollar asset swaps trading?' is meaningless. A bank can only quote the asset swap rate for a specific bond, because every bond will have its own unique combination of maturity date, coupon and price. Second, if an investor buys a bond and enters into an asset swap, and the bond issuer subsequently defaults so that coupons are no longer paid, this does not automatically terminate the asset swap. The investor is still obliged to keep paying the swap counterparty a cash amount equivalent to the bond coupon on each payment date, in return for receiving LIBOR plus the asset swap spread

8.9 CMS and CMT swaps

With a vanilla interest rate swap, the floating rate reference is a short-term rate like three-month or six-month LIBOR, and typically matches the payment frequency. With *CMS* and *CMT swaps*, however, the floating rate reference is a long-term rate like the five-year constant maturity swap (CMS) rate, or the five-year constant maturity treasury (CMT) rate. The reason why these are called *constant maturity* rates is that the swap always references the swap rate of the same tenor each fixing, rather than a swap rate of the same final maturity date. So a five-year CMS traded on 1st February 2011 referencing the ten-year CMS rate will always reference the ten-year swap rate on each fixing date, not a ten-year swap maturing in 2021.

There are certain similarities between vanilla swaps and CMS/CMT swaps, but there are also some important differences.

On each fixing date, a vanilla IRS sets the floating leg for the forthcoming period using the BBA LIBOR fixing at 11am for that currency and tenor. In an analogous way, on each fixing date a CMS sets the floating leg for the upcoming period but uses the ISDAFIX[5] rate posted on the Thomson Reuters and Bloomberg screens for that currency and tenor. For example, if the CMS references the five-year US dollar swap rate, then this is the rate posted shortly after 11am and 3pm New York time every day. Similarly, CMT swaps reference the CMT rates calculated and published by the US Treasury from quotations obtained by the Federal Reserve Bank of New York at the end of each day.

The key difference between a vanilla IRS and a CMS/CMT swap is the mismatch between the payment frequency and the tenor of the reference rates. A vanilla IRS exhibits what is called a *natural time lag* because the gap between fixing date and payment date matches the tenor of the reference rate. For example, a vanilla swap may reference the six-month LIBOR rate on the fixing date, with the floating payment based on this fixing being made six months later – this is the natural time lag. CMS and CMT swaps are different because they reference a long-term rate (e.g. the five-year rate) on the fixing date and then make a payment based on this a short time later. This *unnatural time lag* creates problems when such swaps are hedged, and requires a convexity correction of the kind discussed in section 9.10 of Chapter 9.

CMS and CMT swaps are used for a number of purposes. Life insurance companies have long-term liabilities and therefore have adverse exposure to long-term interest rates. By receiving the floating rate on a CMS, they can hedge their exposure. On the other side, in an environment that features a steeply upward-sloping yield curve, the fixed rate on a CMS will be quite high, reflecting the market's view that swap rates will rise in the future. Financial institutions and other parties which think that swap rates will not rise so fast can benefit by paying the floating rate and receiving the fixed rate.

8.10 Inflation swaps

All the swaps discussed so far have referenced interest rates, but the concept of a swap instrument can be applied to many different underliers. With an *inflation swap*, the floating leg references an inflation index like the CPI in the US, or the ex-tobacco HICP (Harmonised Index of Consumer Prices) in Europe. Inflation swaps come in a number of different flavours:

■ A *zero-coupon* inflation swap (ZCIS) is analogous to a zero-coupon IRS where the swap is settled with a single net payment at maturity. The fixed payer pays the compounded fixed rate over the lifetime of the swap, whereas the floating payer pays the cumulative inflation over the same period.

■ A *year-on-year* inflation swap (YYIS) features regular payments between the swap counterparties who exchange the difference between the fixed rate and the inflation rate for the current period. For counterparties who need regular cash settlements, the year-on-year swap provides this benefit, but does not provide compensation for the cumulative effects of inflation. For example, if inflation over two successive years were 5% per annum, the float-ing legs would provide payments totalling just 10%, even though prices were 10.25% higher.

- A *revenue swap* is effectively a series of zero-coupon swaps with increas-ing maturities that combines the best features of zero-coupon swaps with year-on-year swaps. The revenue swap has periodic settlements to benefit counterparties who prefer regular settlements, but also provides compensa-tion for the cumulative effect of inflation over a longer period.

Typical users of inflation swaps are entities exposed to inflation in the normal course of their business. Insurers and pension funds have liabilities linked to inflation and therefore suffer when inflation is high. Meanwhile, utilities, prop-erty and real-estate companies have assets linked to inflation and benefit from higher inflation. Inflation swaps provide a means for each entity to hedge their inflation risk.

Figure 8.12 illustrates the quotation for five-year euro inflation swaps (using the HICP excluding tobacco inflation index) from March 2008 to March 2011. Note the profound drop in inflation expectations during the fourth quarter of 2008 following the collapse of Lehman Brothers in September that year.

FIGURE 8.12
Euro 5yr zero-coupon inflation swaps 2008–2011

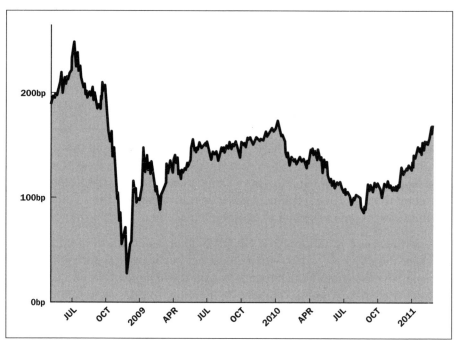

Source: Bloomberg.

8.11 Equity and dividend swaps

In the previous section we saw how the cash flows on one leg of a swap can be linked to an inflation index to create an inflation swap. In an analogous way, the cash flows on one leg of a swap can instead be linked to equity prices to produce an *equity swap*. This equity-linked leg is called the index leg, while the other leg is called the interest leg and is similar to one of the legs on a straightforward interest rate swap, either fixed or floating.

Figure 8.13 illustrates the structure of a typical equity swap, from which you will notice that when the interest leg is floating, a fixed margin is either added to or subtracted from the floating reference, typically LIBOR. Being OTC instruments, there is complete flexibility for the parties to choose the underlying equity price to which the swap is linked. The swap can be linked to a recognised index such as the S&P 500 or the FTSE 100, to an exchange-traded fund (ETF), to a specified basket of stocks, or even to an individual stock.

Equity swaps come in two common flavours. A *price return* swap is one where the index payer pays only the percentage appreciation of the chosen index. In a *total return swap* – which is much more common – the index payer pays not only the appreciation of the index but also the dividends on the underlying stock(s). Equity prices rise much of the time; when they do the direction of the cash flows is just as pictured in Figure 8.13. However, in periods when the underlying equity price falls, the index payer receives the depreciation of the index, and the index receiver therefore ends up paying on both legs of the swap.

When an equity swap transaction is executed, the two parties agree the maturity of the swap, the underlying reference for the equity leg, the basis for the interest leg, the payment frequency and the day count convention. In addition, they agree the size of the notional principal, which is used for calculation purposes, although never exchanged. The notional principal can be fixed throughout the period of the swap, just like a conventional interest rate swap. Alternatively, the principal can be variable, being linked to the underlying equity price. This latter arrangement is more common because it makes the equity swap mimic more closely the performance of an actual equity portfolio.

FIGURE 8.13
Equity swap cash flows

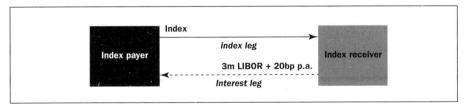

As an example, consider an equity swap having the following characteristics:

Initial principal:	€100,000,000
Index leg:	DAX Index
Interest leg:	EUR LIBOR + 20bp
First floating-rate setting:	1.15%
First DAX setting:	7,180.00
Day count convention (interest leg):	Actual/360
Trade date:	Fri 25th February 2011
Effective date:	Tue 1st March 2011
Maturity date:	Thu 1st March 2012
Payment frequency (index leg):	Quarterly
Payment frequency (interest leg):	Quarterly

We will assume that on the next four setting dates the DAX Index initially rose to 7539.00, then fell to 7312.83, then rose to 8153.81, and finally to 8822.42. We'll also assume that the euro LIBOR fixings on the same dates turned out to be 1.30%, 1.35% and 1.45%. Table 8.3 illustrates the cash flows that would result on each payment date.

TABLE 8.3
Example of cash flows from equity swap

Date	Days	Notional principal	EUR LIBOR + 20bp	Interest leg	DAX Index	Index leg
Tue 01-Mar-11		100,000,000	1.35%		7,180.00	
Wed 01-Jun-11	92	105,000,000	1.50%	345,000	7,539.00	5,000,000
Thu 01-Sep-11	92	101,850,000	1.55%	402,500	7,312.83	–3,150,000
Thu 01-Dec-11	91	113,562,813	1.65%	399,054	8,153.81	11,712,813
Thu 01-Mar-12	91	122,874,930		473,652	8,822.42	9,312,117
TOTAL				1,620,206		22,874,930

Over the course of a year the index receiver would receive €22,874,930 and pay €1,620,206, a net cash inflow of €21,254,725. This is equivalent to the return on a DAX portfolio, financed at euro LIBOR plus 20bp p.a. on the fluctuating principal, showing that the equity swap has replicated the cash flows from such a portfolio of shares.

There are a number of variations on the basic equity swap illustrated here. One variation is to link the index payments to an equity index in another currency. For example, an equity swap could feature index payments linked to the DAX Index, but paid in US dollars, against USD LIBOR plus a margin, also paid in dollars. The conversion from euros to dollars could either be at a single FX rate agreed in advance, or at the FX rates prevailing at the time. In the latter case, a US-based investor gains exposure both to the appreciation of the German stock market as well as to the potential appreciation of the euro.

Another variation is to have both legs linked to equity prices to create an equity basis swap. For example, an investor might elect to pay the appreciation of the FTSE 100 and receive the appreciation of the S&P 500. A further variation is to link the index leg to two or more underlying equity indices, where the index payments could be based on the highest appreciating equity index – a 'best of' swap, or to the average of the underlying indices – a 'rainbow' swap.

Equity swaps can be used in many situations as a substitute for long or short positions in the underlying equities. In some cases equity swaps can provide tax advantages, for example allowing an investor to avoid withholding taxes or stamp duty (in the UK). Swaps can provide ease of market access, especially to emerging market equities, and cost savings by avoiding custody fees. An investor who wishes to hold shares and continue to exercise his voting rights, but to avoid losses in case the share price should fall, can enter into an equity swap as the index payer. Finally, as with many other derivative contracts, users of equity swaps can enjoy greater leverage than is possible with direct investment in the underlying shares.

Before moving on to the next topic, we should also mention *dividend swaps*. Although part of the equity derivatives market they are usually considered as a separate instrument from the equity swaps discussed so far. With a dividend swap, one party makes payments based on the actual level of dividends paid during a specified time period by an underlying stock, a basket of stocks, or an equity index, while the other party makes fixed payments. The notional for a dividend swap is usually defined by specifying the number of shares involved, and the time period specified is usually one year.

Dividend swaps started life in the early 2000s from the desire by banks to hedge the dividend exposures arising from equity structured products and equity-linked notes which they had written. Nowadays, dividend swaps can be used by investors for a number of reasons. One application is to exploit a view of future dividend payments that differs from that of the market. For example, following the Deepwater Horizon oil rig disaster that hit BP in April 2010, the company decided to cancel dividends for the remainder of the calendar year 2010. After the oil spill had been contained, dividend swaps on BP quoted in August 2010 were implying a full-year dividend of 13p for 2011 and 16p for 2012.[6] An investor who believed that dividends would be higher than these levels could elect to be the floating receiver, while another who believed that dividends would turn out lower could enter into the dividend swap as the floating payer.

Dividend swaps can also be used as an alternative asset class to diversify portfolio returns. Dividends exhibit a risk/return profile intermediate between bonds and equities and offer good diversification benefits in a portfolio that may also feature commodities and real estate.[7] In addition, dividends often outperform equities in a bear market, so investors entering into dividend swaps as the index receiver can hedge against a market downturn.

8.12 Commodity swaps

By now it will be clear that the floating leg on a swap transaction can be linked to almost any reference rate or price agreed by the counterparties, so long as it is readily observable and measurable. Not surprisingly, a *commodity swap* is one where the payments are linked to a commodity price such as oil, natural gas, gold and other metals, or an index like the S&P GSCI. According to BIS estimates,[8] the size of the global OTC commodity swaps and forwards market was around $1.8tn at the end of June 2010, with over 80% of this being in contracts linked to the price of oil.

One of the most important practical uses for commodity swaps is to hedge against the fluctuation in commodity prices. As an example, suppose on 25th February 2010 a US-based airline wishes to hedge against the cost of aviation fuel rising, and decides to use a commodity swap linked to crude oil prices as a surrogate hedge. With the spot price of WTI crude oil trading that day at $77.60 per barrel, the airline buys a one-year commodity swap (i.e. enters into the swap as the floating receiver) with the following specification:

Notional (barrels):	1,000,000
Fixed price:	$80.74
Floating price:	WTI Cushing spot price at 4pm ET on 1st business day of each month
Trade date:	Thursday 25th February 2010
Calculation periods:	Monthly from and including the effective date to and including the termination date
Effective date:	Monday 1st March 2010
Termination date:	Tuesday 1st March 2011
Fixing dates:	First business day of each month following the effective date
First fixing date:	Thursday 1st April 2010
Final fixing date:	Tuesday 1st March 2011
Payment frequency:	Monthly
Payment date:	Third New York business day following each fixing date

Table 8.4 shows the resulting cash flows over the ensuing 12 months. The swap has indeed hedged the airline against the general upward trend in oil prices that was experienced at that time, particularly at the beginning of 2011 when unrest in the Middle East led to a sharp hike in oil prices.

Although the swap illustrated in this case proved of substantial benefit to the airline, saving, on average, $3.02 per barrel over the lifetime of the swap, the airline would have still locked into an $80.74 fixed price even if the price of crude oil had fallen over the period.

In addition to vanilla commodity swaps of the kind just described, it is possible to have *basis swaps* where both legs are floating, but linked to different reference rates. An example would be the so-called *crack spread* where one

TABLE 8.4

Example of cash flows from commodity swap

Fixing date	Oil price	Floating receipt	Fixed payment	Net cash flow
Thu 01 Apr 2010	$84.87	$84,870,000	$80,740,000	$4,130,000
Mon 03 May 2010	$86.19	$86,190,000	$80,740,000	$5,450,000
Tue 01 Jun 2010	$72.58	$72,580,000	$80,740,000	–$8,160,000
Thu 01 Jul 2010	$72.95	$72,950,000	$80,740,000	–$7,790,000
Mon 02 Aug 2010	$81.34	$81,340,000	$80,740,000	$600,000
Wed 01 Sep 2010	$73.91	$73,910,000	$80,740,000	–$6,830,000
Fri 01 Oct 2010	$81.58	$81,580,000	$80,740,000	$840,000
Mon 01 Nov 2010	$82.95	$82,950,000	$80,740,000	$2,210,000
Wed 01 Dec 2010	$86.75	$86,750,000	$80,740,000	$6,010,000
Mon 03 Jan 2011	$91.55	$91,550,000	$80,740,000	$10,810,000
Tue 01 Feb 2011	$90.77	$90,770,000	$80,740,000	$10,030,000
Tue 01 Mar 2011	$99.63	$99,630,000	$80,740,000	$18,890,000
TOTAL				$36,190,000

Source: Oil prices from www.wss.com

party makes payments linked to the price of crude oil while the other party makes payments linked to a refined product like gasoline. It is usual for a fixed margin to be added to one of the floating legs.

Another variation of commodity swaps is the *swing swap*, which is a short-term swap – typically one month – where the two parties settle with a single net payment at the end of the month. The net payment is based on the difference between the fixed price agreed at inception and the average of daily prices over the period covered by the swap.

Finally, there is the *multi-fuel* commodity swap, which can be thought of as a variation of the basis swap, but where the two underlying reference rates are in different commodity markets. For example, one party might make payments based on the price of crude oil, while the other party makes payments based on the price of electricity. What makes this different from the basis swap described above is that, being based on two different commodity markets, there will be two different notional amounts. In the crude oil vs. electricity multi-fuel swap, the notional for the crude oil payments would be in barrels whereas that for the electricity payments would be in megawatt-hours.

8.13 Volatility and variance swaps

We have so far explored linking the payments on one or both legs of a swap to references that are either tangible – like equity or commodity prices – or less tangible but familiar – like interest rates and inflation rates. However, as we pointed out at the beginning of the previous section, swap payments can be linked to almost any reference rate or price agreed by the counterparties, so long as it is readily observable and measurable.

Volatility is more difficult to visualise than rates or prices, but there is a way to measure the volatility of a given market variable (the methodology for doing this is explained in section 11.1 of Chapter 11). So that we can picture this now, Figure 8.14 uses that methodology to calculate the experienced volatility of the S&P 500 index during 2010. The peak in volatility that occurs between late April and late June is because the S&P 500 index moved by more than 2% on one day in four during that period, compared with an average daily fluctuation of only ±0.8%. As the figure clearly demonstrates, the more the underlying index fluctuates, the greater is the volatility.

A *volatility swap* is one where the payments are linked to the level of volatility experienced by a particular underlier, which might be an equity index like the S&P 500, an FX rate like the €/$, a commodity price like oil, or even an interest rate. The floating payer might agree to pay $50,000 for every percentage point of volatility experienced over the preceding period, against receiving a fixed payment of $750,000, the latter corresponding to fixed volatility of 15% again at $50,000 per percentage point. In a period where the experienced volatility was 17%, the floating payer would then pay $100,000 net.

Remembering that variance is the square of volatility, a *variance swap* is similar to a volatility swap, except that the parties exchange payments linked to the experienced variance. If the floating payer in the previous example agreed to pay $1,000 per squared percentage point of variance against receiving fixed at

FIGURE 8.14
S&P 500 index and experienced volatility

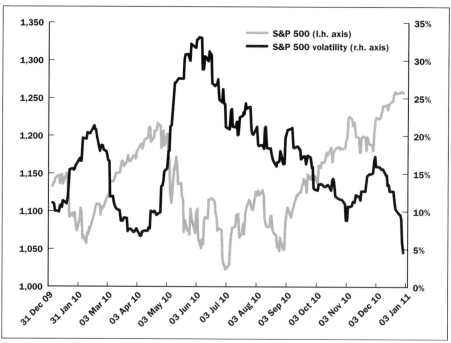

Source: CBOE.

15% squared, in a period where experienced volatility was 17% the fixed payer would receive $64,000 net, calculated as:

$$(17^2 - 15^2) \times \$1,000 = \$64,000$$

The $1,000 per squared percentage point in the above example is called the variance notional $N_{Variance}$, but variance swaps are often quoted in terms of the vega notional N_{Vega}, which can be calculated as:

$$N_{Vega} = N_{Variance} \times 2 \times K$$

where K is the fixed rate (also known as the *strike price*). In the above example, a variance notional of $1,000 on a swap with fixed rate of 15% would have a vega notional of $30,000. As we will see (in Chapter 11), options are sensitive to volatility, and vega measures the sensitivity of an option to a 1% change in volatility. The vega notional of a variance swap measures the sensitivity of a variance swap to changes in volatility in a similar way. In the above example, if volatility were to reduce to 13%, the fixed payer would receive:

$$(13^2 - 15^2) \times \$1,000 = -\$56,000$$

In other words, the fixed payer would pay $56,000. So for a 4% swing in volatility from 13% to 17%, the payout on the variance swap would change by $120,000 (from +$64,000 to –$56,000), exactly four times the variance vega of $30,000.

At first sight, linking swap payments to volatility or variance may seem somewhat esoteric. However, there are at least two practical uses for these instruments.[9] First, investors who want to take a view on volatility can use a volatility swap to express that view. The investor who believes that experienced volatility over the lifetime of the swap will exceed the fixed rate should enter into either a volatility or a variance swap as the fixed payer. Second, these swaps – especially variance swaps – can be used by banks to hedge their book of options against changes in volatility.

8.14 Exotic swaps

Section 8.4 introduced a number of non-standard interest rate swaps. Being OTC derivatives, there are many other possibilities limited only by the demands of users and the imagination of market-makers. In this section, we describe some more exotic variations.

A *cancellable swap* is one which can be terminated by the customer at no extra cost, usually on one or more of the fixing dates. Suppose that a company has arranged a ten-year loan where it pays six-month LIBOR+100bp, reset twice a year. Initially LIBOR is only 3% but the company expects short-term interest rates to rise. The company might therefore enter into a ten-year swap paying fixed at 5% against receiving six-month LIBOR flat, but cancellable after five years. If rates do not rise as expected but look as if they will stay below 5%

for the latter half of the term, the company can exercise its right to cancel the swap at the five-year stage. These swaps are also known as callable or collapsible swaps.

A variation of the cancellable swap is the *extendible swap*. The company in the previous example could instead enter into a five-year swap as the payer of 5% fixed, but with the right to extend the swap after five years for a further five years. In fact, the two alternatives are equivalent. If rates stay low after five years, the ten-year cancellable swap will be cancelled, and the five-year extendible swap will not be extended – either way the company no longer has a swap after five years. (We will explore cancellable and extendible swaps further in section 13.4 of Chapter 13.)

An *index amortising swap* is one where the principal is amortised according to the prevailing level of interest rates using a pre-determined formula. Typically, the lower interest rates go, the quicker the principal is reduced. Such swaps are designed to mimic the pre-payment behaviour of mortgage-backed securities, where the principal also reduces when interest rates decline as borrowers pre-pay existing fixed-rate mortgages and refinance at the lower prevailing rates.

An *index principal swap* is a more general version of an index amortising swap, where the principal can either amortise or accrete according to the level of interest rates.

A *semi-fixed swap* has not one but two fixed rates. At each fixing date, in addition to setting the rate for the floating leg, the fixed rate will be switched between one of two levels according to the level of the floating reference. For example, at a time when vanilla five-year swaps are quoted at 3.4%, a semi-fixed swap might have a trigger of 3.5%, a lower fixed rate of 2.75% (which is 65bp cheaper than the vanilla swap rate) and a higher fixed rate of 4.25% (which is 85bp more expensive than the vanilla swap). Then, if six-month LIBOR on any fixing date was lower than 3.5%, the fixed rate would be 2.75%, but if LIBOR were higher than 3.5%, the fixed rate would be 4.25%. A fixed-rate payer who believes that interest rates will stay below the 3.5% trigger level for most or all of the five-year period may well prefer the semi-fixed swap to a vanilla swap. Such a swap is also known as a double-rate swap.

8.15 ISDA documentation

The International Swaps and Derivatives Association[10] (ISDA) has more than 800 members, including commercial and investment banks, central banks, investing institutions, insurance companies, corporates, exchanges, accounting and law firms, and service providers. ISDA was founded in 1985 originally with a mandate to standardise the legal documentation between parties executing interest rate swaps, but nowadays its activities go further, encompassing efforts to promote sound risk-management practices within the industry, and to advance the understanding and fair treatment of derivatives activities among those responsible for determining public policy and regulatory capital.

The scope of ISDA's legal documentation, comprising Master Agreements, Support Documentation, Definitions, Protocols, Annexes, Addenda, Supplements, Bridges and User's Guides, is huge and whole books[11] have been written about the topic. In this short section we will therefore confine ourselves to a brief summary of the main features.

At the time of writing, the key legal document governing interest rate swaps is still the *2002 ISDA Master Agreement*. Two parties executing swap transactions must first sign the Master Agreement, together with a Schedule which makes certain elections or modifications to the standard terms that the parties have negotiated. Each individual swap transaction is then documented in a Confirmation between the parties. Together, these three documentation elements comprise a single agreement between the parties. The Master Agreement and Schedule provide all the legal definitions (e.g. what is a 'Local Business Day'), while each Confirmation provides the specific details for each individual trade (e.g. the 'Fixed Rate Payer' for this trade is XYZ plc). So-called *short-form* confirmations can rely on the *2006 ISDA Definitions* document, to avoid having to re-state standard terms.

The fact that these documents comprise a single legal agreement is important because it allows payments from one swap transaction to be netted against payments from another swap transaction. This is especially relevant in the event of a swap counterparty becoming insolvent because it ensures that the surviving counterparty's risk is limited to the net cash flows from outstanding transactions, not the gross cash flows.

In addition to signing the ISDA Master Agreement, parties will usually sign an *ISDA Credit Support Annex* (CSA). These were published in 1994 (under New York law) or in 1995 (various other legal jurisdictions), and optionally amended by the *2001 ISDA Credit Support Protocol*. (Alternatively, parties can execute the *2001 ISDA Margin Provisions* instead, although to date there has been little take-up of this option.) These documents set out the legal framework for the depositing of collateral by one counterparty to the other. The idea behind this is to minimise the counterparty credit risk inherent in executing swap transactions.

As an example, suppose that two years have elapsed since two counterparties – ABC and XYZ – entered into a five-year swap contract having a notional principal of $10m and a fixed rate of 4%. Right now the floating rate is just 3% and is likely to remain at that level for the next three years. ABC, the fixed receiver, therefore expects to receive around $100,000 net each year for the next three years from XYZ, the fixed payer. If, however, XYZ were suddenly to default, ABC would lose around $300,000. To avoid this risk, under a CSA XYZ would have already posted collateral with ABC of a similar amount, the exact figure taking into account:

■ the time value of money – discounting the stream of future $100,000 payments back to the present day

- the potential future exposure – taking into account the possibility that floating rates could still rise or fall
- the quality of the collateral posted by XYZ.

The CSA documentation defines who is responsible for calculating the amount of collateral that should be posted, what collateral is eligible, the exact procedures for posting and return of collateral, who actually owns the collateral while posted, how disputes are resolved, and many other aspects of this process.

8.16 Changes in market infrastructure after the credit crisis

When Lehman Brothers collapsed in September 2008, its swaps book comprised more than 66,000 trades across five major currencies and totalled $9tn in notional amounts. Despite this, the majority of counterparties did not lose any money because most of these swap transactions had been cleared through a London-based clearing house called *SwapClear*, owned by LCH.Clearnet.

We have already examined the principles of clearing (Chapter 5) and clearing houses have always been a feature of futures markets. More recently, similar organisations have been created for the OTC derivatives market, and this development has become enshrined in US law with the passing of the Dodd–Frank Act (DFA) in 2010, and similarly in Europe with the European Market Infrastructure Regulation (EMIR), MiFID II and MiFIR legislation timetabled for enactment in late 2012.

The aims of the legislation on either side of the Atlantic are similar: to reduce the systemic risk arising from the huge global market in OTC derivatives, and to increase transparency at all stages of the trading process. To avoid this section becoming even more of an alphabet-soup than it already is, we will focus on the DFA terminology – most aspects of the DFA regulations are mirrored by similar provisions in the European laws but with different abbreviations.

The DFA has two related strands in this regard. The first one mandates that all trading in standardised OTC derivatives be executed either on a *designated contract market* (DCM) or at a *swap execution facility* (SEF). The second one requires that all such trades must be cleared by a *derivatives clearing organisation* (DCO). The standardised OTC derivatives covered by the legislation comprise principally vanilla interest rate swaps as described earlier in this chapter, and credit default swaps (CDS) and credit indices (to be explained in Chapters 14 and 15).

DCMs and SEFs

The intention behind the first strand is to increase the transparency of financial markets operations before and after the trade. Transparency before the trade will be increased by bringing together a larger number of participants, thereby increasing liquidity, reducing bid–offer spreads and making price discovery more efficient. Transparency after the trade will be achieved by more timely reporting and greater access to trade repositories.

As mentioned above, the DFA defines two forums where trading in standardised OTC derivatives must henceforth take place. DCMs are not new – they are exchanges or Boards of Trade (BOTs) under the supervision of the US Commodity Futures Trading Commission (CFTC), and the two most well-known are the Chicago Mercantile Exchange and the Chicago Board of Trade, both now merged within the CME Group. The term SEF is new, however, and is defined by the DFA as:

'a facility, trading system or platform in which multiple participants have the ability to execute or trade swaps by accepting bids and offers made by other participants that are open to multiple participants in the facility or system, through any means of interstate commerce.'[12]

The key concept here is multiplicity. The architects of the DFA want to ensure that derivatives users are presented with a wide range of quotations instead of a single price quoted by just one broker-dealer. The Act requires an SEF to provide multiple-to-multiple interactions, so that requests for quotations (RFQs) are channelled to at least five market participants, and that quotes made available by market-makers are visible to all. This stipulation effectively rules out systems hosted by single market-makers acting on their own. Although DCMs and SEFs have much in common, there are some important differences. DCMs have the rights to:

■ define standardised contract terms

■ require members to meet standardised margin requirements

■ liquidate a member's position or transfer it to another member.

In practice, this means that the DCMs essentially comprise the traditional futures markets, whereas SEFs will provide new exchange-like multilateral trading venues replacing the bilateral OTC markets that have hitherto been the norm for standardised OTC derivatives.

A number of firms currently offer swap execution facilities, especially traditional brokers such as ICAP, Tullett Prebon, GFI and BGC. Most prominent, however, is TradeWeb, which was established in 2005 and with more than 20 liquidity providers reports daily trading volume in excess of $10bn (as of October 2011).

DCOs

The second strand requires standardised OTC derivatives to be cleared through a derivatives clearing organisation, informally known as central clearing counterparties (CCPs). The intention is both clear and sound – to reduce systemic risk by applying the well-established principles of futures clearing to the OTC market. A DCO is defined under US legislation[13] as a clearing house, clearing corporation, or similar organisation that enables each party to the transaction to substitute the credit risk of the DCO for the credit risk of the other party. In addition, DCOs use multilateral netting to reduce the volume of daily settlements, and thus the level of settlement risk.

Chapter 5 (section 5.5) already provides a detailed explanation of how clearing works in the futures market, and the same procedures apply to DCOs working in the OTC derivatives market. The initial deposit of collateral, daily marking-to-market, and daily posting or taking of collateral all apply equally well here.

Most prominent among the DCOs clearing interest rate swaps is the aptly named SwapClear, established in 1999 and owned by LCH.Clearnet. SwapClear clears more than 50% of all OTC interest rate swaps and regularly clears in excess of $1tn every day. As of March 2012, SwapClear had almost $300tn of notional outstanding in more than 1m trades, 17 currencies, and maturities in some currencies extending out to 50 years.

This brings us full circle back to the Lehman Brothers scenario cited at the beginning of this section. The fact that SwapClear had long been established as the main DCO meant that the majority of swap trades where Lehman Brothers was a counterparty had been cleared through SwapClear. When SwapClear managed the ensuing default management process it took just three weeks to resolve the 66,000 outstanding trades. Importantly, no counterparty lost any money, as all exposures were more than adequately covered by the collateral that Lehman had previously posted.

> **'Following the default of Lehman Brothers, LCH.Clearnet was exposed to the risk of sharp market movements across a wide range of products. LCH.Clearnet successfully closed out its positions without using all of the margin it had available to support the post-default process. This illustrates the ability of a clearing house to protect market participants from bilateral counterparty risk, even in the event of default of a major participant.' *Financial Stability Report*, Bank of England, Issue 24, October 2008**

This demonstrates very well both the need for and the effectiveness of derivatives clearing organisations.

Notes

1   At the time of writing (June 2012) there were 43 such banks, comprising a mixture of those EU and international banks having the highest volume of business in the Eurozone money markets.

2   We will prove this as a general statement for all interest rate swaps in Chapter 9 (section 9.5).

3   The extra 37bp is not entirely risk-free though. Although German Bunds are AAA-rated just like US Treasuries, the insurance company faces counterparty risk from the swap counterparty.

4   Using a financial calculator we set PV = 300, N = 10, P/YR = 2, I = 5%, FV = 0, and solve for PMT = 68.6 per year.

5   The ISDAFIX rates are determined in a similar way to LIBOR, with a panel of banks contributing rates for each of the six currencies, and for each of the range of maturities quoted. The published rates are calculated as a simple average of the rates contributed after eliminating the top and bottom four quotes.

6   'BP swaps show 65% lower dividend in 2011 on oil spill', *Bloomberg Businessweek*, 5th August 2010.

7   'Dividend swap market – from A to Z', presentation by Stanislas Ract-Madoux to the September 2008 Eurex and Bloomberg seminar on dividend strategies.

8   *BIS Quarterly Review* (Statistical Annex), March 2011.

9   There are several other applications. Variance swaps are comprehensively reviewed in: 'Variance swaps', a paper produced by JP Morgan Securities Ltd, London, 17 November 2006.

10 The acronym ISDA originally stood for International Swap Dealers Association, but the name was changed in 1993 to reflect the broader scope of ISDA's activities beyond interest rate swaps alone.

11 For example: Harding, Paul (2010) *Mastering the ISDA Master Agreements*, 3rd edition, FT Prentice Hall.

12 MiFID II in Europe defines a multilateral trading facility (MTF) in a very similar way.

13 See 7 USC § 1a (9) of the US Code. All DCOs must register with the CFTC.

9

PRICING AND VALUING SWAPS

The previous chapter introduced a wide range of swaps, from vanilla interest rate swaps to quite unusual non-standard and exotic swaps. This chapter looks at how swaps can be valued and priced. Although we will focus mainly on interest rate swaps, the principles apply in a very similar way across almost all types of swaps.

9.1 Principles of swap valuation and pricing

Nearly all swaps, no matter how complex, are simply a series of cash flows spread over time. There are established techniques – which we will examine shortly – for taking a future cash flow and calculating its present value (PV). If we do this for each cash flow of the payment leg, and likewise for each cash flow of the receipt leg, and then sum the present values, we can determine what each leg is worth. Let's call these values $PV_{payment}$ and $PV_{receipt}$. Valuing a swap means finding the difference between these two amounts.

As we saw in the previous chapter, most swaps are priced so that there is no payment from one counterparty to the other at the outset. This implies that, at inception:

$$PV_{payment} = PV_{receipt}$$

All swaps have a pricing variable quoted by the market-maker. For a vanilla swap it is simply the fixed rate. For a basis swap it is the fixed margin added to one of the floating legs. Pricing a swap means finding the unique value for the pricing variable that equates the present values of payment and receipt legs at the start. For example, with a vanilla swap this means finding the fixed rate that equates the present values of fixed and floating legs at inception.

We can summarise these principles as follows:

- All swaps involve two legs – a payment leg and a receipt leg.
- Swap legs comprise a series of cash flows.
- It is possible to calculate the PV of each leg.
- To price a swap at inception, adjust the pricing variable so that the PVs of both legs are the same.
- To value a swap at any time, calculate the difference between the PVs of the two legs.

The following sections go through the processes involved, step by step. In section 9.2 we introduce the concept of a discount factor and the discount function, and show one way of calculating discount factors from zero-coupon rates. Sections 9.3 and 9.4 go on to demonstrate how discount factors can also be calculated from other sources, such as swap rates and STIR futures prices, and how to generate a complete set of discount factors from a blend of market rates. Section 9.5 discusses how zero-coupon, swap and forward rates are all related to one another. Sections 9.6 and 9.7 then show how all these techniques can be used to value and price swaps. Later sections go on to discuss further aspects of swap pricing and valuation, including cancelling a swap, hedging a swap, the credit risk arising from swap transactions, and the additional complexities created by the introduction of LIBOR–OIS discounting.

9.2 Discount factors and the discount function

The first step in swap valuation and pricing is to determine a set of *discount factors* from market rates. A discount factor is simply a number in the range zero to one which can be used to obtain the present value of some future cash flow.

$$PV_k = v_k \times FV_k \tag{9.1}$$

where:

PV_k is the present value of the future cash flow occurring at time k

FV_k is the future cash flow occurring at time k

v_k is the discount factor for cash flows occurring at time k

The simplest formulae relate discount factors to *zero-coupon rates*. A zero-coupon rate is an interest rate applicable to an investment (or borrowing) which has an initial cash flow, a final cash flow, but none in between. One example of a zero-coupon rate would be the yield on a zero-coupon bond, one which pays no coupons whatsoever over its lifetime. In the context of swap pricing and valuation, however, a more practical example of a zero-coupon rate is LIBOR. As we saw when LIBOR was explained briefly in section 4.3, LIBOR is essentially the interest rate applicable when one bank borrows from another for periods lasting up to one year. However, even for the longest periods, one bank borrows the principal at the outset, repays principal plus interest at maturity, but makes no intervening interest payments.

The only complicating factor is that zero-coupon rates are quoted a little differently depending upon the period concerned. Zero-coupon rates for periods less than or equal to one year are normally quoted assuming simple interest, with no compounding, and equation 9.2 applies. Zero-coupon rates for longer periods assume internal compounding, and equation 9.3 should then be used.

$$v_k = \frac{1}{(1 + z_k t_k)} \tag{9.2}$$

$$v_k = \frac{1}{\left(1 + {z_k}/{F}\right)^{F \times t_k}} \tag{9.3}$$

where:

v_k is the discount factor for cash flows occurring at time k

z_k is the zero-coupon rate for the period to time k

t_k is the time from the value date to time k, expressed in years or fractions of a year

F is the frequency of compounding per year

As an example, Table 9.1 illustrates the discount factors calculated from a set of zero-coupon rates covering periods from three months to five years,[1] while Figure 9.1 depicts the zero-coupon yield curve and the resulting discount factors graphically.

TABLE 9.1
Discount factors calculated from zero-coupon rates

Period	Zero-coupon rate	Discount factor
3 mths	3.50%	0.991326
6 mths	3.75%	0.981595
1 yr	4.10%	0.960615
2 yrs	4.49%	0.915905
3 yrs	4.70%	0.871284
4 yrs	4.80%	0.829001
5 yrs	4.85%	0.789147

The individual zero-coupon rates allow discount factors to be calculated at specific points along the maturity spectrum. However, cash flows may occur at any time in the future, and not necessarily at convenient times such as in three months or after one year. The second step in swap valuation and pricing is to calculate discount factors for every possible date in the future; the complete set of discount factors is called the *discount function*.

The usual technique for finding intermediate values is called *interpolation* and in this context there are two broad possibilities. We could interpolate between known zero-coupon rates to obtain the zero-coupon rate for an in-between date and then calculate the resulting discount factor using equation 9.2 or 9.3. Alternatively, we could interpolate directly between known discount factors to obtain the factor for an intermediate date.

FIGURE 9.1
Zero-coupon yield curve and discount factors

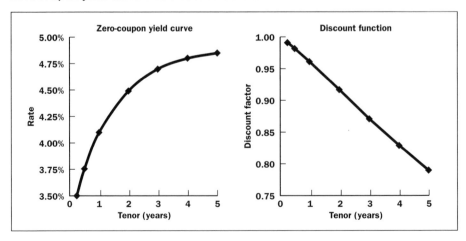

The problem with the first alternative is that we must make an assumption about the shape of the yield curve between adjacent points. Unfortunately, the yield curve can have many shapes: upward-sloping, downward-sloping, flat, convex, concave, humped or dished. Simply assuming that it follows a straight-line path between adjacent points and applying linear interpolation is potentially dangerous, not only because this imposes an arbitrary assumption on the shape of the yield curve but also because it leads to discontinuities when calculating forward interest rates.[2]

A better approach is to use the second alternative – interpolating between discount factors. There are, however, several different ways of doing this. The simplest technique is to interpolate linearly between the two adjacent discount factors, but this has a serious flaw – the discount function is an exponential curve, as this is the shape of the expressions given in equations 9.2 and 9.3.[3] It would therefore be quite wrong to fit a linear curve between two discount factors when the true shape is exponential.

The next technique is to recognise that the discount function is an exponential, and therefore to use exponential interpolation to interpolate between adjacent discount factors. Given any two known points v_1 and v_2 on the discount function, an intermediate point v_t can be interpolated using equation 9.4.

$$v_k = v_1^{\left[\frac{t_k}{t_1}\left(\frac{t_2-t_k}{t_2-t_1}\right)\right]} v_2^{\left[\frac{t_k}{t_2}\left(\frac{t_k-t_1}{t_2-t_1}\right)\right]} \tag{9.4}$$

where:

v_1	is the discount factor at time 1
v_2	is the discount factor at time 2
v_k	is the discount factor at the intermediate time k
t_1	is the time from value date to time 1
t_2	is the time from value date to time 2
t_k	is the time from value date to time k

and all the times are expressed in the same form, e.g. days, or fractions of a year.

At first sight this seems to be much better than anything we have seen so far, but the apparent sophistication of this technique is illusory. It can be demonstrated that exponential interpolation between adjacent discount factors using equation 9.4 is exactly the same as linear interpolation of the (continuously compounded) zero coupon rates, with the same attendant problems.

The best technique is to use *spline* interpolation, which takes a holistic view of a set of data and fits a smooth curve through all the known points. There are actually several ways to implement a spline, but the most commonly used method is the *natural cubic spline*. Figure 9.2 illustrates such a spline, and you can see that the technique does a very good job of creating and fitting a smooth curve through the set of 11 data points (which are called knots). To illustrate more dramatically how splines work, the example shown in Figure 9.2 is not of a discount curve, which can only decrease in value for longer periods of time, but an arbitrary set of data points.

FIGURE 9.2

Example of a natural cubic spline

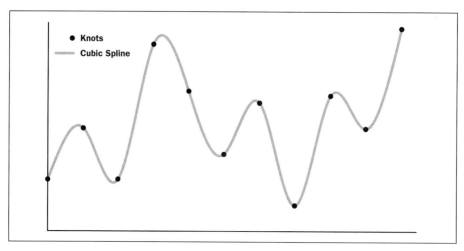

If we apply spline interpolation to the set of discount factors calculated in Table 9.1, we can obtain discount factors for any intermediate date and use these for pricing or valuation purposes. Table 9.2 shows five alternative ways of interpolating between the 2 yr discount factor of 0.915905 and the 3 yr discount factor of 0.871284 to obtain a discount factor for the 2.5 yr point. Using the natural cubic spline interpolation, we obtain 0.893402 as the most appropriate value. While this differs from the value obtained using the other techniques only in the fourth decimal place, this is nonetheless significant. If we use 0.893402 as the 2.5 yr factor, and 0.871284 from Table 9.1 as the 3 yr factor, by using equation 9.13 we can calculate that the mid-market rate for a 30 × 36 FRA should be 5.08%. Using one of the other interpolation techniques would result in an FRA price between 4bp and 8bp higher, a difference worth up to $4,000 on an FRA having a notional of $10m and a contract period of six months.

TABLE 9.2

Discount factors calculated from zero-coupon rates

Method	Discount factor	30 × 36 FRA rate
Linear interpolation of market rates	0.893764	5.16%
Linear interpolation of continuously compounded rates	0.893765	5.16%
Exponential interpolation of discount function	0.893765	5.16%
Linear interpolation of discount function	0.893595	5.12%
Natural cubic spline interpolation of discount function	0.893402	5.08%

9.3 Calculating discount factors from swap and forward rates

The previous section showed how to calculate discount factors from zero-coupon rates. In practice, however, discount factors are calculated from a range of real-life rates, including swap rates and forward interest rates (from STIR futures prices) as well as from zero-coupon rates. We therefore need to develop further formulae that will enable us to calculate discount factors from these alternative market sources.

Let's start by deriving a relationship between swap rates and discount factors. In preparation for this it is first helpful to demonstrate the link between swap rates and the yield on a par bond with the same credit risk. As the name suggests, a par bond is one which trades at par, and this implies that the yield to maturity is the same as the coupon rate. Let the yield and coupon rate be denoted as i. Consider buying 100 nominal of such a par bond. The resulting cash flows are pictured in Figure 9.3.

Now consider financing the purchase of the par bond by borrowing at LIBOR. The cash flows from this financing are shown in Figure 9.4. Combining these two sets of cash flows gives the net flows illustrated in Figure 9.5.

FIGURE 9.3

Cash flows resulting from purchase of par bond

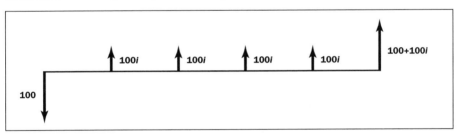

FIGURE 9.4

Cash flows resulting from LIBOR financing

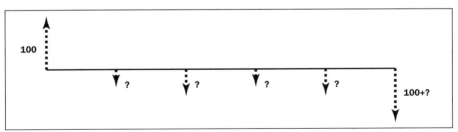

FIGURE 9.5

Net cash flows from par bond and LIBOR financing

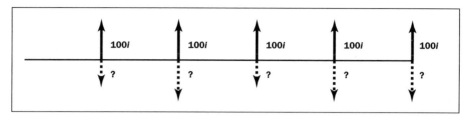

The cash flows from principals cancel out, leaving just the fixed coupons on the par bond and the floating interest payments from the LIBOR financing. Interestingly enough, these are exactly the same cash flows as those of Figure 8.3b for a vanilla interest-rate swap. This finding leads to an important conclusion:

The fixed rate on a vanilla interest-rate swap
is the same as
the yield and coupon on a par bond.

This means that determining the relationship between discount factors and swap rates is the same problem as determining the relationship between discount factors and the coupon rate on a par bond.

If we know the discount factors for each coupon date of a bond, the formula for the present value of a bond is given by equation 9.5.

$$P = \frac{100i_k}{F} v_1 + \frac{100i_k}{F} v_2 + \dots + \frac{100i_k}{F} v_k + 100 v_k \tag{9.5}$$

where:

k	is the total number of coupons
$v_1, v_2, \dots$	are the discount factors on the first, second, etc., coupon dates
F	is the number of times per year that coupons are paid[4]
i_k	is the coupon rate for a k-period bond (expressed as a decimal fraction)
P	is the present value of the bond

For a par bond, however, the present value P must be 100. Substituting $P = 100$ into equation 9.5 and rearranging to solve for i_k gives:

$$i_k = \frac{1 - v_k}{\dfrac{v_1}{F} + \dfrac{v_2}{F} + \dots + \dfrac{v_k}{F}} = \frac{1 - v_k}{\displaystyle\sum_{j=1}^{k} \frac{v_j}{F}} \tag{9.6}$$

Equation 9.6 is important, and provides the means for determining the par yield, and hence the swap rate i_k for a k-period swap. As an example, using the discount factors from Table 9.1 enables us to calculate the three-year annual swap rate as follows:

$$i_3 = \frac{1 - 0.871284}{0.960615 + 0.915905 + 0.871284} = 4.68\%$$

The calculated three-year swap rate is just a little less than the three-year zero-coupon rate of 4.70%.

By rearranging equation 9.6, it is possible to determine the k'th discount factor knowing the k-period swap rate.

$$v_k = \frac{1 - i_k \sum_{j=1}^{k-1} \frac{v_j}{F}}{1 + \frac{i_k}{F}} \tag{9.7}$$

Note that the summation in this case stops at $k{-}1$. This means that, for example, the discount factor for year five can be calculated using the discount factors from year one to year four, and the five-year swap rate. Once the five-year discount factor has been determined, it can be inserted into equation 9.7 together with the six-year swap rate to obtain the six-year discount factor, and so on. Determining discount factors from swap rates in this way is an iterative process colloquially known as 'bootstrapping'.

We have already provided formulae for calculating discount factors from zero-coupon rates either shorter than one year (equation 9.2) or longer than one year (equation 9.3). Inverting these equations enables us to calculate zero-coupon rates from discount factors, either for periods shorter than one year:

$$z_k = \left(\frac{1}{v_K} - 1\right) \times \frac{1}{t_k} \tag{9.8}$$

or for periods longer than one year:

$$z_k = \left[\left(\frac{1}{v_K}\right)^{\frac{1}{F \times t_k}} - 1\right] \times F \tag{9.9}$$

Equations 9.2, 9.3 and 9.6–9.9 give us the means of calculating swap rates from discount factors, discount factors from swap rates, zero-coupon rates from discount factors and discount factors from zero-coupon rates. Together, they provide the mathematical links between swap rates and zero-coupon rates. These links will shortly be illustrated graphically, but there is one further type of rate to consider – forward rates.

Equation 9.2 provided a means of calculating a discount factor from a zero-coupon rate. Suppose that the length of time t_k was a fraction of a year given by $1/F$, in other words, that there were F periods during the year of equal length t_k. Equation 9.2 could then be re-written to give the discount factor v_1 at the end of the first period:

$$v_1 = \frac{1}{\left(1 + \frac{z_1}{F}\right)} \tag{9.10}$$

Equation 9.10 tells us that the present value of 1 after the first period is 1 discounted by the zero-coupon rate using the expression in the denominator of equation 9.10. Once this first discount factor is known, the second discount factor can be obtained by discounting by a similar expression but this time using the *forward rate*.

$$v_2 = \frac{v_1}{\left(1 + \frac{f_{1,2}}{F}\right)} \tag{9.11}$$

where:

$f_{1,2}$ is the forward rate from the end of period 1 to the end of period 2

This formula can be generalised to find the discount factor at any point in time from the previous discount factor and the forward rate:

$$v_k = \frac{v_{k-1}}{\left(1 + \frac{f_{k-1,k}}{F}\right)} \tag{9.12}$$

where:

$f_{k-1,k}$ is the forward rate from the end of period $k-1$ to the end of period k

Equation 9.12 can easily be rearranged to solve for the intervening forward rate, given the discount factors either side:

$$f_{k-1,k} = \left(\frac{v_{k-1}}{v_k} - 1\right) \times F \tag{9.13}$$

As an example, using once again the discount factors from Table 9.1 enables us to calculate the six-month against 12-month forward rate as follows:

$$f_{6\times12} = \left(\frac{v_{6m}}{v_{12m}} - 1\right) \times 2 = \left(\frac{0.981595}{0.960615} - 1\right) \times 2 = 4.37\%$$

With a little more effort, equation 9.12 can be manipulated to solve for the discount factor at time k from all the previous forward rates:

$$v_k = \frac{1}{\left(1 + \frac{f_{0,1}}{F}\right)} \times \frac{1}{\left(1 + \frac{f_{1,2}}{F}\right)} \times \dots \times \frac{1}{\left(1 + \frac{f_{k-1,k}}{F}\right)} = \prod_{j=1}^{k} \left[\frac{1}{1 + \frac{f_{j-1,j}}{F}}\right] \tag{9.14}$$

FIGURE 9.6

'Route map' of links between rates and discount factors

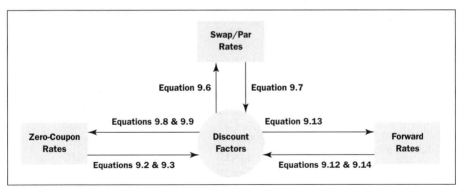

The equations thus developed now give us a versatile means to convert readily between discount factors, swap rates, zero-coupon rates and forward rates. Figure 9.6 provides a 'route map' through the maze and highlights exactly which equation is needed to convert between one set of variables and another.

Note that discount factors are drawn at the centre of the figure. This is the appropriate place because discount factors provide the foundation for swap valuation and pricing. Once the discount factors are known, it is then possible to calculate any other market rate, or to value and price a wide range of financial engineering products.

9.4 Generating the discount function

As we have seen in the last two sections, discount factors can be calculated by combining a number of different market rates. To illustrate how this is done in practice we will use the set of market rates for the US dollar on Friday 25th March 2011 as shown in Table 9.3. These comprise short-term LIBOR rates, STIR futures prices out to two years, and swap rates from 1y through 5y.

Broadly speaking, we will use only those LIBOR rates that are needed to determine the discount factor on the expiry date of the first liquid STIR futures contract. We will then use these STIR futures to generate discount factors until we reach longer maturities when we can use interest rate swaps to provide the necessary data. Using STIR futures prices to generate the discount factors for the shorter maturities is preferable to using LIBOR rates because they are much more liquid, and prices are available almost 24 hours a day.

To obtain the complete set of discount factors out to five years, we will use a number of the techniques that we explored in the last two sections, including the formulae for calculating individual discount factors from market rates, and spline interpolation.

TABLE 9.3

Market rates for US dollars on 25th March 2011

	Maturity	Market rate
LIBOR rates	1w	0.23025%
	1m	0.24825%
	2m	0.28150%
	3m	0.30750%
STIR futures prices	Jun 11	99.6200
	Sep 11	99.5050
	Dec 11	99.3550
	Mar 12	99.1250
	Jun 12	98.8100
	Sep 12	98.4600
	Dec 12	98.1250
	Mar 13	97.8400
Swap rates	1y	0.465%
	2y	0.915%
	3y	1.455%
	4y	1.935%
	5y	2.355%

Source: Complied from wsj.com, CME and ft.com

The specific steps we will take are summarised in Figure 9.7 and comprise:

- Step 1: Calculate discount factors for each of the LIBOR dates until just beyond the expiry date of the first liquid STIR future, in this case the June 2011 contract.

- Step 2: Use spline interpolation of these discount factors to obtain the discount factor for that contract's expiry date, in this case 15 June 2011.

- Step 3: Use the implied forward rates calculated from the STIR contracts to calculate discount factors out to the point where liquidity begins to wane, in this case the two-year point. We now have a set of discount factors corresponding to each of the futures expiry dates, 15 June 2011, 21 September 2011, and so on until the end of the period covered by the last contract used, in this case 19 June 2013, the end of the period covered by the March 2013 contract.

- Step 4: Use a spline to interpolate between these discount factors to produce another set of discount factors corresponding to the quarterly swap payment dates, 29 June 2011, 29 September 2011, and so on until the quarterly date covered by the last futures contract used, in this case 29 March 2013.

- Step 5: Use another cubic spline to interpolate between the annual swap rates, thereby calculating the swap rates for each of these quarterly swap payment dates.

- Step 6: Finally, use the initial set of discount factors from step 4 and the interpolated swap rates from step 5 to calculate the discount factors at each quarterly swap payment date starting with the shortest swap. Where these new discount factors overlap the initial discount factors calculated in step 4, blend the two values.

FIGURE 9.7

Generating a blended discount function

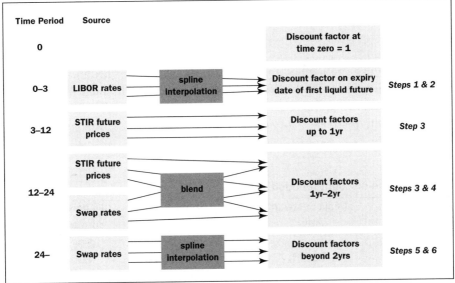

Table 9.4a shows the results of the first two steps. Using the 1m, 2m and 3m LIBOR rates, we first use equation 9.2 to determine the discount factors for these three dates. For example, the first discount factor is calculated thus:

$$v_{1m} = \frac{1}{1 + 0.24825\% \times {}^{31}\!/_{360}} = 0.999786$$

We then fit a natural cubic spline through the four discount factors (including the discount factor of 1 for the spot value date) to obtain the interpolated value of 0.999359 for the discount factor on 15 June 2011. This is approximately half-way between the 31st May and 29th June values of 0.999508 and 0.999215, as you would expect.

TABLE 9.4a

Generating the discount function – steps 1 and 2

Maturity	Date	Days	LIBOR rate	Discount factors from LIBOR rates
Spot	Tue 29 Mar 2011			1
1m	Fri 29 Apr 2011	31	0.24825%	0.999786
2m	Tue 31 May 2011	63	0.28150%	0.999508
3m	Wed 29 Jun 2011	92	0.30750%	0.999215
Jun 2011 contract expiry	Wed 15 Jun 2011			0.999359

Next we use equation 9.12 to calculate the set of discount factors for each futures expiry date out to two years. The figures are shown in Table 9.4b and, for example, the discount factor for 21st September 2011 is:

$$v_{21\,Sep\,2011} = \frac{v_{15\,Jun\,2011}}{\left(1 + \dfrac{f_{Jun\,2011}}{4}\right)} = \frac{0.9993587}{\left(1 + \dfrac{0.380\%}{4}\right)} = 0.9984102$$

Note that we use the implied forward rate of 0.38% from the June 2011 contract, which expires on 15th June 2011, to calculate the discount factor for 21 September 2011. This is because the time period covered by a STIR contract is the three-month period *starting* on the contract's expiry date, a point discussed in Chapter 6.

TABLE 9.4b
Generating the discount function – step 3

Contract	Implied forward rate	Date	DFs from implied forward rates
		Wed 15 Jun 11	0.999359
Jun 11	0.380%	Wed 21 Sep 11	0.998410
Sep 11	0.495%	Wed 21 Dec 11	0.997176
Dec 11	0.645%	Wed 21 Mar 12	0.995571
Mar 12	0.875%	Wed 20 Jun 12	0.993398
Jun 12	1.190%	Wed 19 Sep 12	0.990451
Sep 12	1.540%	Wed 19 Dec 12	0.986653
Dec 12	1.875%	Wed 20 Mar 13	0.982049
Mar 13	2.160%	Wed 19 Jun 13	0.976775

Step 4 involves fitting a cubic spline to these discount factors – which are pinned to the futures contract expiry dates – to determine another set of discount factors corresponding to the quarterly payment dates of interest rate swaps. Table 9.4c shows the results of these calculations. As an example, the interpolated discount factor of 0.986091 for 31 December 2012 is about one-eighth the way along the path between the values of 0.986653 for 19 Dec 2012 and 0.982049 for 20 Mar 2013, as you would expect from the corresponding dates.

TABLE 9.4c
Generating the discount function – step 4

Date	Interpolated DFs from implied forward rates
Tue 29 Mar 2011	1
Wed 29 Jun 2011	0.999238
Thu 29 Sep 2011	0.998317
Thu 29 Dec 2011	0.997051
Thu 29 Mar 2012	0.995406
Fri 29 Jun 2012	0.993143
Fri 28 Sep 2012	0.990113
Mon 31 Dec 2012	0.986091
Fri 29 Mar 2013	0.981550

In step 5 we fit a natural cubic spline to the set of swap rates to create the complete set of swap rates out to five years, in quarterly increments. Finally, to implement step 6 we use equation 9.7 repeatedly to calculate discount factors from these interpolated swap rates, each discount factor providing the information necessary to calculate the next factor. Table 9.4d shows the results of this process.

TABLE 9.4d
Generating the discount function – steps 5 and 6

Date	Interpolated swap rates	Interpolated DFs from implied forward rates	DFs from swap rates	Blended discount factors
Tue 29 Mar 2011		1		1
Wed 29 Jun 2011		0.999238		0.999238
Thu 29 Sep 2011		0.998317		0.998317
Thu 29 Dec 2011		0.997051		0.997051
Thu 29 Mar 2012	0.465%	0.995406	0.995284	0.995345
Fri 29 Jun 2012	0.558%	0.993143	0.992929	0.993036
Fri 28 Sep 2012	0.666%	0.990113	0.989891	0.990002
Mon 31 Dec 2012	0.786%	0.986091	0.986041	0.986066
Fri 29 Mar 2013	0.915%	0.981550	0.981557	0.981554
Fri 28 Jun 2013	1.049%		0.976262	0.976262
Mon 30 Sep 2013	1.186%		0.970166	0.970166
Mon 30 Dec 2013	1.322%		0.963520	0.963520
Mon 31 Mar 2014	1.455%		0.956336	0.956336
Mon 30 Jun 2014	1.582%		0.948722	0.948722
Mon 29 Sep 2014	1.704%		0.940719	0.940719
Mon 29 Dec 2014	1.821%		0.932346	0.932346
Mon 30 Mar 2015	1.935%		0.923612	0.923612
Mon 29 Jun 2015	2.045%		0.914528	0.914528
Tue 29 Sep 2015	2.152%		0.905077	0.905077
Tue 29 Dec 2015	2.256%		0.895414	0.895414
Tue 29 Mar 2016	2.355%		0.885539	0.885539

Once the discount factors are known, any zero-coupon rate, forward rate or swap rate can be calculated. For example, the five-year semi-annually compounded zero-coupon rate can be calculated using equation 9.9:

$$z_5 = \left[\left(\frac{1}{0.885539}\right)^{\frac{1}{2\times5}} - 1\right] \times 2 = 2.45\%$$

The two-year semi-annual swap rate can be calculated using equation 9.6:

$$i_{2y \; semi-annual} = \frac{1 - v_{2y}}{\frac{v_{6m}}{2} + \frac{v_{1y}}{2} + \frac{v_{18m}}{2} + \frac{v_{2y}}{2}}$$

$$= \frac{1 - 0.981554}{\frac{0.998317}{2} + \frac{0.995345}{2} + \frac{0.990002}{2} + \frac{0.981554}{2}} = 0.93\%$$

If the four-year against five-year forward rate were needed, equation 9.13 gives the answer:

$$f_{4y \times 5y} = \left(\frac{v_{4y}}{v_{5y}} - 1\right) = \left(\frac{0.923612}{0.885539} - 1\right) = 4.30\%$$

9.5 Relationship between zero, swap and forward rates

The foregoing equations and the route map of Figure 9.6 provide a symbolic prescription for the relationship between zero-coupon, swap and forward rates. With a little more effort, it is possible to obtain two further equations which enable us to obtain a better feel for the way in which these rates are linked.

By combining and manipulating equations 9.6 and 9.12, it is possible to show that:

$$i_k = \frac{\sum_{j=1}^{k} \frac{f_{j-1,j} v_j}{F}}{\sum_{j=1}^{k} \frac{v_j}{F}} \tag{9.15}$$

Similarly, by using equations 9.3 and 9.14, one can demonstrate that:

$$1 + \frac{z_k}{F} = \left(\prod_{j=1}^{k} \left(1 + \frac{f_{j-1,j}}{F}\right)\right)^{1/F \times t_k} \tag{9.16}$$

The interpretation of these apparently complex equations is actually quite simple.

Equation 9.15 says:

**The *swap rate* is the
weighted arithmetic average of the forward rates.**

This should come as no surprise, and provides an insight into the similarities between an interest-rate swap and a strip of FRAs. Buying an FRA provides a settlement sum to compensate for the difference between the fixed rate originally agreed and the market rate that eventually transpires. If interest rates float higher than the fixed rate agreed, the FRA buyer receives the net payment; if interest rates float lower, the FRA buyer pays. This is directly analogous to the fixed-rate payer under a swap. If the floating rate in any swap period is higher than the fixed rate, the fixed-rate payer receives the net interest payment, while the opposite is true if the floating rate turns out to be lower.

Buying a strip of FRAs to cover multiple periods in the future is therefore virtually the same as entering into a swap agreement for the same period, except for two differences:

a) Each FRA within the strip would normally be executed at a different contract rate, each rate corresponding to the forward rate for that contract period. An interest-rate swap is normally executed with a constant fixed rate.

b) Under an FRA, the settlement sums are normally discounted and paid at the beginning of the contract period. With an interest-rate swap, the net interest payments are normally undiscounted and paid at the end of each period during the life of the swap.

If a single rate could be found to replace the set of individual FRA rates, that single rate would be the swap rate. Common sense would suggest that some kind of average is appropriate, and the mathematics of equation 9.15 shows that it should be a weighted average, the weights being the set of discount factors for each period.

Equation 9.16 says:

> ***One* plus the per-period *zero-coupon rate* is the**
> ***geometric average* of *one* plus the per-period *forward rates*.**

Each of the individual forward rates provides a link between the discount factor at the beginning of a period and the discount factor at the end. To obtain the discount factor at the end of multiple periods, all the individual discount factors must be combined by multiplying them together. By definition, this must give the same result as using the single zero-coupon rate for the entire period.

Swap rates and zero-coupon rates are both therefore averages of the forward rates and therefore will be very similar. The swap rate is the weighted arithmetic average of the forward rates, while (one plus) the per-period zero-coupon rate is the geometric average of (one plus) the per-period forward rates.[5] Although the geometric average of a set of numbers must always be less than or equal to the simple arithmetic average, this does not necessarily follow for a weighted arithmetic average. In fact, it can be proved mathematically that the difference between swap rates and zero rates depends upon the shape of the yield curve. When the yield curve is positively sloped, zero-coupon rates will actually lie slightly above the swap rates, and when the yield curve is negatively sloped, zero-coupon rates will be lower than swap rates.

Table 9.5 illustrates two yield curve scenarios: one with swap rates rising from 1.5% to 4.285% for maturities from one to five years, the other with swap rates falling from 5.2% down to 2.37%. The table shows the zero rates, forward rates and discount factors for each year.

To visualise this information more clearly, Figure 9.8 shows the various interest rates under both scenarios. In each case the swap and zero rates are the cumulative averages of the forward rates. This means that in the positive yield curve environment, for example, the swap and zero rates rise more slowly than the forward rate. Alternatively, one could consider the forward rates rising ever more rapidly than the swap and zero rates. Take the 4-year and $4\frac{1}{2}$-year rates, for instance. The 4-year swap rate of 3.95% is the weighted average of the

TABLE 9.5

Illustration of swap rates, zero rates, forward rates and discount factors

Tenor (yrs)	Positive yield curve				Negative yield curve			
	Swap rates	Zero rates	Forward rates	Discount factors	Swap rates	Zero rates	Forward rates	Discount factors
0.5	1.500%	1.500%	1.500%	0.992556	5.200%	5.200%	5.200%	0.974659
1.0	2.000%	2.003%	2.506%	0.980272	4.700%	4.694%	4.190%	0.954661
1.5	2.450%	2.458%	3.371%	0.964024	4.250%	4.237%	3.325%	0.939047
2.0	2.850%	2.865%	4.094%	0.944688	3.850%	3.830%	2.612%	0.926940
2.5	3.200%	3.225%	4.672%	0.923125	3.500%	3.473%	2.052%	0.917525
3.0	3.500%	3.537%	5.101%	0.900165	3.200%	3.167%	1.646%	0.910034
3.5	3.745%	3.793%	5.339%	0.876760	2.950%	2.913%	1.395%	0.903733
4.0	3.950%	4.010%	5.531%	0.853164	2.730%	2.690%	1.132%	0.898645
4.5	4.130%	4.202%	5.744%	0.829346	2.540%	2.497%	0.963%	0.894341
5.0	4.285%	4.368%	5.875%	0.805680	2.370%	2.325%	0.782%	0.890856

eight preceding forward rates. If the $4\frac{1}{2}$-year swap rate is 18bp higher at 4.13%, the 4-year against $4\frac{1}{2}$-year forward rate must be much higher in order for the addition of one extra forward rate to boost the average that much. If the swap rate were a simple average of nine figures, the 4-year × $4\frac{1}{2}$-year forward rate would need to be nine times 18bp, or 162bp, higher than 3.95% to increase the $4\frac{1}{2}$-year swap rate to 4.13%. This would make the forward rate 5.57%. In fact, with the discount factor weightings, the forward rate turns out to be around 179bp higher at 5.744%.

FIGURE 9.8

Graphical illustration of swap, zero-coupon and forward rates

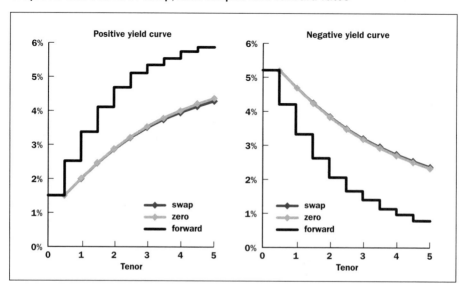

Similar arguments apply to the negative yield curve environment, where all rates fall, but where the forward rates fall much faster than either the swap or zero rates. Note that in this scenario, the zero-coupon rates are a fraction lower than the swap rates, but that this relationship is reversed when the yield curve is positive.

9.6 Valuation and pricing of interest rate swaps

We can now build on these foundations to show how interest-rate swaps of arbitrary complexity can be valued and priced. Let's recap the principles underlying swap valuation and pricing as set out in section 9.1:

- All swaps involve two legs – a payment leg and a receipt leg.
- Swap legs comprise a series of cash flows.
- It is possible to calculate the PV of each leg.
- To price a swap at inception, adjust the pricing variable so that the PVs of both legs are the same.
- To value a swap at any time, calculate the difference between the PVs of the two legs.

The techniques used are fundamentally the same whether one is pricing or valuing a swap. Pricing normally involves finding the correct fixed rate for a new swap such that the NPV is zero. Valuing, on the other hand, normally involves finding the NPV of an existing swap for which the fixed rate has already been set. Thus, in the case of pricing, the NPV is known (to be zero), while the fixed rate is the unknown. In the case of swap valuation, it is the fixed rate which is known, while the NPV has to be determined.

Once we have generated the discount function, swap valuation and pricing therefore proceeds in two steps: identify the cash flows for each leg, then use the discount factors to obtain the present values of these cash flows.

To illustrate the technique, let's start with a $10m vanilla five-year interest-rate swap using the Actual/Actual day count convention and semi-annual payment dates. For market rates we will use the set of swap rates illustrated in Table 9.5 under the positive yield curve environment. What is the net present value of this swap for the fixed-rate payer if it is booked at the prevailing market rate for swaps of this maturity?

If the five-year swap rate is 4.285%, the cash outflows under the fixed leg are simply $428,500 each year or $214,250 every six months. The first floating leg receipt will be at 1.500%, because this is the prevailing six-month rate on the trade date, and the trade date is also the first setting date. However, there is a potential problem: the remaining floating leg receipts are unknown at this stage and will be determined only on the future setting dates. Nevertheless, for valuation purposes we can assume that a bank executing a swap has access to the

STIR futures or FRA markets and could hedge the floating receipts accordingly. For example, the bank expecting to receive 2.506% in the second six-month period could either sell a 6 × 12 FRA or buy a strip of STIR futures. If interest rates in six months turned out to be lower than 2.506%, the profits on the FRA or futures hedge would offset the lower floating interest receipt from the swap. Likewise, if interest rates turned out to be higher than 2.506%, the hedge would make losses equivalent to the extra interest received from the swap. Either way, if the hedge was executed effectively, the combined cash flow from the hedge plus swap floating leg will lock in a floating receipt equivalent to 2.506% for the second period of the swap. Similar hedges could be executed for all the remaining swap periods. We can therefore use the market implied forward rates to value the cash flows of the floating leg of a swap.

Table 9.6 reproduces the market rates and discount factors from Table 9.5, then sets out the resulting fixed payments and floating receipts together with the present values of these cash flows.

The figures show that, at the inception of the swap, the present values of both legs are equal and the net present value is therefore zero. This demonstrates that the swap is correctly priced at 4.285%. The example also illustrates why there is no need for any up-front payment from one counterparty to the other under a vanilla swap.

Of course, it is no real surprise that the swap is found to be fairly priced at 4.285%, because this was the swap rate used to derive the discount factors, which in turn were used to value the swap! Nonetheless, the figures at least prove that the system is self-consistent.

Suppose the swap was executed at 4.285%, and moments later the five-year swap rate moved up to 4.295%. What is the value of the swap to the fixed-rate payer now? Table 9.7 values the swap under the new market rates.

The value of the fixed leg has declined by just $95.12, caused by the higher swap rate reducing five-year discount factor by a small amount. The biggest change, perhaps surprisingly, occurs to the floating leg, which *increases* in value by $4,439.55 despite the weaker discount factor. The explanation follows from the nature of swap rates, which are an average of the component forward rates, as proved in the previous section. The five-year swap rate is the weighted average of the strip of ten six-month forward rates. If the first nine swap rates do not change, then the first nine forward rates must also remain unchanged. The 1bp increase in the five-year swap rate must therefore go hand in hand with a much larger rise in the last forward rate, which here increases by more than 11bp.

The combined effect is for the net present value for the fixed-rate payer to move from zero to $4,534.67. The figures were relatively easy to calculate in this case because we assumed that the swap rate moved immediately after the swap was executed. However, exactly the same method can be used to value a swap at any other time. The only complicating feature is the need to interpolate the discount factors from available market rates to give the discount factors on the dates when the swap cash flows occur.

TABLE 9.6

Valuation of vanilla five-year swap with five-year swap market rates at 4.285%

Years	Swap rates	Zero rates	Forward rates	Discount factors	Fixed payments	Floating receipts	PV of fixed payments	PV of floating receipts
0.5	1.500%	1.500%	1.500%	0.992556	214,250.00	75,000.00	212,655.09	74,441.69
1.0	2.000%	2.003%	2.506%	0.980272	214,250.00	125,313.28	210,023.22	122,841.07
1.5	2.450%	2.458%	3.371%	0.964024	214,250.00	168,545.16	206,542.05	162,481.51
2.0	2.850%	2.865%	4.094%	0.944688	214,250.00	204,676.10	202,399.42	193,355.07
2.5	3.200%	3.225%	4.672%	0.923125	214,250.00	233,583.65	197,779.61	215,626.99
3.0	3.500%	3.537%	5.101%	0.900165	214,250.00	255,063.02	192,860.45	229,598.93
3.5	3.745%	3.793%	5.339%	0.876760	214,250.00	266,957.32	187,845.77	234,057.43
4.0	3.950%	4.010%	5.531%	0.853164	214,250.00	276,571.93	182,790.31	235,961.11
4.5	4.130%	4.202%	5.744%	0.829346	214,250.00	287,181.35	177,687.45	238,172.80
5.0	4.285%	4.368%	5.875%	0.805680	214,250.00	293,744.06	172,616.93	236,663.71
TOTAL							1,943,200.30	1,943,200.30

Principal: $10m   Fixed rate: 4.285%   NPV = 0

TABLE 9.7

Valuation of vanilla five-year swap with five-year swap market rates at 4.295%

Years	Swap rates	Zero rates	Forward rates	Discount factors	Fixed payments	Floating receipts	PV of fixed payments	PV of floating receipts
0.5	1.500%	1.500%	1.500%	0.992556	214,250.00	75,000.00	212,655.09	74,441.69
1.0	2.000%	2.003%	2.506%	0.980272	214,250.00	125,313.28	210,023.22	122,841.07
1.5	2.450%	2.458%	3.371%	0.964024	214,250.00	168,545.16	206,542.05	162,481.51
2.0	2.850%	2.865%	4.094%	0.944688	214,250.00	204,676.10	202,399.42	193,355.07
2.5	3.200%	3.225%	4.672%	0.923125	214,250.00	233,583.65	197,779.61	215,626.99
3.0	3.500%	3.537%	5.101%	0.900165	214,250.00	255,063.02	192,860.45	229,598.93
3.5	3.745%	3.793%	5.339%	0.876760	214,250.00	266,957.32	187,845.77	234,057.43
4.0	3.950%	4.010%	5.531%	0.853164	214,250.00	276,571.93	182,790.31	235,961.11
4.5	4.130%	4.202%	5.744%	0.829346	214,250.00	287,181.35	177,687.45	238,172.80
5.0	4.295%	4.380%	5.988%	0.805236	214,250.00	299,419.37	172,521.82	241,103.26
TOTAL							1,943,105.18	1,947,639.85

Principal: $10m   Fixed rate: 4.285%   NPV = 4,534.67

The real power of these swap valuation and pricing techniques emerges when it comes to non-standard swaps. Consider the following specification:

Description:	4yr accreting margin swap, deferred 1yr
Principal:	$3,000,000 (1st year)
	$5,000,000 (2nd year)
	$7,000,000 (3rd year)
	$10,000,000 (4th year)
Floating rate:	LIBOR+50bp
Day count convention (fixed):	Actual/360
Day count convention (floating):	Actual/360
Trade date:	3rd February 2011
Effective date:	7th February 2012
Maturity date:	8th February 2016
Payment frequency (fixed):	Semi-annual (every 7th Feb and 7th Aug, or modified following business day)
Payment frequency (floating):	Semi-annual (every 7th Feb and 7th Aug, or modified following business day).

Three features distinguish this particular instrument from a vanilla swap. First, there is the deferred start. If the trade date was on Thursday 3rd February 2011, the effective date for a vanilla swap would be Monday 7th February 2011. Deferring this by one year pushes the start of the swap to Tuesday 7th February 2012, and the maturity date four years later falls on Monday 8th February 2016 (rolling from 7th February 2016, which is a Sunday). Second, instead of a constant notional principal this accreting swap has a notional principal of $3,000,000 for the first year, increasing each year until it reaches $10,000,000 in the final year. Finally, the floating reference is not LIBOR flat but LIBOR+50bp.

To price the fixed rate for this non-standard swap, we use the discount factors to value the floating leg, and then find the fixed rate which makes the present value of the fixed leg equal to that of the floating leg.

Table 9.8 summarises the valuation and pricing of the swap, and shows that with the floating margin of LIBOR+50bp, and a fixed rate of 5.7356%, the present values of the fixed and floating legs are indeed identical. The correct price for this particular non-standard swap must therefore be 5.7356%.

Note that, despite the quoted swap rates being the same as those in Table 9.6, the calculated zero-coupon rates, forward rates and discount factors are all a little different. For example, the final forward rate was 5.875% in Table 9.6 but 5.856% here. This is because the day count convention is Actual/360 in this example rather than the simpler Actual/Actual used in the previous example.

The correct swap rate of 5.7356% could have been found by trial and error, but there is a more systematic method. Once again, we start by valuing the floating leg. In general, the present value of the floating leg of a k-period swap is:

TABLE 9.8
Valuation of accreting, margin, deferred start, four-year swap

Date	Swap rates	Zero rates	Forward rates	Discount factors	Notional principal ($m)	Fixed payments	Floating receipts	PV of fixed payments	PV of floating receipts
Mon 08 Aug 11	1.500%	1.517%	1.500%	0.992474	0	0.00	0.00	0.00	0.00
Tue 07 Feb 12	2.000%	2.030%	2.504%	0.980002	0	0.00	0.00	0.00	0.00
Tue 07 Aug 12	2.450%	2.490%	3.374%	0.963567	3	86,990.22	58,750.96	83,820.92	56,610.50
Thu 07 Feb 13	2.850%	2.909%	4.083%	0.943870	3	87,946.15	70,272.51	83,009.73	66,328.11
Wed 07 Aug 13	3.200%	3.269%	4.687%	0.922141	5	144,187.08	130,389.81	132,960.75	120,237.73
Fri 07 Feb 14	3.500%	3.590%	5.089%	0.898763	5	146,576.92	142,829.84	131,737.96	128,370.22
Thu 07 Aug 14	3.745%	3.845%	5.355%	0.875198	7	201,861.91	206,080.16	176,669.07	180,360.87
Mon 09 Feb 15	3.950%	4.075%	5.504%	0.850999	7	207,438.21	217,136.21	176,529.61	184,782.59
Fri 07 Aug 15	4.130%	4.260%	5.781%	0.827221	10	285,187.71	312,295.19	235,913.36	258,337.25
Mon 08 Feb 16	4.285%	4.435%	5.856%	0.803054	10	294,747.07	326,642.98	236,697.69	262,311.81
TOTAL								1,257,339.08	1,257,339.08

Fixed rate: 5.735619%   L+50bp   NPV = 0

$$PV_{float} = \sum_{j=1}^{k} f_{j-1} P_j \frac{d_j}{B} v_j \qquad (9.17)$$

where:

PV_{float}	is the present value of the floating leg
f_j	is the floating rate from time j-1 to time j
P_j	is the notional principal from time j-1 to time j
d_j	is the number of days from time j-1 to time j
v_j	is the discount factor at time j
B	is the day count convention divisor (normally 360 or 365)

In this example, the present value of the first floating receipt is:

$$(3.373690\% + 0.5000\%) \times 3,000,000 \times \frac{182}{360} \times 0.963567 = 56,610.50$$

as shown in the last column of Table 9.8, which also reveals the values for the remaining periods. The total present value of the floating leg is \$1,257,339.08.
    A similar equation provides the present value of the fixed leg:

$$PV_{fixed} = i_k \sum_{j=1}^{k} P_j \frac{d_j}{B} v_j \qquad (9.18)$$

where:

PV_{fixed}	is the present value of the fixed leg
i_k	is the fixed rate for the entire duration of the swap

and the other symbols are as defined for equation 9.17.
    Using equation 9.18, PV_{fixed} for this non-standard swap is:

$$\begin{aligned}
PV_{fixed} = {} & i_k \times \left(3,000,000 \times \frac{182}{360} \times 0.963567 + 3,000,000 \times \frac{184}{360} \times 0.943870 + \right. \\
& 5,000,000 \times \frac{181}{360} \times 0.922141 + 5,000,000 \times \frac{184}{360} \times 0.898763 + \\
& 7,000,000 \times \frac{181}{360} \times 0.875198 + 7,000,000 \times \frac{186}{360} \times 0.850999 + \\
& \left. 10,000,000 \times \frac{179}{360} \times 0.827221 + 10,000,000 \times \frac{185}{360} \times 0.803054\right) \\
= {} & i_k \times 21,921,594.63
\end{aligned}$$

The fixed rate is then obtained by equating the value of fixed and floating legs. Setting PV_{fixed} to 1,257,339.08 gives:

$$1,257,339.08 = i_k \times 21,921,594.63 \qquad \therefore i_k = \frac{1,257,339.08}{21,921,594.63} = 5.7356\%$$

    The methodology described so far thus provides a powerful and flexible technique for valuing and pricing swaps of any type and at any stage in their life.

Once the swap is reduced to its component cash flows, discount factors obtained from market rates can be used to value an existing swap, or to price a new one.

Before extending the technique to currency swaps, there is an interesting short-cut available. The techniques explained so far necessitate two steps in valuing the floating leg of a swap:

a) Forward rates must be calculated in order to determine the size of each floating payment.

b) Each floating payment must then be valued using the appropriate discount factor for that date.

This can be quite a lengthy calculation.

Figure 9.9 recaps what the floating leg cash flows look like to the counterparty receiving the floating rate on a five-year vanilla swap with annual payments. Of course, the size of each cash flow is unknown until the setting date is reached, and therefore the total present value is also unknown at the outset.

Suppose that the counterparty were offered an alternative. Rather than receiving the five floating interest receipts on a notional principal of $1m, the counterparty would receive instead the principal itself, $1m up front, but would have to repay the same $1m in five years' time. The cash flows from this alternative are illustrated in Figure 9.10.

Clearly, the nature of these two alternatives is quite different. The stream of cash flows of Figure 9.9 is regular but uncertain. Those of Figure 9.10 are irregular but known. Which should the counterparty prefer if he had a choice? If the counterparty chose the second alternative, he could invest the initial inflow of $1m for successive periods of one year to earn the 12-month LIBOR rate. At the start of each investment period, the interest rate would be set according

FIGURE 9.9
Cash flows from floating leg of swap

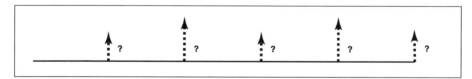

FIGURE 9.10
Replacing floating leg cash flows with exchange of principals

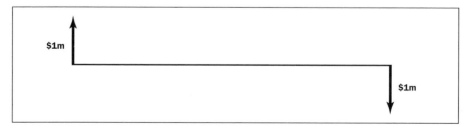

to prevailing market rates and the resulting interest would be received at the end of each period. At the end of the last period, the $1m investment would be returned and would be available to meet the final obligation to repay the $1m. Figure 9.11 summarises the effect of these cash flows.

As should now be apparent from this figure, the two $1m cash flows at the beginning cancel each other out, and so do the two at the end. The net cash flows which are left are exactly the same as those in Figure 9.9. If the investor was to choose the second alternative, and was to invest the principal received at the prevailing LIBOR rates, the end result is to create exactly the same cash flows as those receivable under the first alternative. In other words, despite their apparent differences, the two alternatives are actually equivalent!

This leads to an important finding:

A stream of floating cash flows can be replaced,
***for valuation purposes only*, with an exchange of principals.**

A stream of floating-rate receipts can therefore be replaced, for valuation purposes, with:

- an *inflow* of the notional principal at the start of the first accrual period
- an *outflow* of the notional principal at the end of the final accrual period.

This substitution is much easier to value, as there are only two cash flows and no need to calculate the complete set of forward rates. If the stream of floating-rate receipts starts accruing immediately, the valuation becomes easier still because the present value of a sum paid immediately is the sum itself.

As an example, refer back to Table 9.6 which valued the vanilla five-year swap. The present value of the floating leg was found to be $1,943,200.30 after summing the present values of each of the floating receipts. This result could have been obtained in a single step just by knowing the five-year discount factor, which is 0.8056799699.

$$PV_{float} = 10,000,000 \times 1 - 10,000,000 \times 0.8056799699 = 1,943,200.30$$

FIGURE 9.11
Investing the principals

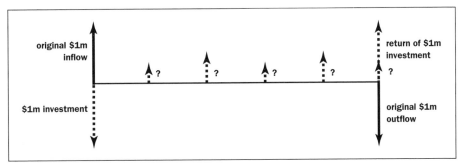

Replacing a stream of floating receipts with an exchange of principals is therefore a useful time-saving technique. However, it is important to emphasise that this replacement is purely a device for calculation and valuation purposes; there is never an actual exchange of principals under an interest-rate swap.

9.7 Valuation and pricing of currency swaps

The principles of valuing and pricing interest-rate swaps can also be applied to cross-currency swaps. Although the foreign exchange element intrinsic to cross-currency swaps may at first sight appear to complicate matters, and the exchange of principals likewise, these design features actually combine to eliminate currency risk and to simplify the resulting structure.

Consider first a vanilla interest-rate swap in one currency, as pictured in Figure 9.12. The swap rate i_1 is such that the swap is fairly priced and thus has a net present value of zero. Now replace the stream of floating-rate receipts with an actual exchange of principals, as explained at the end of the previous section. The resulting cash flows are depicted in Figure 9.13.

Finally, couple this structure with an equal and opposite structure in a second currency, to produce the streams of cash flows depicted in Figure 9.14. The sizes of the two swaps are made equivalent by ensuring that the principals are in

FIGURE 9.12
Vanilla interest-rate swap in one currency

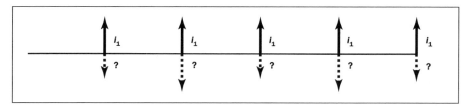

FIGURE 9.13
Interest-rate swap with floating leg replaced by exchange of principals

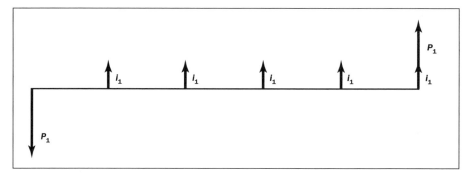

FIGURE 9.14

Fixed-fixed cross-currency swap

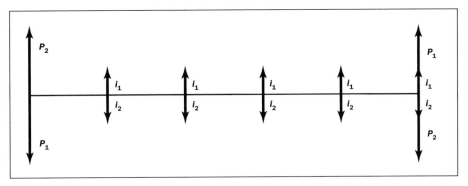

the same ratio as the prevailing spot exchange rate. The swap rate in the second currency i_2 is also the fair market rate for swaps of that maturity, so that the entire structure still has a zero net present value. The result is identical to the fixed-fixed cross-currency swap illustrated in the previous chapter in Figure 8.7. We have therefore built a vanilla cross-currency swap priced fairly with zero net present value measured in either currency. It follows that the two swap rates in a fixed-fixed cross-currency swap should be the same as those for interest-rate swaps in the respective currencies.

For example, suppose that five-year US interest-rate swap rates were 4% for the fixed-rate payer, and five-year euro interest-rate swaps were priced at 5% for the fixed-rate receiver. A €/$ cross-currency swap would be fairly priced if the counterparty paid dollars fixed at 4% against receiving euros fixed at 5%. If there were no initial exchange of principals, the swap would still have a zero net present value. Consider the stream of interest payments and final principal pictured in Figure 9.13, but without the initial outflow of principal. Remembering that the swap rate is the same as the coupon rate on a par bond, and that the par bond by definition is priced at par, the present value of the stream of payments is simply P_1. Similarly, the entire stream of outflows in the second currency shown in Figure 9.14, once again omitting the initial inflow of principal, is $-P_2$. If the exchange rate between the currencies is S, such that one unit of the first currency is equivalent to S units of the second, then $P_2/P_1 = S$ so that the ratio of principals is the same as the prevailing exchange rate. The net present value of the swap in terms of the first currency is then $P_1-(P_2/S) = 0$.

Remember that while the initial exchange of principal is optional, the final exchange is mandatory for a standard currency swap.

A floating-floating cross-currency swap – known as a basis swap – can be constructed in the same way. Figure 9.15 shows one leg of such a swap, including both the initial and final exchange of principals.

To value this structure, we can once again use the ploy of replacing the stream of floating payments with an exchange of principals to produce the structure illustrated in Figure 9.16.

FIGURE 9.15

One leg of a floating-floating cross-currency swap

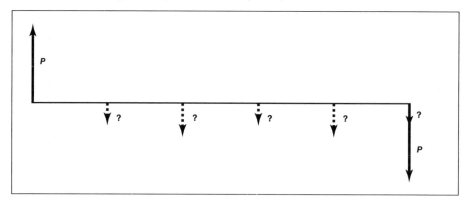

It is obvious from Figure 9.16 that the present value of this structure is zero because the principals at inception and maturity both cancel out, leaving nothing. Each leg of a floating-floating cross-currency swap has zero value initially and, in theory, both legs should therefore be quoted as LIBOR flat.[6] In practice, banks dealing in cross-currency swaps must quote a two-way price with a spread between bid and offer rates, and Table 9.9 provides an illustration of market quotes on 11th January 2010 for cross-currency basis swaps against three-month dollar LIBOR. In every case, the convention is to quote the bid/offer margins for the non-dollar currency against dollar LIBOR flat. As an example, the bank quoting the five-year basis swap in $/¥ is willing to receive Japanese yen LIBOR minus 28bp against paying dollar LIBOR flat, and is also willing to pay Japanese yen LIBOR minus 38bp against receiving dollar LIBOR flat.

In this illustration, most quotations are for LIBOR minus a margin on the non-dollar currency. These biases are due to a number of factors, including credit risk, supply and demand, and also to views or preferences held by banks from time to time. In particular, the negative basis on $/¥ has been a persistent phenomenon for a number of years, and arises because of the perceived credit risk of Japanese banks compared with US banks. If there were no negative basis, a

FIGURE 9.16

Floating payments replaced by exchange of principals

TABLE 9.9

Cross-currency swap quotes on 11th January 2010

Maturity	EUR receive/pay	GBP receive/pay	JPY receive/pay
1 yr	−20.50/−30.50	−6.25/−16.25	−17.25/−26.75
2 yr	−18.50/−23.50	−10.00/−15.00	−20.75/−31.25
3 yr	−16.00/−21.00	−11.00/−16.00	−24.25/−34.25
4 yr	−14.75/−19.75	−11.75/−16.75	−26.50/−36.50
5 yr	−13.75/−18.75	−12.75/−17.75	−28.00/−38.00
7 yr	−12.25/−17.25	−14.75/−19.75	−28.50/−38.50
10 yr	−10.25/−15.25	−16.75/−21.75	−27.50/−37.50
15 yr	−4.75/−9.75	−17.75/−22.75	−24.50/−34.50
20 yr	+0.25/−4.75	−14.75/−19.75	−22.25/−32.75
30 yr	+4.75/−0.25	−7.25/−12.25	−17.50/−27.50

Source: ICAP.

Japanese bank borrowing at yen LIBOR (by definition) could swap the funds into dollar LIBOR and achieve dollar funding at dollar LIBOR flat. In practice, Japanese banks borrowing dollars pay a premium above dollar LIBOR, e.g. dollar LIBOR plus 20bp. This premium would translate to basis swaps either as dollar LIBOR plus 20bp against JPY LIBOR flat or, more conventionally, as dollar LIBOR flat against JPY LIBOR minus 20bp.

The last permutation, a fixed-floating cross-currency swap, presents no new challenges. From the foregoing discussion, we would expect the fixed rate to be identical to the rate for interest-rate swaps of the same maturity, while the floating rate should be quoted the same as the floating leg on a basis swap in that currency. For example, suppose sterling interest-rate swaps were quoted as 3.48–3.43% against sterling LIBOR flat, and floating-floating dollar-sterling swaps were quoted as −13/−18 against dollar LIBOR flat. The bank quoting these rates would then be willing to pay sterling fixed at 3.25% against receiving dollar LIBOR flat, or would expect to receive sterling LIBOR fixed at 3.35% against paying dollar LIBOR flat.

For non-standard cross-currency swaps, pricing and valuation use the same methods that were applied to interest-rate swaps.

To price a non-standard swap, the cash flows in each currency are valued using the set of discount factors derived from market rates in that currency. This gives two net present values, one in each currency. The surplus or deficit in one currency is then transferred into the other currency at the prevailing spot rate. Finally, the swap rate in the latter currency is adjusted to arrive at a zero net present value overall.

Valuing cross-currency swaps follows the same steps, but stops when the balance in one currency is converted to the other; the net present value in the latter currency is the valuation of the swap.

9.8 Cancelling a swap

Although a swap normally commits the two parties to exchange cash flows throughout the life of the swap, a bank counterparty will usually agree to a request by the other counterparty to cancel or terminate the swap earlier. When this happens, however, there will normally be a payment from one party to the other to reflect any non-zero NPV the swap may have at the time.

As an example, let's take the five-year swap we valued in Table 9.6. Paying fixed at 4.285% when the five-year swap rate was also 4.285% gave an NPV at inception of zero, as expected. However, it is quite normal for the NPV to become non-zero thereafter, for two reasons. First, market rates may have moved, as we saw when we revalued this swap in Table 9.7 after five-year swap rates had risen to 4.295%. There we saw that the swap had an NPV of $4,534.67, and this would be the fair cancellation fee payable by the fixed receiver.

Less obvious is the effect of aging. Let's suppose the parties agree to cancel the swap exactly one year after inception, and that market rates have moved exactly as anticipated by the initial set of implied forward rates. This means that six-month LIBOR has now risen from 1.500% to 3.371%, and the four-year swap rate has risen from 3.95% to 4.92%. Under these circumstances, the fixed payer would expect to receive almost $230,000 as a cancellation payment. The reason? The fixed payer is committed to pay only 4.285% for the remaining four years, when four-year swap rates are now 4.92%, 63.5bp higher. Ignoring time-value-of-money considerations for a moment, 63.5bp per year on $10m for four years is worth $254,000. When the prevailing discount factors are applied, the exact PV turns out to be $229,931.70. Looked at another way, after one year the fixed payer has already made net out-payments totalling $228,186.72, equivalent to $229,931.70 when future-valued to the end of the first year. Given that the swap had zero NPV at inception, the fixed payer was therefore anticipating receiving the same amount in net in-payments over the remaining four years, again when valued to the end of the first year, these in-flows arising from the anticipated rise in floating rates well above the 4.285% fixed rate. To compensate the fixed payer for forgoing these positive cash flows, the floating payer should pay a cancellation fee of $229,931.70.

To illustrate this example, Table 9.10 shows the net cash flows from the five-year swap illustrated earlier in Table 9.6, confirms that their initial NPV was zero at the outset, but also shows that re-basing the valuation to the end of year one gives a net outflow of $229,931.70 to date, followed by an expected inflow of the same amount over the remaining four years.

Table 9.11 then re-values the swap at the end of the first year, assuming that interest rates have moved to reflect the initial set of implied forward rates. From Table 9.6 we note that the 1.0–1.5-year forward rate was 3.371%, and we can see that this is now the current six-month rate in Table 9.11; likewise for all the other forward rates. The table shows that the NPV of the swap at this stage is $229,931.70, which would be the cancellation fee payable by the fixed receiver if the swap was terminated at that point.

TABLE 9.10

Valuation of vanilla $10m five-year swap at the one-year stage

Years	Net cash flow	PV of net cash flow	FV of net cash flow after one year	Total FV of net cash flows after one year
0.5	–139,250.00	–138,213.40	–140,994.99	–229,931.70
1.0	–88,936.72	–87,182.15	–88,936.72	
1.5	–45,704.84	–44,060.54	–44,947.28	
2.0	–9,573.90	–9,044.35	–9,226.37	
2.5	19,333.65	17.847.38	18,206.57	
3.0	40,813.02	36,738.47	37,477.85	+229,931.70
3.5	52,707.32	46,211.66	47,141.68	
4.0	62,321.93	53,170.80	54,240.88	
4.5	72,931.35	60,485.35	61,702.63	
5.0	79,494.06	64,046.77	65,335.73	
TOTAL		0.00	0.00	0.00

9.9 Hedging swaps with futures

We know from Chapter 6 that the trading volume for Eurodollar STIR futures regularly exceeds 2 million contracts every day. Earlier in this chapter we saw how STIR futures prices are used as an important source of rate information for swap valuation and pricing. However, merely looking at futures prices doesn't constitute a trade. What does lead to significant futures trading volume is the use that banks make of STIR contracts for hedging the net interest rate exposure arising from their swaps books.

The convenient thing about STIR futures is that each contract covers a relatively short time-span – just three months – and that contracts are listed covering successive quarterly time periods out to ten years. This means that the interest rate exposure arising from even a complex swaps book can be broken down into small three-month maturity buckets, and each bucket precisely hedged with one specific STIR futures contract.

As an example, let's take market rates on 25th March 2011 as shown in Table 9.3, and analyse a five-year pay-fixed swap with semi-annual instalments and a notional of $10m. We can construct a table calculating the change to the swap NPV if market rates change, and Table 9.12 presents the results. The first row measures the sensitivity of the swap to a change in short-term LIBOR rates of 1bp, while the remainder of the table shows the sensitivity of the swap to a 1bp change in each of the STIR futures prices comprising the usual Mar, Jun, Sep, Dec quarterly cycle.

To hedge the pay-fixed swap before the first floating rate is set, the market-maker should buy the 188 contracts specified, perhaps using April 2011

TABLE 9.11

Valuation of vanilla five-year swap after one year

Years	Swap rates	Zero rates	Forward rates	Discount factors	Fixed payments	Floating receipts	PV of fixed payments	PV of floating receipts
0.5	3.371%	3.371%	3.371%	0.983425	214,250.00	168,545.16	210,698.77	165,751.50
1.0	3.729%	3.732%	4.094%	0.963700	214,250.00	204,676.10	206,472.77	197,246.40
1.5	4.036%	4.045%	4.672%	0.941704	214,250.00	233,583.65	201,759.99	219,966.56
2.0	4.293%	4.308%	5.101%	0.918282	214,250.00	255,063.02	196,741.83	234,219.68
2.5	4.492%	4.514%	5.339%	0.894405	214,250.00	266,957.32	191,626.23	238,767.91
3.0	4.654%	4.683%	5.531%	0.870334	214,250.00	276,571.93	186,469.02	240,709.90
3.5	4.798%	4.834%	5.744%	0.846037	214,250.00	287,181.35	181,263.47	242,966.10
4.0	4.920%	4.964%	5.875%	0.821895	214,250.00	293,744.06	176,090.90	241,426.64
TOTAL							1,551,122.98	1,781,054.68

Principal: $10m   Fixed rate: 4.285%   NPV = 229,931.70

contracts to hedge the first stub period. Thereafter, if one of the futures contracts rises in price, then the forward rate for that part of the yield curve will fall. The fixed payer will therefore receive a lower floating payment as a result. On a notional of $10m, a 1bp change in rates over a three-month period is equivalent to $250, but this will become smaller in present value terms the further along the yield curve where the change to the futures price occurs. If the fixed payer has bought the futures contracts at the outset, the 1bp rise in the futures price will generate a profit offsetting the loss on the swap, thereby creating an efficient hedge.

TABLE 9.12
Futures equivalents for $10m five-year swap

Contract	Futures price	Change in NPV for a 1bp rise in futures price	Number of futures contracts to buy
s.t. LIBORs	n/a	–217	9
Jun-11	99.620	–250	10
Sep-11	99.505	–247	10
Dec-11	99.355	–247	10
Mar-12	99.125	–244	10
Jun-12	98.810	–244	10
Sep-12	98.460	–240	10
Dec-12	98.125	–240	10
Mar-13	97.840	–237	9
Jun-13	97.565	–237	9
Sep-13	97.305	–233	9
Dec-13	97.055	–233	9
Mar-14	96.835	–231	9
Jun-14	96.610	–230	9
Sep-14	96.395	–227	9
Dec-14	96.180	–227	9
Mar-15	96.000	–224	9
Jun-15	95.825	–225	9
Sep-15	95.665	–217	9
Dec-15	95.510	–237	9
Mar-16	95.390	–24	1
TOTAL			188

In the preceding analysis, we talked about one of the futures contracts rising in price and the yield curve at that point falling. This isn't a 'chicken and egg' problem, though. It doesn't matter whether the futures price rises followed by the yield curve falling, or whether cause and effect is the other way around. For almost any conceivable change in the yield curve, the change in NPV of the futures hedge should offset the change in NPV of the swap, and the two should cancel out, leaving the swap hedged against changes in market rates.

As time passes, however, the futures hedge will need to be managed. At the outset, the moment the floating rate for the first six-month period is determined, the market-maker should sell the 19 contracts at the top of the table. Early in September, the 10 Sep-11 contracts will need to be rolled before they expire. Then, on 27 September 2011 when the floating rate for the second six-month period is set, the market-maker should sell the rolled September contracts and the 10 Dec-11 contracts, and so on. By the time the last setting date is reached on 25 September 2015, only 19 contracts of the original 188 bought will remain, and these will also be sold once the final floating rate is set. While this hedging strategy using STIR futures is extremely good, it may not be 100% perfect because of the small degree of basis risk[7] arising from the fact that the futures expiry dates do not coincide exactly with the payment dates of the swap. Nonetheless, there is little to beat the flexibility and liquidity of STIR contracts when hedging the net interest rate exposure arising from a swaps book.

9.10 The convexity correction

In many situations in real life, there are second-order effects which create additional complexity within the financial market. The technique of using STIR contracts to hedge a swaps book is one such area where these second-order effects arise.

Let's take the situation where a market-maker who is the fixed payer of a swap then buys STIR contracts to hedge, as illustrated in the previous section. Some time later, interest rates fall and STIR futures prices rise. The loss on the swap is offset by the profit on the futures. Later still, interest rates rise and STIR futures fall, and the profit on the swap is offset by the losses on the futures. This is the first-order effect of the hedging strategy, and is exactly what we want. So far so good, and everything seems fine.

However, we know from section 5.6 that profits and losses arising from futures positions are realised in cash, by credits and debits to the margin account. As such, these futures profits or losses earn or incur interest. However, an uncollateralised swaps position that is simply marked-to-market incurs paper losses or profits, without explicit interest.

In the scenario just described, the fixed payer earns cash profits on the futures position when interest rates fall, but suffers cash losses on the futures hedge when interest rates rise. This means that the fixed payer can invest the futures profits but only when interest rates are low, and must borrow money to fund the futures losses when interest rates are high. This is an undesirable by-product for the fixed payer who buys STIR futures to hedge (a 'long hedger') because it directly leads to an invest-low/borrow-high outcome.

Figure 9.17 charts the net losses for the long-hedger of a $10m five-year swap, and it is clear that the financial outcome features negative convexity. Whether rates rise or fall, the fixed payer loses out, and the more volatile the interest rate

FIGURE 9.17

Net losses arising from pay-fixed $10m five-year swap hedged with STIR futures

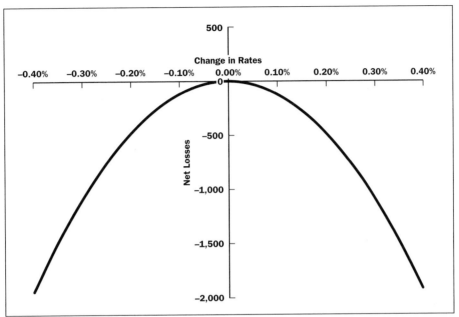

scenario, the greater will be these second-order losses. To restore the balance, the swap market usually applies a *convexity correction* by reducing the fixed rate on a swap a little below the fair rates implied by calculating discount factors from futures prices alone. It can be shown that a suitable correction can be achieved by adjusting each futures price upwards by $0.5\sigma^2t^2$, where σ is the annualised volatility[8] of each forward rate and t is the time to expiry of each contract.

With volatility of 20%, for example, the convexity correction using the futures data from Table 9.12 would be around 4bp. Interestingly, swap rates on 25th March 2011 were 2.34%–2.37%, which is why Table 9.3 uses the mid-rate of 2.355%. However, if one calculates the theoretical swap rate from futures prices alone, you get 2.38%. The market's bid rate of 2.34% for the swap is therefore exactly 4bp lower than the 2.38% calculated direct from the futures price, consistent with a convexity correction of 4bp.

9.11 Credit risk of swaps

At inception, swaps are usually priced so as to create a zero NPV when summing the values of the payment and receipt legs. As we saw in section 9.8, however, it is most unlikely that a swap will remain with an NPV of zero and we explored two factors – aging and the movement of market rates – that together conspire to create non-zero swap NPVs as time moves on.

At any moment during the life of a swap, one party will value the swap with a positive NPV while the other party will value the swap with an equal and opposite negative NPV. Let's refer to these parties as the credit and debit counterparties respectively. Table 9.10 illustrated that one good way of looking at the NPV during the life of a swap was to sum the present values of the remaining expected net cash flows. In that specific example, at the end of the first year the fixed payer expected to receive cash inflows equivalent to $229,931.70 in present value terms, and in the context of that section this was the cancellation fee payable by the fixed receiver at that time.

If the debit counterparty were to default at some time in the future, the credit party would no longer receive the net inflows they were expecting, and this would represent a loss to the credit party. We can therefore say that the NPV of a swap at any time represents the current credit exposure of a swap. One problem associated with assessing swap credit exposure is that it is dynamic and changes over time as the swap ages. Figure 9.18 illustrates the dynamic nature of swap credit exposure by charting the evolution of NPVs over the entire five-year lifetime of this $10m swap. We can see how exposure rises to $229,931.70 after one year, to achieve a peak of $294,806.77 by the end of the second year, before gradually reducing to zero after the last payment is made and the swap terminates.

This is only half the story, though. To arrive at the values for Figure 9.18, we assumed that the six-month rate each period faithfully followed the set of implied forward rates tabulated in Table 9.6, starting at 1.50% at time 0 and eventually rising to 5.875% after 4.5 years. In practice, interest rates are almost never that well behaved and, as economic circumstances evolve, rates will usually follow a different path. For example, on 9th July 2008, the March 2011 Eurodollar future implied a forward rate of 4.455% for the three-month period starting 16th March 2011. On 14th March 2011 (the fixing date for that period)

FIGURE 9.18

Credit exposure for a $10m five-year swap – fixed scenario

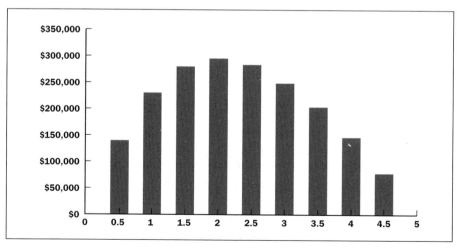

three-month USD LIBOR was only 0.309%, more than 4% lower! A small thing commonly referred to as 'the credit crisis' had intervened.

To arrive at a better estimate of swap credit risk, we need to take into account the myriad possible ways in which interest rates may evolve over time. One technique is to use Monte Carlo simulation to generate a large number of interest rate scenarios, with each scenario generating values for the complete yield curve as it evolves over time. Figure 9.19 illustrates ten sequences for just the six-month rate, always starting at 1.5% (as in Table 9.6) but rising to between 5% and 7% after five years. Remember, however, that the Monte Carlo simulation actually generates the entire yield curve – not just the six-month rate – at six-month intervals over the five-year period shown.

For each rate scenario, we can use the swap valuation techniques illustrated in section 9.8 to value the swap at every six-month point over the five-year lifetime of the swap. Now, instead of a single value for the credit exposure at each six-month interval, we will obtain a distribution of values from which we can derive some useful statistics, and these are summarised graphically in Figure 9.20. The line in the centre of the charts tracks the path of the average exposure over time for the 50,000 rate scenarios generated by the Monte Carlo simulation model used. We see that this starts off at zero, rises to a peak of around $280,000 at the end of the second year, then steadily declines to zero again. These values are very similar to those in Figure 9.18, which showed the credit exposure for the specific rate scenario where six-month rates tracked the original implied forward curve. The medium-shaded area either side of the average exposure line is the ±1σ region, which captures around 68% of the total outcomes. Below this, the bottom edge of the lightly shaded region marks the 1%

FIGURE 9.19
Simulated interest rate paths

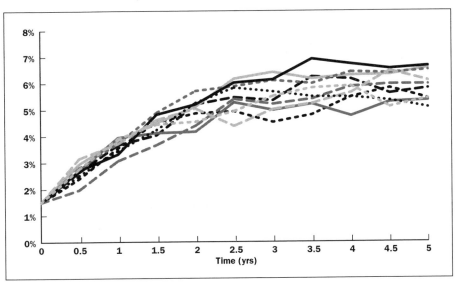

FIGURE 9.20

Credit risk of $10m five-year interest rate swap

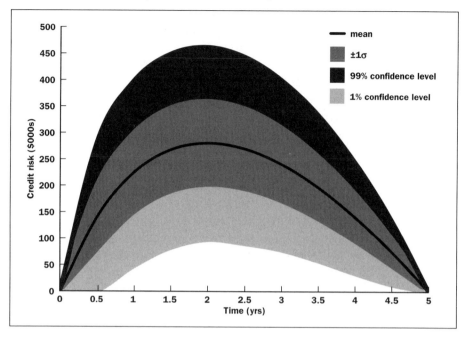

percentile, while the top edge of the darkest region marks the 99% confidence level, so we can be 99% sure that the largest credit exposure at the two-year point will be $462,000 or lower.[9]

A bank executing this swap would therefore need to handle the dynamic credit risk arising from executing this swap. One method is to allocate the credit exposure against the overall credit limit granted to a counterparty, including the swap credit exposure along with actual loans and all the other credit facilities that the bank provides. Security is then provided by the counterparty against the aggregate of all credit risks, regardless of their origin. Another method is for a counterparty's aggregate swap exposure to be collateralised separately from other credit risks. As OTC derivatives trading moves towards clearing through central counterparties, this second approach is likely to become increasingly dominant. Interestingly enough, whether or not a swap is collateralised can lead to another second-order effect on swap pricing, which we will examine shortly.

The inverted U-shape of this chart is typical for the credit exposure of an interest-rate swap. However, the credit risk arising from a currency swap is very different, rising inexorably over time because of one important factor that distinguishes a currency swap from an interest-rate swap – the final exchange of principals but at an exchange rate fixed at the outset. The present value of this exchange depends upon prevailing FX rates, and FX rates have the propensity to drift further and further over time, thereby fuelling the ever-increasing credit exposure as time goes by. Figure 9.21 illustrates the credit exposure arising

FIGURE 9.21

Credit risk of $10m five-year currency swap

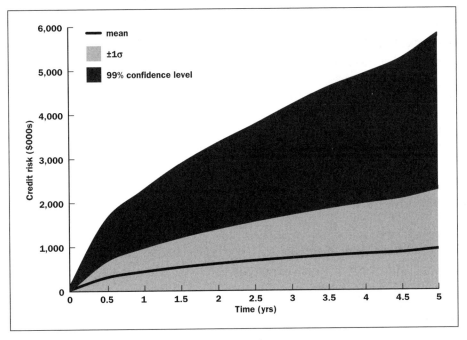

from a five-year €/$ fixed/fixed currency swap with a notional principal of $10m. Potential credit risk is greatest at maturity, with an average of $912,000 and a 99% confidence level of $5.8m, these figures being 3× and 12× the respective exposures for the interest-rate swap illustrated in Figure 9.20.

9.12 Collateralised vs. non-collateralised swaps

We saw in the previous section that one way in which counterparties mitigate the credit risk arising from interest-rate swaps is through the posting of collateral by the debit party to the credit party. This process is governed by a Credit Support Annex (CSA), part of the ISDA documentation summarised in section 8.15 in the previous chapter.

In essence, when a swap is collateralised it is regularly marked-to-market and any gain or loss is mirrored by a transfer of collateral. For example, suppose we are one year into the five-year swap discussed in section 9.8. As Table 9.10 shows, the fixed payer has made two net payments totalling $228,186.72 and the swap now has a mark-to-market NPV of $229,931.70 when cash flows are valued using the set of discount factors shown in Table 9.6. If the swap was collateralised, the fixed receiver would by now have deposited at least $229,931.70, thereby eliminating the credit risk. Figure 9.22 shows all the cash flows over the first year, comprising the net swap payment after six months offset by the initial deposit of $139,250 of collateral, and the cumulative cash flows at the one-year stage. It also demonstrates that the $1,744.99 difference between $228,186.72 and $229,931.70 represents six months' interest at 2.506% (the forward rate implied by the swap curve for the period between six months and one year) on the original $139,250 of collateral posted at the six-month stage.

So far all seems fine and everything seems to balance. There is an issue, however. The calculations here assume that the holder of collateral pays LIBOR when, in fact, the CSA dictates that the holder of collateral pays the *collateral rate* which is defined to be the overnight interest rate in that currency. Prior to the 2007–2008 credit crisis this difference was unimportant. Receiving the overnight rate every day over, say, a three-month period is equivalent to receiving the fixed rate on a three-month OIS and (as we saw in Chapter 8, section 8.5) there used to be little difference between LIBOR rates and OIS rates of the corresponding maturity. So assuming that the holder of collateral receives LIBOR when in fact he receives the compounded overnight rate was reasonable. However, since mid-2007 there has been a significant rift between these two rates and the assumption no longer holds. The solution for collateralised trades is to discount cash flows using OIS rates, and we will examine the necessary changes in the next section.

For swaps which are not collateralised, the net payments shown in Figure 9.22 are not counterbalanced by collateral flows. Outflows will need to be funded, while inflows can be invested. If these interim cash flows can indeed be borrowed or invested at LIBOR, there will be no impact on the valuation and hence fair pricing of the swap. Table 9.13a illustrates the net cash flows from a $10m five-year swap paying fixed at 4.285%. Given the rising yield curve,

FIGURE 9.22

Cash flows in a collateralised swap during first year

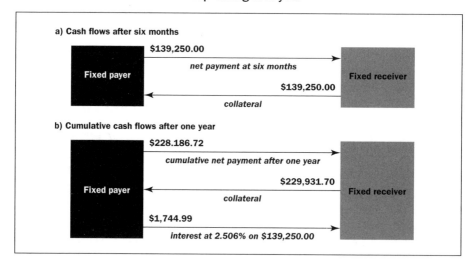

the fixed rate will be higher than the floating rate initially, and net cash flows in early periods will be negative for the fixed payer. If these net outflows can be financed at LIBOR flat, then the net cash flow plus interest accumulates to zero, as the first set of 'cumulative cash flow' figures in the table shows. This is just another way to verify the fair pricing of the swap analysed earlier in Tables 9.6 and 9.10. However, if the fixed payer cannot fund at LIBOR flat, perhaps because of credit or market conditions, and must pay a margin above LIBOR, the swap will no longer be correctly priced at a fixed rate of 4.285%. The final columns of Table 9.13a reveal that the fixed payer would accumulate a deficit of almost $11,000 by the end of the five-year period. Under these circumstances, the fixed payer is paying too much.

The solution in this case is straightforward – the swap needs to be executed with a lower fixed rate. Table 9.13b demonstrates that if the fixed rate is lowered by just 2bp from 4.285% to 4.266%, the cash flows from the swap once again accumulate to zero.

9.13 LIBOR–OIS discounting

Now let's return to the problem of collateralised trades where collateral earns the overnight rate rather than LIBOR. This problem has arisen as a consequence of a number of developments in the market.

- Since the CSA was introduced by ISDA in 1994 (see section 8.15) an increasing number of market participants make use of collateral arrangements. The *ISDA Margin Survey 2012* reports that 78% of interest rate derivative contracts were covered by collateral arrangements.

- LIBOR and OIS rates have diverged since mid-2007, as documented in section 8.5.

- As a result of this divergence, there has been a breakdown in some of the assumptions that are used to form the basis of swap pricing and valuation.

- The collapse of Lehman Brothers in September 2008 revealed discrepancies between the techniques used for the valuation of swaps by different counterparties, including clearing houses. Many counterparties were still using a single curve approach, while others had started to utilise the dual curve method introduced below.

As a result of these events, LCH.Clearnet decided in June 2010 to value collateral requirements using OIS discounting,[10] and rival clearing houses CME Clearing and International Derivatives Clearing Group both followed suit a year later.[11] An increasing number of market participants are now doing the same, and this has become easier as liquidity in the OIS market increases. Maturities for OIS used to be limited to one or two years; now quotations are available out to 10 and 30 years.

TABLE 9.13a
Non-collateralised swaps at 4.285%

Years	Swap rates	Forward rates	Discount factors	Fixed payments	Floating receipts	Net cash flow	Fixed payer funds at LIBOR		Fixed payer funds at LIBOR+1%	
							Interest	Cumulative cash flow	Interest	Cumulative cash flow
0.5	1.500%	1.500%	0.992556	214,250.00	75,000.00	-139,250.00		-139,250.00		-139,250.00
1.0	2.000%	2.506%	0.980272	214,250.00	125,313.28	-88,936.72	-1,744.99	-229,931.70	-2,441.24	-230,627.95
1.5	2.450%	3.371%	0.964024	214,250.00	168,545.16	-45,704.84	-3,875.39	-279,511.93	-5,040.26	-281,373.06
2.0	2.850%	4.094%	0.944688	214,250.00	204,676.10	-9,573.90	-5,720.94	-294,806.77	-7,165.90	-298,112.85
2.5	3.200%	4.672%	0.923125	214,250.00	233,583.65	19,333.65	-6,886.20	-282,359.32	-8,453.99	-287,233.19
3.0	3.500%	5.101%	0.900165	214,250.00	255,063.02	40,813.02	-7,201.94	-248,748.24	-8,762.42	-255,182.59
3.5	3.745%	5.339%	0.876760	214,250.00	266,957.32	52,707.32	-6,640.52	-202,681.44	-8,088.20	-210,563.47
4.0	3.950%	5.531%	0.853164	214,250.00	276,571.93	62,321.93	-5,605.60	-145,965.11	-6,876.41	-155,117.95
4.5	4.130%	5.744%	0.829346	214,250.00	287,181.35	72,931.35	-4,191.85	-77,225.61	-5,230.29	-87,416.89
5.0	4.285%	5.875%	0.805680	214,250.00	293,744.06	79,494.06	-2,268.46	0.00	-3,004.90	-10,927.74

Fixed rate: 4.285%

Principal: $10m

TABLE 9.13b

Non-collateralised swap at 4.266%

Years	Swap rates	Forward rates	Discount factors	Fixed payments	Floating receipts	Net cash flow	Interest	Cumulative cash flow
								Fixed payer funds at LIBOR+1%
0.5	1.500%	1.500%	0.992556	213,301.27	75,000.00	-138,301.27		-138,301.27
1.0	2.000%	2.506%	0.980272	213,301.27	125,313.28	-87,987.98	-2,424.60	-228,713.86
1.5	2.450%	3.371%	0.964024	213,301.27	168,545.16	-44,756.11	-4,998.43	-278,468.39
2.0	2.850%	4.094%	0.944688	213,301.27	204,676.10	-8,625.16	-7,091.92	-294,185.48
2.5	3.200%	4.672%	0.923125	213,301.27	233,583.65	20,282.38	-8,342.62	-282,245.72
3.0	3.500%	5.101%	0.900165	213,301.27	255,063.02	41,761.76	-8,610.27	-249,094.23
3.5	3.745%	5.339%	0.876760	213,301.27	266,957.32	53,656.05	-7,895.22	-203,333.41
4.0	3.950%	5.531%	0.853164	213,301.27	276,571.93	63,270.66	-6,640.30	-146,703.04
4.5	4.130%	5.744%	0.829346	213,301.27	287,181.35	73,880.08	-4,946.55	-77,769.51
5.0	4.285%	5.875%	0.805680	213,301.27	293,744.06	80,442.79	-2,673.28	0.00

Principal: $10m   Fixed rate: 4.266%

Hitherto, swap rates were used both to generate forward cash flows so that the floating leg of a swap could be valued, and also to generate the discount factors used to present-value those cash flows. This is the *single-curve* approach. Under LIBOR–OIS discounting (hereafter just *OIS discounting*), swap rates are still used to generate the forward cash flows, but OIS rates are then used to discount those cash flows. This is the *dual-curve* approach.

The move to OIS discounting affects swap counterparties in several ways. First, the amount of collateral differs when compared with traditional valuation techniques. This mostly affects counterparties like institutional investors who tend to execute swaps in one direction rather than banks which execute swaps in both directions. As we will see shortly, in a rising yield-curve environment fixed-rate receivers benefit because they need to post less collateral than before. Second, mark-to-market values differ when using OIS discounting, and this has important significance when swaps are being terminated, and also for off-market swaps (like asset swaps). Third, the LIBOR–OIS spread is now a source of market risk – as this spread changes, so do the collateral requirements and mark-to-market value of all swaps priced using OIS discounting.

To implement OIS discounting, it is necessary to use two interest curves to generate the set of discount factors and the set of forward rates necessary to value and price an interest rate swap. You will recall that earlier in this chapter we used equation 9.7 to bootstrap a set of discount factors from swap rates, and Table 9.6 provided one of several illustrations of this technique. As the first step in OIS discounting, we bootstrap a set of discount factors, but this time using OIS rates rather than LIBOR swap rates. Table 9.14 provides an example and, for simplicity, assumes a constant 1% LIBOR–OIS spread throughout the maturity spectrum.[12] As the table shows, the discount factors under OIS discounting are slightly higher than those calculated from LIBOR swaps because OIS rates are lower.

TABLE 9.14

Generating the discount function and forward rates

Years	LIBOR swaps	OIS rates	Discount factors from: LIBOR swaps	OIS rates	Forwards calculated from: LIBOR swaps and LIBOR DFs	LIBOR swaps and OIS DFs	OIS swaps and OIS DFs
0.5	1.500%	0.500%	0.992556	0.997506	1.500%	1.500%	0.500%
1.0	2.000%	1.000%	0.980272	0.990062	2.506%	2.504%	1.504%
1.5	2.450%	1.450%	0.964024	0.978496	3.371%	3.364%	2.364%
2.0	2.850%	1.850%	0.944688	0.963650	4.094%	4.081%	3.081%
2.5	3.200%	2.200%	0.923125	0.946363	4.672%	4.653%	3.653%
3.0	3.500%	2.500%	0.900165	0.927456	5.101%	5.077%	4.077%
3.5	3.745%	2.745%	0.876760	0.907886	5.339%	5.311%	4.311%
4.0	3.950%	2.950%	0.853164	0.887910	5.531%	5.500%	4.500%
4.5	4.130%	3.130%	0.829346	0.867494	5.744%	5.707%	4.707%
5.0	4.285%	3.285%	0.805680	0.847020	5.875%	5.834%	4.834%

Next we generate *two* new sets of forward rates, both using the new OIS discount factors we have just calculated, but one based on *LIBOR* swap rates and the other on OIS rates. As the first set is based on a mixture of LIBOR and OIS rates we will call these the *LIBOIS* forwards, while we will refer to the second set based exclusively on OIS rates as the *OISOIS* forwards. We will use the *LIBOIS* forwards to generate the forward cash flows of the swap we are analysing, and we will eventually use the *OISOIS* forwards to calculate interest payments on the collateral posted. By rearranging equation 9.15 we get equation 9.19.

$$i_k \cdot \sum_{j=1}^{k} \frac{v_j}{F} = \sum_{j=1}^{k} \frac{f_{j-1,j} v_j}{F} \tag{9.19}$$

Then, by rearranging 9.19, and replacing the LIBOR-implied forward rates $f_{j-1,j}$ with the OIS-implied forward rates $f_{j-1,j}^{LIBOIS}$ and likewise the LIBOR-generated discount factors v_j with the OIS-generated discount factors v_j^{OIS}, we obtain equation 9.20 for calculating the first set of forward rates from the LIBOR swap rates i_k and the OIS-generated discount factors v_j^{OIS}.

$$f_{k-1,k}^{LIBOIS} = \frac{i_k \cdot \sum_{j=1}^{k} \frac{v_j^{OIS}}{F} - \sum_{j=1}^{k-1} \frac{f_{j-1,j}^{LIBOIS} v_j^{OIS}}{F}}{v_k^{OIS}} \cdot F \tag{9.20}$$

If we now replace i_k with i_k^{OIS} we get equation 9.21 for generating the second set of forward rates exclusively from the OIS rates.

$$f_{k-1,k}^{OISOIS} = \frac{i_k^{OIS} \cdot \sum_{j=1}^{k} \frac{v_j^{OIS}}{F} - \sum_{j=1}^{k-1} \frac{f_{j-1,j}^{OISOIS} v_j^{OIS}}{F}}{v_k^{OIS}} \cdot F \tag{9.21}$$

Note that both of these are bootstrap equations, like equation 9.7 introduced earlier in the chapter. Earlier values of the respective forward rates are used to calculate the later values. As a reminder, the superscript *LIBOIS* describes forward rates calculated using a combination of LIBOR swap rates and OIS discount factors, while the superscript *OISOIS* designates the forward rates calculated from OIS rates and OIS discount factors.

The final two columns of Table 9.14 show these two sets of forward rates, and the previous column compares these with the usual set of forward rates generated from the traditional set of LIBOR swap rates and previously shown in Table 9.6. You will see that the *LIBOIS* forward rates are very similar to the LIBOR-implied forward rates, but just a little lower. This is because the weighted average of the forward rates must always equal the swap rate. Rearranging equations 9.19 and 9.20 gives equation 9.22, which confirms this statement.

$$i_k = \frac{\sum_{j=1}^{k} \frac{f_{j-1,j} v_j}{F}}{\sum_{j=1}^{k} \frac{v_j}{F}} = \frac{\sum_{j=1}^{k} \frac{f_{j-1,j}^{LIBOIS} v_j^{OIS}}{F}}{\sum_{j=1}^{k} \frac{v_j^{OIS}}{F}} \tag{9.22}$$

Therefore, if the OIS discount factors are slightly higher than the LIBOR discount factors, the *LIBOIS* forward rates must be slightly lower than the LIBOR-implied forward rates for the equality to hold.[13] By contrast, the *OISOIS* forward rates are exactly 1% lower than the *LIBOIS* rates because of the 1% spread between LIBOR and OIS rates assumed throughout this example.

Once we have the sets of OIS discount factors and OIS-implied forward rates *LIBOIS*, we can then value a swap. Table 9.15 starts by valuing our vanilla five-year swap using the traditional method in exactly the same way as we did in Table 9.6, arriving at the same NPV for fixed and floating legs of $1,943,200, and a zero NPV for the swap as a whole. To value the swap using OIS discounting we must first use the OIS-implied forward rates *LIBOIS* to determine the floating cash flows and then use the OIS-implied discount factors for all present-valuing. The last three columns of Table 9.15 do this, and arrive at an NPV for each leg of $1,995,491, and a zero NPV overall, as you would expect for a par swap at inception. The individual NPVs under OIS valuation are a little higher than those obtained from the traditional technique, once again because the OIS discount factors are a little higher.

TABLE 9.15

Valuing a $10m pay-fixed five-year par swap at inception

Years	Fixed payments	Floating receipts	Forwards from LIBOR swaps and LIBOR DFs; PVs from LIBOR			Forwards from LIBOR swaps and OIS DFs; PVs from OIS		
			PV of fixed payments	PV of floating receipts	Floating receipts	PV of fixed payments	PV of floating receipts	
0.5	214,250	75,000	212,655	74,442	75,000	213,716	74,813
1.0	214,250	125,313	210,023	122,841	125,188	212,121	123,944
1.5	214,250	168,545	206,542	162,482	168,203	209,643	164,586
2.0	214,250	204,676	202,399	193,355	204,059	206,462	196,641
2.5	214,250	233,584	197,780	215,627	232,668	202,758	220,188
3.0	214,250	255,063	192,860	229,599	253,862	198,707	235,446
3.5	214,250	266,957	187,846	234,057	265,556	194,515	241,095
4.0	214,250	276,572	182,790	235,961	274,976	190,235	244,154
4.5	214,250	287,181	177,687	238,173	285,341	185,861	247,532
5.0	214,250	293,744	172,617	236,664	291,719	181,474	247,092
TOTAL			1,943,200	1,943,200		1,995,491	1,995,491
NPV			0			0	

So far, the impact of OIS discounting has been negligible. However, it is when it comes to calculating collateral and valuing off-market swaps that LIBOR–OIS discounting really makes an impact. We will look at each of these issues in turn.

In the last section we saw that the underlying principle behind collateralisation is that the amount of collateral deposited by a counterparty should equal the mark-to-market loss of an out-of-the-money swap (i.e. one with a negative NPV). Equation 9.23 expresses this algebraically. A positive value for C_k implies collateral received, while a negative value implies collateral posted.

$$C_k = \sum_{j=k+1}^{n} \frac{v_j}{v_k} \cdot CF_j \tag{9.23}$$

where:

C_k is the level of the collateral account at time k
CF_j is the undiscounted swap net cash flow at time j
v_j is the discount factor at time j

As an example, using the data in Table 9.15 for the traditional collateral at the four-year point, we obtain:

$$C_{4y} = \frac{v_{4.5y}}{v_{4y}} \cdot CF_{4.5y} + \frac{v_{5y}}{v_{4y}} \cdot CF_{5y}$$

$$= \frac{0.829346}{0.853164} \cdot (\$287{,}181 - \$214{,}250)$$

$$+ \frac{0.805680}{0.853164} \cdot (\$293{,}744 - \$214{,}250) = \$145{,}965$$

Furthermore, (assuming a 30/360 day count convention for simplicity) the interest paid to the fixed-rate receiver (who posted the collateral) after six months is:

$$\$145{,}965 \times 5.744\% \times 0.5 = \$4{,}192$$

Note that we have used the LIBOR rate in this traditional calculation, as has been the convention in the past. Table 9.16a upholds these figures, as well as the \$229,932 collateral level and \$1,745 interest illustrated earlier in Figure 9.22 at the one-year stage, and extends these examples by showing the complete set of collateral balances, collateral cash flows, swap cash flows and interest paid on collateral balances (at the prevailing LIBOR rate). Importantly, the table confirms that the collateral cash flows every period – principal plus interest – exactly match the swap cash flows, resulting in a zero net cash flow each time.

To determine the level of collateral under OIS discounting, Table 9.16b repeats the exercise, but this time using the *LIBOIS* forward rates to calculate the swap cash flows, and the *OISOIS* forward rates to calculate collateral interest. This time, the level of collateral at the four-year point is:

$$\frac{0.867494}{0.887910} \cdot (\$285{,}341 - \$214{,}250)$$

$$+ \frac{0.847020}{0.887910} \cdot (\$291{,}719 - \$214{,}250) = \$143{,}358$$

Furthermore, the interest paid to the fixed-rate receiver after six months is:

$$\$143{,}358 \times 4.707\% \times 0.5 = \$3{,}374$$

TABLE 9.16a

Calculating collateral using the traditional approach

Years	Collateral	Collateral cash flows	Swap net cash flow	Interest paid on collateral	Net cash flow	PV of swap net cash flow
0.5	139,250	139,250	−139,250	0	0	−138,213
1.0	229,932	90,682	−88,937	−1,745	0	−87,182
1.5	279,512	49,580	−45,705	−3,875	0	−44,061
2.0	294,807	15,295	−9,574	−5,721	0	−9,044
2.5	282,359	−12,447	19,334	−6,886	0	17,847
3.0	248,748	−33,611	40,813	−7,202	0	36,738
3.5	202,681	−46,067	52,707	−6,641	0	46,212
4.0	145,965	−56,716	62,322	−5,606	0	53,171
4.5	77,226	−68,740	72,931	−4,192	0	60,485
5.0		−77,226	79,494	−2,268	0	64,047
TOTAL						0

NB: Forward rates are calculated from LIBOR swaps and LIBOR discount factors, and collateral interest is calculated using LIBOR-implied forwards.

Again we can see that under OIS discounting the net cash flow each period is still zero, which implies that the swap cash flows are exactly balanced by the flows of collateral principal plus interest. However, because (in an upward-sloping yield environment) the OIS-implied forward rates (*LIBOIS*) are a little lower than LIBOR-implied forward rates, the swap cash flows each period are always more negative for the fixed payer, who will pay out more at the outset and receive less back later on. As Table 9.16b confirms, the swap still has an NPV of zero under the OIS discounting method because the smaller positive inflows received later are present-valued using higher OIS discount factors. Nonetheless, the smaller net inflows for the fixed payer later in the life of the swap imply a smaller collateral requirement under OIS discounting, as the last column of Table 9.16b shows. The differences, peaking at a little over $3,000, represent a reduction in collateral of up to 2%. On a $10tn swaps portfolio, the order of magnitude for a major investment bank, this difference equates to more than $1bn in collateral requirements.

Figure 9.23 illustrates the collateral requirements under the two schemes. Note the similarity between this chart and those in Figures 9.18 and 9.20 which pictured the credit risk of an interest-rate swap – the very thing that collateral is designed to obviate.

Finally, let's review the impact of OIS discounting on the valuation of off-market swaps. Suppose that two counterparties have agreed to execute a five-year swap with a fixed rate of 4.285%, like before. Moments later, the five-year swap rate rises by 10bp to 4.385%. This will increase the implied forward rates for the final period and reduce the discount factors for the five-year date. Table 9.17 summarises the impact on the mark-to-market value of the swap under both

TABLE 9.16b

Calculating collateral using the OIS discounting approach

Years	Collateral	Collateral cash flows	Swap net cash flow	Interest paid on collateral	Net cash flow	PV of swap net cash flow	Difference in collateral
0.5	139,250	139,250	−139,250	0	0	−138,903	0
1.0	229,359	90,109	−89,062	−1,047	0	−88,177	−573
1.5	278,117	48,758	−46,047	−2,711	0	−45,057	−1,395
2.0	292,593	14,476	−10,191	−4,285	0	−9,821	−2,214
2.5	279,520	−13,073	18,418	−5,345	0	17,430	−2,840
3.0	245,606	−33,914	39,612	−5,698	0	36,739	−3,142
3.5	199,594	−46,012	51,306	−5,294	0	46,580	−3,088
4.0	143,358	−56,236	60,726	−4,490	0	53,920	−2,607
4.5	75,641	−67,717	71,091	−3,374	0	61,671	−1,585
5.0		−75,641	77,469	−1,828	0	65,618	0
TOTAL						0	

NB: Forwards are calculated from LIBOR swaps and OIS discount factors, and collateral interest is calculated using OIS-implied forwards.

FIGURE 9.23

Collateral for pay-fixed 5yr swap

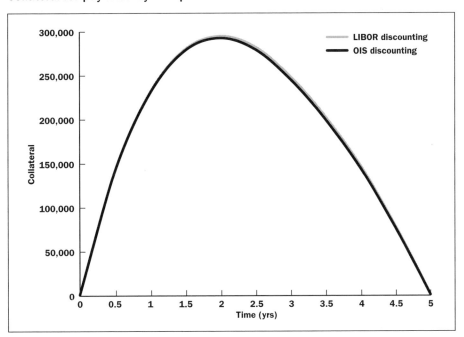

the traditional method and that using OIS discounting. Naturally the swap now has a non-zero NPV under both schemes, but the NPV under OIS discounting is $1,220 higher. This would trigger an immediate collateral payment in favour of the fixed-rate payer, this time larger under OIS discounting. However, detailed calculations reveal that the collateral under the new arrangements would once again reduce to levels slightly below those needed under traditional discounting once the swap entered the second year.

TABLE 9.17

Valuing a pay-fixed off-market swap at inception

Years	Fixed payments	Forwards from LIBOR swaps and LIBOR DFs; PVs from LIBOR			Forwards from LIBOR swaps and OIS DFs; PV from OIS		
		Floating receipts	PV of fixed payments	PV of floating receipts	Floating receipts	PV of fixed payments	PV of floating receipts
0.5	214,250	75,000	212,655	74,442	75,000	213,716	74,813
1.0	214,250	125,313	210,023	122,841	125,188	212,121	123,944
1.5	214,250	168,545	206,542	162,482	168,203	209,643	164,586
2.0	214,250	204,676	202,399	193,355	204,059	206,462	196,641
2.5	214,250	233,584	197,780	215,627	232,668	202,758	220,188
3.0	214,250	255,063	192,860	229,599	253,862	198,707	235,446
3.5	214,250	266,957	187,846	234,057	265,556	194,515	241,095
4.0	214,250	276,572	182,790	235,961	274,976	190,235	244,154
4.5	214,250	287,181	177,687	238,173	285,341	185,861	247,532
5.0	214,250	350,755	171,666	281,040	347,392	180,493	292,657
TOTAL			1,942,250	1,987,576		1,994,510	2,041,056
NPV			45,327			46,546	

Sadly, the changes discussed in this section make the world a more complicated place as a direct consequence of the 2007–2008 credit crisis.

Notes

1 The discount factors are calculated assuming the Actual/Actual day count convention, and annual compounding.
2 Examining equation 4.6 in Chapter 4 shows that the forward rate is proportional to the slope of the yield curve. If the yield curve is interpolated in successive linear segments, any forward rates thus derived will suddenly jump as the slope of the yield curve changes abruptly when moving from one segment to the next. Such jumps are both undesirable and unrealistic.

3   This can be demonstrated by using the Taylor's expansion of equations 9.2, 9.3 and
    the expression e^{-rt}, all of which give similar results.

$$\frac{1}{(1 + zt)} \approx 1 - zt + (zt)^2 - (zt)^3 + (zt)^4 - \ldots$$

$$\approx 1 - \log(1 + zt) + \frac{(\log(1 + zt))^2}{2!} - \frac{(\log(1 + zt))^3}{3!} + \frac{(\log(1 + zt))^4}{4!} - \ldots$$

$$\frac{1}{(1 + z)^t} \approx 1 - t\log(1 + z) + \frac{(t\log(1 + z))^2}{2!} - \frac{(t\log(1 + z))^3}{3!} + \frac{(t\log(1 + z))^4}{4!} - \ldots$$

$$e^{-rt} \approx 1 - rt + \frac{(rt)^2}{2!} - \frac{(rt)^3}{3!} + \frac{(rt)^4}{4!} - \ldots$$

In fact, by substituting $r = [\log(1 + zt)]/t$ into the first expression, and $r = \log(1 + z)$
into the second expression, thereby substituting the continuously compounded rate
r instead of the periodic rate z, all three expressions become identical.

4   To make the terminology a little simpler, the formulae developed in this section
    and in the remainder of this chapter make the implicit assumption that the Actual/
    Actual day count convention is used, and each period is thus of equal length. If any
    of the other day count conventions are used, each occurrence of $1/F$ in the formulae
    must be replaced by a day count fraction of the form d_k/B, where d_k is the assumed
    number of days in period k and B is the assumed number of days in a year (360, 365
    or 366).

5   It is also possible to relate zero-coupon rates and forward rates through another
    kind of average. By transforming the per-period zero-coupon rate z_k and the forward
    rates f_j into their continuously compounded equivalents

$$z'_k = \ln\left(1 + \frac{z_k}{F}\right) \text{ and } f'_j = \ln\left(1 + \frac{f_j}{F}\right), \text{ equation 9.16 becomes a simple}$$

arithmetic average: $z'_k = \frac{1}{t_k}\sum_{j=1}^{k}\frac{f'_j}{F}$. This says that the continuously compounded

per-period zero-coupon rate is the simple average of the continuously compounded
per-period forward rates.

6   A similar conclusion could be reached by building a floating-floating cross-currency
    swap from a fixed-fixed swap and two fixed-floating interest-rate swaps.

7   See section 6.6 of Chapter Six.

8   The concept of volatility is explained in section 11.1 of Chapter 11.

9   In fact, during the 50,000 scenarios simulated here, the single worst credit exposure
    turned out to be around $593,000. This is more than double the peak average
    exposure, and almost 30% larger than the losses experienced at the 99% confidence
    level.

10 'LCH.Clearnet re-values $218 trillion swap portfolio using OIS', *Risk Magazine*
    (online version), 17 June 2010.

11 'CME and IDCG revalue swaps using OIS discounting', *Risk Magazine* (online
    version), 4 October 2011.

12 In practice you would use the full set of OIS quotations for the entire yield curve
    stretching out to ten years and beyond.

13   Although this explanation seems intuitive, there is a fuller and more accurate explanation. As the OIS discount factors are always higher than the LIBOR discount factors, and the difference between them increases with longer maturities, this increases the relative weighting of the more distant *LIBOIS* forwards. In a rising yield-curve environment forward rates rise faster than swap rates. If these later forwards are given a relatively higher weighting, but the weighted average remains the same (being equal to the LIBOR swap rate), the *LIBOIS* forwards must be lower than the LIBOR forwards. The opposite is true with a downward-sloping yield curve.

10

OPTIONS – BASICS AND PRICING

Each of the financial engineering tools discussed so far in this book has, in its own way, made an important contribution to the successful management of financial risk. FRAs, interest rate swaps and STIR futures allow a borrower to secure a guaranteed rate of interest for months or years into the future. A forward currency deal provides a company with foreign currency at an exchange rate fixed, once again, months or even years into the future. All these tools provide certainty, an immunity from future movements in market rates, peace of mind. What more could anyone want?

The trouble is, certainty may not always be the best thing, especially when looking back. With hindsight, a borrower may prefer to have secured certainty if interest rates turned out higher than were expected. Yet the same borrower would naturally prefer to have retained the original exposure to risk if interest rates eventually turned out lower. Achieving certainty with tools such as FRAs, swaps, futures and forwards is sometimes a mixed blessing.

Recall the definition of risk presented in Chapter 1: risk is *any* variation in an outcome. Risk therefore encompasses both adverse and benign developments in market rates. Avoiding risk implies avoiding not only the bad outcomes but also the good ones.

Options are unique among all the tools of financial engineering, for they give the buyer the ability to avoid just the bad outcomes, but to retain the benefit of the good ones. As such, options – and all the products derived from them – seem to provide the best of all worlds. Regrettably for the user, options do not come free. There is a price that must be paid to acquire something that can never be bad. Nonetheless, options frequently provide the ideal solution for controlling risk, for managing risk rather than avoiding it completely.

Although options in one form or another have been used for several centuries, financial options really became established only in the early 1970s, and they were not used widely until the 1980s. Nowadays, options are among the most versatile and exciting of all financial engineering tools. Their flexibility has created a huge range of opportunities, and options are often embedded or hidden within other financial engineering tools (like the structured products we will explore in Chapter 23).

Options are a big subject, so we need to devote several chapters to the subject. This chapter introduces the concept of options and explains how they are priced using several alternative types of model. One of the key pricing variables is *volatility*, and the next chapter considers the different ways of thinking about and measuring volatility, before going on to discuss option 'Greeks', which quantify the behaviour of options under different circumstances. Chapter 12 then goes on to discuss how options can be combined in many different and versatile ways, and Chapter 13 completes the discussion by reviewing the special characteristics of interest rate options and so-called *exotic options*.

Readers who already know the basic terminology can proceed straight away to section 10.4, which discusses the value and profit profiles for options at maturity. Those who wish to skip the more mathematical sections on the behaviour of financial prices, and on the Black–Scholes (B–S) and other models, can avoid sections 10.6–10.10 and jump to the next chapter. We begin, however, by explaining why options are unique.

10.1 Why options are different

All the tools of financial engineering reviewed so far have one thing in common: a 'straight-line' characteristic. As an example, suppose a treasurer buys a 3×6 month FRA on a notional amount of $1m at a price of exactly 5%. The eventual payoff will depend upon the reference rate determined on the fixing date. If the reference rate turns out to be higher than 5%, the treasurer would receive payment under the agreement. If the reference rate was lower, the treasurer would be compelled to pay out. Figure 10.1 graphs the exact relationship between settlement sum and reference rate. As the figure shows, the characteristic is just a straight line:[1] the higher interest rates rise, the larger will be the benefit to the FRA buyer. Conversely, the lower interest rates fall, the larger will be the disadvantage to the FRA buyer.

The same applies to futures, forward FX and swaps. Figure 10.2 shows the same kind of characteristic for the 10yr T-Note futures contract at the CME. This time, however, the figure shows the payoff for both the buyer and the seller of one contract at a market price of exactly 115. Recall from Table 7.3 that the tick size of the 10yr T-Note contract is one-half a 32nd of a point, and the tick value is $15.625, so the profit or loss per full point is $64 \times \$15.625 = \$1,000$.

FIGURE 10.1
Payoff under a forward rate agreement

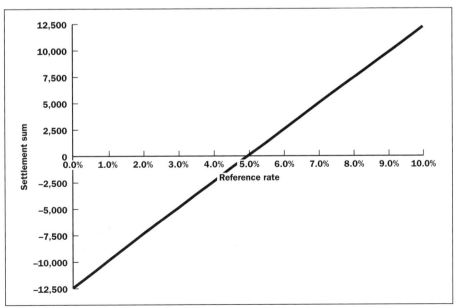

FIGURE 10.2

Payoff for parties under a bond futures contract

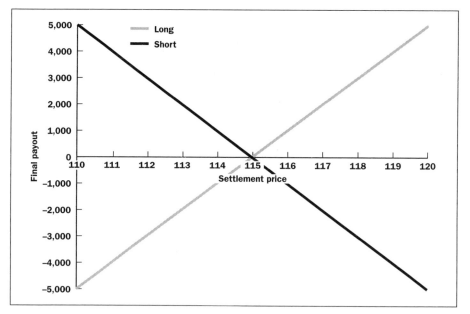

Not only is the linear characteristic evident from this figure, but also the symmetry of payoffs for buyer and seller. The buyer thinks, on balance, that the market price will rise and he will therefore profit. The seller takes the opposite view. If the market price of a bond future is 115, then it follows that the buyer's expected gain from a rise in the market price above that level must be equal to the seller's expected gain from a fall in the market price below that level.

To see that this is true, consider for one moment what would happen if the majority of people, say 60%, thought that potential gains from a long position exceeded potential losses. Buyers would then outweigh sellers, and the law of supply and demand would gradually drive the price higher. As the price rose, more and more people would revise their subjective probability estimates.[2] Eventually, the price would rise to the level where a consensus was reached whereby the expected gains of buyers now equalled the expected gains of sellers. At this point, the number of buyers would equal the number of sellers and the price would stabilise. In an efficient market, the market price at any time will therefore always adjust to this level.

Under these circumstances, both the buyer and seller of a futures contract have an equal chance of gaining and losing, and the expected value of the deal is zero. That is the reason why there is no need for any up-front payment at the outset between buyer and seller. The buyer of an FRA, or a future or a swap simply enters into a binding agreement with the seller; they notionally shake hands on the deal but no entry fee need be involved. The market price is the fair price for both parties to the contract.

Options are quite different. As they allow the buyer to benefit from market movements in one direction, but not to lose from movements in the other direction, there is no longer symmetry between buyer and seller.

Consider an option which gives the holder the right, but not the obligation, to purchase one bond futures contract at 115 on the expiry date of the future. If the price of the bond future turns out higher than 115, the holder will exercise the option, and will benefit from the same payoff as in the top-right quadrant of Figure 10.2. If the price turns out lower than 115, the holder will simply elect not to exercise the option. The resultant payoff for the holder of such an option is illustrated in Figure 10.3, along with the payoff from the counterparty who is short the option.

It is important not to confuse the symmetry between the top and bottom of this figure with the lack of symmetry between left and right. The top and bottom halves must inevitably be mirror images of each other because the buyer's profit must always be the seller's loss. No such symmetry exists between the left and right halves of the figure, unlike that present in Figure 10.2. This means that the holders of long and short positions in this option do not have an equal chance of gaining and losing. The holder of the long position will gain if the market price of the underlying future rises, but will not lose if the price were to fall. Conversely, the holder of the short position can only lose, and can never gain, even if the market price of the future falls below 115. The expected value of this deal is therefore not zero.

FIGURE 10.3

Payoff for parties under option contract

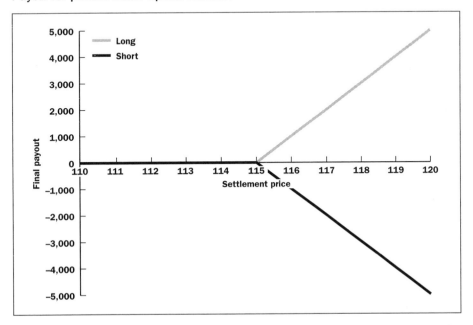

The holder of a long position in options therefore gains an advantage without suffering a disadvantage, a right without an obligation. The option buyer cannot expect to obtain this position without paying something for it. Equally, it would be senseless for someone to sell an option without receiving compensation for entering into a contract where they can only lose or break even.

With options there is thus an up-front payment, from buyer to seller. This rewards the seller for taking on obligations without compensating rights, and is a fair payment for the buyer to make when acquiring rights without offsetting obligations. This is in direct contrast to FRAs, futures and swaps, where the rights acquired by each side are offset by matching obligations, and where an up-front payment is therefore inappropriate.

Thus, what makes options different from all the other financial instruments is the asymmetry of the payoff profile, and the consequent need for an up-front payment between buyer and seller.

10.2 Definitions

Now that the distinguishing features of options have been established, we are ready to define options more precisely. The previous section introduced options by saying that they allow the buyer to benefit from market movements in one direction, but not to lose from movements in the other direction. As an illustration, an option which gave the holder the right to buy one bond futures contract at a price of 115 was described. This is an example of a *call* option.

A *CALL* option is:

■ the right to *BUY*

■ a given quantity of an underlying asset

■ at a given price

■ on or before a given date.

NB: The call option grants a right to the buyer, but does not impose an obligation.

Such an option allows the holder to benefit from a *rise* in the market price of the underlying. In the case of the bond future option, the holder would elect to exercise the option only if the price rose above 115. Suppose, however, that someone in the market wanted to benefit if bond futures prices fell. Perhaps an investment manager holding a portfolio of bonds wanted to construct a hedge against a fall in bond prices. Selling a call option would not provide the protection sought. While the holder of a short position in call options would not lose if the market fell, this is not the same as gaining.

The fundamental asymmetry of options, which respond differently depending upon the direction of the market, means that there needs to be another kind of option, the put option, which is the mirror image of the call option defined above.

A *PUT* option is:

■ the right to *SELL*

■ a given quantity of an underlying asset

■ at a given price

■ on or before a given date.

NB: The put option grants a right to the buyer, but does not impose an obligation.

Put options can sometimes seem confusing at first. The notion of buying a call option is easy to grasp – it confers the right to buy the underlying asset at some future time. If call options can be bought, they can also be sold. If the market price is sufficiently high, the call option will be exercised, and the call buyer receives the underlying from the call seller at an advantageous price, or settles in cash instead.

Put options are just the mirror image of calls. They, too, can be bought or sold. The buyer of a put gains a right, just as the buyer of a call does. In the case of a put, that right is the right to sell the underlying asset. If the market price falls sufficiently, the put option will be exercised, and the put buyer sells the underlying to the put seller at an advantageous price, or can elect to settle in cash.

These definitions of call and put options are very similar to the definition of a futures contract given in Chapter 5 (section 5.2). Indeed, there are many similarities between these two types of derivative instrument, but the key difference is that a futures position always confers both rights and obligations to perform under the contract, whereas an option separates rights from obligations. The holder of a long position in options, whether a call or a put, only has rights but no obligations. Conversely, someone who is short options only has contingent obligations, without any rights. Figures 10.4 and 10.5 illustrate this separation of rights and obligations.

FIGURE 10.4

Futures: rights and obligations go together

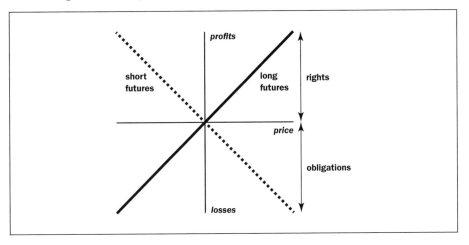

FIGURE 10.5

Options: separation of rights and obligations

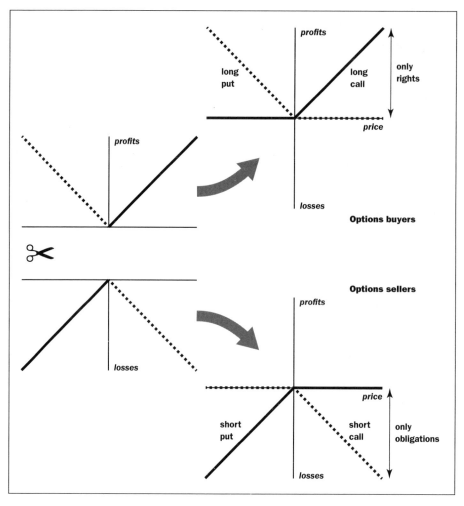

Options are available on a very wide range of underlying instruments, including:

■ shares

■ bonds

■ bills

■ foreign currencies

■ commodities.

They can also be created with other derivatives as the underlying instrument, giving rise to options on:

■ FRAs

■ futures

- stock indices
- swaps
- options.

The last instance, an option on an option, may seem quite esoteric, but there are examples (illustrated in Chapter 19, section 19.4) where such an instrument may turn out to be the optimal choice.

10.3 Options terminology

Being different from other instruments, options introduce a new set of jargon. Table 10.1 provides a concise summary of the nomenclature involved, before each of the key terms is defined in greater detail.

TABLE 10.1

Option terminology

CALL	the right to buy the underlying instrument
PUT	the right to sell the underlying instrument
Option BUYER	the party with the right to exercise the option
Option SELLER	the party with the obligation to perform if the option is exercised
STRIKE or EXERCISE price	the price at which the option can be exercised, normally fixed at the outset
EXPIRY or MATURITY date	the last date on which the option can be exercised
AMERICAN style	an option which can be exercised at any time until maturity
EUROPEAN style	an option which can only be exercised on the maturity date, and not before
PREMIUM	the amount paid by buyer to seller to acquire the option
INTRINSIC VALUE	the value realised if an option were to be exercised immediately, or zero if the option was not worth exercising
TIME VALUE	the amount by which the option premium exceeds the intrinsic value
IN-THE-MONEY	an option which has intrinsic value (i.e. worth exercising)
OUT-OF-THE-MONEY	an option with no intrinsic value (i.e. not worth exercising)
AT-THE-MONEY	an option for which the strike price is equal to the underlying price

CALL, PUT, BUY, SELL

The four combinations – buy a call, sell a call, buy a put, sell a put – can perhaps best be appreciated using a diagram. Figure 10.6 depicts the four possible payoff profiles, following the same conventions as Figure 10.3.

FIGURE 10.6
Basic option payoff profiles

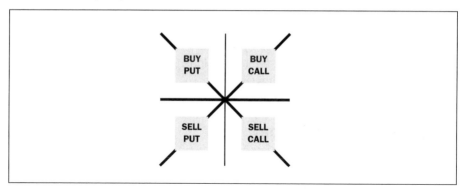

STRIKE or EXERCISE price

As an example, consider a call option to buy 100 shares in ABC plc at a strike price of £5. If the holder of the call decides to exercise the option, he must pay £5 over to the seller for every share purchased. Someone exercising a put option conferring the right to sell XYZ Inc shares at a strike price of $25 would deliver the shares and expect to receive $25 for each one.

AMERICAN or EUROPEAN style

The terms *American* and *European* arose from the conventions once adopted by the options exchanges either side of the Atlantic. Nowadays, geographic location is irrelevant, but the names have stuck. Although a European option cannot be exercised prior to maturity, it can usually be traded. Even for OTC options, it is usually possible to obtain a closing-out price from the original bank, or to find another bank which will agree a price for an offsetting trade.

PREMIUM

We have already established that the asymmetry of option contracts means that the buyer of an option must pay the seller in order to acquire the rights granted under the option. The sum paid is called the premium. The option premium has two components: intrinsic value and time value (sometimes called extrinsic value).

INTRINSIC VALUE

The intrinsic value is the easiest component to understand, for it represents the net positive amount that an option would realise if it were exercised immediately, provided that it was worth exercising. For example, consider a call option struck at 95 on an underlying asset which currently trades at 100. The intrinsic value of this option is simply 5, because the holder of the call could exercise the option and acquire the underlying asset by paying 95, then immediately sell the asset in the open market to realise 100, a net profit of 5. In contrast with the call, a put option struck at 95 would have no intrinsic value because there would be no benefit in exercising it if the underlying asset were priced at 100.

There are two features to note about intrinsic value. First, it is not necessary to know anything about the option premium in order to determine an option's intrinsic value; all one needs to know is the strike price, the underlying price and whether the option is a call or a put. Second, the concept of intrinsic value applies equally to European as well as to American options, even though it is not possible to exercise European options prior to maturity. The intrinsic value is usually defined in just the same way.

However, where a well-developed forward market exists, as in the case of currency options, a little caution must be exercised. In such cases, the intrinsic value of a European option is calculated relative to the forward rate, whereas that of an American option is calculated relative to either the spot or forward rate, whichever gives the largest result. For example, if the spot rate for sterling against the dollar is £1=$1.6000, and the three-month forward rate is £1=$1.5900, the intrinsic value of an American call on sterling struck at $1.5500 would be 5¢ (using the spot rate), while that of an American sterling put struck at $1.6500 would be 6¢ (using the forward rate).

TIME VALUE

In virtually all cases, the option seller will demand a premium over and above the intrinsic value. The excess of total premium over intrinsic value is called the time value because time to maturity is one of the major factors determining the size of the time value. The reason why an option has time value will be discussed in more detail in section 10.5, but for now we can say that it represents the value to the option buyer in being able to decide later whether or not to exercise the option.

To clarify the concepts of total premium, intrinsic value and time value, Figure 10.7 illustrates these amounts for three call options with different strike prices. In each case, the price of underlying asset is 100. In the case of the options struck at 90 and 95, a portion of the premium is intrinsic value, while the remainder is time value. The last option has no intrinsic value, as the strike price and underlying price are the same, so the entire premium comprises time value alone.

IN-, AT- and OUT-OF-THE-MONEY

Once intrinsic value has been defined, defining *in-the-money* and *out-of-the-money* options is straightforward. An option with intrinsic value is said to be in-the-money (ITM) and is worth exercising, while an out-of-the-money (OTM) option is one without intrinsic value and is therefore not worth exercising. For a call, an ITM option is one where the underlying price exceeds the strike price,

FIGURE 10.7

Premium, intrinsic value and time value

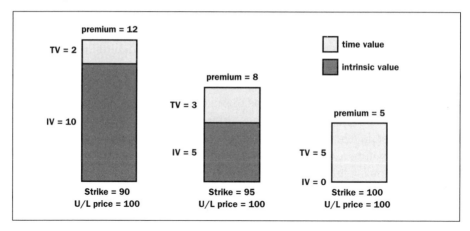

while for a put, the opposite is true. The term *at-the-money* (ATM) is normally used when an option contract is first written, and refers to an option where the strike price is set to the prevailing price of the underlying asset. Figure 10.8 illustrates these terms.

FIGURE 10.8

In-, at- and out-of-the-money options

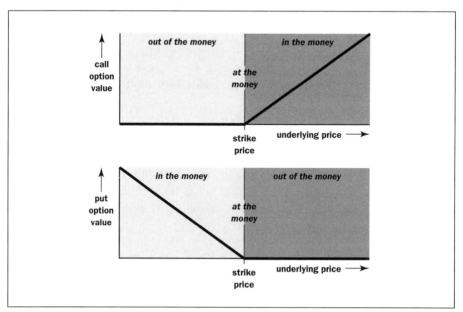

10.4 Value and profit profiles at maturity

With the definitions and terminology in place, we are now ready to explore the price and value characteristics of options. This is an important step in understanding how options can be used in practice.

To start with, consider the value of an option at expiry. As an example, we will take a call option which gives the holder the right to buy one share at a strike price of $100. The left side of Figure 10.9 charts the value of this call option on its expiry date, for values of the underlying share price from 80 to 120.

While the shape of this figure should by now be familiar, this time we can see exactly how much the option value changes when the underlying share price moves. If the shares end up below the strike price of $100 on the expiry date, the call option would expire worthless. Above $100, the value of the call option increases $1 for every $1 rise in the underlying share price. If the shares were trading at $115 on the expiry date, for example, the call option would be worth exactly $15.

This one-for-one relationship is the same for all call options which expire in-the-money, and should not be surprising. When a call option expires in-the-money, it will always be exercised, either to receive the underlying asset or for cash settlement. Either way, the option is replaced by the underlying itself, or its cash equivalent, so the value of an ITM option at expiry must rise in lock-step with rises in the value of the underlying.

In contrast, the right side of Figure 10.9 illustrates the value profile of a put option on the same stock, also struck at $100. Here, the put option expires in-the-money only when the underlying asset price falls *below* the strike price. If the shares ended up trading at $90 on the expiry date of the option, the put would be worth $10. Again there is a one-to-one relationship between the value of a put option which expires in-the-money and that of the underlying asset. For

FIGURE 10.9

Value profile for call and put options

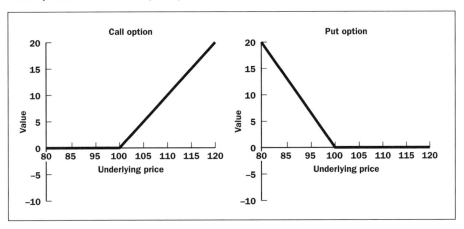

every $1 the share price finishes below the strike price of $100, the put option is worth $1 more at expiry.

While Figure 10.9 illustrates the *value* of options at expiry, it does not show the *profit* from holding these contracts. For this we need to know how much an option cost when it was purchased. The profit is then the difference between the value of the option at expiry and the premium originally paid.

Suppose that these stock options were originally purchased as ATM options with six months to expire, and the premium paid was exactly $5 in each case. Figure 10.10 takes this into account to show the profit profile at expiry.

Now we can see clearly that buying options does not lead to a guaranteed gain, once the premium is taken into account. If the option expires out-of-the-money, and therefore is worthless, the buyer has sacrificed the premium for no gain. The loss incurred is therefore equal to the premium paid. Even if the option expires in-the-money, this does not necessarily secure a profit if the terminal value of the option is less than the premium paid. In fact, in order to break even, the option must expire as much in-the-money as the original premium paid. In this example, this does not occur until the stock price rises above $105 for the call option, or falls below $95 for the put option.

Some people studying this profit diagram for the first time confuse profit and loss with the decision whether to exercise the option or not. Seeing that the call option loses money if the stock price is in the range $100–105 at expiry, they mistakenly think that the call option should not be exercised. Even though the net result is still a loss, that loss would be greater if the option were not exercised. So long as the option has some value at expiry, it should be exercised to release that value. For example, if the stock price was at $102 when the option expired, exercising the option yields $2, reducing the $5 loss to $3, as shown in the figure. At expiry, there are only two factors influencing the decision whether or not to exercise: the underlying price and the strike price. The premium paid originally is irrelevant.

FIGURE 10.10
Profit profile for call and put options

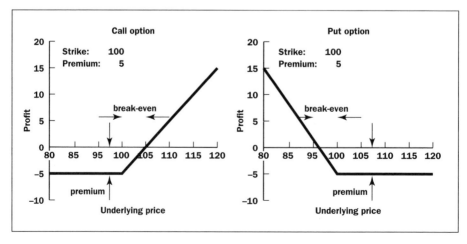

Figure 10.10 shows the profit profile for just one option. It is useful to compare profit profiles for options with different strike prices. Perhaps one option will prove to be better than others? Table 10.2 summarises the premiums paid for five call options with different strike prices ranging from $90 to $110. In each case, the premiums are reasonable market prices for three-month options at a time when the underlying shares were trading at $100.

TABLE 10.2
Option premiums for different strikes

	Strike ($)	Premium ($)
In-the-money	90	12.65
	95	9.22
At-the-money	100	6.44
Out-of-the-money	105	4.31
	110	2.76

Figure 10.11 now shows the profit profiles for each of these options. The shape of each graph is the same in each case: a horizontal section, then a kink, then a diagonal section with a slope of 1:1. As one moves from the most ITM option (the $90 dollar call) to the most OTM option (the $110 call), the position of the kink is higher and further to the right. The vertical position of the kink is governed solely by the option premium: the more expensive the premium, the deeper each line starts. The horizontal position is determined only by the strike price: the bigger the strike price, the further to the right is the kink.

FIGURE 10.11
Profit profiles for five call options with different strikes

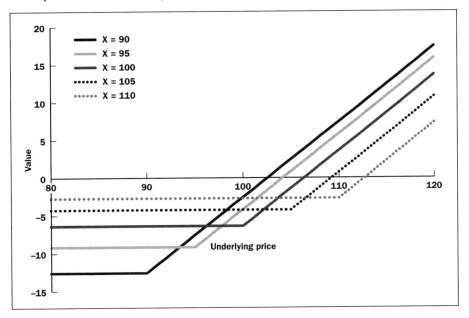

As these are profit profiles, the best option is the one that lies highest in the figure. This implies one which has a small premium, but also a low strike price. Unfortunately, as the figure and table reveal, these two requirements conflict with one another. The smaller the premium, the higher the strike price, and this means accepting some kind of compromise.

Further examination of Figure 10.11 shows that there is no clear choice of one option over another. Take the $90 and $95 strike options as examples. Although the $95 option is $3.43 cheaper, the strike price is $5 higher. For the $95 option, the kink is $3.43 higher, which is better, but $5 to the right, which is worse. The two graphs therefore cross over, meaning that neither option is universally better than the other. If the stock price finishes below $93.43, the option struck at $95 is better. On the other hand, if the underlying ends above $93.43, the $90 strike provides a superior financial result, albeit by just $1.57 at most. This outcome holds true in every case. All the lines in Figure 10.11 exhibit this criss-crossing characteristic, ensuring that no one option totally dominates any other.

If the stock price finishes low, so that all call options expire worthless, the best one (or the least bad) is the $110 strike. This is because the premium on all these options is thrown away if they expire worthless, and the $110 strike option was the cheapest, being the most out-of-the-money. However, if the stock price rallies, so that all call options expire in-the-money, it is now the $90 strike which provides the best result. Despite having the most expensive premium at the outset, the advantage of the $90 strike is that it already starts in-the-money. For every $1 increase in the underlying share price at expiry, this option is worth $1 more. Although the other options eventually exhibit this behaviour as the share price rises through $105 and eventually through $110, the options which are already in-the-money at $100 have a head start. Compare, for example, the options struck at $100 and $105. Although the higher strike option is $2.13 cheaper at the outset, the shares have to rise $5 from the original level of $100 before the $105 option finishes in-the-money. In the meantime, the $100 option has been increasing in value all the time. This is why the $100 option produces $2.87 more profit for any level of the share price above $105.

The conclusion from this is an important one. If fairly priced, no single option can dominate any other option for all possible future outcomes. There will always be some range of outcomes where one option proves better, and another range where it fares worse. With the benefit of hindsight it is, of course, possible to say that one option did outperform another, but with hindsight it is possible to improve on almost every decision in life. In prospect, however, all options offer a reasonable choice. How to make that choice will be discussed in Part II of this book.

For completeness, Figure 10.12 illustrates that the profit profiles for put options demonstrate the same kind of trade-offs as those of call options. The graphs depict the profit characteristics for a set of stock options with the same original maturity and set of strikes as in the previous example, except that these are put options on the stock conferring the right to sell shares at the strike prices indicated.

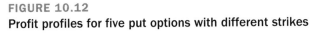

FIGURE 10.12

Profit profiles for five put options with different strikes

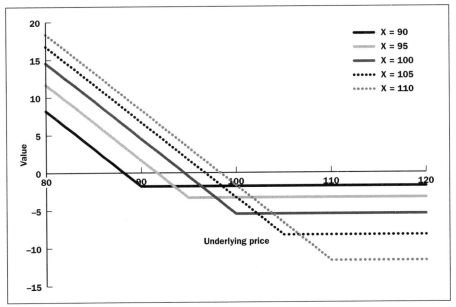

10.5 Pricing options

Profit profiles at maturity are very useful in comparing strategies involving different options, but they rely on one important piece of information: the price of the option when it was originally purchased. While value profiles at maturity are easy to construct, and depend solely on the underlying and strike prices, it is impossible to construct the profit profile – even on the maturity date – without knowing the original premium paid.

For all the derivative products reviewed until now, it has been possible to determine the fair price by constructing a hedging strategy that is both static and riskless. For example, someone selling a bond futures contract can hedge by buying a deliverable bond and financing it under repo. This cash-and-carry process was explained in Chapter 7 (section 7.3). Hedging strategies such as these work because, on the maturity date of the derivative, there is:

a) a rigid relationship between the price of the derivative and prices in the underlying markets

b) a definite procedure that takes place upon maturity.

For options there is also a rigid relationship at maturity between the value of an option and the underlying price, as illustrated by the examples in Figures 10.3 and 10.9. In the case of the call option on the bond futures contract struck at 115, the option was worth nothing if the bond future expired below 115, and

$1,000 for every full percentage point the futures price exceeded 115. This is a rigid relationship, so condition (a) above is also satisfied for options.

What makes options different is the lack of certainty as to what will eventually happen on the maturity date. The holder of an option has the right, *but not the obligation*, to exercise it. This means that the seller of an option cannot know in advance whether or not it will eventually be exercised, and therefore does not know whether he should buy (or sell, in the case of a put option) the underlying asset. Condition (b) is therefore violated by options.

Suppose that a bank sold the above-mentioned call option on the bond futures contract, and chose to hedge by buying the underlying bond future. If the call option expired in-the-money, the holder would exercise it and the bank would simply deliver the bond future that it had been holding. This is no different in principle from hedging futures. But what if the option did not expire in-the-money? In that case, the holder would not exercise the option and the bank would be left carrying the bond future, which may have dropped substantially in price.

The problem for option sellers is not the possibility that the underlying price may move adversely; such eventualities are relatively easy to handle. Rather, the problem arises from the uncertainty of not knowing whether the option will eventually be exercised or not. To see this, compare the seller of a bond future with the seller of a call option if prices fall.

Someone who has bought bonds to hedge a short position in bond futures does not mind if bond prices, and hence bond futures prices, drop. If the hedge has been constructed properly, any loss on the bonds will be offset by a gain on the short futures position. Alternatively, the seller of futures can simply elect to deliver the loss-making bonds against the short futures position. The counterparty who is long futures, and who therefore loses money when bond prices fall, has no choice but to accept these losses, because futures contracts are binding.

Yet someone who has bought the underlying asset against a short position in call options may well mind if prices fall. If a call option expires out-of-the-money and is therefore not exercised, the option seller can no longer offload his losses by delivering the underlying asset. Once the call option moves out-of-the-money, mounting losses from holding the underlying asset are no longer compensated by gains on the options position. Unlike the buyer of a futures contract, the counterparty who is long call options does have a choice and is not compelled to exercise these options if prices have fallen below the strike price.

This uncertainty – whether or not the option will ultimately be exercised – makes options much more difficult to hedge, and therefore much more difficult to price. Though challenging, the problem of pricing an option is, in essence, the task of determining how much the time value is worth. Once you know the time value, just add the intrinsic value of the option, and you have the total premium. Fortunately, determining intrinsic value is a trivial exercise – for an ITM option it is simply the difference between the strike price and the current price of the underlying asset.

So let's come back to time value, the all-important component of the value of an option. Earlier we defined time value as the excess of total premium over and above the intrinsic value. It is what the option buyer must pay in order to get the advantages which an option confers, and the unique benefit that an option provides is that the buyer can decide at the very last moment whether or not to exercise the option. We can therefore say that:

An option buyer has the right to decide later whether or not to exercise the option.

The time value of the option is the value of this right.

What determines time value? It mainly comes back to the same word we have touched on several times already – *uncertainty*. The more uncertain the outcome, the more valuable is the right to defer the exercise decision. After some careful thought, we can say that there are three factors that drive this uncertainty:

- time to option expiry
- volatility of the underlying asset price
- moneyness of the option.

The first two of these are fairly obvious. Consider an option expiring tomorrow with one expiring in one year. We can be pretty sure that the price of the underlying asset tomorrow will be similar to today's price, so we can be fairly certain about the exercise decision. However, a year from now the price of the underlying asset could be significantly different. There is therefore much more uncertainty surrounding the exercise decision for a one-year option compared with a one-day option, so the time value of a one-year option should be a lot higher than that of a one-day option. In a similar way, a three-month option on a more volatile underlier will also have more time value than a three-month option on a more stable underlier, because in the former case there will be more uncertainty surrounding the exercise decision.

The third factor – moneyness – is less obvious at first sight, but a simple example will make this clear. If you examine the price of Microsoft (MSFT) shares over the five-year period from 2006–2010, it never strayed outside the range $25–35. On 21st April 2011, when MSFT shares were trading at $25.52, the premiums quoted for selected call options on MSFT expiring 21st May 2011 are shown in Table 10.3.

TABLE 10.3

Selected option quotations for MSFT on 21st April 2011

Moneyness	Strike ($)	Premium ($)	Intrinsic value	Time value
ITM	21	4.55	4.52	0.03
ATM	25	0.94	0.52	0.42
	26	0.43	0.00	0.43
OTM	30	0.02	0.00	0.02

Source: CBOE.

The $21 strike call is well in-the-money and, with just one month to expiry, there is little doubt that MSFT will remain above the strike price of $21. It is therefore almost certain that this call option will be exercised one month from now. The $30 strike call, however, is well out-of-the-money and, as the share price of MSFT is most likely to remain below $30 over the next month, it is almost certain that this call option will expire worthless. In both cases the respective outcomes are clear – the $21 call will be exercised and the $30 call will not. With little uncertainty about these outcomes, the time values of 3¢ and 2¢ respectively are both small. In contrast, the outcomes for the $25 and $26 strike calls are somewhat unclear. Right now, the $25 call is slightly in-the-money and will be exercised if the share price remains static over the next month, while the $26 is slightly out-of-the-money and will expire worthless under the same circumstances. However, MSFT's share price has to fluctuate only 50¢ or so in either direction to change the eventual outcomes. For this reason, the time values for these close-to-the-money options are much greater, at 42¢ or 43¢, because there is much greater uncertainty as to their eventual outcomes, and so the value of the right to decide later is much greater.

We will shortly examine a number of ways of pricing options but, adapting the previous list, it will not come as a surprise that four of the five key inputs will be:

■ underlying asset price
■ strike price
■ time to option expiry
■ volatility of the underlying asset price.

The first two variables determine moneyness and together with the last two variables these determine the degree of uncertainty regarding the exercise decision, and hence time value. The first two variables also determine intrinsic value, which is part of the premium for an ITM option.

The fifth input – a combination of interest rates and potential earnings on the underlying asset (e.g. dividends on a share) – determines something called 'carry'. With an option, in addition to being able to defer the exercise decision, the option buyer defers the cash flows associated with option exercise. For an ITM call option, the buyer can earn interest on the exercise price until the time when the option is exercised – this is a minor component of time value, but option pricing models must also take this into account.

We have therefore seen that pricing an option essentially involves determining its time value, and time value mainly depends upon the uncertainty surrounding the exercise decision. There are several ways to quantify this uncertainty, and thereby to find the fair price for an option.

One method makes an assumption about the way in which the underlying price behaves over time. From this the expected value of the option at maturity can be estimated. This method can lead to the well-known Black–Scholes model of option pricing. Another method relies upon the possibility of constructing a riskless hedge when an option is first sold and then adjusting this hedge continually until the option expires. This can lead to the so-called binomial model.

A third method is to use Monte Carlo simulation, and a fourth technique uses so-called 'finite differences'. Despite the apparent diversity in these approaches, all these models eventually provide the same answer to the question: what is the fair price for an option?

Professors Fischer Black and Myron Scholes published their seminal paper on option pricing in 1973, and this established for the first time a firm foundation for the pricing of options. Unfortunately, though it is relatively easy to implement, a complete derivation of the B–S model involves some fearsome mathematics which, to the relief of many readers, we shall avoid restating here. Instead, section 10.7 will present a more intuitive explanation of the B–S model and what the various terms mean. However, before coming to the B–S model itself, we first need to study the behaviour of financial prices.

10.6 The behaviour of financial prices

One of the key assumptions underlying the B–S model is that asset prices follow a lognormal distribution. What does this mean? Most people are already familiar with the normal distribution pictured in Figure 10.13.

The normal distribution occurs frequently in nature. For example, if one were to take 1,000 people drawn at random and construct a histogram illustrating how their heights were distributed, the result would be a normal distribution. The distribution would peak at the mean (average) height of the group, but there would be a spread around this mean. The statistical measure for the degree of

FIGURE 10.13
The normal distribution

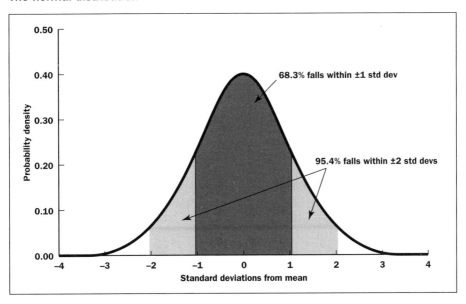

spread is called the *standard deviation*, and a property of the normal distribution is that 68.3% of the distribution lies within ±1 standard deviation of the mean, while 95.4% lies within ±2 standard deviations. In our height illustration, we might find that the mean height was 1.75m and the standard deviation was 0.09m. This would imply that 95.4% of the people in our sample had heights between 1.57m and 1.93m and we could infer that 95.4% of people in the wider population from which our random sample was drawn would also have heights within this range.

With the normal distribution being so common in nature, it would be tempting to assume that financial prices also follow a normal distribution. Such an assumption would create several problems, however, not least of which is the possibility for a variable which is normally distributed to take on negative values, something which most financial prices can never do.

It turns out that, while prices themselves are not normally distributed, returns mostly are. An investor buying a share at 100 and expecting to break even is just as likely to see a return of –10% as a return of +10%. However, we need to be extremely careful what is meant by 'return'.

At first sight, one would think that an investor should not be upset if his investment first went up by 10% and then down by 10%; he would simply be back where he started. Or would he? A 10% increase takes the value of his shares from 100 up to 110, but the subsequent 10% decrease brings it from 110 down to 99. The reason why the investor ends up with less than he started arises from the way in which return has been measured here. The rise from 100 to 110 is an increase of 10 on a starting price of 100, or +10%. The fall from 110 to 99 is a decrease of 11 on a starting price of 110, or –10%. The size of the price change differs, despite the fact that the percentage price change itself is the same in both cases, because the basis for measuring the percentage has altered.

The problem with using straight percentages in this way is that one is tempted to add successive percentage changes to obtain the overall result. This leads to the wrong result, as the above example illustrates, because 10% – 10% = 0%, but the end result was patently a loss of 1%. The correct result is obtained, not by adding percentage changes but by multiplying *price relatives*. A price relative is simply the ratio of successive prices. In the above example, the two price relatives are 110/100 = 1.10 and 99/110 = 0.90. The product of the price relatives is 1.10 × 0.90 = 0.99, which gives the correct result, namely that the final price is 0.99 times the original price.

Fortunately, there is a mathematical device which enables us once again to use addition rather than multiplication. Adding the logarithms[3] of two numbers gives the logarithm of the product of those numbers. Applying this technique here gives the following result:

$\ln(110/100) =$	0.0953	or	+9.53%
$\ln(99/110) =$	−0.1054	or	−10.54%
$\ln((110/100) \times (99/110)) =$	−0.110	or	− 1.01%

The decrease from 110 to 99 is shown for what it is, a greater effective reduction than the original increase from 100 to 110. That is why the end result is negative, implying an overall price decrease. To find out exactly what the final price implied by the −1.01% figure is, we need to use the opposite of logarithms, exponents. As logarithms to the base e have been used, we must take $e^{-0.0101}$ to obtain 0.99 or 99%. The calculation therefore implies that the final price should be 99, which we know is the correct answer.

Summarising the argument so far, we have demonstrated that taking the logarithm of price relatives gives a more consistent method for calculating returns than taking the price relatives themselves. In other words, defining return as:

$$return = \ln\left(\frac{S_{t+1}}{S_t}\right) \tag{10.1}$$

is more consistent than using the more traditional definition:

$$traditional \ return = \left(\frac{S_{t+1}}{S_t} - 1\right) \tag{10.2}$$

where S_t is the market price at time t, and S_{t+1} is the price one period later.

Using this method, what happens to the price if the return in the first period is +10%, and in the next period −10%? Starting at a price of $S_0 = 100$, we obtain:

$$S_1 = 100 \times e^{+0.10} \quad = 110.52$$

$$S_2 = 110.52 \times e^{-0.10} = 100.00$$

This time the price does return to its original level following a 10% increase, and then a 10% decrease, just as common sense would dictate.[4]

Consider the effect on price if the return was +10% every year for seven years. Starting at 100, the price would increase as follows:

100, 110.52, 122.14, 134.99, 149.18, 164.87, 182.21, 201.38

In absolute terms, the price doubles over seven years, with every successive price change being greater than the previous one. Now consider the effect of seven years of price decreases, also starting at 100:

100, 90.48, 81.87, 74.08, 67.03, 60.65, 54.88, 49.66

In this case, the price halves over the seven-year period, with every successive price change being smaller than before. If we plotted these two series on a horizontal scale, showing how the prices progressed over time, we would obtain a diagram like that of Figure 10.14. This shows very clearly the ever-expanding series of prices on the right side of the figure and the compression of prices on the left.

We can now return to the concept of financial returns being normally distributed. If the returns follow a symmetric normal distribution, the distribution

FIGURE 10.14

Successive price movements over time

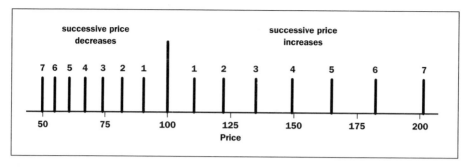

of prices will follow a distorted normal distribution, distorted in the same way as Figure 10.14 with the left side being compressed and the right side being stretched. This is clear from a comparison of Figure 10.15, which depicts normally distributed returns having a mean of 10% and a standard deviation of 30% in absolute terms, with Figure 10.16, which depicts the resulting distribution of prices.

The distribution of prices illustrated in Figure 10.16 is called a *lognormal distribution*, because the logarithm of the variable – prices in this case – is normally distributed. To better understand the relationship between returns and prices, let us start with the distribution of returns.

FIGURE 10.15

Normal distribution of returns

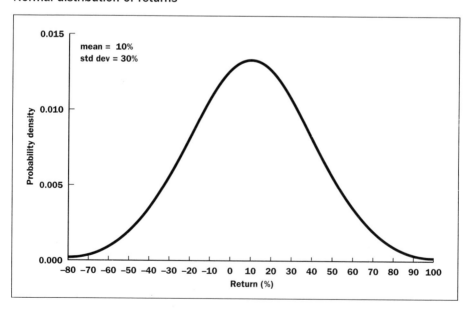

FIGURE 10.16
Lognormal distribution of prices

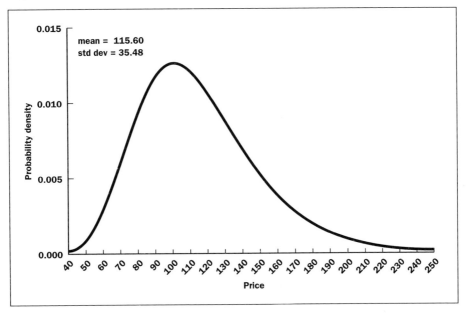

Returns are defined as the logarithm of the price relatives, and are assumed to follow the normal distribution such that:

$$\ln\left(\frac{S_t}{S_0}\right) \sim N(\mu t, \sigma\sqrt{t}) \qquad (10.3)$$

where:

S_0	is the price at time 0
S_t	is the price at time t
$N(m,s)$	is a random normal distribution with mean m and standard deviation s
μ	is the annual rate of return
σ	is the annualised standard deviation of returns

and the symbol ~ has the meaning 'is distributed according to…'

It follows directly from equation 10.3 that the logarithm of the prices is normally distributed, because:

$$\ln(S_t) \sim \ln(S_0) + N(\mu t, \sigma\sqrt{t}) \qquad (10.4)$$

and S_0 is a constant. Prices are therefore lognormally distributed, and follow the relationship:

$$\frac{S_t}{S_0} \sim e^{N(\mu t, \sigma\sqrt{t})} \qquad (10.5)$$

From equation 10.3 it also follows that the expected return is simply μt:

$$E\left[\ln\left(\frac{S_t}{S_0}\right)\right] = \mu t \tag{10.6}$$

where:

E[.] is the expectation operator

The graph in Figure 10.15 was obtained by setting μ = 10%, σ = 30% and t = 1 year. In an average year the return would therefore be 10%, giving rise to a price relative of $e^{0.10}$ or 1.1052. Starting at 100, the price at the end of that average year would then be 110.52. Surprisingly, this differs from the mean or expected price of 115.60 shown in Figure 10.16. To understand why the return in an average year does not produce the average price, one needs to consider what happens across the entire spectrum of possible returns.

In a bad year, the return might fall to –20%, one standard deviation below the mean, leading to a price relative of 0.8187. However, the return might rise to +40% in a good year, one standard deviation above the mean, and this would result in a price relative of 1.4918. As returns are normally distributed with a mean of +10%, there is an equal chance of finding returns of –20% and +40%, and therefore of finding price relatives of 0.8187 and 1.4918.

If we take the geometric average of 0.8187 and 1.4918, we obtain $(0.8187 \times 1.4918)^{0.5}$ = 1.1052. In other words, if a bad year was followed by a good year, the price would end up the same as if two average years had followed one another. This is a direct consequence of the way we have defined returns, and is perfectly consistent.

However, if we wish to obtain an estimate of the expected price after one year, we must take an arithmetic average of all the possible price relatives, not the geometric average. The arithmetic average of a typical bad year and a typical good year is now (0.8187 + 1.4918)/2 = 1.1553, which is somewhat larger than the value of 1.1052 obtained before (and very close to the price relative of 1.1560 implied by Figure 10.16). In fact, it is a well-known property that the arithmetic mean of a set of numbers is always greater than or equal to the geometric mean.

The expected price relative is therefore going to be more than $e^{\mu t}$, and it is possible to prove[5] that the expected price relative is, in fact:

$$E\left[\frac{S_t}{S_0}\right] = e^{\mu t + \frac{\sigma^2 t}{2}} \tag{10.7}$$

In the above example, the expected price relative is therefore $e^{0.10 + 0.09/2}$ = 1.1560. If the original price were 100, the expected price is then 115.60, which is the mean of the price distribution shown in Figure 10.16.

The average price is therefore greater than the price obtained from average return. Though paradoxical, the reason lies once again in the asymmetry of the lognormal distribution. For returns below the mean, the price distribution is compressed, while for above-average returns the price distribution is stretched. While good and bad returns are symmetrical and cancel out, the prices resulting from these returns are not symmetrical and do not cancel out. In general, if the return in a good year is $\mu+\delta$, and the return in the corresponding bad year is $\mu-\delta$, the average price relative from these two years is:

$$\frac{e^{\mu+\delta} + e^{\mu-\delta}}{2} = e^{\mu}\left(\frac{e^{\delta} + e^{-\delta}}{2}\right) = e^{\mu} \cosh(\delta) \geq e^{\mu}$$

because $\cosh(\delta)$ is always greater than 1 for all δ. This means that the expected price relative will always exceed e^{μ}. In the arithmetic example given previously, μ was 10% and δ was 30%, giving an average price relative of 1.1553, very close to the correct expected price relative of 1.1560. Equation 10.7 tells us that the bigger the variance σ^2, the bigger will be the asymmetry of the price distribution, and the bigger the expected price relative will be.

We have thus seen that:

- returns should be measured by taking the natural logarithm of price relatives (equation 10.1)
- returns follow a normal distribution (equation 10.3)
- price relatives, and hence prices follow a lognormal distribution (equation 10.5)
- the expected price relative is greater than the price relative from the expected return (equation 10.7).

Before seeing how these findings lead to the B–S model, let us return to an assertion made at the beginning of this section and repeated here: that returns follow a random normal distribution. Much empirical research has been undertaken within each of the major financial markets and, to a large extent, most rates and prices most of the time[6] follow a random walk according to equation 10.5. Note that this does not preclude trends or patterns from emerging. The existence of a trend is recognised explicitly by the drift term μt, while patterns may appear in the same way as people identify objects from a Rorschach ink blot.

As an example, consider the four lines depicted in Figure 10.17. One of the lines shows the evolution of the €/$ exchange rate between 2008 and 2010. The other three lines start with the same initial value, and have similar means and variances, but are streams of prices generated completely at random using equation 10.5. It is difficult, if not impossible, to determine, just by looking, which line represents the real data. This is by no means proof of the random walk nature of financial prices, but demonstrates visually that random data looks real, and real-life data looks random. Which line was the real data? The answer lies at the end of this chapter.[7]

The lognormal behaviour of financial prices is an important assumption upon which the B–S model rests. The next section explains how this assumption can be used to determine a fair price for options.

FIGURE 10.17
Random walk nature of financial prices

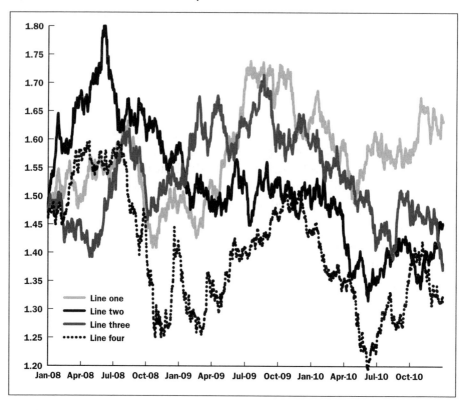

10.7 The Black–Scholes model

The fair price for any financial asset is its expected value. For example, if a share has a 30% chance of achieving a price of 40, and a 70% chance of achieving a price of 50, the fair value would be:

$$(0.30 \times 40) + (0.70 \times 50) = 47$$

The same principle applies to options. The fair value of an option at expiry is the sum of the products of every possible value it could achieve multiplied by the probability of that value occurring. In the simple example given above, there were just two discrete outcomes. Options, however, can take on almost any value, so it is necessary to use continuous rather than discrete probability distributions. Figure 10.18 illustrates three discrete and one continuous distribution. With a discrete distribution, the probability of a particular outcome can be measured directly from the height of the bar. For continuous distributions, the probability of a particular range of outcomes is measured by taking the area beneath that section of the curve.

FIGURE 10.18
Discrete and continuous distributions

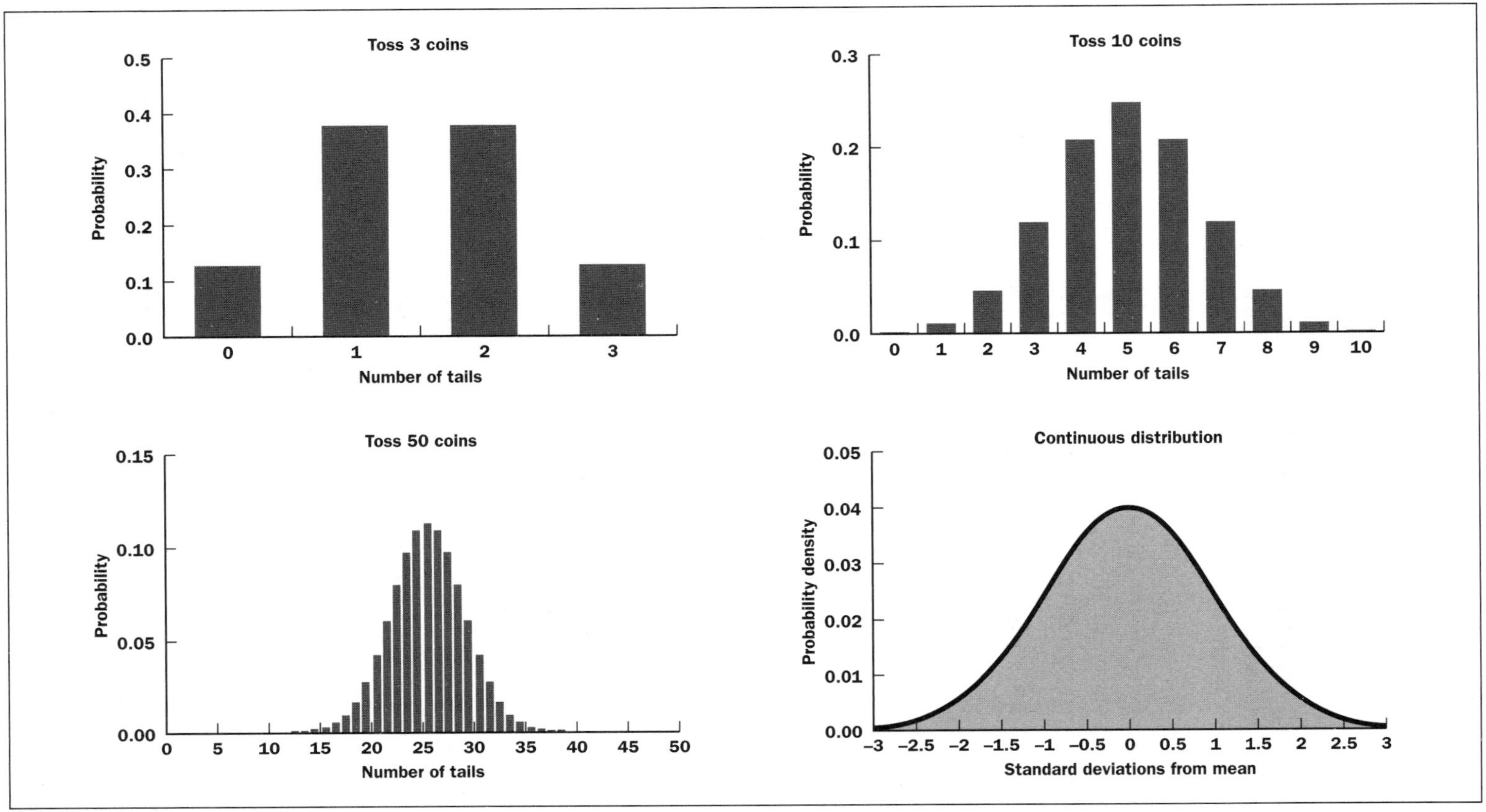

From the definition of a call option, the expected value of the option at maturity is:

$$E[C_T] = E[\max(S_T - X, 0)] \tag{10.8}$$

where:

$E[C_T]$ is the expected value of the call option at maturity
S_T is the price of the underlying asset at maturity
X is the strike price of the option

There are two possible situations that can arise at maturity. If $S_T > X$, the call option expires in-the-money, and $\max(S_T - X, 0) = S_T - X$. If $S_T < X$, the option expires out-of-the-money, and $\max(S_T - X, 0) = 0$. If p is defined as the probability that $S_T > X$, equation 10.8 can be rewritten:

$$\begin{aligned} E[C_T] &= p \times (E[S_T \mid S_T > X] - X) + (1 - p) \times 0 \\ &= p \times (E[S_T \mid S_T > X] - X) \end{aligned} \tag{10.9}$$

where:

p is the probability that $S_T > X$
$E[S_T \mid S_T > X]$ is the expected value of S_T given that $S_T > X$

Equation 10.9 gives us an expression for the expected value of the call at maturity. To obtain the fair price at the inception of the contract, the expression must be discounted back to its present value to obtain the following:

$$C = p \times e^{-rt} \times (E[S_T \mid S_T > X] - X) \tag{10.10}$$

where:

C is the fair price for the option at inception
r is the continuously compounded riskless rate of interest
t is the length of time until maturity

The problem of pricing an option has been reduced to two slightly simpler problems:

a) determine p – the probability that the option ends in-the-money such that $S_T > X$

b) determine $E[S_T \mid S_T > X]$ – the expected value of the underlying asset given that the option ends in-the-money.

The solution for both of these problems can be found in the lognormal distribution of financial prices. Figure 10.19 shows the same lognormal price distribution as that of Figure 10.16, but highlights the part of the distribution for which the price exceeds 120. This will be of interest if we wish to price an option whose strike price was set at 120. The area of the shaded part is 39.19% of the area under the graph as a whole, so the probability that the final price will exceed 120 is 0.3919. The expected value of the shaded part[8] is 150.51. If continuously

FIGURE 10.19

Lognormal distribution for in-the-money outcomes

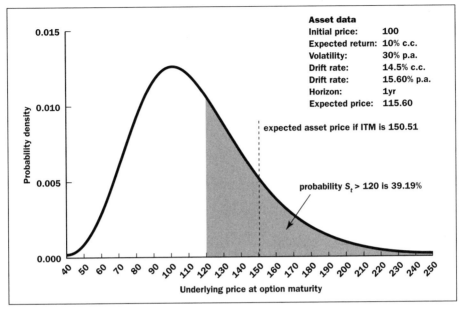

compounded interest rates are 14.5%, the fair price for the option struck at 120 is:

$$C = 0.3919 \times e^{-0.145} \times (150.51 - 120) = 10.34$$

This is, in fact, exactly the value of the option as suggested by the B–S model, as we will see shortly.

How were the values of 0.3919 and 150.51 calculated? It is relatively straightforward to derive an expression for the probability p, but rather more difficult to do so for the expectation expression $E[S_T | S_T > X]$. We therefore will show here how the probability can be calculated, but not how the expectation can be derived; for the latter we will merely state the end result. Combining the two expressions will give us the formula for the B–S model itself.

Finding the probability p that the underlying price at maturity S_T will exceed some critical price X is the same as finding the probability that the return over the period will exceed some critical value r_X. This is an easier problem to solve because returns are assumed to follow a normal distribution, and normal distributions are easier to work with than lognormal distributions. Remembering that returns are defined according to equation 10.1 as the logarithm of the price relatives means that we must find the probability p such that:

$$p = \text{Prob}[S_T > X] = \text{Prob}\left[return > \ln\left(\frac{X}{S_0}\right)\right] \tag{10.11}$$

where S_0 is the underlying price at the outset.

In general, the probability that a normally distributed variable x will exceed some critical value x_{crit} is given by:

$$\text{Prob}[x > x_{crit}] = 1 - N\left(\frac{x_{crit} - \mu^*}{\sigma^*}\right) \qquad (10.12)$$

where:

μ^* is the mean of x
σ^* is the standard deviation of x
$N(.)$ is the cumulative normal distribution

In the context of equation 10.11, we need to find expressions for μ^* and σ^*, the mean and standard deviation of returns. Equation 10.7 provided an expression for the expected value of the price relative S_T/S_0. If we define r such that:

$$r = \mu + \frac{\sigma^2}{2} \qquad (10.13)$$

we can then rewrite equation 10.7 in a simpler way:

$$E\left[\frac{S_T}{S_0}\right] = e^{rt} \qquad (10.14)$$

The new variable r is not only convenient shorthand for the expression $\mu + \sigma^2/2$, it is actually the continuously compounded riskless rate of interest. It may seem surprising that this is the relevant interest rate to use when valuing risky investments like options, but the answer to this conundrum lies in the risk neutrality argument.

The basis for the risk neutrality argument is the possibility of constructing a riskless portfolio combining an option with some proportion of the underlying asset. In fact, this approach is the foundation of the binomial method for option valuation discussed in the following section. A riskless portfolio is one that has the same financial outcome regardless of events, and therefore future cash flows should be discounted at the riskless interest rate. With such a portfolio, investors' risk preferences are irrelevant, and the portfolio should be worth the same whether being valued by risk-averse or by risk-neutral investors. Since it is easier to value the portfolio at the riskless rate used by risk-neutral investors, we may as well choose the riskless rate.

Note that the risk neutrality argument does not imply that all financial assets actually do grow at the riskless rate implied by equation 10.14. What the argument says is that the same answer for the price of an option will be obtained whether we choose the riskless rate or some higher interest rate. If a higher rate were selected, the underlying asset would grow at a faster rate, but the payoffs from an option on this asset would also have to be discounted back at a higher rate, and the two effects cancel out.

Another way to consider this is to remember that the option price is determined in proportion to the price of the underlying asset; double both the underlying asset price and the strike price, and the option price will also double. If the underlying asset price happens to be depressed because risk-averse investors are discounting future cash flows at a particularly high rate, the price of the option will also be depressed since it is calculated in proportion, but this is just as it should be. To be consistent, the same investors should discount future cash flows from the option at the same high rate.

Equation 10.6 now becomes:

$$E\left[\ln\left(\frac{S_t}{S_0}\right)\right] = \mu t = \left(r - \frac{\sigma^2}{2}\right)t = \mu^* \tag{10.15}$$

which gives an expression for μ^*, the mean return. Equation 10.3 already defined the standard deviation of returns as $\sigma\sqrt{t}$. Combining equations 10.11, 10.12 and 10.15, we now have:

$$\text{Prob}[S_T > X] = \text{Prob}\left[return > \ln\left(\frac{X}{S_0}\right)\right] = 1 - N\left(\frac{\ln\left(\frac{X}{S_0}\right) - \left(r - \frac{\sigma^2}{2}\right)t}{\sigma\sqrt{t}}\right) \tag{10.16}$$

The symmetry of the normal distribution means that $1 - N(d) = N(-d)$, so:

$$p = \text{Prob}[S_T > X] = N\left(\frac{\ln\left(\frac{S_0}{X}\right) + \left(r - \frac{\sigma^2}{2}\right)t}{\sigma\sqrt{t}}\right) \tag{10.17}$$

Substituting the values in the previous example, we have:

$$\text{Prob}[S_T > X] = N\left(\frac{\ln\left(\frac{100}{120}\right) + \left(0.145 - \frac{0.30^2}{2}\right) \times 1}{0.30\sqrt{1}}\right) = N(-0.2744) = 0.3919$$

and this is the value for the probability p obtained before.

Finding a formula for the expression $E[S_T | S_T > X]$ involves integrating the normal distribution curve over the range X to ∞. When this is done,[9] the result is:

$$E[S_T | S_T > X] = S_0 e^{rt}\frac{N(d_1)}{N(d_2)} \tag{10.18}$$

where:

$$d_1 = \frac{\ln\left(\frac{S_0}{X}\right) + \left(r + \frac{\sigma^2}{2}\right)t}{\sigma\sqrt{t}} \text{ and } d_2 = \frac{\ln\left(\frac{S_0}{X}\right) + \left(r - \frac{\sigma^2}{2}\right)}{\sigma\sqrt{t}} = d_1 - \sigma\sqrt{t} \quad (10.19)$$

Now we have expressions for p (equation 10.17) and $E[S_T | S_T > X]$ (equation 10.18) we can insert these into equation 10.10 to obtain the complete formula for a call option:

$$C = N(d_2) \times e^{-rt} \times \left(S_0 e^{et} \frac{N(d_1)}{N(d_2)} - X\right)$$
$$\therefore C = S_0 N(d_1) - Xe^{-rt} N(d_2) \quad (10.20)$$

This is the famous Black–Scholes model. It provides a single formula, which enables the fair price for a call option to be calculated. As the foregoing derivation has demonstrated, the formula can be interpreted as measuring the expected present value of the option based on the key assumption that prices follow a lognormal distribution.

By inserting into equation 10.10 the values for the probability of exercise, the expected asset price if the option expires in-the-money, and the rate of interest, we obtained a value of 10.34 for the fair option premium. In practice, we can't easily observe or measure these probabilities and expected prices, so equation 10.10 would be difficult to work with in practice. However, the information needed by the B–S formula of equations 10.19 and 10.20 is readily observable and we can therefore obtain the fair option premium of 10.34 much more readily, as follows:

$$d_1 = \frac{\ln\left(\frac{100}{120}\right) + \left(0.145 + \frac{0.30^2}{2}\right)1}{0.30\sqrt{1}} = 0.025595, \text{and } d_2 = d_1 - \sigma\sqrt{t} = -0.274405$$

$$N(0.025595) = 0.510210, \quad N(-0.274405) = 0.391887, \text{and } e^{-0145\times1} = 0.865022$$

$$C = S_0 N(d_1) - Xe^{-rt} N(d_2)$$
$$= 100 \times 0.510210 - 120 \times 0.865022 \times 0.391887$$
$$= 51.0210 - 40.6789$$
$$= 10.3421$$

Although the existence of normally distributed returns and hence lognormally distributed prices is one of the principal assumptions underlying the B–S model, there are a number of other assumptions which it relies upon:

■ The underlying asset can be bought and sold freely, even in fractional units.

■ The underlying asset can be sold short, and the proceeds are available to the short seller.

- The underlying asset pays no dividends or other distributions before maturity.
- Lending and borrowing are possible at the same riskless interest rate, which accrues continuously in time.
- The option is European style and cannot therefore be exercised prior to maturity.
- There are no taxes, transactions costs or margin requirements.
- The underlying price is continuous in time, with no jumps or discontinuities.
- Variability of underlying asset prices and interest rates remain constant throughout the life of the option.

While many of these conditions are not strictly true in practice, the basic model can be adjusted – in many cases quite simply – to handle departures from these assumptions. Take, for example, a currency option, where the underlying asset – a foreign currency – does pay a distribution, namely the interest that can be earned on a currency deposit. To price such an option, the standard B–S formula of equation 10.20 can be modified thus:

$$C = Se^{-r_b t} N(d'_1) - Xe^{-r_p t} N(d'_2) \qquad (10.21)$$

where:

S is the spot exchange rate

r_b is the continuously compounded interest rate in the base currency

r_p is the continuously compounded interest rate in the pricing currency

and:

$$d'_1 = \frac{\ln\left(\frac{S}{X}\right) + \left(r_p - r_b + \frac{\sigma^2}{2}\right)t}{\sigma\sqrt{t}} \text{ and } d'_2 = d'_1 - \sigma\sqrt{t} \qquad t \ o$$

arrive at the so-called Garman–Kohlhagen model for currency options. Merton arrived at an almost identical model for pricing stock options on dividend-paying stocks where d, the dividend yield, replaces r_b in the above formula.

The great virtue of the B–S model is that it is relatively easy to calculate and it produces reasonable and consistent pricing. For this reason it has been adapted to cope with many different types of options.

We have concentrated on pricing call options and so far ignored the problem of pricing puts. Fortunately, there is no need to develop a separate model because the price of a call option and the price of a put option are inextricably linked through a relationship called the *put–call parity theorem*.

To illustrate put–call parity, consider executing the following transactions:

a) Sell one call option with time to maturity t and strike price X.

b) Buy one put option on the same underlier, with the same maturity date and strike price.

c) Buy the underlying asset.

d) Borrow a sum of money Xe^{-rt}, where r is the continuously compounded riskless interest rate.

If S_0 is the original price of the underlying asset, C the premium of the call, and P the premium of the put, the total cash flow generated through carrying out these transactions is:

$$C - P - S_0 + Xe^{-rt}$$

At maturity, whatever the price of the underlying asset, the borrowing will need to be repaid, and this will lead to an outflow of X. What happens next depends upon the underlying asset price.

Consider first what happens at maturity if $S_t > X$. The call option expires in-the-money and is exercised against the seller, who therefore delivers the underlying asset (which he already holds) and receives the strike price X. This provides exactly the cash required to repay the original borrowing. The put expires worthless. The net cash flow is therefore exactly zero.

Now consider the situation at maturity if $S_t < X$. This time the call option expires worthless, but the put can now be exercised. This gives the buyer the right to sell the underlying asset (which he already holds) and receive the strike price X, which is exactly the cash flow required to repay the borrowing. Once again the net cash flow is zero.

In the unlikely event that $S_t = X$ at maturity, both options expire worthless. This time the underlying asset can be sold in the market at its prevailing price to receive X and the proceeds used to repay the borrowing. The net result: a zero cash flow once more.

In other words, this set of transactions will produce a zero net cash flow whatever happens. If the final value of the portfolio must always be zero, then the initial value must also be zero. If it were less than zero, an opportunity for riskless profit would arise. If it were greater than zero, the reverse set of transactions could be executed to secure a riskless profit. This means that:

$$C - P - S_0 + Xe^{-rt} = 0$$

Therefore:

$$P = C - S_0 + Xe^{-rt} \qquad (10.22)$$

This provides a formula for pricing a put option from a call, and there is therefore no need for a separate pricing model for put options.

The model developed by Professors Black and Scholes established a milestone in finance. For the first time it provided a reliable means for pricing options on stocks, and variations developed since have extended the formula to cover a wide range of option types and underlying assets. Models like the original B–S model and its descendants are called *closed-form* models; this description means that they all produce a formula which can be solved in a single pass using relatively straightforward arithmetic. Closed-form models have the advantage that they are easy to implement, are quick to execute and produce an exact answer.

Unfortunately, there are some options for which there are no closed-form solutions. For these, alternative methods must be used, like the binomial model, Monte Carlo simulation, or finite difference methods. Each of these alternatives will be explained in the following sections.

10.8 The binomial approach

In introducing option pricing, section 10.5 referred to a method which relies upon the possibility of constructing a riskless hedge when an option is first sold and then adjusting this hedge continually until the option expires. If such a riskless hedge can be found, then pricing options becomes similar to pricing other financial derivatives such as futures. The only difference is that, as we shall see, the options hedge will need constant revision whereas hedges like the cash-and-carry futures hedge can be set up and then left alone.

To see how this hedging process works, we must first suspend belief for a little while and suppose that at any given moment in time, a financial asset can move up or down by only a pre-specified proportion. If the asset price is S at time t, it can either move up to uS or down to dS at time $t + \Delta t$. Suppose there is a call option on this asset with a price C at time t. If the underlying asset moves up to uS, the option will move up to C_{up}, but if the underlying asset moves down to dS, the option will move down to C_{down}. Figure 10.20 illustrates these parallel movements. As the financial asset can achieve only two possible prices, the sequence is appropriately called a binomial process. The scenario described thus far is completely general, as we have not yet specified values for any of the variables.

For the sake of illustration, suppose that $S = 100$, $u = 1.20$ and $d = 0.90$, and that the call option is struck at 100 and has one period to mature. Under these circumstances we now know that if the underlying asset moves up to 120, the option will be worth 20 at maturity, but if the asset goes down to 90, the option will expire worthless. Figure 10.21 depicts this specific scenario.

FIGURE 10.20

One-period binomial process – general case

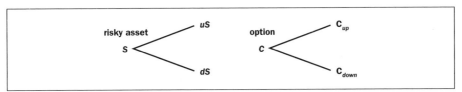

FIGURE 10.21

One-period binomial process – specific case

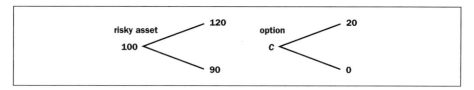

The only unknown in Figure 10.21 is C, the value of the call option one period prior to maturity. We will demonstrate that a suitable value for C can be determined by forming a riskless hedge between the option and the underlying asset. Consider a portfolio comprising:

a)   Sell three call options at price C each.

b)   Buy two of the underlying assets at 100 each.

c)   Borrow 163.64 at 10% over the period.

The net cash flow at the outset will thus be $3C - 200 + 163.64 = 3C - 36.36$. At maturity, there are two possible outcomes, and the financial impact of each situation is summarised in Table 10.4.

TABLE 10.4

Outcome from portfolio of options and underlying assets

	UP	DOWN
Proceeds from selling asset	2 × 120 = 240	2 × 90 = 180
Payout on short call position	3 × (–20) = –60	3 × (0) = 0
Repay borrowing	–180	–180
Net cash flow	0	0

The amazing result is that this particular combination of underlying asset, borrowing and options has the same financial outcome whether the underlying asset goes up or down in price. This is a riskless hedge. If the outcome of this particular portfolio is always zero, then the fair price for acquiring the portfolio at the outset must also be zero. This means that $3C - 36.36 = 0$, so $C = 12.12$.

We have therefore determined a fair price for an option on a risky underlying asset one period before maturity. The only information required is the extent to which the underlying asset could move up or down, and the riskless rate of interest. Knowing the probability of an up-move or a down-move is, surprisingly enough, not necessary.

The concept of the riskless options hedge has been illustrated by means of a specific example, but the technique is universal. In the general case, consider the portfolio comprising:

a) Selling one call option.

b) Buying h units of the underlying asset (h is called the hedge ratio).

c) Borrowing an amount B.

At maturity, we wish to select values of h and B such that the financial outcome is zero whether or not the underlying asset price moves up or down. This can be achieved if we set:

$$huS - C_{up} - BR = 0$$
$$hdS - C_{down} - BR = 0 \tag{10.23}$$

where R is e^{it} and i is the continuously compounded riskless interest rate. This is a pair of equations in two unknowns, and with a little algebra the solutions for h and B are:

$$h = \frac{C_{up} - C_{down}}{S(u - d)} \text{ and } B = \frac{dC_{up} - uC_{down}}{R(u - d)} \tag{10.24}$$

Setting the initial cash flow to zero gives the condition:

$$C - hS + B = 0 \tag{10.25}$$

Substituting the values for h and B from equation 10.24, we obtain:

$$C = \frac{(R - d)C_{up} + (u - R)C_{down}}{R(u - d)} \tag{10.26}$$

Finally, making the substitution:

$$p = \frac{R - d}{u - d} \tag{10.27}$$

gives a slightly more manageable expression for the value of a one-period option:

$$C = \frac{pC_{up} + (1 - p)C_{down}}{R} \tag{10.28}$$

The terms p and $(1 - p)$ look like probabilities, because they always fall in the range zero to one, and they provide a ready interpretation of equation 10.28: the option value at each step is simply the sum of the present values of the expected outcomes, each outcome being weighted by the probability of its occurrence.

To illustrate how these equations work, we can insert the values from the previous example to obtain:

$$h = \frac{20 - 0}{100(1.20 - 0.90)} = 0.6667 \text{ and } B = \frac{0.90 \times 20 - 1.20 \times 0}{1.10 \times (1.20 - 0.90)} = 54.55$$

and therefore:

$$C = hS - B = 0.6667 \times 100 - 54.55 = 12.12$$

This technique for valuing a one-period option can readily be extended in order to value options with a longer time to maturity. To illustrate this, we can examine the case of a two-period option. Figure 10.22 extends the example illustrated in Figure 10.21 for an additional period. The initial price is still 100, $u = 1.20$ and $d = 0.90$, just as before. If the price rises two periods in a row, the final price will be $100 \times 1.20 \times 1.20 = 144$. Similarly, if the asset price falls both periods, it will finish at 81. Finally, if the asset rises and then falls, or falls and then rises, the price will eventually turn out to be 108.

The way to value the two-period option is to break the big problem into a series of little problems, a 'divide and conquer' approach. We can start with the top right of Figure 10.22, which is reproduced separately in Figure 10.23. This is exactly the same problem as valuing a one-period option. We can apply equations 10.24 and 10.28 to find the hedge ratio and C_{up}, which turn out to be 1 and 29.09 respectively. The bottom-right branch of Figure 10.22 can be evaluated in a similar way to calculate the hedge ratio as 0.30, and C_{down} as 4.85. We now have the values of the option one period before maturity. If these figures are inserted into Figure 10.22, the final step is to value the left-hand branch, which is now illustrated separately in Figure 10.24.

This is once again just like valuing a one-period option, and so the previous formulae can be applied once more to find that the hedge ratio for this branch is 0.81,

FIGURE 10.22
Two-period binomial option pricing

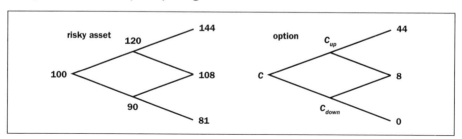

FIGURE 10.23
Two-period binomial pricing – top-right branch

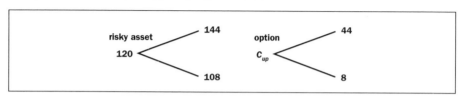

and the option price is 19.10. Figure 10.25 illustrates the complete two-period model, with all the values inserted. In the two-period model, there are three nodes in the lattice where the price may move up or down. Each node can be valued by using equation 10.24 to form a riskless hedge between the option and the underlying asset. The hedge ratio will differ from node to node, but this is an essential feature of the binomial model, and reflects the reality that practitioners hedging a book of options constantly have to re-balance their hedges to restore risk-neutrality. In the two-period example of Figure 10.25, the option could be hedged with 0.81 of the underlying asset. If the asset price then moved down, 0.51 would need to be sold to bring the hedge ratio down to 0.30. On the other hand, if the asset price moved up, another 0.19 would be purchased to increase the hedge ratio to 1.

If the one-period model can be extended to two periods, it can be extended to any number of periods, to obtain the full lattice structure pictured in Figure 10.26. Each point in the lattice represents the underlying asset price at one moment in time. At every step, the price may move up or down. Starting with the current market price at the left, the lattice gradually expands to cover every possible price that the underlying asset may achieve as time passes. The longer the time to maturity, and the more volatile the underlying asset, the wider the lattice will be.

FIGURE 10.24

Two-period binomial pricing – left-hand branch

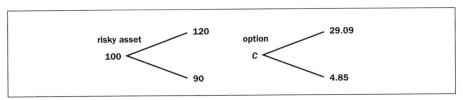

FIGURE 10.25

Two-period option pricing – complete tree

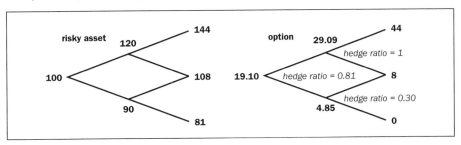

FIGURE 10.26
The binomial lattice

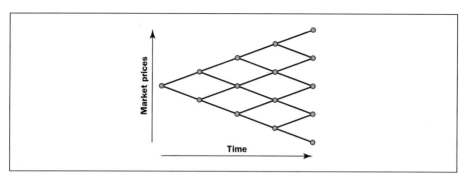

Worked example 10.1

As an illustration of the binomial technique, Tables 10.5 and 10.6 provide the full set of asset prices and option values using an eleven-step binomial model to price the option discussed in the previous section.

TABLE 10.5
Eleven-step binomial pricing – asset prices

0	1	2	3	4	5	6	7	8	9	10	11
											270.47
										247.08	
									225.71		225.71
								206.19		206.19	
							188.36		188.36		188.36
						172.07		172.07		172.07	
					157.19		157.19		157.19		157.19
				143.59		143.59		143.59		143.59	
			131.17		131.17		131.17		131.17		131.17
		119.83		119.83		119.83		119.83		119.83	
	109.47		109.47		109.47		109.47		109.47		109.47
100.00		100.00		100.00		100.00		100.00		100.00	
	91.35		91.35		91.35		91.35		91.35		91.35
		83.45		83.45		83.45		83.45		83.45	
			76.23		76.23		76.23		76.23		76.23
				69.64		69.64		69.64		69.64	
					63.62		63.62		63.62		63.62
						58.12		58.12		58.12	
							53.09		53.09		53.09
								48.50		48.50	
									44.30		44.30
										40.47	
											36.97

TABLE 10.6

Eleven-step binomial pricing – option values

0	1	2	3	4	5	6	7	8	9	10	11
											150.47
										128.65	
									108.83		105.71
								90.84		87.76	
							74.52		71.48		68.36
						59.90		56.72		53.64	
					47.12		43.76		40.31		37.19
				36.27		32.85		29.16		25.16	
			27.34		24.04		20.44		16.37		11.17
		20.20		17.20		13.96		10.36		6.07	
	14.66		12.06		9.33		6.42		3.30		0.00
10.47		5.63		6.12		3.92		1.79		0.00	
	8.31		3.95		2.37		0.97		0.00		0.00
		2.52		1.41		0.53		0.00		0.00	
			0.84		0.29		0.00		0.00		0.00
				0.16		0.00		0.00		0.00	
					0.00		0.00		0.00		0.00
						0.00		0.00		0.00	
							0.00		0.00		0.00
								0.00		0.00	
									0.00		0.00
										0.00	
											0.00

To obtain these figures, the following steps were taken:

1 Start at the left of the asset price lattice with the initial price of 100.

2 Working left to right, insert successive asset prices by multiplying the previous price either by u or d. In this example $u = 1.094670$ and $d = 0.913517$ (why these figures were used will be explained shortly). The highest price achieved after 11 successive moves up is therefore $100 \times 1.094670^{11} = 270.47$.

3 For each of the terminal asset prices, evaluate the value of the option at expiry. With a strike price of 120 the top-right option value will be $270.47 - 120 = 150.47$.

4 Now work right to left through the option value lattice applying equations 10.27 and 10.28, the one-period option pricing model, each time. R in this example was 1.013269, and again this value will be justified shortly. This choice of values makes $p = 0.550650$ and $(1 - p) = 0.449350$.

5 The option value at the start of the lattice is the fair price for the option at the outset.

In this example, the 11-step binomial model produces an answer of 10.47 as the fair price for the option, about 1% higher than the B–S value of 10.34 for the same option. Even with just 11 steps, the binomial model produces an answer consistent with the Black–Scholes model. In practice, however, it is usual to use a much larger number of steps than we have illustrated here, otherwise the answers produced by the binomial model may not be sufficiently accurate. Figure 10.27 illustrates the answers obtained by using binomial models with steps ranging from as little as one up to 500. Many commercial pricing models use around 300 steps as a reasonable compromise between reliability and calculation speed.

The binomial model is flexible enough to work with underlying assets whose prices follow any distribution of returns. By inserting the appropriate values for u and d, which could alter at different parts of the lattice if desired, any progression of prices may be simulated. The most common choices in practice for u and d are those which enable the binomial model to approximate the lognormal distribution of prices found in practice. With a little algebra[10] it is possible to show that:

$$u = e^{\sigma\sqrt{\frac{t}{N}}}$$

$$d = e^{-\sigma\sqrt{\frac{t}{N}}} \tag{10.29}$$

$$R = e^{i\left(\frac{t}{N}\right)}$$

where:

σ is the annualised standard deviation of returns
t is the time to maturity (expressed as a fraction of a year)
i is the continuously compounded riskless interest rate
N is the number of binomial steps used

Inserting $\sigma = 30\%$, $t = 1$ year, $i = 14.5\%$ and $N = 11$ steps gives $u = 1.094670$, $d = 0.913517$ and $R = 1.013269$, the figures cited in the worked example above to create the 11-step model illustrated in Tables 10.5 and 10.6. Note that the larger the volatility of the underlying asset, the larger σ will be. This will make u bigger and d smaller, and the resulting binomial lattice will exhibit a wider spread of prices, just as one would expect.

Figure 10.28 illustrates how the binomial model eventually approaches the lognormal distribution when this choice for u, d and r is made. Even when as few as ten steps are used, the skewed lognormal shape appears, and this becomes very obvious by the time a 50-step process is used.

It is at this point that our belief, which had to be temporarily suspended at the beginning of this section, can be reinstated. The whole discussion about the binomial model started by our assuming that prices at each step could move up or down by only pre-determined amounts. While this seems an unrealistic assumption at first, if the steps are made small enough, and if sufficient steps

FIGURE 10.27

Reliability of binomial model

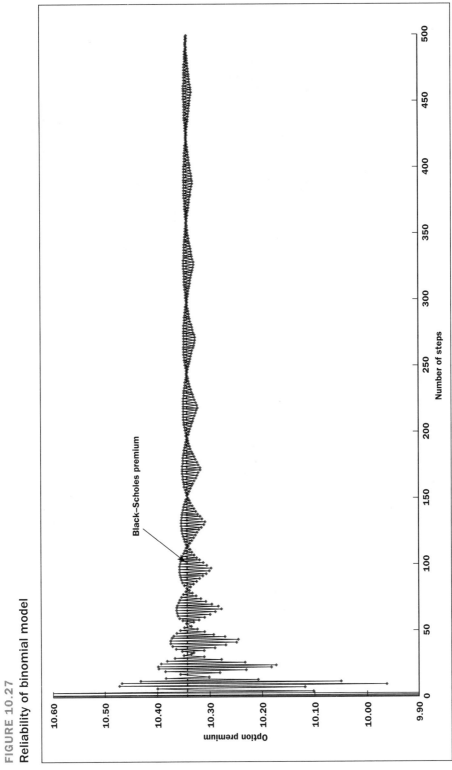

FIGURE 10.28
1-step, 10-step and 50-step binomial, and lognormal models

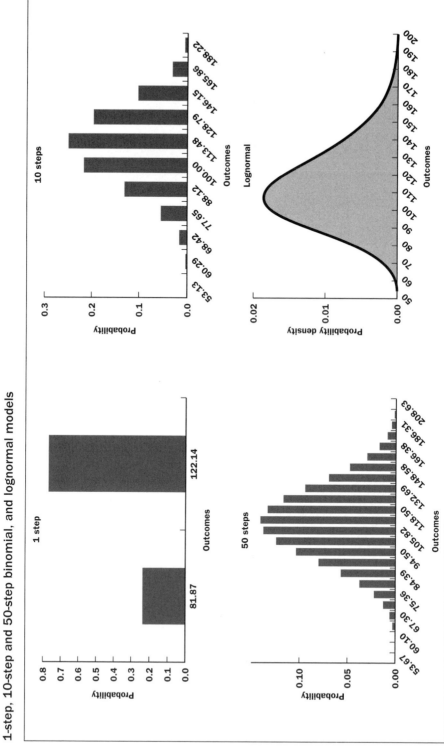

are combined, the evolution of prices generated by the binomial model will become more and more realistic. A good analogy is to think of digital photography. Print or display a picture at only 10 dots per inch and you will only get a crude representation of reality; increase the resolution to 300 dots per inch and the picture comes to life. The initial assumptions made by the binomial model are therefore reasonable, provided that a large number of small steps is used.

As the number of binomial steps gets larger and larger, and eventually approaches infinity, the binomial model ultimately becomes identical to the B–S model. This poses the question: why use the binomial model at all when it involves an iterative process that is time-consuming to calculate? The answer is that the binomial model has few restrictions, and can be used to price options where the B–S model cannot easily be applied. For example, pricing American-style options, or stock options for which the underlying stock has an irregular dividend payout, requires the B–S to undergo difficult contortions. In these situations, the binomial model may prove an easier method to use.

10.9 The Monte Carlo approach

Although the binomial model is very flexible, it has one potential weakness when it comes to pricing certain types of options, for example so-called path-dependent options. We will examine such options in more detail in Chapter 13 but also we can briefly summarise here. A path-dependent option is one where the payout at maturity depends not only on the final underlying asset price achieved but also on the particular sequence of underlying asset prices over time. An example of such an option is an average price option, where the payout at maturity is the difference between the strike price and the average of underlying asset prices over a pre-specified averaging period. This path-dependent feature makes the application of the binomial model impractical, as we will now see.

To price the simplest of options using the binomial model, it is only necessary to evaluate the payouts at each of the terminal nodes of the lattice pictured in Figure 10.26 and Tables 10.5 and 10.6. For an n-step tree there are $(n+1)$ such terminal nodes. For slightly more complex options, such as American-style options, it is necessary to perform calculations for all the nodes apart from the terminal nodes. For an n-step tree it is easy to show that there are $0.5 \times n \times (n+1)$ such nodes, and this implies that 45,150 calculations are necessary for a 300-step tree. Although this sounds daunting at first, with desktop computers capable of performing 20bn calculations each second, almost 500,000 such options could be priced every second, so this presents no problem in the modern world.

However, valuing a path-dependent option using the binomial model would require the computer to evaluate each individual path, and there are 2^n such paths in an n-step tree. Even at 20bn calculations per second, it would take a desktop computer 3×10^{72} years to complete the process for a 300-step tree. As the universe will probably have come to an end long before then, it looks as if we will need to find another approach, and this is where the Monte Carlo methodology provides an alternative and viable solution.

A Monte Carlo model generates a large number of possible scenarios, and evaluates and collates the outcomes. If the scenarios are representative of the real world, then so will be the outcomes. Just like a market research company can extrapolate the opinion of the wider population from a much smaller sample, so a Monte Carlo model can estimate the price of a path-dependent option with 2^{300} possible paths by walking down just 50,000 or 100,000 of them.

As an illustration of the Monte Carlo approach, Figures 10.29 and 10.30 show the results when pricing the vanilla call we illustrated earlier in sections 10.7 and 10.8. The behaviour of the underlying financial asset was simulated by a computer over 100,000 trials. In each trial, the return was sampled at random from a normal distribution with mean $\mu = 10\%$ and standard deviation $\sigma = 30\%$. If the return in a given trial turned out to be ψ, the price S_t after a period of time t would be given by $S_t = S_0 e^{\psi t}$, and the present value of the option would be $(S_t - X)\, e^{-rt}$ if $S_t > X$, and 0 otherwise.

Starting always with an initial price of 100, this experiment gave rise to the distribution of prices after one year illustrated in Figure 10.29. This has a mean of 115.60 and a standard deviation of 35.48, exactly that predicted by equation 10.7 and illustrated in the theoretical distribution of Figure 10.16. The probability of the underlying price being below 120 was 0.6081, the same as the theoretical figure of 0.6081 $(1.00 - 0.3919)$ predicted by equation 10.17.

FIGURE 10.29
Distribution of underlying asset prices

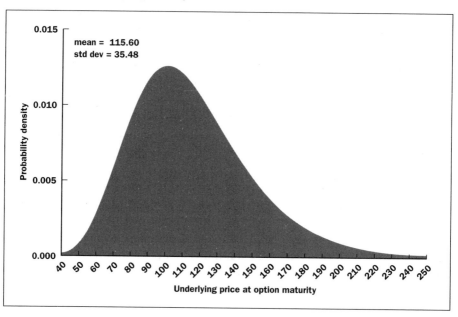

FIGURE 10.30
Distribution of option values

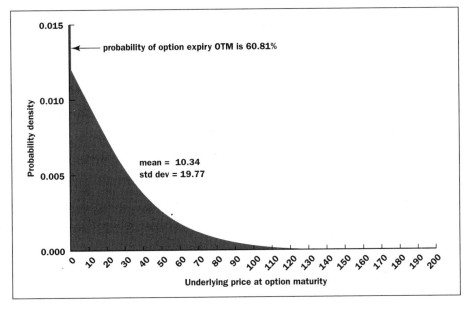

Underlying price at option maturity

The corresponding distribution of option prices is illustrated in Figure 10.30. The option expired out-of-the-money in 60.81% of the trials, while in the remainder of cases it expired in-the-money with values ranging from just above zero to as high as 285.49. The mean of this very wide distribution was 10.34, exactly the price calculated using the B–S model in equation 10.20.

Thus, starting only with an assumption of returns which are normally distributed, and using nothing other than very simple arithmetic, the Monte Carlo simulation arrives at the same answer for the expected value of the vanilla option as the B–S model. If the Monte Carlo methodology works so well with a vanilla option, whose value we can verify against models like the B–S model, then it is reasonable to expect that the Monte Carlo model will also work well when pricing options for which there may be no other viable alternative.

10.10 Finite difference methods

In section 10.7 we used an intuitive approach to get to the B–S equation for pricing a call option, although one important mathematical step – the formal derivation of equation 10.18 – was deliberately omitted. In fact, the original B–S model was actually derived in a different way, by solving the following partial differential equation[11] (PDE):

$$\frac{\partial C}{\partial t} + rS\,\frac{\partial C}{\partial S} + \frac{1}{2}\,\sigma^2 S^2\,\frac{\partial^2 C}{\partial S^2} = rC \tag{10.30}$$

where all the symbols are the same as previously defined.

As we have seen earlier, the option premium C is a function of a number of variables, including the underlying asset price S and the time to maturity t, and we can represent this by referring to $C(S,t)$. To make the explanation of finite difference methods easier, let's now define the option premium in terms of the natural logarithm of the underlying price, so:

$$w(y,t) = C(S,t) \qquad (10.31)$$

where $y = \ln(S)$. So w and C give the same answers, except C uses the underlying asset price directly, while w uses the log of that price. Once this transformation has been made, the PDE becomes:

$$\frac{\partial w}{\partial t} + \left(r - \frac{\sigma^2}{2}\right)\frac{\partial w}{\partial y} + \frac{1}{2}\sigma^2\frac{\partial^2 w}{\partial y^2} = rw \qquad (10.32)$$

There are a number of ways to solve PDEs, and one of these is to use a numerical technique called the finite difference method. This constructs a rectangular grid containing the values of the variable being studied – in this case the option premium $w(y,t)$ – at different levels of the underlying asset price and at various points of time. Figure 10.31 represents this grid; for each dot there will eventually be a value for the option price. For example, the dot half-way down the first column represents $w(\ln(S_0),T)$, the value of the option at the outset when the underlying asset is at its initial value S_0, and the option has T years to expire. (The meaning of the shaded cells will be explained shortly.)

To complete the grid, we first make equation 10.32 discrete:

$$\frac{\Delta w}{\Delta t} + \left(r - \frac{\sigma^2}{2}\right)\frac{\Delta w}{\Delta y} + \frac{1}{2}\sigma^2\frac{\Delta^2 w}{\Delta y^2} = rw \qquad (10.33)$$

FIGURE 10.31
Finite difference grid

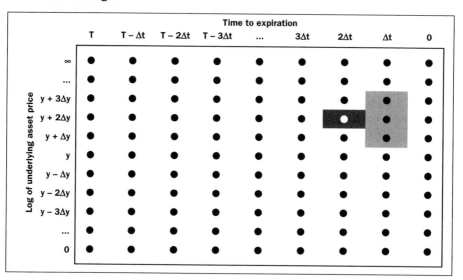

Using finite differences, the three partial differentials can be approximated as follows:

$$\frac{\Delta w}{\Delta t} = \frac{w(y, t + \Delta t) - w(y, t)}{\Delta t}$$

$$\frac{\Delta w}{\Delta y} = \frac{w(y + \Delta y, t + \Delta t) - w(y - \Delta y, t + \Delta t)}{2\Delta y} \qquad (10.34)$$

$$\frac{\Delta^2 w}{\Delta y^2} = \frac{w(y + \Delta y, t + \Delta t) - 2w(y, t + \Delta t) + w(y - \Delta y, t + \Delta t)}{\Delta y^2}$$

Substituting the expressions from equation 10.34 into equation 10.33 gives us the following:

$$w(y, t) = \frac{p_u w(y + \Delta y, t + \Delta t) + p_m w(y, t + \Delta t) + p_d w(y - \Delta y, t + \Delta t)}{1 + r\Delta t}$$

where:

$$p_u = \frac{\Delta t}{2}\left(\left(\frac{\sigma}{\Delta y}\right)^2 + \frac{\left(r - \frac{\sigma^2}{2}\right)}{\Delta y}\right)$$

$$p_m = 1 - \frac{\sigma^2}{\Delta y^2}\Delta t \qquad (10.35)$$

$$p_d = \frac{\Delta t}{2}\left(\left(\frac{\sigma}{\Delta y}\right)^2 - \frac{\left(r - \frac{\sigma^2}{2}\right)}{\Delta y}\right)$$

Equation 10.35 now gives us a method for inserting values into the grid. If we know the values of the option at time $t + \Delta t$ for three adjacent levels of the market $y + \Delta y$, y, and $y - \Delta y$ (these are the light-shaded cells in Figure 10.31), we can determine $w(y,t)$ – the value of the option at time t (this is the dark-shaded cell in Figure 10.31).

To start the process, we must choose the size of the grid, and the price and time intervals Δy and Δt. If the grid has M price steps and N time intervals, it follows that $\Delta t = T/N$ and it can be shown that a good choice for Δy is $\sigma\sqrt{(3\Delta t)}$. The value of the underlying asset will then range from $S_0 e^{-(M/2)\Delta y}$ to $S_0 e^{+(M/2)\Delta y}$ and with this we can complete the right-most column by filling in the values of the option at expiry. For a call option, the top-right cell in the grid will be $\max(S_0 e^{+(M/2)\Delta y} - X, 0)$, and the rest of that column can be completed in a similar way.

We can then work through the grid right to left, completing one column at a time using the formulae in equation 10.35. There is a slight problem, however, in determining the top and bottom items in each successive column because equation 10.35 would need to know values for the option outside the grid. For example, $w(y_M, \Delta t)$ would need a value for $w(y_{M+1}, 0)$ and $w(y_0, \Delta t)$ would need a value for $w(y_{-1}, 0)$, both of which lie beyond the grid boundaries. Fortunately, there is a solution in both cases. Provided that the grid is big enough, the option will be completely in-the-money at one boundary and completely out-of-the-money at the other. If we are completing the grid for a call option, the value at the top of the column will be the value of the option in the cell immediately below, plus the amount by which the underlying asset price has increased (because an option that is completely in-the-money rises 1:1 with the underlying asset price). Conversely, for a call option, the value of the option at the bottom of the column will be zero, because the underlying asset price will itself be close to zero at the bottom of the grid.

By repeating this process for each column, we gradually complete the grid of option prices, and the value in the centre of the left-most column will be the value of the option at inception – the very thing we are trying to determine. Table 10.7 provides an illustration of the finite difference methodology to price the call option discussed earlier in sections 10.7 through 10.9. Using a 20 × 20 grid, time-to-maturity of exactly one year, strike price of 120, volatility of 30%, and a continuously compounded rate of interest of 14.5%, we obtain the following parameters:

$$
\begin{aligned}
\Delta t &= 0.05 \\
\Delta y &= 0.116190 \\
p_u &= 0.188183 \\
p_m &= 0.666667 \\
p_d &= 0.145150
\end{aligned}
$$

To illustrate exactly how the table was completed, we'll take the following examples:

- $w(y_{20},0) = 199.60$ – this value of the option at expiry is simply the underlying asset price in state 20 of 319.60 less the strike price of 120. Using this rule, we can calculate the final column of the grid.

- $w(y_{20},0.05) = 200.47$ – this uses the rule discussed earlier for a completely in-the-money option and is the value of the option immediately below, namely $w(y_{19},0.05) = 165.41$ plus (319.60–284.54). Using this rule, we can calculate the top row of the grid.

- $w(y_0,0.05) = 0$ – this uses the rule for a completely out-of-the-money option and is defined to be zero. Using this rule, we can calculate the bottom row of the grid.

- $w(y_{19},0.05) = 165.41$ – this uses equation 10.35 and calculates the value as follows: $(0.188183 \times 199.60 + 0.666667 \times 164.54 + 0.145150 \times 133.33)/(1+14.5\% \times 0.05) = 165.41$. Using this rule, we can complete every remaining cell in the grid.

Using these rules, the values for all the cells in the grid can be determined, although only those values in the grey-shaded cells of Table 10.7 are eventually used.

The premium for the option turns out to be 10.37, the value $w(10,1)$ half-way down the first column of the table, and is just 0.3% different from the true

TABLE 10.7

Explicit finite difference method using log transformation

State	T	T−Δt	T−2Δt	T−3Δt	⋯											⋯	3Δt	2Δt	Δt	0	Price at expiry	ln(S)
	1.00	0.95	0.90	0.85	0.80	0.75	0.70	0.65	0.60	0.55	0.50	0.45	0.40	0.35	0.30	0.25	0.20	0.15	0.10	0.05	0.00		
20	215.82	215.06	214.30	213.53	212.75	211.97	211.19	210.40	209.61	208.80	208.00	207.18	206.37	205.54	204.71	203.87	203.03	202.18	201.33	200.47	199.60	319.60	5.77
19	180.76	180.00	179.24	178.47	177.70	176.92	176.13	175.34	174.55	173.75	172.94	172.13	171.31	170.48	169.65	168.82	167.97	167.12	166.27	165.41	164.54	284.54	5.65
18	149.56	148.80	148.03	147.26	146.49	145.71	144.92	144.13	143.33	142.53	141.73	140.91	140.09	139.27	138.44	137.60	136.76	135.91	135.06	134.20	133.33	253.33	5.53
17	121.81	121.05	120.28	119.50	118.72	117.94	117.15	116.35	115.55	114.75	113.94	113.12	112.30	111.48	110.65	109.81	108.97	108.12	107.27	106.41	105.54	225.54	5.42
16	97.21	96.43	95.65	94.86	94.07	93.27	92.47	91.66	90.85	90.04	89.22	88.40	87.57	86.74	85.91	85.07	84.23	83.38	82.53	81.67	80.80	200.80	5.30
15	75.53	74.74	73.93	73.12	72.31	71.49	70.66	69.83	68.99	68.15	67.30	66.46	65.61	64.76	63.91	63.05	62.20	61.35	60.50	59.64	58.77	178.77	5.19
14	56.69	55.88	55.05	54.21	53.37	52.52	51.65	50.78	49.90	49.01	48.12	47.21	46.31	45.39	44.48	43.56	42.66	41.77	40.89	40.03	39.16	159.16	5.07 ⋯
13	40.71	39.89	39.05	38.20	37.34	36.47	35.58	34.67	33.76	32.82	31.87	30.89	29.90	28.89	27.86	26.81	25.74	24.66	23.59	22.57	21.70	141.70	4.95 y+3Δy
12	27.68	26.88	26.07	25.25	24.41	23.55	22.68	21.80	20.89	19.96	19.00	18.02	17.01	15.96	14.87	13.72	12.50	11.20	9.76	8.13	6.16	126.16	4.84 y+2Δy
11	17.61	16.89	16.16	15.42	14.67	13.91	13.14	12.35	11.55	10.73	9.90	9.05	8.17	7.28	6.35	5.39	4.40	3.36	2.28	1.15	0.00	112.32	4.72 y+Δy
10	10.37	9.78	9.19	8.59	7.99	7.39	6.79	6.18	5.58	4.97	4.37	3.78	3.19	2.61	2.05	1.51	1.01	0.57	0.22	0.00	0.00	100.00	4.61 y
9	5.60	5.16	4.73	4.31	3.89	3.47	3.07	2.68	2.30	1.94	1.60	1.27	0.97	0.70	0.47	0.28	0.13	0.04	0.00	0.00	0.00	89.03	4.49 y−Δy
8	2.74	2.46	2.18	1.92	1.67	1.43	1.20	0.99	0.80	0.62	0.47	0.34	0.22	0.14	0.07	0.03	0.01	0.00	0.00	0.00	0.00	79.26	4.37 y−2Δy
7	1.21	1.05	0.89	0.75	0.62	0.51	0.40	0.31	0.23	0.16	0.11	0.07	0.04	0.02	0.01	0.00	0.00	0.00	0.00	0.00	0.00	70.57	4.26 y−3Δy
6	0.48	0.40	0.32	0.26	0.20	0.15	0.11	0.08	0.05	0.03	0.02	0.01	0.00	0.00	0.00	0.00	0.00	0.00	0.00	0.00	0.00	62.83	4.14 ⋯
5	0.17	0.13	0.10	0.08	0.06	0.04	0.03	0.02	0.01	0.01	0.00	0.00	0.00	0.00	0.00	0.00	0.00	0.00	0.00	0.00	0.00	55.94	4.02
4	0.05	0.04	0.03	0.02	0.01	0.01	0.01	0.00	0.00	0.00	0.00	0.00	0.00	0.00	0.00	0.00	0.00	0.00	0.00	0.00	0.00	49.80	3.91
3	0.01	0.01	0.01	0.00	0.00	0.00	0.00	0.00	0.00	0.00	0.00	0.00	0.00	0.00	0.00	0.00	0.00	0.00	0.00	0.00	0.00	44.34	3.79
2	0.00	0.00	0.00	0.00	0.00	0.00	0.00	0.00	0.00	0.00	0.00	0.00	0.00	0.00	0.00	0.00	0.00	0.00	0.00	0.00	0.00	39.47	3.68
1	0.00	0.00	0.00	0.00	0.00	0.00	0.00	0.00	0.00	0.00	0.00	0.00	0.00	0.00	0.00	0.00	0.00	0.00	0.00	0.00	0.00	35.14	3.56
0	0.0007	0.0004	0.0002	0.0001	6E-05	2E-05	9E-06	2E-06	5E-07	6E-08												31.29	3.44

Option values over time / Underlying asset

Black–Scholes value of 10.34 determined earlier. Although we have achieved remarkable accuracy with just a 20×20 grid, in practice you would normally use at least 100 steps, and more likely 300–500 steps. As with the binomial and Monte Carlo models discussed earlier, if finite difference models can generate similar option prices to those generated by the B–S model for simple options where the results can be compared, we can be reasonably confident that finite difference models will do a good job in pricing more complex options where no closed-form model exists.

The methodology described in this section is, in fact, just one of several finite difference methods, the so-called Explicit Finite Difference method using the Log Transformation, and is one of the easiest to implement. There are other finite difference methods, including the Explicit Finite Difference, the Implicit Finite Difference and the Crank-Nicolson methods. Several of the books cited below provide further information about these techniques.[12]

Further reading on option pricing

Those readers wishing to delve deeper into option pricing would do well to start with the original 1973 article by Professors Black and Scholes. Each of the following references then offers a different perspective on this fascinating subject.

Black, Fischer and Scholes, Myron (1973) 'The pricing of options and corporate liabilities', *Journal of Political Economy*, 81, pp. 637–54.

Haug, Espen Gaarder (2007) *The Complete Guide to Option Pricing Formulas*, McGraw-Hill, 2nd edition.

Hull, John C. (2008) *Options, Futures, and other Derivative Securities*, Prentice-Hall, 8th edition.

James, Peter (2003) *Option Theory*, Wiley.

Jarrow, Robert and Rudd, Andrew (1983) *Option Pricing*, Irwin.

Wilmott, Paul (2001) *Paul Wilmott Introduces Quantitative Finance*, Wiley.

Notes

1   The payoff for FRAs is, in fact, very slightly curved due to discounting, in this case deviating from the truly linear by about 2.5% when the reference rate is 500 basis points higher than the contract rate. Nonetheless, FRA payoffs are, to all intents and purposes, linear.

2   Subjective probability is the human perception of likelihood; objective probability is the statistical measurement of likelihood. The objective probability of a fatal airline crash is infinitesimal, but for the passenger with a fear of flying it is the subjective probability that counts. Although one can analyse past market data, it is only subjective probability that matters when considering the future development of market prices.

3   Logarithms to any base could be used, but in finance it is most useful to use natural logarithms (logarithms to the base e).

4   Seeing a 10% return leading to what seems like a 10.52% increase in price should not appear too strange. Exactly the same result would arise if a bank paid interest at 10% per annum but paid interest continuously rather than at discrete intervals. Paid just twice a year, 10% per annum would compound to an effective return of 10.25%, to 10.47% if paid monthly, to 10.5156% daily, and finally to 10.5171% if paid continuously.

5   Equation 10.7 follows from the relationship between the logarithm of an expectation, and the expectation of a logarithm. If x is a random variable, then: $\ln(E[x]) = E[\ln(x)] + 0.5 \times \text{var}[\ln(x)]$.

6   ... but not all rates and prices all of the time. Markets often feature a 'fat-tailed' distribution, with occasional quirky outliers. Section 11.2 explains how this is handled in practice.

7   Line four depicts the real data.

8   If you were to take a piece of wood cut out in the shape of the shaded part, it would balance at exactly the point corresponding to 150.51.

9   See Jarrow and Rudd, p. 94, cited in the further reading section above.

10 See James, pages 78–79, cited in the further reading section above.

11 In mathematics, a differential equation is one which involves a function and its derivatives (the word 'derivative' here being used in the context of calculus). A partial derivative is a derivative of a function where one variable changes and the others are held constant.

12 A short paper by Professor D Chance entitled 'Teaching Note 97–02: Option pricing using finite difference methods', available on the internet, is also very useful.

11

OPTIONS – VOLATILITY
AND THE GREEKS

This chapter starts with an extensive discussion of volatility, introduced in the previous chapter, and an essential ingredient for pricing options. Later we will introduce the 'Greeks', most of which measure how sensitive the option premium is to changes in the pricing variables. Finally we look at the way in which banks use *delta hedging* to manage their option books, and show how the costs of so doing compare with the premiums they receive.

11.1 Volatility

No matter which model we use, whether a closed-form model like Black–Scholes, a binomial model, a Monte Carlo simulation or a finite difference method, we will always need the same basic five inputs that we first listed in the previous chapter (section 10.5).

- underlying asset price
- strike price
- time to option expiry
- 'carry' (a combination of interest rates and potential earnings on the underlying asset)
- volatility of the underlying asset price.

Four of these five inputs are easy to obtain. The underlying asset price and the level of interest rates can be read directly from any quote screen. The strike price and time to maturity are negotiated when the option terms are discussed and are written into the contract. Potential earnings on the underlying asset are either known with certainty (e.g. bond coupons), or can be predicted with considerable accuracy (e.g. forthcoming dividends on shares). The fifth variable, however, is definitely more obscure: the variability of the underlying asset, or *volatility*.

Volatility has already been defined as the *annualised standard deviation of returns* (it was one of the parameters of equation 10.3 in the previous chapter). Note that this definition does not refer to the variability of the prices directly but to the variability of the returns that generate these prices. As an illustration of how volatility may be calculated, Table 11.1 provides a full illustration, and is based on the £/$ exchange rate during March 2011.

Price relatives are calculated from the raw prices by taking the ratio of successive prices. The returns are then calculated according to equation 10.1 in the previous chapter as the logarithm of the price relatives. The mean and standard deviation of returns follow standard statistical procedures using the formulae:

$$\mu = \sum_{i=1}^{N} \frac{x_i}{N} \text{ and } \sigma = \sqrt{\sum_{i=1}^{N} \frac{(x_i - \mu)^2}{N - 1}}$$

where x_i is the i'th price relative and N is the total number of observations. These formulae are built into Excel as the AVERAGE and STDEV functions.

Using the latter, the standard deviation or volatility of daily price relatives is 0.4599%. To convert this to an annual figure, it is necessary to multiply this by the square root of the number of working days in a year, normally taken to be 252. This gives an annualised volatility of 7.30% for the £/$ FX rate during the month of March 2011.

TABLE 11.1
Calculating historic volatility

Date	£/$ rate	Price relatives	Log price relatives
28 Feb	1.6226		
01 Mar	1.6285	1.003636	0.3630%
02 Mar	1.6312	1.001658	0.1657%
03 Mar	1.6273	0.997609	−0.2394%
04 Mar	1.6266	0.999570	−0.0430%
07 Mar	1.6244	0.998647	−0.1353%
08 Mar	1.6162	0.994952	−0.5061%
09 Mar	1.6207	1.002784	0.2780%
10 Mar	1.6115	0.994323	−0.5693%
11 Mar	1.6029	0.994663	−0.5351%
14 Mar	1.6141	1.006987	0.6963%
15 Mar	1.6051	0.994424	−0.5591%
16 Mar	1.6062	1.000685	0.0685%
17 Mar	1.6137	1.004669	0.4659%
18 Mar	1.6179	1.002603	0.2599%
21 Mar	1.6282	1.006366	0.6346%
22 Mar	1.6382	1.006142	0.6123%
23 Mar	1.6249	0.991881	−0.8152%
24 Mar	1.6156	0.994277	−0.5740%
25 Mar	1.6077	0.995110	−0.4902%
28 Mar	1.6003	0.995397	−0.4613%
29 Mar	1.5977	0.998375	−0.1626%
30 Mar	1.6044	1.004194	0.4185%
31 Mar	1.6057	1.000810	0.0810%

Source: FX rates from www.oand.com, and author's calculations.

Standard deviation of log price relatives (using Excel STDEV) = 0.4599%

Annual volatility = 0.4599% × $\sqrt{252}$ = 7.30%

In performing these calculations there is a compromise over how many observations to include. The reliability of the answer will improve the more observations are included. However, figures taken from the distant past may no longer be relevant in calculating today's volatility. Commonly, between 20 and 50 observations provide a reasonable balance

There are a number of adjustments that can be made to this method. One is to weight recent price relatives more heavily. Another is to use an alternative formula which includes the day's range as well as successive closing prices. However, no matter how sophisticated the method used, all the calculations produce a figure for *historic volatility* which, of course, is backward-looking. What is required, though, is a figure for *future volatility*. After all, it is the future variability of returns that is relevant for pricing an option expiring in the future, not the past variability.

The problem is that future volatility cannot ever be measured directly because the variability of returns needed for the calculation has yet to happen. Although future volatility cannot be measured directly, the subjective market consensus can be observed indirectly. Market-makers must use some figure for volatility in order to price an option. If option prices can be calculated from volatility, then volatility can also be determined from option prices. The idea is to use an option pricing model 'backwards', as depicted in Figure 11.1.

Normally, an option pricing model calculates the option price from volatility and other information. Used in the opposite sense, the model can calculate the volatility implied by the option price. Not surprisingly, volatility measured in this way is called *implied volatility*. The only problem is that there is no way to invert a closed-form model like the B–S formulae of equations 10.19 and 10.20 in the previous chapter. Instead, it is necessary to use a trial-and-error approach, and gradually iterate towards the right answer.

As an example, on 29th April 2011 Microsoft shares were trading at $25.92 and paying a dividend yield of 2.47%. The calls expiring 16th July 2011 and struck at $26 were trading at a premium of $0.79. At the time, three-month US dollar interest rates were 0.273%. By using a modified closed-form model which takes dividends into account, and a trial-and-error approach, we can arrive at an implied volatility of 18.58% after just three iterations, as Table 11.2 shows. The first two iterations of 20% and 15% were guesses, while the final one was obtained by linear interpolation and proved to be exactly correct. Since quotations for option prices are readily available, and most participants in the market use similar or identical pricing models, evaluating implied volatility is therefore relatively straightforward and is much more appropriate than using historic volatility.

FIGURE 11.1

Calculating implied volatility using an option pricing model

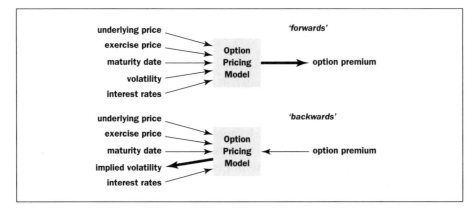

TABLE 11.2
Calculating implied volatility for a MSFT call option

Iteration	Volatility	Option premium
1	20%	0.8573
2	15%	0.6199
3	18.58%	0.7900

So, historic volatility is backward-looking, while implied volatility is forward-looking. As they are looking in opposite directions, we should not expect them to be the same. To illustrate the contrast between historic and implied volatility, Figure 11.2 shows how these compare in the period January 2009 to April 2011 for the S&P 500 stock market index. Historic volatility was calculated by looking back over the previous month's S&P 500 closing prices, and performing the same calculation as that shown in Table 11.1. For implied volatility, the chart uses the 30-day VIX, a well-known volatility index based on the S&P 500, and described later in this chapter. The broad trends in the two charts are similar – a

FIGURE 11.2
Comparison of historic and implied volatility for the S&P 500

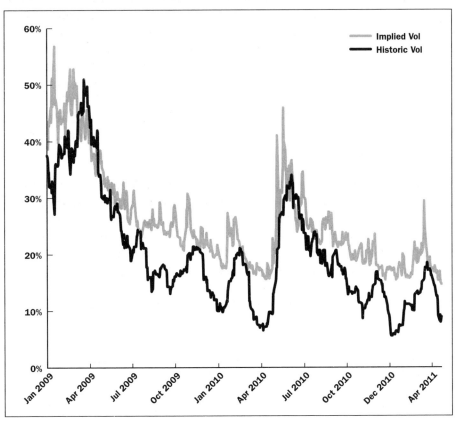

Source: Implied volatility data from CBOE, historical volatility data from www.finance.yahoo.com, and author's calculations.

gradual fall from April 2009 to April 2010, a spike into mid-May, then another fall to the end of 2010 – and the correlation between them was 0.89. However, the actual figures were somewhat different. On average, over the period under observation, implied volatility was around 5.6% higher than historic volatility, and the standard deviation of the difference between the two volatilities was 4.4%. We will see at the end of the chapter why it is usually the case that implied volatility is systematically higher than historic volatility.

While volatility refers directly to the variability of returns, it is nonetheless possible to use volatility to make inferences about the distribution of prices. If annual returns are normally distributed with mean μ and standard deviation (or volatility) σ, we can make the following statements:

a) The mean price at time t is $S_0 e^{(\mu + \sigma^2/2)t}$.

b) The median price at time t is $S_0 e^{\mu t}$.

c) There is a 68.3% chance that prices will fall in the range $S_0 e^{\mu t - \sigma \sqrt{t}}$ and $S_0 e^{\mu t + \sigma \sqrt{t}}$.

d) There is a 95.4% chance that prices will fall in the range $S_0 e^{\mu t - 2\sigma \sqrt{t}}$ and $S_0 e^{\mu t + 2\sigma \sqrt{t}}$.

To illustrate this, consider once again the example where $\mu = 10\%$, $\sigma = 30\%$ and $S_0 = 100$. After one year, the mean price will be 115.60 as determined before, while the median price will be 110.52. Some people get confused between means and medians, as they are both averages of a sort. Consider taking 1,000 different shares, all starting at a price of 100, and all having returns normally distributed with μ and σ as above. The arithmetic average of the 1,000 share prices at the end of the year would be 115.60; this is the mean price. However, half the shares would have a price below 110.52, while half would have a price above 110.52; this is the median price. If prices were distributed normally, the mean and the median would be the same, but as they follow an asymmetric lognormal distribution, the mean and the median will be different.[1]

Also after one year, it is likely that 683 of the share prices will fall in the range 81.87–149.18. The figure of 683 comes from a property of the normal distribution, where 68.3% of the distribution falls in the range ±1 standard deviation. Similarly, 954 of the share prices should fall in the range 60.65–201.38, the proportion of 95.4% also being a property of the normal distribution.

Figure 11.3 illustrates the 'volatility envelope' resulting from a Monte Carlo simulation of the evolution of these asset prices in this example over one year. The bars mark the 68.3% confidence interval over time, while the central line shows the growth in the median price.

11.2 Volatility smiles and skews

One of the key assumptions behind the B–S option pricing model is that the returns on financial assets follow a normal distribution, and asset prices them-

FIGURE 11.3
Volatility envelope

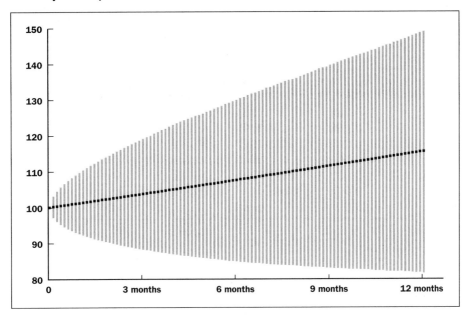

selves therefore follow a lognormal distribution. (The mathematics behind this was explored at length in section 10.6 in the previous chapter.) It's now time to explore whether or not this assumption is true.

To illustrate this here we picked just one market – the equities market – and just one underlier – Microsoft. However, extensive research by others demonstrates that what we found with Microsoft's share price over the 11-year period from 2000–2010 inclusive applies to nearly all other financial instruments across a wide range of markets.

We took 2,767 daily closing prices for Microsoft's share price from 3rd January 2000 to 31st December 2010, adjusted these for dividend payments, and calculated the 2,766 log price relatives just like we did in Table 11.1. The average daily volatility was 2.21% of the 11-year period, and the mean return was virtually zero. If the returns on Microsoft's shares were normally distributed, then 68.3% of the 2,766 values should fall in the range ±2.21% or ±1σ, and we should therefore expect to see 1,888 such occurrences. In fact, we counted 2,175 observations falling within this range, about 15% more than expected. Compensating for this, however, was the outcome in the 1σ–2σ range, where 752 occurrences were expected but only 448 observed in practice. Combine these two results, and the actual outcomes over the entire ±2σ range almost exactly match the expectations. So far so good, you may think, but the sting is in the tail, as Table 11.3 shows.

TABLE 11.3

Behaviour of MSFT stock price from 2000–2010

Standard deviations	Probability	Odds	Expected frequency	Number of occurrences	
				Expected	Actual
0–1	68.27%	2 in 3	most days	1,888	2,175
1–2	27.18%	1 in 4	1 week	752	448
2–3	4.28%	1 in 23	1 month	118	101
3–4	0.26%	1 in 379	1.5 yrs	7	25
4–5	0.01%	1 in 15,931	63 yrs	0	8
5–6	0.00%	1 in 1.75m	6,900 yrs	0	5
6–7	0.00%	1 in 507m	2m yrs	0	0
7–8	0.00%	1 in 391bn	2bn yrs	0	3
8–9	0.00%	never		0	1

Table 11.3 divides up the returns distribution into nine bands, and compares the actual number of observations occurring in each band with what would be expected if the returns were normally distributed. We have already discussed the $0\sigma–1\sigma$ band, which runs from -1σ to $+1\sigma$, and the $1\sigma–2\sigma$ band, which is in two parts from -2σ to -1σ and from $+1\sigma$ to $+2\sigma$, and have seen that actual outcomes match expectations for the aggregate of these two bands. The $2\sigma–3\sigma$ band also presents few surprises. However, things begin to go wrong in the $3\sigma–4\sigma$ band, where we would expect to see such outcomes on average once every $1\frac{1}{2}$ years or so, around 7 over the 11-year observation period – but we witnessed 25 such outcomes.

It gets worse. You would expect to experience a $4\sigma–5\sigma$ outcome (let's call this a 4σ event for brevity) only once in a working lifetime, so it would be somewhat unlikely to happen in the arbitrary 11-year period we selected – but it happened 8 times in our sample. A 5σ event is even less likely, and should only happen once every 6,900 years or so. We would have to journey back to pre-biblical times to witness the last such event, and it would be very odd for such a rare outcome to happen even once in the current 11-year period, but 5 such events occurred! Although it so happens that no 6σ events happened in our sample, this is more than made up by the surprises that follow. A 7σ event is so rare that it should occur only once every 2bn years – that's just twice since the planet Earth was formed around 4.5bn years ago. To witness three such events just in the last 11 years is astonishing. Finally, an 8σ event is so incredibly extraordinary that, according to the normal distribution, it should never occur, not since the beginning of time. Yet one did, on 19 October 2000 as it happens, to the MSFT share price that day when the company posted unexpectedly good earnings figures that day.

Clearly, something odd is happening, and a glance at Figure 11.4 illustrates the problem. The histogram is the distribution of actual asset returns for MSFT over the 11-year period, while the line depicts the closest normal distribution that can be fitted to the actual distribution. The most prominent feature of the histogram is the tall peak in the middle, but the real problem arises from the

FIGURE 11.4

Actual distribution of asset prices

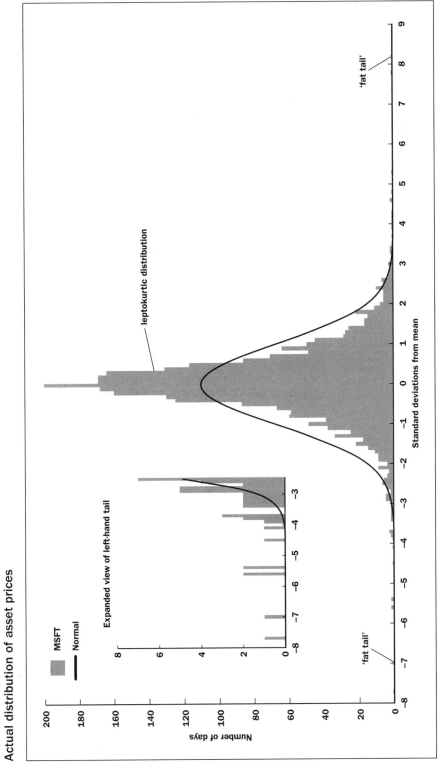

Source: Microsoft share price data from finance.yahoo.com, and author's calculations.

little 'blips' in the tails, which are pictured more clearly in the inset chart which focuses on the left-hand tail. *Fat tails* and a tall centre region are features of a leptokurtic distribution, where kurtosis is the property of a statistical distribution which measures its shape.

Now that we have established that returns are not, in fact, normally distributed but have a fat-tailed distribution, let's explore the implications for option pricing. Recall from section 10.7 in the previous chapter that a key component of calculating the premium of an option is to determine the probability of exercise. Get that wrong, and the option premium will be wrong. Unfortunately, the results tabulated in Table 11.3 clearly demonstrate that if we assume that returns are normally distributed, we will get the probabilities wrong, especially for out-of-the-money options.

To illustrate the problem, let's price some options on Microsoft assuming that daily volatility is 2.21%, like that experienced over the 2000–2010 period. Multiplying this by $\sqrt{252}$ gives an annual volatility of 35.08% which we will round to 35% for convenience. Let's also assume a three-month interest rate of 0.24% p.a. and an annual dividend yield of 2.47%. Using an adapted version of equation 10.13 in the previous chapter we can calculate $\mu = r - d - \sigma^2/2 = -8.35\%$. Assuming that we start with an initial share price of $25, a -2σ move corresponds to a drop in price down to:

$$\$25 \times e^{-8.35\% \times 0.25 - 2 \times 35\% \sqrt{0.25}} = \$17.25$$

Likewise, -3σ and -4σ moves correspond to asset prices of 14.48 and 12.16. Using a modified version of the closed-form model of equation 10.21 in the previous chapter, Table 11.4 prices three out-of-the-money puts at these strike levels. We can also adapt equation 10.17 to determine the probability of exercise of these puts as $1 - N(d_2)$, and these probabilities are also shown in the table. Finally, remembering that the analysis presented in Table 11.3 was based on 2,766 observations, we can estimate on how many occasions the respective puts would be exercised over the 11-year period, and these are shown in the penultimate row of Table 11.4 as 'Expected # occasions'.

Starting with the $17.25 strike put, the option pricing model produces a premium of 2.41¢, a 2.27% probability of exercise, and exercise on around 63 occasions. This agrees quite well with the empirical results from Table 11.3, where there were 143 events larger than 2σ, of which half would be -2σ events and the other half $+2\sigma$ events, hence the figure of 71.5 in Table 11.4 as the 'Actual # occasions'. However, the option pricing model appears to break down when it comes to pricing the other two puts. At 0.09¢ the premium for the $14.48 strike put is tiny, and the $12.16 strike put is virtually free (around 1/1000th of a cent). Worse, these options would respectively be around 6× and 100× more likely to be exercised in practice than the model expects. A bank

TABLE 11.4

Pricing MSFT put options with a smile

	Basic data	Constant volatility			Adjusted volatility		
Spot	25.00						
Time to maturity	0.25						
Interest rate	0.24%						
Dividend yield	2.47%						
Strike		17.25	14.48	12.16	17.25	14.48	12.16
Moneyness		−2.0σ	−3.0σ	−4.0σ	−1.9σ	−2.4σ	−2.7σ
Volatility		35.0%	35.0%	35.0%	35.9%	42.7%	49.9%
Premium		0.0241	0.0009	0.0000	0.0286	0.0072	0.0026
Probability of exercise		2.27%	0.13%	0.00%	2.58%	0.76%	0.31%
Expected # occasions		62.8	3.7	0.1	71.5	21.0	8.5
Actual # occasions		71.5	21.0	8.5	71.5	21.0	8.5

selling these options at the premiums suggested by the option pricing model would almost certainly lose money.

The problem arises, of course, because option pricing models like the B–S model assume that asset returns are normally distributed when in practice the distribution is fat-tailed. One way of handling this is to tweak the model inputs to adjust for this when pricing out-of-the-money options. In the right-hand side of Table 11.4 we have increased the volatility input so that the probability of exercise predicted by the model matches the empirical figures found in practice. For example, Table 11.3 showed that there were 17 events more severe than 4σ, and we can assume that half or 8.5 were more negative than −4σ. By increasing the implied volatility from 35% to 49.9%, the option pricing model matches this figure. An important consequence of this adjustment is that the premium for this put option increases from virtually zero to a more respectable 0.26¢. This might not sound much, but it is almost 200 times larger than before, and is the kind of premium a bank would need to charge in order not to suffer from these tail events.

This adjustment to the volatility input is exactly what is done in practice. Banks increase the implied volatility input when pricing out-of-the-money options to cope with the fact that, in practice, freak events happen more frequently (pun intended) than the normal distribution suggests. This most readily can be seen if one draws a chart of implied volatility against strike price, when a U-shaped curve can easily be seen. This is called the *volatility smile* and is illustrated in Figure 11.5, which plots the set of volatility smiles for Microsoft options on 29th April 2011. On that date MSFT shares were trading at $25.92, so we used OTM puts struck at $25 and below to plot the left-hand side of the curve, and OTM calls struck at $26 and above to plot the right-hand side.

FIGURE 11.5

Volatility smiles for MSFT on 29 Apr 2011

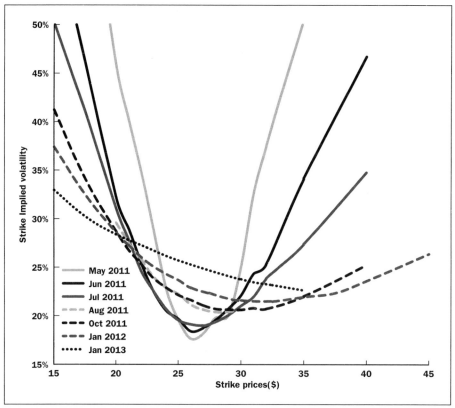

Source: Option price data from CBOE, plus author's calculations.

Two other features of implied volatility are evident from Figure 11.5. One aspect is that some of the curves – particularly those relating to the longer-dated options – are skewed to the left. The implied volatility for deep out-of-the-money puts appears to be somewhat higher than that for deep out-of-the-money calls. This *volatility skew* is a feature of many financial markets, and is almost always negative (skewed to the left) for equity options like the ones pictured in Figure 11.5. This follows from the typical behaviour of the equity market; if there is a sudden move in equity prices it is more likely to be a sharp drop than a sharp rise. Market-makers are therefore at greater risk when selling OTM put options than when selling OTM calls, and the option premiums – and hence implied volatilities – reflect this.

The second aspect is that the curves differ for options having different maturity dates. For the ATM options struck at $26, implied volatility is higher the longer the maturity. It appears that there is a term structure of volatilities analogous to the term structure of interest rates (i.e. the yield curve) first mentioned in Chapter 2. This arises in the options world because the market perceives that uncertainty increases as you look further and further into the future, and so tends to price longer-dated options at a higher implied volatility than shorter-dated options. While we all expect that the premium for a long-dated option should be more expensive than that for the equivalent short-dated option, all option pricing models explicitly take care of this without needing to manually change the volatility input. For example, in the B–S model, the volatility term σ is always multiplied by $\sqrt{t}$, wherever it appears. The tendency nonetheless to use higher implied volatilities for pricing longer-dated options reflects the higher subjective risk associated with these options.

Instead of displaying the volatility smile for each maturity as a separate line, one can combine all the implied volatilities into a single 3D volatility surface, like the one pictured in Figure 11.6. This shows the smile characteristic as the x-axis (left-to-right) and the term structure feature as the z-axis (depth of chart). Constructing a smooth 3D surface allows one to interpolate a value for implied volatility between specific strikes and maturity dates, so that any arbitrary option on that underlier can be priced.

Some of the implications of the volatility smile may seem a little bizarre. If one thinks of volatility in the literal sense as being the extent to which the underlying asset price fluctuates, then how can two options on the same underlier with the same maturity date have two different volatilities? There is more than one answer to this apparent conundrum.

First, one can simply accept that option pricing models are good representations of reality, but are not perfect. In order to handle one of their deficiencies – the assumption of normally distributed returns in a non-normal world – tweaking the volatility input is a pragmatic solution. This has best been summarised by Riccardo Rebonato when he said that 'implied volatility is the wrong number to put in the wrong formula to obtain the right price'.[2]

A second approach is to think of the volatility smile as a way to use the tool we have – option pricing models that assume a normal distribution of returns – in the real world where market returns have a leptokurtic distribution. Instead of using just a single normal distribution, let's combine several, as depicted in Figure 11.7. For at-the-money options we will use the tall-thin normal distribution (low implied volatility), labelled ND1. For slightly out-of-the-money options we will switch to the slightly shorter and wider normal distribution (intermediate implied volatility), labelled ND2. Finally, for very out-of-the-money options we will use the short and very wide distribution (high implied volatility) labelled ND3. The composite result, shown with a black line, is a passable likeness to the fat-tailed real-world distribution shown earlier in Figure 11.4.

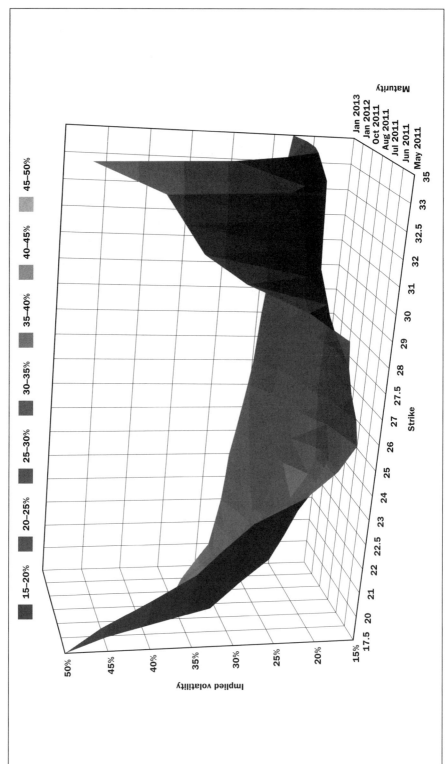

FIGURE 11.6
Volatility surface for MSFT on 29 Apr 2011

FIGURE 11.7

Synthesising a fat-tailed distribution

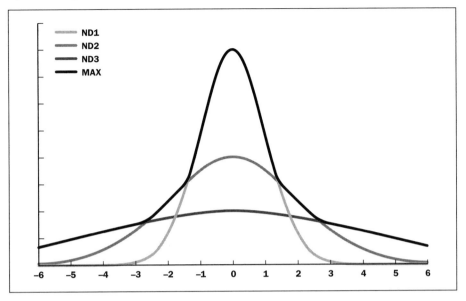

11.3 The VIX

The VIX volatility index was introduced to the world by the Chicago Board Options Exchange (CBOE) in 1993 and has since become a widely quoted index. It is often dubbed the 'investor's fear gauge' because the price and implied volatility of equity options is closely connected with the market's uncertainty (= fear) about the future.

The VIX was originally defined as the average implied volatility of eight 30-day ATM options on the S&P 100. As it would be most unusual on any given day to find options which had strike prices exactly ATM and maturities of exactly 30 days, the methodology used a two-step interpolation process. First, two strike prices straddling the ATM level and two maturities straddling the 30-day target maturity were selected. At each of the four strike–maturity combinations CBOE calculated the simple average of the implied volatilities of the put and the call. At each maturity, CBOE then interpolated between the implied volatilities at the two strikes to find the ATM volatility. Finally, CBOE interpolated between the ATM implied volatilities at the two maturities to find the 30-day implied volatility, and hence the VIX. If you review this process, you will see why eight options were needed: a put and a call at each of two strikes and two maturities.

In 2003, CBOE revised the methodology for calculating the VIX, making three important changes. First, the calculations are now based on S&P 500 options, which is a broader-based stock index. Second, all OTM options are used, provided their bid prices are non-zero, rather than just ATM options. This makes the new VIX reflect the entire volatility curve, including smile and skew effects. Finally, a completely different model is used to perform the actual calculations. Rather than deduce volatility by using a B–S model, the new VIX calculates volatility as the weighted average of actual option premiums. The framework was first suggested in a research note published in 1999 and provides a more solid foundation for the practical use of the VIX as the underlier for various derivative contracts.[3] In fact, shortly after the methodology was introduced, the CBOE launched futures and options contracts on the VIX, and trading volume in these derivatives exceeds 100,000 contracts every day.

In the context of comparing historical and implied volatility, Figure 11.2 already illustrated the behaviour of the VIX over a two-year period from 2009 to 2011. From a different perspective, Figure 11.8 compares the VIX with the underlying S&P 500 index over an 11-year period from 2000 to 2011. This figure vividly shows the negative correlation between these two indices, in both the long term and the short term. Three long-term trends which are clearly visible are the rise in the S&P 500 from 2003 to 2007, the collapse from 2007 to 2009, and the subsequent recovery since then. These are accompanied by a fall in the VIX from around 35% in 2003 down to 10% in 2007, followed by a sharp rise to 80% in 2009, and then another fall to around 15% in mid-2011 as confidence continued to return to the market. Short-term correlation is also evident. For example, when the S&P 500 dropped by 9.2% on 29th September 2008 amidst the turmoil of the credit crisis, the VIX rose by 27% the same day. These figures also highlight another feature of the VIX – the index itself is very volatile. In 2010, the annualised volatility of the VIX was 116%, compared with just 18% for the S&P 500 itself.

More recently, volatility indices have been introduced to other global stock markets. For example, in 2005 Eurex introduced VSTOXX, VDAX-NEW and the VSMI volatility indices, based respectively on the Euro STOXX 50, DAX and SMI stock indices, followed later by a range of tradable futures and options.

As indices like the VIX, VSTOXX and others have gained visibility and acceptance, derivative products based on volatility – both exchange-traded and OTC – have grown in importance. Starting as an input into an option pricing model, volatility nowadays is considered an asset class in its own right, and volatility derivatives such as VIX futures and the volatility swaps introduced in Chapter 8 can be traded just like derivatives on equities, bonds and commodities.

11.4 Value profiles prior to maturity

Together, this chapter and the previous one have so far introduced options, reviewed several different models for determining the fair premium, and discussed the importance of one pricing variable in particular – volatility. Early in the previous chapter we reviewed the hockey-stick payoff profile of an option at maturity illustrated, for example, in Figure 10.9. With all this work behind us, we can now explore the payoff profile of an option prior to maturity.

FIGURE 11.8
VIX and SPX compared

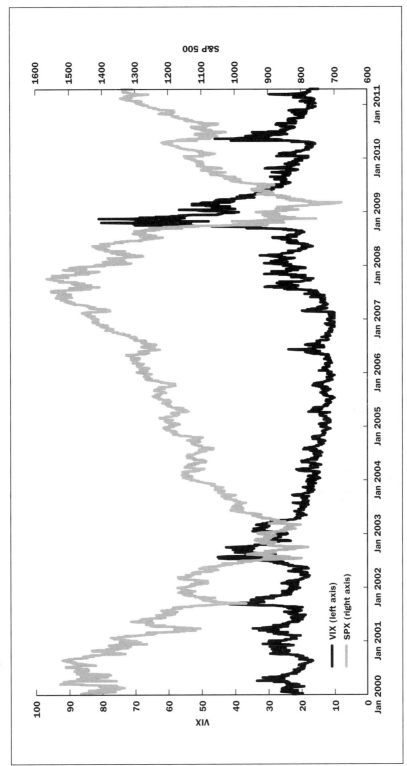

Source: CBOE.

Recall that all option pricing models require the same five inputs, as reviewed at the beginning of section 11.1:

- underlying asset price
- strike price
- time to option expiry
- carry
- volatility of the underlying asset price.

Note that there is no need to make any assumption about the future expectations for the price of the underlying asset. In an efficient market, these expectations will already have been taken into account, and will be reflected in the current price of the underlying asset. To consider them again would be double counting.

Using any of the models described in the previous chapter, it is now possible to derive a satisfactory and fair price for an option prior to maturity. Figure 11.9 shows what a typical call option looks like six months prior to expiry, two months prior to expiry and at the expiry date itself, for various values of the underlying asset price. To create the curves, we used the standard B–S model of equations 10.19 and 10.20 in the previous chapter, and priced a call option similar to the one that we have priced several times before, with these characteristics:

- Underlying asset price: 100
- Strike price: 100
- Continuously compounded rate: 14.5% p.a. (implies an annual carry cost of 15.6%)
- Volatility: 30%

This happens to be based on an equity option, and this and the remaining sections in this chapter use this specific option as the principal example. However, the findings are quite general and can be applied to options on almost any underlying asset.

The pair of straight lines that was typical for the profile of an option at maturity is now replaced with a curve. The option with 180 days to expiry features quite a smooth curve, but as time passes, the smooth curve gradually approaches the straight line profile characteristic of an option at maturity. Not surprisingly, longer-dated options are more expensive than shorter-dated ones.

As we already know, the total premium of an option can be split into two components, intrinsic value and time value, and Figure 11.10 portrays the value of the 180-day option in a different way to emphasise these two components.

When we first looked at option pricing (in section 10.5) we saw that the art and science of pricing an option prior to maturity is really a question of pricing the time value. Figure 11.10 makes this clear – for a given strike and underlying price, an option's intrinsic value is the same both at and prior to maturity.

FIGURE 11.9

Value of an option prior to maturity

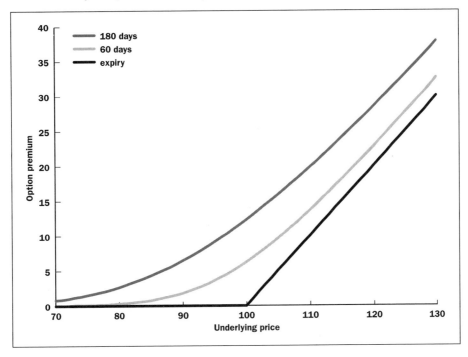

FIGURE 11.10

Intrinsic value and time value for call option

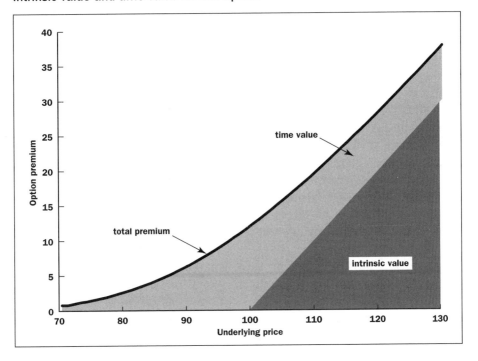

The same figure also confirms what we saw earlier, that time value is greatest for ATM options. Interestingly enough, the figure reveals something else, that time value is greater for the illustrated ITM option than for the corresponding OTM option.

In section 10.5 we introduced the conceptual foundation of time value:

**An option buyer has the right to decide later whether
or not to exercise the option.
The time value of the option is the value of this right.**

In fact, just as an option premium can be split into two components – intrinsic value and time value – time value itself can be split into two components. The dominant aspect of time value is the one defined above – the value to the owner in being able to decide later whether or not to exercise the option. From the viewpoint of the holder of an option, this aspect of time value invariably has a positive value. It is always advantageous to be able to delay until the last moment the decision whether or not to exercise, because it provides the opportunity for the holder to change his mind if he so wishes. As we saw in the example in Table 10.3, there is not so much benefit in the case of options which are deep in-the-money or deep out-of-the-money, because it is already fairly clear which way the decision will go. In contrast, the ability to defer the decision is of greatest benefit to the holder of an ATM option because the ultimate decision could easily go either way. This explains why time value is greatest for ATM options and less for OTM and ITM options.

The second component of time value is common to a number of derivative instruments:

**The value to the option buyer in being able to defer the cash flows
arising from the sale or purchase of the underlying asset when the
option is exercised.**

This is effectively the cost-of-carry, and there is a difference here between OTM and ITM options, between calls and puts, and between options on cash instruments and options on derivatives. To explain all this, let's first assume that interest rates are higher than any earnings (e.g. dividends) generated by the underlying asset, so that there is a cost (rather than a benefit) in carrying the underlying asset – negative carry.

When a market-maker writes an ITM call option, there is a more than likely chance that the option will be exercised, and the market-maker therefore needs to buy some of the underlying asset as a hedge. In a negative carry world, this will incur a net financing cost. In contrast, when writing OTM options it is not so necessary to buy the underlying asset, and the net financing cost is therefore not so great. This explains why ITM call options have a greater time value than the corresponding OTM options.

With this component of time value, however, there is a difference between European-style calls and puts. When a call is exercised, the holder pays over a sum of money equal to the strike price and receives the underlying asset. The holder gains an advantage in deferring this cash flow because the money can be invested to earn interest in the meantime. This advantage to the holder (and disadvantage to the writer) is reflected in a larger time value for ITM calls. In contrast, when a put is exercised, the holder delivers the underlying asset and receives a sum of money equal to the strike price. Delaying exercise is a disadvantage for the holder of a put option because it is now the writer of the option who can earn interest on the strike price.

In a negative carry world, this second component of time value is therefore *positive* for ITM calls on cash instruments and *negative* for ITM puts. This difference can be seen by comparing Figure 11.10, which showed time value for a call option, with Figure 11.11, which illustrates time value for the corresponding put option.

It is interesting to note that, for values of the underlying asset below \$92, this put option has negative time value. The put option gives the holder the right to sell the underlying asset and receive cash. As the underlying asset price falls progressively below the strike price, it becomes more and more likely that the put will be exercised. The magnitude of the first component of time value therefore becomes progressively smaller and smaller. As this option was priced in an environment where carry costs 15.60% p.a., it becomes an increasing disadvantage for the holder to have to wait before being able to exchange the underlying asset for cash and earn the 15.60% carry. The second component of time value

FIGURE 11.11
Intrinsic value and time value for put option

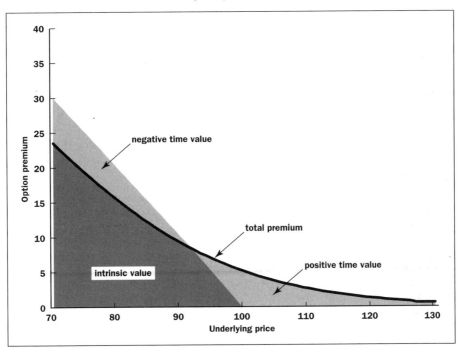

is therefore negative in this case and becomes progressively larger as the under-lying asset price falls. At \$92 the two components cancel out, while below this point the negative second component dominates the positive first component, and the net time value is negative.

The second component of time value, the cost-of-carry, is predominantly a feature for options on cash instruments, for which there is an explicit interest cost involved in holding the underlying asset. With options on derivative instru-ments, for example options on futures or options on swaps, there is little or no such cost. For these options, only the first component of time value is sig-nificant, and there will be an almost perfect symmetry between OTM and ITM options,[4] and also between calls and puts.

Before leaving the topic of value profiles, we should pause to consider American-style options. Until now, we have concentrated solely on the pricing of European-style options. At first sight, it would seem that an American option should be worth more than its European counterpart, because it gives the holder the right to exercise the option at any time, including the maturity date, whereas exercising a European option can be done only on the maturity date itself. Since an American option gives the holder everything a European option offers, plus more, the American option should be worth more. Whether this is actually the case will turn upon the answer to the question: is it ever rational for the holder of an option to exercise it prior to maturity?

The simple answer is no. When an option is exercised, the holder receives only the intrinsic value. If, on the other hand, the option is *sold*, the holder receives the full value of the option, including the time value. In almost all cir-cumstances, as the holder of an option will receive more if the option is sold rather than exercised, it is irrational to exercise an American option prior to maturity. This is captured in the aphorism that an option is worth more alive than dead. The one quality that distinguishes an American from a European option is the ability to exercise it prior to maturity, but if it is not rational to do so, there is then no reason why an American option should be worth more than its European counterpart after all.

In most circumstances, an American option is worth just the same as a European option with the same characteristics. Models like the B–S model, which were designed to price only European options, can usually be used to value and price American options as well.

There are exceptions, however, and one situation arises whenever an option, if it were European, would have a negative time value. In those circumstances, the option is worth more dead than alive and it does become rational for early exercise to take place.

The phenomenon of negative time value has already been discussed earlier in this section, and can arise under certain conditions when a European option is deep in-the-money fairly close to maturity. Under these circumstances the first component of time value – the value of deferring the decision whether or not to exercise – will be a small positive value. However, the second component – the value of deferring the cash flows upon exercise – may be a larger negative value. There are a number of examples where this can occur.

(a) When carry is negative (interest rates higher than dividend yields), deep ITM puts may have negative time value.

(b) When carry is positive (interest rates lower than dividend yields), deep ITM calls may have negative time value.

(c) In the case of currency options, negative time value can arise for European puts on low interest-rate currencies or European calls on high interest-rate currencies. When these options are exercised, the holder can exchange a low rate currency for a high rate currency, and so there is a disadvantage in deferring exercise.

(d) Negative time value can also arise for European options on futures when these are deep in-the-money. When a futures option is exercised, the holder receives the underlying futures contract marked-to-market at the prevailing price. Any profit on the future is then realised in cash, which can be invested to earn interest. There is therefore a disadvantage for holders of both calls and puts in deferring the exercise of a deep-in-the-money futures option, because the opportunity to earn interest on the variation margin is lost.

When valuing American options under these circumstances, the potential for early exercise needs to be taken into account. Figure 11.12 illustrates the similarity between European and American calls in a negative carry environment, but the divergence between the pricing of European and American puts in the same situation, where the possibility of early exercise makes the American put always more valuable than the European put. It is worthwhile noting from the chart that the European put has negative time value when the underlying asset price falls below $92. However, the potential for early exercise ensures that the American put can never have negative time value; while it is zero below $80 when the American put just trades at its intrinsic value, the time value is never negative. In all cases the options are struck at $100 and have one year to mature in an environment where the continuously compounded interest rate is 14.5% p.a. (implying an annual carry cost of 15.60%).

Since the possibility for early exercise is taken into account when valuing an American option, the prospect of negative time value consequently disappears. However, there will be a range of prices when such an option has positive time value and is still in-the-money. This raises the question: if an American option has a positive time value, should it ever be exercised in practice?

Again the simple answer is no, because it will usually be better to sell the option than to exercise it. However, there can be exceptions. When an American option is exercised before maturity, any time value is lost, but the present intrinsic value is captured. If instead the holder exercises the option at maturity, the intrinsic value at that time is realised. If it is expected that the intrinsic value may fall, and this decline is greater than the time value sacrificed, early exercise may be warranted. This may happen if the underlying asset is expected to make

FIGURE 11.12

Contrast between prices of American and European options

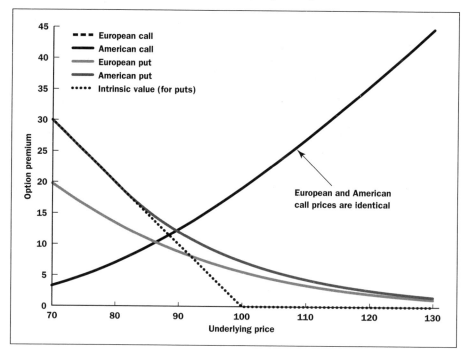

a cash distribution, for example when a share pays a dividend. Holders of the share itself will receive the benefit, but holders of the call option do not, and suffer moreover from the drop in share price when the share goes ex-dividend. Exercising an American call option may be advantageous just prior to a dividend payment if the time value sacrificed is less than the dividend received.

11.5 How options behave – the Greeks

As readers must by now appreciate, options are probably the most complex of financial instruments to price. Compare the problems faced by a treasurer managing a book of swaps, or a book of bond futures, with one managing a portfolio of options.

While pricing a swap is not easy, any swap on the treasurer's books responds mainly to just one market variable – the swap rate – and that response is almost perfectly linear. Similarly, while equation 7.8 for pricing a bond future requires many inputs, bond futures prices track the cheapest-to-deliver bond, and little else matters. In other words, the treasurer needs to keep his eye on only one market rate, and there is generally a linear relationship between that variable and the derivative instrument. This linear relationship means, for example, that if swap rates increasing by one basis point causes a particular swap to appreciate by \$450, then an increase of ten basis points should cause the swap to appreciate by ten times as much.

Options are not so simple, for two reasons. First, options respond not only to the price of the underlying asset changing but also to volatility, the passage of time and changes in interest rates. Second, this response is not always linear. At first sight it may seem a super-human task to follow the behaviour of just one option in a changing market, let alone a whole portfolio of options. Fortunately there is a solution to this seemingly intractable problem.

Rather than trying to understand how an option will behave when everything changes at once, we will examine how the price and value of an option behaves when one thing at a time changes. These separate effects can eventually be put together.

Recall from the previous section that the price of an option depends upon just five variables:

■ underlying asset price

■ strike price

■ time to option expiry

■ carry (but here we will mainly focus on interest rates)

■ volatility of the underlying asset price.

One of these, the strike price, is normally fixed in advance and therefore does not change. That leaves the remaining four variables. We can now define four quantities, each of which measures how the price of an option will change when one of the input variables changes while all the others remain the same. The definitions are as follows:

Delta is the change in premium for a unit change in the underlying asset price.

Theta is the change in premium for a unit change in the time to maturity (usually the passage of one day).

Vega is the change in premium for a unit change in volatility (usually 1%).

Rho is the change in premium for a unit change in interest rates (usually 1%).

These are the Greek letters that users of options often refer to.[5] In fact, there are several others as well, of which the most common is:

Gamma is the change in delta for a unit change in the underlying asset price.

But you may also encounter:

Lambda is the *percentage* change in premium for a percentage change in the underlying asset price.

Phi is the change in premium for a unit change (usually 1%) in the underlying asset yield (e.g. dividend yield); confusingly, some also use lambda for this concept.

We shall now examine each of these in turn.

Delta

This is undoubtedly the most important measure of option price sensitivity, for it defines exactly how much the option price will move when the underlying asset price changes, and it is this sensitivity that most concerns all users of options. If the underlying asset price moves up by 100¢, an option with a delta of 0.40 will move up by 40¢, while an option having a delta of –0.70 would move down 70¢. Figure 11.13 shows the value profiles again for two call options struck at $100, but this time the graphs are annotated with the values for delta at a number of key points.

For both the 30-day and 180-day options, the delta starts at zero when the options are well out-of-the-money. By the time the options are at-the-money, the deltas have reached values of around 0.5. Finally, when they are deep in-the-money, the delta reaches 1.0. In the case of the 180-day option, this transition is very smooth, but this is in contrast to the 30-day option where delta only moves away from zero at around $80 and all but reaches unity at $120.

There are two important interpretations of delta. One that follows directly from its definition is that delta is the slope of the premium/underlying asset price curve. This is readily visible from the graph in Figure 11.13. A second interpretation is that delta is the hedge ratio that should be used when hedging an option with the underlying asset, which we will explore in the next section.

FIGURE 11.13
Value profile showing deltas

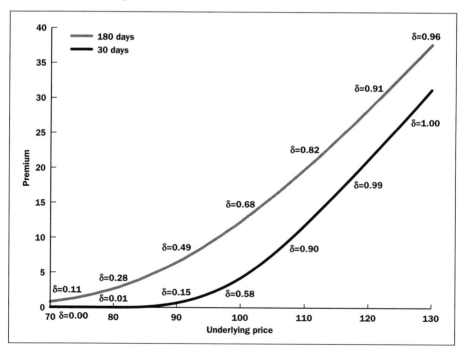

Put another way, the delta describes numerically how similar the option behaves to the underlying asset. When delta is close to zero, the option will hardly respond to movements in the underlying asset price; in other words, the option behaves nothing like the underlying asset. On the other hand, when delta approaches unity, the option moves almost one for one with the underlying asset and therefore behaves very much like it. Given this interpretation of delta, it is not surprising why this measure is considered so important.

Theta

This expresses how the option behaves over time. Long-dated options have more time value than short-dated ones. Therefore, as an option ages and approaches maturity, the time value will gradually erode. Theta defines exactly how much time is lost from day to day, and is a precise measure of *time decay*. To illustrate this concept, Figure 11.14 charts the time value of three call options as they approach maturity. All of them start with 180 days to mature, and were written at a time when the underlying asset price was $100. One option is struck at the money, while others have strikes of $80 and $120.

ITM and OTM options have less time value to start with, so it is not surprising that the decay of this time value is smaller. In the illustration, theta starts at –0.0340 for the OTM option struck at $120 and at –0.0354 for the ITM option

FIGURE 11.14
Time decay and theta

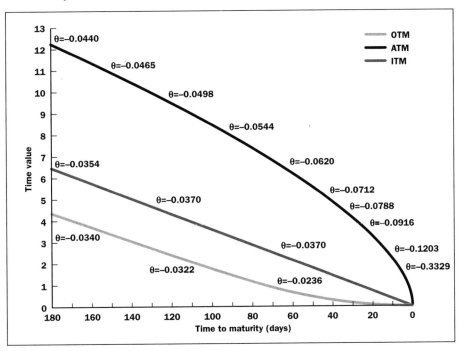

struck at \$80, which means that these options lose about 3½¢ each day, and there is an almost linear decay of time value as they approach maturity.

The ATM option starts with a much larger time value and a higher value for theta of –0.0440. Perhaps surprisingly, time decay stays almost constant for almost two-thirds of the option's life, when it gradually begins to pick up. By the time the ATM call has reached 30 days prior to expiry, time decay has increased to –0.0788 per day. Beyond this point, theta accelerates quite rapidly reaching –0.3329 the day before expiry. This phenomenon gives rise to a parabolic shape for the decay of time value, whereby 70% through the life of an option it still retains around half its original time value, but this disappears quite quickly thereafter.

Time decay is therefore principally a feature of ATM options close to maturity. For other options at other times, time decay is less of an issue. The nature of theta has significant implications for buyers of ATM options, who stand to lose time value fastest in the last few weeks of the option's life. We will review the reasons for this in the next section when we look at delta hedging.

Vega

This defines the response of an option to volatility. Since higher volatility means more uncertainty, and uncertainty manifests itself as the first component of time value, options become progressively more expensive with higher volatility. This is evident from Figure 11.15, which charts value against volatility for two at-the-money options, one with 180 days to expire and the other with 30 days.

Vega is essentially a property of longer-dated options, in contrast to theta, and – for the ATM option pictured – is also quite linear. Across almost the entire spectrum of volatility levels pictured in Figure 11.15, for every rise in volatility of 1% the 180-day option increases in value by around 25¢, while the 30-day option increases likewise by 11¢.

Rho

This is probably the least used measure of sensitivity, perhaps because interest rates are relatively stable, and when they do move they don't change by very much. There is therefore less need to monitor how the option premium will move when interest rates change. For completeness, Figure 11.16 shows the option premium for different levels of interest rates together with values of rho at three key points. Like vega, rho is more prominent for longer-dated options. Phi is sometimes used to measure the analogous sensitivity of the premium to changes in the other component of carry – dividend yield in the case of a stock option, or the base currency interest rate in the case of a currency option. Phi and rho are very similar, but have opposite signs.

FIGURE 11.15
Sensitivity to volatility – vega

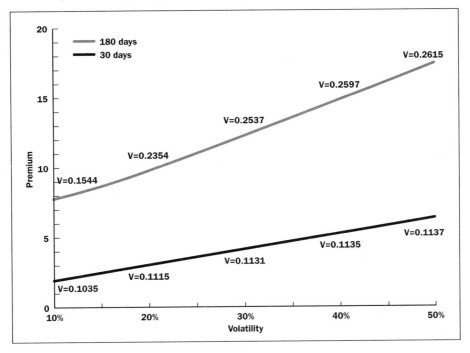

FIGURE 11.16
Sensitivity to interest rates – rho

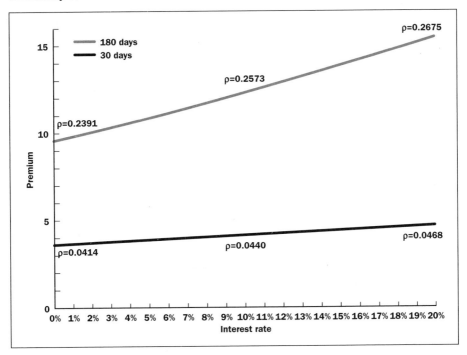

All of the sensitivity measures so far have had one thing in common: they all express how much an option's premium will change for a unit change in one of the pricing variables. Since they measure changes in premium, the values of delta, theta, vega and rho will all be expressed in the same units as the option premium. In the case of the stock options used in all the examples in this section, the units will therefore all be dollars and cents.

Lambda

This is similar to delta in measuring how the option premium changes when the underlying price changes. However, instead of expressing this in absolute terms, lambda measures the *percentage change* in the premium for a *percentage change* in the underlying asset price, and can be calculated by multiplying delta by the ratio of the underlying asset price over the option premium. Lambda is thus an expression of the gearing or leverage of an option, and it is an easy matter to demonstrate that lambda must always be greater than one. Figure 11.17 shows the same set of option prices as those in Figure 11.13, but annotated this time with values for lambda.

As the numbers show, even the most ITM options illustrated have a gearing of at least three times. This means that if the underlying asset price was to rise, an investor could obtain three times the benefit if he were to invest, say, $100,000 in stock options rather than in shares directly. Of course, gearing works both ways. The same investor could lose at least three times more with options than with the shares if the underlying asset price fell.

FIGURE 11.17
Option gearing – lambda

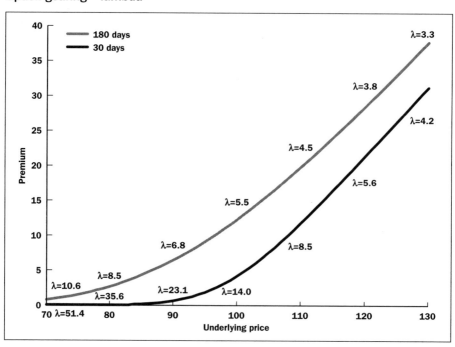

Some of the gearing numbers are astronomical for OTM options, but these can be misleading, for a number of reasons. First, as we saw in section 11.2, a market-maker pricing such OTM options is likely in practice to use a much higher implied volatility, but the graphs in Figure 11.17 were constructed assuming volatility stays constant throughout. If the ATM $100 strike options are priced using 30% volatility, an OTM option struck at $125 may well be priced at 45% volatility. For a 30-day option this makes a big difference: instead of the theoretical premium of 2.41¢ and a delta of 0.0086, which gives rise to a lambda of 35.6, the actual premium would be 32¢ with a delta of 0.06 thereby halving the lambda to 18.8. Second, an investor would be unwise to commit his entire wealth in buying OTM options in the hope of making a quick fortune. Even if the market were deep enough, the most likely outcome for any OTM option is that it will expire worthless and the investor would lose everything.

Gamma

This is the 'odd one out' because it is the only Greek letter that does not measure the sensitivity of the option's premium. Instead, gamma measures how the option's delta changes when the underlying asset price moves. As delta is the single most important measure of an option's sensitivity, it makes sense to track how delta is affected by movements in the underlying asset price. Figure 11.18 once again repeats the option prices illustrated in Figure 11.13, but shows the values for gamma. In practice, gamma can be expressed in a number of different ways depending upon the conventions in different markets,[6] but the figures in Figure 11.18 show the absolute change in delta for a unit change in the underlying price.

The simplest interpretation for gamma is that it measures the *curvature* of the option premium when graphed against the underlying price. The graph of the 180-day option illustrated in Figure 11.18 is mostly quite a smooth and shallow curve, so gamma for this option is relatively small – about 0.01 or 0.02 – and does not change much over quite a wide range of underlying prices. In contrast, the premium curve for the 30-day option has three distinct regions: a straight part below $85, a very curved part between $85 and $115, and then another straight part above $115. The gamma reflects this, being close to zero for levels of the underlying asset below $85 and above $115, but being much larger in between, especially when the option is at-the-money.

Recalling that the delta of an option is the hedge ratio, the gamma therefore expresses how much the hedge ratio changes when the underlying asset price moves. Options with a small gamma are therefore easier to hedge because the hedge ratio will not change much when the underlying asset price fluctuates. Those with a high gamma cause problems, however, because the market-maker will constantly have to readjust the hedge in order to avoid risk. As we will see in the next section, this is costly, and is further justification for ATM options, which have the highest gamma, being the most expensive.

FIGURE 11.18

Sensitivity of delta – gamma

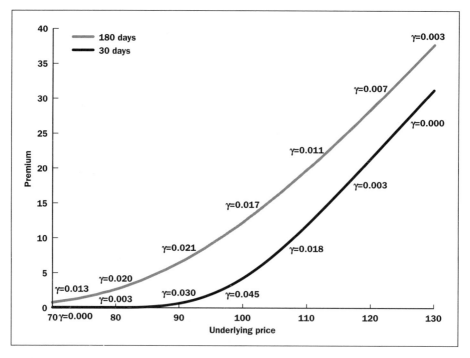

We have so far reviewed each of the Greek letters separately. Figure 11.19 illustrates four of the key measures – delta, gamma, theta and vega – all together, so that comparisons can easily be drawn. Each graph shows one of the measures plotted against the underlying asset price, but for an option at five moments in its life: 180 days to expiry, 90 days, 30 days, 15 days and finally one day before expiry.

The graphs of delta show quite clearly how the smooth nature of a longer-dated option gradually grows more acute as it approaches maturity, until delta becomes virtually a zero–one variable when the option has just one day to mature. This reflects the gradual resolution of the key issue affecting any option, whether it will be exercised or not. With many months to mature, the issue is largely unresolved even when the underlying price is away from the strike price. The hedge ratio does not stray far from 0.50 as the option 'hedges its bets' so to speak. As maturity approaches, there is less and less time for any significant move in the underlying price, so it becomes more and more apparent whether the option will expire in-the-money or out-of-the-money.

The behaviour of gamma follows directly from that of delta. Not only does gamma measure the curvature for the premium/underlying price curve, it is the slope of the delta/underlying price graph. Far from maturity, delta does not change much, and gamma remains small, even for ATM options. As maturity approaches, delta becomes unstable at-the-money, with correspondingly large

Comparison of delta, gamma, theta and vega

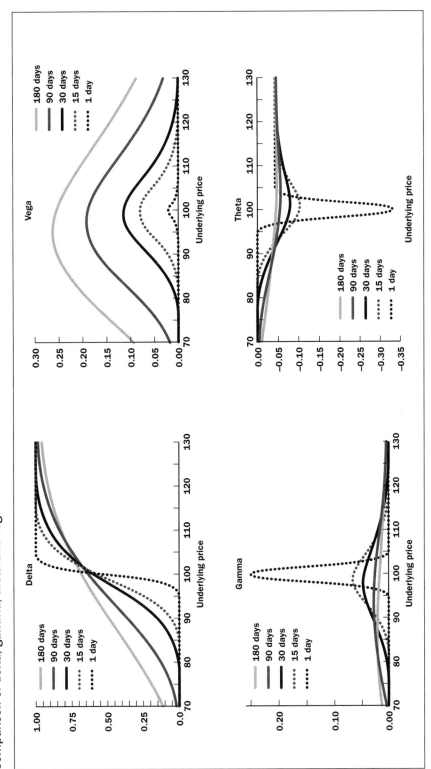

values of gamma. Away from the strike price, though, delta approaches either zero or one with a stable and flat characteristic, so gamma once again takes on small values.

The shape of theta is very similar to that of gamma, though it is upside down. Like gamma, theta is predominantly a feature of ATM options near maturity. Unlike gamma, there is a slight asymmetry between OTM and ITM options. This reflects carry, which becomes an issue only when hedging and pricing ITM options.

In these graphs vega is the odd one out. With the other three Greek letters illustrated in Figure 11.19, it is the characteristics of the short-dated options that dominate the picture. Sensitivity to volatility, however, is the preserve of longer-dated options, and the largest values of vega are achieved by longer-dated options across quite a wide range of underlying prices.

So far we have described and illustrated the behaviour of the Greeks and provided a number of numerical examples, but how are the values of the Greeks determined? When using a closed-form model, the easiest way is to develop a formula for calculating the Greeks directly. As an example, with the original Black–Scholes model defined in equation 10.20 in the previous chapter, we can use calculus to produce a simple and exact formula for delta:

$$\delta = \frac{\partial C}{\partial S} = N(d_1) \tag{11.1}$$

In a similar way, formulae can be developed for all the other Greeks. Although some of the expressions can be complex, the formulae do provide a quick and exact way of calculating values for the different Greeks.

If no closed-form model is available, an alternative technique is to perturb ('tweak') the inputs of the pricing model and measure the impact on the calculated option premium. As an example, let's take a six-month ATM call option on an underlying asset priced at 100, when six-month interest rates are 15.6% and volatility is 30%. With these values, we can use an option pricing model to calculate the following premiums:

Underlying asset price (S)	Premium
S = 100.1	12.3309
S = 100.0	12.2631
S = 99.9	12.1954

Remembering that the delta is defined as the change in premium for a unit change in the underlying asset price, we can calculate delta to be:

$$\frac{12.3309 - 12.1954}{100.1 - 99.9} = 0.677$$

This value agrees with the Black–Scholes value calculated from equation 11.1:[7]

$$d_1 = \frac{\ln\left(\frac{100}{100}\right) + \left(0.15025 + \frac{0.30^2}{2}\right) \times 0.5}{0.30\sqrt{0.5}} = 0.4602, \text{ and } N(0.4602) = 0.677$$

It also agrees with the value for delta of 0.68 shown in Figure 11.13 for the 180-day option when the underlying asset price is 100.

Now that we have seen what the Greeks are and how they can be calculated, let's look at a simple example of how they can be used. Consider someone holding an ATM option with the following characteristics:

option type:	Call	premium:	12.26
strike price:	$100	delta:	0.6773
underlying price:	$100	theta:	–0.0440
time to maturity:	180 days	vega:	0.2537
volatility:	30%	rho:	0.2573
interest rate:	15.6%	gamma:	0.0169

Suppose after one week the underlying price was to rise to $105, interest rates to fall 1% and volatility to fall 2%. What effect would this combination have on the price of the option? This can be answered by using the Greek letters to assess the effect of each separate influence and combining the result. Table 11.5 analyses the separate impacts and shows that the combined effect is for the premium to rise by 2.31. This would imply that the premium would be 12.26 + 2.31 = 14.57.

TABLE 11.5
Using the Greek letters

Influence	Greek letter	Change × sensitivity	Effect
Change in underlying price	delta	5 × 0.6773	+3.3866
Passage of time	theta	7 × (–0.0440)	–0.3080
Change in volatility	vega	–2 × 0.2537	–0.5075
Change in interest rate	rho	–1 × 0.2573	–0.2573
Total			+2.3138

In fact, if the option is re-priced using the B–S model with all the inputs changed to reflect the new conditions, the premium turns out to 14.79, an actual increase of 2.53. The true answer is a little different because of second-order effects. Some of the Greeks are accurate for only small changes in the inputs. In fact, the gamma of this ATM option implies that delta should increase by about 0.0846 by the time the underlying price reaches $105. If we take this into account, the delta averages 0.6773 + 0.0846/2 = 0.7196, and the predicted effect of the rise in underlying price increases from the +3.3866 shown in Table 11.5 to +3.5980, and this means that the option is now predicted to rise by 2.53 – exactly what happens.

In this case, after using gamma to modify delta, the change in premium predicted by the Greeks proves to be perfectly correct. Unfortunately, this happy result is a little fortuitous. Had we considered a rise in volatility of 2% rather than a fall, the actual rise in premium would have been 3.46, but the Greeks would have predicted a rise in premium of 3.54, even after applying the gamma correction. The reason why the result is not quite so accurate this time is because there are other second-order Greeks as well as gamma.[8] Not only does delta change when market conditions change, but so do the other Greeks. For example, vega falls from 0.2537 to 0.2276 or 0.2371 in the two scenarios we have considered here, but in Table 11.5 we have implicitly assumed that vega and the other Greeks stay constant.

To illustrate the dynamic nature of the Greeks, Figure 11.20 provides a set of 3D charts for delta, gamma, vega and theta, and shows how these Greeks change as the underlying asset price changes as well as how they change over time. The top-right 3D chart of vega shows how vega falls, not only as the option approaches expiry but also as the underlying asset price moves away from the strike price of $100.

Nonetheless, using the Greek letters makes it possible to perform quick calculations to determine with reasonable accuracy what will happen to an option when various market conditions change. However, where the Greek letters really come into their own is in evaluating the impact of market fluctuations on an entire portfolio of options. By taking the weighted sum of the deltas, thetas, vegas and gammas of the individual options, the behaviour of the entire options portfolio can be summarised in just four numbers. Then, instead of having to re-price perhaps 1,000 options when market rates change, a calculation similar to the one presented in Table 11.5 will reveal reasonably accurately what the combined effect is.

It is possible to extend this idea. To make an entire options portfolio immune to changes in the underlying asset price, it is necessary only to ensure that the portfolio delta sums to zero, making the portfolio *delta-neutral*. This is the essence of delta hedging and we will explore this in detail in the next section.

11.6 Delta hedging

When we introduced the concepts behind option pricing in section 10.5 in the previous chapter we saw that, unlike with other derivative products, it is not possible to create a hedging strategy that is both static and riskless. The principal reason, as discussed in that section, is because we do not know what will eventually happen at maturity: maybe the option will get exercised, and maybe it won't. This leads to the inevitable conclusion that hedging an option is a dynamic and ever-changing process.

When we discussed the binomial approach to pricing options in section 10.8 we explained how the technique relies on creating a series of riskless hedges that change over time. In that section the hedge ratio – the proportion of the underlying asset to buy or sell – was given the symbol h defined in equation 10.24. Finally, in the previous section, we stated that the hedge ratio of an option was its delta.

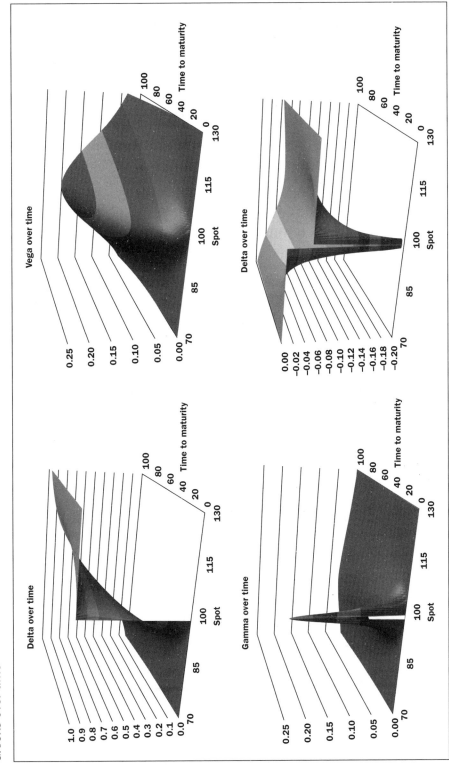

FIGURE 11.20

Greeks over time

Let's now explore delta hedging in more detail. To illustrate the concept, consider a bank which has sold one-year OTM call options struck at 120 on 1,000 shares – in fact, the same option that we used in the examples in sections 10.7–10.10 in the previous chapter. We know from those earlier examples that if the underlying asset is trading at 100, the fair premium is 10.34, and we can calculate that the option has a delta of 0.510 initially. This means that a bank must buy 510 shares in order to create the initial delta hedge, which is illustrated in Figure 11.21. In that figure the pale grey line shows the profit and loss from the call sold, the dark grey line is that from the 510 shares bought, and the black line is the profit and loss from the combined position. Note that the solid black line is absolutely flat at the initial share price of 100. This is because the positive slope of the shares bought exactly matches the negative slope of the call sold. This is exactly what a delta-neutral hedge is intended to achieve – no exposure to the price of the underlying asset.

Unfortunately, the hedged portfolio will not stay delta-neutral for ever. Once the underlying asset price moves away from its initial value, the delta of the option will change and the portfolio will no longer be delta-neutral. Consider first what would happen if the share price was to rise to 105. In this case, the call delta will rise to 0.574 and the bank would need to buy 64 more shares in order to stay delta-neutral. If it did not, it would be under-hedged, and the resulting position would no longer be delta-neutral but delta-negative. Being net short shares on a rising market would cause the bank to lose money. Now consider what would happen if the share price was to fall to 95. Then the call delta would

FIGURE 11.21
The initial delta hedge

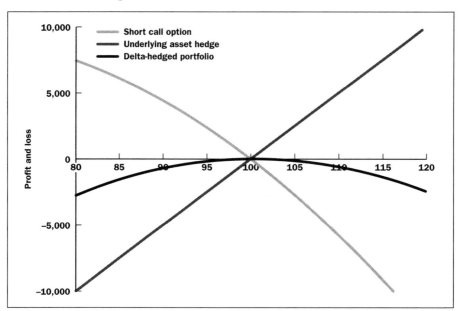

fall to 0.442 and the bank would need to sell 68 shares to stay delta-neutral. If it failed to do so, the bank would be over-hedged, delta-positive and net long shares on a falling market, and again the bank would lose money. That's why the solid black line, while flat in the middle, droops down on either side of the figure.

To avoid these losses, the bank should dynamically adjust the size of the hedge, buying and selling shares to remain delta-neutral as the underlying asset price changes. This is pictured in Figure 11.22 but unfortunately there is a problem with this strategy. When a bank sells an option, it will generally result in a gamma-negative position. The concept of 'gamma-negative' can be pictured in two ways. First, and most easily, we saw in the previous section that gamma is the curvature of the premium or profit/loss curve. Negative gamma means negative curvature – a curve that is flat in the middle and is lower at each side. Second, gamma measures the change in delta, so negative gamma means a delta that decreases as you move from left to right in the figure. The problem with delta-hedging a gamma-negative portfolio is that the bank must buy shares when the underlying asset price rises and sell shares when the underlying asset price falls. This is a buy-high and sell-low strategy, one that is guaranteed to cost money.

To explore how much this delta-hedging strategy costs, Table 11.6 shows the buying and selling decisions arising from a simulated sequence of underlying asset prices, assuming that the bank adjusts the hedge 20 times over the one-year lifetime of the option introduced earlier in this section.

FIGURE 11.22
Dynamic delta hedging

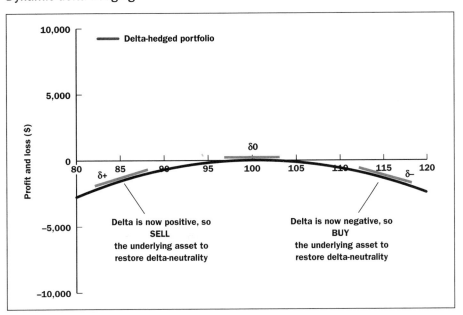

TABLE 11.6
Dynamically managing a hedge for a short-call option

Step	Underlying	Hedge ratio	Asset traded	Value of asset held	Hedging cash flow	Option cash flow	Total cash flow	PV of cash flow
0	100.00	0.5102	510.2	51,020.97	-51,020.97	10,342.09	-40,678.88	-40,678.88
1	101.41	0.5166	6.4	52,386.68	-647.14		-647.14	-642.46
2	103.32	0.5299	13.3	54,744.84	-1,371.38		-1,371.38	-1,351.64
3	95.21	0.4003	-129.6	38,110.20	12,339.44		12,339.44	12,073.95
4	92.97	0.3503	-50.0	32,567.01	4,646.76		4,646.76	4,513.94
5	80.58	0.1625	-187.8	13,095.52	15,131.60		15,131.60	14,592.91
6	77.66	0.1143	-48.2	8,875.79	3,744.07		3,744.07	3,584.70
7	85.40	0.1852	70.9	15,818.06	-6,057.03		-6,057.03	-5,757.30
8	77.62	0.0832	-102.0	6,456.08	7,921.32		7,921.32	7,474.95
9	86.31	0.1559	72.7	13,455.07	-6,276.47		-6,276.47	-5,880.00
10	84.75	0.1167	-39.2	9,892.06	3,320.01		3,320.01	3,087.83
11	89.07	0.1455	28.7	12,956.55	-2,560.13		-2,560.13	-2,363.89
12	89.10	0.1212	-24.2	10,802.39	2,157.71		2,157.71	1,977.92
13	87.85	0.0834	-37.9	7,323.84	3,326.79		3,326.79	3,027.56
14	84.25	0.0355	-47.9	2,989.40	4,034.65		4,034.65	3,645.23
15	85.40	0.0255	-10.0	2,180.01	850.18		850.18	762.58
16	88.66	0.0243	-1.2	2,152.84	110.53		110.53	98.42
17	82.53	0.0015	-22.8	120.15	1,883.63		1,883.63	1,665.21
18	79.93	0.0000	-1.4	1.77	114.60		114.60	100.58
19	79.87	0.0000	0.0	0.00	1.77		1.77	1.54
20	82.02	0.0000	0.0	0.00	0.00		0.00	0.00
TOTAL								-66.87

At inception, with a hedge ratio of 0.5102, the bank must buy 510.2 shares, resulting in an initial cash outlay of around 51,020. Next period, the underlying asset price has risen to 101.41 and the hedge ratio to 0.5166. This means that a further 6.4 of the underlying asset must be bought at the higher price, generating a further outlay of around 647. When the asset price drops substantially in period three, the hedge ratio drops in sympathy, and 129.6 shares need to be sold to realise a cash inflow of 12,339.44. The NPV of all 21 cash flows is just –66.87, or just $0.07 per share. Put another way, charging the initial premium of $10.34 per share has more or less covered the dynamic delta-hedging costs.

The figures in Table 11.6 provide just one example of the cash flows that would arise if that particular sequence of underlying prices were to occur. Of course, the price of the underlying asset could follow many different paths in practice. Figure 11.23 illustrates a fuller example where the bank hedges twice a day, 500 times over the lifetime of the one-year option. Note how the size of the delta hedge (shown as the shaded bars on the right-hand scale) follows closely the path of the underlying asset price (shown as the solid line on the left-hand scale).

Some of the possible paths will lead to higher hedging costs, while other paths might lead to lower costs. The key determinant is the amount of experienced volatility. If the underlying asset price fluctuates more, then there will be more buying high and selling low, and this will prove to be more expensive for the bank which has sold the option. On the other hand, if the underlying asset price turned out to be more stable, then there would be less need to adjust the delta hedge, resulting in less buying high and selling low, thereby cheapening the cost of running the delta hedging operation.

Why do banks delta hedge when they sell options? Why go to all the trouble, inevitably incurring buy-high/sell-low costs? The answer to these questions is that they want to reduce risk, and delta hedging achieves this. To illustrate this, we will look at a situation where a bank sells the 120 strike one-year call discussed earlier in this section, and collects the fair premium of 10.34. We then explore two strategies – one in which the bank dutifully delta hedges the short options position twice a day until the option expires, and the other in which the bank simply does nothing. To assess these strategies, a Monte Carlo simulation was used to create 100,000 possible price paths for the sequence of underlying asset prices over the ensuing year, assuming that the returns on the underlying asset followed a normal distribution with a mean of 10% and volatility of 30%. The resulting statistics are summarised in Table 11.7.

TABLE 11.7
Comparing option hedging strategies

Statistic	No delta hedging	Delta hedging
Mean	0.00	0.00
Worst result	–246.20	–3.28
Best result	+10.34	+2.61
Standard deviation	19.80	0.48

FIGURE 11.23
Dynamic delta hedging – 500 step example

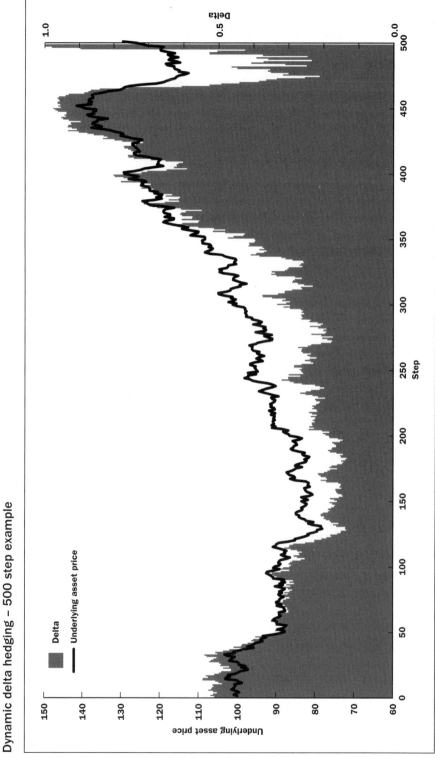

In one respect, the two strategies are identical – the average outcome is to break even. This interesting result confirms the effectiveness of the Black–Scholes option pricing model in calculating the correct premium for this option. Assuming that the 30% volatility experienced exactly matches the 30% implied volatility used to price the option, the hedging costs are covered exactly. Put another way, the buy-high/sell-low costs associated with dynamic delta hedging should not be considered as a surcharge to be added to the option premium – these hedging costs are what the option premium is intended to cover. Of course, in real life no bank would be content just to break even. In practice, a bank would always want to price an option using an implied volatility higher than it expects to experience so that it can generate a reasonable profit margin and cover the transaction costs associated with buying and selling the underlying asset – something that the above simulation has ignored.

However, the average result is the only aspect where the two strategies are equivalent. A quick glance at the figures in Table 11.7 reveals the very considerable risk to which an option seller is exposed if they did not delta hedge. The worst outcome is for the option seller to lose more than $246 on an original income of around $10 – a 25-fold loss. This most unfortunate outcome arose in at least one scenario where the price of the underlying asset rose from $100 at the beginning of the year to around $376 by the end of the year. The call struck at 120 would be exercised by the holder who will hand over $120 and expect to receive one share. Not having delta hedged, the bank is forced to buy the share in the market spending $376. The net loss is therefore the $376 cost of the share, less the strike price of $120 and the original premium of $10.34 received at the outset, leading to the net loss of around $246.

Compare this worst result of $246.20 with the worst result of just $3.28 if the bank delta hedges: the delta hedging strategy is 75 times safer! Alternatively, compare the standard deviations of the two strategies, $19.80 without delta hedging against just $0.48 with delta hedging; using this measure, delta hedging is more than 40 times safer!

Figure 11.24 charts the distribution of hedging results, making the difference in risk characteristics of the two strategies plain to see.

Let's first examine the result without delta hedging. The spike on the right represents the situations where the call option expires worthless and the bank keeps the $10.34 premium. You cannot see the top of the spike because the chart's vertical axis has been deliberately truncated, but it is more than 12 times the height of the chart representing the 61% chance of this happening. Unfortunately, the remaining 39% of the time the call option expires in-the-money, and the bank has to pay out sums ranging from just a few cents to hundreds of dollars. The chart's horizontal axis has also been deliberately truncated because the left-hand tail extends to three times the width of the chart. So there is a considerable chance the bank makes more than $10 profit, but this is counterbalanced by a very small chance the bank makes a loss of several hundred dollars. On average the bank breaks even, but this is an average of extreme results and doesn't reflect the huge relative risk which the bank faces.

FIGURE 11.24

Distribution of hedging results

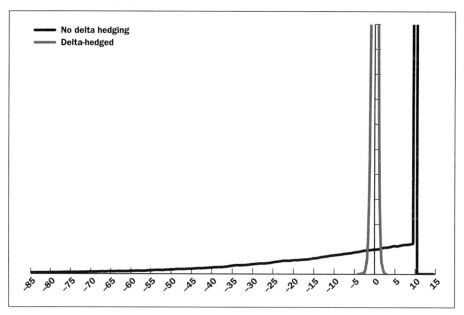

Compare this with the delta-hedged result. Now there is a tall spike centred on the break-even result. Again, the spike is too tall to fit on the chart and is, in fact, 11 times the height of the chart. This time, however, the dispersion is minimal, and the distribution is virtually symmetrical, with no adverse left-hand tail. Provided the markets remain liquid and do not exhibit sudden jumps in price, banks delta hedging their options books can avoid the nasty sting in the tail.

This analysis suggests that delta hedging is a no-brainer. For the same net profit, the bank which delta hedges its book of options can reduce risk by a considerable multiple. In reality, while transaction costs and bid–offer spreads will lessen the relative advantage of the delta-hedging strategy, larger banks can exploit economies of scale. It is not necessary to hedge each individual option; instead an entire book of options on, say, Microsoft, can be hedged with a single purchase or sale of Microsoft shares. The bigger the book of options, the more efficiently it can be hedged.

Notes

1   As another example, consider a bag containing six green balls, four blue balls and one red ball. You are allowed to pick a ball unseen, and will receive 1 if you pick a green ball, 2 if you pick a blue one and 19 if you pick the red one. The median payoff is 1, the mean (or average) payoff is 3, but there is less than a 10% chance of receiving the average payoff or more.

2 Rebonato, Riccardo (1999) *Volatility and Correlation in the Pricing of Equity, FX and Interest-rate Options*, Wiley.

3 See Demeterfi, Kresimir; Derman, Emanuel; Kamal, Michael and Zou, Joseph (1999) *More than you ever wanted to know about volatility swaps*, Goldman Sachs Quantitative Strategies Research Notes, March. A detailed worked example can be downloaded from the CBOE website (www.cboe.com/micro/VIX/vixwhite.pdf) and a comparison between the methodologies is presented by Carr, Peter and Wu, Liuren (2006) 'A tale of two indices', *Journal of Derivatives*, 13.

4 For deep ITM European-style options on futures, time value will eventually become negative. See the discussion on American options at the end of section 11.4 for a fuller explanation.

5 Actually, the term vega is an impostor because there is no Greek letter of that name. The sensitivity of an option's price to changes in volatility is sometimes called kappa, which really is a Greek letter, but almost all option experts prefer the alliteration of vega/volatility to the classical perfection of sticking consistently to the Greek alphabet.

6 In the FX options market, for example, gamma is normally expressed as the change in delta for a 1% change in the underlying FX rate (rather than a unit change in the FX rate).

7 A six-month interest rate of 15.6% is equivalent to a continuously compounded rate of 15.025%.

8 For example, *vanna* is the change in vega when the underlying asset price changes, and also the change in delta when volatility changes. *Volga* is the change in vega when volatility changes, and there are several other curiously named second-order Greeks as well.

12

OPTIONS – FROM BUILDING
BLOCKS TO PORTFOLIOS

One of the main reasons why options have enjoyed such extraordinary growth since the 1980s is their tremendous versatility – options can be assembled in myriad combinations and permutations. As such, they can be thought of as elemental building blocks which can be put together to form a wide range of financial structures. This chapter demonstrates how options can form the basic building blocks for a number of financial structures, and reviews some of the most common option combinations.

12.1 The building block approach

Consider an investor who simultaneously buys some asset and also an at-the-money put option on the same asset. If the asset price subsequently falls so that the option expires in-the-money, the investor will exercise the option, deliver the asset and receive the exercise price. As the option was originally struck at-the-money, receiving the exercise price exactly offsets the price paid to acquire the asset originally. This sequence will occur for any asset price below the strike price of the put, fixing the net loss for the investor at the original premium paid for the put. On the other hand, if the asset price finishes at any level above the strike price, the put option will expire out-of-the money and will not be exercised. The investor can then sell the asset on the open market to receive the prevailing price, yielding net proceeds of the gain in the market price less the original premium paid. Summarising the outcomes: the net proceeds at maturity are a constant loss if the asset price finishes below the strike price of the put option, and rise one-for-one if the underlying asset price finishes above the strike.

Compare this with the outcome if the investor did not buy the asset itself, but bought an at-the-money call option on the asset instead. If the underlying asset price finished below the strike, the call would not be exercised and the net loss would be the premium paid for the call. If the asset price rose, however, the option would expire in-the-money, producing a net profit equal to the gain in the underlying asset price less the premium paid. Again, the net proceeds at maturity are a constant loss if the asset price finishes below the strike, and rise one-for-one otherwise.

Qualitatively, the payoffs from these two strategies are the same. In fact, if the options are fairly priced, by applying the principle of put–call parity introduced in Chapter 10, section 10.7, one can show that the payoffs are *exactly* the same. In other words, combining an asset with a put option gives exactly the same effect as a call option at the same strike price. Figure 12.1 shows the corresponding profit profiles, illustrating this 'option arithmetic' pictorially. For outcomes below the strike, the downward diagonal profile of the long asset position is exactly cancelled by the upward diagonal profile of the put option, leaving a level result identical to that of the call option. Above the strike, the flat profile of the put does not affect the diagonal profile of the long asset position, and the result is an unchanged diagonal profile again mirroring that of the call.

FIGURE 12.1

Option arithmetic

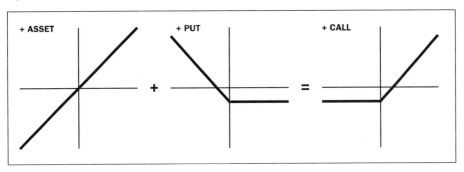

We can express this kind of arithmetic symbolically as well. Let an outcome with a negative slope be denoted as {–1}, one with a positive slope as {+1} and one with a level result as {0}. Where payoffs are different under different circumstances, they can be listed sequentially separated by commas. The result from buying a call option would then be symbolised as {0, +1}, indicating the level outcome {0} if the option expires out-of-the-money, and a positive slope {+1} otherwise.

Using this nomenclature, the relationship depicted in Figure 12.1 becomes:

Buying an asset:	{+1,	+1}
Buying a put option:	{–1,	0}
Net result:	{0,	+1}

which is equivalent to the payoff from a call option.

What would the result be if an investor bought an asset and sold a call option on the same asset? Using this system we obtain:

Buying an asset:	{+1,	+1}
Selling a call option:	{0,	–1}
Net result:	{+1,	0}

which is the same as selling a put. Figure 12.2 illustrates this combination.

There are two other basic combinations, both of which now involve selling the underlying asset:

Selling an asset:	{–1,	–1}	
Buying a call option:	{0,	+1}	
Net result:	{–1,	0}	(equivalent to buying a put)

FIGURE 12.2

More option arithmetic

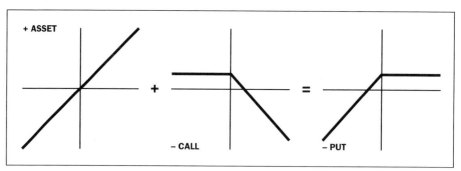

and:

Selling an asset:	{–1,	–1}
Selling a put option:	{+1,	0}
Net result:	{0,	–1}　(equivalent to selling a call)

These simple examples show that it is possible to combine the underlying asset with an option of one type and obtain the exact equivalent of the other type of option. So far, however, nothing new has been created, but then we have hardly begun to explore the possibilities. By putting the elementary building blocks together in different ways, entirely novel structures can be created.

In all, there are just six basic building blocks, and these are illustrated in Figure 12.3. In a similar way as a child with a Lego® set can build an enormous range of structures and objects, it is possible to create an almost unlimited number of financial instruments simply by combining long or short positions in call options, put options and the underlying asset. Just as with Lego®, the possibilities are limited solely by the imagination of the user.

The next four sections describe some of the more common structures found in practice. For convenience, these have been organised under the following headings:

a) spreads – comprising the purchase of one option and the sale of another option of the same type but with a different strike price and/or time to maturity.

b) Volatility structures – usually designed to take advantage of an anticipated shift in volatility.

c) Range structures – which generate profits if the underlying asset remains range-bound.

d) Arbitrage structures – which seek to profit from a temporary mispricing.

Some of these combinations are awarded their own name, acknowledging that the resultant products are important enough to warrant treatment as instru-

FIGURE 12.3

Basic building blocks

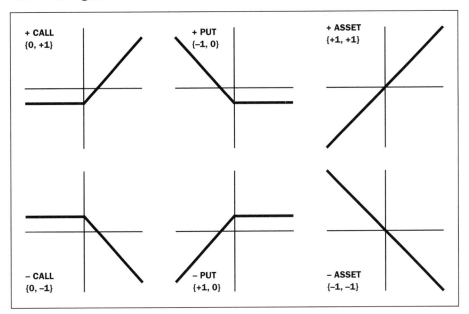

ments in their own right. A good example is the interest rate cap discussed in the next chapter, which is simply a strip of options, but which is invariably packaged as a product in its own right. The selection presented in this chapter is by no means exhaustive, and Part II of this book will provide illustrations of other option-based structures, often packaged with a proprietary name.

To provide a concrete example here, the spread, volatility and arbitrage structures are all illustrated using European-style options on a particular equity which is currently trading at a price of exactly 100. Expiry takes place in 270 days, volatility over this period is expected to be 20%, the nine-month interest rate is 5% per annum and the dividend yield is expected to be 1% per annum. Table 12.1 summarises the premiums for most of the options used.

TABLE 12.1

Option premiums

Strike	Calls	Puts
80	22.63	0.49
90	14.51	2.00
100	8.28	5.41
110	4.21	10.97
120	1.92	18.32

While this provides a specific example, the structures illustrated are completely general, and can be applied equally well to currency options, interest rate options or options on almost any underlying asset or derivative.

Although the basic building blocks are easiest to understand by thinking of the straight-line shapes shown in Figure 12.3, or of the equivalent nomenclature {–1, 0, +1} introduced earlier, this simplicity can often be misleading for it represents the characteristic of the option only on its maturity date. While this may be good enough for structures intended to be held until that date, many structures are designed to be bought and sold prior to maturity. For this reason, all the ensuing figures show the characteristics of these structures as they change over time, not just on the maturity date. In addition, to illustrate the behaviour of volatility structures properly, they are pictured not just over time but over a range of volatility levels.

12.2 Option spreads – vertical, horizontal and diagonal

A *spread* position in options is defined as a long position in one type of option and a matching short position in the same type of option, but with a different strike price and/or a different maturity date. If both options are calls, the result is a call spread. If both option positions involve puts, the combination is, not surprisingly, a put spread.

Many published tables of option prices are organised with different maturity dates as the column headings, and different strike prices as the row headings. If a dealer's position is recorded in such a table, it can show at a glance where he is long options and where he is short. Spread positions can be identified by adjacent cells having opposite positions, as illustrated in Figure 12.4.

It is now clear from this illustration how horizontal, vertical and diagonal spreads got their name:

■ A *vertical spread* is the purchase of one option, and the sale of a similar option but with a different strike price.

FIGURE 12.4
Vertical, horizontal and diagonal spreads

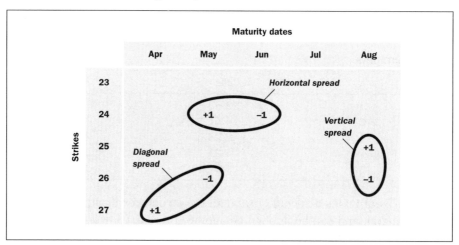

- A *horizontal spread* is the purchase of one option, and the sale of a similar option but with a different maturity date.

- A *diagonal option* is the purchase of one option, and the sale of a similar option but with a different strike price and maturity date.

We shall now examine each type of spread in turn.

Vertical spreads

If the option purchased has a lower strike price than the option sold, the result is a *bull spread*. If, however, the option purchased is the one with the higher strike price, the resulting structure is called a *bear spread*. Figure 12.5 shows the profit profile resulting from buying the 90 call and selling the 110 call. The different lines highlight the evolution of the profile from the smooth curve at inception, 270 days from the maturity of the options, to the zigzag shape that develops at the maturity of the options (i.e. with 0 days to expiry).

The zigzag shape of the profit profile at maturity is characteristic of any bull spread, and can easily be explained by combining the contribution from each of the options:

Buying a call with lower strike:	{0,	+1,	+1}
Selling a call with higher strike:	{0,	0,	−1}
Net result:	{0,	+1,	0}

FIGURE 12.5
Profit profile for bull call spread

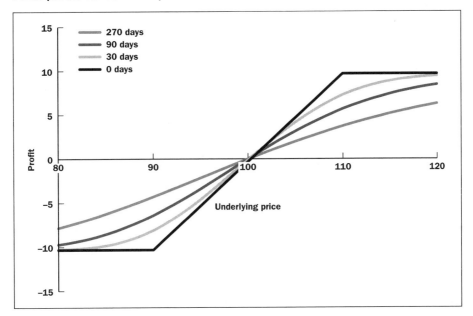

The {0, +1, 0} profile implies a characteristic starting flat, then rising with a positive slope, and then becoming flat again, just as illustrated in Figure 12.5.

The bull spread is a strategy often favoured by those who believe that the underlying asset price will rise, who wish to obtain a geared return through using options, but who do not wish to incur the full expense of buying an ATM option. Selling the call option with a higher strike price brings in premium income, thus reducing the net premiums paid. In the example of the 90–110 spread featured in Figure 12.5, contrast the premium of 14.51 for the 90 call with a net cost of 10.31 for the bull call spread, a reduction of 29%. This net cost is a little more than the premium of 8.28 for the ATM 100 call, but the result for the spread dominates that of the simple option strategy over a wide range of underlying asset prices at maturity. As Figure 12.6 shows, the profit from the spread is greater if the underlying asset finishes anywhere between 92 and 118.

The main sacrifice in buying a bull spread is the profit potential forgone if the underlying asset rises higher than the second strike. At that point, increasing profits on the long call with the lower strike are exactly offset by losses on the short call with the higher strike. This means that the profits with a bull spread are limited, in fact, to the difference between the strike prices less the original net premium paid, 9.69 in this example (20.00 – 10.31). This contrasts with the potentially unlimited profits available from buying a call.

Against this slight drawback, the bull spread has one distinct benefit – its time decay characteristic. A close study of Figure 12.5 reveals that the lines tracing out the profit profile tend to cluster together near the mid-point between the strike prices. Moreover, above a certain underlying price, around 101 in this illustration, time decay appears to benefit the holder. To the right of this point

FIGURE 12.6
Comparison of bull call spread with simple option strategy

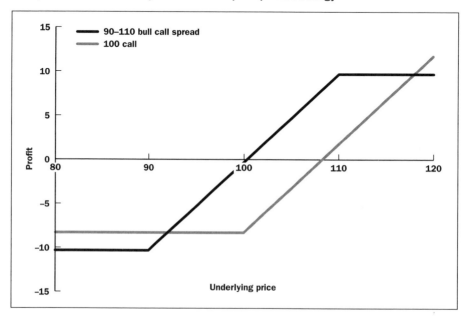

the profit actually rises as one moves from the initial line (270 days to maturity) towards the final line showing the profit at maturity. The explanation for this is in two parts. First, the time decay of the option sold works in favour of the holder of the bull spread, counteracting the negative time decay of the ITM option. Second, this effect becomes more prominent as the underlying asset approaches the higher strike price of the option sold.

A clearer picture of this beneficial time decay is evident if we plot theta for the entire portfolio, and Figure 12.7 does this both for the 90–110 bull call spread, and for the simple 100 call option strategy. At the current underlying asset price of 100, compare the theta of around –0.02 for the simple call, implying a loss of more than 50¢ a month, with the negligible theta for the bull spread.

FIGURE 12.7
Theta for bull call spread compared to simple call strategy

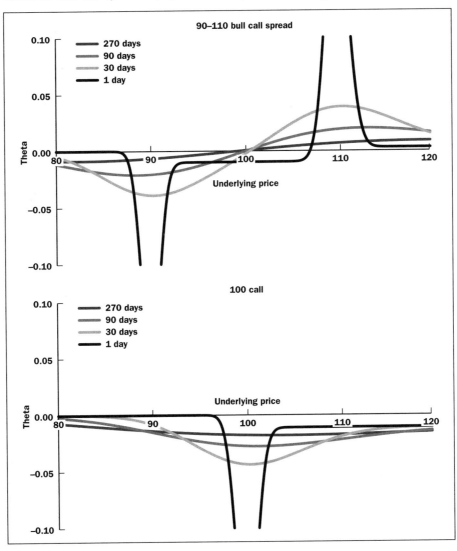

The bull spread can also be constructed with put options in just the same way. A straightforward analysis of the portfolio gives an identical result to that for the bull call spread:

Buying a put with lower strike:	{−1,	0,	0}
Selling a put with higher strike:	{+1,	+1,	0}
Net result:	{0,	+1,	0}

In fact, it matters little to the final result whether a bull spread is built with calls or with puts. Not only is the broad characteristic of {0, +1, 0} exactly the same, the precise financial results throughout the life of the strategy are almost the same, as Figure 12.8 demonstrates.

The only minor differences between this figure and Figure 12.5 for the bull call spread are the exact profit figures as expiry approaches. In every case, the bull put spread produces a result 0.72 below that for the bull call spread. For example, the maximum profit attained with the bull call spread is 9.69, compared with 8.97 for the bull put spread.

The explanation for this difference is quite straightforward. The bull call spread will always result in a net premium cost, because the call option sold is at a higher strike price, more out-of-the-money than the option purchased, and therefore cheaper. Conversely, the bear put spread will always result in a net inflow of premium, because the put option sold, also at the higher strike price, is now more in-the-money. In this example, the net premium outflow for the

FIGURE 12.8
Profit profile for bull put spread

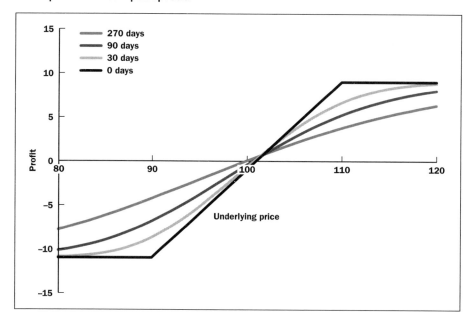

call spread is 10.31, compared with an inflow of 8.97 for the put spread. The difference in premiums is thus 19.28, in favour of the put spread. If this saving of 19.28 is invested at 5% for 270 days, the interest earned is 0.72. The bull put spread must therefore underperform by exactly this amount when compared to the bull call spread.

Bear spreads can be constructed in just the same way as bull spreads, except that the option sold must now be the one with the lower strike price. Figure 12.9 shows the resulting profit profile from a bear put spread. This is simply the mirror image of the bull call spread illustrated in Figure 12.5, with similar time decay characteristics working in favour of the holder, but this time when the underlying price falls.

In selecting the options to create either a bull or bear spread, an investor or speculator must weigh up:

- the net premium cost
- the likely strength of any directional move in the underlying asset price
- timing.

If a significant price move was expected, a speculator may prefer options with widely separated strike prices, to produce a profile with an extended diagonal middle section. Any benefit will be offset, to some extent, by a more expensive premium, and higher adverse time decay until the market moves. All option strategies involve a compromise.

FIGURE 12.9
Bear put spread

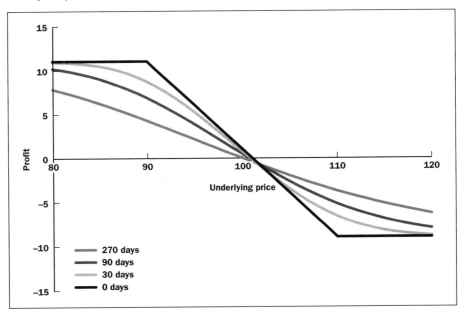

Horizontal spreads

These spreads involve buying and selling options with the same exercise price, but with different times to maturity. This means that it is impossible to hold such a spread until the final maturity of both options because one of the options will already have matured earlier. This means that any analysis based on maturity profiles, like the {0, +1} nomenclature introduced earlier, is inappropriate here. Instead, it is necessary to analyse the characteristics of the component options prior to maturity.

Consider a horizontal spread which comprises the purchase of a long-dated option and the sale of a short-dated option, both at-the-money. If there is little movement in the underlying asset price, both options will exhibit time decay. The long position in the long-dated option will therefore lose value for the spread holder, and the short position in the short-dated option will gain value. However, as time decay will be greater for the short-dated option, and this decay works in favour of the holder, the spread as a whole will make money as time passes. Figure 12.10 illustrates the characteristics of this spread, built using 270-day and 90-day options.

The paler two lines in Figure 12.10 show the profit profile 90 days and 30 days prior to the expiry of the short-dated option, while the solid black line shows the

FIGURE 12.10
Horizontal spread

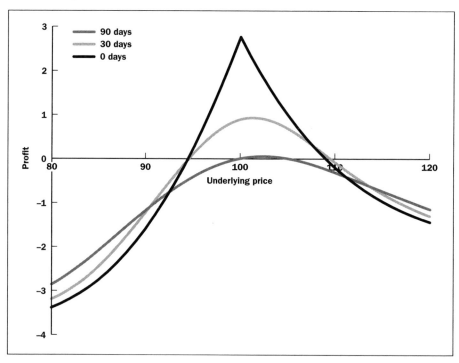

result upon expiry. Unlike with previous profit profiles, the black line is curved, not straight, because the long-dated option still has 180 days to mature and therefore exhibits a curved characteristic.

The y-axis scale of Figure 12.10 shows that there is not much to be gained or lost from a horizontal spread, largely because rather similar options have been bought and sold. The strategy will make money in a relatively static market through the beneficial effect of time decay, and will remain profitable even if the underlying price drops to 95 or rises to 109, a relatively wide range.

Of course, it is possible to create a horizontal spread with the opposite profile, by buying the short-dated option and selling the long-dated one. The profit profile would be the same as Figure 12.10, only upside down. Such a strategy would lose through the action of time decay, but would gain if there was a shift in the market, and also from the possibility to earn interest on the net premiums received.

Diagonal spreads

A vertical spread has a definite direction but little time decay. A horizontal spread has little directional bias, but exploits time decay. As one might imagine, a diagonal spread is a mixture of the two, and features both a directional bias and time decay. Figure 12.11 illustrates two different diagonal spreads. The first involves selling a short-dated 100 call and buying a long-dated 90 call at a net premium cost of 10.04. The second spread involves switching the strikes: selling a short-dated 90 call and buying a long-dated 100 call for a net premium inflow of 3.16.

The first diagonal spread is relatively expensive to establish, because the option bought is long-dated and in-the-money, while the option sold is short-dated and at-the-money. In return, the spread is profitable if the short-date option expires while the underlying asset is anywhere above 96. This reflects the bullish directional slant arising from buying the call option with the lower strike, just like a vertical spread. Maximum profits are achieved if the asset finishes at exactly 100, reflecting the beneficial action of time decay at the strike price of the short-dated option, just like a horizontal spread. The flavours of both vertical and horizontal spreads come clearly through.

The second diagonal spread actually brings in premium income, because the premium income of 11.44 from the ITM option, despite its short time to maturity, exceeds the premium expense of 8.28 from the ATM longer-dated option. Selling the call option with the lower strike gives this diagonal spread its distinctly bearish tendency, as is evident from the diagram. Profits now emerge if the underlying asset finishes below 100, and maximum profits occur at the strike price of the short-dated option, 90.

FIGURE 12.11

Diagonal spreads

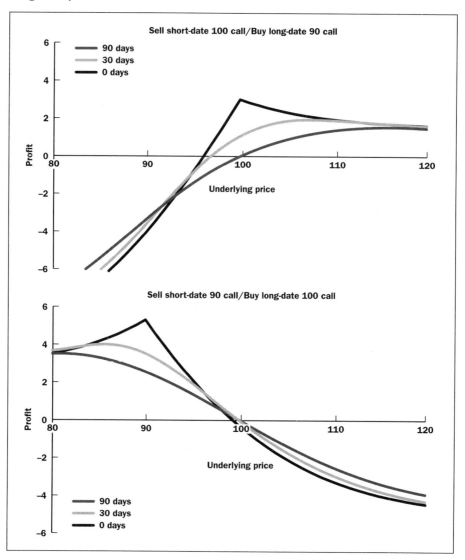

12.3 Volatility structures

Certain combinations of options are designed to react to a shift in volatility, but the concept of a 'shift in volatility' can mean different things to different people. Some view it as a significant movement in the market price of some asset, for example a jump in interest rates, or the sudden devaluation of a currency. Others view this concept as meaning a change in the implied volatility of options. We will examine both viewpoints initially by reference to the most common volatility structure, the straddle.

Straddles

A *long straddle* is the purchase of a put option and a call option with identical characteristics: the same strike price, the same time to maturity, and the same underlying asset, of course. We can obtain an idea of the resulting profile by combining the individual characteristics of the two options:

Buying a put option:	{−1,	0}
Buying a call option:	{0,	+1}
Net result:	{−1,	+1}

implying a 'V' shape. At first sight, it might appear that buying an ATM put and call creates a combination that cannot possibly lose. If the underlying asset drops in price, the put expires in-the-money, while if the asset rises in price, the call expires in-the-money. Unless the underlying asset price is exactly equal to the strike price at maturity, an unlikely outcome, one or other of the options must provide the straddle holder with a payoff, and one that grows in size the further away the asset price deviates from the strike price at maturity.

Unfortunately, this simple vision ignores the premiums that must be paid to acquire the options in the first place. Furthermore, if ATM options are chosen, the premiums will be relatively large because time value is greatest for options struck at-the-money. Figure 12.12 provides a more complete illustration, showing not only the V-shaped characteristic at maturity but also the behaviour of the straddle over time.

FIGURE 12.12
Long straddle

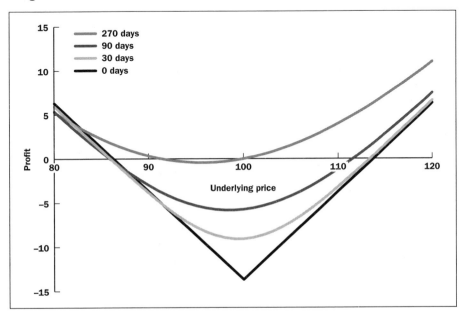

In this illustration, with both options struck at 100, the total premium amounts to 13.69. This means that the underlying asset price must move up or down by at least this amount if the straddle is to prove profitable at maturity. The break-even asset prices are therefore at 86.31 and 113.69, where the solid black line crosses the zero profit axis in the figure. If the underlying asset price finishes between these points at maturity, the straddle will end up losing money for the holder.

A straddle held to maturity would therefore require a significant shift in the market price of the underlying asset in order to prove profitable, one that is statistically less than likely to occur. In fact, by applying equation 10.17 from Chapter 10, it is possible to calculate that in this case there is only a 43.1% chance of the straddle earning money. When interest on the premiums is taken into account, the break-even prices move even further away and the chance to make a profit drops to just 41.4% here.

Another feature evident from Figure 12.12 is the aggressive time decay when the underlying asset price stays at 100. Initially, the straddle loses around 0.2% of the initial premium paid every day. By the time 180 days have elapsed, the options have lost almost 42% of their value and the rate of loss each day increases to 0.3%. One month prior to expiry, the straddle has lost two-thirds of its value, which now erodes at 0.6% per day. Straddles are therefore an expensive option portfolio to hold over an extended period of time.

This first view of 'a shift in volatility' – as being equivalent to a significant move in market prices – does not place the straddle in such a flattering light, as we can see. To examine the alternative interpretation, that a shift in volatility means a change in implied volatility, it is necessary to construct a different kind of profit profile, one that illustrates how straddles respond to implied volatility.

Before we do this, however, there is a problem with the straddle we have been examining so far. An investor wishing to take a view of implied volatility does not want any other exposures, but a glance at Figure 12.12 shows that there is an exposure to the underlying asset price. When the straddle is first created, the 270-day line is not flat when the underlying asset is at the initial price of 100; instead there is a small positive slope. For a ±1% change in the underlying asset price, the straddle exhibits a ±0.2% change in value. The reason for this is that the deltas of the two options are opposite in sign, but not quite equal. The call delta is +0.60 while the put delta is –0.40. The combined delta of +0.20 explains the ±0.2% change in straddle value for a ±1% change in the underlying asset price.

To address this problem, the most common solution is to buy or sell the appropriate amount of the underlying asset in order to create a *delta neutral straddle*. In this case, selling 20% of the underlying asset will hedge the residual exposure to the underlying asset price and create the straddle pictured in Figure 12.13. Note that the 270-day line now sits squarely on the x-axis. For small movements in the asset price, either up or down, the delta-hedged straddle makes neither a profit nor a loss. This is exactly how a delta-neutral portfolio should be.

FIGURE 12.13

Delta-neutral straddle

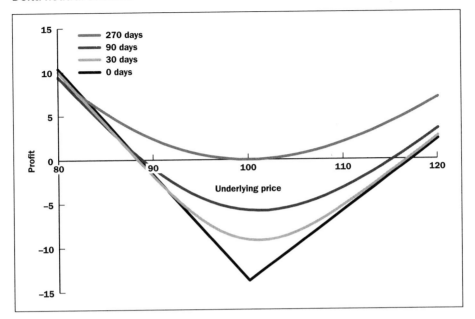

In principle, another way to create a delta-neutral straddle would be to ratio the amount of puts to calls. In practice, this would be a more awkward approach because delta hedging is likely to be an on-going process rather than a one-off task. Although the hedged portfolio remains delta neutral for small movements in the underlying asset price, this is not the case for larger movements. As Figure 12.13 shows, once the underlying asset price fluctuates by more than a few percentage points from the original price of 100, the 270-day line curves away from the zero profit/loss line. For example, if the underlying asset price reaches 105 the straddle generates a profit[1] of 0.53 and has a delta of +0.21. This exposure to the underlying asset price can be avoided by constantly delta hedging, using the technique explained in section 11.6 in the previous chapter, and this is more easily accomplished by executing single trades in the underlying asset than having to execute pairs of option trades to re-balance the put–call ratio.

Now that we have created a delta-neutral straddle, we can examine its response to changes in implied volatility. The charts in Figures 12.12 and 12.13 looked at the option portfolio at different times to maturity keeping implied volatility constant. Figure 12.14, meanwhile, examines the straddle at one moment in time, but for different levels of implied volatility.

Since we are now examining profit profiles far from maturity, the V-shape that many people associate with a straddle disappears. Instead, each of the curved profit profiles traces out the profits earned by the straddle at a specific level of volatility. If implied volatility was to rise by 5%, the profit profile moves from the solid black line up to the dark grey line of Figure 12.14. At inception, no matter

FIGURE 12.14

Volatility profit profile for delta-neutral straddle

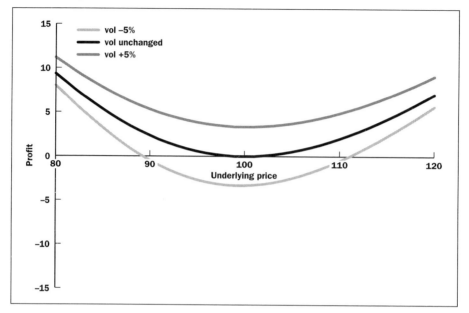

where in the 80–120 range the underlying price ends up, the gap between these two lines is between 1.61 and 3.33 – the profit from a 5% rise in volatility. Of course, there would be a similar loss were volatility to fall. If implied volatility were to decline by 5%, then the profit profile would move down to the light grey line.

If someone had the opposite view, that implied volatility might fall in the future, the opposite position could be adopted. A short straddle, obtained by selling puts and calls at the same exercise price, gives exactly the opposite profile to those illustrated previously. Figure 12.15 provides an explicit illustration of a delta-hedged short straddle, showing profit profiles over time and profit profiles with changes in volatility.

Strangles

A common alternative to the straddle is the *strangle*, and this is constructed in a similar way but using options with different strike prices. Usually, strangles employ OTM options, to lower the premium cost. The resultant profile will look very similar to the V-shaped straddle, except for a flat bottom between the two strike prices:

Buying a put with lower strike:	{−1,	0,	0}
Buying a call with higher strike:	{0,	0,	+1}
Net result:	{−1,	0,	+1}

FIGURE 12.15
Short delta-neutral straddle

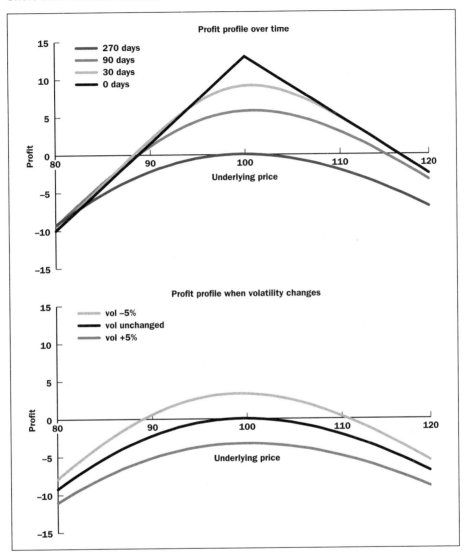

Figure 12.16 pictures the time and volatility profit profiles for a delta-hedged long strangle built by buying equal amounts of 90 puts and 110 calls, and then executing a delta hedge by selling 19% of the underlying asset. As both these options are out-of-the-money, the premium in this case is considerably less than for the straddle, only 6.21 compared with 13.69.

If the strangle were held to maturity, two conflicting factors influence the break-even levels for the underlying asset price. On the one hand, the strangle premium is much lower, which tends to lessen the amount by which the underlying asset price must move. On the other hand, the asset price must move a certain amount in either direction before one or other of the options becomes

FIGURE 12.16

Long delta-neutral strangle

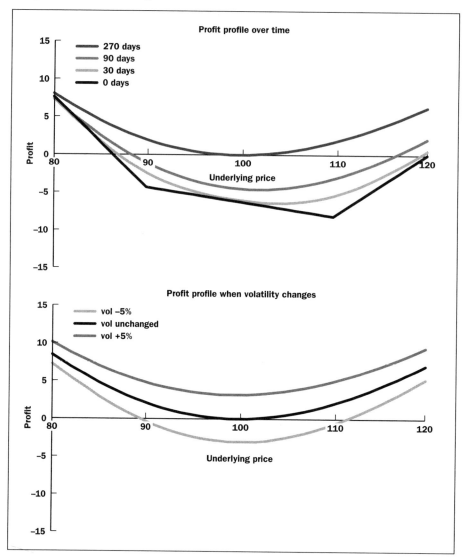

in-the-money. This 'dead space' tends to increase the amount that the asset price must move before the strangle breaks even. The net effect is to make the gap between break-even points equal to twice the premiums paid plus the gap between the strike prices, plus an additional factor dependent upon the size of the delta hedge, and this gap will always be wider than that for the equivalent straddle.[2] In this example, the underlying asset must move below 86.39 or above 119.99, and this will occur with a statistical probability of only 34.3%. In fact, there is a 56.5% chance that the underlying asset will finish in between the strike prices, so that both options expire out-of-the-money.

Comparing a strangle with a straddle thus far, the strangle has the disadvantage that it is less likely to result in a profit if held to maturity, and is quite likely to end up worthless. Counteracting this, the strangle has the advantage of being much cheaper than the straddle, minimising the initial outlay and the amount that can be lost if the asset price remains static.

However, compare the volatility profile of the strangle shown in the second part of Figure 12.16 with that for the straddle in Figure 12.14 – they are virtually identical. This means that a strangle is almost as efficient at taking advantage of a change in implied volatility as a straddle, though it may cost only half as much. For an explanation of this, refer back to Figure 11.19 in the previous chapter which showed, among other things, the vega of options with different maturities. For long-dated options, the vega is much the same for options slightly in-the-money or slightly out-of-the-money as it is for an at-the-money option. This means that the sensitivity of a strangle built with OTM options will be much the same as that for a straddle constructed from ATM options. In these examples, the vega for the straddle was 0.66 compared with 0.56 for the strangle – 85% of the volatility sensitivity for just 45% of the premium.

12.4 Range structures

So far we have explored spread structures, which generally allow an investor to exploit a directional view of the underlying asset price, and volatility structures, which can be used to exploit a view on implied volatility. But what if an investor believes that the underlying asset will neither increase nor decrease but remain range-bound? As we will see in this section, the flexibility of options is such that there are a number of structures which generate the greatest payoff when the underlying asset price remains static. These include butterflies, condors and ratio spreads, and we will explore each in turn.

Butterflies

The *butterfly spread* is a little more complex than the spreads reviewed earlier in this chapter because it involves buying and selling options with three different strike prices, equidistant from one another. A long butterfly can be built by buying one option at the lowest strike price, selling two options at the middle strike price, and buying one option at the highest strike price. If the options are fairly priced, the butterfly can be constructed either from puts or from calls, giving exactly the same result.

The classic shape of a long butterfly, an inverted 'V' with wings, can be predicted by combining the characteristics of its components, illustrated here with call options:

Buying a call with lower strike:	{0,	+1,	+1,	+1}
Selling two calls with middle strike:	{0,	0,	–2,	–2}
Buying a call with higher strike:	{0,	0,	0,	+1}
Net result:	{0,	+1,	–1,	0}

The profit and volatility profiles are illustrated in the example of Figure 12.17, which uses strike prices of 90, 100 and 110. Since the same number of options are being bought as sold, the net premium paid will be quite small, an outflow of just 2.15 in this case. Note from the figure that the classic butterfly shape does not emerge until very close to maturity. At all other times, the butterfly spread is almost riskless, as the very flat curves showing time to expiry from 270 days down to 30 days demonstrates.

The maximum loss to the holder of a long butterfly occurs either if all the options expire out-of-the-money, or if they all expire in-the-money. This will occur if the underlying asset price finishes below the lowest strike price, or above the highest strike price. In both cases, this maximum loss is limited to the net premium paid, and is therefore quite small. On the other hand, a long butterfly makes money if the asset price remains range-bound, and maximum profits are earned if the asset price equals the middle strike price at expiry. Note that this is in the opposite sense to the behaviour of a long straddle or strangle, which loses money if the underlying asset remains static. Once again, this is because the long butterfly has an inverted V-shape, while a long straddle is V-shaped, but the right way up.

FIGURE 12.17
Long butterfly

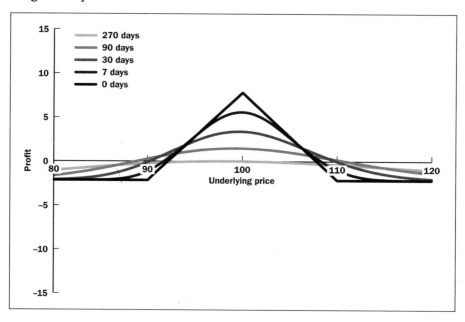

A corollary of the low net premium for the butterfly is that the break-even points are much closer together than those of the corresponding straddle. Here the gap is the difference between the lowest and highest strike prices less twice the net premium paid. Compare the break-even points of 92.15 and 107.85 for the butterfly with 86.31 and 113.69 for the straddle reviewed earlier. Unfortunately, this narrower range works against the long butterfly investor, because here the profitable region is within the break-even range, whereas the long straddle is profitable outside the break-even range. The chance of at least breaking even with the butterfly is only 35%, compared with 43% for the straddle.

On the other hand the low premium leads to a high potential reward-to-cost ratio. In general, the profit earned when the underlying asset finishes at the middle strike is half the break-even range defined above. In the example illustrated here, the maximum profit of 7.85 for an investment of 2.15 gives a reward-to-cost of 3.6 times.

Another contrast with straddles or strangles is the almost complete lack of the butterfly's response to changes in implied volatility. Since vega for long-dated options is fairly flat over a wide range of underlying asset prices, the positive vega contributed by the options bought will be almost perfectly offset by the negative vega of the options sold. As maturity approaches, vega for all options declines, so the vega for the entire portfolio will remain small.

Where butterfly spreads are most commonly used is close to maturity, where they provide a low-cost and low-risk means of profiting either from a range-bound market – by using a long butterfly – or from a market expected to shift up or down very soon – by using a short butterfly spread.

Condors

A condor is very similar to a butterfly spread, except that there are two middle strike prices rather than one. This is analogous to the relationship between a straddle and a strangle. Specifically, a long condor is assembled by buying an option at the lowest strike, selling an option at the next strike, selling another option at the next strike, and buying an option at the highest strike. As with the butterfly spread, there is no difference between using call options all the way through, or put options. A condor incurs about the same net premium cost as the equivalent butterfly, so the maximum potential loss and the gap between break-even points is similar. The maximum potential profit is slightly less for the condor, as it has a flattened top, but this maximum profit is earned over the range of asset prices between the middle strikes rather than at a single point. Figure 12.18 illustrates the characteristics of the condor, from which it is evident that there is not much to choose between a condor and a butterfly spanning the same range of strike prices.

FIGURE 12.18
Long condor

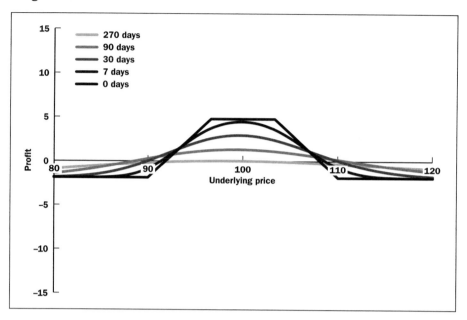

Ratio spreads and backspreads

There is a whole family of spreads involving buying one type of option and selling a multiple of the same type at a different strike price. The term *ratio spread* is reserved for portfolios where more options are sold than bought, while *ratio backspreads* apply where more options are bought than sold. Whether there is a net premium inflow or outflow will depend upon the gap between strike prices and the ratio of contracts bought and sold. However, ratio spreads are normally designed to incur a net premium cost (by buying options which are more in-the-money than the options sold), while backspreads usually bring in net premium (by buying options more out-of-the-money than the options sold). Depending upon whether calls or puts are used, four different permutations are possible, and these are illustrated in Figure 12.19.

As is evident from the figure, ratio spreads have unlimited loss potential because more options are sold than bought. Conversely, ratio backspreads have unlimited profit potential.

Ratio spreads and backspreads have both directional and volatility characteristics. To illustrate the generic behaviour of these ratio spread structures, the call ratio spread will be used as an example here, and the findings can then be generalised to cover the other three permutations. The simplest call ratio spread

FIGURE 12.19

Ratio spreads and backspreads

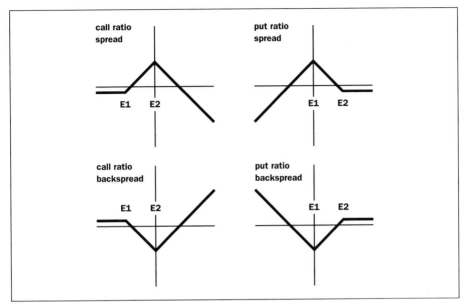

comprises buying one call at a lower strike price, and selling two calls at a higher strike:

Buying a call with lower strike:		{0, +1, +1}
Selling two calls with higher strike:		{0, 0, −2}
Net result:		{0, +1, −1}

The {0, +1, −1} characteristic confirms the profile pictured at the top-left of Figure 12.19: a flat profile, a rising section, and finally a falling section. Figure 12.20 illustrates this with a specific example, using options struck at 90 and 102. In this particular example, there is actually a very small net inflow of premium amounting to 0.08.

Until maturity is imminent, the behaviour of this call ratio spread is similar to that for a simple short call position, with limited profits if the market falls, and mounting losses if the market rises. In the few weeks just prior to maturity, however, time decay becomes highly favourable to the holder if the asset price is close to the higher strike price, with maximum profits being achieved at the higher strike price itself. This latter feature is reminiscent of a short straddle position, and this can also be seen from the volatility profile in the lower half of Figure 12.20, showing rising profits for a decline in implied volatility.

FIGURE 12.20

Call ratio spread

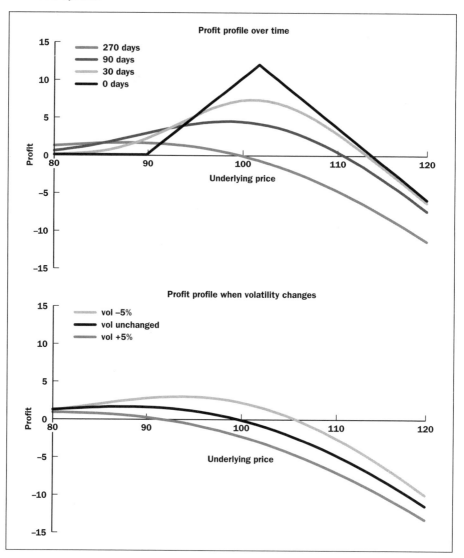

The call ratio spread is therefore of benefit to someone who feels that the market will either be stable or, if it moves, is more likely to fall. The other ratio spreads and backspreads would be suitable depending upon the combination of views as to market stability or instability, and the likely direction of any move. Table 12.2 summarises the possible permutations.

Generally, ratio backspreads are preferred when the market is expected to be unstable, so that the holder can benefit either from the net premiums received if all options expire out-of-the-money, or from the unlimited profit potential if the favoured directional move occurs. On the other hand, ratio spreads benefit

TABLE 12.2
Ratio spread and backspread strategies

	price more likely to fall	price more likely to rise
market expected to be stable	call ratio spread	put ratio spread
market expected to be unstable	put ratio backspread	call ratio backspread

either from price stability, so that the holder benefits from the beneficial time decay of the options sold, or once again from the expected directional move.

12.5 Arbitrage structures

When the basic building blocks were introduced at the beginning of this chapter, some basic relationships were defined between calls, puts and the underlying asset. These can be restated as follows:

Buying a call option:	{0,	+1}
Selling a put option:	{+1,	0}
Net result:	{+1,	+1} (equivalent to buying the underlying asset)

and:

Selling a call option:	{0,	−1}
Buying a put option:	{−1,	0}
Net result:	{−1,	−1} (equivalent to selling the underlying asset)

These relationships are just another way of expressing the put–call parity theorem introduced in Chapter 10. Rearranging equation 11.22 gives a straightforward relationship between the price of calls and the price of puts on non-interest bearing assets:

$$C - P = S - Xe^{-rt} \qquad (12.1)$$

where:

C is the call premium
P is the put premium
S is the underlying asset price
X is the strike price
r is the continuously compounded riskless rate of interest
t is the time to maturity (expressed as a fraction of a year)

There are similar expressions for options on currencies:

$$C - P = Se^{-r_b t} - Xe^{-r_p t} \qquad (12.2)$$

where:

   S is the spot exchange rate
   r_b is the continuously compounded interest rate in the base currency
   r_p is the continuously compounded interest rate in the pricing currency

and the other symbols are as defined before. For options on futures where premiums are paid up-front, the expression is:

$$C - P = (F - X)e^{-rt} \qquad (12.3)$$

where:

   F is the futures price

and the other symbols are as defined before. If the premium payments are deferred, the relationship is even simpler:

$$C - P = F - X \qquad (12.4)$$

If prices for calls, puts and the underlying asset ever deviate from these relationships, a riskless arbitrage would be possible, and the sequences of transactions that would profit from such a mispricing are called conversions and reversals.

A *conversion* comprises the strategy of selling a call, buying a put with the same strike price and time to maturity, and buying the underlying asset. The characteristic is perfectly flat, because the combination of a short call and long put creates a synthetic short position in the underlying asset, which is then offset by the long position in the asset itself:

Selling a call option:	{0,	−1}
Buying a put option:	{−1,	0}
Buying the underlying asset:	{+1,	+1}
Net result:	{0,	0}

The *reversal* is the opposite strategy: buying a call, selling a put and selling the underlying asset, and this will have the same flat characteristic.

To see if conversions or reversals can be exploited as a means to make money, we will take as one example the closing price for the December CME 10yr T-Note futures on 19th August 2011, which was 129-275. There was a wide range of options on these futures, and the December 131 calls closed at 1-21 while the December 131 puts closed at 2-30. Remembering that the futures are priced in 1/32nds and one-half 1/32nds, and the options in 1/64ths, expressing all these prices as decimal fractions, we have:

   Dec future   129.859375
   Dec 131 call   1.328125
   Dec 131 put   2.46875

The last trading date for these options was 25th November 2011, a period lasting 98 days. Taking three-month US interest rates as 0.303%,[3] applying equation 12.3 gives the expected difference between call and put prices as:

$$C - P = (129.859375 - 131)\, e^{-0.0030288 \times (98/360)} = -1.1397$$

The actual difference in prices is –1.1406, which is almost identical, differing by only 0.0009. In this case, no riskless arbitrage is possible, by executing neither a conversion nor a reversal. Although this may disappoint those who wanted to profit from potential mispricings, the *possibility* to execute conversions and reversals serves to ensure that the prices for calls, puts and the underlying asset all trade within a very narrow range defined by equations 12.1–12.4, thus guaranteeing the efficiency of the markets.

Although it seems that a conversion or a reversal is unlikely to be profitable when executed as a simultaneous set of trades, they may instead be the end product of a sequence of trades executed at different times, even though the original intention might have been otherwise.

For example, suppose that an investment manager holds shares currently priced at 100, financed by borrowing at 5%. He believes that the share price will remain static, and decides to write some OTM European-style call options against those shares in the expectation that he can collect the premium income without the options being exercised against him. He sells nine-month calls struck at 110 to bring in premium income of 7.90. Table 12.3 shows the initial position, together with progressive valuations as time passes.

TABLE 12.3
Illustration of conversion

	Initial position t = 0	Shares rally t = 3 mths	Buy puts t = 3 mths	Final position t = 9 mths
Shares	+100.00	+120.00	+120.00	}
Call option	–7.90	–17.24	–17.24	} +110.00
Put option			+4.55	}
Borrowing	–92.10	–92.10	–96.65	–96.65
Interest		–1.15	–1.15	–3.60
Net value	0.00	+9.51	+9.51	+9.75

Unexpectedly, after three months the share price rallies to 120. The calls are now in-the-money, and are valued at 17.24. The profit for the investment manager at this point is the gain in the shares of 20, less the loss on the options of 9.34, less financing costs of 1.15, a net profit of 9.51. The investment manager feels that the rally will be short-lived and the share price will eventually fall back. He therefore wishes to lock in the profits realised so far. One way to do this would be to buy back the calls, liquidate the shares and repay the borrowing. The net proceeds of 9.51 could then be invested for six months, growing to 9.75. However, executing two trades might incur unnecessary transaction costs.

The other alternative is for the investment manager to buy puts with the same strike price and maturity as the calls originally sold, thereby creating a conversion. The puts are fairly valued at 4.55, and the cost of acquiring these will slightly increase the financing requirement from 92.10 to 96.65.

With the conversion in place, it does not matter what the share price is when the options expire. If the share price is above the strike price, the call will be exercised against the investment manager, who can deliver the shares against the short call position to receive 110. If the share price is below the strike price, the investment manager will exercise the puts and deliver the shares, again receiving 110. This can be used to repay the borrowing plus interest, leaving a net balance of 9.75, exactly the same as if the portfolio had been liquidated at the three-month stage. The conversion, acquired in stages, has had the desired effect of neutralising the portfolio against any further developments in the price of the underlying asset.

A final variation on arbitrage structures is the *box*, which is a combination of a conversion at one exercise price and a reversal at another exercise price. Since each component is already riskless, the box is also a riskless structure, but built entirely with options. Conventionally, a long box is a conversion at the higher strike coupled with a reversal at the lower strike. This can also be viewed as the combination of a bull call spread and a bear put spread.

Boxes most often arise in a similar way to the conversion illustrated in the previous example, as a sequence of separate transactions. For example, someone originally having a bullish view of the market might have bought a bull call spread. Later, when the market was about to turn, he may have found that buying a bear put spread at a different strike price was slightly more profitable than reversing the original transactions, but was equally effective at locking in the profit.

Notes

1 Although making a profit might seem unobjectionable, a short straddle would generate a loss under the same circumstances. Generally speaking, those taking positions in straddles want to focus on implied volatility and not have to worry about anything else.

2 This is because the gap in premiums between two similar options having different strike prices is always less than the gap between the strike prices. This is evident by examining Figures 10.11 and 10.12.

3 This converts to a continuously compounded rate of 0.30288%.

13

OPTIONS – INTEREST RATE AND EXOTIC OPTIONS

This chapter focuses on two further and important option topics – interest rate options and exotics. It starts by explaining why interest rate options are different from options on other underliers, and then goes on to show how strips of single-period options can be combined to create multi-period products such as caps, floors, collars and swaptions. The last of these is an example of an option on a derivative, in this case an option into a swap, but options can also be written on other options to create a *compound* option, which we will also review here. The chapter then examines the definitions and characteristics of exotic or 'second-generation' options, including path-dependent, digital and multivariate options. We will see how these add another dimension of versatility when compared with the 'plain vanilla' (or just 'vanilla') options introduced in Chapter 10. The chapter finishes by exploring some of the ways in which options can be found embedded within other financial products.

13.1 Why interest rate options are different

The previous chapters on options have mainly drawn on examples from the equities market, because stock options are probably the easiest to understand. Nevertheless, the principles apply almost exactly to most other underliers such as currencies and commodities. The principles also apply in large part to interest rates, but there are one or two important differences.

First, those wishing to minimise exposure to adverse movements in interest rates most often seek protection over an extended period of time rather than the rate prevailing on a single date. Consequently most interest rate options are structured to cover a period of time rather than a single moment in time, as we shall see in the very next section.

Second, the nature of interest rates is somewhat different from most other underliers. To demonstrate this, Table 13.1 compares four market prices – the Fed Funds rate, the share price of Apple Inc. (adjusted for dividends and stock splits), the $/¥ exchange rate and the price of WTI Oil – over the period 1985–2011.

TABLE 13.1
Comparison of market rates 1985–2011

	Fed Funds	AAPL ($)	$/¥	Oil ($)
July 1985	7.88%	1.81	241.14	27.33
July 1990	8.15%	9.87	149.04	18.64
July 1995	5.85%	11.18	87.40	17.30
July 2000	6.54%	25.41	108.21	29.77
July 2005	3.26%	42.65	111.86	58.70
July 2010	0.18%	257.25	87.60	76.37
July 2011	0.07%	390.48	79.42	97.19

Source: www.wsj.com

Now think where the $/¥ exchange rate could be in the year 2035 – ¥70, ¥60, ¥50 or even ¥30? What about the AAPL share price – $1000, $2000, $5000, $20,000 or even back down to $100? How about the price of oil – $50, $100, $200 or even $300? Now think about the Fed Funds rate – 1%, 5%, 8%? The differences between interest rates on the one hand, and other market rates on the other hand, should now be clear. Share prices, exchange rates and commodity prices can drift upwards or downwards almost without limit, but interest rates in a major economy are seldom outside the range 0% to 8%.

As we saw in sections 10.6 and 10.7 of Chapter 10, option pricing models like the original Black–Scholes model assume that market prices follow a random walk, and Figure 11.3 showed the resultant envelope of asset prices expanding ever wider over time. Such models are not really appropriate for modelling interest rates, and most practitioners now use one of a range of models designed explicitly for pricing interest rate options. The references at the end of this chapter provide recommended further reading for those interested in finding out more about the development and use of these models. Suffice it to say here that it is the unique behaviour of interest rates that warrants the separate treatment of interest rate options compared to options on other underliers.

13.2 Caps, floors and collars

Most of the option combinations considered in the previous chapter have involved mixing options of different types or different strike prices, but usually with the same maturity date. This section discusses an important group of instruments used quite extensively to hedge interest rate risks: caps, floors and collars. As we shall shortly see, caps and floors are strips of options of the same type, usually with the same strike price, but covering a series of non-overlapping periods. Collars combine a cap and a floor.

If a borrower required finance for a single short period in the future and wished to protect against a rise in interest rates, there are a number of choices available. One strategy would be to fix the interest rate now, either by borrowing directly at a fixed rate, by buying FRAs or by selling STIR futures. This has the benefit of avoiding risk, but the borrower then loses the opportunity to benefit if rates decline in the future. An alternative strategy would be to buy an option providing interest rate protection. A call on an FRA, sometimes called an *interest rate guarantee*, would provide the right, but not the obligation, to buy an FRA on the date when the borrowing rate was fixed. If rates had risen above the strike rate by then, the call option would be exercised, and this would cap the borrowing rate at the strike level. Buying a put option on an interest rate future would have a similar effect. However, if rates had fallen, the borrower would simply let the option expire, and could take advantage of the lower borrowing rates.

If the borrower's need were longer term, finance would normally be available on a floating-rate basis, where the term would be split into a number of periods, and the interest rate for each successive period would be fixed at the start of that period. A borrower wishing to obtain protection under these circumstances could fix the rate by buying a strip of FRAs, or by selling a strip of futures. Each FRA or future would cover one interest period during the lifetime of the loan. Of course, there is a tailor-made product that provides the equivalent of a strip of FRAs, namely the interest rate swap explained in Chapter 8. Once again, while this solution provides certainty, it denies the borrower the opportunity to benefit from any decline in interest rates during the lifetime of the loan. The alternative is to buy a strip of call options on FRAs (or put options on interest rate futures), the option expiry dates matching the fixing dates of the loan. At each fixing date, the borrower would compare the prevailing interest rate to the strike rate, and would exercise the relevant option if it were in-the-money, or let it expire otherwise.

Just as the swap is a tailor-made product equivalent to a strip of FRAs, an *interest rate cap* is a customised product equivalent to a strip of call options on FRAs, each one being known as a *caplet*. Table 13.2 summarises the relationship between FRAs, swaps, IRGs and caps.

TABLE 13.2

Classification of interest rate products

	single period	multiple periods
guaranteed interest rate	FRA or future	swap
protection against higher rates plus ability to benefit from lower rates	IRG or futures option	cap

A borrower buying an interest rate cap obtains protection against higher rates, but can enjoy the benefits if interest rates fall. Figure 13.1 illustrates the effect of a 5% three-year cap. At each reset date, if interest rates are below the cap rate, the borrower simply pays the prevailing market rates, and takes advantage of these lower rates. On the other hand, if the interest rates on any reset date are higher than the cap rate, the cap will provide a payoff to offset the consequence of the higher rate, effectively limiting the borrowing rate to the cap level.

As with any option-based product, the borrower gains protection against the downside (higher interest rates) while benefiting from the upside (lower interest rates). With the particular sequence of rates pictured in Figure 13.1, the borrower would pay interest based on LIBORs of: 4.5%, 5% (capped from 5.25%), 5% (capped from 5.75%), 4.875%, 5% (capped from 5.25%) and 5% (capped from 5.5%). The simple average of these capped rates is 4.896%, while the weighted average is almost the same at 4.891%. If the borrower had used a swap instead, he would pay a constant rate throughout, and would not benefit in any period when the market rate fell below the swap rate. If the market had

FIGURE 13.1

Example of protection afforded by interest rate cap

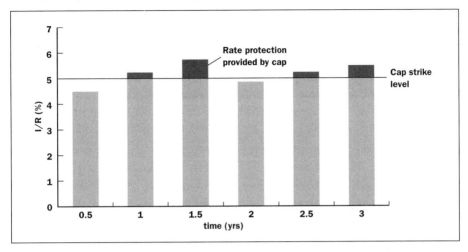

been able to foretell the strange sequence of interest rates that occur in this illustration, the swap rate would have been 5.178%. On the face of it, the cap works out about 29bp cheaper, but then we have not yet considered what the cost of the cap would have been in this case.

We will explore some basic methods of pricing caps and other interest rate derivatives in section 13.5 later in this chapter. As we will see, by using those techniques, together with assumptions about interest rate volatilities in the prevailing economic environment, we can generate a set of up-front premium quotations for interest rate caps of different maturities and with different strikes, like those illustrated in Table 13.3. These quotations are always expressed as a percentage of the notional principal. As an example, a borrower with a five-year floating rate $10m loan who wanted to cap the interest rate at 5% would need to pay a premium of 180bp or $180,000 up-front, which is equivalent to 40bp p.a. on an amortised basis.

TABLE 13.3

Example cap and floor premiums

Maturity	Swap rate	Up-front cap premiums (bp)					Up-front floor premiums (bp)			
		3.0%	3.5%	4.0%	4.5%	5.0%	2.5%	3.0%	3.5%	4.0%
2yr	2.85%	73	38	17	7	2	5	27	64	116
3yr	3.50%	245	165	104	61	33	5	27	66	122
4yr	3.95%	455	333	231	151	94	5	28	66	125
5yr	4.29%	687	524	384	268	180	5	28	67	128
7yr	4.81%	1193	957	745	563	414	5	28	68	133

Table 13.3 also shows the premiums for *interest rate floors*. If an interest rate cap is equivalent to a strip of calls on FRAs (caplets), then a floor is equivalent to

a strip of puts (called floorlets). Caps go into the money when interest rates rise above the strike rate, while floors go into the money when interest rates fall below the strike rate. Taking another example from Table 13.3, a five-year floor struck at 3.5% would involve an up-front premium of 67bp, equivalent to 15bp p.a.

One use for interest rate floors is by investors hedging against a fall in future interest rates. By buying a floor, the investor ensures that the income each period cannot go below the strike rate, because the floor will compensate for the difference between the market rate and the strike in any period when interest rates are low.

Another use for floors is in conjunction with a cap. Borrowers using interest rate caps often seek to lower the cost of protection – whatever it turns out to be – by selling a floor at a lower strike rate. The combination of buying a cap at a higher strike rate, and selling a floor at a lower strike rate, is called a *collar*. Using the figures already discussed, a borrower might buy a five-year cap struck at 5% and sell a floor struck at 3.5%. This combination lowers the cost from 180bp for the cap alone to a net cost of 113bp, a saving of 37%. With this collar in place, the borrower's costs are collared between 3.5% and 5%. In any period when rates are higher than the call strike of 5%, the collar will compensate the borrower for the extra interest cost incurred, but in a period when interest rates are lower than the floor strike, the borrower must pay the collar counterparty the difference between the floor strike of 3.5% and the rates prevailing. The borrower is thus protected from interest rates above the call strike, but cannot benefit from a fall in interest rates once the floor level is reached.

Collars are popular tools for hedging interest rate risk over an extended period, because they provide protection against a rise in rates, and some benefit from a fall in rates. By setting the cap rate at or below the borrower's threshold of pain, and the floor rate high enough to bring in sufficient premium income, the collar can be tailored to provide a reasonable compromise between interest rate protection and cost.

By juggling with the cap and floor rates, it is also possible to create a *zero-premium collar* – one for which there is no net premium to pay. Table 13.3 shows that a three-year cap struck at 5% would have an up-front premium of 33bp in the economic environment illustrated, while a three-year floor struck at 3% would involve a premium of 27bp. By moving the floor strike up to 3.09% the premium rises to 33bp, matching that of the cap. This enables us to create a three-year zero-cost collar with a cap at 5.00% and a floor at 3.09%. The borrower would neither pay anything for the collar up-front, nor over the life of the borrowing, but would be guaranteed a borrowing rate over the five years no higher than 5.00%, and no lower than 3.09%. For many, this would be a more attractive solution than entering into a three-year swap paying fixed at 3.50%, particularly if they felt that short-term rates were not going to rise as high as the forward curve predicted. Chapter 19 discusses collars and other tools for hedging interest rate risk in much more detail. In the meantime, Figure 13.2 illustrates the effective cost for a borrower with and without this particular collar in place.

FIGURE 13.2

Effective rate with a zero-premium interest rate collar

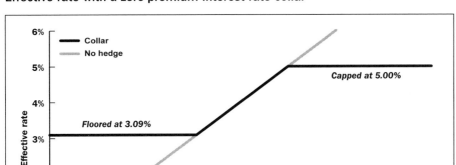

13.3 Swaptions

An alternative form of long-term interest rate protection is the *swaption*. As the name suggests, a swaption is an option to enter into an interest-rate swap on some future date. A *payers swaption* is the right to pay the fixed rate on the swap, while a *receivers swaption* is the right to receive the fixed rate.

Swaptions are very similar to other options, but instead of the underlying instrument being some tangible asset like a share or an amount of some foreign currency, the underlying instrument in a swaption is an interest rate swap. The strike price of the swaption is the fixed rate of the underlying swap, while the expiry date is the date upon which the swaption may be exercised into the underlying swap or cash-settled. In practice, swaptions are invariably cash-settled if in-the-money at expiry. This avoids potential credit-risk issues[1] arising later if the alternative – exercise into the underlying swap – was done. Swaption premiums, like those on caps and floors, are normally quoted as a percentage of the notional principal and are also paid up-front.

As a payers swaption gives the right to pay the fixed rate, this becomes more valuable the higher interest rates are at expiry. This means that payers swaptions go into the money when swap rates are above the strike rate. Conversely, as receivers swaptions confer the right to receive the fixed rate, such a swaption goes into the money when swap rates are below the strike rate. Figure 13.3 illustrates the payoff profiles for two swaptions, one a payers and the other a receivers, both with an initial premium of 133bp, and both being exercisable one year from now into the underlying five-year swap – so called one-year into five-

FIGURE 13.3

Swaption payoff profiles

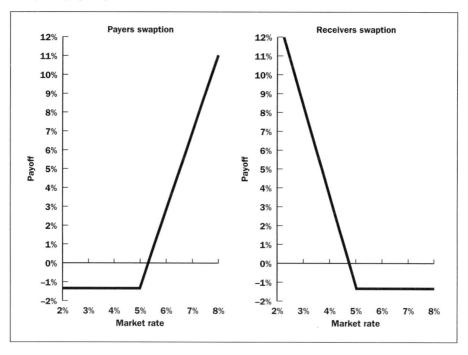

year swaptions. You can see that the profile for a payers swaption is analogous to that for a call option, while that for a receivers swaption is analogous to that of a put option.

Barely visible from the charts is the slight convexity exhibited by both swaptions. When a swaption is cash-settled, the payment is calculated by summing the present values of the benefits from the off-market swap. For example, if the five-year swap rate was 6% at expiry, the payers swaption struck at 5% would be 1% p.a. in the money, which is worth around 434bp in present-value terms. If the five-year swap rate was 7% at expiry, the 5% payers swaption would be 2% p.a. in the money, but present-valued at the higher rate of 7% this is not worth 868bp (twice 434bp) but only about 845bp. This means that the profile for the payers swaption rises more and more gradually on the right of the chart. Receivers swaptions exhibit the opposite effect, with the payoff profile rising more and more steeply to the left of the chart, because as rates fall the stream of payments is present-valued at lower and lower rates.

European swaptions can be cash-settled (or exercised) solely on the expiry date of the swaption. American and semi-American[2] swaptions are also available, and these come in two varieties. In a *variable swaption*, the underlying swap has a fixed tenor, no matter when the swaption is exercised. In a *wasting swaption*, the underlying swap has a fixed maturity date, so the tenor of the underlying swap becomes shorter the later the swaption is exercised.

Swaptions provide another financial engineering tool for handling interest rate risk and are therefore often compared with swaps and caps. A good way to understand how swaptions relate to these other products is to consider an example. Suppose that a construction company knows that it will have to borrow floating rate funds (with semi-annual resets) for five years, but starting in one year rather than immediately. It faces the risk that interest rates may fluctuate over the five-year period of the loan, and some of the ways in which the company may meet this problem are:

a) Do nothing: this is the simplest strategy. If rates rise during the loan itself, it will be forced to pay the higher rate, though the company will benefit whenever rates fall.

b) Enter into a deferred-start swap: the company could enter into a five-year swap deferred one year, whereby it pays the fixed rate and receives the floating rate. This will lock the company into a rate fixed now. The company is completely protected against a rise in rates, but cannot benefit from a fall in rates.

c) Buy a deferred-start cap: buying a five-year cap deferred one year will provide protection against any rise in rates during the life of the loan, while also allowing the company to benefit if rates fall.

d) Buy a swaption: the company could buy a one-year payers swaption into a five-year swap. In one year, the company would exercise the swaption if swap rates had risen above the strike rate, or would allow the swaption to expire otherwise.

Assuming that swaption volatility was 12%, Tables 13.4 and 13.5 provide a comparison between these different alternatives.

TABLE 13.4

Example swap rates

5yr swap	4.29%
6yr swap	4.57%
5yr swap deferred 1 yr	5.16%

TABLE 13.5

Example cap and swaption premiums

	Swaption	Deferred-start cap
strike = 5.16%	1.33%	2.56%
strike = 6.00%	0.29%	1.32%

Note from Table 13.4 the difference between, on the one hand, the regular swap rates for five-year and six-year maturities, and on the other hand the five-year swap deferred by one year. The deferred swap rate is considerably higher because of the steepness of the yield curve used. The cash flows under the deferred swap are similar to those of the regular five-year swap, except that the first two semi-annual payments are omitted. Since these would involve substantial net payments by the fixed-rate payer, their omission has to be offset by higher fixed payments over the remaining periods.

Table 13.5 gives a comparison between the swaption and the deferred-start cap, for two different strike rates. The strike at 5.16% was chosen to be at-the-money for the deferred-start swap, while the 6.00% strike was set at a reasonable point out-of-the-money. In each case the cap premiums are substantially more expensive than those for the swaption, and this highlights two very important distinctions between these two products.

First, a swaption provides protection against movements in interest rates only during the initial exposure period. In the case of the one-year swaption into a five-year swap, the exposure period is just one year long. By contrast, the cap provides protection against interest rate movements right up to the expiry date of the last caplet. In the current example, this extends out to five-and-a-half years.

Second, a swaption can be exercised only once, whereas a cap has multiple exercise dates. This gives the holder a greater deal of protection. For example, consider what would happen if interest rates stayed low for the first two years, then rose sharply thereafter. The swaption would expire worthless after one year, and so would the first two caplets. However, the remaining caplets would continue to provide protection, and would limit the borrower's costs for the last four years of his commitment.

For these reasons, namely a longer exposure period and multiple exercise dates, caps include more time value than the equivalent swaption. Neither product is superior. The cap costs more but offers the buyer more options, quite literally. The choice between a swaption and other products depends upon the objectives of the buyer, and this will be reviewed further in Chapter 19 (sections 19.4 and 19.5).

13.4 Cancellable and extendible swaps

Once a user enters into a vanilla swap, he is obliged to continue exchanging payments all the way until the maturity of the swap, even if this proves to be disadvantageous. Imagine a company which is borrowing money for five years, fears a rise in interest rates and therefore wishes to lock into a fixed rate. The simplest choice is for the company to enter into an interest rate swap as the fixed-rate payer. However, if interest rates remained low, the swap payments might prove an undesirable obligation, and prevent the company from benefiting from the continuing low rates. An alternative would have been for the company to hedge its interest rate exposure by using an interest rate cap, but these involve paying a potentially expensive premium up-front, whereas the swap avoids this. Is there a way for the company to have the best of both worlds? Is there a solution which provides some of the future flexibility of an interest rate cap, but without such an expensive up-front premium? A *cancellable swap* provides exactly this compromise.

A cancellable swap is where one party has the right, but not the obligation, to cancel or terminate the swap on one specific date prior to the final maturity date of the swap, without incurring any further cost. For example, a company could enter into a five-year swap paying fixed at 4.50%, but with the right to cancel the swap at the end of the third year.

Cancellable swaps can be created by combining a vanilla interest rate swap with a swaption. In the example just cited, the cancellable swap could be created by combining a vanilla five year swap with a three-year receivers swaption into a two-year swap struck at the fixed rate of the vanilla swap. To see how this works, consider what might happen in three years' time. If two-year interest rates turn out higher than the fixed-rate on the swap, the company will simply continue paying fixed on the original swap for the remaining two years of its life. On the other hand, if two-year rates were lower than the fixed-rate on the swap, the company would exercise the receivers swaption which – struck at the same rate as the swap – would then be in-the-money. If the swaption was exercised into an underlying swap, the resulting receive-fixed swap would exactly offset the original pay-fixed swap. Alternatively, if the swaption was cash-settled (the usual choice), then the money received would exactly cover the cancellation costs[3] of the original pay-fixed swap. Either way, the swaption has allowed the company to cancel the original five-year swap after three years without further cost.

Using the same economic environment as in the previous section, five-year swap rates are 4.29%, and the up-front premium for a three-year into a two-year receivers swaption struck at 4.29% is 16bp. The company could either pay this as an explicit premium when entering into the original vanilla swap or, more neatly, the premium could be financed by modifying the fixed rate of the vanilla swap. In this case, by raising the swap rate paid by the company from the vanilla rate of 4.29% to the off-market rate of 4.33% the company would normally receive 18bp as compensation (this is the PV of 4bp p.a. for five years). Raising the strike rate of the receivers swaption from 4.29% to 4.33% increases the premium cost from 16bp to 18bp, matching the up-front payment on the off-market swap. The two up-front payments therefore cancel out, which means that the company simply pays fixed at 4.33% for five years, with the embedded right to cancel the swap after three years, with neither up-front nor cancellation payment. Figure 13.4 pictures the evolution of the vanilla swap plus receivers swaption with up-front payment into an off-market swap plus receivers swaption with no up-front payment.

There is actually a second way in which a cancellable swap can be created. Instead of entering into a five-year vanilla swap as the fixed-rate payer and implementing the cancellation feature by buying a three-year into a two-year receivers swaption, the company could instead pay fixed on just a three-year swap, and acquire the right to extend the swap by buying a three-year into a two-year payers swaption. The result is just the same. Although the vanilla three-year swap rate in the same environment is just 3.50%, the payers swaption struck at this rate would cost 361bp up-front. To avoid the up-front premium payment for the swaption, the rate for the three-year swap needs to be

FIGURE 13.4

Creating a cancellable swap

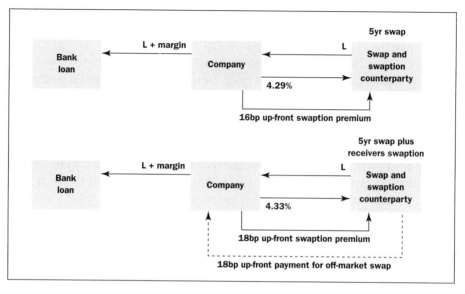

increased to 4.33%, so that the 236bp up-front payment for the off-market swap funds the reduced swaption premium of 236bp for a three-year into a two-year payers swaption struck at 4.33%. Table 13.6 summarises the key numbers for both implementations – the 5yr swap cancellable after three years, and the 3yr swap extendible after three years.

TABLE 13.6

Cancellable and extendible swaps

	Vanilla swap		Off-market swap			Swaption	
					Up-front	Struck at vanilla swap rate	Struck at off-market swap rate
	Maturity	Rate	Maturity	Rate	payment		
Cancellable swap (receivers swaption)	5yrs	4.29%	5yrs	4.33%	18bp	16bp	18bp
Extendible swap (payers swaption)	3yrs	3.50%	3yrs	4.33%	236bp	361bp	236bp

13.5 Pricing interest rate options

We mentioned earlier that interest rate caps are actually strips of options, each covering one of the sub-periods within the overall lifetime of the cap. Pricing a cap is actually done by working out the price of each of the individual options within the cap structure as a whole. Figure 13.5 provides a schematic represen-

FIGURE 13.5
Schematic representation of three-year cap

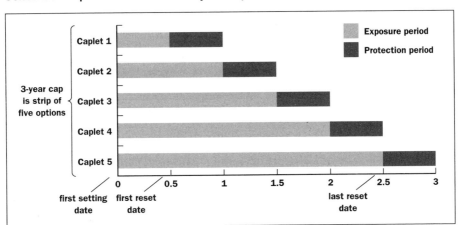

tation of a three-year semi-annual cap, showing that it comprises five separate options or *caplets*.

It is not usual to include the first interest period for two reasons. First, if the borrowing starts immediately, the interest rate for the first period is already known, because the cap trading date and the first setting date are one and the same. An option covering the first period would have zero time to expiry, and therefore zero time value. Second, the strike rate for most caps is set such that the first interest period is out-of-the-money. An option covering the first period would therefore have no intrinsic value either.[4]

Each caplet involves two periods of time, the exposure period and the protection period. The exposure period for a caplet starts when the cap is purchased, and finishes on the interest reset date of the underlying borrowing period. The exposure periods therefore vary in length, the first one being one interest period long, and the last one being equal to one interest period less than the cap's term. The protection period for a caplet corresponds to one of the interest periods of the underlying borrowing, and is normally three, six or twelve months long. The protection periods therefore are usually all of similar length, differing only because one period may be a few days longer or shorter than the next owing to calendar effects.

Figure 13.6 shows the exposure and protection periods in detail for a single caplet, and assumes that the cap is arranged on the same day as the borrowing facility. The figure shows four explicit dates:

A   is the trading date.
B   is the value date when interest starts accruing on the borrowing facility.
C   is the date when interest starts accruing on the period protected by the caplet.
D   is the date when interest stops accruing on that period.

FIGURE 13.6

Detailed diagram of caplet

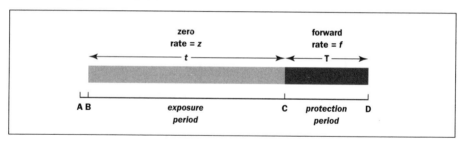

The exposure period of length t is the period between B and C, while the protection period of length T runs from C to D.

As explained in section 13.1, nowadays most practitioners use a special interest rate option pricing model to calculate the appropriate premium for interest rate derivatives, and the references at the end of this chapter provide suggestions for further reading. Nonetheless, it is possible to make some simple modifications to the standard Black–Scholes (B–S) model and obtain a reasonable formula for valuing caplets, floorlets and swaptions. While the answers generated may not be precise enough for real-world use, they are sufficiently accurate to produce the illustrations and comparisons we show here.

The B–S model was presented in the previous chapter, but for convenience, we will reproduce the formula and symbols here:

$$C = S\,N(d_1) - Xe^{-rt}N(d_2) \tag{13.1}$$

and:

$$d_1 = \frac{\ln\left(\frac{S}{X}\right) + \left(r + \frac{\sigma^2}{2}\right)t}{\sigma\sqrt{t}} \text{ and } d_2 = d_1 - \sigma\sqrt{t} \tag{13.2}$$

where:

C is the value of a call option
S is the current price of the underlying asset
X is the strike price
r is the continuously compounded riskless rate of interest
t is the time to maturity
$N(.)$ is the cumulative normal distribution function
σ is the volatility of the underlying asset returns

To use this formula to price a caplet, it is first necessary to replace S and X with values suitable here. If a caplet is exercised, the holder should receive a sum of money at the end of the protection period sufficient to compensate for the extra interest paid on the borrowing facility. We can write this sum as follows:

$$caplet\ payment = A \times (i - x) \times T \tag{13.3}$$

where:

A   is the principal amount
i   is the interest rate at the reset date of the protection period
x   is the cap strike rate
T   is the length of the protection period (expressed as a fraction of a year)

This is equivalent to the caplet holder paying out AxT and receiving AiT. Compare this to the exercise of an ordinary call option where the holder pays out the strike price and receives the underlying asset – there is a direct analogy. The quantity AxT is comparable to the strike price of an ordinary option, and AiT is similar to the underlying asset. While there are close parallels, we are not quite ready to substitute these expressions into equation 13.1.

The strike price of an ordinary option is paid over when the option expires, but the payment of AxT is deferred until the end of the protection period. It is therefore necessary to discount the caplet payment back to the beginning of the protection period. The appropriate rate to use is the forward rate for the protection period, which is the rate at which a bank could secure a riskless hedge. We can therefore make the following substitution for X in equation 13.1:

$$X \equiv \frac{AxT}{(1 + fT)} \tag{13.4}$$

where:

f   is the forward rate over the protection period

In the B–S model, S is the current price for the underlying asset, but the expression AiT refers to the amount received at the very end of the protection period. To make the two equivalent, we must first substitute the forward rate f for the future interest rate i, and then discount the expression back to the present time. This gives us the following substitution:

$$S \equiv \frac{AfTe^{-zt}}{(1 + fT)} \tag{13.5}$$

where:

z   is the continuously compounded zero coupon rate over the exposure period

Making these substitutions into equations 13.5 and 13.6, we obtain the following expression for the caplet premium:

$$CAPLET = \frac{Te^{-zt}}{(1 + fT)}[fN(d_1) - xN(d_2)] \tag{13.6}$$

and:

$$d_1 = \frac{\ln\left(\frac{f}{x}\right) + \left(\frac{\sigma^2}{2}\right)}{\sigma\sqrt{t}} \text{ and } d_2 = d_1 - \sigma\sqrt{t} \qquad (13.7)$$

where:

CAPLET	is the caplet premium expressed as a percentage of the principal amount
T	is the length of the protection period (expressed as a fraction of a year)
t	is the length of the exposure period (expressed as a fraction of a year)
z	is the continuously compounded zero coupon rate over the exposure period
f	is the forward rate over the protection period
x	is the cap strike rate
σ	is the volatility of the forward interest rate

Note that z is the appropriate rate to use as the riskless rate, and has been substituted for r throughout. Also, A has disappeared because the caplet premium is normally quoted as a percentage of the principal rather than as an absolute amount.

Equations 13.6 and 13.7 therefore provide a means of pricing each individual caplet within a cap. The cap premium as a whole is simply the sum of the separate caplet premiums. Table 13.7 illustrates the pricing of a full interest rate cap with a strike rate set at 5%.

TABLE 13.7

Cap pricing example

Interest period	Exposure period (yrs)	Swap rate (%)	Zero rate (%)	Protection period (yrs)	Forward rate (%)	Volatility (%)	Caplet premium (%)
1				0.0 – 0.5	1.500%		
2	0.0 – 0.5	1.500%	1.500%	0.5 – 1.0	2.506%	15	0.00%
3	0.0 – 1.0	2.000%	2.002%	1.0 – 1.5	3.371%	14	0.00%
4	0.0 – 1.5	2.450%	2.458%	1.5 – 2.0	4.094%	14	0.02%
5	0.0 – 2.0	2.850%	2.865%	2.0 – 2.5	4.672%	13	0.10%
6	0.0 – 2.5	3.200%	3.225%	2.5 – 3.0	5.101%	13	0.21%
7	0.0 – 3.0	3.500%	3.537%	3.0 – 3.5	5.339%	12	0.27%
8	0.0 – 3.5	3.745%	3.793%	3.5 – 4.0	5.531%	12	0.33%
9	0.0 – 4.0	3.950%	4.010%	4.0 – 4.5	5.744%	12	0.40%
10	0.0 – 4.5	4.130%	4.202%	4.5 – 5.0	5.930%	12	0.46%
TOTAL							1.80%

The table shows the zero-coupon and forward rates for each six-month caplet period, and also the swap rates for completeness. Using these rates, and the implied volatility figures given, equations 13.6 and 13.7 have been used to calculate the caplet premiums for each period within the cap. Note that there is a term structure of volatilities, just as there is a term structure of interest rates, and it is usual for the volatility of short-term rates to be higher than the volatility of longer-term rates.

With a cap strike rate of 5%, the 6–12-month forward rate at 2.506% is so out-of-the-money that the first caplet premium covering the second interest period is negligible. The same is true of the 12–18-month period where the forward rate is 3.371%. Thereafter, the caplet premiums in this example grow in size, because the forward rates gradually rise through the strike rate, and also because the exposure periods become longer.

The total cap premium amounts to an up-front payment of 1.80% (180bp) of the amount borrowed, and this agrees with the quotation for the five-year 5% cap given in Table 13.3. This might seem a sizeable premium for a 5% cap when prevailing short-term rates are just 1.5%, but there are two significant factors.

First, while the current six-month interest rate is just 1.5%, the forward rates suggest that interest rates will have risen to 5.93% by the end of the cap period. Although the first few caplets are out-of-the-money compared with the forward rates for the periods concerned, the latter ones are in-the-money. For this reason, the appropriate rate to compare with the strike rate is not the current short-term rate, but rather the swap rate for the cap period. In this example, the five-year swap rate is 4.29%, so the cap is only slightly out-of-the-money.

Second, the 1.80% is an up-front premium covering the entire five-year period. This is a bit like saying that the interest on a five-year loan is 25%, when it was really only 5% per annum. If the cap premium were amortised over the lifetime of the cap rather than being paid in one instalment up-front, the premium paid semi-annually in arrears would be just 0.40% per annum (i.e. 0.20% of the principal paid each half-year). This may be a fairer way of assessing cap premiums.

Floorlets can be priced using a similar formula, related to the caplet equation through put–call parity. In fact, extending the idea of put–call parity to the entire cap and floor gives rise to a similar parity equation: cap–floor parity. We saw in section 12.5 of Chapter 12 that:

$$+\text{CALL} -\text{PUT} \equiv +\text{ASSET}$$

In other words, buying a call and selling a put (same underlier, same maturity and same strike) is equivalent to being long the underlying asset. In a similar way we can say that:

$$+\text{CAP} -\text{FLOOR} \equiv +\text{SWAP}$$

In other words, buying a cap and selling a floor (same underlying interest rate, same maturity and same strike) is equivalent to paying the fixed on an interest rate swap of the same maturity. To illustrate this, if we priced a floor also struck at 5% using the same rates environment, and also included the first six-month period (because the floorlet would be in-the-money) the floor premium would be 5.02% up-front, equivalent to 1.11% per annum. The combination of buying a cap and selling a floor, both struck at 5%, is therefore equivalent to paying 5% per annum fixed for five years, less 71bp per annum (1.11% received less 0.40% paid), or 4.29%, which is exactly the same as the five-year swap rate.

Swaptions can be priced using a methodology similar to that used for pricing caplets.[5] If a payers swaption is exercised, the holder enters into the underlying swap paying the strike rate of the swaption and receiving the floating rate. If s is the current swap rate for a deferred swap matching the underlying swap, receiving the floating rate is equivalent to receiving s instead. Exercising the swaption is therefore equivalent to paying the strike rate and receiving s. The present value of paying the strike rate is:

$$x\sum_{i=t_1}^{i=t_2}\frac{v_i}{F}$$ (13.8)

where:

x	is the strike rate for the swaption
v_i	is the discount factor at the end of the i'th period from now
t_1	is the period from now when the deferred swap would start
t_2	is the period from now when the deferred swap would end
F	is the number of times per year that coupons are paid

In the above example of a one-year swaption into a five-year semi-annual swap, $t_1 = 3$, $t_2 = 12$ and $F = 2$, so the discount factors v_3 to v_{12} would be used. The expression in equation 13.8 can therefore be substituted for the expression Xe^{-rt} in equation 13.1. Similarly, the present value of receiving s can be written as:

$$s\sum_{i=t_1}^{i=t_2}\frac{v_i}{F}$$ (13.9)

where:

s	is the swap rate for the deferred swap matching the underlying swap

and this expression can be substituted for S in equation 13.1. This gives the full formula for a payers swaption as:

$$payers = [sN(d_1) - xN(d_2)]\sum_{i=t_1}^{i=t_2}\frac{v_i}{F}$$ (13.10)

and a similar expression for the receivers swaption:

$$receivers = [xN(-d_2) - sN(-d_1)]\sum_{i=t_1}^{i=t_2}\frac{v_i}{F}$$ (13.11)

The formulae for d_1 and d_2 are as given in equation 13.7, except that s should be substituted where f appears.

Using equations 13.10 and 13.11 we can calculate that, using the same rates environment as pictured in Table 13.7, a one-year into a five-year payers swaption struck at 5% would have an up-front premium of 168bp, while the receivers swaption at the same strike would be priced at 100bp. If the strike rate were raised to 5.16%, which is the swap rate for a five-year swap starting in one year, the two swaption premiums would both be 1.33%.

13.6 Compound options

If it is possible to buy an option on a swap, then why not an option on a cap? There is no reason why not, and such a product is known, not surprisingly, as a *caption*. There are no prizes for guessing what *floortions* and *collartions* are. All of these are examples of options on an option, sometimes called a *compound option*.

Compound options come in four possible configurations: a call on a call, a call on a put, a put on a call, and a put on a put. The first two give the holder the right to buy the underlying option, while the second two confer the right to sell. The underlying option can itself, of course, be a call or a put. Most compound options are struck at-the-money, so that the strike price agreed at the outset is the same as the premium quoted for the underlying option.

There are two main reasons why compound options are bought: to provide protection in a contingency situation when protection may or may not be needed, and as a form of risk insurance cheaper than buying options outright.

As an example of the first application, consider a German company tendering for a sizeable project for a US client. The tender process will take two months. If the company is successful in winning the tender, the project will eventually result in payment of a fixed amount of $1.4m one year from now. The German company is concerned about the resultant currency risk, for if it wins the tender, and if the dollar should fall thereafter, the revenues converted back into euros may prove insufficient to cover costs. The company cannot load the quotation with a margin to cover potential currency fluctuations, because this would almost certainly make its tender uncompetitive.

One solution would be for the company simply to buy a conventional put option on US dollars (call on euros) expiring in one year. This may, however, prove too expensive. Using the following market rates:

€/$ spot rate:	1.4000	Euro one-year interest rate:	3%
Volatility:	12%	Dollar one-year interest rate:	2%

a one-year at-the-money put on the dollar would cost €0.0300 per dollar. Even for a $1.4m project, spending €42,000 may be rather too much to commit merely at the tendering stage. Of course, if the company was unsuccessful in winning the tender, it could always sell the option back after two months. If the €/$ exchange rate remained where it was, the action of time decay would reduce the value of the option to €0.0277 per dollar, a loss of over 7% of the premium spent. If, however, the euro weakened to $1.3500, something very possible, the option would fall to €0.0178 per dollar, a drop in value of more than 40%. The problem here is that a currency option is exposed to currency movements, by its very nature. If there is an underlying currency position which the option is hedging, the currency exposure from the option and the underlying position should net to zero. If the underlying position fails to materialise, though, then the exposure from the option can create rather than solve problems.

A compound option may prove to be just the tool in such circumstances. In this example, there are two conditional events necessary for the company to suffer a loss: 'If the company is successful in winning the tender...' and 'If the dollar should fall thereafter...' A compound option mirrors this structure by offering two occasions when the holder can exercise a choice. The first occasion is the expiry date of the compound option. If the company was successful in winning the tender, it could exercise the compound option, pay over the strike price and receive the underlying option.[6] The second occasion would arise if the company had been successful, had bought the underlying option, and found that the dollar had fallen below the strike price. Under these circumstances, the company could exercise the underlying option, and sell its dollar proceeds for euros at the guaranteed rate.

Using the same market rates, the company could buy the requisite compound option having the specification set out in Table 13.8. The strike price for the compound option is set to the current premium of the underlying option, making it at-the-money. This reflects normal market practice, though it is quite feasible to set the strike price at any reasonable level. Note that the premium for the compound option is just €0.0067 per dollar, less than one-quarter the price of the underlying option. Protection at the tendering stage can therefore be achieved at a fraction of the cost.

TABLE 13.8

Compound option specification

	Compound option	Underlying option
Type	Call on one-year dollar put	Put on US dollar/Call on euros
Maturity	Two months from now	One year from now
Strike price	€0.0300 per dollar	$1.4000 per euro
Notional	$1.4m	$1.4m
Premium	€0.0067 per dollar	€0.0300 per dollar

It is important to remember, however, that if the compound option is exercised, the strike price of €0.0300 must be paid over in order to acquire the underlying option. A total of €0.0367 will have been spent to acquire an option that would originally have cost only €0.0300 to buy. This is not a special feature of compound options, though. Whenever an out-of-the-money or an at-the-money option is exercised, the total price paid to acquire the underlying asset will be more than the cost if the asset had been bought originally instead of the option. What an option provides in compensation is the opportunity to avoid losses if the underlying asset falls in price.

13.7 Exotic options

Nowhere is the tremendous versatility offered by options more evident than in the profusion of 'second-generation' or exotic options, which vary one or more of the conditions or features of vanilla options. Many of these products service a genuine need, and provide a valuable extension to the range of financial engineering tools available for managing risk. Others are novel and innovative, but perhaps will prove to be short-lived. One or two are certainly interesting, but are probably solutions for which a problem has yet to be found.

The diverse nature of some exotic options makes it difficult to categorise them. However, in discussing the various products, we will organise exotic options under four headings:

a) Path-dependent options.

b) Digital options.

c) Multivariate options.

d) Time-dependent options.

We will explain each of these in the following sections.

13.8 Path-dependent options

With a vanilla option, there are only two things that determine the value on the maturity date: the underlying asset price at expiry and the strike price. How the underlying asset price got there is not important. As an illustration, Figure 13.7 shows three possible sequences for an asset price over time. In each case the asset price starts at 100 and finishes at 130. In each case a vanilla call would be worth 30 at expiry. A *path-dependent* option is different, however, because its value would be influenced by not only the final underlying asset price but also the particular path taken by the asset price over time.

There are many different types of path-dependent option, including barriers, average price options, lookbacks, ladders, cliquets and others. They all have one thing in common – their value depends upon the way in which the underlying asset price evolves over time. Probably the most important of these path-dependent options is the barrier option, so we will start by looking at its features, applications and behaviour.

FIGURE 13.7

Possible price paths

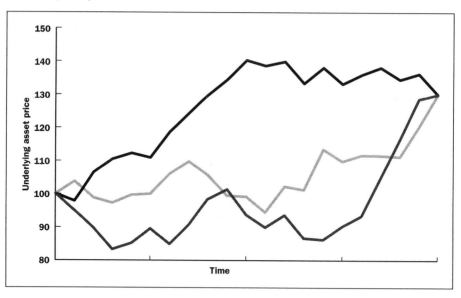

Barrier options

With a barrier option there are two price levels established at the outset. One is the normal strike price, but the other is a specified barrier or trigger level. What happens if and when the underlying asset price should touch or move through the barrier level depends on the type of barrier option. A *knock-out* option starts out like an ordinary option, but is extinguished if the barrier level is breached. A *knock-in* option is activated if and when the barrier is touched. Barrier options occasionally give the buyer a pre-specified rebate if the option is knocked out, or if it fails to knock-in.

These characteristics of barrier options mean that although the buyer always pays a premium at inception, he may not actually own an option at expiry. If the underlying asset price ever trades through the barrier of a knock-out option, the buyer will receive nothing at expiry, regardless of whether the option would have been in-the-money. Similarly, the buyer of a knock-in option will also receive nothing at expiry if the underlying asset price fails to trade through the barrier at some stage in the lifetime of the option.

Figure 13.8 illustrates a typical scenario. Suppose that an investor pays a premium and buys an ATM call struck at 100 but knocked-out at 95. Initially the underlying asset price rises and the option moves into the money. After a while, however, the asset price starts to fall and the option starts to move out of the money. Unfortunately, in our scenario the asset price falls still further and eventually trades through the barrier. At this point this option gets knocked-out and ceases to exist.

FIGURE 13.8
Illustration of barrier options

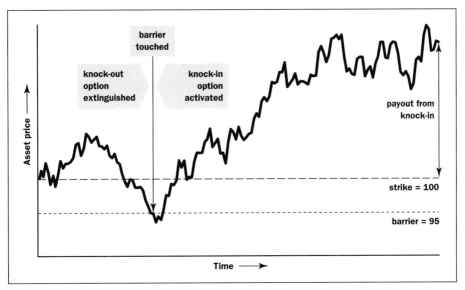

Now consider an alternative scenario. Suppose the same investor had instead bought a knock-in option with the same strike and barrier level. This time he would have paid a premium (usually different from that of the equivalent knock-in option) but would only own a dormant, deactivated option. Only when the underlying asset price trades through the barrier does this option become activated, and thereafter behaves like a vanilla option.

You may wonder why anyone would want to pay money for an option that might not exist at maturity. The answer is simple – barrier options are invariably cheaper than their vanilla counterparts. As an example consider the option premiums shown in Table 13.9 for three-month ATM call options struck at 100, and with a barrier level of 95. When compared with the 6.44 premium for the vanilla call, the two alternative barriers offer savings of 36% and 64%. This could be attractive for option buyers, although they would have to weigh up the benefit of the premium savings against the risk that the option might not exist at expiry. In Part II we will explore further the use of exotic options, including barriers.

TABLE 13.9
Barrier option premiums

Type	Premium	Saving
Vanilla	6.44	
Knock-out call	4.11	36%
Knock-in call	2.33	64%

Barrier options conventionally have their barrier set in the out-of-the-money direction, as in the above example. This means that a barrier event – when the underlying asset price moves through the barrier – is relatively benign because the option is out-of-the-money when this happens, and therefore has comparatively little value. The owner of a knock-out loses relatively little when his option is extinguished, and the seller of a knock-in also loses relatively little when the knock-in is activated and suddenly becomes a liability.

It is also possible to set the barrier in the in-the-money direction to create so-called *reverse knock-out* and *reverse knock-in* options. These can potentially be more dangerous because the barrier event occurs when the option is in-the-money and therefore has a considerable amount of intrinsic value. Table 13.10 re-prices the same barrier options as those in Table 13.9, except that this time the barrier level is set at 105. In this case, the reverse knock-out call is almost worthless because as the underlying asset price rises through the strike, the rise in option value that would normally be seen with a vanilla (or ordinary knock-out) call is completely offset by the approaching in-the-money barrier. This just needs to be touched once, and any value the reverse knock-out option would have had immediately becomes destroyed. Conversely, the reverse knock-in call with a 5% in-the-money barrier is almost as expensive as a vanilla call because any scenario where the option would have a reasonable value at expiry is one in which the barrier would have been traversed at some stage in the life of the option.

TABLE 13.10
Reverse barrier option premiums

Type	Premium
Vanilla	6.44
Reverse knock-out call	0.02
Reverse knock-in call	6.42

Some practitioners use an alternative nomenclature to describe knock-out or reverse knock-out options, and their complementary cousins the knock-ins. They refer instead to 'down-and-out call options', or 'up-and-in put options', and so on. The first word – 'down' or 'up' – refers to the position of the barrier in relation to the current market price, while the second word – 'out' or 'in' – refers to what will happen if the barrier is hit. So the options in Table 13.9 are down-and-out and down-and-in calls, while those in Table 13.10 are up-and-out and up-and-in calls.

The observant reader may have noticed an interesting property from Tables 13.9 and 13.10; when you add the premiums for a knock-out and a knock-in option with the same specification (same underlier, strike, maturity and barrier) the sum is equal to the premium of the corresponding vanilla option. For example, taking the values from Table 13.9 you get:

$$4.11 + 2.33 = 6.44$$

This feature is explained in section 13.12 later in this chapter.

In addition to the standard and reverse barrier options discussed so far, there are quite a number of other variations:

- A *window* barrier is in place for a pre-specified time window only, for example, the last month of a three-month period, or on each annual anniversary date of a five-year option.

- An *outside* barrier is one which references an underlier different from the one that determines the potential payout at maturity, for example, a currency option that would be knocked-out if the price of oil were to trade through the specified barrier level.

- *Double* barriers are where there are two barriers: one set in the OTM direction and the other set in the ITM direction. They are usually both of the same type, giving rise to double knock-out or double knock-in options. Trading through either barrier triggers the barrier event.

- A *Parisian* barrier is one which is triggered only if the underlier trades through the barrier and then remains there for a pre-specified contiguous length of time. For example, the contract may stipulate that the underlier must cross the barrier and remain there for five consecutive days before the barrier event is triggered.

- A *Parasian* barrier is similar to the Parisian barrier just discussed, except that the pre-specified length of time is defined in terms of cumulative days rather than consecutive days.

- A *soft* barrier is one where the principal reduces gradually depending upon *how long* the underlier spends on the 'wrong' side of the barrier. For example, the notional might reduce by 20% for each day the underlier remains beyond the barrier level.

- A *fluffy* barrier is also one which has a progressive effect, but this time linked to the *amount* by which the underlier has moved through the barrier level. For example, an S&P 500 call struck at 1,500 might have a knock-out barrier starting at 1,400 that reduces the notional size of the contract by 10% for every 10 points below 1,400 that the index subsequently falls.

While some users of barrier options are simply attracted by the lower premiums, others choose them because the characteristics of the barrier option agree with their strategy or view. As an example, suppose that a British company is about to export goods to the United States and has fixed the selling price in US dollars. The proceeds from the sale will be received in three months' time. Suppose that the exchange rate is £1=$1.5000 spot, and £1=$1.4890 three months forward. The company is adversely exposed to a rise in the British pound, and would make insufficient profits if the pound rose above $1.6000. However, if the pound fell to $1.4500 at any time, the company would immediately wish to lock in its additional profit by selling its dollars forward. Under these circumstances, a down-and-out call on the pound (put on the dollar) with the barrier set at $1.4500 would prove ideal, because it would provide exactly the protection required at a lower cost than for a vanilla call option. If the pound never fell to the barrier level, the call would behave just like a vanilla call, providing a payout if the pound was above $1.6000 at expiry. If the pound ever touched $1.4500, the option would be extinguished, but the company would execute the forward trade, thus rendering the option unnecessary thereafter.

Average-rate, average-price or Asian options

For a vanilla option, the payoff on maturity is the difference between the strike price and the underlying price on the expiry date. With an average-price option, instead of using the underlying price solely on the expiry date, the average of the underlying asset prices over a period of time is used. There are many permutations for the averaging process:

- The samples can be taken monthly, weekly, daily or over any other pre-specified cycle.
- The averaging period can cover the entire life of the option, or some sub-period.
- Either an arithmetic or a geometric average can be calculated.[7]

Which method is used will normally be determined by the user's underlying exposure. For example, consider a company buying fixed quantities of goods from a foreign supplier on the last day of each month over a six-month period. A six-month average-rate option, with monthly arithmetic averages being calculated using the spot rate prevailing at 11am on the last day of each month, would probably afford the most suitable protection. Average-price options are cheaper than vanilla options, because the average of the underlying asset price over a period of time is less volatile than the underlying price on a specific date, and this reduces the option's risk and hence its time value. Figure 13.9 illustrates an example of an average-price option involving averaging once a week over the last six weeks of the option's life.

Average-strike options

This is similar to the average-price option in that the underlying price over a period of time is averaged. This time, however, the strike price of the option is set to the average price, and the payout is the difference between the strike and the asset price on the maturity date. Figure 13.10 illustrates the averaging process for an average-strike option, showing how the payout at maturity is calculated.

To clarify the difference between a vanilla option, an average-price option and an average-strike option, we can express the payout from a call option in each case as follows:

vanilla option: $\max(0, S_T - X)$
average-price option: $\max(0, S_A - X)$
average-strike option: $\max(0, S_T - S_A)$

FIGURE 13.9

Illustration of average-price (average-rate) option

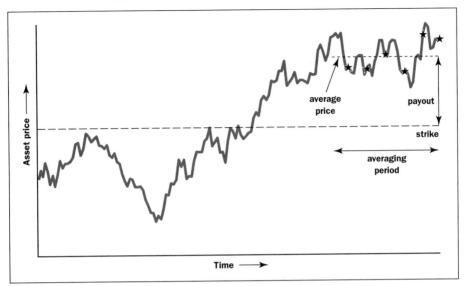

where S_T is the underlying price on the expiry date, S_A is the average of the underlying prices over the averaging period and X is the strike price. The nature of the underlying risk exposure will define which of these payout schemes, and hence which type of average option, is most suitable. To illustrate this, consider three different US companies, each of which sells goods in Europe.

FIGURE 13.10

Illustration of average-strike option

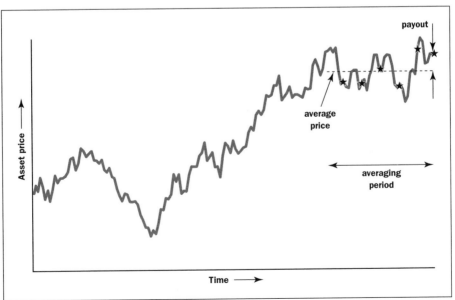

a) Company A makes occasional and irregular exports. The goods cost $1m to manufacture, and the company needs to make at least a 20% profit margin. Price competition fixes the selling price in Europe at €1m. There is a six-month gap between receiving the order and eventually receiving payment in euros. Company A should buy a vanilla put option on €1m (call option on $1.2m) struck at €1 = $1.2000.

b) Company B makes regular shipments to Europe over a one-year period and is paid in euros on the last day of every month. These remittances are immediately exchanged into US dollars at the prevailing spot rate. It faces the same cost and pricing structure as Company A. Company B should therefore consider buying at the start of the year a 12-month average-rate put option on €1m (call option on $1.2m), with a strike price of €1 = $1.2000, and with the payout at maturity being determined by the average of the exchange rates at the end of each month. Then if the average exchange rate turned out to be below $1.2000, the average rate put would ensure that the total dollar proceeds over the year would be sufficient.

c) Company C has its manufacturing facility in the Eurozone itself. Each month, the plant incurs expenses of €833,333 which are remitted by the parent company using a spot €/$ FX trade executed every month at the prevailing rate. The plant is engaged on a large project which will be completed at the end of the year, whereupon payment of €12m will be received, and the company plans to convert this back into US dollars by executing another spot FX transaction at the then prevailing rate. The profit in US dollars is therefore exposed to the exchange rate at the end of each month and, most particularly, at the end of the year. In this case, the company could consider buying a 12-month average-strike put option on €12m. Such an option would pay out if the final exchange rate at the end of the year (which governs the company's revenues) was lower than the average exchange rate during the year (which governs the company's costs). This would ensure that the company's end-year revenue exceeded the company's costs by at least 20%.

In the case of Companies A and B, their costs in US dollars are fixed at the outset, and this dictates the fixed strike price of €1 = $1.2000. The dollar costs for Company C are not known until the end of the year, which is why the strike price for its option must be determined by the average of the exchange rates.

Lookback options

These are similar in some respects to average-strike options, in that the strike price for a lookback is also set when the option expires. However, rather than use the average of the underlying asset prices, the holder of a lookback option can look back and choose the best price achieved during the lifetime of the option. For a lookback call, the strike price will therefore be the minimum price seen during the option's life, while for a lookback put the maximum price is used.

Lookback options may seem to provide a significant advantage over American-style options because the holder never needs to worry that he might miss the best time to exercise the option. The lookback will always be exercised at the best possible price. Furthermore, the lookback option can never expire out-of-the-money. The worst that can ever happen is that the price on the expiry date is the lowest seen during the lifetime for a lookback call (or the highest price seen for a lookback put) and the lookback then expires at-the-money. Unfortunately, because the payoff for a lookback option will almost always be greater than that for an ATM vanilla option, lookbacks are much more expensive, and seldom worth the price in practice. Moreover, there are few situations in real life which create an underlying exposure matching the payoff from a lookback.

Cliquet and ladder options

The strike price for a cliquet option is set initially, but is then reset to match the prevailing asset price on a set of predetermined dates. Whenever the strike price is reset, any intrinsic value is locked in. For example, if the initial strike price was 100, and the price rose to 110 on the first reset date, the strike price would be reset to 110 and gains of 10 would be locked in. If the underlying price subsequently fell to 95 on the next reset date, the strike would again be reset; although no additional gains would be added, the 10 earned in the first period would still be safe. A rise to 103 by the following reset date would lock in additional gains of 8. Although the market has only risen from an initial price of 100 to reach 103, the cliquet now has a locked-in gain of 18. This is because a cliquet option ratchets in gains when the market price moves in the in-the-money direction between resets, but preserves the accumulated profits even when the market moves in the out-of-the-money direction – this is why they are also known as ratchet options. A cliquet, illustrated in Figure 13.11, can be priced as a strip of short-term delayed options, which are explained later in this chapter in section 13.11.[8]

A ladder option works in a similar way to a cliquet, but for one detail. With a cliquet option, what triggers the reset of the strike price and the locking-in of intrinsic value is the calendar. The counterparties don't know where the market will be on reset dates, but they do know when these will occur. With a ladder option, what triggers the reset and lock-in is the level of the market. At the outset, the counterparties agree a number of ladder levels, for example, 100, 110, 120, ..., 150. Whenever the market reaches the next ladder level, the strike price is reset and the intrinsic value is locked-in. Here the counterparties do know where the market will be on reset dates, but they don't know when these will occur. A ladder option, illustrated in Figure 13.12, can be constructed from a strip of reverse knock-out options with rebates.[9]

FIGURE 13.11

Illustration of cliquet option

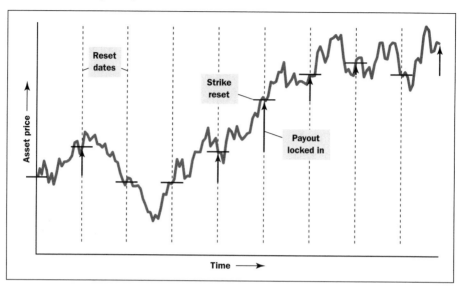

FIGURE 13.12

Illustration of ladder option

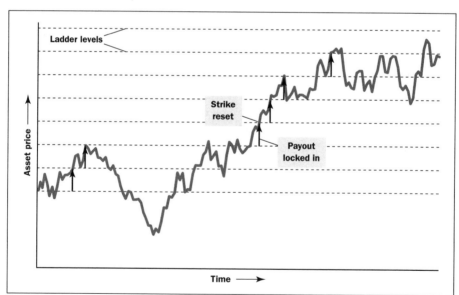

13.9 Digital options

The payoff with a vanilla option depends upon the amount by which the option is in-the-money at expiry. A call, for example, will pay out $\max(0, S - X)$, where S is the underlying price at expiry and X is the strike. A digital option pays out a pre-determined fixed amount A if the option is in-the-money at expiry, and zero otherwise. The extent to which the digital option is in-the-money is therefore not relevant. Figure 13.13 sketches the payoff from a vanilla option compared with that from a digital option.

Digital options can come in two flavours: *all-or-nothing* and *one-touch/ no-touch*. An all-or-nothing digital option pays out only if it is in-the-money at expiry, while a one-touch digital option will pay out so long as the option was in-the-money at some stage during its life. In the latter case, the payout can either be paid immediately the option goes in-the-money (pay-at-touch, or PAT) or be deferred until normal maturity (pay-at-maturity, or PAM). A no-touch option is the opposite of the one-touch, and pays out at maturity only if the option was never in-the-money at any time during its life. One-touch and no-touch digital options are therefore path-dependent, with the one-touch akin to a knock-in and the no-touch analogous to a knock-out, except with digital payouts. In addition to the digitals already mentioned, it is possible to find *double one-touch* (DOT) and *double no-touch* (DNT) options. These are like their one-touch and no-touch cousins, except they have two triggers – one above the current underlying asset price and the other below; if the market price trades through *either* trigger level, the DOT will pay out while the DNT will be extinguished.

By themselves, digital options are not that useful. However, combined with other options, either vanilla or exotic, they become an invaluable building block for creating other attractive products. An example is the *pay-later* or *contingent premium* option. This is an option for which there is no premium payable unless the option is exercised. However, the option must be exercised if it is

FIGURE 13.13

Payoffs from vanilla and digital options

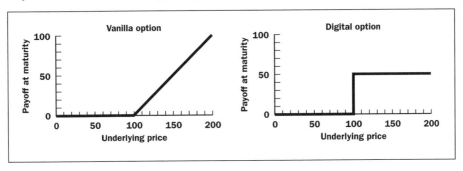

FIGURE 13.14

Contingent premium options

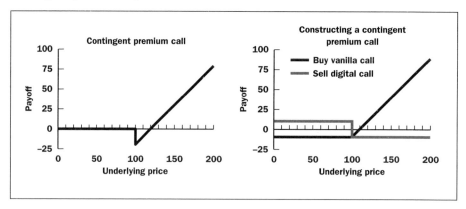

in-the-money at expiry, even if the intrinsic value is less than the premium payable. The advantage to the option buyer, who is reluctant to spend money on buying an option that he believes will not be needed, is that no premium is ever payable if the option expires out-of-the-money. This is a little like a hypothetical car insurance policy where no premium would be payable if there was no claim in a given year. However, the disadvantage is that the deferred premium, if payable, is typically double that of the corresponding vanilla option for an at-the-money structure.

Figure 13.14 pictures the payout profile for a contingent premium call and shows that buying this option is equivalent to buying a vanilla option and selling an all-or-nothing digital option. The premium of the digital is set to match that of the vanilla option by adjusting the digital payout accordingly, and the digital payout becomes the deferred premium. The reason why the deferred premium is around double that of the vanilla premium is because the ratio of premium to payout for a digital option is roughly equal to the probability of exercise, and this is around 50% for an at-the-money option.

13.10 Multivariate options

A *multivariate option* is one where the final payoff depends upon the prices of two or more underlying assets. The complicating feature here is that the value of the option depends upon the correlations between the different underliers, which is why they are also known as *correlation* options. There are a number of examples of these multivariate or correlation options, and some of them are discussed in the following paragraphs.

Rainbow or outperformance options

The payoff from a rainbow call is determined by the highest price achieved by two or more underlying assets, while that from a rainbow put is calculated from the worst performer. Symbolically, the call payoff is max $(0, \text{max } (S_1, S_2, ..., S_n) - X)$, where S_1, S_2, etc., are the asset prices of the n assets on the expiry date, and X is the strike price. For example, a rainbow call option might offer an investor a return equal to the maximum gain from the FTSE 100, CAC 40, DAX and S&P 500 stock indices.

Basket options

These could be considered a variation of a rainbow option, except that the payoff here is the weighted average of the prices within the basket of underlying assets. An example could be an OTC option to cover a specific basket of shares held by an investor. The advantage for the investor is that a basket option is almost always cheaper than a basket of vanilla options. As an example, suppose that an investor owns $5m of Microsoft shares and $5m of Intel shares, and wants to protect the $10m portfolio against a fall in value of more than 10%. As Table 13.11 shows, buying a one-year basket put struck at $9m would almost always be cheaper than buying two 10% OTM one-year vanilla put options on the constituents.

TABLE 13.11

Basket option premiums

Type	Correlation	Premium
Vanilla puts	n/a	7.25%
Basket put	+1.0	7.25%
	+0.5	5.94%
	0.0	4.36%
	–0.5	2.44%
	–1.0	0.00%

The example illustrated assumes an equally weighted basket, one-year interest rates of 1% p.a., dividend yields on both stocks of 2% p.a., and one-year volatility of 30% p.a., again for both stocks. The only instance where the basket option is not cheaper than the pair of vanilla puts is in the extreme case where correlation between the prices of both stocks is +1. In the other extreme case where the correlation is –1 the basket option is free; this is because in such a world it would be impossible for the basket to fall in value at all, let alone by 10%.

Spread options

The payoff in this case is the difference between a pair of asset prices. As an example, an option could pay the difference between sterling and euro six-month interest rates.

Quanto options

In a quanto option, the payoff depends on one underlying price, but the size or value of the exposure depends upon another. Most often, quanto products manifest themselves in options quoted in one currency upon an underlying asset denominated in another. An example would be an option on the Nikkei stock index, with a payout in dollars, so that the index expiring at 11,000 on a call option struck at 10,000 would pay out $1,000.

It may not be immediately apparent why an option on a foreign stock index should result in a variable exposure to the underlying asset – after all, an index is just a dimensionless number. The reason becomes clear, however, when one considers what the option writer must do to hedge such an option. For a Nikkei stock-index option, the underlying asset is a market-weighted basket of Japanese stocks. In order to hedge the call option sold, the option writer should therefore buy delta times the value of this underlying basket. However, the value of the underlying asset in terms of the payout currency will depend upon the $/¥ exchange rate. Suppose that, close to maturity, the Nikkei has moved up to 11,000 and the delta of the stock index option is now 100%. To hedge the now ITM option the writer owns ¥1,100,000 worth of shares that might originally have been bought for ¥1,000,000. If the FX rate is $1 = ¥100, the profit on the hedge exactly matches the size of the $1,000 payout. However, if the dollar then strengthened to $1 = ¥105, the value of the shares held would decline to $10,476 leaving just a $476 profit to finance a $1,000 payout.

Of course, the option writer could try to hedge the FX exposure arising from the yen-denominated hedge and the dollar-denominated liability, but the problem is that the size of the FX hedging transaction depends upon the level of the Nikkei and the delta of the stock index option. With the Japanese index at 11,000 and the option having a delta of 100%, the size of the hedge is ¥1,100,000. However, if the index fell to 10,000 and the delta to 50%, then the size of the hedge would only be ¥500,000. A standard FX forward or FX option is therefore not suitable. Instead, the option writer would need a **quant**ity-adjusting FX **o**ption to hedge, hence the name 'quanto'.

13.11 Other exotic options

We have so far reviewed the most important types of exotic options: path-dependent, digital and multivariate. There are a few others worthy of note, and some of these can be categorised as options where one of the standard contract terms – for example, the strike price, or even the option type – is not decided at inception but later. In this short section we provide two specific examples.

Delayed or forward-starting option

This is an option where the strike price is only determined on a specific future date – the *grant date* – by reference to the prevailing market prices at the time. The most usual arrangement is for the strike price to be set to 100% of the underlying asset price on the grant date.

Chooser option

This variation allows the holder to choose on some future date (the choose date) whether the option is a put or a call. This is similar to a straddle, but cheaper, because after the choice is made the holder has only one type of option, whereas the holder of a straddle continues to have both a call and a put right up to maturity.

13.12 Pricing exotic options

The pricing of exotic options is, unfortunately, much more complex than pricing vanilla options. There are three broad methods available.

Closed-form solutions

For most exotic options, there is actually a *closed-form* solution. In other words, formulae exist which express the fair option price as some function of the input variables. However, these formulae are usually much more complex than the Black–Scholes equation. As just one example, consider the formula for a down-and-out currency call option, with the barrier set below the strike:

$$C_{do} = \max\left[\left(Se^{-r_bt}N(x_1) - Xe^{-r_pt}N(x_2)\right) - \left(Se^{-r_bt}\left(\frac{S}{H}\right)^{-2\lambda}N(y_1) - Xe^{-r_pt}\left(\frac{S}{H}\right)^{-2\eta}N(y_2)\right),0\right]$$

(13.12)

where:

- S is the spot exchange rate
- X is the strike price of the option
- H is the barrier price
- r_b is the continuously compounded interest rate in the base currency
- r_p is the continuously compounded interest rate in the pricing currency
- t is the length of time until maturity

and:

$$x_1 = \frac{\ln\left(\frac{S}{X}\right) + \lambda\sigma^2 t}{\sigma\sqrt{t}} \qquad \text{and } x_2 = x_1 - \sigma\sqrt{t}$$

$$y_1 = \frac{\ln\left(\frac{H^2}{S \cdot X}\right) + \lambda\sigma^2 t}{\sigma\sqrt{t}} \qquad \text{and } y_2 = y_1 - \sigma\sqrt{t}$$

$$z = \frac{\ln\left(\frac{H}{S}\right) + \gamma\sigma^2 t}{\sigma\sqrt{t}}$$

$$\lambda = \frac{r_p - r_b}{\sigma^2} + 0.5 \qquad \eta = \lambda - 1 \qquad \mu = \sigma^2\eta \qquad \gamma = \frac{\sqrt{\mu^2 + 2r_p\sigma^2}}{\sigma^2}$$

If you compare this with equation 10.21 in Chapter 10 you will note that there are certain similarities and symmetries, but equation 13.12 is obviously more intricate. The complexity doesn't stop here, though. As another example, the closed-form solution for a double no-touch option involves summing an infinite series. Closed-form formulae have been developed by various authors over an extended period of time, but Espen Haug's book (cited in the references at the end of Chapter 10) provides an excellent summary.

Unfortunately, in a few cases – such as an arithmetically averaged average-price option – there is no known closed-form solution which provides an exact answer, although approximations do exist. We then have to turn to other methods, like the binomial model or Monte Carlo simulation.

Binomial models

Any option can be valued using the binomial technique, but the problem becomes much more complex for path-dependent options, because every possible path through the binomial lattice must be evaluated individually. Suppose that, at each step, the underlying asset price can either rise by a factor of 1.1000 or fall by a factor of 0.9091. Two possible paths after four steps are:

$$100, 110, 121, 110$$

and $$100, 110, 100, 110$$

In each case, there are two up-moves and one down-move, so the final price is the same for each path. A vanilla option would have the same value whichever path was chosen, because the terminal value of the option only depends upon the underlying price at expiry, not upon how the price got there. An average-price option would have two different terminal values, however, because the average price over the first path is 110.25, but only 105 over the second path, even though the terminal values are the same.

Path-dependent options therefore have the unfortunate effect of exploding the size of the binomial lattice, as pictured in Figure 13.15. In general, for n steps, the standard lattice needs just $(n + 1)$ terminal valuations, while the

FIGURE 13.15

Binomial lattices for vanilla and path-dependent options

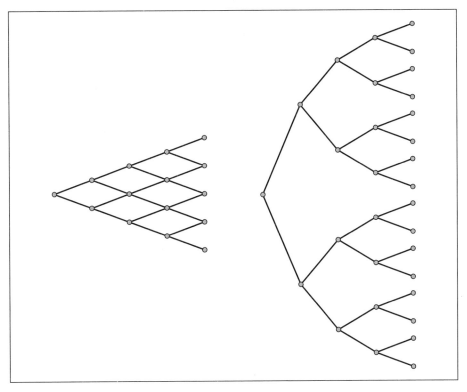

path-dependent option needs 2^n. There are over one million different paths to evaluate when pricing a path-dependent option using a 20-step binomial model, and this makes the task quite time-consuming even with a powerful computer.

As an illustration of what is involved, Figures 13.16 and 13.17 show the calculations involved in pricing an average-price option with the following characteristics:[10]

Underlying price:	100	Number of steps:	4
Strike price:	100	r	1.024114
Time to maturity:	360 days	u	1.105171
Volatility:	20%	d	0.904837
Interest rate:	5%	p	0.595389

The rightmost column of Figure 13.17 shows the terminal values of the average-price option at expiry, using the arithmetic average of the five observed underlying asset prices. This is then folded back using the technique described in Chapter 10 (section 10.8). The answer of 5.64 in this simple four-step binomial model is remarkably close to the answer of 5.75 obtained using a more accurate analytical model. In practice, a binomial model with more time steps would need to be used to obtain better precision.

FIGURE 13.16

Binomial pricing asset values

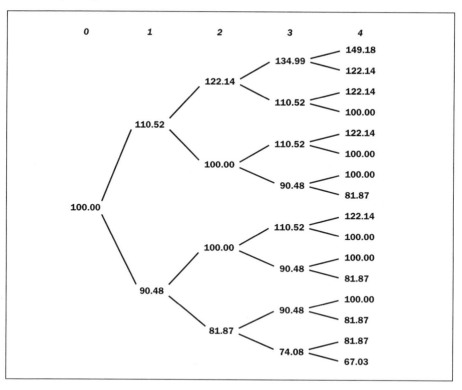

Monte Carlo simulation

When all else fails, it is possible to value any option using a Monte Carlo simulation approach, like the examples illustrated in the previous chapter. This involves simulating the path of the underlying asset at random over thousands of trials, and valuing the option on each occasion. The mean of all the results provides a reasonable estimate for the fair value of the option. For some path-dependent options, especially barrier options, it may be necessary to carry out tens of thousands of simulations, each with small time steps, in order to obtain a sufficiently reliable answer. Figure 13.18 shows the result of one such Monte Carlo simulation where the same average-price option was simulated over 50,000 trials, with each trial itself involving 250 steps. The mean value obtained was 5.73, very close to the previous answers obtained with the other techniques.

In addition to the problems of modelling and pricing, multivariate options introduce a new difficulty, that of estimating the anticipated *correlation* between two or more financial variables. It is difficult enough anticipating the volatility of single prices, but far more complicated to produce reliable estimates for the way in which two or more variables move in relation to one another. For example, what is the relationship between exchange rates and interest rates,

FIGURE 13.17

Binomial pricing – option values

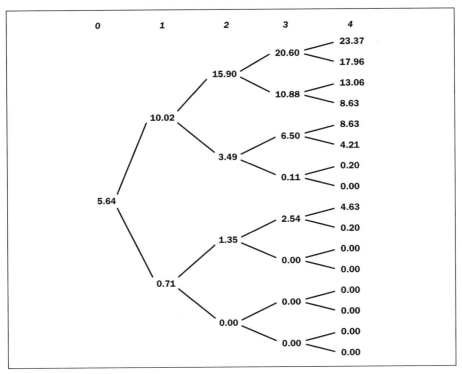

FIGURE 13.18

Monte Carlo pricing of average-price option

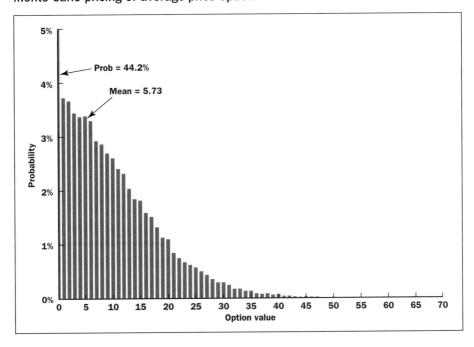

or between either of these and stock-index levels, and will these relationships remain stable over time? Unfortunately, the pricing of multivariate options relies to a considerable extent on values for these correlations.

13.13 Price comparisons between exotic options

The vast range of choice between different kinds of exotic options, each one having several permutations, means that there is a wide spectrum of option prices available. In order to allow some kind of comparison, Table 13.12 shows the premiums for 14 exotic options at three different strike prices.

All the options shown have the same general specification:

Option type:	Call
Underlying asset price:	100
Time to maturity:	90 days
Three-month interest rate:	5%
Dividend yield:	1%
Volatility:	20%

TABLE 13.12
Comparison of exotic option prices

		$X = 95$ (ITM)	$X = 100$ (ATM)	$X = 105$ (OTM)
Vanilla call		7.52	4.47	2.38
Vanilla put		1.60	3.49	6.34
Average-price call	Avg. prd. 90 days	6.03	2.61	0.79
	Avg. prd. 30 days	7.19	4.03	1.96
Down-and-out call	Barrier: 92.50	6.76	4.20	2.30
	Barrier: 95.00	5.55	3.61	2.06
	Barrier: 97.50	3.35	2.32	1.40
Up-and-out call	Barrier: 105	0.49	0.07	–
	Barrier: 110	2.03	0.66	0.09
	Barrier: 115	4.02	1.82	0.56
Pay later call		10.67	8.70	7.29
Compound	Call on call	1.77	1.33	0.87
(30-day maturity)	Put on call	1.74	1.31	0.86
Lookback call	(observed minimums)	9.21	8.19	8.19
Chooser	Choose date: 30 days	7.94	6.30	7.21
Forward-starting call	Grant date: 30 days	–	3.58	–

Starting with the average-price options, these show considerable savings, with the first ATM option being about half the price of the vanilla option premium. Premiums for two averaging periods are shown, one starting immediately and lasting throughout the life of the option, while the other covers just the last 30 days. As the averaging period becomes shorter, the average-price option becomes more like a vanilla option, and the premiums rise accordingly.

The down-and-out call options show savings of between 6% and 48% for the ATM options, depending upon where the barrier is set. The table shows option prices for three barrier levels: 7.5%, 5% and 2.5% below the current underlying asset price. Premiums are cheaper the closer the barrier is set to the current underlying price because this increases the chance that the option will be extinguished.

Although prices for down-and-in options are not shown, it is easy to prove that:

$$C_{vanilla} = C_{do} + C_{di} \qquad (13.13)$$

where:

$C_{vanilla}$	is the premium for a vanilla option
C_{do}	is the premium for a down-and-out option
C_{di}	is the premium for a down-and-in option

To see why, consider owning a portfolio of one down-and-out option and a similar down-and-in option. If the barrier is never touched, the 'in' option is never activated, but the 'out' option remains alive until expiry to behave just like a vanilla option. If the barrier is touched, the 'out' option is extinguished, but the 'in' option is activated to remain in existence until expiry. Either way, the owner ends up holding one vanilla option at maturity. The combination of the two barrier options therefore gives the same payout as a vanilla option at maturity, and must therefore be equivalent in value at any time prior. Thus, knowing the price of any 'out' option and that of the corresponding vanilla option means that the price of the 'in' option can be readily calculated. This relationship is called *barrier parity*.

The up-and-out call options show even greater savings, in one case of more than 98%. While these options are very cheap, they offer little promise of substantial gains. As the underlying asset price rises above the strike to create intrinsic value, it also approaches the lethal barrier. Touching this just once at any time during the option's life extinguishes the option. For these options to have any value at maturity, the underlying asset price must rise above the strike, but not by very much, and this feature severely limits their value.

The premiums for pay-later options are all more expensive than their vanilla counterparts, the at-the-money pay-later option being approximately twice as expensive. In fact, it can be shown that the fair price for a pay-later option is approximately the premium for a vanilla option divided by the probability of exercise (whose value is similar to the delta of the vanilla option). This is why the contingent premium of the out-of-the-money pay-later option is so high, being some three times the premium of its vanilla counterpart. This pricing provides proof, if proof were needed, of Milton Friedman's maxim that 'there's no such thing as a free lunch'.

Some of the cheapest options are the compound options illustrated, all of which have their exercise price set to the original cost of the vanilla option. It must be remembered that the premium shown does not buy the underlying option itself, just the option-on-option. If the underlying option is eventually required, the strike price must be paid over when the compound option is exercised. For example, if the call option into the ATM vanilla call option was acquired, and this compound option was later exercised to receive the underlying option, a total premium of 5.80 would have been paid instead of the 4.47 to acquire the vanilla option at the outset.

The lookback options are some of the most expensive, a buyer having to pay almost double the cost of a vanilla in order to acquire the advantages of a lookback option; few circumstances in real life would warrant such a premium. Likewise, the choosers are all rather more costly than the more expensive of the two vanillas, albeit less than the sum of the vanilla premiums.

Finally, the forward-starting call illustrated has a premium 20% cheaper than the corresponding ATM vanilla, and the 3.58 premium illustrated here is identical to that for a two-month ATM vanilla call.

To provide a visual comparison of the different exotic options discussed here, Figure 13.19 analyses nine 90-day options with a strike price, where relevant, of 100: a vanilla call, an average-price call with the averaging process taking place throughout the life of the option, a down-and-out call with the barrier set at 95, an up-and-out call with the barrier set at 115, a pay-later option, a compound option with 30 days to expiry, a lookback call, a chooser with a choose date after 30 days, and a forward-starting option with a grant date after 30 days. The graphs show the fair premiums for underlying prices extending from 80 to 120. In addition to the points already made, notice how similar the profile of the down-and-out option is to that of an option near expiry. As the barrier approaches, so does the option's imminent demise, and so it is not surprising that the option behaves like one just about to expire.

Finally, to provide another illustration of why these options are called 'exotic', take a look at Figure 13.20 which illustrates some of the Greeks for selected exotics compared with those of the equivalent vanilla option. Note the following examples of their strange behaviour:

Deltas – the delta of the down-and-out options stays much higher than that of the vanilla call, even increasing a little as the underlying asset price approaches the barrier, before crashing down to zero. That of the up-and-out starts positive, as you would expect with a call option, but swings round to negative as the asset price keeps increasing; this is because the option eventually starts to lose value as the underlying asset price rises to the barrier level.

FIGURE 13.19

Comparison of exotic option premiums

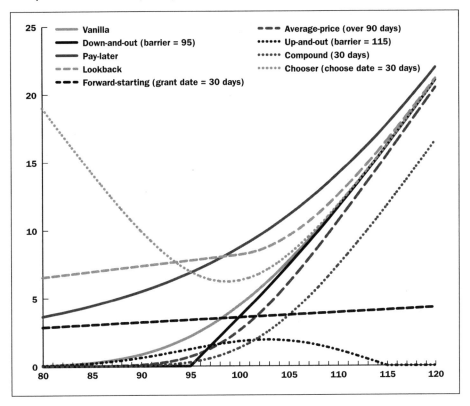

Legend:
- Vanilla
- Down-and-out (barrier = 95)
- Pay-later
- Lookback
- Forward-starting (grant date = 30 days)
- Average-price (over 90 days)
- Up-and-out (barrier = 115)
- Compound (30 days)
- Chooser (choose date = 30 days)

Thetas – vanilla options generally have negative theta, losing value as time elapses. The theta of an up-and-out call, however, swings around to positive value once the option is in-the-money. This is because with every day that elapses, there is one day less for the option to be at risk of being extinguished and therefore of surviving intact to maturity. The digital option has a similar pattern. If the digital is out-of-the-money, every day that passes means one day less opportunity for the option to move in-the-money, so the digital option loses value and exhibits negative theta. However, once in-the-money, every day that passes means a greater chance of reaching maturity and realising the fixed payout, so the digital option gains value and has positive theta.

Vegas – vanilla options always have positive vega because the bigger the volatility, the greater and greater potential gains from an in-the-money expiry more than offset the fixed losses from an out-of-the-money expiry. However, if the up-and-out call is in-the-money but below the barrier, bigger volatility increases the threat both from the higher barrier and the lower strike. Similarly, with bigger volatility the ITM digital call gains nothing from a higher underlying price, but can lose if the underlying asset moves below the strike. Both these options would actually prefer the underlying asset price to remain where it is; hence they both exhibit negative vega.

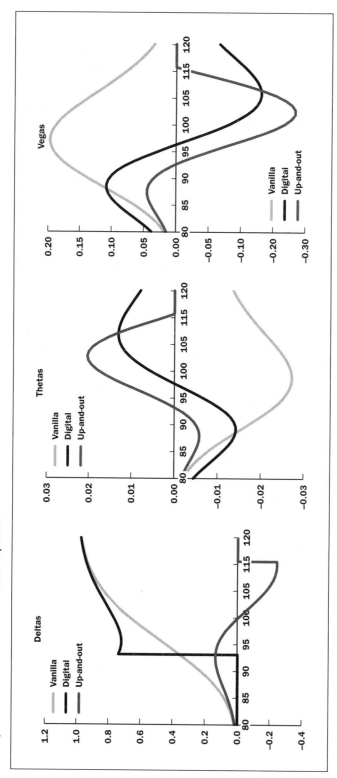

FIGURE 13.20

Examples of Greeks for some exotic options

Banks which must manage the risks arising from their option books are therefore faced with a greater challenge from exotic options. Exotics' Greeks often behave completely differently from those of vanillas, in many cases having the opposite sign, and in some cases changing their value abruptly. That's why they are exotic!

13.14 Embedded options

Many financial instruments include option-like properties. Here are some examples:

- A convertible bond confers the right to exchange the bond for a specified number of common shares of the issuer.
- A mortgage-backed security securitises a portfolio of residential fixed-rate mortgages, each of which grants the mortgager the right but not the obligation to pre-pay the debt. Pre-payments will accelerate when interest rates fall, because borrowers are able to refinance themselves at a lower cost.
- A callable bond is one which allows the issuer to call back the bond on certain dates prior to the normal maturity. As with the mortgage-backed security, a borrower may opt to do this if interest rates fall sufficiently.
- A puttable bond is one that the investor can put back to the issuer, which may be attractive if interest rates have risen since the bond was issued.

The option feature is readily apparent in all these cases. However, there are other products which do not appear to have option-like qualities, but do. Consider these:

- A 'guaranteed income' investment which offers 120% of the gain in the FTSE 100 stock index over five years, or the investor's money back in full if the FTSE falls.
- A 'participating forward' which allows a UK company to buy US dollars at a guaranteed exchange rate, but to share in any savings if sterling should strengthen beyond the fixed rate.

In some cases, option technology has improved our understanding of how existing financial instruments should be priced. In other cases, developments have opened up new opportunities, allowing innovative financial engineering products to be created. The last two examples are cases in point. These, and many other tools, will be explained further in Part II.

Further reading

Listed below are a number of books which provide further information on interest rate option models and on the pricing and hedging of exotic options.

Interest rate options

Rebonato, Ricardo (1998) *Interest-Rate Option Models: Understanding, Analysing and Using Models for Exotic Interest-Rate Options*, Wiley, 2nd edition.

Rebonato, Ricardo, McKay, Kenneth and White, Richard (2009) *The SABR/LIBOR Market Model: Pricing, Calibration and Hedging for Complex Interest-Rate Derivatives*, Wiley.

Wilmot, Paul (1998) *Derivatives: The Theory and Practice of Financial Engineering*, Wiley.

Exotic options

Bouzoubaa, Mohamed and Osseiran, Adel (2010) *Exotic Options and Hybrids: A Guide to Structuring, Pricing and Trading*, Wiley.

De Weert, Frans (2008) *Exotic Options Trading*, Wiley.

Notes

1 The credit risk of swaps was explored in section 9.11 of Chapter 9.

2 A semi-American or Bermudan option has an exercise style in between that of a European option and an American option, allowing exercise to take place only on specific dates during the option's life.

3 The costs associated with cancelling a vanilla swap were explained in Chapter 9, section 9.8.

4 If the strike rate was such that the first period was in-the-money, the additional cost of the cap can be calculated by using the same formula as is used to determine the settlement sum of an FRA (see equation 4.2).

5 Recall again that while the model presented here is a reasonable one, especially for swaptions having an option period short in comparison with the maturity of the underlying swap, in real-life applications a more advanced yield-curve model should be used.

6 Actually, the rational decision – whether or not to exercise the compound option – does not depend upon the result of the tender. If the tender was successful, but option prices had fallen below the strike price of the compound option, it would be more sensible to buy the required option in the open market. Conversely, if the tender was unsuccessful but the compound option was in-the-money at expiry, it should be cash-settled or exercised and the underlying option immediately sold.

7 The arithmetic average is the most popular because it is easier to understand and calculate, and is the method of averaging which most commonly reflects the underlying risk exposure. Unfortunately, valuing arithmetic average-price options is much more difficult than valuing those using a geometric average.

8 As an example, for a cliquet with one-month resets the first option would simply be an ATM vanilla call, the second option would be a two-month delayed call option with the strike price determined at the one-month date, the third option would be a three-month delayed call option with the strike price determined at the two-month date, and so on.

9 In the example given, the first option would be an RKO call struck at 100, knocked-out at 110, and with a rebate of 10. The second option would be an RKO call struck at 110, knocked-out at 120, also with a rebate of 10, and so on.

10 See Chapter 10 for an explanation of the variables and methodology used.

14

INTRODUCING CREDIT DERIVATIVES

The evolution of derivatives has been a steady progression spanning more than a century. Some of the earliest derivatives were commodity futures traded on the Chicago Board of Trade from the middle of the nineteenth century. Equity options have also been traded for more than 100 years, although they did not make a formal debut until 1973 when the Chicago Board Options Exchange opened its doors, coincidentally just a few weeks after Professors Black and Scholes published their famous options pricing model. Currency futures were introduced on the Chicago Mercantile Exchange, followed by interest rate futures in 1975, and stock-index futures in 1982. By the time that interest rate swaps made their debut, also in 1982, the derivatives markets allowed the trading and hedging of commodity risk, equity risk, currency risk and interest rate risk. What other risks are there?

Well, probably one of the oldest financial risks is credit risk, which has been around ever since one person borrowed from another. For commercial banks it is the single biggest risk. Credit derivatives can therefore be seen as the next step in the progression of risk management tools. This chapter introduces credit derivatives, and then focuses on the workings of credit default swaps (CDS) – the single largest component of the credit derivatives market. The next chapter then explores the pricing of CDS, as well as explaining credit indices – the second biggest segment of the market.

14.1 Development of the credit derivatives market

JP Morgan is acknowledged as being the first to devise and execute a credit derivative transaction. In 1994 Exxon, one of its major customers, sought a $5bn line of credit to help fund the liabilities arising from the 1989 Exxon Valdiz disaster. At the time, JP Morgan was reluctant to take on the risk, not least because of the regulatory capital that it would need to reserve. How could JP Morgan provide the credit line, thereby keeping its client happy, while avoiding the need to set aside additional capital? The answer came from a brainstorming session during an offsite meeting held at Boca Raton in June of that year.

Blythe Masters, one of those attending the meeting, marketed the idea to the European Bank of Reconstruction and Development (EBRD). JP Morgan would extend the credit line to Exxon, but pass on the resulting credit risk to EBRD in exchange for a fee. This is illustrated in Figure 14.1. Now everyone is happy! Exxon has the credit line it needs. JP Morgan has a satisfied client, and EBRD has earned fees for taking on the credit risk of Exxon, which it perceived as being a low and acceptable risk.

What this example illustrates is a common feature of all credit derivatives – the transfer of credit risk between two parties, a protection buyer and a protection seller, and this is illustrated in Figure 14.2. The example also demonstrates the separation of funding and credit risk. Here, JP Morgan provided the funding while EBRD took on the credit risk. For five centuries – since Monte de

FIGURE 14.1

The first credit derivatives transaction

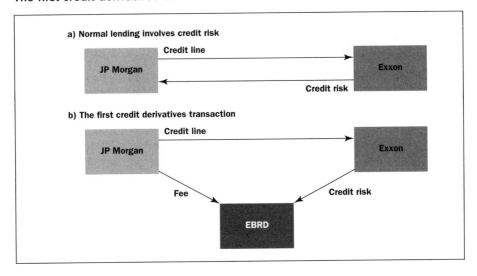

Paschi de Siena was established in 1492 as the world's first bank – until the late twentieth century – the two were inextricably intertwined. Now a bank could lend without necessarily being exposed to the credit risk of the borrower.

From this initial trade, the credit derivatives market grew steadily, reaching around $600bn in notional principal outstanding by 1999. The first real break-through came in that year when ISDA published the first standardised legal documentation for credit default swaps which, as we shall see shortly, is the most common type of credit derivative. From this point onwards the market grew dramatically, doubling in size every year until 2007, by which time notional outstandings had reached over $60tn. Compare these figures with the underlying corporate bond market which in the US was less than $8tn in size at the end of 2011.

However, as Figure 14.3 shows, the size of the credit derivatives market appears to have shrunk since then. This apparent contraction is illusory though, because from 2008 onwards major credit derivatives users instigated a number of compression cycles, where sets of offsetting trades between two or more counterparties are cancelled. For example, bank A may have bought protection from B, who bought protection from C, who in turn bought protection from D,

FIGURE 14.2

Credit derivatives and the transfer of credit risk

FIGURE 14.3

Growth of the credit derivatives market

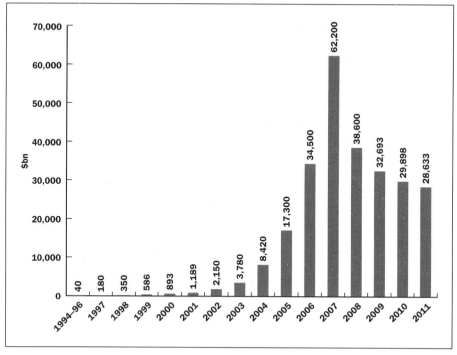

Credit derivatives in this chart comprise credit default swaps referencing single names, indexes, baskets and portfolios.

Source: British Bankers Association Credit Derivatives Survey 2006; ISDA Market Surveys 2001 to 2008, BIS 2009 onwards.

who finally bought protection from A. These trades would not have originally been executed simultaneously, but may have accumulated over time as a result of banks offsetting the risks of one transaction with another. After all the offsetting trades are cancelled, the respective positions of the various users remain unchanged, but the total size of the market will have shrunk. Such compression cycles, orchestrated by firms like TriOptima and Markit, totalled $35tn in 2008 and $60tn in 2009. These compression cycles are also run for interest rate derivatives, and TriOptima compressed $62tn of OTC derivatives in 2011.

Even after compression reduced the size of the notional outstandings to around $30tn in 2010, this is still a huge market, around four or five times the size of the equity derivatives market.

Credit derivatives reference a wide range of borrowing entities, with sovereigns and financial institutions currently topping the list, but with consumer goods and services, telecoms and technology, and industrials also featuring strongly. Figure 14.4 shows the breakdown of outstanding transactions by reference entity for the week ending 28 October 2011. At the time, the risk arising from sovereign debt – especially that of certain European issuers – was a great concern to many investors, as was the knock-on effect on those financial institutions which were major holders of that debt. The fact that there was more than

FIGURE 14.4

Analysis of reference entity types

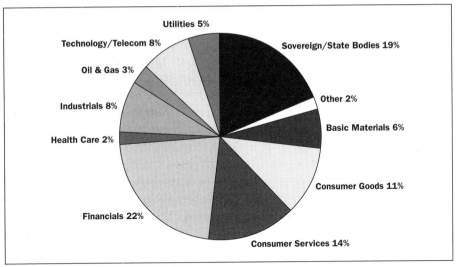

Source: DTCC Week ending 28 October 2011.

$6tn of credit derivatives outstanding on just these two groups of debt issuers alone indicates how important these instruments are to those interested in managing credit risk or taking a view on future trends in credit.

14.2 Motivations for using credit derivatives

When the credit derivatives market started in the mid-1990s, and continuing into the early 2000s, the prime motive for users was the most obvious one – to protect investors from the losses arising from bonds in their portfolio that may default.

As an example, suppose that early in 2001 an investor held $10m face value of bonds issued by Pacific Gas and Electric and was concerned about the possibility of the company defaulting. The investor could have hedged this risk by buying a credit default swap with a notional of $10m referencing PG&E. When PG&E did file for bankruptcy on 6th April 2001 the investor could have handed over the bonds to the protection seller and would have received $10m in cash. As such, the credit default swap would have provided an effective hedge against the losses which the investor would otherwise have realised.

As the years went by, however, credit derivatives began to be used more and more for another purpose – to hedge against or position for a change in perceived credit quality, as manifest by a widening or tightening of credit spreads.[1]

As a simplified example, on 15th August 2011 suppose that an investor believes that a worsening economy will reduce discretionary expenditure and, as a result, the annual premium cost for credit default swaps on bonds issued by the Walt Disney Company (DIS) – then trading at 40bp p.a. – is going to increase. The investor could buy five-year protection on Walt Disney on a notional principal of $10m, agreeing to pay $40,000 per year for the next five years. One month later, on 15th September 2011, premiums had indeed widened to 48bp p.a. The investor could execute a second transaction, selling five-year protection on Walt Disney for the same notional principal and expiry date as the first transaction, thereby agreeing to receive $48,000 per annum for five years. The difference between these two sets of cash flows amounts to some $40,000 in total[2] ($8,000 each year for five years). This is the net profit from these trades, and is the motivation for executing the two transactions in the first place.

Situations like this – where an investor executes credit derivative transactions to position for an anticipated change in credit quality – are the main factor that has driven the huge growth in volumes witnessed since the early 2000s. In Chapter 22 we provide many other examples of such opportunities. In the meantime the remainder of this chapter explores the principal credit derivative instrument – the CDS – in more detail.

14.3 Introducing credit default swaps (CDS)

Although we have touched on the credit default swap earlier in this chapter, it is now time to introduce the CDS more formally.

A single-name CDS is a derivative contract involving two counterparties. The protection buyer agrees to transfer to the protection seller the credit risk of a particular third-party borrower on a given notional principal amount for a specified period of time and, in so doing, agrees to pay the protection seller an annual fee for the duration of the contract. The third-party borrower is called the *reference entity*, and may be a corporation like AT&T Corporation, a financial institution like Deutsche Bank, or a sovereign like the French Republic. The standard period of time covered by a CDS is five years, but CDS contracts can cover any period from one to ten years, or even longer. The annual fee is quoted in basis points per annum as a percentage of the notional principal. This annual rate is called the premium or the spread, but is actually paid in quarterly instalments. In the unlikely event that the reference entity experiences a credit event, like bankruptcy, the protection seller compensates the protection buyer for the financial loss incurred.

All these important concepts:

- the protection buyer
- the protection seller
- the notional principal
- the reference entity
- the period of time covered by the CDS
- the annual premium rate (spread)

- the series of quarterly premium payments
- the contingent payment following a credit event

are illustrated in Figures 14.5a and 14.5b.

As an example, suppose that InvestCo Inc., an investment company, owns $10m face value of five-year bonds issued by ABC Corporation, a manufacturing conglomerate, and seeks to protect its investment should ABC go bankrupt. InvestCo therefore buys five-year protection referencing ABC on a notional of $10m from BankCo, a large investment bank, agreeing to pay BankCo 150bp p.a. on $10m for the next five years.

FIGURE 14.5
How CDS work

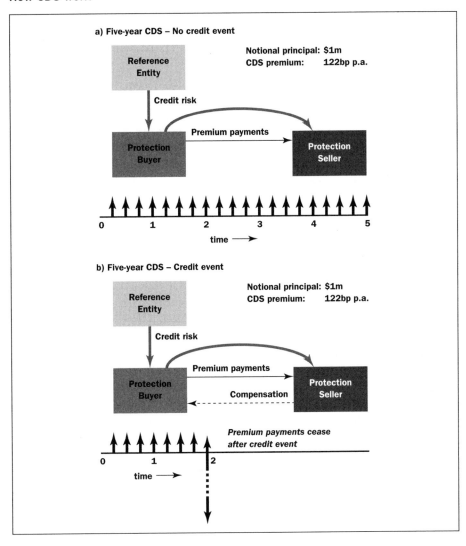

Two years later, ABC files for bankruptcy following plummeting sales, and its bonds drop in value to just 20% of their face value; InvestCo's bonds are therefore worth just $2m. Fortunately, following the credit event, BankCo pays InvestCo $8m to compensate the latter for the losses incurred, and InvestCo is 'made whole' as a result. At this point the CDS terminates and premium payments thereafter cease.

In this example:

- the protection buyer is InvestCo
- the protection seller is BankCo
- the notional principal is $10m
- the reference entity is ABC Corporation
- the period of time covered by the CDS is five years
- the annual premium rate (spread) is 150bp
- the series of quarterly premium payments is equivalent to approximately $37,500 every three months[3]
- the contingent payment following the credit event is $8m.

Described in this way, CDS sound very similar to insurance contracts. InvestCo was exposed to risk, bought protection, paid a regular premium, and was able to claim compensation following a credit event. However, it is important to emphasise that CDS are not insurance contracts, and are not regulated as such. One important difference between a CDS and an insurance contract is that a *CDS contract has value*, and this value changes as market conditions change.

To illustrate this, let's consider an alternative scenario for InvestCo. This time, although ABC suffers a decline in sales, it is not disastrous and ABC stays in business. However, as a result of the worsening business climate, credit spreads on ABC's bonds (which now have three years to mature) widen by 1% and the price of the bonds therefore falls to 97.30, resulting in a $270,000 loss for InvestCo. However, under the terms of the standard CDS contract, this does not constitute a credit event, and so the protection seller need not and does not make any compensating payment to the protection buyer. Fortunately for the protection buyer, premiums on CDS contracts referencing ABC also widen by 100bp p.a., equivalent to $100,000 per year on the $10m notional. Using the ISDA CDS Standard Model, which is explained in section 15.4, this makes the CDS contract worth around $270,000 in present-value terms. If InvestCo sold the bonds and cancelled the CDS contract, both with three years remaining until maturity, the rise in value of InvestCo's CDS would compensate it for the loss in value on its bonds.

As the latter example illustrates, it is solely because CDS contracts have value that ABC can use them to hedge against the losses caused by a widening of credit spreads on their bonds. Insurance contracts do not have value in the same way.

Another important difference between a CDS and an insurance contract is that a protection buyer does not need to own ABC's bonds in order to buy protection. By contrast, the buyer of insurance needs to have *insurable interest* in the entity insured; in other words, the insurance buyer must be adversely affected by the occurence of the insured event. As an example of this, you can buy insurance on your own car but you can't buy insurance on your neighbour's car.

14.4 Market conventions

Now that we have introduced the credit default swap, we will examine exactly how they work in more detail.

The most common CDS maturity is five years, although market-makers will also quote for standard maturities of one, three, seven and ten years. The termination date is normally set to the anniversary of the next CDS Date (defined below), so a five-year CDS traded on 9th November 2011 would mature on 20th December 2016. The reason for this standardisation of termination dates is to make it easier for a five-year CDS traded on one day to be offset by another five-year CDS traded several days or weeks later; with this convention in place both CDS would have the same termination date.

Although premiums are quoted on an annual basis, usually in basis points per annum, the premium payments are actually made quarterly in arrears on four *CDS Dates*: 20th March, 20th June, 20th September and 20th December. If any of these dates falls on a weekend or public holiday, the *Adjusted CDS Date* is the following business day. Premium payments are calculated on an Actual/360 basis, starting with and including the previous Adjusted CDS Date and finishing with and excluding the following Adjusted CDS Date. (For the very last period the final Adjusted CDS Date is included in the calculation.) The use of the Actual/360 convention means that the amount paid each quarter is a little more than 25% of the annual premium.

For example, on a CDS with an annual premium rate of 100bp and a notional principal of $10m, the premium payable on 20th June 2011 would be $25,277.78. There are 91 days in the premium accrual period which runs from and including 21st March 2011 (the 20th March 2011 was a Sunday) until and excluding 20th June 2011. The premium is therefore:

$$\frac{91}{360} \times \$10\text{m} \times 1\% = \$25,277.78$$

For CDS traded in-between Adjusted CDS Dates, premiums start accruing on the *Effective Date*, which is the day immediately following the trade date (irrespective of whether the effective date is a working day or not), and stop accruing on the *Termination Date*.

Before 2009, CDS contracts were usually executed at the market rate prevailing on the trade date. So if the premium for a five-year swap was quoted at 150bp, the protection buyer would pay premiums at that rate for the duration of the contract.

In 2009 however, the market changed to a system of *standardised premiums*. In most geographical locations all CDS on investment grade[4] issuers are fixed at 100bp p.a. while those on high-yield issuers are fixed at 500bp p.a.[5] To compensate for the difference between the market rate quoted at the time the trade is executed, the so-called *par spread*, and the standardised premium, one party makes an *up-front payment* to the other. An example will make this clearer.

On 5th September 2011, premiums for five-year protection on Dell Inc. terminating on 20th December 2016 were quoted at 122bp p.a. (the par spread), but because of the 100bp p.a. standardised premium, the protection buyer will only pay a running premium of 100bp p.a. for the five-year duration of the trade. On a transaction with a $10m notional, this 22bp p.a. underpayment is approximately $22,000 per year, or around $110,000 over the five-year period. In fact, the protection buyer in this instance must pay a little less – $109,334 – to compensate the protection seller for the shortfall in premium instalments over the five-year period.

There are three reasons why the up-front payment is $109,334 instead of exactly $110,000:

- There are actually 1933 days (5.37 years) inclusive between the effective date of 6th September 2011 and the termination date of 20th December 2016.

$$5.37 \times \$22,000 = \$118,127.78.$$

- However, these cash flows are spread out over time. $22,000 receivable in the fifth year is not the same as $22,000 right now. To account for this, each quarterly underpayment needs to be present-valued by multiplying it by the appropriate discount factor, as introduced in Chapter 9 (section 9.2).
- The underpayment of around $22,000 each year is predicated on the survival of Dell Inc., the reference entity, for the lifetime of the CDS. If Dell were to experience a credit event at any time during the five-year period, the CDS would terminate and the premium payments would cease. To handle this, each underpayment must also be multiplied by the appropriate survival probability, in other words, the probability of the reference entity (Dell Inc.) surviving until that moment in time.

Combining these three factors – the first of which increases the up-front payment while the last two decrease it – leads to the actual figure of $109,334. Exactly how this amount is determined will be explained in section 15.4 when we look at CDS pricing. In the meantime, Figure 14.6 shows a screen-shot of the markit.com implementation of the ISDA CDS Standard Model, and depicts the Dell Inc. example just discussed.

As you will see from this figure, the protection buyer actually pays just $87,667, which is $21,667 less than the figure just discussed. This represents accrued premium and arises because of a second aspect of standardisation. Since 2009, on each Adjusted CDS Date protection buyers always pay the premium for the entire quarter just ended. If protection had been bought prior to the start of the quarter, then this is entirely fair. However, if the contract started

FIGURE 14.6

Up-front fee calculator using ISDA CDS Standard Model

Source: Markit Group.

at some point during the current quarter, then the protection buyer would be overpaying. It would be like buying car insurance on 30th June, and paying a full year's premium even though the policy expires on 31st December.

To handle this, a second component of the up-front premium is the premium accrued since the last Adjusted CDS Date. In the example of Dell Inc., there are 78 days between 20th June 2011 (the previous CDS Date) and 6th September 2011 (the effective date). The protection seller must therefore reimburse $21,667 of accrued premium to the protection buyer:

$$\$10,000,000 \times 100\text{bp} \times \frac{78}{360} = \$21,667$$

This is fair to both parties, because on 20th September 2011 the protection buyer will have to pay $25,556 to the protection seller, being the full 92 days of premium from 20th June to 20th September. However, the $21,667 rebate for the 78 days accrued since 20th June reduces the net premium payment to $3,889, equivalent to 14 days of premium, corresponding to the 14-day period from 6th–20th September over which the protection buyer enjoys protection.

Let's summarise the important details relating to CDS premiums:

- CDS premium payments are made four times a year, on the Adjusted CDS Dates.

- CDS premium rates are standardised, usually at 100bp p.a. or 500bp p.a., irrespective of the rates quoted at the time the transaction is executed.

- The payments are calculated on an Actual/360 basis for the full three-month period, irrespective of when the CDS was traded.

- An up-front payment is made to compensate the parties for:
  - The difference between the market rate on the trade date (the par spread) and the standard premium rate. Let's call this the 'off-market' payment.
  - The accrued premium since the last Adjusted CDS Date.

In general, if the par spread is higher than the standardised premium, the protection buyer makes the off-market payment to the protection seller to compensate the latter for being underpaid during the lifetime of the CDS; if the par spread is lower, then it is the seller who makes the off-market payment. However, the protection seller always makes the accrued premium payment to the protection buyer, because in paying a full quarter's premium the buyer always overpays the seller.

In the Dell example cited earlier, the two components of the up-front payment are:

- an off-market payment of $109,334 from the protection buyer to the protection seller

- an accrued premium of $21,667 from the protection seller to the protection buyer

which together lead to the net payment of $87,667 from buyer to seller.

14.5 Credit events and determination committees

The 2003 ISDA Credit Derivatives Definitions specify six types of credit events – situations that can trigger payment by the protection seller – and these are:

- bankruptcy
- failure to pay
- restructuring
- obligation acceleration
- obligation default
- repudiation or moratorium.

Most CDS contracts select only a subset of these six events, as will be explained shortly, but if one of these selected events occurs then it will potentially trigger payment from the protection seller to the protection buyer. We will see how this works in section 14.7, but first we will summarise what each of these credit events means.

Bankruptcy

Every country's legal system includes legislation relating to the bankruptcy of individuals or corporations. In the US, the Bankruptcy Reform Act of 1978 includes Chapter 7 (for liquidation of bankrupt entities) and Chapter 11 (for reorganisations). In the UK, the Insolvency Act of 1986 sets out the procedures for a variety of insolvency circumstances, and there are similar Acts as part of the legal codes in other jurisdictions. If a creditor petitions for the bankruptcy of the reference entity, or if the latter itself files for bankruptcy, this will potentially trigger a bankruptcy credit event. Note that such bankruptcy legislation does not apply to sovereigns themselves; they cannot be dissolved after defaulting nor wind themselves up.

Failure to pay

If a reference entity fails to make a scheduled interest or principal payment on borrowed money on the due date, or within a grace period (typically 7 or 14 days) immediately thereafter, this will potentially trigger a 'failure to pay' credit event. Note that such a payment failure is limited to borrowed money – trade or other credit obligations are excluded. The amount in question must also be greater than a stipulated amount, often $1m.

Restructuring

A restructuring is where an obligor, under deteriorating financial circumstances, agrees with all its creditors to:

■ reduce or postpone payment of interest or principal
■ change the seniority of an obligation so that it becomes subordinated
■ change the currency or composition of a material debt obligation to a currency other than that of a G7 member or an OECD member with a AAA credit rating.

Obligation acceleration

This occurs if one or more obligations become prematurely due and payable following a default by the reference entity.

Obligation default

This may happen if a reference entity, without failing to pay, nonetheless breaches a debt covenant.

Repudiation or moratorium

This may arise if a sovereign entity (or an authorised officer of a non-G7 corporate) repudiates one or more outstanding debt obligations or declares a moratorium on payments.

In practice, obligation acceleration and obligation default are almost never used, and repudiation/moratorium are only found in sovereign CDS. For corporate CDS, that potentially leaves just the first three types of credit event as potential triggers of CDS. Bankruptcy and failure to pay feature in all such contracts, whereas it is the norm for CDS contracts on European and Asian corporates also to include restructuring while those on North American corporates do not. The latter are often known as NR (No Restructuring) or XR (eXcluding Restructuring) contracts.

So far we have been careful in referring to the above circumstances as *potentially* triggering a payment from the protection seller to the protection buyer. In fact, one of the aspects of the 2009 ISDA Supplement[6] was to set out the procedure whereby a *Determination Committee* (DC) must rule in every instance whether a credit event has occurred.

There are five DCs, one for each of the following regions:

- Americas
- Europe, Middle East and Africa (EMEA)
- Asia excluding Japan
- Japan
- Australia and New Zealand.

Each DC comprises 15 voting members and 3 non-voting members, in each case with dealers (such as Barclays and Goldman Sachs) forming two-thirds of the numbers and non-dealers (like Citadel and PIMCO) forming the remaining third. Most members are global, sitting on all five regional DCs, but one or more of the 15 members of each DC are regional.

Determination Committees are responsible for deciding on:

- Credit events – answering the question 'Did reference entity X experience or trigger a credit event?' In the majority of cases the answer is straightforward, and the ruling by the DC is a mere formality. In some situations, particularly those involving restructurings, the DC must weigh up the circumstances and decide accordingly. Either way, a credit event cannot happen without the relevant regional DC's ruling.

- Auctions – as explained in section 14.7, following a credit event an auction of the reference entity's debt obligations is normally held to determine their post-default value, and hence the resulting payout by the protection seller. However, it is the DC's prerogative to decide whether or not such an auction should be held and also which obligations are deliverable.

- Succession events – suppose there are two entities, A and B, and they merge to form a new entity AB. After the merger, the original entities A and B no longer exist, so what happens to counterparties with CDS contracts in A or B? Do they now own contracts referencing AB? The complementary situation may also arise where entity JK splits to form two new entities J and K. Do counterparties with contracts in JK now have two new contracts in J and K? In all these cases, the regional DC interprets the rules set out in the ISDA legal documentation and decides accordingly.

- Substitute reference obligations – as we will see in the next section, most CDS contracts designate a *reference obligation*, a specific debt obligation of the reference entity, typically a specific bond. What happens if the reference obligation matures, is called, or repaid before the expiry of the CDS? In such situations the DC decides which other debt obligation should take its place.

14.6 Capital structure, recovery rates, reference and deliverable obligations

When a corporation raises finance by issuing more than one instrument, the question arises as to the relative seniority of one instrument compared to another. The sources and prioritisation of these financial obligations is referred to as the *capital structure* of the organisation. Figure 14.7 shows a typical hierarchy showing senior debt at the top, followed by junior debt, preferred equity, and eventually common equity. Within senior debt there is often a distinction between secured debt – collateralised by assigning specific assets to cover the bonds issued or the loans granted – and unsecured debt, which is a general obligation of the issuer. Other distinctions are between senior and subordinated debt, and between senior and junior debt; in both comparisons the latter ranks lower.

FIGURE 14.7
Capital structure and seniority

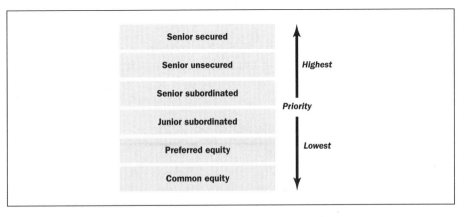

This hierarchy becomes significant in the event of corporate distress and bankruptcy, where the capital structure defines a strict pecking-order governing which investors have priority over the liquidation of a company's assets and the distribution of the resulting cash. First, in fact, are the company's *preferential creditors*, typically employees and the taxation authorities. After these obligations have been discharged, the funds are applied successively to each level of the capital structure, starting with senior secured creditors, then senior unsecured creditors, next the subordinated debt holders, and so on. As each level in the hierarchy is reached, if there is sufficient cash to cover all the obligations, then all the creditors at that level receive a 100% payout. If there is some cash remaining, but not sufficient to pay everyone at that level in full, then there is a *pro rata* distribution, with each creditor at that level receiving the same proportional payout. This is what is meant by *pari passu* – literally 'with equal pace' – every creditor at the same level of seniority or subordination ranks equally. Once this level is reached, any lower levels receive nothing.

This means that the *recovery rate* for creditors – the proportion of the amount owed that they are likely to receive following a bankruptcy – depends very much on the seniority of the debt, and upon whether or not it is secured. The results of a detailed study by Moody's are summarised in Table 14.1 and show clearly the deterioration in recovery rates as you descend through the capital structure.

TABLE 14.1

Average Corporate Debt Recovery Rates Measured by Post-Default Trading Prices

Lien Position	Issuer-weighted			Volume-weighted		
	2011	2010	1982–2011	2011	2010	1982–2011
1st Lien Bank Loan	70.9%	70.9%	66.0%	77.8%	72.3%	59.9%
2nd Lien Bank Loan	66.2%	18.1%	29.7%	66.2%	18.1%	28.1%
Senior Unsecured Bank Loan	23.1%	–	47.1%	43.0%	–	40.2%
Senior Secured Bond	64.1%	62.5%	51.5%	57.8%	54.7%	50.3%
Senior Unsecured Bond	40.4%	49.5%	36.8%	56.1%	63.8%	37.8%
Senior Subordinated Bond	36.7%	37.5%	30.9%	31.5%	42.8%	25.6%
Subordinated Bond	35.4%	33.7%	31.5%	35.2%	32.2%	25.3%
Junior Subordinated Bond	–	–	24.7%	–	–	17.1%

Source: *Annual Default Study: Corporate Default and Recovery Rates 1920–2011*, Moody's, February 2012.

Fitch also publishes data on recovery rates, and this is summarised in Table 14.2. Although the categories do not match exactly, the figures are broadly comparable.

TABLE 14.2

Median recovery rates on high-yield debt 2006–2011

	2006	2007	2008	2009	2010	2011	Average
Senior secured	96.9%	93.9%	29.5%	25.4%	55.3%	74.7%	50.6%
Senior unsecured	60.0%	74.6%	25.1%	31.0%	81.6%	22.0%	24.4%
Senior subordinated	26.0%	44.4%	7.3%	14.9%	16.9%	23.1%	19.2%

Source: *Fitch US High Yield Default Insight*, Fitch Ratings, October 2012.

Recovery rates are important because they determine the size of the payout that a protection buyer will receive following a credit event, and hence the potential liability faced by the protection seller. This means that recovery rates form one of the inputs to the ISDA CDS Standard Model when deciding the correct premium to quote. However, premiums are fixed at the outset, while recovery rates will only be determined if a credit event occurs. Moreover, as the figures in Table 14.2 reveal, there is considerable variation in recovery rates from year to year. For these reasons, rather than estimating the recovery rate on a contract-by-contract basis, the CDS market has chosen a set of standardised recovery rates for use when pricing CDS contracts, and these are summarised in Table 14.3.

TABLE 14.3

Standardised recovery rates

	Senior	Subordinated
North American Corporate and Sovereign	40%	20%
Western European Corporate	40%	20%
Western European Sovereign	40%	20%
Eastern and Central European Corporate and Sovereign	25%	25%
Japanese Corporate and Sovereign	35%	15%
Asian Corporate and Sovereign	40%	20%
Latin American Corporate and Sovereign	25%	25%
Middle Eastern Corporate and Sovereign	25%	25%
Australian Corporate and Sovereign	40%	20%
New Zealand Corporate and Sovereign	40%	20%

Source: Markit Group Ltd, Credit Derivatives Glossary, May 2011.

Recall that the original purpose of CDS was to provide investors with protection against the losses arising from bonds in their portfolio that default. Now that we can see the importance of seniority in influencing recovery rates, and hence the compensation a protection buyer should receive following a credit event, it is vital that there is no ambiguity or misunderstanding between CDS counterparties as to where in the capital structure protection is provided. Most CDS contracts clarify this by designating a *reference obligation*, a specific debt obligation of the reference entity, typically one specific bond.

The purpose of the reference obligation is to define by means of example the level of seniority in the borrower's debt structure covered by the CDS. Any bond ranking *pari passu* with the reference obligation (or higher in the capital structure) is then defined to be a *deliverable obligation*, and these include:

■ the reference obligation itself, or any other direct obligation of the reference entity, so long as it ranks *pari passu* with the reference obligation, or higher

■ obligations of one of the reference entity's subsidiaries

■ obligations of a third party guaranteed by the reference entity.

As explained in the next section, following a credit event deliverable obligations are then used in one of two ways:

- Most commonly, a bond auction is arranged shortly after a credit event, and deliverable obligations are the securities traded in that auction. The result of the auction is then used to calculate the cash settlement due to CDS protection buyers.

- If *physical delivery* is used instead, deliverable obligations are the ones exchanged between the CDS counterparties.

So to recap, seniority affects the recovery rates on defaulted bonds, and hence the losses experienced by an investor. The reference obligation defines seniority by demonstrating which bonds are deliverable obligations, and deliverable obligations determine the amount of financial compensation a protection buyer receives, whether by auction or physical delivery, alternatives which we will now discuss.

14.7 Settlement methods and auctions

When CDS were introduced, the main rationale for their use by protection buyers was to nullify losses on their bond portfolio if an issuer were to default. In those days the most popular settlement method following a credit event was physical delivery, which is pictured in Figure 14.8, and this was the default method incorporated into every standard CDS contract.

With physical delivery, the protection buyer delivers to the protection seller a deliverable obligation and in return receives the face value in cash. The great advantage of this method is that it avoids any conflict between protection buyer and protection seller over what the deliverable obligation is worth. Suppose an investor had originally bought bonds in ABC Corporation at par, and had also bought CDS protection on ABC, and then a credit event occurs. Regardless of what the bonds are worth post-default, the investor delivers the bonds (which he owns) to the protection seller and receives their face value in cash in return. This mechanism automatically ensures that the investor is 'made whole' following a credit event, one of the original objectives of CDS.

As CDS trading volume increased in the years 2001–2005, the volume of CDS contracts outstanding soon began to outstrip the volume of physical bonds issued by a reference entity. More and more users started to trade CDS contracts in order to express a credit view rather than to protect the value of bonds held. When Delphi Corporation filed under Chapter 11 in October 2005 it is estimated that the notional value of CDS contracts referencing Delphi exceeded the

FIGURE 14.8
Settlement using physical delivery

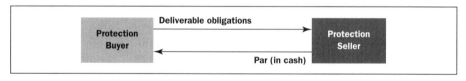

bonds issued by Delphi by a factor of 100 to 1. Although physical delivery would not have been impossible – protection sellers could have recycled delivered bonds back into the market in a grandiose version of 'musical chairs' – it would clearly have been extremely challenging.

Fortunately the market had by then evolved an alternative system. Starting with the 2005 credit event of Collins & Aikman, ISDA issued an Auction Protocol. Anyone with a credit derivatives position could sign up to the protocol, with two consequences. First, their obligation to settle CDS contracts using physical delivery was irrevocably exchanged for an obligation to settle in cash. Second, the size of the cash settlement was to be determined by an auction process whose objective was to establish the prevailing market value of the reference obligation and other *pari passu* bonds. Between 2005 and 2009 more than 30 such auctions took place, and the method became the *de facto* standard for the settlement of CDS contracts following a credit event. The 2009 ISDA Supplement[6] made Auction Settlement *the* standard by hard-wiring this methodology into all pre-existing and new CDS contracts.

The reason why auctions are necessary is because it is impossible to determine the *actual* recovery rate within the one-month timescale set by the standard CDS contract. If the trigger was a Chapter 11 filing (or the equivalent in non-US countries) the company still continues in operation, and usually re-emerges after a year or more without a formal liquidation of assets. In such cases the actual recovery rate will never be known. Even in the case of a Chapter 7 filing (or the equivalent) the liquidation process can take years. For example, at the time of writing, more than ten years after the bankruptcy of Enron in late 2001, the court cases continue and creditors are still awaiting final settlement. Instead, what a credit event auction seeks to determine is the *expected* recovery rate based on information available at the time the auction is held.

The auction process evolved over the first half-dozen auctions held between 2005 and 2006, and is now enshrined in the 2009 ISDA Supplement to the 2003 ISDA Credit Derivative Definitions. The procedures create a completely fair method for determining the fair price for the reference entity's defaulted obligations, and are designed to eliminate the risk that any of the interested parties could in some way manipulate the result of the auction.

The auction involves a two-step process comprising an *Initial Auction* and a *Final Auction*, both held on the same day and separated by a 90-minute interval. It is a real auction in the sense that bonds previously issued by the reference entity are bought and sold, thereby establishing a fair price. The Initial Auction establishes the *Inside Market Midpoint* – a first estimate of the auction's final result – together with discovery of the *Open Interest* – the net amount that interested parties wish to buy and sell. The Final Auction then establishes the *Auction Final Price*, which is the single price used for all bond transactions during the auction, and for the cash settlement of all CDS contracts immediately thereafter. Figure 14.9 illustrates that with cash settlement the protection seller discharges his obligation and compensates the protection buyer by means of a single cash payment, as determined by the auction.

FIGURE 14.9

Cash settlement

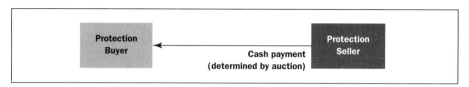

Case study 14.1

To illustrate how auction settlement works, we will examine the General Motors Auction that took place on 12th June 2009. The key dates involved with the GM credit event were:

- 1st June 2009: GM files for bankruptcy under Chapter 11 of the US Bankruptcy Code.

- 1st June 2009: the Determination Committee is petitioned and votes unanimously that a Bankruptcy Credit Event has occurred to General Motors Corporation, and that an auction should be held.

- 1–10th June 2009: the list of Deliverable Obligations to be auctioned is finalised. This turns out to be a list of 21 different bonds, all issued by GM or associated companies, with maturity dates ranging from 1st June 2009 (the date when they filed for bankruptcy) to 15th March 2036.

- 10th June 2009: the list of Participating Bidders is published. This comprises 13 of the major banks most active in the CDS market, from (alphabetically) Bank of America/Merrill Lynch to UBS.

- 12th June 2009: the auction is held using an internet-based system administered by Creditex and Markit.

- 18th June 2009: the Auction Settlement Date for all transactions executed in the auction, and for all CDS cash settlements

As mentioned above, the Initial Auction determines the Inside Market Midpoint and the Open Interest. To start the ball rolling, each Participating Bidder submits a bid and offer price for a $5m trade in any of the Deliverable Obligations. These executable two-way prices are quoted to the nearest 0.125%, and the largest permitted spread is 2%. Table 14.4 shows the actual prices submitted, ranging from 8.50–10.50 by Credit Suisse to 12.00–14.00 by RBS.

These prices are then sorted in numerical order, with bids ranging from high to low, and offer prices from low to high. Table 14.5 shows the result of this sorting process, but also reveals the three pairs of prices which either touch or cross. It turns out that the 12.00 bid by RBS crosses the 10.50 offered by Credit Suisse, and likewise for BNP Paribas' bid with JP Morgan's offer. Furthermore, HSBC's bid of 11.00 touches Goldman Sachs' offer at the same price. These three pairs of quotes will be eliminated from further consideration.

TABLE 14.4

Dealer inside market for the GM auction

Dealer	Bid	Ask	Dealer
Bank of America/Merrill Lynch	10.25	12.25	Bank of America/Merrill Lynch
Barclays	10.00	12.00	Barclays
BNP Paribas	11.00	13.00	BNP Paribas
Citibank	9.75	11.75	Citibank
Credit Suisse	8.50	10.50	Credit Suisse
Deutsche Bank AG	10.00	12.00	Deutsche Bank AG
Goldman Sachs	9.00	11.00	Goldman Sachs
HSBC Bank	11.00	13.00	HSBC Bank
JP Morgan Chase Bank, N.A.	8.75	10.75	JP Morgan Chase Bank, N.A.
Morgan Stanley	9.00	11.00	Morgan Stanley
The Royal Bank of Scotland	12.00	14.00	The Royal Bank of Scotland
Société Générale	10.25	12.25	Société Générale
UBS	10.50	12.50	UBS

Data source: Creditex Group Inc.™ and Markit Group Limited™. © Creditex Group Inc.™ and Markit Group Limited™.

TABLE 14.5

Dealer inside market sorted by price

Dealer	Bid	Ask	Dealer
The Royal Bank of Scotland	12.00	10.50	Credit Suisse
BNP Paribas	11.00	10.75	JP Morgan Chase Bank, N.A.
HSBC Bank	11.00	11.00	Goldman Sachs
UBS	10.50	11.00	Morgan Stanley
Bank of America/Merrill Lynch	10.25	11.75	Citibank
Société Générale	10.25	12.00	Barclays
Barclays	10.00	12.00	Deutsche Bank AG
Deutsche Bank AG	10.00	12.25	Bank of America/Merrill Lynch
Citibank	9.75	12.25	Société Générale
Goldman Sachs	9.00	12.50	UBS
Morgan Stanley	9.00	13.00	BNP Paribas
JP Morgan Chase Bank, N.A.	8.75	13.00	HSBC Bank
Credit Suisse	8.50	14.00	The Royal Bank of Scotland

Source: Adapted from table 14.4, Creditex Group Inc.™ and Markit Group Limited™. © Creditex Group Inc.™ and Markit Group Limited™.

To determine the Inside Market Midpoint, we take the simple average of the best half of the remaining prices, as highlighted by Table 14.6. It turns out that the simple average of the ten numbers ranging from 10.00 to 12.25 is exactly 11.00 – this is the *Inside Market Midpoint* for the GM auction. Notice how the process avoids any Participating Bidder, whether by accident or otherwise, distorting the result of the Initial Auction by posting either too high or too low a price. First, the crossing or touching quotes are eliminated completely, on the basis that the bid(s) must have been too high and/or the offer(s) too low. Second, only the best remaining prices – the highest bids and the lowest offers – are included in the final averaging process. This step also ensures that any lowball or highball numbers are excluded from the calculation.

TABLE 14.6

Determining the Inside Market Midpoint

Dealer	Bid	Ask	Dealer
The Royal Bank of Scotland	12.00	10.50	Credit Suisse
BNP Paribas	11.00	10.75	JP Morgan Chase Bank, N.A.
HSBC Bank	11.00	11.00	Goldman Sachs
UBS	**10.50**	**11.00**	**Morgan Stanley**
Bank of America/Merrill Lynch	**10.25**	**11.75**	**Citibank**
Société Générale	**10.25**	**12.00**	**Barclays**
Barclays	**10.00**	**12.00**	**Deutsche Bank AG**
Deutsche Bank AG	**10.00**	**12.25**	**Bank of America/Merrill Lynch**
Citibank	9.75	12.25	Société Générale
Goldman Sachs	9.00	12.50	UBS
Morgan Stanley	9.00	13.00	BNP Paribas
JP Morgan Chase Bank, N.A.	8.75	13.00	HSBC Bank
Credit Suisse	8.50	14.00	The Royal Bank of Scotland

Source: Adapted from table 14.4. Data Source: Creditex Group Inc.™ and Markit Group Limited™.© Creditex Group Inc.™ and Markit Group Limited ™.

To determine the Open Interest, as a second part of the Initial Auction each Participating Bidder submits a single number representing their *Physical Settlement Request* (PSR) – the amount of deliverable bonds they would either like to buy or to sell in the Final Auction. These PSRs can either originate from the Participating Bidder's customers, or from their own trading book. Table 14.7 shows the actual PSRs submitted for the GM auction. It turns out that nine of the Participating Bidders wanted to buy a total of $994.098m of GM's bonds, while the four remaining Participating Bidders wished to sell a total of $465m. This means that there was a net Open Interest of $529.098m to buy GM bonds.

TABLE 14.7

Physical Settlement Requests for the GM auction

Dealer	Bid/Offer	Size ($m)
Credit Suisse	Sell	407.000
HSBC Bank	Sell	0.000
Morgan Stanley	Sell	18.000
UBS	Sell	40.000
BNP Paribas	Buy	9.900
Bank of America/Merrill Lynch	Buy	21.146
Barclays	Buy	86.779
Citibank	Buy	126.000
Deutsche Bank AG	Buy	108.635
Goldman Sachs	Buy	144.200
JP Morgan Chase Bank, N.A.	Buy	237.438
The Royal Bank of Scotland	Buy	240.000
Société Générale	Buy	20.000

Data source: Creditex Group Inc.™ and Markit Group Limited™. © Creditex Group Inc.™ and Markit Group Limited™

The Initial Auction, which takes just 15 minutes, is almost over, but there is one final step. Recall from Table 14.5 that there were three crossing or touching quotes that were initially eliminated from the calculation of the Inside Market Midpoint because they were either too high or too low. However, now that we know that the Open Interest is to buy (rather than to sell) GM bonds in the Final Auction, we can be almost certain that the price will eventually be bid up (rather than down). As a result we cannot now say that the crossing or touching bids of 11.00 and 12.00 were too high, nor can we say that the touching offer of 11.00 by Goldman Sachs was too low because it matches the Inside Market Midpoint, but we can now be confident that the offers of 10.50 by Credit Suisse and 10.75 by JP Morgan were on the low side. Of all the prices submitted in the Initial Auction, these two were on the wrong side of the Inside Market Midpoint, being lower than 11.00 when we know that the Auction Final Price will be higher.

As a result, the auction process calls for *Adjustment Amounts* – small financial penalties – to be levied on any Participating Bidder whose prices are eventually found to be lower (higher) than the Inside Market Midpoint when the Open Interest is to buy (sell). These Adjustment Amounts are calculated by multiplying the $5m quote size by the difference between the offending price and the Inside Market Midpoint. In the case of the GM auction, Credit Suisse therefore paid $25,000 ($5m × 0.5%) while JP Morgan paid $12,500 ($5m × 0.25%).

The Final Auction takes place 90 minutes after the Initial Auction, and also lasts just 15 minutes. During the Final Auction, Participating Bidders submit limit orders either on their own behalf or that of their customers with a view to fulfilling the Open Interest. In the case of the GM auction, these limit orders will all be selling orders in order to offset the Open Interest to buy $529.098m of GM's bonds. In addition to these new limit orders, the Final Auction also includes all the executable quotes from the Initial Auction; in the case of the GM auction these will be all the offers, adjusted to the Inside Market Midpoint if (like the two mentioned in the previous paragraph) they were on the wrong side. Table 14.8 provides a list of the relevant orders, each one being designated as one of the following:

■ PSR Buy or PSR Sell – these are the 13 Physical Settlement Requests submitted by Participating Bidders in the Initial Auction, as originally listed in Table 14.7. These give rise to the $529.098m residual Open Interest to buy shown in the last column at the end of the second block of the table.

■ Inside Market Offer – one of the original offers for $5m submitted by Participating Bidders in the Initial Auction, as originally listed in Table 14.5.

■ Adjusted Inside Offer – these two original offers were adjusted from 10.50 and 10.75 to the Inside Market Midpoint of 11.00 as a result of the adjustment process described in the previous paragraph.

■ Limit Offer – a new offer to sell a specified amount of GM bonds at a specific price. These can improve on the Initial Market Midpoint by up to 1% (as illustrated by the 10.00 limit order submitted by Goldman Sachs to sell $1m of GM deliverable bonds).

When all the limit orders are received they are sorted by price and the auction mechanism sweeps through the list, starting from the best price (in this case the lowest offer at 10.00) and gradually working through the list. As each offer is processed, it reduces the residual open interest. In the GM example illustrated in Table 14.8 you will see that by the time we get to the two offers at 12.375 there is just 56.138m open interest remaining. If all the offers at the next higher offer of 12.500 were executed, then it would more than cover the open interest; the order size in this last price band is therefore scaled down – in this case to 95.15% of the original amount – so that executing the last three orders at 12.500 exactly matches the total sell orders with the original $994.098m of buy orders, thus ensuring that the auction is successful. This market-clearing price of 12.500 is then the Auction Final Price.

▶

TABLE 14.8

Limit orders for the GM auction

Dealer	Order type	Size ($m)	Limit	Cumulative
BNP Paribas	PSR Buy	9.900		9.900
Bank of America/Merrill Lynch	PSR Buy	21.146		31.046
Barclays	PSR Buy	86.779		117.825
Citibank	PSR Buy	126.000		243.825
Deutsche Bank AG	PSR Buy	108.635		352.460
Goldman Sachs	PSR Buy	144.200		496.660
JP Morgan Chase Bank, N.A.	PSR Buy	237.438		734.098
The Royal Bank of Scotland	PSR Buy	240.000		974.098
Société Générale	PSR Buy	20.000		994.098
Credit Suisse	PSR Sell	407.000		587.098
HSBC Bank	PSR Sell	0.000		587.098
Morgan Stanley	PSR Sell	18.000		569.098
UBS	PSR Sell	40.000		529.098
Goldman Sachs	Limit Offer	1.000	10.000	528.098
Credit Suisse	Adjusted Inside Offer	5.000	11.000	523.098
JP Morgan Chase Bank, N.A.	Adjusted Inside Offer	5.000	11.000	518.098
Goldman Sachs	Inside Market Offer	5.000	11.000	513.098
Morgan Stanley	Inside Market Offer	5.000	11.000	508.098
BNP Paribas	Limit Offer	11.960	11.000	496.138
Deutsche Bank AG	Limit Offer	5.000	11.000	491.138
Citibank	Inside Market Offer	5.000	11.750	486.138
Barclays	Limit Offer	25.000	11.875	461.138
Deutsche Bank AG	Limit Offer	25.000	11.875	436.138
Barclays	Inside Market Offer	5.000	12.000	431.138
Deutsche Bank AG	Inside Market Offer	5.000	12.000	426.138
Citibank	Limit Offer	60.000	12.000	366.138
Barclays	Limit Offer	25.000	12.000	341.138
Citibank	Limit Offer	50.000	12.000	291.138
Deutsche Bank AG	Limit Offer	25.000	12.000	266.138
Citibank	Limit Offer	50.000	12.125	216.138
Bank of America/Merrill Lynch	Inside Market Offer	5.000	12.250	211.138
Société Générale	Inside Market Offer	5.000	12.250	206.138
Citibank	Limit Offer	50.000	12.250	156.138
Goldman Sachs	Limit Offer	25.000	12.250	131.138
Citibank	Limit Offer	50.000	12.375	81.138
Goldman Sachs	Limit Offer	25.000	12.375	56.138
UBS	Inside Market Offer	5.000	12.500	51.138
Citibank	Limit Offer	50.000	12.500	1.138
Credit Suisse	Limit Offer	4.000	12.500	−2.862
Citibank	Limit Offer	75.000	12.625	
Citibank	Limit Offer	130.000	12.750	
Citibank	Limit Offer	75.000	12.875	
Deutsche Bank AG	Limit Offer	25.000	12.875	

... and 72 more offers

Being a single-price auction, *all* trades executed in the auction are done so at the Auction Final Price. Participating Bidders who made lower offers are therefore not penalised, but instead succeed in having 100% of their order filled at the Auction Final Price. Those who offered at that price get partial execution, while those who submitted higher offers are not filled at all. At the same time, all CDS contracts are cash settled by receiving an amount of cash equal to:

$$\text{Notional Contract Size} \times (100\% - \text{Final Auction Price})$$

Importantly, the auction process ensures that an investor owning bonds issued by the reference entity who had bought protection via a CDS contract is guaranteed to be made whole, thus honouring one of the original objectives of credit default swaps. To illustrate this, suppose that an investor owned $10m face value of GM bonds originally purchased at par, and subsequently bought protection on GM by buying a CDS with a notional value of $10m. Following the credit event, the investor would have placed his bonds into the auction via one of the Participating Bidders, and would then receive $1.25m as a result of the bond sale. However, the Auction Final Price of 12.5% would then lead to an $8.75m cash settlement under the CDS contract. The investor would thus receive $10m in total, enjoying 100% compensation despite the credit event. This is pictured in Figure 14.10.

FIGURE 14.10
Using the auction

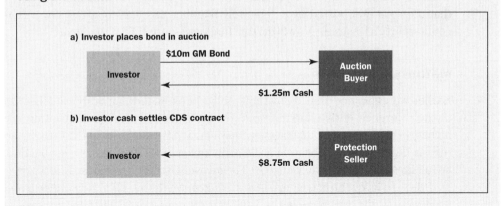

14.8 Other aspects of CDS

In this section we will briefly explore four additional aspects of CDS: swap execution facilities and central counterparties, maturity limitations, recovery CDS, and CDS on loans and US municipalities.

Swap execution facilities and derivatives clearing organisations

We first introduced the establishment of Swap Execution Facilities (SEFs) and Derivatives Clearing Organisations (DCOs) in Chapter 8 (section 8.16) as they apply to the interest rate swap market. Immediately after the credit crisis of 2007–2008 the credit derivatives market also started to evolve central counterparties, well before legislators brought out laws like the Dodd Frank Act in the United States, and EMIR and MiFID II in Europe. However, the relative proportion of CDS trades currently being executed on SEFs and cleared through DCOs is much smaller than that for interest rate swaps, largely because a much greater proportion of the latter are standardised.

SEFs are provided by several firms including MarketAxxess and TradeWeb, but trading volumes at the time of writing are low in comparison to those executed in the traditional OTC market for CDS. However, with the trend in financial markets firmly in the direction of electronic trading over traditional methods it is likely that the role of SEFs will increase in the future.

DCOs have been more successful, though, with ICE Clear Credit and ICE Clear Europe being the market leaders in the US and Europe respectively, and exchanges like the CME and Eurex also offering credit derivatives clearing services under the banners of CME Clearing, CME Clearing Europe and Eurex Clearing. From their launch in mid-2009 until May 2012, ICE Clear Credit and ICE Clear Europe have together cleared almost 900,000 trades totalling $27.1tn across 88 credit derivative indices, 253 corporate single names and 4 sovereigns. In addition to the collateral posted by members, ICE also maintains a CDS Guaranty Fund designed to provide an additional safety measure in the event that the collateral posted by a defaulting member was inadequate to cover that counterparty's losses. In May 2012 this fund was more than $7bn in size.

Maturity limitations

Earlier we explained that deliverable obligations include any direct obligation of the reference entity ranking *pari passu* with the reference obligation (or higher). This means that all bonds at the same level of seniority in the debt structure as the reference obligation are equally deliverable. This raises the question: are all these bonds equally valuable? The answer to this question is: it depends.

If the credit event is triggered by a bankruptcy filing, all bonds at the same level of seniority will receive the same payoff once the bankruptcy process is complete. They are therefore equally valuable, trade at similar heavily discounted prices, and it is not necessary to make any distinction between them when it comes to CDS contracts. However, if the credit event is triggered by a restructuring, the bankruptcy laws do not apply, and so the *pari passu* property of the bonds no longer guarantees equal treatment and equal value. Under these circumstances longer-maturity bonds tend to trade at deeper discounts than short-dated bonds. Investors reason that the restructuring process will probably give the issuer some breathing space, at least for a few years, and so short-dated bonds are likely to be repaid. However, the bond issuer may face further problems in the medium term, making it somewhat less certain that long-dated bonds will be repaid in full. These bonds therefore tend to trade lower than their shorter-maturity cousins.

The original 1999 ISDA Credit Derivatives Definitions did not acknowledge this phenomenon, and made no distinction between the triggers of a credit event, nor between deliverable bonds of different maturities. It wasn't long, however, before the nascent credit derivatives market realised its mistake. In September 2000, a US financial services company called Conseco restructured $900m of some of its loans, agreeing with its bankers to extend the maturity by 15 months, and to increase the rate of interest from LIBOR+50bp to LIBOR+250bp. Some of Conseco's other outstanding loans were repaid in full, as were Conseco's short-term bonds maturing at about the same time. As a result, Conseco's restructured short-term loans were trading at 92% of their face value in the secondary market, reflecting the optimism that these would be repaid when due 15 months later. Conseco's long-term debt was trading much lower, however, at around 68% of face value.[7]

As the restructuring was unequivocally a credit event, CDS contracts on Conseco were triggered. Banks owning the restructured debt who had previously bought protection were able to buy long-dated bonds in the market and deliver these to CDS protection sellers, receiving par in exchange. Despite losing on the restructured loans only 8% of their face value, the lenders were able to collect compensation of 32% of their face value, four times as much. This probably went against the spirit of the CDS agreement, if not the letter of the contract.

To prevent this happening again, ISDA brought out a Restructuring Supplement in 2001 which was later incorporated into the 2003 Credit Derivatives Definitions. This had the effect of capping the maturity of deliverable obligations, but only in situations where the protection buyer triggered payment following a Restructuring Credit Event. In such circumstances, the maturity of deliverables was limited to the earlier of:

a) 30 months following the credit event

b) the maturity of the longest-dated restructured obligation

unless the CDS maturity date was longer, in which case the CDS maturity date was used as the maturity cap. This scheme was called *Modified Restructuring*, and CDS contracts which adopted this were labelled MR. Modified Restructuring was adopted by CDS counterparties as the norm from 2001 until 2009 for contracts on North American, Australian and New Zealand reference entities.

For European reference entities, a further modification extended the maturity cap to the later of:

a) the CDS maturity date

b) 60 months (if a restructured obligation is delivered) or 30 months (for other deliverables) following the credit event.

This modification of the modified restructuring clause became known as *Modified Modified Restructuring* and is abbreviated to MM.

These modifications, and modifications of modifications, have led to a multiplicity of contract terms. However, since 2009 the market has generally converged on the following standards, dependent on where the reference entity (not the CDS counterparties) are domiciled:

- MR – is used principally for Australian and New Zealand names.

- MMR – is used principally on European names.

- Old-R (also known as FR and CR) – is principally used for Japanese and emerging markets names, and also for CDS on sovereign entities. It stands for 'Old Restructuring' (or Full Restructuring, or Complete Restructuring) and means that the contract is written according to the original 1999 rules, with no restrictions on what may be delivered following a restructuring credit event.

- XR (or NR) – is used principally for US names, and stands for eXcluding Restructuring (or No Restructuring). This means that restructuring is excluded as a trigger for these CDS contracts.

Recovery CDS

The credit derivatives market has evolved three new products, each one related to the traditional CDS, but with variations based on recovery rates.

A *fixed recovery CDS* is just like a vanilla CDS, except that the protection seller pays the buyer a fixed sum when a credit event occurs rather than one which depends upon the recovery rate determined at the auction. The fixed sum, and hence the fixed recovery rate implied by the contract, is agreed by the counterparties at inception. Figure 14.11 contrasts the cash flows of a vanilla CDS with those of a fixed recovery CDS. Neither party is exposed to the recovery rate – the only factor that influences the value of a fixed recovery CDS is the perceived probability of default.

The other two products – *recovery locks* and *recovery swaps* – are the complete opposite of the fixed recovery CDS; with these the eventual recovery rate means everything. Recall from Table 14.3 that the credit derivatives market uses

FIGURE 14.11
Fixed recovery CDS

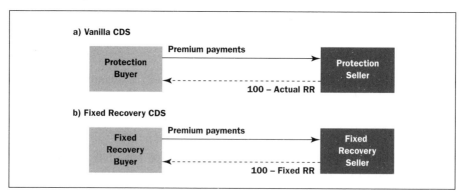

a set of standard recovery rate assumptions when pricing CDS, and this is reasonable when a credit event is still a remote possibility. However, when pricing a CDS on a reference entity in severe financial difficulties, the emphasis changes. Instead of considering the probability of default, which will move towards 100%, the market instead starts to weigh up what the recovery rate will be following the likely default.

Market participants who want to take a view on the recovery rate can use a *recovery lock* which is illustrated in Figure 14.12. This differs from a regular CDS in two ways. First, no regular premium payments are made between the parties. Second, if a credit event occurs, the recovery lock seller pays the buyer the excess of the actual recovery rate (as determined at the auction) over the fixed recovery rate agreed at the outset. To see how this might work, suppose that recovery locks on XYZ Inc. are being quoted at 20%, but an investor thinks that the actual recovery rate following a potential credit event is more likely to be 30%. The investor could monetise this view by buying the recovery lock. If a credit event occurred and the recovery rate did indeed turn out to be 30%, the investor would receive 10% of the notional principal. Note that, under a recovery lock contract, if no credit event occurs then neither party makes any payments at any time.

Recovery swaps are almost identical to recovery locks. The only difference is that a recovery lock is executed as a single transaction, whereas a recovery swap is executed as two separate transactions which can later be unwound separately if desired. As Figure 14.13 illustrates, the buyer of a recovery swap sells a vanilla CDS and buys a fixed recovery CDS. The premium flows cancel, and the buyer

FIGURE 14.12
Recovery locks

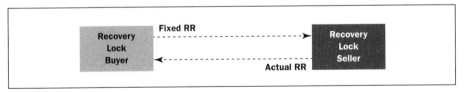

FIGURE 14.13
Recovery swaps

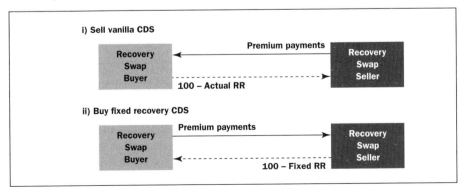

will receive the excess of the actual recovery rate over the fixed recovery rate, exactly like the buyer of a recovery lock.

CDS on loans and municipals

The underliers (or deliverables) for a normal CDS are bonds issued by the reference entity. Of course, borrowers can also raise finance through ordinary bank loans, and the larger borrowers through syndicated loans involving a number of banks. Consequently, a market for CDS contracts based on syndicated loans started in 2003 and evolved slowly, but it wasn't until 2006 when ISDA published standard documentation to cover LCDS (loan-only credit default swaps) that trading volumes started to grow. LCDS are similar to CDS, except that the underlier is a syndicated secured loan rather than a bond. Note that loans usually rank senior to bonds in the debt structure of a company and are usually secured, while bonds are usually unsecured. As a result, the recovery rate following loan defaults is usually much higher than that for bond defaults. Table 14.1 earlier in this chapter contrasted the average 66% recovery rate for 1st lien (senior secured) bank loans with 36.8% for senior unsecured bonds.

In an analogous way, an MCDS is a credit default swap where the underlier is a US municipal bond rather than a corporate or sovereign bond. The market for MCDS also started in 2003, but grew more strongly after 2007–2008 following the downgrades of monoline insurers. These monolines (like AMBAC and MBIA) had traditionally been responsible for insuring against the default of municipal bond issuers, but suffered in the aftermath of the credit crisis. This meant that investors in municipal bonds suffered increasing credit exposure, and turned to the MCDS market as an alternative. The bankruptcy process of municipalities in the US is somewhat different from that applying to corporates; as a consequence there are just two credit events that can trigger an MCDS: failure to pay (after a grace period) and restructuring. Owing to the higher recovery rates witnessed following muni defaults in the past, the MCDS market assumes a recovery rate of 80% rather than the 40% applying to most of the corporate CDS market.

Despite some recent growth, both LCDS and MCDS markets are small compared with the mainstream CDS market, each comprising around 1% of the total credit derivatives market.

Notes

1 Until credit derivatives came along, the term credit spread typically referred to the difference between the yield on a (risky) corporate bond and the yield on a (assumed riskless) government bond of the same maturity. Nowadays the term credit spread typically refers to the premium of a credit default swap, i.e. the annual cost of buying credit protection on the same issuer.

2 As we will see in the next chapter, the actual profit will be a little less than this, not least because of the need to present-value the stream of cash flows.

3 As we will see in the next section, the actual cashflows will be different owing to the system of standardised premiums introduced in 2009.

4 Investment grade is a rating of BBB- (S&P and Fitch), Baa3 (Moody's), or better. A rating lower than this is said to be 'high yield'.

5 CDS on Japanese issuers can also feature a 25bp p.a. standardised premium, while those on European issuers can feature 25bp and 1000bp as well.

6 2009 ISDA Credit Derivatives Determinations Committees and Auction Settlement Supplement to the 2003 ISDA Credit Derivatives Definitions (published on March 12, 2009).

7 Such caution was warranted. Conseco filed for protection under Chapter 11 in late December 2002.

15

CDS PRICING AND CREDIT INDICES

The first part of this chapter explores in some depth the pricing of single-name credit default swaps. We'll start by developing a simple CDS pricing model – this will enable us to establish the underlying principles and identify the key pricing variables. We can then progress to the full-blown ISDA CDS Standard Model, now the universally accepted model used for pricing and valuing CDS contracts, and for determining the up-front payment when contracts are initiated. The second part of the chapter will then examine credit index products, including tranches.

15.1 A simple CDS pricing model

Consider a bank which has been asked to sell protection on a reference entity for a single period and wants to know how much premium it should charge. The *fair premium* would be the one that, if charged, would be fair to both sides of the transaction, with neither party expected to make or lose money from the transaction. In other words, the fair premium equates to the expected losses. A key word in the previous two sentences is 'expected' and we use this here in the statistical sense, meaning a long-run expectation. For example, if I buy a £1 lottery ticket in the UK National Lottery, statistically I 'expect' to get back about 45p, but this is a long-run average based on the design of the game, and I cannot make any firm predictions about a specific lottery draw. In fact, there is a 98.1% chance I will win nothing, a 1.8% chance I will win £10, and a 0.1% chance I will win a bigger prize, possibly even the jackpot.

In a similar way, any CDS pricing model can only calculate the statistically fair premium based on probabilities. The outcome from any specific CDS contract is, however, a binary event. The most likely outcome is that no credit event will occur, and the protection seller will collect the relatively small premium payments over the lifetime of the contract. The alternative is that a credit event occurs, and the protection seller pays a big cash settlement far in excess of the premiums collected on that particular contract. So there is a large probability of a small profit, and a small probability of a large loss. Although a protection seller cannot predict in advance what the final profit or loss will be on a specific CDS contract, if he charges the fair premium across a CDS portfolio the protection seller should expect to break even. Of course, in practice the bank selling protection needs to make a living, and so must charge a premium slightly higher than the fair premium in order to build in a reasonable profit. Likewise, if the bank was buying protection it would in practice do so at a premium slightly lower than the fair premium. Nonetheless, the bank needs to determine the fair premium so that the bid and offer quotes for buying and selling protection can be positioned around it.

To calculate the fair premium, the bank needs to have answers to the following statistical questions:

1 What is the probability of a credit event occurring?
2 If a credit event occurs, how much is the protection seller likely to pay?
3 If a credit event occurs, when will this happen?

The last question is relevant because CDS premiums are accrued on a daily basis. The later the credit event occurs, the more premium will be collected before the eventual payout.

Suppose that the bank does some research and comes up with the following answers, at least to the first two questions.

1 The probability of default (*PD*) is 5%.

2 The loss given default (*LGD*) is 60%, which implies a recovery rate *R* of 40%.

To keep the model simple, we will deal with the third question by assuming that if a credit event occurs, it can only do so at the very end of the period.

We can now develop our simple CDS pricing model step by step. To calculate the fair premium, we need to determine the expected cost of losses, and equate the two. To make it easier to understand, Table 15.1 develops the model both algebraically and with a specific numerical example based on a portfolio of 100 identical credits, each one having the same values of 5% for the *PD* and 60% for the *LGD*.

TABLE 15.1
Developing the simple CDS pricing model

	Specific numerical example	Algebraic formula
DATA		
Probability of default	5%	PD
Loss given default	60%	LGD
Recovery rate	100% − 60% = 40%	R
Number of names	100	N
Principal on each name	$1m	P
ANALYSIS		
Expected number of losses	5% × 100 = 5	$PD \times N$
Expected cost of losses	5 × $1m × 60% = $3m	$PD \times N \times P \times LGD$
Fair premium for entire portfolio	$3m	$PD \times N \times P \times LGD$
Fair premium per name (in $)	$30,000	$\dfrac{PD \times N \times P \times LGD}{N}$
Fair premium per name (in bp)	300bp	$\dfrac{PD \times N \times P \times LGD}{N \times P}$ $= PD \times LGD = PD \times (1-R)$

The final result is the one we are looking for. It tells us that the fair CDS premium should be:

$$CDS = PD \times LGD = PD \times (1 - R) \qquad (15.1)$$

Of course, this is only a simple one-period CDS pricing model with restrictive assumptions. However, it will form the basis of the more complex ISDA CDS Standard Model, as we will see shortly.

In order to use this equation, we need two inputs: the probability of default PD, and the recovery rate R. From our discussions earlier, we know that the CDS market assumes the standard recovery rates shown in Table 14.3. We will now explore where default probabilities can be found.

15.2 Obtaining default probabilities

There are actually two broad sources from which default probabilities can be derived. The most important nowadays is the CDS market itself. However, it is immediately obvious that if we were to use CDS premiums to infer default probabilities, and then use these default probabilities to derive CDS premiums, we would have a circularity. We will address this issue later in this section. For now we will avoid this issue by using an external source: the bond market

The yield generated by owning a corporate bond can be split into two components: a risk-free rate traditionally assumed to be the yield on an assumed riskless government bond of the same maturity and currency, and a credit spread specific to that bond. Intuitively we can say that the greater the perception of default risk, the bigger the credit spread must be in order to reward investors for taking on the additional credit risk

Let's suppose that a risk-neutral[1] investor invests \$1 in a bond for t years and is indifferent between:

a) receiving a riskless rate of return of z per annum

b) receiving a more beneficial return of $(z + r)$ per annum, but where the bond issuer has a probability of default of PD and a recovery rate of R if a default occurs.

Assuming continuous compounding, and with some other simplifying assumptions, we can say that the total proceeds after t years are:

$$e^{zt}$$

from the riskless investment, and:

$$(1 - PD)e^{(z+r)t} + PD \cdot R \cdot e^{(z+r)t}$$

from the risky corporate bond. If our risk-neutral investor is indifferent between these alternatives we can equate them:

$$(1 - PD)e^{(z+r)t} + PD \cdot R \cdot e^{(z+r)t} = e^{zt}$$

and solve for PD to obtain:

$$PD = \frac{1 - e^{-rt}}{1 - R}$$

As an example, if t = 4 years, r = 0.85% and R = 40%, we can solve the above equation to obtain a cumulative probability of default of 5.57% for the four-year period. Likewise, if the five-year yield was 0.95%, we obtain a cumulative probability of default of 7.73% for the whole five-year period. If we wanted to know the probability of default for the fifth year alone, we just subtract these numbers to get 2.16%. Now that we have market-derived data on default probabilities, we can proceed to build a more comprehensive model.

15.3 Developing a multi-period framework

One of the deficiencies of our one-period model is that it doesn't reflect the reality of CDS contracts – that there are multiple time periods. To remedy this, we will construct a multi-period framework like the one in Figure 15.1.

At any time, the reference entity can be in one of two states, the survival state or the default state, designated respectively by S and D. At the inception of a CDS contract, the reference entity is obviously still around, so starts in state S_0. In the first period, however, there is a possibility that it might default, and we label this probability q_1. So by the time we get to the end of the first period there are two possible alternatives. Either the entity defaulted and ended up in state D_1, or it survived and ended in state S_1, with probabilities q_1 and $(1-q_1)$ respectively. If the entity defaulted in the first period, the protection buyer receives cash settlement from the protection seller and the CDS terminates. That's why the state diagram shows the path leading to D_1 terminating there. On the other hand, if the entity survives the first period it then goes on to the second period, where the same two possibilities exist, this time with probabilities q_2 and $(1 - q_2)$. Note that these probabilities are both *conditional probabilities*, in both cases conditional on the entity surviving to reach S_1.

To determine the unconditional probability of the entity surviving until the end of the second period we must invoke the laws of conditional probability and multiply the conditional probability $(1 - q_2)$ by $(1 - q_1)$, the chance of the entity reaching S_1. Continuing this process, the unconditional probability that the entity makes it to the very end and reaches S_N is the product of all the single-period survival terms:

$$PS_N = (1 - q_1) \times (1 - q_2) \times (1 - q_3) \times (1 - q_4) \times \ldots \times (1 - q_N)$$

FIGURE 15.1
Multi-period framework

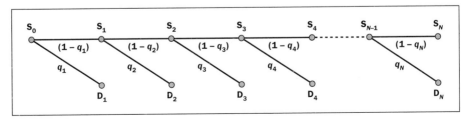

We can also write an expression for PS_N in terms of PS_{N-1}:

$$PS_N = PS_{N-1} \times (1 - q_N)$$

Likewise we can write an expression for the unconditional probability of default in any period:

$$PD_N = PS_{N-1} \times q_N = PS_{N-1} - PS_N$$

Now that we have expressions for the unconditional probabilities of default and survival, we can apply one of the basic laws of probability and state:

$$PS_N + \sum_{i=1}^{N} PD_i = 1$$

In other words, summing the probabilities of all possible outcomes gives 1. We will now use this set of unconditional probabilities to develop the ISDA CDS Standard Model.

15.4 The ISDA CDS Standard Model

When we developed our simple single-period CDS pricing model, we equated the premiums collected to the expected losses, and obtained the premium rate to be $PD \times (1 - R)$, as given in equation 15.1. The same principle applies in our multi-period framework. The fair premium rate is the one that equates the stream of premiums collected to the expected value of losses. Figure 15.2 illustrates the cash flows for a protection seller in two particular scenarios:

a) No credit event occurs – in which case the protection seller collects premiums at the end of each period for the entire lifetime of the CDS contract.

b) A credit event occurs during period 4 – in which case the protection seller collects full premiums for the first three periods, and then a partial premium representing the premium accrued until the credit event determination date. In the figure, k represents the fraction of the period that has elapsed before the credit event, and AR the actual recovery rate following the auction.

However, as we are dealing with the uncertainty of whether and when a credit event will occur, in practice none of the cash flows is certain, neither the premiums collected nor the potential losses paid out. Figure 15.3 pictures all the *possible* cash flows that may arise, but these are all drawn as dotted lines rather than solid lines in order to highlight their probabilistic nature. For example, the accrual premium cash flow can only happen once in practice during the life of a CDS contract, if and when a credit event arises, and may not happen at all; likewise for the contingent loss payments. In order to combine these we will need the probabilities of survival and default for each period and use these to probability-weight all the possible cash flows that may arise from a CDS contract.

FIGURE 15.2

Cash flows in a deterministic environment

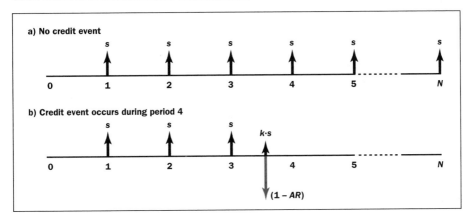

To understand how this probability weighting works, consider a simple game where a fair coin is tossed. If heads appears, the player receives $2, but if tails appears he pays $1. A moment's reflection will reveal that this game is worth entering because of the asymmetric payoffs in favour of the player. To analyse this more scientifically, we can sum the probability-weighted values of the outcomes like this:

Heads: 50% × (+2)   =   +1.00
Tails: 50% × (−1)   =   −0.50
Total: +0.50

As the outcomes are mutually exclusive, we can sum their probability-weighted outcomes to arrive at 50¢ as the expected value of the coin-tossing game. While no single iteration of the game can yield a payout of 50¢, this will be the average return to the player over a large number of repetitions. For example, after taking

FIGURE 15.3

Cash flows in a probabilistic environment

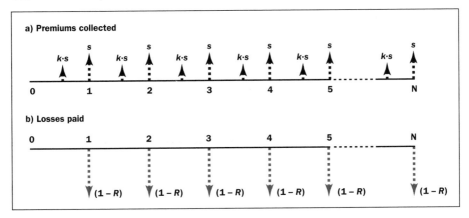

HANDBOOK OF FINANCIAL ENGINEERING

part in 100 games the player expects to pay out a total of $50 on the 50 instances where tails appears, but to receive a total of $100 on the 50 instances when heads appears. The net receipt is $50 across the 100 games, or 50¢ per game.

In a similar way we will sum the probability-weighted cash flows for the protection seller starting with the premiums collected, as shown at the top of Figure 15.3. As we are working with multiple periods stretching over time, we will also need to use discount factors to bring each probability-weighted cash flow to the present day before summing them. Equation 15.2 provides an expression for *PVS*, the expected present value of premiums collected for a CDS contract with a notional principal of $1:

$$PVS = \sum_{j=1}^{N} s_N T_{j-1,j} v_j PS_j + \sum_{j=1}^{N} s_N \frac{T_{j-1,j}}{2} v_j PD_j \qquad (15.2)$$

where:

s_N is the CDS premium rate per annum for an *N*-year CDS
$T_{j-1,j}$ is the length of time of period *j* (expressed as a fraction of a year)
v_j is the discount factor at the end of period *j*
PS_j is the probability of survival through period *j*
PD_j is the probability of default during period *j*

The equation comprises two summations across all the CDS periods, and each summand consists of four terms multiplied together.

Each summand in the first summation provides the expected present value of premiums collected provided that no credit event occurs in the given period. To arrive at this number, the first two terms simply give us the dollar amount of the premium payment for period *j*, being the product of the annual premium rate s_N and the day-count fraction $T_{j,j-1}$, similar to the example given at the beginning of section 14.4. This is multiplied by the third term v_j to give the present value of this premium instalment, and finally by the fourth term PS_j to give the probability-weighted present value of this cash flow.

Each summand in the second summation provides the expected present value of the possible accrual premiums if a credit event does occur in the given period, and is identical to the first summation apart from two differences. First, the day-count fraction used is exactly half that used in the first summation. This is because the ISDA CDS Standard Model makes the reasonable assumption that if and when a credit event occurs, on average it will happen half-way through a period, and so the protection seller will receive half that period's premium income. Second, because the accrual premium only applies in the period when a credit event occurs, the probability used in the second summation is PD_j rather than PS_j.

The two summations together give us the *expected* present value of premiums collected for a CDS contract with a notional principal of $1. Although it may seem that in some way adding the two components is double-counting the premium flows, the methodology used in equation 15.2 is identical to that used in the coin-tossing game discussed earlier which also summed payouts for both the heads and tails outcomes. Using the appropriate probability weighting ensures that equation 15.2 nonetheless gives us the correct result.

We will now sum the probability-weighted cash flows arising from the potential loss payments illustrated in the bottom half of Figure 15.3. In any period j where a credit event may occur, the present value of the payout will be:

$$(1 - R) \times v_j$$

assuming a recovery rate of R and a discount factor v_j. Probability-weighting this by PD_j and summing then gives us PVD, the expected present value of losses paid out on the CDS contract:

$$PVD = (1 - R) \sum_{j=1}^{N} v_j PD_j \tag{15.3}$$

To find the fair premium we set PVS equal to PVD to obtain the result in equation 15.4:

$$\sum_{j=1}^{N} s_N T_{j-1,j} v_j PS_j + \sum_{j=1}^{N} s_N \frac{T_{j-1,j}}{2} v_j PD_j = (1 - R) \sum_{j=1}^{N} v_j PD_j \tag{15.4}$$

Finally, rearranging this and solving for s_N gives us:

$$s_N = \frac{(1 - R) \sum_{j=1}^{N} v_j PD_j}{\sum_{j=1}^{N} T_{j-1,j} v_j PS_j + \sum_{j=1}^{N} \frac{T_{j-1,j}}{2} v_j PD_j} \tag{15.5}$$

Equation 15.5 is essentially the ISDA CDS Standard Model[2] adopted as the industry standard since the 'CDS Big Bang' of March 2009.[3]

To illustrate the application of this formula, Table 15.2 sets out a worked example assuming that we know the set of default and survival probabilities for a specific reference entity, and the set of discount factors for the currency in which payments will be made. The items in the last three columns enable us to calculate the numerator of equation 15.5 (Term 1), and the denominator (Term 2 and Term 3).

To calculate the CDS premium for a five-year contract, we therefore sum the items in the last three columns to obtain:

$$s_N = \frac{0.0698}{4.6378 + 0.0148} = 150\text{bp}$$

15.5 Bootstrapping default probabilities

In the previous section we were able to use equation 15.5 to calculate the fair CDS premium given the set of default and survival probabilities relating to the entity in question. We also showed earlier that it is mathematically possible to

TABLE 15.2

Pricing a CDS using default and survival probabilities

Period	Dates	Day count	Day count fraction	Discount factors	Default probability	Survival probability	Term 1	Term 2	Term 3
0	19 Dec 2011					100.0000%			
1	20 Mar 2012	92	0.2556	0.998603	0.6369%	99.3631%	0.0038	0.2536	0.0008
2	20 Jun 2012	92	0.2556	0.996038	0.6328%	98.7303%	0.0038	0.2513	0.0008
3	20 Sep 2012	92	0.2556	0.992855	0.6288%	98.1016%	0.0037	0.2489	0.0008
4	20 Dec 2012	91	0.2528	0.988881	0.6180%	97.4836%	0.0037	0.2437	0.0008
5	20 Mar 2013	90	0.2500	0.988062	0.6074%	96.8762%	0.0036	0.2393	0.0008
6	20 Jun 2013	92	0.2556	0.987261	0.6170%	96.2592%	0.0037	0.2429	0.0008
7	20 Sep 2013	92	0.2556	0.986460	0.6130%	95.6462%	0.0036	0.2411	0.0008
8	20 Dec 2013	91	0.2528	0.985669	0.6025%	95.0437%	0.0036	0.2368	0.0008
9	20 Mar 2014	90	0.2500	0.983335	0.5922%	94.4515%	0.0035	0.2322	0.0007
10	20 Jun 2014	92	0.2556	0.980901	0.6015%	93.8500%	0.0035	0.2353	0.0008
11	22 Sep 2014	94	0.2611	0.978420	0.6106%	93.2394%	0.0036	0.2382	0.0008
12	22 Dec 2014	91	0.2528	0.976024	0.5874%	92.6520%	0.0034	0.2286	0.0007
13	20 Mar 2015	88	0.2444	0.972335	0.5645%	92.0875%	0.0033	0.2189	0.0007
14	22 Jun 2015	94	0.2611	0.968411	0.5992%	91.4883%	0.0035	0.2313	0.0008
15	21 Sep 2015	91	0.2528	0.964627	0.5763%	90.9120%	0.0033	0.2217	0.0007
16	21 Dec 2015	91	0.2528	0.960858	0.5727%	90.3393%	0.0033	0.2194	0.0007
17	21 Mar 2016	91	0.2528	0.955675	0.5691%	89.7702%	0.0033	0.2169	0.0007
18	20 Jun 2016	91	0.2528	0.950520	0.5655%	89.2047%	0.0032	0.2143	0.0007
19	20 Sep 2016	92	0.2556	0.945336	0.5681%	88.6366%	0.0032	0.2141	0.0007
20	20 Dec 2016	91	0.2528	0.940236	0.5584%	88.0782%	0.0031	0.2093	0.0007
TOTAL							0.0698	4.6378	0.0148

derive these probabilities from corporate bond spreads. In practice, however, the corporate bond market is usually rather less liquid than the CDS market, so it doesn't make much sense to derive probabilities from the less liquid bond market and use these to price CDS contracts traded in a more liquid market. Fortunately it is possible to re-work equation 15.5 to address this issue.

As presented, equation 15.5 is designed to solve for s_N given PD_N. With some effort it is possible to rearrange the formula to solve for PD_N given s_N, and equation 15.6 is the end result:

$$
PD_N = \frac{s_N \left[\displaystyle\sum_{j=1}^{N-1} v_j T_{j-1,j} PS_j + \sum_{j=1}^{N-1} v_j \frac{T_{j-1,j}}{2} PD_j + v_N T_{N-1,N} PS_{N-1} \right] - (1-R) \displaystyle\sum_{j=1}^{N-1} v_j PD_j}{v_N \left[s_N \dfrac{T_{N-1,N}}{2} + (1-R) \right]}
$$

$$(15.6)$$

If you look carefully at this formula it is evidently more complex than its alter ego, not just because it has more terms, but also because it is a *bootstrap* formula. With equation 15.5, the calculation of the CDS premium s_N did not involve knowing the premium for shorter periods like s_{N-1}. Equation 15.6 is different, however. Here, the value of PD_N does depend on the values of PD_{N-1} and PS_{N-1}, and these in turn depend upon PD_{N-2} and PS_{N-2} and so on. This means that you cannot simply use the CDS premium s_N to calculate PD_N in a single operation. Instead, you must follow a step-by-step process starting with the calculation of PD_1. The steps are shown in Table 15.3. In each case we use the results from one step to provide the inputs needed for the next step until we finally arrive at the value for PD_N.

TABLE 15.3

Calculating PD_N

To calculate...	You need to know...
PD_1 and PS_1	s_1
PD_2 and PS_2	s_2 as well as PD_1 and PS_1
PD_3 and PS_3	s_3 as well as PD_1, PD_2 and PS_1, PS_2
... and so on	
PD_{N-1} and PS_{N-1}	s_{N-1} as well as PD_1, PD_2, ..., PD_{N-2} and PS_1, PS_2, ..., PS_{N-2}
PD_N and PS_N	s_N as well as PD_1, PD_2, ..., PD_{N-1} and PS_1, PS_2, ..., PS_{N-1}

Table 15.4 provides an example of the bootstrap calculation, using a CDS premium of 150bp p.a. for all maturities. The five columns headed 'Term 1' to 'Term 5' refer to the five terms in equation 15.6 (four in the numerator and one in the denominator). As we will need the values of PD and PS at every stage, the entries in each row for Terms 1, 2 and 4 perform the summation as a running total in each row, rather than at the bottom of the table.

TABLE 15.4

Bootstrapping default and survival probabilities using CDS premiums

Period	Dates	Day count	Day count fraction	Discount factors	CDS premium	Term 1	Term 2	Term 3	Term 4	Term 5	Default probability	Survival probability
0	19 Dec 2011											100.0000%
1	20 Mar 2012	92	0.2556	0.998603	150	0.0038	0.0000	0.0038	-0.0038	0.6011	0.6369%	99.3631%
2	20 Jun 2012	92	0.2556	0.996038	150	0.0076	0.0000	0.0038	-0.0076	0.5995	0.6328%	98.7303%
3	20 Sep 2012	92	0.2556	0.992855	150	0.0113	0.0000	0.0038	-0.0113	0.5976	0.6288%	98.1016%
4	20 Dec 2012	91	0.2528	0.988881	150	0.0150	0.0000	0.0037	-0.0150	0.5952	0.6180%	97.4836%
5	20 Mar 2013	90	0.2500	0.988062	150	0.0186	0.0001	0.0036	-0.0186	0.5947	0.6074%	96.8762%
6	20 Jun 2013	92	0.2556	0.987261	150	0.0222	0.0001	0.0037	-0.0223	0.5942	0.6170%	96.2592%
7	20 Sep 2013	92	0.2556	0.986460	150	0.0258	0.0001	0.0036	-0.0259	0.5938	0.6130%	95.6462%
8	20 Dec 2013	91	0.2528	0.985669	150	0.0294	0.0001	0.0036	-0.0295	0.5933	0.6025%	95.0437%
9	20 Mar 2014	90	0.2500	0.983335	150	0.0328	0.0001	0.0035	-0.0330	0.5918	0.5922%	94.4515%
10	20 Jun 2014	92	0.2556	0.980901	150	0.0364	0.0001	0.0036	-0.0365	0.5904	0.6015%	93.8500%
11	22 Sep 2014	94	0.2611	0.978420	150	0.0399	0.0001	0.0036	-0.0401	0.5890	0.6106%	93.2394%
12	22 Dec 2014	91	0.2528	0.976024	150	0.0434	0.0001	0.0035	-0.0435	0.5875	0.5874%	92.6520%
13	20 Mar 2015	88	0.2444	0.972335	150	0.0467	0.0001	0.0033	-0.0468	0.5852	0.5645%	92.0875%
14	22 Jun 2015	94	0.2611	0.968411	150	0.0501	0.0001	0.0035	-0.0503	0.5829	0.5992%	91.4883%
15	21 Sep 2015	91	0.2528	0.964627	150	0.0535	0.0002	0.0033	-0.0536	0.5806	0.5763%	90.9120%
16	21 Dec 2015	91	0.2528	0.960858	150	0.0567	0.0002	0.0033	-0.0569	0.5783	0.5727%	90.3393%
17	21 Mar 2016	91	0.2528	0.955675	150	0.0600	0.0002	0.0033	-0.0602	0.5752	0.5691%	89.7702%
18	20 Jun 2016	91	0.2528	0.950520	150	0.0632	0.0002	0.0032	-0.0634	0.5721	0.5655%	89.2047%
19	20 Sep 2016	92	0.2556	0.945336	150	0.0664	0.0002	0.0032	-0.0666	0.5690	0.5681%	88.6366%
20	20 Dec 2016	91	0.2528	0.940236	150		0.0002	0.0032		0.5659	0.5584%	88.0782%

So, to calculate the probability of default in the last three-month period, we sum the items in the last row for Terms 1 to 4, and then divide by the Term 5 entry:

$$PD_N = \frac{0.0664 + 0.0002 + 0.0032 - 0.0666}{0.5659} = 0.005584 = 0.5584\%$$

The probability of survival through to the end of this last three-month period can be calculated by adding up the default probabilities for all the periods to date, and subtracting this from 100%:

$$PS_N = 100\% - (0.6369\% + 0.6328\% + \ldots + 0.5681\% + 0.5584\%) = 88.0782\%$$

In this way we can use CDS premiums to imply default and survival probabilities for the reference entities quoted in the liquid CDS market.

15.6 Calculating up-front payments

We saw in Chapter 14 (section 14.4) that the CDS market now uses a system of standardised premiums and up-front payments. To see how the up-front payment can be calculated, let's first value the cash flows from a CDS assuming that the parties simply paid the par spread rather than the standardised premium. Table 15.5 takes the par spread of 150bp p.a., bootstraps the default and survival probabilities in exactly the same way as Table 15.4, and then calculates *PVS* and *PVD* as in equations 15.2 and 15.3. These respectively give values for the expected present value of premium receipts, and the expected present value of losses paid out. Not surprisingly, these are equal in this case because the bootstrapping equation 15.6 is derived by assuming that *PVS* = *PVD*.

However, if the protection buyer paid a standardised premium of only 100bp p.a. rather than the par spread of 150bp p.a., *PVS* would be correspondingly smaller while *PVD* would stay the same. The protection seller would therefore need compensation equal to the difference between these two values, and the up-front payment is simply this difference. Table 15.6 repeats the calculations, but this time with the protection buyer paying 100bp p.a. rather than 150bp p.a. Note that we still need to bootstrap the default and survival probabilities using the unchanged market quotation of 150bp p.a., so the resulting figures for these probabilities do not change between Table 15.5 and Table 15.6. What changes is the premium rate paid by the protection buyer, not the level of credit risk exhibited by the reference entity.

The last figure in Table 15.6 of –2.33% is 0.0465 less 0.0698, the cumulative values for *PVS* and *PVD*. Expanding this to five decimal places, the number is actually 2.32627%, so on a CDS contract with a notional principal of $10m the up-front payment by protection buyer to seller would be:

$$2.32627\% \times \$10,000,000 = \$232,627$$

TABLE 15.5

Expected present values of CDS cash flows with par spread of 150bp p.a.

Period	Dates	Day count fraction	Discount factors	Par spread	Default probability	Survival probability	PVS	PVD
0	19 Dec 2011					100.0000%		
1	20 Mar 2012	0.2556	0.998603	150	0.6369%	99.3631%	0.0038	0.0038
2	20 Jun 2012	0.2556	0.996038	150	0.6328%	98.7303%	0.0076	0.0076
3	20 Sep 2012	0.2556	0.992855	150	0.6288%	98.1016%	0.0113	0.0113
4	20 Dec 2012	0.2528	0.988881	150	0.6180%	97.4836%	0.0150	0.0150
5	20 Mar 2013	0.2500	0.988062	150	0.6074%	96.8762%	0.0186	0.0186
6	20 Jun 2013	0.2556	0.987261	150	0.6170%	96.2592%	0.0223	0.0223
7	20 Sep 2013	0.2556	0.986460	150	0.6130%	95.6462%	0.0259	0.0259
8	20 Dec 2013	0.2528	0.985669	150	0.6025%	95.0437%	0.0295	0.0295
9	20 Mar 2014	0.2500	0.983335	150	0.5922%	94.4515%	0.0330	0.0330
10	20 Jun 2014	0.2556	0.980901	150	0.6015%	93.8500%	0.0365	0.0365
11	22 Sep 2014	0.2611	0.978420	150	0.6106%	93.2394%	0.0401	0.0401
12	22 Dec 2014	0.2528	0.976024	150	0.5874%	92.6520%	0.0435	0.0435
13	20 Mar 2015	0.2444	0.972335	150	0.5645%	92.0875%	0.0468	0.0468
14	22 Jun 2015	0.2611	0.968411	150	0.5992%	91.4883%	0.0503	0.0503
15	21 Sep 2015	0.2528	0.964627	150	0.5763%	90.9120%	0.0536	0.0536
16	21 Dec 2015	0.2528	0.960858	150	0.5727%	90.3393%	0.0569	0.0569
17	21 Mar 2016	0.2528	0.955675	150	0.5691%	89.7702%	0.0602	0.0602
18	20 Jun 2016	0.2528	0.950520	150	0.5655%	89.2047%	0.0634	0.0634
19	20 Sep 2016	0.2556	0.945336	150	0.5681%	88.6366%	0.0666	0.0666
20	20 Dec 2016	0.2528	0.940236	150	0.5584%	88.0782%	0.0698	0.0698

TABLE 15.6

Expected present values of CDS cash flows with standardised premium of 100bp p.a.

Period	Dates	Day count fraction	Discount factors	Par spread	Default probability	Survival probability	PVS	PVD	Up-front payment
0	19 Dec 2011					100.0000%			
1	20 Mar 2012	0.2556	0.998603	150	0.6369%	99.3631%	0.0025	0.0038	−0.13%
2	20 Jun 2012	0.2556	0.996038	150	0.6328%	98.7303%	0.0051	0.0076	−0.25%
3	20 Sep 2012	0.2556	0.992855	150	0.6288%	98.1016%	0.0076	0.0113	−0.38%
4	20 Dec 2012	0.2528	0.988881	150	0.6180%	97.4836%	0.0100	0.0150	−0.50%
5	20 Mar 2013	0.2500	0.988062	150	0.6074%	96.8762%	0.0124	0.0186	−0.62%
6	20 Jun 2013	0.2556	0.987261	150	0.6170%	96.2592%	0.0148	0.0223	−0.74%
7	20 Sep 2013	0.2556	0.986460	150	0.6130%	95.6462%	0.0173	0.0259	−0.86%
8	20 Dec 2013	0.2528	0.985669	150	0.6025%	95.0437%	0.0196	0.0295	−0.98%
9	20 Mar 2014	0.2500	0.983335	150	0.5922%	94.4515%	0.0220	0.0330	−1.10%
10	20 Jun 2014	0.2556	0.980901	150	0.6015%	93.8500%	0.0243	0.0365	−1.22%
11	22 Sep 2014	0.2611	0.978420	150	0.6106%	93.2394%	0.0267	0.0401	−1.34%
12	22 Dec 2014	0.2528	0.976024	150	0.5874%	92.6520%	0.0290	0.0435	−1.45%
13	20 Mar 2015	0.2444	0.972335	150	0.5645%	92.0875%	0.0312	0.0468	−1.56%
14	22 Jun 2015	0.2611	0.968411	150	0.5992%	91.4883%	0.0335	0.0503	−1.68%
15	21 Sep 2015	0.2528	0.964627	150	0.5763%	90.9120%	0.0358	0.0536	−1.79%
16	21 Dec 2015	0.2528	0.960858	150	0.5727%	90.3393%	0.0380	0.0569	−1.90%
17	21 Mar 2016	0.2528	0.955675	150	0.5691%	89.7702%	0.0401	0.0602	−2.01%
18	20 Jun 2016	0.2528	0.950520	150	0.5655%	89.2047%	0.0423	0.0634	−2.11%
19	20 Sep 2016	0.2556	0.945336	150	0.5681%	88.6366%	0.0444	0.0666	−2.22%
20	20 Dec 2016	0.2528	0.940236	150	0.5584%	88.0782%	0.0465	0.0698	−2.33%

Figure 15.4 illustrates the same pricing[4] using the version of the ISDA CDS Standard Model found on the Markit website. You may also note from this screen-shot that the market also quotes the 'clean price' of 97.67%. This is simply 100% less the up-front payment of 2.33%. CDS prices are related to CDS premiums in a similar way that bond prices are related to bond yields; the higher the CDS premium, the lower the CDS price. Furthermore, like a bond price, the CDS price is related directly to what the protection buyer pays up-front. When par spreads are higher than the standardised premium, as in the above example, the CDS price will be lower than par, and the protection buyer must make the off-market payment to the protection seller. From the protection seller's view-point this is like buying a bond at par (100%) when it is only worth 97.67%, so he must receive 2.33% up-front to compensate. When par spreads are lower than the standardised premium, the opposite is true, and the CDS price will be higher than par.

FIGURE 15.4

Up-front fee on 150bp CDS using ISDA CDS Standard Model

UPFRONT FEE CALCULATOR

Trade Date	Maturity Date	Convert From
19-Dec-2011	Buyer ▾	20-Dec ▾	2016 ▾	Conventional Spread ▾	150 bps

Recovery Rate	Running Coupon	Notional	Currency		Convert
40%	100 bps	10 MM	USD ▾		

Settlement

T+3 (transaction Date + 3 Day) ▾

Results Clear

Conventional Spread	Clean Price	Cash Settlement Amount	Accrued Amount	Days Accrued	Settle Date		
150.00000000000 bps	97.67348422224%	-232,652	0.00	0	22-Dec-2011	Share	Print

Chart   Table

Interest Rate Curve 22-Jan USD

Type	Tenor	Rates		
Deposit	1M	0.2849%	Spot Date	21-Dec-2011
Deposit	2M	0.4139%	MM Day Count Convention	ACT/360
Deposit	3M	0.5632%	Swap Day Count Convention	30/360
Deposit	6M	0.7880%	Float Day Count Convention	ACT/360
Deposit	9M	0.9467%	Swap Payment Frequency	6M
Deposit	1Y	1.1104%	Float Payment Frequency	3M
Swap	2Y	0.7235%	Bad Day Convention	M
			Holidays	none

This application (version 2.2) is based on the ISDA CDS Standard Model (version 1.7), developed and supported in collaboration with Markit

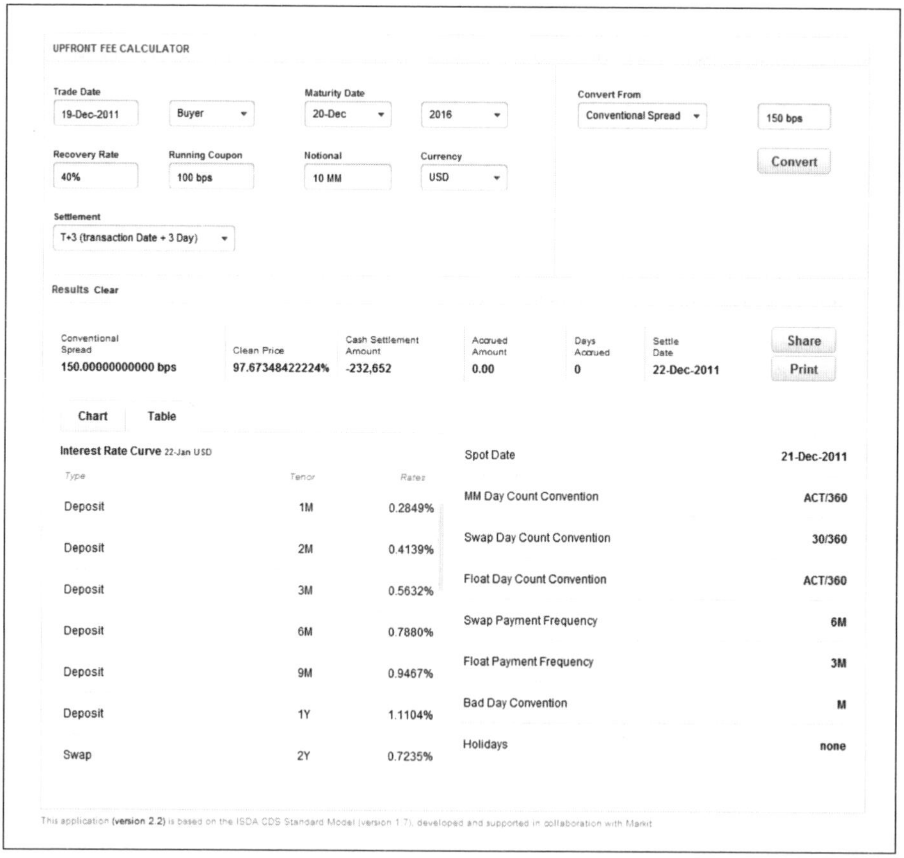

Source: Markit Group.

We can easily adapt equation 15.4 to calculate the up-front payment *UFP* for the protection buyer as follows:

$$UFP = PVD - PVS = (1 - R)\sum_{j=1}^{N} v_j PD_j - \hat{s}\left(\sum_{j=1}^{N} T_{j-1,j} v_j PS_j + \sum_{j=1}^{N} \frac{T_{j-1,j}}{2} v_j PD_j\right)$$

(15.7)

where $\hat{s}$ is the standardised premium, and a positive value for UFP means that the up-front payment is made by the protection buyer to the protection seller.

15.7 Mark-to-market and CDS valuation

Once a CDS contract is in place between two counterparties, its value will fluctuate as market prices change. To determine the mark-to-market profit at any time, we can use an extension of the technique presented in the previous section.

Suppose that an investor has just bought protection on XYZ Inc. using a five-year CDS contract on a $10m notional at a time when the market was quoting a 150bp p.a. premium. As we saw from Table 15.6, with a standardised premium of 100bp p.a. the protection buyer would need to make an up-front payment to the protection seller of $232,627. Later that same day premiums on XYZ have risen to 151bp p.a. and the protection buyer immediately decides to close out the position by entering into another CDS contract, this time selling protection for five years on a $10m notional at 151bp. This time our investor will receive the up-front payment, and to calculate this we must once again bootstrap the default and survival probabilities from the credit curve, and this is shown in Table 15.7.

If you compare the figures from Tables 15.6 and 15.7 you will see that:

- the default probabilities are now higher – for example, PD_{20} has risen from 0.5584% to 0.5616%
- the survival probabilities are now lower – for example, PS_{20} has fallen from 88.0782% to 88.0037%
- *PVS* is now fractionally lower, having fallen from 0.04652550 to 0.04650642
- *PVD* is now higher, having risen from 0.06978824 to 0.07022470.

This is because higher CDS premiums are consistent with and imply higher default probabilities and lower survival probabilities, which increases *PVD* and lowers *PVS* accordingly. The result is that the up-front payment which our investor will receive is now $237,183.

The difference of $4,555.26 between the $232,627 paid on the first trade and the $237,183 received on the second is the actual profit that would be realised if both trades were executed, or if the investor sought to unwind the first trade with the original counterparty. Alternatively, if the investor simply wanted to determine the mark-to-market profit after CDS premiums had risen, then this would also be $4,555.26.

TABLE 15.7

Expected present values of CDS cash flows with par spread of 151bp p.a.

Period	Dates	Day count fraction	Discount factors	Par spread	Default probability	Survival probability	PVS	PVD	Up-front payment
0	19 Dec 2011					100.0000%			
1	20 Mar 2012	0.2556	0.998603	151	0.6411%	99.3589%	0.0025	0.0038	0.13%
2	20 Jun 2012	0.2556	0.996038	151	0.6370%	98.7219%	0.0051	0.0076	0.26%
3	20 Sep 2012	0.2556	0.992855	151	0.6329%	98.0890%	0.0076	0.0114	0.39%
4	20 Dec 2012	0.2528	0.988881	151	0.6220%	97.4670%	0.0100	0.0151	0.51%
5	20 Mar 2013	0.2500	0.988062	151	0.6113%	96.8557%	0.0124	0.0187	0.63%
6	20 Jun 2013	0.2556	0.987261	151	0.6209%	96.2348%	0.0148	0.0224	0.76%
7	20 Sep 2013	0.2556	0.986460	151	0.6169%	95.6178%	0.0173	0.0261	0.88%
8	20 Dec 2013	0.2528	0.985669	151	0.6064%	95.0115%	0.0196	0.0296	1.00%
9	20 Mar 2014	0.2500	0.983335	151	0.5959%	94.4156%	0.0220	0.0332	1.12%
10	20 Jun 2014	0.2556	0.980901	151	0.6053%	93.8103%	0.0243	0.0367	1.24%
11	22 Sep 2014	0.2611	0.978420	151	0.6144%	93.1959%	0.0267	0.0403	1.36%
12	22 Dec 2014	0.2528	0.976024	151	0.5910%	92.6049%	0.0290	0.0438	1.48%
13	20 Mar 2015	0.2444	0.972335	151	0.5679%	92.0369%	0.0312	0.0471	1.59%
14	22 Jun 2015	0.2611	0.968411	151	0.6028%	91.4341%	0.0335	0.0506	1.71%
15	21 Sep 2015	0.2528	0.964627	151	0.5798%	90.8543%	0.0357	0.0540	1.82%
16	21 Dec 2015	0.2528	0.960858	151	0.5761%	90.2781%	0.0379	0.0573	1.93%
17	21 Mar 2016	0.2528	0.955675	151	0.5725%	89.7056%	0.0401	0.0606	2.05%
18	20 Jun 2016	0.2528	0.950520	151	0.5689%	89.1368%	0.0423	0.0638	2.16%
19	20 Sep 2016	0.2556	0.945336	151	0.5714%	88.5653%	0.0444	0.0671	2.26%
20	20 Dec 2016	0.2528	0.940236	151	0.5616%	88.0037%	0.0465	0.0702	2.37%

15.8 PV01 and SDV01

We have just seen that, in the example above, a 1bp shift in market rates led to a change in the value of our $10m CDS of $4,555.26. This measure of CDS value sensitivity is called the *SDV01*, which stands for Spread Dollar Value of an 01. The SDV01 for a CDS contract is directly analogous to the DV01 for a bond. The SDV01 measures the sensitivity of a CDS's value to a 1bp change in credit spreads (i.e. CDS premiums) while the DV01 measures the sensitivity of a bond's value to a 1bp change in interest rates.

We can calculate the SDV01 for a particular CDS contract empirically in the same way as we have done just now, namely, by valuing the CDS at the current level of the market, moving the curve by 1bp, revaluing the CDS, and taking the difference. More generally, however, we can write a formula for the SDV01. If we adapt equation 15.7, we get an expression for the expected present value *EPV* of a CDS position where the protection buyer pays the standardised premium $\hat{s}$, and the default and survival probabilities *PD* and *PS* are bootstrapped from the current market rate s_N:

$$EPV = (1 - R)\sum_{j=1}^{N} v_j PD_j - \hat{s}\sum_{j=1}^{N} T_{j-1,j} v_j \left(PS_j + \frac{PD_j}{2} \right) \qquad (15.8)$$

If we now move the market rate up by 1bp to s'_N such that:

$$s'_N = s_N + 1\text{bp}$$

we get a revised value for *EPV'*, where the new level of CDS premiums s'_N leads to revised default and survival probabilities *PD'* and *PS'*:

$$EPV' = (1 - R)\sum_{j=1}^{N} v_j PD'_j - \hat{s}\sum_{j=1}^{N} T_{j-1,j} v_j \left(PS'_j + \frac{PD'_j}{2} \right) \qquad (15.9)$$

The SDV01 is the difference between *EPV'* and *EPV*.

From equation 15.4 we know that *PVS = PVD*, so:

$$s_N \sum_{j=1}^{N} T_{j-1,j} v_j \left(PS_j + \frac{PD_j}{2} \right) = (1 - R)\sum_{j=1}^{N} v_j PD_j \qquad (15.10)$$

and likewise that *PVS' = PVD'*, so:

$$(s_N + 1\text{bp}) \sum_{j=1}^{N} T_{j-1,j} v_j \left(PS'_j + \frac{PD'_j}{2} \right) = (1 - R)\sum_{j=1}^{N} v_j PD'_j \qquad (15.11)$$

If we substitute the right-hand side of equations 15.10 and 15.11 into the expressions for *EPV* and *EPV'* in equations 15.8 and 15.9, we obtain a formula for the SDV01:

$$\text{SDV01} = \left[(s_N + 1\text{bp} - \hat{s})\sum_{j=1}^{N}T_{j-1,j}v_j\left(PS'_j + \frac{PD'_j}{2}\right)\right]$$
$$-\left[(s_N - \hat{s})\sum_{j=1}^{N}T_{j-1,j}v_j\left(PS_j + \frac{PD_j}{2}\right)\right] \tag{15.12}$$

Using the figures from Tables 15.6 and 15.7 we obtain:

$SDV01 = (0.0051 \times 4.650642 - 0.0050 \times 4.652550) \times \$10,000,000 = \$4,555.26$

which is exactly the same figure as the market-to-market profit at the end of the previous section.

There is a similar, but slightly different, CDS sensitivity measure – the PV01. This is defined as the value of a risky 1bp cash flow at *current* market rates:

$$\text{PV01} = \left[(s_N + 1\text{bp} - \hat{s})\sum_{j=1}^{N}T_{j-1,j}v_j\left(PS_j + \frac{PD_j}{2}\right)\right]$$
$$-\left[(s_N - \hat{s})\sum_{j=1}^{N}T_{j-1,j}v_j\left(PS_j + \frac{PD_j}{2}\right)\right] \tag{15.13}$$
$$= 1\text{bp} \times \sum_{j=1}^{N}T_{j-1,j}v_j\left(PS_j + \frac{PD_j}{2}\right)$$

Again, using the figures in Table 15.6 we obtain:

$\text{PV01} = 0.0001 \times 4.652550 \times \$10,000,000 = \$4,652.55$

The formulae for SDV01 and PV01 given in equations 15.12 and 15.13 are very similar, differing only in their first terms. Both express the value of a basis point for a CDS, but the PV01 does this by changing the cash flows while keeping the credit curve the same, whereas the SDV01 does this by changing the credit curve while keeping the cash flows the same. Each measure has its uses:

■ The PV01 is ideal for valuing an off-market CDS against the current credit curve, and the most common application for this is in determining the up-front payment. In the example above, a PV01 of \$4,652.55 means that the up-front payment involved when executing a CDS at the standardised premium of 100bp when the par spread is 50 points higher at 150bp is:

$50 \times \$4,652.55 = \$232,627.48$

which is indeed the up-front payment we calculated earlier for this CDS contract.

■ The SDV01 is ideal for calculating the profit or loss arising on an existing CDS position after market rates change. In the example above, an SDV01 of \$4,555.26 means that if market rates rise by 1bp, the profit or loss arising from a \$10m CDS contract should be \$4,555.26. We saw earlier that the actual profit when revaluing the CDS contract following a 1bp rise in CDS rates was indeed \$4,555.26.

FIGURE 15.5
SDV01 and PV01 compared

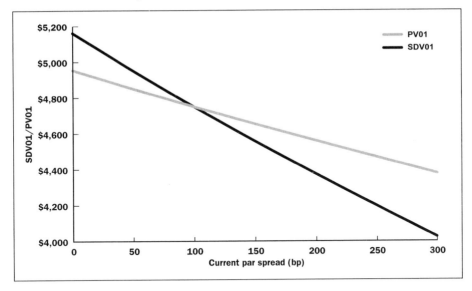

Figure 15.5 charts the values of PV01 and SDV01 at different levels of market rates. The values are broadly similar throughout, but are only identical when par spreads (i.e. market rates) are the same as the standardised premium rate.[5]

15.9 How credit indices developed

There have been indices based on stocks since the late nineteenth century, the earliest being the Dow Jones Industrial Average launched in 1896. Stock indices are invaluable because they inform investors and other interested parties about not just the level of a single stock price, but that of the stock market as a whole (or at least a very substantial part of it). Initially, stock indices were simply purveyors of information; they told you what was happening to the stock market, but you couldn't actually use them to express a view. When financial markets eventually evolved products like stock index futures and ETFs, it became possible to trade these indices allowing investors to express their views.

There are many parallels between stock indices and credit indices like the CDX and iTraxx families which we will shortly introduce. Just as the S&P 500 index indicates the direction and level of the majority of the US stock market, so the CDX indices do the same for the majority of the US credit market. Moreover, both stock indices and credit indices can be traded, allowing investors to hedge existing exposures or to express a view of future developments of their respective markets.

Credit indices started life as a multiplicity of bespoke products, each one created by a different investment bank. The first tradable credit index was called

FIGURE 15.6

Development of credit indices

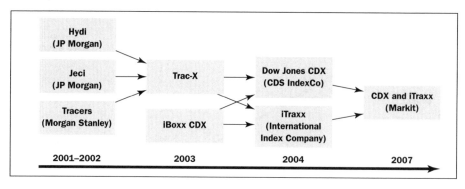

Hydi (High Yield Debt Index) and was launched by JP Morgan in 2001. Hydi was closely followed in 2002 by Jeci (JP Morgan European Credit Index) and Morgan Stanley's Tracers (Tradable Custodial Receipts). It wasn't long before the two competing firms decided that market liquidity would be improved if both agreed on a common credit index product, and so in 2003 Hydi, Jeci and Tracers merged to form Trac-X, administered by Dow Jones. Shortly afterwards, a consortium of around a dozen other banks launched another credit index family under the iBoxx CDX name. In 2004 the competing parties agreed to merge their products into the CDX series of indices (managed by CDS IndexCo) and the iTraxx series of indices (managed by the newly formed International Index Company). Finally, in 2007 Markit Group acquired iTraxx and CDX and is now responsible for the management of all credit indices. Figure 15.6 illustrates the evolution and consolidation of the credit indices market.

15.10 The CDX and iTraxx credit indices

The CDX and iTraxx families are by far the most liquid of all the credit indices available, currently accounting for more than 95% of the total volume of index trading. The indices span a wide range of geographical regions, credit qualities, industry sectors, seniorities and maturities. Table 15.8 summarises the matrix of categories, but not every combination is actually available, so Table 15.9[6] lists the specific indices that actually trade. Most of the terminology in these tables should already be clear, but two terms probably warrant qualification:

- *High volatility* – at first, such a label may sound pretty dangerous, but in fact this group comprises investment grade companies, but those at the lower end of the credit quality spectrum, typically those with ratings of BBB and A.

- *Crossover* – these are companies that are mostly below investment grade but the category can sometimes include borderline investment grade companies, or those with split ratings (where one rating agency rates the company as investment grade while another rates it as high yield).

TABLE 15.8

CDX and iTraxx index categories

Region	Credit quality	Sector	Seniority	Maturity
North America (NA)	Investment grade (IG)	All industries	Senior	1yr
Europe	High volatility (HVOL)	Financials	Subordinated	2yr
Japan	Crossover (XO)	Non-financials		3yr
Asia excluding Japan	High yield (HY)			5yr
Australia	BB rated (HY.BB)			7yr
Emerging Markets	B rated (HY.B)			10yr
	Sovereign			

TABLE 15.9

CDX and iTraxx indices traded

Family	Region	Quality	Maturities	Other	Names
CDX	NA	IG	1, 2, 3, 5, 7, 10		125
CDX	NA	HVOL	3, 5, 7, 10		30
CDX	NA	HY	3, 5, 7, 10		100
CDX	NA	HY.BB	5		varies
CDX	NA	HY.B	5		varies
iTraxx	Europe	IG	3, 5, 7, 10		125
iTraxx	Europe	HVOL	3, 5, 7, 10		30
iTraxx	Europe	XO	3, 5, 7, 10		50
iTraxx	Europe	IG	5, 10	Financials, Senior	25
iTraxx	Europe	IG	5, 10	Financials, Subordinated	25
iTraxx	Japan	IG	5		50
iTraxx	Asia excluding Japan	IG	5		40
iTraxx	Australia	IG	5		25
CDX	Emerging Markets	Sovereign	5		15

With only one exception (CDX.EM) all these indices are an equally weighted basket of single-name CDS contracts. For example, the CDX.NA.IG – the world's most liquid credit index – comprises a basket of CDS contracts on 125 equally weighted investment-grade companies domiciled in North America.

Although we have drawn parallels with stock market indices, there are two important aspects about credit indices that make them different (see Table 15.10).

First, a new edition or *series* of every index is launched every six months, on 20th March and 20th September of each year, except for the CDX.NA.HY indices which roll one week later. When this happens, the majority of liquidity switches to the new 'on-the-run' series, but the previous series doesn't disappear. For example, in the week ending 27th January 2012, 53% of all trading in the CDX.NA.IG was focused on the series 17 contract which was launched in September 2011, but the other 47% of trading volume continued in 13 of the previous series (notably series 9, for historical reasons).

Second, credit indices have static membership. Once a series is launched, the constituents remain in place until the index matures. The only exceptions are if a credit event occurs to one of the reference entities within a series or if a succession event occurs. If a credit event occurs, once the appropriate cash settlement has been made by the protection seller to the protection buyer, the defaulting entity is removed but is not replaced. Instead, the series continues with one fewer name, and is referred to as Version 2 of that series. If a second credit event occurs within a series, that entity is also removed, and the series continues as Version 3, and so on. Every time an entity is removed following a credit event, the notional size of each contract is reduced pro rata, and the weightings of the surviving entities adjusted accordingly. Note that a significant change to an entity's credit rating is not grounds for removal from an existing series. For example, if an entity in an IG index is downgraded to high yield it is not removed from that series, although it may not be eligible for inclusion in a later IG series.

Table 15.10 summarises the key differences between credit and stock indices.

TABLE 15.10
Credit and stock indices compared

Credit indices	Stock indices
A new series is launched on a regular twice-yearly timetable.	Changes to stock indices like the S&P 500 only occur on a when-needed basis.
Previous (off-the-run) series continue to trade alongside the latest on-the-run series.	It is only possible to view and trade the index as currently constituted.
Nearly all credit indices are equally weighted. Each constituent is equally important.	Most stock indices are weighted by market capitalisation.
If a constituent is removed following a credit event, it is not replaced. That series continues with fewer names.	Whenever a constituent is removed for any reason, it is always replaced. The S&P 500 always comprises 500 companies!

The roll process every March and September follows a strict set of rules. The default starting point for a new series is the complete set of existing entities, but then deletions and additions are applied to ensure that all the names in the new series meet the appropriate criteria of credit quality and liquidity. For the CDX.NA.IG the following steps take place:

- **12 business days prior to the roll date** – Markit removes names that are no longer eligible because:
  - the reference obligation is no longer rated investment grade by the majority of the three rating agencies S&P, Moody's and Fitch which have assigned a rating.
  - a merger, acquisition or other corporate action has occurred (or has been announced) that renders the entity no longer suitable for inclusion

- the outstanding debt is less than $100m
- a credit event is under consideration or in progress
- the entity is a market-maker.

■ **9 business days prior to the roll date** – Markit notifies Eligible Members (market-makers in the index) of:

- the list of excluded entities as determined above
- a list of entities to be excluded because of illiquidity
- a list of potential new entities based on liquidity.

The liquidity criteria are determined by using the previous six months of trading data on market risk activity as published by the Depository Trust & Clearing Corporation (DTCC) from its Trade Information Warehouse.

■ **8 business days prior to the roll date** – Markit organises a call with the Eligible Members to verify that the roll process has been executed accurately.

■ **7 business days prior to the roll date** – Markit publishes the final composition of the new series.

As an example, Table 15.11 lists the updated provisional list of changes announced by Markit on 9th September 2011 in relation to the roll of the CDX.NA.IG index from series 16 to series 17 that eventually took place on 20th September 2011. The final list of 125 entities included within the CDX.NA.IG17 spanned the entire spectrum of business and commerce, and Figure 15.7 charts the number of constituents in each industry sector.

TABLE 15.11

Changes from CDX.NA.IG16 to CDX.NA.IG17

Ratings-based removals	Ratings-based additions
R.R. Donnelley & Sons Company Toll Brothers, Inc.	
Liquidity-based removals	**Liquidity-based additions**
The TJX Companies, Inc.	Macy's, Inc. The Gap, Inc. Boston Scientific Corporation
Affiliate removals	**Affiliate additions**
AT&T Mobility LLC Progress Energy, Inc. Capital One Financial Corporation	Capital One Bank (USA), National Association
Subsequent liquidity-based removals	**Subsequent liquidity-based additions**
	Nabors Industries, Inc. H.J. Heinz Company

Source: Markit Group.

FIGURE 15.7

Industry distribution of entities within CDX.NA.IG Series 17

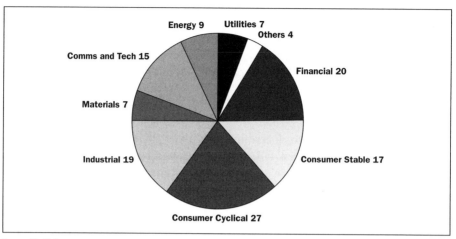

Source: Markit Group.

As an example of re-versioning following credit events we can look at the somewhat turbulent history of the CDX.NA.HY17 index in the four months following its launch in September 2011. The bankruptcy filings of Dynergy Holdings, PMI Group and Eastman Kodak during this period resulted in the CDX.NA.HY17 quickly reaching Version 4. Table 15.12 summarises these changes. This is not the most extreme example, though. The high-yield index CDX.NA.HY11, which was launched in October 2008 in the middle of the worst period of the 2007–2008 credit crisis, had reached Version 21 by May 2012. In other words, more than 20% of the original 100 entities within that series had experienced a credit event in the three or so years that followed.

TABLE 15.12

Credit events and CDX.NA.HY17

Event Determination Date	Version	Event
20 Sep 2011	1	(*initial composition of index*)
08 Nov 2011	2	Dynergy Holdings Bankruptcy Credit Event
23 Nov 2011	3	PMI Group Bankruptcy Credit Event
19 Jan 2012	4	Eastman Kodak Company Bankruptcy Credit Event

Credit indices use the exact same trading conventions as single-name CDS. Investment grade indices like CDX.NA.IG, CDX.NA.HVOL, iTraxx Europe and others trade with a 100bp standardised premium, while high-yield indices like CDX.NA.HY and iTraxx Europe Crossover trade with a 500bp standardised premium. As a result, just as with single-name CDS contracts, every time a credit index position is opened or closed, there is an up-front payment between buyer and seller as documented earlier in this chapter. In fact, credit indices have used fixed premiums since their early days; it is single-name CDS that have copied this convention from credit indices rather than the other way around

If a credit event occurs to any entity with a credit index, the usual consequence will be that the relevant DC will instigate an auction. Remember that credit indices are a basket of liquid single-name CDS contracts, so if a credit event occurs to an index entity it must also have triggered the underlying single-name CDS contracts. Following the auction, the index protection seller will pay 100 minus the Auction Final Price on the pro-rata notional of that name. Thereafter, the protection buyer continues to pay the standardised premium, but on a notional amount reduced to reflect the removal of the affected entity, as mentioned earlier.

Figure 15.8 provides an illustration of the impact of the first credit event on a 125-name investment grade index like the CDX.NA.IG where the original principal was $100m. If the recovery rate was 12.5%, as in the GM Auction for example, the protection seller would pay the protection buyer $0.7m, calculated thus:

$$\frac{\$100m}{125} \times (100\% - 12.5\%) = \$0.7m$$

Thereafter, the protection buyer would pay the 100bp on the reduced principal of $99.2m:

$$\$100m \times \frac{124}{125} = \$99.2m$$

FIGURE 15.8
Cash flows following a credit event

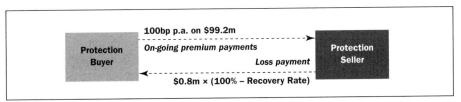

15.11 Market quotations and statistics

Table 15.13 illustrates some credit index quotations for the major indices traded. As with the CDS pictured in Figure 15.4, it is technically possible to quote credit indices either by using the par spread or by quoting the 'price' as 100 minus the up-front payment. For example, on 3rd February 2012 the market was quoting the five-year CDX.NA.IG at 94.43bp p.a., equivalent to an up-front receipt by the protection buyer of 26.1bp and a 'price' of 100.261. In fact, the market convention for the CDX family is to quote investment grade indices by using spreads and high yield indices by using prices, whereas for the iTraxx family all quotations use spreads, and these are the figures shown in bold in Table 15.13.

TABLE 15.13

Credit index spreads and prices on 3rd February 2012

Index	Maturity	Coupon	Spread	Price
CDX.NA.IG	5yr	100	**94.43**	100.261
CDX.NA.HVOL	5yr	100	**202.59**	95.406
CDX.NA.HY	5yr	500	530.94	**98.744**
CDX.NA.HY.BB	5yr	500	330.11	**107.370**
CDX.NA.HY.B	5yr	500	505.84	**99.761**
iTraxx Europe	5yr	100	**127.45**	98.752
iTraxx Europe HiVol	5yr	100	**195.73**	95.765
iTraxx Europe Crossover	5yr	500	**550.20**	98.063
iTraxx Europe Senior Financials	5yr	100	**196.23**	95.744
iTraxx Europe Subordinated Financials	5yr	500	**341.14**	106.863
iTraxx Japan	5yr	100	**157.83**	97.330
iTraxx Asia excluding Japan	5yr	100	**172.17**	96.729
iTraxx Australia	5yr	100	**150.67**	97.683
CDX.EM	5yr	500	256.37	**110.900**

Source: Markit Group.

To provide an idea of which index products are the most liquid, Table 15.14 presents a summary of trading volumes and open positions collated from the DTCC Trade Information Warehouse database for the week ending 27th January 2012. It is clear that the two 125-name indices – CDX.NA.IG and iTraxx Europe – are by far the most actively traded. Close behind in terms of trading volume are the CDX High Yield index and the iTraxx Europe Crossover index, which is the European equivalent of CDX.NA.HY. This reflects the on-going concern at the time about the risk arising from the underlying entities. Recall from Table 15.12 that three such high-yield names had defaulted in the short period from November 2011 to January 2012 alone. In addition, the volume of contracts traded in the iTraxx Europe Financials indices revealed an active interest in the strength of European financial institutions, no doubt precipitated by the European sovereign debt crisis and the prevailing exposure to Greek debt.

Credit indices are a major part of the credit derivatives market, and Table 15.15 compares the volume of index trading with that of single-name CDS, again during the week ending 27th January 2012. It is evident that these two strands of the credit derivatives market are comparable in size. While the number of single-name contracts traded and their open positions outstanding dominates that of index products, the dollar-equivalent volume of index trading was four times that of single-name contracts during the week in question. This liquidity highlights the advantage of index products for any market participant who wants either to hedge exposure to the general level of credit risk, or to take a view on the future evolution of credit spreads.

TABLE 15.14

Index trading volumes and open positions for the w/e 27th January 2012

	Trading volume		Open positions	
Index	Gross notional ($bn)	Contracts	Gross notional ($bn)	Contracts
CDX.NA.IG	229.7	2,537	2,862.4	17,647
CDX.NA.HY	55.2	2,073	639.5	10,182
iTraxx Europe	197.2	2,613	3,059.8	24,701
iTraxx Europe HiVol	1.4	39	146.3	1,372
iTraxx Europe Crossover	25.4	1,764	359.4	11,285
iTraxx Europe Senior Financials	52.3	1,069	510.9	10,747
iTraxx Europe Subordinated Financials	6.2	366	191.7	4,222
iTraxx Japan	1.3	87	109.2	5,437
iTraxx Asia excluding Japan	1.7	79	115.0	6,816
iTraxx Australia	1.3	85	138.5	7,397
CDX.EM	2.7	236	151.2	10,062
Other untranched indices	18.8	2,732	1,080.2	40,824
TOTAL	593.3	13,680	9,364.1	150,692

Source: DTCC.

TABLE 15.15

Market volumes and open positions for the w/e 27th January 2012

	Trading volume				Open positions			
Market sector	Gross notional ($bn)		Contracts		Gross notional ($bn)		Contracts	
Single-name CDS	155.8	20.3%	27,686	66.1%	14,834.1	56.1%	2,123,283	91.9%
Untranched indices	593.3	77.1%	13,680	32.7%	9,364.1	35.4%	150,692	6.5%
Tranched indices	20.4	2.6%	521	1.2%	2,250.4	8.5%	36,018	1.6%
TOTAL	769.5	100.0%	41,887	100.0%	26,448.6	100.0%	2,309,993	100.0%

Source: DTCC.

The two previous tables mention 'untranched indices' and 'tranched indices'. We will explain these two items at the very end of this chapter.

15.12 Other credit indices

As Table 15.14 reveals, the CDX and iTraxx family of indices together represent over 96% of the trading volume in credit indices, and almost 90% of the open interest outstanding, as measured by gross notional values. Nonetheless, there are a number of other indices that trade, and these include the following:

- **SovX** – a family of indices on sovereign CDS covering countries around the globe. At the time of writing the family comprises three members which actually trade:

  - iTraxx SovX Western Europe – comprising 15 names from the Eurozone region plus Denmark, Norway, Sweden and the UK

  - iTraxx SovX CEEMEA – comprising 15 names in Central and Eastern Europe, Middle East and Africa

  - iTraxx SovX Asia Pacific – comprising ten names from the Asia and Oceania regions.

  In addition, there are four others whose prices are quoted but are not tradable.

- **LCDX** – an index referencing 100 LCDS, each LCDS in turn referencing a first-lien loan listed on the Markit Syndicated Secured List.

- **LevX** – another index on first-lien LCDS, this one comprising 40 liquid LCDS traded on the European Leveraged Loan CDS market.

- **MCDX** – an index referencing 50 single-name MCDS.

- **CMBX** – an array of seven indices, each one referencing a basket of 25 commercial mortgage-backed securities (CMBS) with a specific credit rating ranging from AAA down to BB. Unlike CDS and other similar products where a single credit event (like bankruptcy) can trigger payment by the protection seller, the CMBX operates on a Pay As yoU Go (PAUG) basis. In any period where there is a shortfall of interest or principal on the underlying mortgage pool, or if there is a write-down, the protection seller makes a payment to the protection buyer in order to make good the loss of revenue or principal. As this can happen more than once during the lifetime of the CMBX contract, it is more like a 'swap' than a conventional CDS.

- **ABX.HE** – a family of indices launched at the height of the sub-prime credit boom. Like the CMBX family, each ABX.HE member references a basket of 20 securities with a specific credit rating ranging from AAA down to BBB-. These underlying securities were Collateralised Debt Obligations (CDOs) on a portfolio of sub-prime home-equity loans. Sadly, the sub-prime market collapsed in 2007–2008, and with it the ABX.HE family. While the ABX.HE indices are still quoted and traded, none has rolled since July 2007.

- **PrimeX**, **TRX.NA**, **IOS**, **PO** and **MBX** – these are specialised indices on structured finance products. PrimeX references non-agency Prime RMBS (Residential Mortgage-Backed Securities) and TRX.NA references Total Return Swaps (TRS) on CMBS. IOS and PO are families of indices referencing respectively the interest-only and principal-only component of fixed-rate FNMA mortgage pools, while each member of the MBX family of indices is simply a combination of the corresponding IOS and PO indices.

Trading volumes and positions outstanding for these other credit indices are much smaller than those for the mainstream CDX and iTraxx markets, being just 3% and 12% respectively (weighted by gross notional) as Table 15.14 shows. Table 15.16 analyses the trading volumes and open positions of these other credit indices, and it is clear that the most liquid of these are the CMBX, the iTraxx SovX Western Europe, the iTraxx SovX CEEMEA and the IOS.

TABLE 15.16

Other index trading volumes and open positions for the w/e 27th January 2012

Index	Trading volume		Open positions	
	Gross notional ($bn)	Contracts	Gross notional ($bn)	Contracts
iTraxx SovX Western Europe	4.3	611	235.7	6,362
iTraxx SovX CEEMEA	3.1	265	102.6	8,508
iTraxx SovX Asia Pacific	0.1	4	11.0	793
CMBX.NA	4.6	1,073	144.3	9,775
ABX.HE	1.1	111	84.4	3,220
PrimeX	0.3	23	11.5	944
TRX.II	0.5	375	1.6	454
IOS	4.3	229	93.2	3,315
PO			3.1	36
MBX			31.3	829
LCDX.NA	0.1	20	79.9	1,935
iTraxx LevX Senior			5.1	233
MCDX.NA	0.3	21	28.2	2,031
Index swaptions			227.7	1,713
Other untranched indices			20.4	676
TOTAL	18.8	2,732	1,080.2	40,832

Source: DTCC.

15.13 Index tranches

In a normal credit index contract, protection sellers are exposed to losses arising on the underlying reference portfolio, and each seller's liability is apportioned simply according to the notional principal of each contract. In other words, the loss payout per $1m of notional principal is the same for all protection sellers. For example, suppose that 100 investors each sell $1m of protection on the 125-name CDX.NA.IG index, and one index name then defaults with a recovery rate of 25%. The resulting total loss of $0.6m is shared equally among the 100 investors, with each one paying out $6,000 to their respective protection buyer. Put another way, each protection seller pays out:

$$\frac{\$1m}{125} \times (100\% - 25\%) = \$6,000$$

If there was a second, third or fourth credit event, all with the same recovery rate, each protection seller would again pay $6,000 on each loss

With a tranched index contract, however, losses are not divided equally. Instead, potential losses are grouped into *tranches*, like the ones set out in Table 15.17. Investors selling protection on a specific tranche are also exposed to the loss experience of the underlying reference portfolio, but only for losses lying within the specified range of that tranche. For example, sellers of protection on the 3–7% tranche would pay out nothing if portfolio losses were less than 3%, that tranche's *attachment point*. However, once portfolio losses exceeded 3%, those investors alone would be fully responsible for meeting losses until they reached 7% of the portfolio, the *detachment point* of that tranche. At this stage, protection sellers would have lost 100% of their investment, and further losses would be handled by the next tranche.

TABLE 15.17
Standard credit index tranches

CDX.NA.IG	CDX.NA.HY	iTraxx Europe
0–3%	0–10%	0–3%
3–7%	10–15%	3–6%
7–15%	15–25%	6–9%
15–100%	25–35%	9–12%
	35–100%	12–22%
		22–100%

Source: Markit Group, May 2011.

To illustrate this, let's return to our example of 100 investors each selling $1m of protection, but this time on successive tranches of the CDX.NA.IG index. Three of the investors might therefore each sell $1m of protection on the 0–3% tranche, and thereafter be responsible for the first $3m of losses on the reference portfolio. Another four investors might each sell $1m protection on the 3–7% tranche, and be responsible for the next $4m of losses, and so on. Figure 15.9 illustrates how this looks.

If no losses occur on the reference portfolio, then all investors walk away happy, having collected premiums over the life of the contract, but paying out nothing. Suppose, however, one loss occurs, again with a 25% recovery. This time the net loss of $0.6m would not be shared among all 100 investors, but would be met solely by the three investors who had sold protection on the 0–3% tranche, destroying 20% of their original

FIGURE 15.9

Credit index tranche structure

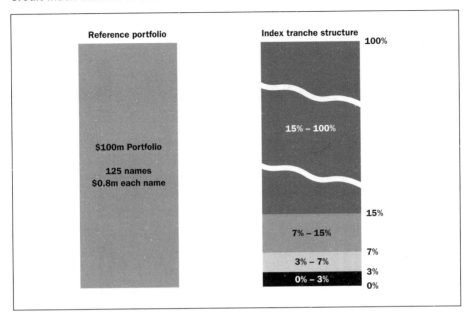

$3m aggregate investment. If four credit events occurred, again with the same recovery, the net loss of $2.4m would eliminate 80% of their investment, and if five credit events occurred, their $3m would be wiped out completely. The sixth loss would then begin to affect the sellers of the 3–7% tranche, who would have to pay out the excess $0.6m loss not covered by the 0–3% tranche, thereby losing 15% of their aggregate investment of $4m. Figure 15.10 illustrates the impact of losses on the various tranches, while Table 15.18 tabulates the loss experience of each tranche both in absolute dollar losses and in terms of percentage loss.

It is clear from this example that investing in tranches is potentially much more risky than investing in the index as a whole. It is inconceivable that all 125 names in the CDX.NA.IG would experience credit events and, even then, protection sellers would not suffer a total loss because of potential recoveries. So the chance of a total loss for the whole index investor is virtually zero. However, it would only take a handful of credit events to create 100% losses for the 0–3% tranche, even with the recovery rate being non-zero.

Why do potential investors trade tranched indices? There are actually a number of reasons:

- **Return** – given the level of risk associated with tranche investing, protection sellers demand and receive a correspondingly high premium especially for the lower tranches. This is intended to compensate them for the high level of potential losses.

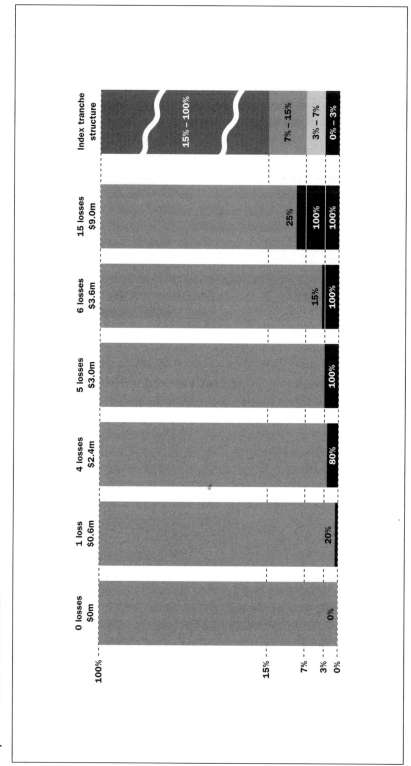

FIGURE 15.10
Impact of losses on tranches

TABLE 15.18

Impact of losses on CDX.NA.IG tranches

Number of losses	Losses ($m) Gross	Net	Tranche losses ($m) 0–3%	3–7%	7–15%	15–100%	Tranche losses (%) 0–3%	3–7%	7–15%	15–100%
0	0.0	0.0	0.0	0.0	0.0	0.0	0%	0%	0%	0%
1	0.8	0.6	0.6	0.0	0.0	0.0	20%	0%	0%	0%
2	1.6	1.2	1.2	0.0	0.0	0.0	40%	0%	0%	0%
3	2.4	1.8	1.8	0.0	0.0	0.0	60%	0%	0%	0%
4	3.2	2.4	2.4	0.0	0.0	0.0	80%	0%	0%	0%
5	4.0	3.0	3.0	0.0	0.0	0.0	100%	0%	0%	0%
6	4.8	3.6	3.0	0.6	0.0	0.0	100%	15%	0%	0%
7	5.6	4.2	3.0	1.2	0.0	0.0	100%	30%	0%	0%
8	6.4	4.8	3.0	1.8	0.0	0.0	100%	45%	0%	0%
9	7.2	5.4	3.0	2.4	0.0	0.0	100%	60%	0%	0%
10	8.0	6.0	3.0	3.0	0.0	0.0	100%	75%	0%	0%
11	8.8	6.6	3.0	3.6	0.0	0.0	100%	90%	0%	0%
12	9.6	7.2	3.0	4.0	0.2	0.0	100%	100%	2.5%	0%
13	10.4	7.8	3.0	4.0	0.8	0.0	100%	100%	10.0%	0%
14	11.2	8.4	3.0	4.0	1.4	0.0	100%	100%	17.5%	0%
15	12.0	9.0	3.0	4.0	2.0	0.0	100%	100%	25.0%	0%
16	12.8	9.6	3.0	4.0	2.6	0.0	100%	100%	32.5%	0%
17	13.6	10.2	3.0	4.0	3.2	0.0	100%	100%	40.0%	0%
18	14.4	10.8	3.0	4.0	3.8	0.0	100%	100%	47.5%	0%
19	15.2	11.4	3.0	4.0	4.4	0.0	100%	100%	55.0%	0%
20	16.0	12.0	3.0	4.0	5.0	0.0	100%	100%	62.5%	0%

- **Expressing a view on credit risk** – the losses experienced by the various tranches are highly sensitive to the level of losses experienced by the reference portfolio. For example, an increase in the probability of default from 0.8% to 1.6% increases the expected losses on the portfolio from 0.6% to 1.2%, and on the 0–3% tranche from 20% to 40%. An investor who wants to monetise their view on credit quality can use this 33.3× leverage to magnify their exposure.

- **Expressing a view on correlation** – the loss experience of tranches is affected not only by the level of defaults on the underlying reference portfolio but also by the correlation between defaults. If losses are uncorrelated, their sporadic occurrence will mainly affect the 0–3% tranche. However, if the occurrence of losses is correlated, then they will tend to bunch together, increasing the chance that enough defaults will occur over a short period of time to wipe out the 0–3% tranche and then cause losses for the higher tranches. Paradoxically, higher correlation is actually beneficial to the 0–3% tranche, because it also increases the chance that all the reference entities will survive, resulting in fewer losses being experienced by the lowest tranche.

To illustrate the impact of correlation on tranches, consider the experience of a 125-name reference portfolio, where each name has a probability of default of 0.8% per annum, and a recovery rate of 25%. The expected number of defaults on the portfolio each year is therefore 1. If default correlation was zero, the expected outcome over a 100-year period would be one loss every year, 100 in total. Investors selling protection on the 0–3% tranche would therefore expect, on average, to pay out on losses amounting to 0.6% of the value of the portfolio each year. This corresponds to 20% of their investment each year, and so they would need to be paid premiums in excess of 20% p.a. to take on this obligation. On the other hand, investors in the 3–7% tranche would expect to pay out nothing, as the number of losses is expected to be just one each year, leading to monetary losses below the attachment point.

Now suppose correlation was not zero, but 1. This time the behaviour of the portfolio over a 100-year period is quite different. In 99 of those years the portfolio would experience no losses at all, but in one particular year all the entities would default. The total number of losses experienced by the portfolio is still 100 over the 100-year period, but this time they are all bunched together. Note that this is consistent with a default probability of 0.8%; over a 100-year period the expected total number of losses on a 125-name portfolio should indeed be 100:

$$125 \times 0.8\% \times 100 = 100$$

This behaviour is also consistent with a correlation of 1, which implies that all the entities always behave alike. In 99 of the 100 years they all survive, and in 1 of the 100 years they all default. In no year does any entity behave differently from all the others.

In this correlation environment the 0–3% tranche investor now fares much better than before. For this investor the expected loss has fallen from 20% p.a. to 1% p.a. (a 100% loss just once in 100 years). The 3–7% tranche investor fares worse though, because his expected loss has risen from 0% to 1% (again, a 100% loss once in 100 years).

This example demonstrates clearly that index tranches are exposed to the impact of default correlation. In practice, more sophisticated models are used to assess the impact of correlation in a probabilistic environment. However, despite their complexity such models require one key input – default correlation – and this can only be estimated but never observed.

Notes

1 A risk-neutral investor is one that does not expect to be rewarded for taking on financial risk. A simple example of a risk-neutral investor would be one who would be indifferent between receiving $1 for sure, or instead receiving $2 or $0 depending upon the flip of a coin. In the long run, both alternatives are statistically equivalent, and most readers would probably be risk-neutral for the example just given. However,

replace the payoffs with $10m, $20m and $0m respectively, and most of us in practice would be risk-averse, preferring the certain $10m rather than risk losing a possible $20m on the flip of a coin.

2 Source code and example spreadsheets of the complete model can be downloaded from: www.cdsmodel.com. In fact, the full ISDA CDS Standard Model is very slightly different from formula 15.4, as end-note 4 below explains. The subtle differences might produce a 1bp difference in calculations of up-front payments or CDS mark-to-mark valuations.

3 See: *The CDS Big Bang: Understanding the Changes to the Global CDS Contract and North American Conventions*, Markit Group, 13 March 2009.

4 The up-front figure of $232,652 shown on the screen is fractionally different from the figure of $232,627 calculated here owing to the detailed way in which the computer algorithm distributed by ISDA executes the bootstrapping process. The computer program uses an iterative search technique called *Brent's Method* to bootstrap default probabilities assuming a constant continuously-compounded conditional default probability (i.e. a constant hazard rate). The discrete approach presented here gives an almost identical result.

5 Strictly speaking from equations 15.12 and 15.13, PV01 and SDV01 are only the same when $s_N = \hat{s} - 1\text{bp}$.

6 In addition to the indices listed in Table 15.9, in September 2012 Markit launched a new 20-name index referencing Latin American Corporate debt (CDX.LATAM.CORP), and in November 2012 they launched a sub-index of CDX.EM to exclude European constituents (CDX.EM.ex-EU).

PART II

TECHNIQUES

16

APPLICATIONS FOR FINANCIAL ENGINEERING

This chapter sets out the main applications where financial engineering techniques may profitably be employed. One use in particular – hedging – is explored in greater depth, reviewing the sources of financial risk, setting hedging objectives and measuring hedge efficiency. A final section discusses whether a company's finance division should act merely as a service for other parts of the company, or whether it should be counted as a profit centre in its own right.

16.1 Applications of financial engineering

The applications for financial engineering can be summarised under four main headings: hedging, speculation, arbitrage and structuring.

Hedging

This is where an entity already exposed to risk attempts to eliminate the exposure by adopting an opposing position in one or more hedging instruments. A simple example is the case of a borrower who buys an FRA to hedge against the effects of fluctuating interest rates. A perfect hedge is one where the hedging instrument matches the original exposure perfectly in every detail. If such an instrument is available, risk can be eliminated completely, as illustrated in Figure 16.1.

FIGURE 16.1
Illustration of a perfect hedge

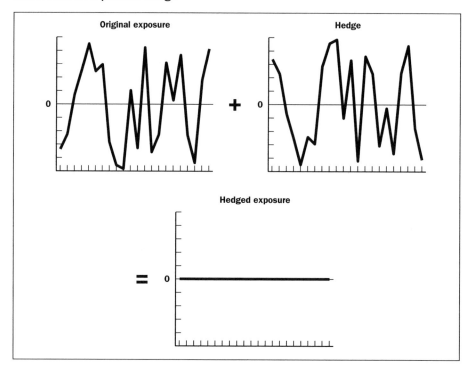

In practice, such perfect correlation between the original exposure and the hedging instrument may not always be obtainable, and the hedge may prove to be less than perfect. Nonetheless, almost any properly designed hedge will provide a much safer overall result than having no hedge at all. It would be a poor hedge indeed that created more risk than the original exposure.

The hedge illustrated in Figure 16.1 matched every fluctuation of the original exposure, hedging both adverse and beneficial movements in the underlying price; the end result was absolute certainty. Others exposed to risk may prefer a hedge which eliminated only the bad outcomes. Such a hedge is illustrated in Figure 16.2, where the hedge compensates against adverse swings in the original exposure beyond a certain level, but allows any beneficial swings to pass through unchanged. The end result is a capped exposure.

Speculation

This is where someone wishing to take advantage of a particular view of the market can speculate on anticipated changes, thus creating an exposure where none existed before. Speculation often takes the straightforward form of buying something whose price is expected to rise, or selling something whose price is expected to fall. Some of the biggest examples of such trades were those executed by a small number of traders and firms in the period 2005–2008 speculating on

FIGURE 16.2
Illustration of a hedge producing a capped exposure

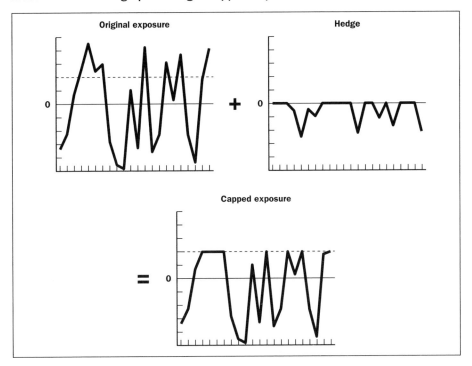

the imminent collapse of the sub-prime market.[1] Those who speculated against the overvalued mortgage market made billions in profits; sadly, those who did not see it coming lost billions, sometimes tens of billions. It is not always necessary to use derivative instruments in order to speculate. For example, some who shorted the sub-prime market did so by using one of the oldest techniques in the financial markets, namely shorting the shares of banks who were actively involved in sub-prime loans. Nonetheless, the tools of financial engineering can prove advantageous for a number of reasons.

a) **Gearing**. Most derivatives offer tremendous gearing or leverage, because they allow positions to be adopted with the minimum of capital outlay. For example, a speculator can bet on a rise in the US stock market through buying E-mini S&P 500 futures contracts at the CME. A position in $1m in stocks can be achieved for an outlay of around $75,000, and this initial margin could be deposited in interest-bearing securities rather than cash.[2] This gearing of around 13× is by no means unusual with derivative instruments.

b) **Ability to assemble complex strategies**. Using derivatives as basic building blocks, it is possible to create highly tailored exposures that would be difficult to achieve any other way. For example, a speculator could bet on a narrowing in the interest differential between euros and US dollars, or could position himself to take advantage of the market moving to within a specific range of prices.

c) **Ability to create exposures impossible otherwise**. Some views are simply impossible to take advantage of without using derivatives. The speculator who believes that market volatility will decline has little choice but to use options or other volatility-based derivatives.

Arbitrage

There is a profusion of inter-related financial products, and in many cases it is possible to synthesise one product from a combination of others. FRAs and interest rate futures are very similar to one another. Interest rate swaps are similar to a strip of FRAs. Caps and swaptions are tightly bound to their underlying instruments. Close mathematical relationships therefore exist linking the prices of comparable instruments.

Under normal circumstances, the actual prices of related products will follow these mathematical relationships almost exactly. As an illustration, consider the example cited in Chapter 6 (at the very end of section 6.2), where the quoted prices for dollar FRAs matched the respective futures prices for dollar interest rate contracts within a fraction of a basis point.

Occasionally, however, prices may slip out of line for a short while. This may happen in turbulent markets, or when there is a physical separation between markets as, for example, in the case of stock index futures quoted in Chicago against cash equities quoted in New York. When this happens, arbitrageurs – usually driven by high-speed computer algorithms – will quickly intervene, buying in the market where the price is cheap, and selling where the price is dear. They aim to profit from any difference in prices, but without assuming any risk. The action of arbitrageurs is actually beneficial on the whole because, in driving up underpriced instruments and driving down overpriced ones, it rapidly restores market prices to their natural equilibrium.

For all practical purposes, we can therefore assume that market prices of related instruments are exactly in line with one another. Users of the widely quoted financial engineering tools like FRAs, caps, swaps and so on, should therefore not spend too much time shopping around for mispriced instruments. Such bargains rarely exist. It is more fruitful to spend time instead on selecting the most appropriate financial strategy. Of course, for the unusual or exotic products which are individually priced, it does make sense to compare the quotations from two or three different market-makers. Where there are price differences, it does not necessarily imply that arbitrage profits are possible. The spreads involved in creating a riskless arbitrage may eliminate any apparent arbitrage profits, as may the risk of executing several deals simultaneously before the prices have moved. Alternatively, one cheap quote may simply reflect the preferences or underlying position of one particular market-maker.

Structuring

Financial engineering can be used to restructure the characteristics of a particular transaction or exposure. As a simple example, a bond issuer may use an interest-rate swap to switch the stream of floating-rate obligations into fixed-rate payments. A sophisticated investor who believes that oil prices over the next two years will remain range-bound, not dropping below today's price and not rising more than $20, may use a structured note to enjoy an above-market yield for every day during the two-year period that his view holds true. Another investor with a view that six-month dollar interest rates will stay at around 3.5–4% may convert a regular FRN into a reverse floating-rate note paying 11%–LIBOR to gain an immediate yield advantage of at least 3%. All these are examples of structured finance techniques which exploit the versatility of financial engineering tools to alter cash flows and financial exposures according to the needs of users.

Most of Part II of this book will be devoted to hedging, the first of the applications discussed here. Successive chapters will show how financial engineering can help to manage and hedge currency risk, interest rate risk, equity risk, commodity risk and credit risk. Speculation will not be covered as a separate topic, although some of the hedging examples will feature users having speculative leanings. Arbitrage will not be considered further, other than to assume that the activities of arbitrageurs help to ensure that prices of similar instruments are comparable. Finally, one chapter will be devoted entirely to structured products, and will demonstrate how financial engineering techniques can be used to better meet the preferences of investors, borrowers and other participants in the financial marketplace.

16.2 Sources of financial risk

Risk is all-pervasive, affecting individuals, companies and governments in almost every area of their activities. Financial risk is the impact on the financial performance of any entity exposed to risk. It is difficult to draw up a foolproof classification, but the principal effects of financial risk can be categorised under the following major headings.

Currency risk

This arises from exposure to movements in exchange rates. Currency risk is often sub-divided into transaction risk, where currency fluctuations affect the proceeds from day-to-day transactions, and translation risk, which affects the value of assets and liabilities on the balance sheet. An example of transaction risk would be the purchase by a British manufacturer of machined components produced by a Swiss company and invoiced in Swiss francs. Translation risk would affect the published accounts of a Dutch-based industrial conglomerate with subsidiaries in the United States. Chapter 17 will examine how currency risk can be managed.

Interest-rate risk

This arises from the impact of fluctuating interest rates, and will directly affect any entity borrowing or investing funds. The most common exposure is simply to the level of interest rates, but some entities may be vulnerable to the shape of the yield curve. The management of interest-rate risk is a large subject, and Chapters 18 and 19 are devoted to this topic.

Equity risk

This affects anyone holding a portfolio containing one or more shares, which will rise and fall with the level of individual share prices in particular, and with the level of the stock market in general. In addition, companies whose shares are publicly quoted may face difficulty in obtaining finance or in bidding for orders if their shares fall significantly in value. Equity risk will be discussed in greater detail in Chapter 20.

Commodity risk

This risk arises from any change in commodity prices. Commodities include 'soft' commodities like foodstuffs, and 'hard' commodities like metals. A coffee manufacturer like Kraft Foods will find that the price of processed coffee will depend to a large extent on the price of coffee beans. A collapse in supply, perhaps caused by a blighted crop, will push up prices and lead to a slump in demand. Commodity risk may have a wider impact than at first meets the eye. A firm like Delphi Automotive, which produces a wide range of components for car manufacturers, would be adversely affected by a rise in oil prices, because this might discourage people from driving and lead to a cut in car production. Also affected, though perhaps one step removed, would be the out-of-town shopping centre or a drive-in cinema, both of which rely on people using their cars.

Credit and counterparty risk

These two risks are closely related, both arising from the non-performance of a counterparty in a financial transaction. *Credit risk* occurs when the original transaction was a loan, and on a scheduled payment date the defaulting counterparty fails to repay interest, principal or both. *Counterparty risk* also arises from the failure of a counterparty to honour a financial commitment, but one other than a loan. For example, if an interest rate swap counterparty fails to pay the net interest due on the designated payment date, this is a manifestation of counterparty risk. The magnitude of credit risk depends on the total amount outstanding at any time, while counterparty risk depends upon the size of all outstanding positions with a particular counterparty, the size of transactions due for settlement on a particular day, and whether or not any netting arrangements are in force.

When it comes to counterparty risk, practitioners often distinguish between *settlement risk*, which is the loss that can arise from the settlement of transactions on a given day, and *replacement risk*, which is the potential loss if a transaction has to be replaced prior to its maturity date. As an example, suppose that a customer some time ago executed a forward deal buying £10m against dollars at a rate of £1 = $1.6000. With one month left to mature the one-month forward price for sterling is £1 = $1.5000. If the customer were to declare bankruptcy, the replacement cost of the deal would be $1m. On the other hand, if the customer were to declare bankruptcy on the settlement date after receiving the £10m, but before paying the $16m, the settlement risk would be the full $16m.

Derivative transactions usually involve less risk than cash market transactions, because the principal amounts are not normally exchanged. Among derivatives, futures are the least risky, because of the financial standing of the clearing house and the daily settlement of gains and losses through the margining mechanism. However, following the 2007–2008 credit crisis, the movement of the OTC market towards central counterparties has brought similar advantages to the trading of OTC instruments like interest rate and credit default swaps.

Liquidity risk

This is the potential risk arising when an entity cannot meet payments when they fall due. It may involve borrowing at an excessive rate of interest, or facing penalty payments under contractual terms, or selling assets at below-market prices (this is sometimes classified as *forced-sale* risk). Banks in particular are concerned about liquidity risk, because their successful operation depends absolutely upon trust and confidence, and failure to meet payments at the appointed time could destroy that confidence. A prime example of this is the rapid collapse of Northern Rock in the late summer of 2007. As a bank, it had pursued an aggressive lending policy in the UK sub-prime market, and eventually experienced severe loan losses on this portfolio when the sub-prime market collapsed. However, it was not these bad debts that precipitated the failure of Northern Rock, but the drying up of its access to the interbank market and other wholesale sources of funds. Northern Rock depended in large part on funding from the wholesale money markets, as its retail deposits dropped from 62% of total liabilities in 1997 to just 22% at the end of 2006.[3] When confidence in sub-prime lending began to wane, money market investors were the first to pull their deposits in an attempt to avoid credit risk if Northern Rock eventually became insolvent. Without access to liquidity, Northern Rock could not survive, and had to be rescued by the UK government.

Operating risk

This is commonly defined as 'the risk of direct or indirect loss resulting from inadequate or failed internal processes, people, and systems, or from external events'. Put simply – if anything can go wrong, it will! (Murphy's Law.) An obvious operating risk is that arising from fraud, and all institutions must undertake procedures to prevent or minimise this threat. Over the years there have been a number of well-publicised 'rogue trader' stories, including Nick Leeson, who in 1995 single-handedly bankrupted Barings Bank, and Kweku Adoboli, who in 2011 lost over $2bn at UBS. However, operating risk can occur in other ways, and a potentially mounting problem stems from the increasing reliance on technology, and the occasionally accident-prone interface between man and machine. So-called 'fat-finger' mistakes can prove expensive, as the following two examples illustrate.

- In July 1998, a London-based trader working at Salomon Brothers leaned on the keyboard and his elbow accidentally depressed the F12 'instant sell' key. The computer's auto-repeat functionality then duplicated the order 145 times before the errant elbow was moved, unintentionally selling 10,000 T-Bond contracts on the French Matif futures exchange. The mistake cost Salomon several million dollars.

- In December 2005, a broker working at Mizuho Securities accidentally tried to sell 610,000 shares in a newly issued company called J-Com for ¥1. What he meant to do was to sell one share at ¥610,000, and the mistake cost Mizuho ¥40.7bn at the time (although the TSE later refunded ¥10.7bn). As Julia Roberts famously said in the movie *Pretty Woman*, 'Big mistake. Big. Huge!'

Other market risk

There are many residual market risks which come under this heading. Among these are *volatility* risk, which affects option traders, and *basis risk*, which has a far wider impact. In general, basis risk arises whenever one kind of risk exposure is hedged with an instrument that behaves in a similar, but not necessarily identical, way.

One example would be a company using three-month interest rate futures to hedge its commercial paper or euronote programme. Although LIBOR rates, to which futures prices respond, are well correlated with commercial paper rates, they do not invariably move in lock step. If commercial paper rates moved up by 50bp, but futures prices dropped by only 35bp, the 15bp gap would be the basis risk in this case.

Another example is the use of proxy currencies as hedging instruments. Liquidity in some currency pairs, for example the euro/Polish zloty (EUR/PLN), is greater than in some others, like the euro/Hungarian forint (EUR/HUF), but the two currency pairs are highly correlated. Banks and companies can therefore use trades in the EUR/PLN as a proxy to hedge exposures in EUR/HUF.

Model risk

Some of the latest financial instruments are heavily dependent on complex mathematical models for pricing and hedging. If the model is incorrectly specified, is based on questionable assumptions, or does not accurately reflect the true behaviour of the market, banks offering these instruments could suffer extensive losses.

16.3 Accounting and economic risk

When assessing risk exposure, it is vital to distinguish between *accounting risk* and *economic risk*.

Accounting risk is the risk which can be measured from an entity's financial accounts. Information about transactional cash flows, the location and denomination of assets and liabilities, and the maturity structure of the balance sheet, enable an objective assessment of the magnitude of the risks which are faced. Accounting risk is therefore largely a backward-looking concept, looking at how cash flows, assets and liabilities have been affected by risk in the past, or how they may be affected by changes that take place right now.

Economic risk goes much further, and is concerned with the broader impact of risk upon an entity's entire operations. As such, economic risk is often concerned with second- and third-order effects, as the impact of risk ripples through the economic system.

As one example of the distinction between accounting and economic risk, consider what effect a rise in interest rates would have upon a typical manufacturing company. The accounting risk will be relatively easy to quantify. Any floating-rate liabilities, bank borrowing facilities for example, will incur greater costs, while floating rate assets, perhaps a deposit account, will earn more interest. If the company has used any financial engineering tools to hedge its exposure, these will show profits or losses depending upon the nature of the hedge.

The economic risk, however, is wider but less obvious in its impact. Suppliers faced with higher interest costs will demand payment sooner, while customers may take extended credit and pay later. This will worsen the company's cash flow, leading to more borrowing, and yet higher interest costs. Worse, higher interest rates may slow down economic activity, resulting in less demand for the company's goods. In addition, the higher rates may encourage overseas investors, leading to a temporary increase in the strength of the domestic currency. This will reduce the price of imported goods in terms of the domestic currency, while at the same time increasing the price of exported goods in foreign currency terms. The net effect: a worsening of the company's competitive position, and a further reduction in the company's fortunes.

This discussion of economic risk has focused on interest rate risk, but economic risk can be even more subtle when it comes to currency exposure. As another example, consider a mythical manufacturing company based in St Louis, Missouri, having the following operating features:

- All raw materials are purchased from local suppliers and paid for in US dollars.
- All labour and other production costs are incurred in US dollars.
- All production machinery is purchased from machine-tool manufacturers based in the United States and paid for in dollars.
- All finished goods are sold in the US mid-west, and priced in US dollars.
- All financing is in dollar-denominated borrowings from local banks.

It seems fairly obvious that the one problem this company does not face is currency exposure. It operates in the very centre of the United States, far from any foreign shores. All its costs are based in US dollars, and all its revenues likewise.

Looking deeper, however, one important factor has been omitted from this analysis – competition. We operate in a world market, and even if our mythical company is not interested in exporting outside the United States, companies elsewhere may be very interested in importing their goods into the States. If the dollar strengthens against other world currencies, the price of imported goods in the United States becomes cheaper, and this could well threaten the cosy existence of our mythical mid-west manufacturer.

Although we have illustrated the economic risk arising from currency exposure with an invented example, there are many real-life stories. As an example, Table 16.1 shows that for the Benetton Group in 2009–2010, economic FX risk was the dominant component of the company's total FX risk.

TABLE 16.1
Economic vs. accounting risk for Benetton

Net foreign currency hedging (losses)/gains	2010 (€m)	2009 (€m)
Economic exchange risk	12.3	(1.4)
Transaction exchange risk	2.3	(1.3)
Translation exchange risk	0.8	(0.2)
Other	(3.3)	0.3
Total	12.1	(2.5)

Source: Benetton Group 2010 Annual Report.

16.4 Defining hedging objectives

When hedging was defined earlier in this chapter, two different hedging examples were illustrated. In one, dubbed the 'perfect' hedge, a hedging instrument was found which exactly mirrored the underlying risk. By combining the two, a completely flat and riskless result was obtained. In the second example, the hedge only came into effect when the underlying risk exceeded a predetermined threshold of pain. This had the effect of capping the risk, thereby limiting the adverse fluctuations, but allowing the benefits from benign fluctuations to pass through.

These two illustrations demonstrate that hedging can take on a number of forms, and one person's 'perfect' hedge may be another's straitjacket. Before any hedging scheme can be designed, and certainly before any hedging decisions are implemented, it is vital to clarify what the scheme is meant to achieve. The answers to four key questions will help to define what a particular client's hedging objectives actually are:

- Does the client simply wish to obtain complete protection against *any* movements in price?
- If a degree of risk is to be tolerated, how does the desire to obtain upside savings compare with the wish to avoid downside risk?
- How averse is the client to paying for risk protection?
- What is the client's view of the likely direction, magnitude and timing of market movements?

Complete protection

Risk has already been defined as *any* variation in an outcome, so complete protection against *any* movements in price implies hedging against both adverse and benign outcomes. Nonetheless, for some clients, absolute certainty may be exactly what they want. If this is the case, the appropriate financial engineering tools to use are those with straight-line or symmetric characteristics[4] like FRAs, forwards, futures or swaps. When coupled with the underlying exposure, all of these tools attempt to guarantee a particular financial outcome, thus securing as complete protection as possible against market price risk.

Upside vs. downside

Other clients may wish to have the best of both worlds – protection against the downside while enjoying the benefits of the upside. In these cases, options or option-based risk management solutions are likely to be the preferred choice, but the number of possible permutations is infinite. To narrow the choice, the client needs to indicate the balance between his dislike of downside losses and his liking for upside savings. For many clients, the trade-off will not be symmetrical, because the desire to avoid losses for most companies is greater than the desire to realise savings.

As an example, consider the following non-exclusive propositions:

- paying a £200 insurance premium to avoid a 1-in-100 chance of losing £10,000
- paying £200 to buy a lottery ticket with a 1-in-100 chance of winning £10,000.

The situations are very similar, but most people would agree to pay the £200 premium to avoid the £10,000 loss, but would not buy the £200 lottery ticket giving them an equivalent chance to gain £10,000.[5] Many financial engineering solutions reflect this reality, by providing stronger protection against the downside than opportunities to benefit from the upside, but any structure can be tailored to suit the exact preferences of each client.

Paying for protection

Ironically, while individuals and companies are quite prepared to pay insurance premiums on risks like fire and theft, there is often a marked reluctance to pay for protection against financial risks. This can partly be explained by the fact that traditional insurance is a centuries-old business, and many people take for granted the need to buy insurance, while financial risk management techniques have only been developed since the 1980s, and have yet to become as firmly established as insurance. Another reason is that some financial engineering tools, especially option-based ones, may appear expensive in relation to the perceived risk. The truth is that many individuals underestimate the true extent and impact of financial risk, because it is less tangible than physical risk. They may therefore believe that a financial risk premium is excessive, when in reality it may be fairly priced in relation to the true level of risk.

Financial risk is very real, though. One of the most frequently occurring financial risks is that arising from fluctuations in FX rates, and there are numerous examples of companies reporting losses amounting to tens or hundreds of millions of US dollars arising from unhedged currency exposures. As an example, in just one three-month period from July to September 2011, Crisil Research reported that the depreciation of the Indian rupee had cost 42 of the 50 companies in the Indian Nifty index around $1bn in FX losses on their foreign-currency denominated debt, leading to an 8% reduction in their pre-tax profits.

Nonetheless, banks have responded to the aversion of clients who prefer to pay little, if anything, for hedging against financial risk, and have devised a wide range of low-cost and zero-cost risk management solutions. For example, a bank can buy a portion of the client's profit opportunities in return for selling the requisite level of protection, and by striking a balance between the two can arrive at a net cost of zero. The chapters which follow are replete with examples.

View of the market

Many clients have their own view of what may happen to market rates in the future. For example, they may believe it likely that the pound sterling will strengthen against the euro, or that interest rates in Japan will rise, or that dollar interest rates may rise but more slowly than the implied forward rates predict. In all these circumstances, such views can and should be incorporated into the hedge design. A client who believes it most unlikely that interest rates will fall will be easily persuaded to sell a floor in order to finance the purchase of a cap. On the other hand, a client who thinks that the dollar will almost certainly rise will be reluctant to pay for protection against the dollar falling.

Once the client's attitudes, views and preferences are known, one or more hedging schemes can be designed appropriate for his needs. After the scheme is implemented, the client will be concerned to see how well the hedge is performing, and the next section discusses how this can be assessed.

16.5 Measuring hedge efficiency

Measuring hedge efficiency is not the same as measuring hedge profitability, although many users may equate the two.

Consider the scenario of a US pharmaceutical company which exports its products to Germany. Orders result in shipment three months later, and the goods are invoiced and paid for in euros one month after shipment. The company therefore knows four months in advance what its sales proceeds in euros will be and, being prudent, decides to hedge its currency exposure by selling the euros four months forward for US dollars. Suppose that the forward rate is €1 = $1.3000, thus fixing the amount of dollars received at $1.3m on a sale of €1m. Four months later, out of curiosity, the company decides to check the spot exchange rate prevailing on the day the euros are actually received. It turns out that the euro has weakened, and the spot euro is trading at €1 = $1.2000. The manufacturer is well pleased that it had decided to hedge, because the forward deal resulted in proceeds $100,000 greater than would have been received had the company simply sold its €1m on the spot market – a $100,000 'profit'.

Following its successful experience with hedging, the manufacturer repeats the strategy on receiving the next order. By coincidence, the forward rate once again is €1 = $1.3000. On this occasion, however, it is the euro's turn to strengthen and four months later the euro is trading at €1 = $1.4000. The manufacturer is now upset, because the hedge has now resulted in a 'loss' of $100,000.

Is the company justified in being upset? Did it first profit by $100,000 and then lose $100,000? How efficient was the hedge? The answers to all these questions depend entirely upon the hedging objectives which the company established at the outset. If the company's original goal was to realise proceeds of $1.3m from the transaction, then the forward deal producing this cash flow is a perfect hedge, and therefore 100% efficient. The company really is not justified in being upset if the spot rate later turns out to be more advantageous. In terms of achieving its objective of $1.3m, looking at the spot rate is irrelevant for the company. So, too, are the concepts of gaining or losing $100,000 in this example.

Of course, it is an understandable human reaction to regret setting up a hedge if the market rate eventually goes in favour of the original exposure, but it is always easy to fault a decision with the benefit of hindsight.[6] What matters when judging the quality of a hedging decision are the original objectives and the information available at that time.

With this in mind, we can now define five alternative measures of hedge efficiency. The choice of the right one to use depends upon the hedging objectives.

1. Objective: Achieve a target financial result; more is better, less is worse

This is typical of many hedging situations. The particular result may be a target investment rate, or target financial proceeds from a business transaction. The hedge efficiency can be defined simply as:

$$Hedge\ efficiency = \frac{T_{ACT}}{T_{TGT}} \qquad (16.1)$$

where:

T_{ACT} is the actual financial result
T_{TGT} is the target financial result

For example, if funds were actually invested at 4.82%, and the target rate was 5.00%, the hedge efficiency would be 96.40%.

2. Objective: Achieve a target financial result; less is better, more is worse

This is similar to the previous case, except that the exposure is in the opposite direction. Examples would include a target borrowing rate, or target project costs. In this case, the formula can be rearranged thus:

$$Hedge\ efficiency = \frac{T_{TGT}}{T_{ACT}} \qquad (16.2)$$

As an illustration, if target project costs were $6.8m, but actual costs after hedging turned out to be $7.1m, the hedge efficiency would be 95.77%.

3. Objective: Achieve a target financial result subject to a minimum acceptable result

This is also similar to the first case, except that there is a second threshold which sets the minimum acceptable result. The hedge efficiency in this case can be calculated thus:

$$Hedge\ efficiency = \frac{T_{ACT} - T_{MIN}}{T_{TGT} - T_{MIN}} \qquad (16.3)$$

where:

T_{MIN} is the minimum acceptable financial result

and the other symbols are as defined before.

Suppose that the target proceeds from a financial transaction are £5m, and the break-even proceeds were £4m, thereby setting the minimum acceptable result. If actual proceeds turn out to be £5.2m, the hedge efficiency would be 120%.

4. Objective: Achieve a target financial result subject to a maximum acceptable result

This is like the previous example, except that the conditions are reversed once again with the imposition of a maximum acceptable result. The hedge efficiency here is:

$$Hedge\ efficiency = \frac{T_{MAX} - T_{ACT}}{T_{MAX} - T_{TGT}} \qquad (16.4)$$

where:

T_{MAX} is the maximum acceptable financial result

and the other symbols are as defined before.

A company's borrowing facility is due to be renewed shortly. The target borrowing rate is 5%, with a maximum permissible rate of 6%. After hedging, the company manages to borrow at 5.10%, giving rise to a hedge efficiency of 90%.

5. Objective: Maintain the status quo

This is different from the hedging objectives discussed so far. In this case, *any* deviation from the present situation is deemed undesirable. In the four previous situations, there was always a directional preference, and this meant that hedge efficiencies greater than 100% could be recorded if the target was bettered.

502 HANDBOOK OF FINANCIAL ENGINEERING

Many banks run portfolios of financial instruments which they wish to hedge from any deviations in market rates. Perfection here is a hedged portfolio whose value is totally unaffected when market prices change. A portfolio which is imperfectly hedged leaves it exposed to possible gains or losses if market rates move. Although a movement of rates in one direction could lead to fortuitous profits from an imperfectly hedged portfolio, the bank would rightly argue that the market could just as easily have moved in the other direction.

The appropriate measure of hedge efficiency in this case is:

$$Hedge\ efficiency = \min\left(1 - \frac{\Delta T}{\Delta U}, 1 + \frac{\Delta T}{\Delta U}\right) \tag{16.5}$$

where:

ΔT is the change in the total value of the hedged portfolio
ΔU is the change in the total value of the unhedged portfolio

For example, suppose a bank is hedging a portfolio of FRAs with interest rate futures. Following a shift in the yield curve, the value of the hedged portfolio increases by $1,512 while the FRAs alone lose $20,000. The hedge efficiency is 92.44% in this case.

Note that the definition of hedge efficiency given in equation 16.5 precludes efficiencies greater than 100%. The best result attainable is an efficiency of 100%, and this is achieved when $\Delta T = 0$, i.e. when the hedged portfolio does not change in value at all. For any deviation in portfolio value, whether positive or negative, $\Delta T \neq 0$, and the efficiency will decline from 100%. If the hedge is totally ineffective, $\Delta T = \Delta U$, and the hedge efficiency will be zero. It is possible for negative efficiencies to be recorded if the hedge actually exaggerates the effect of market rate fluctuations.

It is important to set proper hedging objectives, and then to measure hedge efficiency correctly. Failure to do so may lead to the wrong decisions being taken, either before or after the event. As a particular illustration of this, consider the problem which beset the German national airline Lufthansa in the mid-1980s. It had placed an order with the Boeing Corporation for delivery of 20 jets approximately one year later, to be paid for in US dollars. At the time, the dollar was uncharacteristically strong. Lufthansa believed that the most likely scenario was for the dollar to weaken over the following year. However, it was worried. If the market appeared to be acting irrationally in overpricing the dollar when the aeroplanes were ordered, what if the market were even more irrational when it came to paying for them? Lufthansa reviewed the alternatives:

a) Buy dollars forward.
b) Buy a currency option (call on dollars/put on D-marks).
c) Do nothing now, and buy dollars spot when the aeroplanes were due for delivery.

Since Lufthansa already thought that the dollar was overpriced when it placed the order, it was reluctant to buy dollars at what it considered was an inflated price. This ruled out the first alternative. As for using currency options, because Lufthansa believed that the dollar was eventually going to weaken, it expected that the dollar call would expire worthless, and that the option premium (about 6% of the notional) would therefore be thrown away. This was seen as an unnecessary waste. Alternative (c) seemed attractive if Lufthansa's view held, but this strategy would be abhorrent for a conservative company. After all, failure to hedge a known currency exposure is tantamount to speculation.

In fact, Lufthansa executed a fourth strategy:

d) Buy half the required dollars forward.

The company reasoned as follows. If the dollar weakens, as it expected, Lufthansa would gain by 50% of any such move, since half the original exposure was left unhedged. If the dollar were to strengthen unexpectedly, any resultant costs would be halved, for similar reasons.

What happened? The dollar fell substantially, just as Lufthansa had believed. As it was able to buy half the required dollars in the spot market at a much lower price, the company saved a great deal compared to the cost of the jets one year earlier. One would think that the executives responsible should have been amply rewarded for their astuteness, but no. They lost their jobs amid what nearly became a national scandal. Why? The accounts that year reported separately (i) the purchase of jets, and (ii) the forward purchase of dollars. There was no recognition that the aeroplanes had been purchased some 25% cheaper as a result of the fall in the dollar, but the forward purchase of dollars was recorded as a currency loss of sizeable magnitude. Even though the combination of the hedge with the underlying exposure saved money for Lufthansa, the accounts did not couple the two results, nor did they reflect the rationale behind the hedging strategy.

If there is a moral to be learned, it is this. If a hedge is designed against a specific exposure, then the financial results of the two should be reported together, as one indivisible entity. The exposure and the hedge should metaphorically be placed together in a box, the lid slammed tightly shut, and the temptation to peek inside to see how each separate item is doing should be firmly resisted. It looks as if Lufthansa has learned this lesson. Its 2010 Annual Report states:

'Derivative financial instruments are used exclusively for hedging underlying transactions. The market value of the derivatives must therefore be seen in connection with the hedged items.'

16.6 The finance division as a profit centre

With increasing attention being focused on the financial performance of a company's operating divisions, the finance division in some companies is now considered as a profit centre. There is nothing wrong with this in principle, but it does raise some important questions of profit measurement.

How should the transfer prices be set?

In any company where one division provides materials or services to another, the tricky issue of transfer pricing arises. Sometimes these can be determined fairly rationally, but in many instances transfer prices can be set quite arbitrarily. Suppose the finance division exchanges euros for sterling on behalf of a British-based operating division, or raises SwF5m for five years at a fixed rate in order to finance a new factory near Zurich. Should it add a margin to whatever spot FX rate it receives from the bank? Should it charge a fixed fee? Should it charge interest in floating sterling, and treat any difference between floating sterling coupons and fixed SwF coupons as profit or loss? Unless the company can establish a clear policy so that these issues can be fairly resolved, the concept of the finance division as a profit centre becomes meaningless.

How does one measure the economic value of hedging?

A simple strategy for a finance division would be to cover all known exposures using forward deals, thereby fixing costs. Against this would be the valid criticism that a number of opportunities to save on costs may be missed. For example, fixing the cost of a five-year dollar loan at 4% when current six-month rates are only 1.7% incurs an immediate cost of 2.3%. Worse, if a prudent hedge is implemented, and subsequently the market moves in favour of the original position, the hedge loses money when looked at in isolation. It is situations like these that grab the headlines, as the following examples testify:

■ Shares in Cathay Pacific dropped 5% in January 2009 on the news that the airline lost almost $1bn on fuel hedges following the plunge in oil prices from $147 to just $40 a barrel over a six-month period from July 2008 to January 2009. (Curiously, at around the same time Ryanair reported its first ever loss, in part because it *didn't* hedge against rising fuel prices in the first half of 2008.)

■ China Eastern, another Asian airline, lost over $900m in 2008, again as a result of the plummeting price of oil at that time.

■ Agrium is a major supplier of agricultural products and services to the Americas. The company's 2012 Q1 profits fell almost 10% compared with the same period in 2011, and part of this was attributed to a $13m loss on natural gas hedges.

■ Hartford Financial Services' profits for the same period fell by 81% owing to losses of $378m from a combination of currency and equity market hedges.

What is common with all these examples is that derivatives-based hedges are blamed when their losses offset profits on an underlying risk exposure. However, it seems that in most cases this is a modern-day repeat of the same thing that afflicted Lufthansa in the 1980s, as discussed in the previous section. The *Wall Street Journal* was perceptive in its reporting of the Cathay Pacific loss:

'Common hedging methods lock in fuel prices, protecting airlines when prices rise. But when prices fall, financial accounts often list the price differences as losses, though the losses are usually noncash ones.'

'Hedging bites Cathay Pacific', *WSJ*, 12 March 2009

Once again, we emphasise that it is important for the financial results from any hedging operation to be reported together with those of the underlying position, and not placed separately under the microscope.

It is even more important for entities to have a consistent hedging policy. When situations arise like those just highlighted, it is not uncommon for companies to refrain from hedging, justifying this decision by a temporarily benign trend in market prices on their underlying exposure. An example of this is Southwest Airlines whose oil price hedging strategies proved extremely successful since they started in the mid-1990s, and which are analysed in Chapter 21. However, like Cathay Pacific and China Eastern, their oil price hedges generated losses in 2008 Q4 of $56m, and Southwest reportedly then unwound almost all its hedges as a result.

One way to avoid the problems caused by using swaps as hedging tools is to use options instead. As we will see in Chapters 17 and 19, these allow an entity to hedge only the downside while preserving the upside. Keeping to the airline theme, Qantas Airways provides a useful example of this:

'Australia's Qantas Airways Ltd., for example, used relatively expensive hedges involving options that allowed it to walk away from unprofitable contracts. For these hedges it paid fees of roughly $12 a barrel, compared with around $3 a barrel for less-flexible hedges, Chief Executive Alan Joyce said recently. Mr Joyce said that as a result, 85% of Qantas's fuel needs now benefit from falling prices.'

'Hedging bites Cathay Pacific', *WSJ*, 12 March 2009

On the whole, the correct use of derivatives can lead to substantial benefits – certainly in terms of reducing the variability of earnings, and often in terms of generating net profits. However, commercial companies should look to their prime areas of business activity, whether it be flying planes or manufacturing widgets, for the means to generate profits. While the more sophisticated companies may well create a profit centre out of their finance division, this should not get to the stage where the pursuit of profits leads to disaster. At what point does deliberate under- or over-hedging cease to be 'taking a prudent view of the markets' and become outright speculation?

Like many powerful tools, derivatives can deliver tremendous benefits when used properly, but can prove dangerous if placed in the wrong hands. The next few chapters show how, used correctly, derivatives can form the basis for the sound, prudent and profitable management of market risk.

Notes

1 A number of books have been written about this, including Lewis, Michael (2010) *The Big Short*, Norton, and Zuckerman, Gregory (2009) *The Greatest Trade Ever*, Penguin.

2 This calculation uses data as of 10th February 2012 when the E-mini contracts were trading at around 1340 and involved an initial margin per contract of $5,000.

3 Milne, A. and Wood, G. (2008) 'Banking crisis solutions: old and new' *Review* (Federal Reserve Bank of St Louis), September/October, pp. 517–30.

4 Refer back to Chapter 10 (section 10.1) for a discussion of symmetric vs. asymmetric characteristics.

5 Objectively, you should neither buy the lottery ticket nor the insurance contract. The probability-weighted value of the lottery ticket is only £100, so it is irrational to pay £200 for such a ticket. Likewise, the probability-weighted value of the risk exposure is a loss of only £100, so it is also irrational to pay £200 for the insurance. However, as most individuals are risk averse, in practice they buy insurance to avoid even a small chance of a big loss. Having said this, many people do buy lottery tickets costing £1 that offer only a 1 in 10 million chance to win £5m; the ratio of stake to expected payout is just the same as the first lottery example (2-to-1) but one can afford to be irrational if the stake costs just £1 instead of £200.

6 Interestingly enough, the break-forward deal was created in the late 1980s to exploit just this feeling of regret. This deal, which allows the client to break the transaction if it becomes too unfavourable, is explained in Chapter 17 (section 17.12).

17

MANAGING CURRENCY RISK

Chapter 1 has already portrayed the extent of currency volatility since the breakdown of fixed exchange rates in the early 1970s (see section 1.3 in Chapter 1). Although a small number of currency pairs remain closely linked, like the Chinese yuan against the US dollar, the major world trading currencies are free to float. FX transactions involving the US dollar, the Japanese yen, the euro and the pound sterling are all subject to currency risk. Even the euro itself, which was created to replace the disparate legacy currencies within Europe with a single European currency, is subject to the risk that it may break apart.

Under these circumstances, managing currency risk is vital for any organisation exposed to the influence of fluctuating exchange rates, and this is not limited solely to those executing FX transactions. Economic risk affects a much wider cross-section of companies, including the mythical St Louis-based manufacturing company discussed in the previous chapter, whose every transaction was denominated in US dollars.

This chapter starts with a brief review of managing currency risk using 'straight-line' products such as forwards. The bulk of the discussion, however, is devoted to option-based risk management strategies, which permit a rich assortment of objectives to be achieved.

17.1 Forwards and futures solutions

If the client's objective in managing currency risk is to eliminate the impact of *any* fluctuation in exchange rates, the answer is a forward exchange contract of some kind. Such an instrument will establish a firm price today for a foreign exchange deal to take place at some time in the future. There is a range of choices available here, and the choices can be sub-divided into two headings: cash instruments and exchange-traded futures.

Cash instruments

Into this category fall all the traditional tools of the FX market. The simplest is the outright forward, which fixes the rate for the exchange of agreed amounts of each currency on a particular date in the future. A variation is the option-dated forward, which allows the client to execute the exchange on any date within a pre-specified range. Long-term foreign exchange (LTFX) deals are one or more outright forward deals, but for dates further than one year into the future. Finally, the foreign exchange swap is the exchange of agreed amounts of each currency on one date, and the re-exchange on another date. Most commonly one date is spot, and the other forward, but forward-forward deals are done regularly where both dates are forward.

The great advantage of these cash instruments is that they are all OTC products, and every aspect of the transaction can be tailored to meet the specific needs of each customer. Deals can be arranged of almost any size –

whether round or odd amounts, for almost any value date – whether standard or odd-dated, and between almost any pair of currencies – whether major, minor or 'exotic'.

A French-based customer due to pay $1.73m in ten weeks can thus obtain a firm quotation for an outright forward deal, fixing the amount of euros to be paid in exchange for the dollars that he needs. If the exact timing is unknown, but will definitely fall in the range 8–12 weeks from now, the bank can quote for the option-dated forward. If the French company is contracted to pay $500,000 annually for the next five years, an LTFX deal will convert the dollar obligations into a fixed euro liability on each date. Finally, if the company decides to make a short-term investment of $1m repayable after eight months, a swap will fix the euro amounts both at the outset and at the maturity of the deal.

Exchange traded futures

Although currency futures were the very first kind of financial futures created, trading volumes have never approached those of other futures contracts, largely due to the depth and flexibility of the OTC market. Competition between banks, and the wide and rapid dissemination of FX prices, have ensured the narrowness of the spreads quoted. One of the prime advantages of futures markets – price transparency – is therefore equalled by the OTC market, while the need to manage daily futures margins is often considered an administrative burden by customers. The end result is that FX futures trading volumes represent only about 2–3% of the global FX market.

The common feature of both these solutions is that they enable the user to fix the rate for an exchange of currencies to take place on some future date. This eliminates the uncertainty, and hence the risk, arising from the volatility of spot rates. However, fixing the rate removes not only the downside risk, but also the possibility to benefit from advantageous movements in the spot rate. To take advantage of these, while maintaining protection against adverse fluctuations, option-based techniques must be used.

17.2 Options are chameleons

The chameleon is a small lizard that has the interesting ability to change the colour of its skin to match its surroundings. If it rests on a leaf, it looks like a leaf. If it crawls on the ground, it looks like the ground. In other words, the chameleon can behave like different things.

Options have a similar feature. A deep in-the-money option behaves just like the underlying asset. If the underlying asset changes by one point, so will the option. A deep out-of-the-money option, meanwhile, behaves like nothing at all.[1] If the underlying asset price moves, the option just sits there and does nothing.

As you compare options with different strike prices ranging from totally out-of-the-money to completely in-the-money, their nature changes smoothly from complete inertness to complete emulation of the underlying. In fact, the delta of an option measures precisely how similar the option is to the underlying asset.

Figure 17.1 illustrates this property by showing the profit profiles at expiry for various call options on the euro against US dollars. Each option is identical except for the strike price, which varies in 10¢ steps from $1.0000 to $1.6000. The options are all fairly priced with 270 days to maturity at a time when the 270-day forward euro was trading at €1 = $1.3000. Implied volatilities are assumed to range from 10% for the ATMF (at-the-money-forward) option to 13% for the OTM options, thereby incorporating the volatility smile explained in Chapter 11 (section 11.2). Finally, we assume nine-month interest rates of 1% p.a. for the US dollar, and 2% p.a. for the euro. The graphs show the profits to one who buys a call option on €1m and holds the option until maturity. As a comparison, the final line on the chart shows the profit profile for someone buying €1m nine months forward at the fixed price of $1.3000, as opposed to a call option on €1m.

At one extreme is the option struck at $1.0000, deep in-the-money. The characteristic for this option is the mostly diagonal line from near the bottom-left to top-right, with a break-even point at €1 = $1.2980, a fraction below the forward

FIGURE 17.1

The chameleon-like behaviour of options

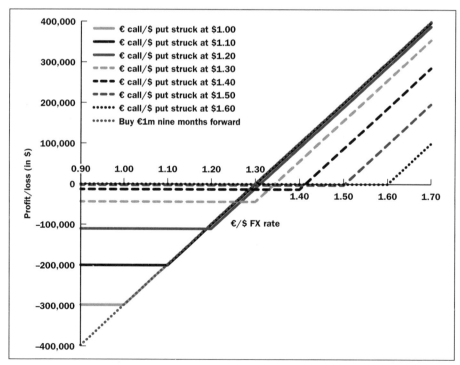

price of $1.3000. The shape is virtually identical to the diagonal profit profile of simply buying €1m rather than a call option on €1m, because under almost all circumstances the option will end up being exercised, so the profile looks simply like being long €1m. The only difference (from €1 = $1.0000 upwards) is the barely visible constant gap of +$2,000 between the option strategy and the simple one of being long the underlying. This reflects the small negative time value of the very deep in-the-money option, amounting to 0.20¢ per euro, or $2,000 in total. This negative time value is caused by a combination of two factors. First, there is the advantage to the option holder of being able *not* to exercise the option in the unlikely event that the euro falls below $1.0000; this is worth 0.02¢ per euro to the option buyer. Second, the option costs almost 30¢ per euro right now, and the cost to the option buyer of financing this premium over a 270-day period is around 0.22¢. The net of these is the 0.20¢ per euro negative time value of this option.

At the other extreme is the out-of-the-money option struck at $1.6000, whose profile is the mostly flat line just below the x-axis. The shape of this characteristic is virtually identical with doing nothing, except for the constant gap this time of 0.13¢ per euro between the option's result and zero for all values of the euro below the strike price of $1.6000. Once again, this is just the time value of the out-of-the-money option, which is the value to the holder of being able to buy euros at $1.6000 in the unlikely event that the euro should rise above this level.

In between lie all the other option profiles, each one sharing some component of the diagonal characteristic from the underlying asset (long €1m), and some element of the flat characteristic from the 'do-nothing' strategy. The at-the-money option struck at $1.3000, for example, displays equal amounts of each.

While Figure 17.1 shows the profile for seven specific strike prices, there is in fact a complete continuum of profiles ranging smoothly from deep out-of-the-money to deep in-the-money. Figure 17.2 illustrates this using a three-dimensional representation of the profit profiles.

There are separate axes for original strike price (middle-front to back-left), underlying price at maturity (middle-front to back-right), and profit or loss (bottom to top). At the back-left of the figure is the horizontal line showing the completely flat profit profile of the deep out-of-the-money option struck at $1.7000. As one moves towards the front-right of the picture, the strike price moves lower and further into the money, until one reaches the totally diagonal profile at the very front-right for the deep in-the-money option struck at $1.0000. In between there is the classic hockey-stick profile of a call option at maturity. In this diagram the flat region goes from the front-left towards the middle of the figure until the €/$ exchange rate hits the strike price; the chart then bends diagonally upwards from there towards the back-right.

One of the themes that will permeate this chapter is the way in which the nature of the hedge will change depending upon the degree of 'moneyness' of the options used. With deep out-of-the-money options, the hedge will be almost

FIGURE 17.2
Continuum of profiles

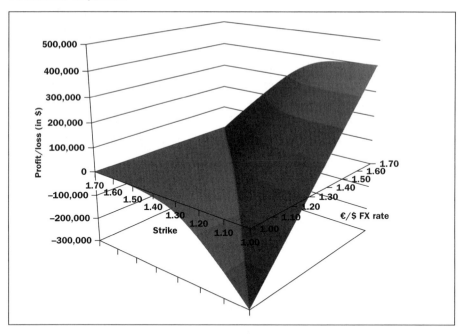

non-existent, and the full extent of the underlying exposure will come through. With deep in-the-money options, all the techniques illustrated will behave in the same way as a simple forward contract, and the ability to benefit from benign movements in the market price will disappear. Only between these two extremes will the distinctive features of each technique be realised.

17.3 How FX options are different

In the previous section we referred several times to a call option on €1m at various strike prices denominated in US dollars. For example, we can think of a call option on €1m struck at $1.25, and this is pictured in Figure 17.3a. If the option buyer exercises the option, he or she will pay the strike price of $1.25 per €1, paying a total of $1.25m for the €1m called. As a comparison, Figure 17.3b shows a put on $1.25m struck at €0.80 per $1. If the option buyer exercises this option, he or she will deliver the $1.25m, receiving €0.80 per US dollar, a total of €1m. Study the figures closely and you will see that the two options are identical. In other words, every FX option is both a call and a put! For this reason, it is conventional in the FX options market to refer to such an option as a 'call on euros/put on US dollars' or, more briefly, as a 'euro call/US dollar put'.

FIGURE 17.3

FX options are both calls and puts

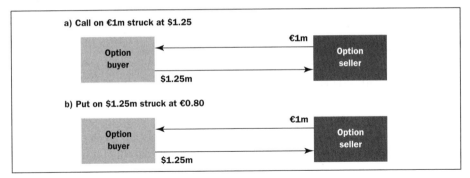

Another consequence of the underlier being money (rather than an object like a barrel of oil or a share in a company) is that the option premium can be quoted in four different ways:

- in terms of the pricing currency
- as a percentage of the base currency
- in terms of the base currency
- as a percentage of the pricing currency.

Taking once again the example of a call on euros struck at $1.25, Table 17.1 shows how the starting figure of $0.0739 per €1 obtained from an option pricing model can be converted to all the other quotations at a time when spot is trading at €1 = $1.3097.

TABLE 17.1

Quoting FX options in different ways

Quotation style	Quotation	Conversion
In terms of the pricing currency	$0.0739 per €1	None needed
As a percentage of the base currency	5.64% of €1	$\dfrac{\$0.0739}{\$1.3097} = €0.0564$ per €1 = 5.64%
In terms of the base currency	€0.0451 per $1	$\dfrac{\$0.0739}{\$1.3097 \times \$1.25} = €0.0451$ per $1
As a percentage of the pricing currency	5.91% of $1	$\dfrac{\$0.0739}{\$1.25} = \$0.0591$ per $1 = 5.91%

The original quotation of $0.0739 is for a call option on €1. To express this as a percentage of the base currency we merely need to divide by the *spot price* to convert the dollar-denominated premium of $0.0739 into a euro-denominated premium of €0.0564 or 5.64%. To convert this to a put option on $1 priced in euros we need to divide again by the *strike price*, because we need to convert from a put option on $1.25 (€1) to a put option on $1, giving us €0.0451. Finally, to express this as a percentage of the pricing currency, we need to multiply the €0.0451 by the spot rate of $1.3097 to get a dollar-denominated premium of $0.0591or 5.91%. Alternatively, we can start with the original $0.0739 premium for a call on €1 and divide by $1.25 to obtain the dollar-denominated premium for a put option on $1.

These are all equivalent quotations for exactly the same option. A US customer with a euro payable would probably prefer the option quoted as a call on the euro priced in US dollars ($0.0739 per €1), or expressed as a percentage of the pricing currency, namely 5.91%. On the other hand, a European customer with a dollar receivable would usually prefer the option quoted as a put on the US dollar priced in euros (€0.0451 per $1), or expressed as a percentage of the base currency, namely 5.64%.

17.4 The scenario

To illustrate the various approaches to hedging currency risk, we will take the case of a US-based company which is due to pay €1m in 270 days' time. As hedging objectives, the company wishes:

- to prevent excessive losses in case the euro rises
- to benefit, if at all possible, should the euro weaken
- to minimise the cost of providing protection against adverse movements in the euro, while obtaining an adequate degree of protection.

The euro is currently trading at €1 = $1.3097 spot, and at $1.3000 nine months forward. Nine-month interest rates are 2% and 1% respectively for the euro and dollar, while implied volatility ranges from 10% to 13% depending on the strike price. The company has no particular view as to the direction of future market movements, but feels that it is most unlikely for the euro to stray outside the range $1.1000–$1.5000 over this period.[2] This range will therefore form the horizon of possible exchange rate movements that the company will contemplate.

Table 17.2 summarises the premiums for European-style options at various strike levels, all quotations being in US dollar points per euro. As an example, the ATMF options cost 446 points, or $0.0446 per €1. Notice that the market-maker has quoted premiums with a higher implied volatility for in- and out-of-the-money options, compared with the implied volatility used for at-the-money options, reflecting the volatility smile mentioned earlier.

TABLE 17.2
Option premium quotations

Strike ($)	Call on € (Put on $)	Put on € (Call on $)	Implied volatility
1.0000	2980	2	12.00%
1.0500	2488	7	11.50%
1.1000	2003	18	11.00%
1.1500	1538	50	10.75%
1.2000	1110	117	10.50%
1.2500	739	243	10.25%
1.3000	446	446	10.00%
1.3500	259	755	10.25%
1.4000	142	1135	10.50%
1.4500	75	1564	10.75%
1.5000	38	2024	11.00%
1.5500	22	2503	11.50%
1.6000	13	2990	12.00%
1.6500	8	3482	12.50%
1.7000	5	3975	13.00%

Using this set of quotations, we will now explore various ways for the US company to manage its currency risk, while bearing in mind the hedging objectives just defined. In nearly every case, we will assume that the company wishes to set up a hedge, and then to leave it until maturity. For this reason, the graphs will show the results solely at maturity rather than beforehand. Section 17.16 towards the end of this chapter will, however, review dynamic hedging strategies.

17.5 Comparing hedging strategies

The clearest way to compare different hedging strategies is to draw the resulting payoff profiles, and the best place to start is to look at the US company's original exposure to the euro, which is charted in Figure 17.4. Recall that the company has a €1m payable, and so is effectively short the euro. If the euro were to weaken all the way down to parity with the dollar the €1m would only cost $1m to finance, but if the euro were to strengthen all the way up to €1 = $1.6000 then the €1m would cost $1.6m. We have arranged the y-axis to show the actual dollar cash flow so that the more dollars the US company pays out, the more negative is the cash outflow, which then appears lower down the chart. This ensures that the visual message conveyed by the chart makes sense – better outcomes appear higher (fewer dollars paid out) while worse outcomes appear lower (more dollars paid out) – and the resultant exposure profile goes from top-left to bottom-right as the euro becomes stronger. This is consistent with the US company's short position in euros.

FIGURE 17.4

Original exposure to €1m payable

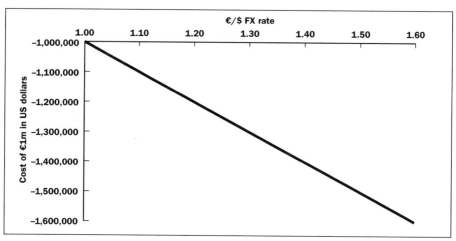

To avoid this currency risk, the company could buy an at-the-money call on the euro (put on the dollar) struck at $1.3000, for a total cost of $44,600. Figure 17.5 graphs the original exposure, the profit profile of the option at maturity, and the combined result. The dark grey diagonal line representing the original exposure is the same as in the previous figure, while the pale grey profile of the option has the familiar shape characteristic of long a call. Finally, the black line showing the total result is just the arithmetic sum of the two components.

To explain the shape of the total result, we will divide the graph into two regions. First, to the left of the strike price at $1.3000 the call expires worthless, so the total result is the same as that of the original exposure, less the $44,600 option premium. The black line showing the hedged exposure tracks the dark grey original exposure, but $44,600 lower. Second, if the euro finishes to the right of the $1.3000 strike price the option expires in-the-money with a payout which increases at exactly the same rate as the mounting losses from the original exposure. In this region, the rising profile from the option and the falling profile from the original exposure cancel out to leave a flat result – the company always pays $1,344,600 for the €1m it needs.

You can arrive at the capped $1,344,600 cost in one of two ways:

a) The US company buys the euros it needs by physically exercising the euro call option, paying the strike price of $1,300,000 and receiving the €1m in exchange. Adding the original premium of $44,600 gives the all-in cost of $1,344,600.

b) The US company cash-settles the option. For example, if the euro was trading at $1.4000 at expiry the option would be 10¢ in-the-money and be worth $100,000 at expiry. The company would have to buy the euros it needed in the spot FX market and pay the then prevailing price of $1.4000 per euro, or $1,400,000 in total. However, the $100,000 cash settlement from the option

FIGURE 17.5
€1m payable hedged by $ call/€ put struck at $1.30

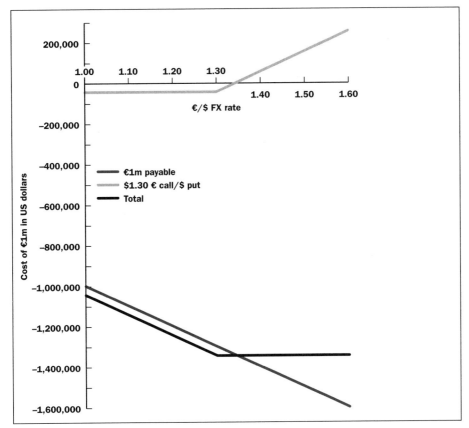

would reduce the effective cost of the euros at expiry to $1,300,000. Adding the option premium cost of $44,600 once again gives us the same all-in cost of $1,344.600.

17.6 Basic option hedges

The US company in our scenario is obligated to pay euros in nine months' time and is therefore adversely exposed to the risk that the euro may strengthen when the time comes to buy the €1m required. The simplest and most obvious option-based hedge is for the company to buy a nine-month call option on the euro (put on the US dollar), just like the example discussed above. The only issue which needs to be resolved is to select an appropriate strike price.

At one extreme is the most in-the-money option struck at $1.0000 at a premium cost of $0.2980 per euro. At first sight, this option seems to guarantee that the US company could buy its euros at a price no higher than $1.2980 (the $1.0000 strike price plus the $0.2980 premium), with a total cost *less* than the prevailing forward rate of $1.3000. However, this simple calculation does not take into account the timing of the cash flows involved. The option premium is paid up front, but the exercise price would be paid only at the expiry of the contract. With a straight-forward forward contract, the cash flows all take place at maturity. To place everything on the same basis, we need to allow for the cost of financing the option premium over the nine-month time span. With US interest rates at 1% per annum, the interest adds another $0.0022 per euro to the cost of the option hedge, bringing the maximum all-in cost to $1.3002. The extra $0.0002 compared with the forward price of $1.3000 is the value to the company of being able *not* to buy its euros under the option contract in the unlikely event that the euro falls below $1.0000.

At the other extreme is the $1.7000 strike option which costs very little, only $0.0005 per euro, $500 in all, but which affords very little protection. The euro would have to climb by 40¢ before the option even began to have any value at expiry. By this time, the company would have paid out an extra $400,000 to purchase its €1m.

The complete range of alternatives is graphed in Figure 17.6, which shows the total cost of €1m using options with strike prices ranging from $1.0000 to $1.6000. All the figures have been adjusted for the cost of financing the premiums over the nine-month period. When you do this, the correct all-in cost of the €1m using the $1.30 euro call is therefore $1,344,935 rather than the $1,344,600 referred to earlier.

FIGURE 17.6
Basic option hedges

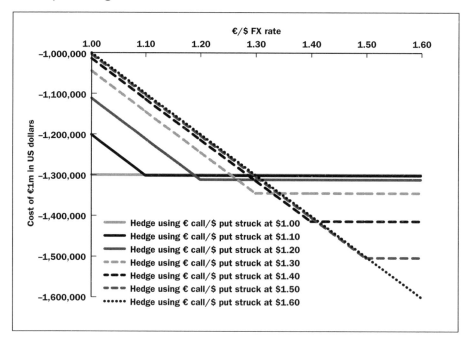

The extreme cases discussed so far establish two boundaries. The in-the-money options struck at $1.0000 and $1.1000 have completely flat characteristics over the company's horizon, and deliver profiles almost exactly the same as that from hedging completely by buying euros forward. The profiles of the out-of-the-money options struck at $1.5000 and $1.6000 are diagonal throughout the company's horizon, and virtually identical to the company's original exposure. In other words, they are tantamount to doing nothing. This reflects the chameleon-like nature of options discussed earlier in this chapter, with in-the-money options behaving like the underlying asset, and out-of-the-money options behaving like nothing at all.

In between these two extremes lie all the other possibilities, demonstrating once again the continuum of profiles possible with different strike levels.

As the strike price decreases from $1.6000, the options provide a greater degree of protection. The region where costs are capped becomes wider and, perhaps even more importantly, the level at which costs are capped becomes less. Contrast, for example, the $1.2000 strike with the $1.4000 strike options. The first option limits exposure above $1.2000 to a maximum all-in cost of $1,311,833 (including interest). The second option only limits the exposure over a narrower range starting at $1.4000, and costs can rise as high as $1,414,307. It therefore seems that the more in-the-money options with lower strike prices are definitely better, because they set a lower ceiling on costs over a wider range.

Unfortunately, nothing in this world comes free, and the additional protection from options which are more in-the-money carries with it a higher price tag. With an initial premium of $0.1110 per euro, the option struck at $1.2000 costs almost eight times as much as the one struck at $1.4000 whose initial premium is only $0.0142. This has implications for the company's costs if the euro should fall. Suppose that the euro was trading at just $1.1000 at the end of nine months. In that case, both these options would expire worthless. However, the company would have incurred additional costs of $97,526 in premium and financing costs if it bought the $1.2000 rather than the $1.4000 option.

None of the options considered is superior to any other. The additional protection provided by options further in-the-money is desirable, but their additional cost is not. The cheapness of out-of-the-money options is attractive, but their relative ineffectiveness is not. If the euro rises, the best options are the ones that are most in-the-money. If the euro falls, the low-cost out-of-the-money options perform best.

Right in the middle is the option struck at-the-money forward, and this offers a real compromise. It caps costs at the present level of the forward exchange rate, so once the company pays the premium, any rise in the euro is immediately neutralised by the payout from the option. Conversely, any fall in the euro will see the option expire out-of-the-money, and so the company is not locked into buying euros at the current forward price, but can buy them cheaper at the then prevailing rates. The compromise nature of the $1.3000 option is evident from Figure 17.6, where its characteristic lies right in the middle of the diagonal lines on the left of the figure, and again in the middle of the flat lines on the right of the figure.

Once again, however, there is a price to be paid. The option struck at-the-money is the one with the highest time value. The entire $44,600 premium paid at the outset is time value, and all of this will inevitably be lost when the option expires. With interest, the effective cost of this option is $44,935. If the option expires out-of-the-money, the company will end up paying $44,935 more than if it had not hedged. On the other hand, if the option expires in-the-money, the company will also pay $44,935 more than if it had hedged with a forward contract. This is the price of compromise.

There is therefore no ideal choice when considering a basic option hedge. A balance must be sought between the degree of protection provided, and the cost of acquiring that protection. There are no right and wrong answers, and companies exposed to risk need to select the particular compromise which best satisfies the hedging objectives which they have set.

17.7 Selling options within a hedging programme

When marketing option-based solutions, one of the principal problems which banks experience is the cost of the products they are selling. Companies don't like paying up-front for protection against currency fluctuations, and they don't like paying sizeable premiums. For example, in the case of the US company, the up-front premium of $44,600 for the at-the-money option is 3.4% of the amount at risk. Some companies, especially those working to tight margins, may find this excessive.

Suppose the company in our scenario is buying the goods from Germany at a cost of €1m in order to sell them in the United States at a fixed price of $1,500,000. If the company uses a forward contract to guarantee the exchange rate, it secures a $200,000 profit, equivalent to 15.4%. If it hedges with the $1.3000 option, the premium and financing costs of $44,935 consume 22.5% of the company's profit margin. If it chooses the $1.4000 option instead, while the hedging costs of $14,307 are slashed by 68%, the company faces increased currency exposure. Should the euro rise to $1.4000 or higher, the company's profits would decline to just $85,694, wiping out 57% of the original $200,000 profit margin.

From the company's viewpoint, this seems to present a dilemma. It may be reluctant to buy option-based protection, because option premiums look too high. On the other hand, it cannot afford to go unhedged, because of the consequences of a rise in the euro. If it chooses the forward contract, the company secures a certain profit margin, but gives up any opportunity to benefit from a decline in the euro.

The answer to this problem is to tailor the option-based hedge so that it provides the benefits required, but no more. The trouble with the basic option hedge is that there is a single point at which the characteristic changes. Once the underlying asset price moves through the strike and makes the option in-the-money, the option provides unlimited protection against further adverse movements in the underlying asset, no matter how bad they become. On the other hand, once the underlying asset price moves the other way so that the option is out-of-the-money, the client can benefit to an unlimited extent from beneficial movements in the underlying asset, no matter how big these movements are. Figure 17.7 shows this graphically for the US company buying the at-the-money option. There is unlimited protection against increases in the euro above $1.3000, regardless of how high it goes, and there is unlimited potential for the company to benefit if the euro falls below $1.3000, regardless of the depths to which it might descend.

Such unlimited protection against a rise in the euro, and such unlimited potential to benefit from a fall, are not what the US company necessarily wants. In setting out its objectives, the company stated that it did not think the euro would move outside the range $1.1000 to $1.5000. Why then pay for protection or opportunities outside this range?

In fact, the bank can tailor a hedge to operate solely within this range, and not outside. If the company buys protection against a rise in the euro from $1.3000 up to $1.5000, but no higher, this will be less expensive than buying a protection which operates for all values of the euro above $1.3000. Similarly, if the company sells off its opportunity to benefit from a fall in the euro below $1.1000, it can use the proceeds to lessen the cost of protection. The resulting profile could, in principle, look like the one pictured in Figure 17.8.

FIGURE 17.7
Unlimited protection and potential from basic option hedge

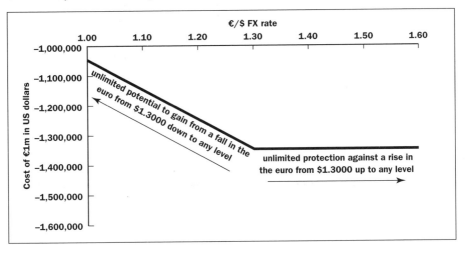

FIGURE 17.8

Tailored hedge

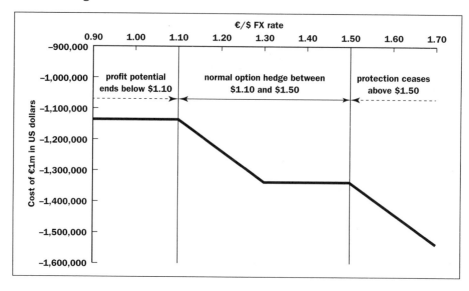

Using the nomenclature defined in Chapter 12 (section 12.1), we can characterise the shape of this profile as {0, –1, 0, –1}, while that of the basic option hedge of Figure 17.7 is {–1, –1, 0, 0}. Using the building block approach, the tailored hedge can be created using the following steps:

Underlying exposure:	{–1,	–1,	–1,	–1}
Buy a call with intermediate strike:	{ 0,	0,	+1,	+1}
Basic option hedge:	{–1,	–1,	0,	0}
Sell a put with a low strike:	{+1,	0,	0,	0}
Sell a call with a high strike:	{ 0,	0,	0,	–1}
Net result:	{ 0,	–1,	0,	–1}

The basic hedge has unlimited profit potential as the underlying asset, the euro in this case, goes lower and lower. The US company can sell off this potential by selling a put option on the euro at a lower strike price, and use the premium income to offset the cost of the euro call being purchased. Through this euro call, the basic hedge also provides unlimited protection for an ever-higher euro. This protection can therefore be stopped at a particular level by selling a euro call at a higher strike price. Again, the premium income from selling this euro call can be used to offset the expense of the euro call being purchased.

The essence of this technique is to tailor the protection profile to suit the particular needs of the client. Options are purchased to provide protection where it is needed. Options of the same type can then be sold in order to turn off the protection where it is not needed, and options of the opposite type can also be sold in order to sell off profit potential where it is not wanted.

Some companies have an almost pathological fear of selling options, perhaps after hearing horror stories of multi-million pound losses on option trades that have gone awry. However, there is the world of difference between a company selling options as part of a tailored option-based hedge, and selling options as a risky way of gaining premium income. As part of a well-designed hedge, option sales are balanced by option purchases elsewhere, or by the underlying exposure. In the example of Figure 17.8, the euro calls sold are balanced by the euro calls purchased at a lower strike price, while the euro puts sold are balanced by the beneficial underlying exposure to a falling euro. Nowhere in the resulting profile is the company's risk any greater after having sold options than it was from its original position.

To avoid the complexity of assembling option-based hedges, and overcome any aversion among companies to buying or selling options, banks often construct a complete package and give it a proprietary name. The next few sections discuss some of the many permutations available, such as participations, ratio-forwards, break-forwards and flexi-forwards. In many cases, these packages are carefully designed such that the premium income from the options sold is exactly equal to the premium expense of the options purchased, creating a zero-premium risk management solution. One of the best known among these is the zero-premium collar, explained in the next section.

17.8 Collars, range-forwards, forward-bands and cylinders

Collars, range-forwards, forward-bands and cylinders are different names for the same product, one which allows exposure over a defined range, but which collars the exposure outside this range.

A *collar* is usually constructed by buying an option of one type to limit the downside risk, and selling an option of the opposite type to limit the upside potential. Both options are normally out-of-the-money, which leaves a range either side of the current forward price within which the hedge is inactive. Figure 17.9 illustrates three different collars suitable for the US company in our scenario. All have a cap set at $1.4000, but floors ranging from $1.1500 to $1.2500. In each case, the collar is built by buying a call on €1m struck at $1.4000, and selling a put also on €1m struck at the respective floor levels. Table 17.3 summarises the net premiums involved.

All the collars have the same broad shape: a diagonal section in the middle, and flat sections either side. The diagonal section corresponds to the original exposure, with lower costs if the euro should fall, and higher costs if the euro rises. The only difference is the net premium paid. The $1.2000/$1.4000 collar is interesting in this regard, because the premium from the put sold almost matches the premium of the call purchased. At just $2,500 the tiny net premium here means that the diagonal section of this collar differs from the underlying exposure by just $2,500 in this central range. The $1.1500/$1.4000 collar has a

FIGURE 17.9

Example of collars

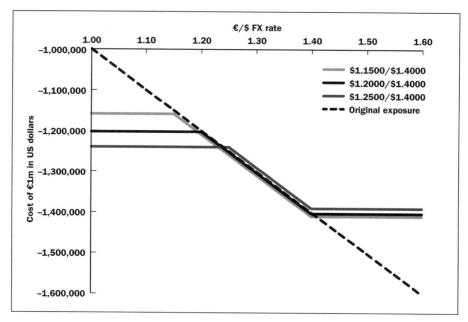

somewhat greater net premium making its profile just a little more expensive, both in the diagonal section and in the capped part. The $1.2500/$1.4000 collar, meanwhile, actually involves the bank paying a net premium of $10,100 to the company, which improves the profile in the diagonal and capped sections, but the higher floor strike prevents the company from benefiting so much if the euro falls.

TABLE 17.3

Net premiums for collars

collar range ($)	premiums paid (+)/received (−) in $			
	call	put	net	net with interest
1.1500/1.4000	+14,200	−5,000	+9,200	+9,269
1.2000/1.4000	+14,200	−11,700	+2,500	+2,519
1.2500/1.4000	+14,200	−24,300	−10,100	−10,176

There are three factors which a client can specify when requesting a quotation for a collar:

- the strike price for the cap
- the strike price for the floor
- the net premium to be paid.

These are inter-related, and for a given level of underlying forward price, interest rates and volatility, specifying two of these items automatically determines the third. A company will typically choose to set the strike price for the cap and the net premium, and then ask the bank to quote for the strike price of the floor. The cap strike level usually corresponds to the maximum level of financial risk which the company finds acceptable, and the net premium is commonly specified to be zero in order to create a zero-premium hedge. Table 17.4 sets out the floor levels for various zero-premium collars, while Figure 17.10 graphs the resulting profiles including one for a nominal $1.3000 cap.

Once again, the continuum of profiles is clearly evident from the figure. At one extreme, the $1.3000 cap results in a completely flat profile equivalent to hedging by buying €1m nine months forward. The reason for this is that a $1.3000 cap is at-the-money forward, so the floor level must also be struck at the same price in order to create a zero-premium collar. Buying a call and selling a put option at the same strike price and expiry date creates a synthetic long position in the underlying asset, so the zero-premium collar in this special case is equivalent to a simple forward contract.

At the other extreme, the profile from the $1.7000 cap is a diagonal line almost identical to the profile from the unhedged original exposure. Setting the cap level so high means that the floor level can be moved all the way down to $1.0349 in order to establish a zero-premium collar. Unless the euro breaks out of this range, both options will expire out-of-the-money, and so the option hedge will be non-existent to all intents and purposes. This leaves the €1m liability effectively unhedged.

TABLE 17.4
Floor levels for zero-premium collars

cap level	floor level
$1.4000	$1.2121
$1.5000	$1.1362
$1.6000	$1.0826
$1.7000	$1.0349

In between, the other zero-premium collars allow a reasonable compromise between the maximum cost if the euro should rise, and the minimum cost if the euro falls. For example, with the $1.1362/$1.5000 collar, the maximum cost to the US company to buy €1m is $1,500,000 while the minimum cost is $1,136,200. This protects the company from any rise in the euro of more than 15.4%, while allowing the company to benefit from any weakening of the euro of up to 12.6%.[3]

FIGURE 17.10

Zero-premium collars

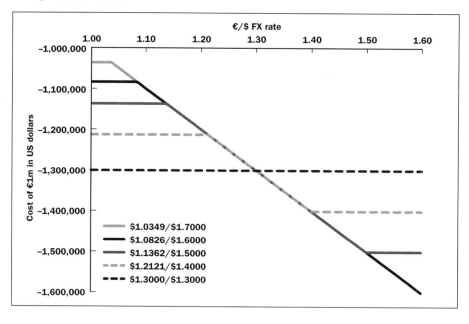

Zero-premium collars have proved to be a very attractive product to companies, for a number of significant reasons:

- They provide protection against an adverse move in FX rates beyond a
  certain point.
- They allow the company to benefit from beneficial currency movements, up
  to a certain point.
- They are 'free'.

17.9 Spread hedges

As we have just seen, the profile of a collar consists of a diagonal section in the
centre, and two flat sections either side. A *spread hedge* is just the opposite, with
a flat central part, and diagonal characteristics elsewhere. Whereas the idea of a
collar is to permit exposure within a defined band, but to eliminate risk outside this
range, the spread hedge creates certainty within the range, but allows exposure
outside. A collar was created by selling off unwanted profit opportunities in order
to finance the protection needed. A spread hedge is created by buying options to
obtain the protection required, and then selling options of the same type, but more
out-of-the-money, in order to sell off the protection where it is not needed.

To illustrate how spread hedges work, we will examine three alternatives with
different permutations of strike price and amounts of notional. Table 17.5 summarises the components of each one, and compares the structure with a simple
at-the-money call.

TABLE 17.5

Net premiums for spread hedges

	call purchased ($)	call sold ($)	net premium ($)	net premium with interest ($)
spread hedge	1.2000	1.4155	99,255	100,000
spread hedge	1.3000	1.4700	38,800	39,091
ratio spread hedge	1.4000	1.5000*	0	0
simple call	1.3000		44,600	44,935

*call sold on 3.74 times the underlying amount

It is not normally possible to create a zero-premium spread hedge because the option sold is always more out-of-the-money than the option purchased. However, there are two ways to create a spread hedge having effectively a zero cost. One method is to use a combination of an in-the-money option and an out-of-the-money option, setting the strike price of the OTM option sold so that the premium matches the *time value* component of the ITM option purchased. The net premium paid is then equal to the intrinsic value of the ITM option, because the time values cancel out. If this option is eventually exercised, the total amount paid out will then be equal to the original forward price, thus making the effective cost of the option strategy zero. The first of the spread hedges in Table 17.5 has been designed with this objective in mind.[4] The second way to achieve a zero cost is for the option sold to be based on a multiple of the underlying exposure, as illustrated by the third example in Table 17.5. The problem with this alternative is that the resulting exposure will be greater in size than the original exposure, gearing up the potential for losses. This alternative must therefore be treated with caution.

Figure 17.11 shows the three spread hedges specified in Table 17.5, and compares them with the profile from the basic strategy of buying an at-the-money call struck at $1.3000. To provide further references, the figure also shows the diagonal profile of the original exposure, and the flat profile from the riskless hedge using a forward purchase of euros at $1.3000.

Each of the spread hedges illustrated has the shape described at the beginning of this section: a flat central section with diagonal profiles on either side. The flat section of the $1.2000/$1.4155 spread hedge provides the US company with €1m at the fixed price of $1.3000, provided that the euro ends up somewhere in the range between the two strike prices. This is the same price as could be fixed with a forward contract. If the euro drops below $1.2000, the company begins to benefit, and would save $200,000 if the euro fell to $1.0000, a 30¢ fall from the forward price of $1.3000. However, if the euro ends up higher than $1.4155 the spread hedge offers no further protection, and the company would begin to pay more and more for its euros. Nevertheless, the loss will always be less than if the company had not hedged, because the losses only begin to accumulate once the euro exceeds the higher strike price of $1.4155.

FIGURE 17.11

Examples of spread hedges

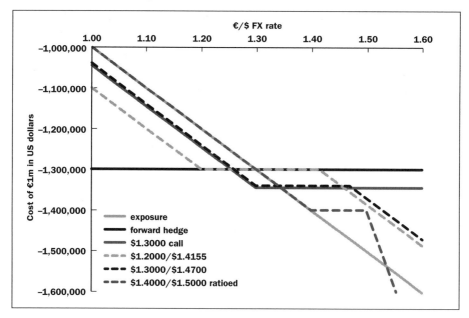

The second example illustrates a spread hedge using options which are less in-the-money. It offers a region without risk if the euro ends up anywhere between $1.3000 and $1.4700, allowing the company to buy its euros at an effective cost of $1.3391, only slightly worse than the forward rate of $1.3000. Compared with the first spread hedge, the $1.3000/$1.4700 strategy incurs an initial outlay of less than 40% of the premium, and outperforms the previous example for most outcomes of the euro, apart from a central region between $1.2650 and $1.4550. The second spread strategy also outperforms the simple call hedge for any terminal value of the euro below $1.4758.

The final example is of a ratioed spread hedge using euro calls struck at $1.4000 and $1.5000. However, instead of both calls being based on an underlying asset size of €1m, the calls sold are for a multiple of 3.74 times. This particular strategy has been designed so that the net premium outlay is zero, and only fares worse than the unhedged exposure for values of the euro beyond $1.5365, an 18% rise over nine months. However, the danger is that losses begin to grow rapidly once the euro exceeds the $1.5000 strike level, because of the ratio gearing.

17.10 Participating forwards

We have now examined a number of cases where the purchase of one option has been financed by the selling of another. In all but one instance, the underlying amount of the option sold has matched that of the option purchased, which in turn is equal to the size of the original exposure. The variables until now have been the strike prices, and hence the net premium paid.

With a *participating forward*, the strike price of the option sold is made equal to the strike price of the option bought, and is therefore fixed. The variable here is the underlying amount of the option sold, which is adjusted so as to create a zero-premium product. Of course, the options bought and sold must be of opposite types – one a call and the other a put – as there would be no sense in buying and selling the same type of option at the same strike price and maturity date.

A participating forward works only if the option purchased is out-of-the-money,[5] so that the option sold will be in-the-money and therefore more valuable. This means that the underlying amount can thus be ratioed down in order to make the net premium zero.

One way to look at the participating forward is to regard it as an adaptation of the zero-premium collar discussed earlier. Let us start with the first collar itemised in Table 17.4, which had a cap struck at $1.4000, and the floor level adjusted to $1.2121 so that the net premium was zero. Now consider what would happen if the cap level and zero net premium were kept the same, but the strike price of the floor was gradually raised. As the level of the floor increased, the value of the option sold would also rise, allowing the floor's underlying amount to be reduced in order to maintain a zero net premium. Table 17.6 shows the floor premiums at various strike prices from $1.2121 up to $1.4000, and analyses the underlying amount necessary to cover the cost of the cap premium. As the figures show, the ratio of floor amount to cap amount is simply the ratio of cap to floor prices.

The effect of gradually reducing the size of the underlying floor amount is to reduce the proportion of profit opportunities sold off. Starting with the zero-premium collar, the floor:cap ratio of 1.00 means that 100% of the company's ability to profit from a weaker euro is transferred away. As the floor is raised, the floor:cap ratio decreases. By the time the floor strike is raised to match the strike price of the cap this ratio declines to 0.125, and only 12.5% of the profits are given away, allowing the company to participate in the remaining 87.5%. An 87.5% participating forward has thus been created. Figure 17.12 graphs this gradual transition.

TABLE 17.6
Creating a participating forward from a zero-premium collar

cap strike ($)	cap price ($ per €)	cap amount (€)	floor strike ($)	floor price ($ per €)	cap:floor price ratio	floor amount (€)
1.4000	0.0142	1,000,000	1.2121	0.0142	1.000	1,000,000
1.4000	0.0142	1,000,000	1.2500	0.0243	0.584	584,362
1.4000	0.0142	1,000,000	1.3000	0.0446	0.318	318,386
1.4000	0.0142	1,000,000	1.3500	0.0755	0.188	188,079
1.4000	0.0142	1,000,000	1.4000	0.1135	0.125	125,110

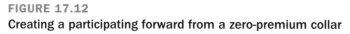

FIGURE 17.12

Creating a participating forward from a zero-premium collar

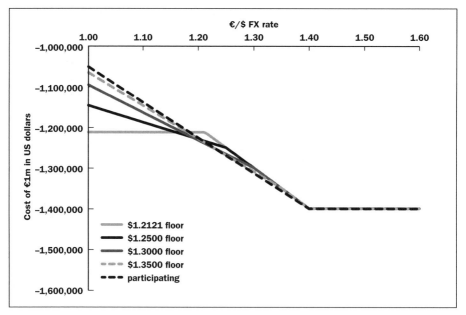

A 100% participation in profits would be shown as a diagonal line with a 45° slope, assuming that the graph was drawn with both axes on the same scale. An 87.5% participating forward would therefore have a slope of 0.875 × 45°, or about 39°. Another way to measure the participation is to examine the company's savings if the euro falls below the $1.4000 level. With the euro at $1.2000, for example, the company would pay $1,225,000 for its €1m, making the effective FX rate $1.2250. This is a $0.1750 saving for a $0.2000 fall in the FX rate, equivalent to an 87.5% profit participation.

This is just one example of a participating forward, which gives the company an 87.5% participation in any gains from the euro finishing below $1.4000. There are, of course, an infinite number of variations, just as with the zero-premium collar. The company can choose either the degree of participation, or the strike level at which the participation starts. The closer the strike level to the prevailing forward rate, the lower will be the degree of participation. Table 17.7 illustrates this by setting out the strike levels for a selection of participation rates.

At the extreme, the strike level could be set equal to the forward rate, but the participation rate would be zero. This is because the forward rate is the equilibrium price at which potential gains and losses are exactly balanced, and a bank selling a participating forward struck at this rate could not therefore afford to give away any of its profits. As the strike level moves away from the forward rate, the company is dealing at a slightly disadvantageous rate, and so the bank can now afford to let the company share in the potential profits. For example,

TABLE 17.7

Price levels and participation rates

Participation rate	Strike level ($)
0%	1.3000
10%	1.3048
25%	1.3131
50%	1.3319
75%	1.3654
90%	1.4117
99%	1.5408

if the strike level is set at $1.3319, which is only about 2.5% away from the forward rate, the company can obtain a 50% share of the bank's profits should the euro fall below this strike rate.

The effect of having different strike prices and participation rates is more clearly seen in Figure 17.13, which graphs the resulting profiles for all the participations listed in Table 17.7.

The now familiar continuum is once again in evidence. At one extreme, the 0% participation at $1.3000 is exactly the same as a simple forward deal and has the flat profile characteristic of a complete hedge. As the strike moves to the right, the company locks in protection, but at a progressively off-market rate.

FIGURE 17.13

Various participating forwards

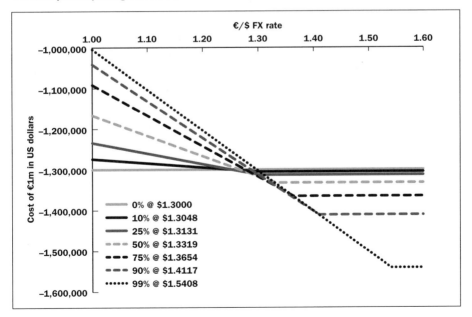

The flat part of successive profiles therefore sinks lower in the diagram reflect-ing the extra cost of dealing at a higher exchange rate. For example, the 50% participation struck at $1.3319 fixes the maximum cost at $1,331,900. However, in return for paying a higher maximum price, the company can reap savings at a progressively greater rate when the euro falls below the strike price. At the other extreme, the 99% participation in profits from a very off-market price of $1.5408 has the diagonal profile characteristic of a non-existent hedge, which is effectively what such a participation would be.

Participating forwards thus provide another very attractive tool for currency hedging:

- They fix the company's maximum cost in case of adverse movements in FX rates.

- They allow the company to benefit from beneficial currency fluctuations, with no limitation on the savings that can be made.

- They are 'free'.

17.11 Ratio forwards

Consider what would happen if one started with a participating forward but moved the strike price to the other side of the forward rate. The option bought would now be in-the-money, and the option sold would be out-of-the-money. In order to construct a zero-premium product, options would have to be sold on a multiple of the original exposure. This is perfectly possible, and the resulting product is called a *ratio forward*.

The advantage of a ratio forward is that the buyer acquires an in-the-money option free, enabling him to buy the underlying asset at a price better than the current market price. The disadvantage is that the buyer has had to sell a mul-tiple of the out-of-the-money options in order to finance the option purchased. If these options eventually expire in-the-money, the ratio forward buyer may have to pay out on a multiple of the underlying exposure, and this could cost a great deal.

As an illustration of what is possible, Table 17.8 lists the strike levels for vari-ous gearing ratios. For example, by selecting a gearing of 3:1, the US company in our example could buy euros at the fixed rate of $1.2506, which is almost five 'big figures' better than the current market rate. The downside is that the com-pany will begin to *lose* if the euro drops below the strike level, because the 3:1 gearing effectively reverses and doubles the direction of the company's expo-sure to a falling euro. As Figure 17.14 shows, if the euro falls to $1.2000, the company would pay $1.3518 for its euros, and a further fall of 10¢ to $1.1000 sees the company's costs rise by 20¢ to $1.5518 per euro.

TABLE 17.8
Price levels and gearing ratios

Gearing ratio	Strike level ($)
1:1	1.3000
1.5:1	1.2818
2:1	1.2688
3:1	1.2506
4:1	1.2378
5:1	1.2279

The situation becomes even worse with higher gearing ratios. While there is an attractive benefit from being able to obtain the underlying asset at a price better than the forward rate, this benefit diminishes very rapidly. Note how the flat sections of the profiles in Figure 17.14 become progressively closer. More importantly, the adverse gearing becomes more and more severe, leading to potentially catastrophic losses.

For this reason, the ratio forward is a product to be used with extreme caution, owing to the limited upside and the unlimited downside. As with the ratioed spread hedge, the ratio forward is a product which can increase the buyer's risk. It should be used only if the company has a very firm view of the market's likely direction, if the gearing ratio is strictly limited, and if the company puts in place a stop-loss strategy to limit the downside if the market goes the wrong way.

FIGURE 17.14
Various ratio forwards

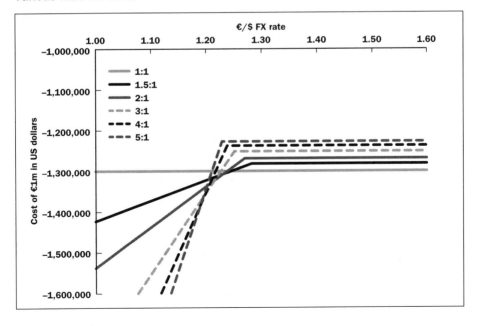

17.12 Break-forwards, FOXs and forward-reversing options

Break-forwards and the other terms are all alternative names for the same concept: a forward contract which can be broken, a **f**orward contract with **o**ptional e**x**it (FOX), a forward contract that can be reversed. The idea is to package with a forward deal the ability for the client to break out of the commitment should market rates go in favour of the original exposure, and against the forward.

The spark for creating the concept probably arose out of the regret that many companies experienced at having hedged when the market eventually moved in their favour. 'If only we hadn't hedged ...', 'If only we could get out of this wretched forward deal ...', no doubt are sentiments which have been voiced innumerable times. The proper establishment of hedging objectives and the correct measurement of hedge efficiency (both discussed in the previous chapter) should avoid these later pangs of regret. However, it is an understandable human reaction to exploit hindsight in criticising earlier decisions, and the break-forward provides an answer.

Building a break-forward is actually quite simple. The bank is selling the customer an option to reverse the forward deal, but is not charging an explicit premium. The cost of the option, plus any financing costs, must therefore be loaded into an off-market forward rate.

To illustrate how this works, we can return to our example of the US company which needs €1m. It can buy these euros forward at the market price of $1.3000, but now wants an option to sell them should the euro fall below a certain price. Suppose it chooses $1.2000 as the break price. The normal price of the put on euros struck at this level is $0.0117 per euro. With financing costs, this rises to $0.0118. Packaging these together, and building the $0.0118 premium into an off-market forward rate, we have the following:

- Company buys €1m at $1.3118.

- Company has the right to break the forward contract without penalty and buy its euros on the spot market if the euro falls below $1.2000 in nine months' time.

Note that in this example the company is always obligated to buy euros at the contracted rate of $1.3118. What the break-forward allows is for the company to break out of the commitment at the break price, but it effectively loses the ability to benefit from the decline in the euro from $1.3118 to $1.2000. The latter is just an opportunity cost, because the company was presumably happy to pay the guaranteed price of $1.3118, and the break-forward allows it to benefit once the euro moves below the break price of $1.2000. Nonetheless, one can still imagine the complaints of some companies when the exchange rate finishes anywhere below the off-market forward rate: 'If only we hadn't hedged ...'!

To illustrate something of the range of possibilities available, Table 17.9 lists combinations of break prices and off-market forward rates, while Figure 17.15 illustrates the resulting profiles.

TABLE 17.9
Break prices and forward rates

Break price ($)	Forward rate ($)
1.3000	1.3449
1.2500	1.3245
1.2000	1.3118
1.1500	1.3050
1.1000	1.3018
1.8000	1.8002
0.8000	1.3000

The higher the break price, the sooner the company can break out of the forward contract and profit from a lower euro. This advantage is balanced by the company dealing at a forward rate further away from the current market price. For example, if the break price is set to the prevailing forward rate of $1.3000, the off-market rate offered to the company rises to $1.3449, around 3.5% higher. As the break price is set lower, the opportunity to reverse the forward contract recedes, but the company is able to deal at a forward rate closer to the true market rate. A break price of $1.2000 allows the company to execute the forward deal at $1.3118, less than 1% higher than the actual forward rate.

FIGURE 17.15
Various break-forward contracts

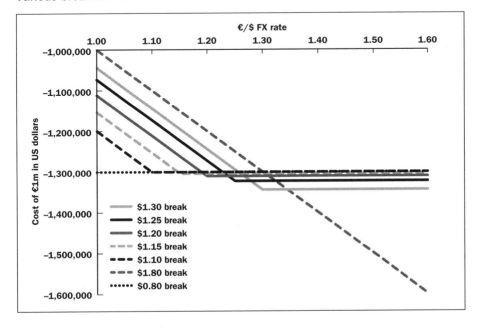

The continuum of possibilities is once again in evidence, and is made clearer in Figure 17.15 by the inclusion of break-forward contracts at the extreme prices of $0.8000 and $1.8000. With the break price set to $0.8000, the chance of the contract being broken is infinitesimal, so the company deals at the true forward rate of $1.3000, and the break-forward degenerates to the completely flat profile of a regular forward contract. At a high break price of $1.8000, the contract will almost always be broken, so the company will almost inevitably deal at the prevailing spot rate. The off-market rate is then set very high, but very close to the break price. In the example shown, the off-market rate at $1.8002 is just a fraction above the break price of $1.8000. Since the forward contract is almost invariably broken, the hedge becomes virtually non-existent, and the diagonal profile of the original exposure dominates.

If looking at Figure 17.15 gives some readers a strange feeling of *déjà vu*, then there is a perfectly valid explanation. The profiles illustrated here are virtually identical to those of Figure 17.6, which showed the profiles from hedging with a simple call. A moment's reflection will reveal that the combination of buying the underlying asset and buying a put creates a synthetic call. The only difference between the break-forward and hedging with a real call is the timing of the premium. In the case of the break-forward, the option premium is effectively paid in arrears, and added to the price of the asset at maturity. The $1.3000/$1.3449 break-forward could therefore be replicated by letting the company buy a $1.3000 call, and lending the company the $0.0446 premium for nine months at an all-in cost of $0.0449.

17.13 Flexi-forwards

Flexi-forwards are documented as forward contracts, but give the client a very attractive choice at the maturity of the contract. They can either execute the FX transaction at a fixed rate (plus a margin) or at the prevailing spot rate (plus the same margin). Table 17.10 provides some illustrative quotations.

TABLE 17.10
Flexi-forward rates

Fixed rate ($)	Margin ($)
1.3000	0.0449
1.3500	0.0261
1.4000	0.0143
1.4500	0.0076
1.5000	0.0038

Let's suppose that the client chose the fixed rate of $1.3000, which would be accompanied by the margin of $0.0449. If, nine months later, the spot rate was higher than $1.3000, the client would buy the €1m at the rate of $1.3449.

FIGURE 17.16
Flexi-forward contracts

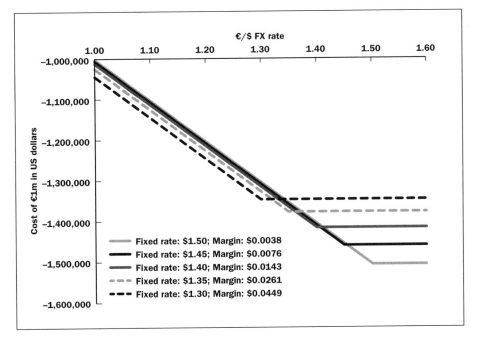

On the other hand, if the spot rate was lower, the client would be able to buy the €1m at the spot rate prevailing plus the $0.0449 margin. Figure 17.16 charts the various alternatives.

Once again there is the feeling of *déjà vu*. These profiles are very similar to those shown in Figure 17.15 for the various break-forward contracts, and the specific case of the $1.30 break-forward is identical to the $1.30 flexi-forward. Both contracts involve the client effectively borrowing money to buy an option. In the case of the break-forward, the option bought (in conjunction with an ordinary outright forward) is typically an OTM option which goes into the money if the FX rate moves in the direction of the original exposure – in our scenario OTM euro puts with strikes starting at $1.3000 and then going lower. In the case of the flexi-forward, the option bought is typically an OTM option of the opposite type which moves into the money if there is an adverse move in the spot rate. In this scenario the options are OTM euro calls with strikes starting at $1.3000 and then going higher.

17.14 Using exotic options

Chapter 13 (section 13.7 onwards) reviewed a variety of exotic options and gave some examples of their practical use. Of the wide range of exotics available, we will single out the three which are most commonly used.

Average-rate options

These are suited for hedging applications where the underlying exposure is not linked to a transaction taking place on a single date, but to a series of transactions which take place over a period of time. They are also known as average price options and as Asian options, and are the ideal hedging vehicle if a company is regularly paying or receiving funds denominated in another currency. Case 17.1 illustrates the position of a UK-based wine importer in just this situation, while Chapter 13 (section 13.8) has already provided some other short illustrations showing how both the average-rate and the more unusual average-strike options could be used in managing exposure to fluctuating exchange rates on multiple transactions.

In addition to handling transaction risk, average-rate options would be appropriate for a company hedging its balance sheet against translation risk, so long as the company used average rather than year-end rates when drawing up its accounts. Another source of currency exposure, economic risk, is an even better candidate for the use of average-rate options, because the factors which give rise to economic risk operate over an extended period of time, and are sensitive to the average exchange rate over a period rather than on a single day.

Case study 17.1

Using average-rate options

American Wine Importers Ltd (AWI) is a UK-based company specialising in the importation of fine Californian wines into the United Kingdom. On 31st January 2011, the company is preparing its annual budget for shipments to take place between March 2011 and February 2012. The company is entering into a contract to import 2,000 crates of wine per month at the fixed price of $320 per crate, the amount to be paid on the last business day of each month.

The pound has risen steadily since the beginning of the year, from £1 = $1.5606 to today's level of £1 = $1.5848. AWI's finance director believes that, while the pound may continue to strengthen for a little while, it will more likely fall back to around $1.5000. If so, the company's profitability would be threatened, since the minimum acceptable profit margin on the consignment would be breached if the pound fell to $1.5200 or below.

AWI considers three possible alternatives offered by its bank:

i)   A strip of forward contracts, fixing the exchange rate at £1 = $1.5700 for each monthly consignment.

ii) A strip of vanilla calls on the dollar (puts on the pound) struck at £1 = $1.5200, each on $640,000, costing an average of £0.0104 per $1, or £79,872 in total.

iii) An average-rate call on the dollar (put on the pound), struck at £1 = $1.5200, and priced at £0.0081 per $1, or £62,208 in total, 22% cheaper than the strip of vanillas.

AWI decides to go for the average-rate option, on the basis that the forward contract does not allow the company to benefit from the current strength of the pound, and the 22% saving in premium costs when compared to the strip of vanillas.

The details of the average-rate option are as follows:

Type:	Average-rate deferred start call on $/put on £
Strike price:	£1 = $1.5200
Premium:	£0.0081 per $1
Underlying amount:	$7,680,000
Total premium:	£62,208
Expiry date:	Wed 29th February 2012
Averaging period:	Tue 1st March 2011 to Wed 29th February 2012
Averaging method:	Arithmetic average of closing spot rates on last business day each month (12 observations)
Payout:	On Friday 2nd March 2012 based on difference between strike and average price

Over the 12-month period covered by the contract, the pound initially rose on fears of a stagnant US economy, reaching a high point of $1.6702 at the beginning of May 2011. Sentiment then reversed with increasing confidence in US economic growth, with the pound reaching a low point of $1.5319 on 15th January 2012. Table 17.11 summarises the exchange rates and resulting cash flows. As can be seen, the strength of the pound (especially in the first six months) meant that AWI was able to benefit by using the prevailing FX spot rate at the end of each month, which was always better than either the fixed forward rate of $1.5700, or the option strike rate of $1.5200.

TABLE 17.11

Cash flows for American Wine Importers Ltd

Date	FX rate (£/$)	Invoice amounts ($)	Using strip of forwards (£)	Using strip of vanillas (£)	Using average-rate option (£)
Thu 31-Mar-2011	1.6032	$640,000	£407,643	£405,858	£404,386
Fri 29-Apr-2011	1.6666	$640,000	£407,643	£390,671	£389,199
Tue 31-May-2011	1.6472	$640,000	£407,643	£395,194	£393,722
Thu 30-Jun-2011	1.6018	$640,000	£407,643	£406,207	£404,735
Fri 29-Jul-2011	1.6331	$640,000	£407,643	£398,549	£397,077
Wed 31-Aug-2011	1.6349	$640,000	£407,643	£398,117	£396,645
Fri 30-Sep-2011	1.5625	$640,000	£407,643	£416,256	£414,784
Mon 31-Oct-2011	1.6126	$640,000	£407,643	£403,531	£402,059
Wed 30-Nov-2011	1.5557	$640,000	£407,643	£418,046	£416,574
Fri 30-Dec-2011	1.5425	$640,000	£407,643	£421,567	£420,095
Tue 31-Jan-2012	1.5696	$640,000	£407,643	£414,403	£412,931
Wed 29-Feb-2012	1.5848	$640,000	£407,643	£410,492	£409,020
TOTAL	1.6003	$7,680,000	£4,891,720	£4,878,891	£4,861,227
Saving compared to forward:				£12,829	£30,493

▶

The average exchange rate over the period was £1 = $1.6003, which meant that the average rate option expired out-of-the-money. Nonetheless, the cost of buying $7,680,000 at this rate was only £4,799,019; adding the premium cost of £62,208 comes to an all-in cost of £4,861,227. This is £17,664 cheaper than the solution using a strip of vanilla options, and £30,493 cheaper than using a strip of forwards.

In general, the advantage of using options is that the company can benefit from a benign movement in the spot rate, something that would be denied to a company using forwards. In particular, as AWI was exposed to an *average* FX rate over a range of dates, the average rate option was cheaper, simpler and more appropriate than a strip of vanilla options.

Barrier options

These are attractive because they are always cheaper than standard options, but a note of caution must be sounded here. Cost savings for knock-out options become significant only when the barrier is brought relatively close to the prevailing market rate, but this increases the chance that the option will be extinguished and the protection conferred will disappear. Similarly, knock-in options are cheaper when the barrier is set relatively far from the present market rate, but then there is a strong likelihood that the option will never be activated.

The most appropriate hedging applications for barriers involve using knock-outs where the movement in the spot rate that causes the option to be extinguished is benign for the underlying exposure, allowing the user to take advantage of better prevailing spot rates when the knock-out is triggered. Case 17.2 illustrates just such a strategy as used by a British high-technology company.

Case study 17.2

Using barrier options

Videotech Ltd is a British company producing state-of-the-art digital image processing equipment used in television studios. It has just won an order to deliver a $5m system to a New York TV company. Delivery and invoicing (in US dollars) will take place in six months' time. Right now, spot sterling is trading at £1 = $1.5600 (equivalent to $1 = £0.6410), and the six-month forward rate is quoted as £1 = $1.5528 (equivalent to $1 = £0.6440).

Videotech is adversely exposed to a rise in the British pound. The company's treasurer believes that the British economy will eventually stage a strong recovery, making a rise in the pound quite likely in the not-too-distant future. One easy solution would be for Videotech to sell its $5m receivable at the forward rate, thereby receiving £3,220,000 in six months' time. This would provide the company with a satisfactory return, since this amount exceeds the company's minimum benchmark income of £3.15m from the deal.

However, the treasurer is tempted by the possibility to gain in case the pound should dip further at any time over the next six months. With economic uncertainty in Britain, he believes that such a possibility in the short term is quite likely. The obvious choice is for Videotech to buy an ATMS put on the dollar (call on pound) struck at $1 = £0.6410, which would protect it against a rise in sterling but allow the company to profit from any fall. Unfortunately, the price of this option is considered too expensive at £0.01773 per dollar, because the proceeds net of premium costs would be only £3,116,350 if the option were exercised, and this is less than the company's benchmark of £3.15m.

Videotech goes instead for an ATMS knock-out put on the dollar (call on pound), with a strike price at $1 = £0.6410, and a barrier set at $1 = £0.6575 (which corresponds to an exchange rate of £1 = $1.5210 quoted in the more usual way, 2.5% lower than spot). The premium quoted is £0.0108 per dollar, which is 39% cheaper than the standard option. At the same time, Videotech leaves instructions with its bank to sell its dollars forward should the spot rate fall to $1.5210 (dollar appreciates to £0.6575) at any time. This strategy ensures that Videotech covers its exposure in the event that the option is extinguished. There are now two possible scenarios.

i) Sterling never drops to $1.5210 and the option stays alive. In this case, the knock-out option behaves like a standard put on the dollar (call on the pound). If the pound is below the strike price at expiry, the option expires worthless, and Videotech executes a spot deal to buy pounds and sell dollars. If the pound is above $1.5600, Videotech exercises its option, and receives £3,205,000 at maturity. When the option premium of £54,000 is deducted from this, Videotech is left with £3,151,000. This is the smallest possible sterling amount which the company can receive, and is just above the benchmark of £3.15m.

ii) Sterling drops below $1.5210, the option is extinguished, and Videotech executes a forward deal to sell dollars and buy pounds. Suppose this happens after three months have elapsed, and the forward rate which Videotech receives is $1 = £0.6590. This leads to eventual sterling proceeds of £3,295,000, or £3,241,000 after the option premium is taken into account, £21,000 more than from the simple forward deal first considered by the company.

Digital options

Chapter 13 (section 13.9) provided a simple example of one application for an embedded digital option: to create a *pay-later* or *contingent premium* option. Recall that with such an option the buyer does not pay any premium at inception, but only pays at maturity if the option expires in-the-money, but then the pay-later premium is typically double that of the original vanilla option. Here we explore another interesting application, the *stepped premium* option. Like the pay-later option, no premium is paid up-front. Instead, premium is only payable if spot moves in the out-of-the-money direction at any time during the option's life. Unlike the pay-later option, however, a stepped premium option involves the buyer making these premium payments in instalments, each one triggered by the spot rate moving further and further out-of-the-money. Case 17.3 provides an example that should make this clearer.

Case study 17.3

Using digital options

German Car Imports Inc. (GCI) is a US-based company which imports and distributes Mercedes, BMW and other prestige German cars. In three months' time, GCI is due to pay €4,000,000 for the import of 80 cars. For some time there has been considerable uncertainty about the euro, and as a result GCI does not want to face the risk of a rising euro pushing up the cost of the cars it is about to import.

▶

With spot at €1 = $1.3000, three-month vanilla ATMS euro calls (dollar puts) are currently quoted at $0.0243 per €1, or 1.87% of the notional. GCI considers this too high a price to pay for three-month protection, but nonetheless wants a solution that provides protection against a stronger euro, while allowing GCI to benefit from a weaker euro. This objective rules out using a simple forward FX transaction.

GCI's bank then comes up with the following quotation for a *stepped premium* option with the following specification:

Strike:	$1.3000	
Maturity:	three months	
Initial premium:	zero	
1st premium instalment:	0.93%	(if spot €/$ falls below $1.2850)
2nd premium instalment:	0.93%	(if spot €/$ falls below $1.2700)
3rd premium instalment:	0.93%	(if spot €/$ falls below $1.2550)

Figure 17.17a shows the payoff profile for this stepped-premium call on €1. Note that there are multiple lines on this chart representing the four different 'states of the world' possible during the lifetime of the option:

- spot remains above $1.2850
- spot falls below $1.2850 but remains above $1.2700
- spot falls below $1.2700 but remains above $1.2550
- spot falls below $1.2550.

The payoff profile starts with the pale grey line, and will remain there provided spot does not fall below $1.2850. If it does, then the payoff profile drops down to the black line, and so on. If spot eventually drops below $1.2550, the payoff profile drops to the dashed line.

The key advantage of this stepped-premium option is that if the spot rate remains at $1.3000 or moves higher, GCI enjoys the benefits of a free call on the euro, protecting the company against any rise in the value of the euro. GCI's costs under these circumstances cannot rise above $5,200,000. In fact, spot can even fall by 1.15% to $1.2850 and GCI still pays no premium. A free option, especially when it eventually expires in-the-money and is therefore needed to compensate for higher currency costs, is very appealing.

If the spot rate falls below the $1.2850 level at any time over the three-month period of the hedge, then GCI must immediately pay the first premium instalment of 0.93%, and a further 0.93% instalment if spot falls further to below $1.2700. Even if this happens, the total cost of the first two instalments is still less than the original 1.87% quoted for the vanilla euro call. Only if spot were to fall below $1.2550 would GCI pay the third and final premium, bringing total premium costs to 2.79%. Even then, GCI has cause to celebrate, because it could buy the €4m that it needs at the prevailing spot rate which will be at $1.2550 or lower. This is 3.46% cheaper than the original $1.3000 spot rate, which means that the savings in costs are greater than the cumulative cost of the stepped-premium option.

This is clear from Figure 17.17b which shows the total cost of buying €4m hedged with the stepped-premium option. Even though the cost suddenly jumps (chart suddenly drops) every time a premium instalment is paid, the costs jump to successively smaller amounts. Immediately after paying the first instalment, total dollar costs rise from $5,140,000 to $5,188,400. Immediately after paying the second instalment, the costs rise from $5,128,400 to $5,176,800. Costs have indeed jumped, but to a figure that is $11,600 better than after the previous hike. Once again, this is because the premium instalments of 0.93% are less than the 1.15% gap between the premium trigger levels.

FIGURE 17.17

Using a stepped-premium option

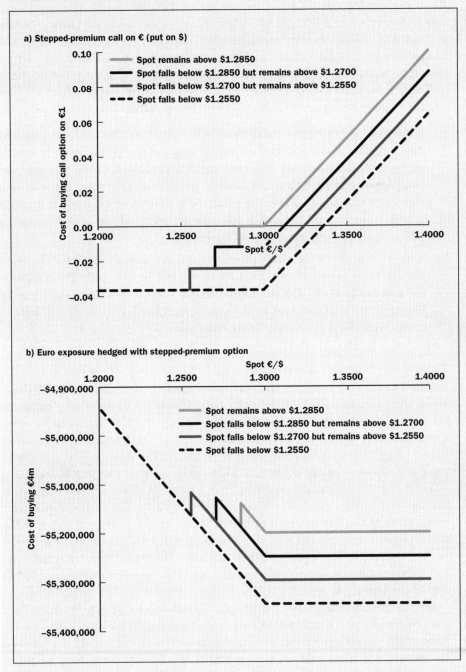

a) Stepped-premium call on € (put on $)

- Spot remains above $1.2850
- Spot falls below $1.2850 but remains above $1.2700
- Spot falls below $1.2700 but remains above $1.2550
- Spot falls below $1.2550

b) Euro exposure hedged with stepped-premium option

- Spot remains above $1.2850
- Spot falls below $1.2850 but remains above $1.2700
- Spot falls below $1.2700 but remains above $1.2550
- Spot falls below $1.2550

17.15 Selling options outside a hedging programme

In every case considered so far, whenever options were sold, the motivation was to generate funds in order to pay for other options being purchased. Selling options with no position in the underlying asset can be risky, because of the unlimited potential for losses. However, a company with an existing exposure does have an underlying position. What if options were sold against that position?

The US company in our scenario has a need for euros – its position is short €1m. If it sells a put option on €1m there are two possible outcomes at maturity:

a) If the euro is below the strike price, the option will be exercised against the company, which will end up buying euros at the strike price. Normally an option seller loses out when an option is exercised, but in this case the company needs euros anyway, and so benefits in two ways if the option expires in-the-money. First, the company is able to buy the euros it needs at a fixed price, and second, it has already received the option premium which lowers the effective cost of the euros.

b) If the euro is above the strike price, the option expires worthless. The company gets to keep the premium received, but has no protection against the rise in the euro. The premium income therefore softens the blow by lowering the effective cost of the euros purchased, but the option fails to compensate for a progressively stronger euro.

As a specific example, suppose the company sells the euro put struck at $1.3000 for an initial consideration of $0.0446 per euro. This premium can be invested to earn interest over the nine-month period, and will be worth $0.0449 when the option expires. If the euro ends up below $1.3000, the company receives €1m through the exercise of the option, but the premium received lowers the effective cost to $1.2551, a saving of 3.5%. If the euro ends up higher than $1.3000, the company must buy its euros on the open market, and must pay the going rate. The effective cost will then be the spot rate less $0.0449.

Figure 17.18 illustrates the profiles from a strategy of selling euro puts, using five different strike prices, and compares these with the flat profile from buying euros forward and the diagonal profile of the original exposure. The lower the strike price of the euro put sold, the less likely it is to be exercised, and so the profile approaches that of the original exposure. The higher the strike, the more likely the option is to expire in-the-money, and the more the profile approaches that of the forward hedge.

It must be emphasised that selling options outside a hedging programme does not provide any protection whatsoever, only a dilution of the risk. The US company might consider the strategy as a possible way to reduce costs if it believed the market was most likely to remain static. However, the company would be well advised to buy an out-of-the-money euro call option as a kind of 'disaster insurance' to provide protection in case the market were to move sharply against the original position. Interestingly enough, this amendment would create a collar, bringing us full circle in our review of strategies.

FIGURE 17.18

Selling options outside a hedging programme

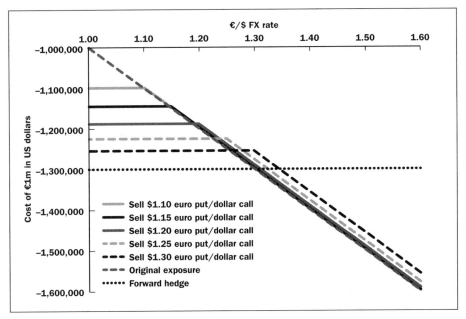

17.16 Dynamic hedging

Companies using options to hedge their currency exposure often employ a static hedging technique. This involves designing a hedging strategy, implementing it at the outset and then leaving it alone. The option's maturity is designed to match the timing of particular transactions or exposures. When this particular time comes, in-the-money options are cash-settled or exercised, and the option payoff compensates for any adverse market movements which have occurred.

There are a number of circumstances when a dynamic hedging programme is more beneficial:

■ if options of sufficiently long maturity are not available or are too expensive, so that a rolling hedge must be used[6]

■ if the underlying exposures are changing constantly

■ if the company wishes regularly to optimise the hedge.

Banks must continuously balance and re-balance their books as market rates change, as new deals are executed, as old deals mature and as their view of the market changes. In particular, they will usually aim to *delta hedge* their portfolio to remove any exposure to movements in the underlying asset prices, as explained in Chapter 11 (section 11.6). If possible, they may attempt to *gamma hedge* the book, to minimise the need for constantly re-balancing, and to immunise their position against the effect of step changes in market rates.

There is normally less need for corporate users of options to employ dynamic hedging, but companies which wish to exploit movements in FX rates during the lifetime of a hedge can take advantage of beneficial swings to improve the profile of their hedge.

A method frequently employed is to *roll up* or *roll down* the hedge when rates move in favour of the original exposure. It is easiest to illustrate this technique with a basic option hedge, but it can just as easily be applied to most of the other hedges illustrated in this chapter.

To illustrate rolling down a hedge, let us return to the US company introduced at the beginning of this chapter which had a €1m payable in nine months. Assume that it starts with a basic option hedge and buys a call on the euro struck ATMF at $1.3000 for an up-front premium of $0.0446 per euro.

Three months later, the euro falls so that the spot rate stands at $1.2562 and the forward rate is now at $1.2500. While the value of the call has declined to $0.0163, a loss of $0.0283, the underlying position makes the company 5¢ per euro better off. At this point the company could roll the hedge down to a strike price of $1.2500 by liquidating the existing $1.3000 call and buying one struck at $1.2500. The new premium payable would be $0.0351, resulting in a net outlay of $0.0188 per euro.

Suppose that the euro falls again, and three months later the spot euro is trading at $1.2030 and the forward euro at $1.2000. The company could repeat the process, and roll the hedge down from $1.2500 to $1.2000. This time, the option it is holding will have fallen to just $0.0071, and the new option bought will cost $0.0239, a net outlay of $0.0168 per euro. We can now summarise the transactions that have taken place.

At t = 0:	Buy 9m call struck at $1.3000 @$0.0446	−44,600
At t = 3 months:	Sell 6m call struck at $1.3000 @$0.0163	+16,300
	Buy 6m call struck at $1.2500 @$0.0351	−35,100
		−18,800
At t = 6 months:	Sell 3m call struck at $1.2500 @$0.0071	+7,100
	Buy 3m call struck at $1.2000 @$0.0239	−23,900
		−16,800

The company started with an at-the-money option struck at $1.3000, for an outlay of $0.0446. Ignoring the cost of financing the premium, the initial strategy therefore established the maximum rate for purchasing euros as $1.3446. After rolling down the hedge, the company ended up with an option struck at $1.2000 for a total cost of $0.0802, so that the most the company can now pay for its euros is $1.2802. The effect of this strategy is therefore to lock in gains from favourable movements in the underlying asset price, thereby establishing a new ceiling to the company's costs.

Figure 17.19 illustrates the strategy by showing the initial profile, the result after the first roll, and the final result after the second roll. As a reference, the figure also shows the profiles from the forward hedge and the original exposure. It is interesting to note that after the first roll, the option strategy establishes a maximum cost (of $1.3134 per euro) comparable with that of the forward hedge (of $1.3000 per euro). After the second roll, the company cannot pay more than $1,280,470 when premium financing costs are taken into account, which is 1.5% cheaper than the original forward rate. Furthermore, the company stands to benefit from any decline in the euro below $1.2000.

Although the strategy of rolling a hedge has been illustrated with a basic option hedge, the principle works equally well with collars, spread hedges, participations and other hedging structures. If the underlying asset price has moved in favour of the original exposure, options with strikes more in-the-money can be financed from the gains made, locking in savings and establishing a new ceiling for maximum costs. Although dynamic hedging may involve additional cash outflows prior to maturity, these will be more than offset by inflows at maturity. Alternatively, if the underlying asset price has moved against the original exposure, hedgers using structures like the spread hedge may prefer to buy back options sold as part of the hedge, in order to avoid further losses if the market continues in the same direction.

FIGURE 17.19
Rolling down a hedge

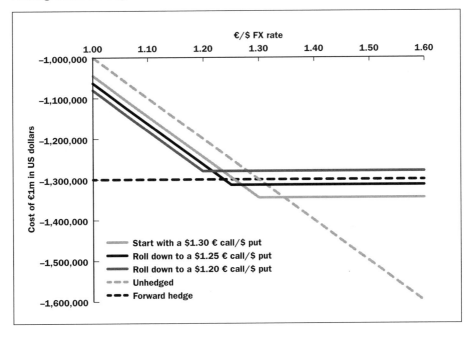

17.17 Which strategy is best?

This chapter has perhaps presented a bewildering array of financial engineering techniques to handle currency risk. The reader may be tempted to ask: Which technique is best? Unfortunately, the answer to this question is that no one technique is best for everyone. It depends upon the nature of the exposure, the risk preferences of the user, and his view of the market. Defining the user's hedging objectives carefully (as set out in Chapter 16, section 16.4) will narrow down the selection, and the summary presented in Table 17.12 may help to clarify the choices available.

TABLE 17.12

Comparison of hedging structures

Strategy	Advantages	Disadvantages
Forward	No premium payable Provides guaranteed outcome	No ability to benefit from upside
Basic option hedge	Provides unlimited protection Unlimited ability to benefit from upside	Premium may be too expensive
Collar	Provides unlimited protection Limited ability to benefit from upside Smaller or zero-cost premium	Some losses if market moves adversely
Spread hedge	Price certainty over central range Unlimited ability to benefit from upside if market moves significantly	Protection ceases after a certain point
Participating forward	Unlimited ability to benefit from upside	Forward component is at off-market rate
Ratio forward	Ability to execute forward deal at better-than-market rate	Potential to suffer large losses from highly geared position
Break-forward	Ability to benefit if market moves significantly	Forward deal is at off-market rate
Flexi-forward	Provides unlimited protection without payment of an up-front premium At maturity the ability to execute an FX trade at the better of the prevailing spot rate and a fixed rate agreed at inception	FX trade executed at expiry always involves paying a margin

Notes

1 Well, perhaps it behaves like a dead chameleon.

2 Taking 'most unlikely' to mean outside the range ±2 standard deviations, which captures 95.4% of possible outcomes under the assumption of normal returns, 10% annual volatility implies a range of prices from $1.0933 to $1.5458 after 270 days. See the discussion on volatility in Chapter 11 (section 11.1) for an explanation of how this range can be calculated.

3 This apparent asymmetry arises from the underlying assumption of most option pricing models, that returns are normally distributed while prices are lognormally distributed.

4 For this to work properly, the net premium paid out should be made equal to the *present value* of the ITM option's intrinsic value, rather than to the intrinsic value itself. The $1.2000/$1.4155 spread hedge illustrated here does this.

5 If the option bought is in-the-money, the product becomes a ratio forward, discussed in the next section.

6 A rolling hedge comprises buying shorter-dated options and then rolling them at or just before maturity into new shorter-dated options. For example, to cover a two-year period, you could start by buying a six-month option. Four months later, as the first option begins to approach maturity, buy another six-month option, and repeat the process. By rolling the options two months before expiry, you avoid the potentially aggressive negative time decay that affects ATM options in the last few weeks before expiry.

18

MANAGING INTEREST RATE RISK USING FRAS, FUTURES AND SWAPS

The term *interest rate risk* implies an exposure to movements in interest rates, but this is a very general concept. As we saw in Chapter 9, there are swap rates, zero-coupon rates, forward rates and par yields, all of which are interest rates. Even after focusing upon just one type of rate, there is a range of different maturities from as short as one day, to as long as for ever. So in its widest sense, interest rate risk can encompass exposure to any type of interest rate at any point on the maturity spectrum. In practice, however, nearly all exposures fall into one of three much narrower categories.

First, there is exposure to a short-term rate of a specific maturity, but covering a single period in the future. A company treasurer who needs to borrow for three months, but starting in six months' time, is a prime example. His exposure is to the three-month rate, but six months forward from now. This is exposure to a *short-term forward rate*.

The second exposure is also to a short-term rate of a specific maturity, but over a number of future periods. An investor who has just purchased a five-year FRN having coupons reset every six months is exposed to the six-month rate over the next ten periods. The exposure here is to *a strip of short-term forward rates*.

Finally, there is exposure to an interest rate of one specific maturity. A pension fund which has purchased a 20-year fixed-income bond is exposed to movements in 20-year bond yields. A bank having executed a five-year swap is exposed to five-year swap rates. In both these illustrations, the exposure is to *spot yields*, namely yields covering the period from now until a specified future date.

Forward rates and spot rates are closely linked, of course, and formulae for converting from one to the other were developed in Chapter 9 (section 9.5). Nonetheless, in reviewing interest rate risk we shall distinguish between different exposures according to which rate is the most prominent. For example, the investor with the five-year FRN will be thinking about the trend in future six-month rates, and may consider entering into a swap to convert the floating receipts into a fixed stream. His focus will initially be on short-term forward rates. If the investor executes a five-year swap with his bank, the bank will subsequently focus on the five-year swap rate when managing the interest rate risk. Although the two risks are substantially the same, the viewpoints are different.

In dealing with interest rate risk, this chapter will concentrate on techniques which seek to guarantee a particular result, thereby eliminating all uncertainty. The principal tools used here will be FRAs, futures and swaps. The next chapter will then examine how option-based tools can be used to manage interest rate risk more selectively, providing protection against the downside, together with the possibility to benefit from the upside.

18.1 Using FRAs

A full description of FRAs appeared in Chapter 4, together with a simple illustration of their use in hedging. FRAs cover a single specified period in the future, and are therefore suitable for hedging exposures to short-term forward rates. In practice, FRAs are readily available in all major currencies, covering standard contract periods up to one year in length, and up to two years into the future. In addition to all the standard contracts, like 1×4 or 3×9, banks are normally prepared to quote for odd-dated periods like a $3\frac{1}{2}$ month contract period $4\frac{1}{2}$ months in the future. In the case of non-standard contracts, however, banks will usually quote a wider bid/offer spread to cover the extra cost of hedging.

If a user's interest rate exposure is LIBOR-linked, and if the period covered exactly matches the dates of one of the standard contracts, an FRA can provide a perfect or near-perfect hedge. Case 18.1 studies a German industrial company using FRAs to lock in a particular rate. The FRA hedge proved perfect in practice, because the company was borrowing under a LIBOR-linked facility over a standard period. The company therefore achieved precisely the borrowing rate it expected when the hedge was set up. Note that hedging with FRAs guarantees a particular outcome, whether this is for better or worse. In the example illustrated, once the company has bought the FRA, its effective borrowing rate is inextricably linked to the FRA contract rate. If interest rates eventually fall below this rate, the company will not be able to benefit.

If there is any mismatch between the period of the risk exposure and the period covered by a standard FRA, or between the interest rate bases used, the user has three broad choices. The easiest route is for the user to exploit the flexibility of the OTC market and obtain a customised quotation from a bank. The advantage of this alternative is that the resulting contract can be tailored to fit the specification of the underlying risk exposure, once again resulting in a near-perfect hedge. Against this is the slightly higher cost of entering into a non-standard FRA contract, which is usually reflected in a rate just a little removed from the theoretically fair market rate.

The second alternative is to hedge with the closest available standard FRA contracts and accept the residual basis risk, namely that the hedge will perform slightly differently from the underlying exposure. Depending upon the gap between the original exposure and a standard FRA, the basis risk will not be large, and will almost invariably be just a fraction of the unhedged risk exposure.

The last alternative is to hedge with standard FRA contracts, but to manage the basis risk. Since users of futures contracts face exactly the same problems, methods have been developed within the futures market to minimise basis risk. These techniques are examined in detail in the next section and, to avoid repetition, will not be repeated here. FRA users who have non-standard exposures, but wish to use standard FRAs, can apply the same techniques.

Using FRAs to lock in a borrowing rate

Craft Industrial Components Inc. (CICI) is a medium-sized US-based industrial company pro-ducing high-quality machined components for other manufacturing companies. In January 2011, CICI's Director of Finance is planning the company's budget for 2011, and anticipates a seasonal borrowing requirement from July 2011 to January 2012 of $5m.

US interest rates have been kept very low in order to stimulate the economy, but as growth begins to pick up there are expectations that the Fed will begin to raise rates in the foreseeable future. To obtain a more precise idea of the structure of interest rates, the Finance Director contacts his bank, and obtains the following quotations for cash and FRA rates on 14th January 2011.

LIBOR rates		FRA rates			
1m	0.26125%	1 × 4	0.350%	1 × 7	0.395%
2m	0.28250%	2 × 5	0.372%	2 × 8	0.422%
3m	0.30313%	3 × 6	0.405%	3 × 9	0.455%
6m	0.45594%	4 × 7	0.437%	4 × 10	0.488%
9m	0.61656%	5 × 8	0.465%	5 × 11	0.519%
12m	0.78219%	6 × 9	0.498%	6 × 12	0.563%
		9 × 12	0.627%		

Source: LIBOR rates from BBA, FRA rates from Garban ICAP.

The upward-sloping yield curve in the cash market and rising prices in the FRA market both point to expectations of higher interest rates in the US over the next year, but CICI's Finance Director believes that rates may rise sooner and more quickly than the market antici-pates. He therefore decides to lock in the six-month forward rate by buying an FRA with the following specification:

Notional principal:	$5,000,000	Fixing date:	Thu 14th Jul 2011
Dealing date:	Fri 14th Jan 2011	Settlement date:	Mon 18th Jul 2011
Spot date:	Tue 18th Jan 2011	Final maturity date:	Wed 18th Jan 2012
Contract rate:	0.563%	Contract period:	184 days

On 14th July 2011, US LIBOR fixes at 0.416%%. It turns out that rates stayed low; in fact dropping slightly from the 0.456% prevailing at the outset, and certainly lower than the 0.563% rate agreed in the FRA contract. As a result, the settlement sum CICI paid on 18th July 2011 was $3,748.70, calculated according to equation 4.3 thus:

$$\frac{(0.00416 - 0.00563) \times 5,000,000}{\left(\frac{360}{184}\right) + 0.00416} = -3,748.70$$

CICI would have to finance the settlement sum at 0.416% costing an extra $7.97 in inter-est, bringing the total cost of the FRA to $3,756.67 by the final maturity date. On 14th July, CICI was able to borrow the $5,000,000 it needed at the prevailing rate of 0.416% plus its normal borrowing margin of 30bp. This facility was drawn down on 18th July 2011 and repaid 184 days later on 18th January 2012. On this final maturity date, the cash flows were as follows:

	$
Total cost of FRA	3,756.67
Interest payable on $5m borrowed for 184 days at 0.716%	18,297.78
Total borrowing costs after adding FRA cost	22,054.45

The total borrowing cost of $22,054.45 gives an effective borrowing rate of 0.863%, which is the FRA contract rate plus CICI's 30bp margin, exactly what was expected. The FRA has therefore enabled CICI to lock in the precise borrowing rate it anticipated when setting up the hedge.

Although in this example the borrower would have been better without the FRA hedge, to regret having bought the contract would be the same as a homeowner regretting the purchase of house insurance because his house didn't burn down last year. People buy house insurance because they want or need protection against adverse events. Here CICI would have been protected against higher interest rates had they materialised. In fact, whatever rate eventually transpires, CICI always pays the same effective rate of 0.863%. What FRAs do is achieve certainty.

18.2 Using short-term interest rate futures

One of the key differences between FRAs and futures is the flexibility of the former compared with the standardisation of the latter. It is possible, in theory at least, for a client to ask a bank to design an FRA tailored to match the exact features of a particular interest rate exposure. With futures there is no such choice, and users have to accept the standard features of the contracts quoted. This means that there are a number of headings under which differences may arise between a risk exposure and the particular futures contract used to hedge. Table 18.1 summarises the potential problem areas.

TABLE 18.1

Potential problem areas caused by standardisation of futures

Problem area	Description
Principal at risk	Contract size is fixed, e.g. $1m
Exposure period	Contract length is fixed, e.g. three months
Exposure date	Contracts mature on fixed dates, e.g. third Wednesday of March, June, September and December
Exposure basis	Contract settlement linked to one market rate, e.g. LIBOR
Settlement sum	Futures tick value is constant, e.g. $25
Margin flows	Maintaining the margin account leads to unpredictable cash flows through life of contract

Fortunately, for every problem area, there is a solution. Apart from the timing problem caused by a mismatch between the exposure date and the futures expiry date, all of the other difficulties itemised in Table 18.1 can be solved by calculating the futures hedge ratio properly. Section 18.3 explains exactly how this should be done. In some circumstances, using a strip hedge can further reduce the basis risk arising from any mismatch in the exposure period, and section 18.4 compares the use of the strip with the more common stack hedge. There is even a way of dealing with the one outstanding difficulty – the exposure date problem – and section 18.6 presents a practical solution.

Methods therefore exist which circumvent the problems caused by standardisation of futures contracts. However, it should be pointed out that many of the techniques reviewed are merely refinements enabling the hedger to approach perfection ever more closely. Once the basic hedge ratio is calculated, and this depends solely on the amount of principal at risk and the length of the exposure period, a simple futures hedge will normally neutralise at least 80% of the risk exposure.

Whether a user needs to go to the trouble of applying some of the more sophisticated techniques depends upon how important it is to achieve 100% hedge efficiency. For many companies, the effort involved may simply not be worthwhile. In the case of very large risks run by other companies, or the tiny profit margins that some banks operate within, the quest for the perfect futures hedge may be the *sine qua non* of success.

18.3 Calculating the hedge ratio

With a customised FRA hedge, the characteristics of the FRA can be adjusted to match the original risk exposure. Once this is done, the behaviour of the hedge should mirror that of the underlying risk. In particular, the change in market value of the hedge should offset exactly the change in value of the exposure. In other words, the basis point values should be the same.[1]

There is no such flexibility for the futures contract, whose basis point value (i.e. the tick value) is always constant. If it is not possible to tailor an individual contract so that its basis point value matches that of the underlying risk, the alternative is to adjust the number of standard contracts used. The essence of calculating the correct hedge ratio is then to determine how many futures contracts must be bought or sold such that the aggregate basis point value of the hedge portfolio matches that of the underlying risk.

By taking the appropriate factors into account, the hedge ratio can adjust for:

- the principal at risk
- the exposure period
- the exposure basis

- settlement sum

- margin flows.

The first two factors are of paramount importance, and no futures hedge can be constructed without taking these into account. The remaining factors add further layers of sophistication, and would only be necessary for large or rate-critical hedges. To reflect this, we will define the hedge ratio as having two major components:

$$HR = HR_{basic} \times HR_{advanced} \qquad (18.1)$$

where:

HR	is the final hedge ratio
HR_{basic}	is the component of the hedge ratio adjusting for principal at risk and exposure period
$HR_{advanced}$	is the component of the hedge ratio adjusting for exposure basis, settlement sum and margin flows

Each of the hedge ratio's major components can in turn be broken into its constituents thus:

$$HR_{basic} = HR_{principal} \times HR_{period} \qquad (18.2)$$

and:

$$HR_{advanced} = HR_{expbasis} \times HR_{settlement} \times HR_{margin} \qquad (18.3)$$

where:

$HR_{principal}$	is the component of the basic hedge ratio adjusting for principal at risk
HR_{period}	is the component of the basic hedge ratio adjusting for the length of the exposure period
$HR_{expbasis}$	is the component of the advanced hedge ratio adjusting for the exposure basis
$HR_{settlement}$	is the component of the advanced hedge ratio adjusting for the settlement sum
HR_{margin}	is the component of the advanced hedge ratio adjusting for margin flows

For non-critical applications, it is possible to set $HR_{advanced} = 1$ and use just the basic hedge ratio. Alternatively, if one or two of the components of $HR_{advanced}$ are important, they can be calculated properly, and the remaining component(s) set to unity.

We will now show how each of these hedge ratio components can be calculated, and then illustrate the construction of a futures hedge with a specific example.

Principal at risk

This is one of the easiest components to calculate, and is simply the ratio of principal at risk to the notional principal of the futures contract.

$$HR_{principal} = \frac{Principal\ of\ underlying\ risk\ exposure}{Notional\ principal\ of\ futures\ contract} \quad (18.4)$$

For example, if the underlying risk exposure was a $50m borrowing, and this was being hedged with the three-month Eurodollar contract, which has a notional principal of $1m, $HR_{principal}$ would simply be 50.

Exposure period

This is also straightforward to calculate, and is the ratio of the length of time covered by the underlying risk to the length of time covered by the deposit underlying the futures contract.

$$HR_{period} = \frac{Period\ covered\ by\ underlying\ risk}{Period\ covered\ by\ deposit\ underlying\ futures\ contract} \quad (18.5)$$

Note that the denominator has nothing to do with the time from now until expiry of the futures; rather it is the fixed period specified as part of the contract definition. For example, if a one-year borrowing commitment was being hedged by the three-month Eurodollar contract, the fixed period would of course be three months, and HR_{period} would be four.

Exposure basis

Nearly all futures contracts are based on three-month rates, the most popular being the contracts on Eurodollars, Euribor and three-month sterling. There are very few exceptions, the most notable being the thirty-day Fed-funds contract at the CBOT, and the one-month Eurodollar contract at the CME. However, compared with the trading volumes of the three-month contracts, activity in the Fed-funds contract is much lower, and that in the one-month Eurodollar contract is negligible.

In non-dollar currencies, the choice is therefore limited to the respective three-month contract, while the relative lack of liquidity in the very short-term dollar contracts may limit their usefulness.[2] This practical constraint may not present a problem if the underlying exposure is directly linked to the three-month LIBOR rate in one of the above-mentioned currencies, but there are many situations where the risk exposure may differ, for example:

- borrowing linked to bank base rates or prime rates
- borrowing or investment linked to commercial paper rates
- borrowing denominated in a currency where no interest rate futures contract exists.

One solution in all these examples is to use a related futures contract, and to adjust the hedge ratio according to the relationship between the Eurocurrency rate underlying that contract, and the interest rate underlying the risk. As an example, consider the case of a US company whose borrowing is linked to prime rate. Eurodollar rates and prime rate tend to move together, but if the company is to use Eurodollar futures successfully as a hedge, the inter-relationship between these rates must be defined more closely. Fortunately, there is a statistical technique which can determine the nature of this association. By performing a *regression analysis* on past observations of Eurodollar rates and the prime rate, it is possible to obtain an equation of the form:

$$PRIME = \alpha + \beta \times EURO \qquad (18.6)$$

In relation to futures hedging, the most important aspect of this equation is the β coefficient, which defines the extent to which prime rate moves when the Eurodollar rate changes. Another important by-product of the regression analysis is the correlation coefficient, normally given the symbol ρ, which measures the reliability of the relationship as defined by the equation.

To illustrate how regression analysis works, Figure 18.1 shows a scatter diagram of more than 3,000 daily observations on Eurocurrency and prime rates over a 12-year period.[3] The leftmost point, for instance, represents one particular observation on 15th June 2011 when three-month LIBOR was 0.245% and the prime rate was 3.25%. The line of best fit, defined by equation 18.6, is also shown in the figure.

With the data used in this particular illustration, the regression analysis produces the following formula linking prime rate with Eurodollar rates:

$$PRIME = 2.79\% + 0.9854 \times EURO$$

This formula means that, whenever Eurodollar rates change by 100bp, prime rate moves in the same direction by 98.54bp. In addition to determining the values for the coefficients α and β, the regression analysis also calculated the value of the correlation coefficient as being 0.9865 (giving an R^2 of 0.9731). This indicates a very strong link between the two sets of observations in this case.

What we have been looking for is a suitable value for $HR_{expbasis}$ – the factor which specifies how the hedge ratio should be amended to adjust for the exposure basis. In fact, $HR_{expbasis}$ is simply the β coefficient from the regression analysis. In other words:

$$HR_{expbasis} = \beta \qquad (18.7)$$

If the US company was hedging a borrowing facility linked to prime rate, the number of futures contracts required must be scaled by a factor of 0.99 to allow for the finding that the prime rate tends to move just a little less than the Eurodollar rate. If the company did not make this adjustment, it would end up being slightly over-hedged.

FIGURE 18.1

Link between prime and LIBOR rates

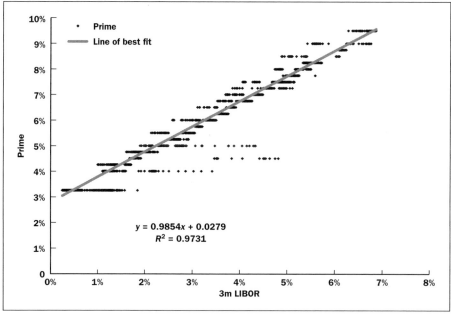

Source: Interest rates from FRED® – Economic and Financial Database (St Louis FRB).

Settlement sum

The settlement sum for an FRA[4] explicitly takes into account the number of days in the contract period, and is discounted to allow for the sum being paid at the beginning of the contract period rather than on the final maturity date. If the settlement sum for interest rate futures contracts were calculated in the same way, the tick value could be as low as $11.53 for the three-month Eurodollar contract, as discussed in Chapter 6 (section 6.1). Tick values, however, are constant for any particular type of short-term interest rate futures contract, regardless of day counts or discounting conventions. The Eurodollar contract on the CME, for example, always has a tick value per half basis point of $12.50. This means that the settlement sum can be as much as 8.5% too large or 7% too small if this anomaly is not taken into account. To adjust for this feature, the hedge ratio can be modified by $HR_{settlement}$ defined thus:

$$HR_{settlement} = \frac{1}{t\left[\dfrac{BASIS}{DAYS} + 1 - \dfrac{FP}{100}\right]} \tag{18.8}$$

where:

t is the nominal length of the futures contract (in years)

$BASIS$ is the day count convention (e.g. 360 for dollars, 365 for sterling)

DAYS   is the actual number of days in the futures period (usually 91, but not always)

FP   is the current futures price

For example, if Eurodollar futures were trading at 98, $HR_{settlement}$ would be 1.006. As an alternative example, if three-month sterling futures were trading at 97, $HR_{settlement}$ would be 0.990. In both cases we are assuming that the contract length is 91 days; however, the values for $HR_{settlement}$ would be significantly different from 1 in the rare instance when quirks in the calendar create an 84-day or a 98-day contract period.

Equation 18.8 provides the correct hedge ratio adjustment assuming that the futures contract is held until maturity. If it is planned that the hedge will be liquidated prior to the maturity of the contract, a modified version of the formula must be used:

$$HR_{settlement} = \frac{1}{t\left[\dfrac{BASIS}{DAYS} + \left(1 - \dfrac{FP}{100}\right)\left(1 + \dfrac{T}{DAYS}\right)\right]} \tag{18.9}$$

where:

T   is the number of days prior to maturity that the futures position will be closed out

Margin flows

Having to manage the daily mark-to-market process, and the attendant flows of variation margin, is a mixed blessing. Apart from the administration involved, paying or receiving variation margin prior to the liquidation or maturity of the futures position can distort the result of a futures hedge. It is not the flows of margin *per se* which causes this distortion, but the interest paid or earned on these flows. Whether the flows of margin are positive or negative, the effect of interest will increase the magnitude of the flows, and so the size of the futures hedge must be scaled down accordingly

Suppose that a user has taken into account all preceding adjustments, and has calculated that the number of contracts required is N. Ignoring the interest on variation margin, the sum that will eventually be received when the contracts mature or are liquidated is:

$$VM_{total} = N \times (F_T - F_0) \times TV \tag{18.10}$$

where:

VM_{total} is the total variation margin paid or received, ignoring interest
N is the number of futures contracts
F_0 is the futures price at inception
F_T is the futures price at maturity or liquidation
TV is the tick value of the contract

Let us make the assumption that the futures price moves in a linear fashion from F_0 to F_T, so that the flow of variation margin on any day t will be given by:

$$VM_t = \frac{N \times (F_T - F_0) \times TV}{D_H} \tag{18.11}$$

where:

VM_t is the variation margin on day t

D_H is the number of days in the hedging period

Let us now assume that the user can either borrow or invest at a rate of interest i. The variation margin flow on day t will now result in interest of $VM_t \times i \times [(D_H - t)/BASIS]$ on the remaining days until maturity. Summing this expression over the lifetime of the hedge, and simplifying, gives:

$$VM_{total} = \sum_{t=1}^{D_H} \left[VM_t \left(1 + i \frac{(D_H - t)}{BASIS)} \right) \right]$$

$$= N \times (F_T - F_0) \times TV \left[1 + \frac{i}{2} \frac{(D_H - 1)}{BASIS} \right] \tag{18.12}$$

$$= VM_{total} \times \left[1 + \frac{i}{2} \frac{(D_H - 1)}{BASIS} \right]$$

where:

i is the rate of interest for short-term lending or borrowing

In other words, the variation margin actually paid or received is increased by the factor on the right of equation 18.12. To allow for this, the hedge ratio must therefore be decreased by this factor, giving:

$$HR_{margin} = \frac{1}{\left[1 + \frac{i}{2} \frac{(D_H - 1)}{BASIS} \right]} \tag{18.13}$$

Adjusting the hedge ratio in this way is known as *tailing the hedge*. Note that equation 18.13 does not include either F_0 or F_T, because these variables cancel out. It is therefore not necessary to guess where the futures price may ultimately settle, nor even whether variation margin will be paid or received. The only information needed is the prevailing interest rate i and the length of the hedging period D_H. Although the rate of interest for lending and borrowing will differ in practice, this makes very little difference to the calculation of HR_{margin}.

To illustrate the construction of an adjusted futures hedge, Case 18.2 looks nrate exposure on a dollar-denominated investment fund being rolled into commercial paper.

Using futures with an adjusted hedge ratio

Fund Management Company Ltd (FMC) runs a number of investment funds, each one denominated in one of the world's major currencies. On 28th March 2011, FMC was reviewing strategy for its dollar-based money market fund. The $50m proceeds from a maturing investment are due to be received on Tuesday 13th March 2012, and FMC wishes to invest this in three-month A1/P1-rated financial commercial paper.

CP rates have been painfully low over the past three years, and although STIR futures are pricing-in a rise in three-month rates to 4% by 2015, FMC believes that rates will stay low for a considerable time. FMC therefore decides to use CME Eurodollar futures, both to hedge against a potential fall in rates and to take advantage of the higher rates being priced-in, and proceeds to calculate the appropriate hedge ratios based upon the following details (all references to 'futures' apply to the March 2012 Eurodollar contract):

Today's date:	Mon 28th Mar 2011	Current CP rate:	0.26%
Investment date:	Tue 13th Mar 2012	Current 3m LIBOR:	0.307%
Hedging period:	351 days	Current futures price:	99.09
Expiry date of future:	Wed 21st Mar 2012	Futures period:	91 days
Investment size:	$50,000,000	CP maturity:	91 days
Contract size:	$1,000,000		
Regression equation:		$CP = -0.1144 + 0.9902 \times ED3$	

Using the relationships defined in equations 18.4, 18.5, 18.7, 18.9 and 18.13, FMC was able to calculate the following hedge ratios:

$HR_{principal}$	50.0000	HR_{basic}	50.0000
HR_{period}	1.0000	$HR_{advanced}$	0.9980
$HR_{expbasis}$	0.9902		
$HR_{settlement}$	1.0086	HR	49.90
HR_{margin}	0.9991		

HR in this example turns out to be no different from $HR_{principal}$, because $HR_{period} = 1$ and the deviations from unity for the various components of $HR_{advanced}$ cancel each other out. In other situations, especially when hedging an exposure of length different from three months, or when interest rates are higher, HR may differ considerably from $HR_{principal}$.

FMC therefore buys 50 March 2012 Eurodollar contracts at a price of 99.09. The futures price of 99.09% implies a LIBOR of 0.91%, and therefore an implied CP rate for FMC of 0.79%.

Although US interest rates began to rise very slowly through 2011, on 25th January 2012 Fed Chairman Ben Bernanke extended his pledge to keep US interest rates low until 2014. This immediately quashed any upward pressure on rates, which thereafter began to ease back down. FMC's initial expectations about lower rates were vindicated.

▶

On 13th March 2012, FMC received the expected $50m proceeds from maturing investments and immediately purchased a similar quantity of three-month A1/P1 financial commercial paper to yield just 0.30%, little higher than the 0.26% rate prevailing at the outset. However, FMC was able to close out its futures position, selling its 50 contracts at 99.525 and making a total profit of $54,375 over the almost one-year hedging period. In fact, as these hedging profits were credited to FMC's margin account throughout this time, FMC was able to earn some interest, although with overnight rates lower than 20bp, the total interest earned was only around $50. FMC was then able to invest the $54,425.90 thus accumulated for a further three months (the 91-day investment period) earning an additional $65.16.

The total futures profits plus interest of $54,491.06 effectively adds 43bp to the rate of return earned on the CP, more than doubling it from 30bp to 73bp. This compares favourably with the 79bp anticipated by the hedge at the outset. Using equation 16.1 the hedge efficiency was 93%. The 6bp shortfall in this case was mainly due to a breakdown in the relationship between CP and LIBOR rates at the time. The regression model on which $HR_{expbasis}$ was calculated had an R^2 of 99.6% over the 12-year period from 2000 to 2012, but this dropped to just 14% in the last three years from 2010 to 2012. Nonetheless, the end result was more than satisfactory.

18.4 Stack vs. strip hedges

The methodology discussed in the previous section defines *how many* futures contracts should be bought or sold. It does not, however, specify *which* contracts should be used. The answer depends upon two factors:

- the liquidity of the particular futures market
- the period covered by the underlying risk exposure.

For some contracts on some futures exchanges, liquidity only exists in the nearest contract. In such cases, there is really only one choice: use the nearest contract regardless of the underlying risk exposure's properties. Where liquidity exists across a range of futures maturity dates, and in particular where it extends beyond the final maturity date of the underlying risk, there are two strategies available – the stack hedge and the strip hedge.

To illustrate the difference between these two techniques, consider hedging a $10m six-month borrowing which commences at the beginning of March. Using equations 18.2, 18.4 and 18.5, the basic hedge ratio is 20, implying that 20 futures contracts must be sold.

The *stack hedge*, as the name implies, involves using a stack of futures contracts all with the same maturity date. The contract selected should be the first one maturing *after* the rate is fixed on the underlying risk exposure. There is no point in buying a contract which matures earlier, because the position will need to be rolled into the later contract to preserve the hedge. In the case of the $10m borrowing, this means selling 20 March contracts right now, and then liquidating them in early March, the moment the rate is fixed on the loan.

The *strip hedge*, also self-evident from its name, involves using a strip of futures contracts which covers the underlying exposure as closely as possible. Once again, the first contract in the strip should mature after the rate is fixed on the underlying risk, while the period covered by the last contract in the strip will normally extend beyond the underlying exposure. To hedge the $10m borrowing with a strip hedge will therefore entail selling 10 March and 10 June contracts.

A strip hedge is therefore only relevant for underlying exposures whose maturity is longer than the period covered by a single futures contract. In practice, this normally means an exposure having a maturity which is some multiple of the futures period. For shorter maturities, or in the case of illiquid futures markets, the stack hedge is the clear choice. Figure 18.2 illustrates both techniques, and should help to make the distinction between them somewhat clearer.

The stack hedge is easier to implement, because it involves executing a trade in only one futures contract, whereas a strip hedge will involve trades in several. The drawback, however, is that the stack hedge introduces another *basis risk*. Hedging a six-month rate with three-month futures contracts relies on the implicit assumption that three-month and six-month rates move together. If this assumption is valid, then futures prices will track the three-month rate, which in turn will move in step with changes in the six-month rate. The three-month futures would then be a reasonable hedge for an exposure linked to the six-month rate. If, however, the assumption is not valid, the stack hedge will be less than perfect, and the strip hedge will prove more reliable.

FIGURE 18.2
Stack vs. strip hedges

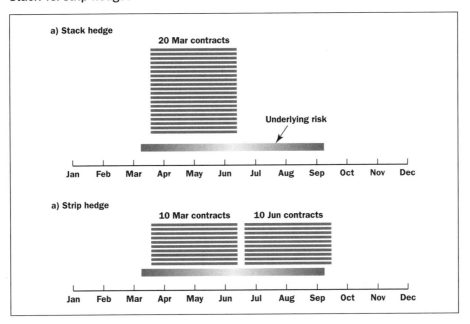

The reason why a strip hedge minimises this particular basis risk lies in the way that strips of futures combine to give a single forward rate. If $f_1, f_2, \ldots, f_n$ are the individual forward interest rates implied by a strip of n consecutive futures contracts, then the single forward rate f_{strip} implied by the entire strip is given by equation 18.14 where the period covered is less than or equal to one year:

$$(1 + ntf_{strip}) = (1 + tf_1) \times (1 + tf_2) \times \ldots \times (1 + tf_n) \qquad (18.14)$$

or by equation 18.15 for periods greater than a year:

$$(1 + f_{strip})^{nt} = (1 + tf_1) \times (1 + tf_2) \times \ldots \times (1 + tf_n) \qquad (18.15)$$

where:

f_{strip} is the futures strip rate
f_n is the interest rate implied by the nth futures contract
n is the number of contracts in the strip
t is the nominal length of the futures contract (in years)

Given the efficiency of financial markets in general, and of futures markets in particular, f_{strip} will closely follow the forward rate over the strip period. If this were not the case, an arbitrage opportunity would open up. For example, if the futures strip rate were lower than the market forward rate, arbitrageurs could sell futures and sell the equivalent FRAs and capture the profit from any gap between the prices.

In the case of the Mar–Jun strip illustrated in Figure 18.2, the strip of two three-month contracts will follow the six-month forward rate from mid-March to mid-September. Most important is what happens when the March contract finally matures. At that time, the relationship between three-month and six-month rates will not matter, because the strip rate will match the prevailing six-month rate. For example, if the yield curve was positive, so that six-month rates were higher than three-month rates, the forward rate implied by the June contract will lie above the March implied rate.[5] This will price the strip rate above the three-month rate, and arbitrage will ensure that it matches the six-month rate. The opposite would be true if the yield curve were negative: the six-month rate would lie below the three-month rate but still be matched by the strip rate.

The implication is that hedgers using stack hedges will be exposed to a basis risk. If the slope of the yield curve changes between the time the hedge is established and the time when the hedge is liquidated, the stack hedge will not be 100% efficient. A strip hedge, if available, would minimise this basis risk, because the strip rate would follow the exposure rate much more closely.

To see whether this basis risk is significant in practice, Figure 18.3 plots the evolution of LIBOR rates from 2000 until 2011, and shows maturities ranging from overnight to one year. Despite the volatility of interest rates over that decade, at first glance they all appear to move in unison, as a tightly packed bunch. Indeed, a statistical analysis shows that the correlations between movements in rates with adjacent maturities, for example three-month and six-month

FIGURE 18.3

LIBOR rates 2000–2011

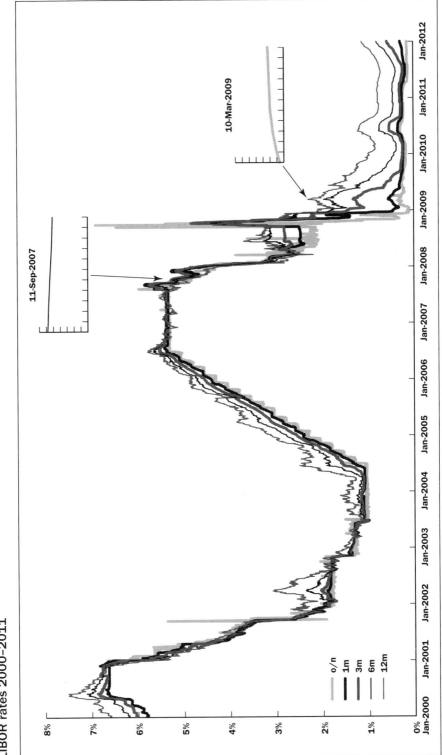

Source: Interest rates from FRED® – Economic and Financial Database (St Louis FRB).

rates, are all in excess of 0.99. Even the correlation between seven-day and one-year rates is as high as 0.97.

Despite this appearance, it is nonetheless possible for the basis to change very substantially. The two thumbnail sketches within Figure 18.3 illustrate this by showing the yield curves on two dates just 18 months apart. On 11th September 2007, the yield curve was downward-sloping with one-year rates around 72bp below one-month rates. By 10th March 2009, the yield curve had normalised but become very steep, and the one-year rate was now 1.73% above one-month rates, and almost 2% above overnight rates. This degree of twist could have wreaked havoc with a stack hedge.

Even when the yield curve does not change direction so dramatically, but just alters its slope, a stack will be less efficient than a strip hedge. Case 18.3 provides a concrete example of just such a situation which arose after expectations about interest rates in the US changed during the latter part of 2011 and early part of 2012.

To summarise: a strip hedge is the ideal choice when the length of the underlying exposure is a multiple of the futures period, and if there is acceptable liquidity in the later futures contracts. If the exposure period is shorter, if the back contracts are illiquid, or if the application is not so critical that 100% hedge efficiency is the goal, then the stack hedge is an acceptable and simpler alternative.

Case study 18.3

Stack vs. strip hedge

FMC, the fund management company introduced in Case 18.2, believes that US interest rates will remain low, and wants to use the futures market to take advantage of the higher rates currently being priced into Eurodollar contracts, as well as hedging against an actual fall in rates. This time, however, it is planning to make a LIBOR-linked one-year investment of $50m on 13th March 2012. Today, 28th March 2011, market rates are as follows:

LIBOR rates		Eurodollar futures prices	
3m	0.30700%	Mar 12	99.09
6m	0.46050%	Jun	98.76
12m	0.77950%	Sep	98.40
		Dec	98.06

Using equation 18.14, the one-year forward rate implied by the futures strip is 1.43%, which is 65bp up compared with the prevailing 12-month rate of 0.78%, but FMC believes that US rates will not reach anything like these levels by March next year.

Using the techniques previously described, FMC needs to buy 200 futures contracts altogether. The company then considers two alternative strategies:

a) Implement a stack hedge by buying 200 Mar 12 contracts.
b) Implement a strip hedge by buying 50 Mar 12, 50 Jun 12, 50 Sep 12 and 50 Dec 12 contracts.

After reviewing the potential basis risk inherent with the stack hedge, and encouraged by the depth and liquidity of the market in Eurodollar futures, FMC decides to execute the strip hedge, and achieve a one-year rate of 1.43% in March 2012.

On 13th March 2012, FMC agreed to invest its $50m for value on 15th March at the prevailing 12-month LIBOR rate of 1.055%. At the same time, the company liquidated the futures hedge at the following prices:

Mar 12	99.525	Sep	99.485
Jun	99.520	Dec	99.440

The futures hedge gained $457,500, equivalent to 91.5bp on a $50m one-year investment. The effective yield was therefore 1.97%, 54bp higher than the 1.43% one-year rate anticipated by the original futures strip. The extra 54bp arises because of the credit risk associated with LIBOR rates as compared with STIR futures, as discussed extensively in Chapter 6. On 13th March 2012 there was a 55bp gap between the one-year strip rate of 0.508% calculated from the futures contracts, and the 12-month LIBOR rate of 1.055%. Taking this into account, the hedge efficiency with the strip hedge was almost 100%.

Had FMC chosen the stack hedge instead, the futures hedge would only have generated $217,500 in profits, less than half that of the strip hedge, and equivalent to 43.5bp on the $50m investment. The effective investment rate would only have been 1.49%, and the hedge efficiency would therefore have dropped to 77%. In this example, the strip hedge proved both more suitable and more effective at hedging the one-year interest rate risk.

18.5 Different kinds of basis risk

The term *basis risk* has been used a number of times already in this chapter in a number of different contexts. In general, basis risk arises when there is a difference between the behaviour of the underlying exposure and that of the hedging instrument. There are, however, a number of distinct causes of basis risk, and it is now appropriate to categorise them properly. Two of the following headings have already been discussed, while the third one will be analysed in the next section.

Exposure basis

This form of risk arises when the basis for determining the interest rate differs between the exposure and the hedge. A good example would be an investor hedging rate risk on a 91-day T-Bill portfolio by using three-month STIR futures contracts. Although both rates cover a similar duration, there will be discrepancies between fluctuations in Treasury bill yields and movements in Eurocurrency rates. Section 18.3 showed how the hedge ratio can be adjusted to allow for this form of basis risk, but there is no way of eliminating this particular risk.

Period basis

As the name suggests, this risk occurs when the duration of the exposure and hedge differ. When the exposure is a multiple of the length of the hedging instrument, this basis can be minimised or even neutralised completely using a strip hedge, as explained in the previous section. If the exposure period is shorter than the hedging instrument, the hedge ratio can also be adjusted using equation 18.5, but this time a residual basis risk will remain.

Convergence basis

The price of a short-term interest rate derivative like an FRA or a future will usually differ from the prevailing cash market rate, because the derivative reflects the forward interest rate while the cash market reflects the spot interest rate. When the derivative is a futures contract, the gap between futures and cash prices is called the basis, and this was defined in Chapter 6 (section 6.3). Basis in this context is governed by the shape of the yield curve, for it is the slope of the yield curve which determines the relationship between spot and forward interest rates. As a derivative approaches maturity, the basis will gradually decline until it reaches zero on the maturity date itself. If the design of a hedge involves holding a derivative until maturity, there is no risk that the hedge result will differ from the market rate underlying the hedging instrument. If, however, the hedge design necessitates liquidating the hedge prior to its normal maturity, there will be a risk that basis will not have converged as expected. This would happen if the yield curve changes shape after the hedge is established.

All three types of basis risk thus relate to different aspects of the yield curve. Exposure basis arises when there are two different yield curves: one for the exposure and the other for the hedging instrument. Period basis and convergence basis are both caused by changes in the shape of a single yield curve, but at different points in the maturity spectrum. Period basis occurs when the yield curve changes shape between the tenor of the futures contract and the tenor of the exposure, and is therefore affected by slightly longer-term rates. In contrast, convergence basis arises from the short-term yield curve bending. Section 18.4 explained how the period basis could be handled with a strip hedge; the next section analyses how convergence basis can be reduced using spreads.

18.6 Managing the convergence basis

To see how convergence basis can be managed, it is first necessary to understand exactly how it arises in the first place, and this is most easily done with a specific illustration. Suppose that time $t = 0$ is mid-December, and the short-term yield curve is defined by the rates tabulated in Table 18.2.

TABLE 18.2
Example yield curve at $t = 0$

Tenor (months)	Zero-coupon rate
1	3.18%
2	3.35%
3	3.48%
4	3.60%
5	3.68%
6	3.73%
7	3.77%
8	3.80%
9	3.82%
10	3.85%
11	3.86%
12	3.88%

Using the techniques explained in Chapter 9 (sections 9.4 and 9.5), it is possible to calculate a set of discount factors from any yield curve, and then to derive a set of forward rates for any specific date in the future. Figure 18.4 shows the initial yield curve at $t = 0$, and projected yield curves for the following three months. In this example, the final almost-flat yield curve in mid-March when $t = 3$ is a stable rate structure such that all future projected yield curves will be the same. In particular, the three-month rate at $t = 3$ is projected to be 3.94%, and all futures maturing in mid-March or thereafter will be priced at 96.06. As the figure shows, the yield curves are projected to rise steadily over the next three months, so that three-month rates starting at 3.48% will increase to 3.73%, 3.87% and finally to 3.94%. With March futures at 96.06, the basis is therefore projected to be +46bp at $t = 0$, +21bp at $t = 1$, +7bp at $t = 2$, and finally zero at $t = 3$.

FIGURE 18.4
Projected yield curves

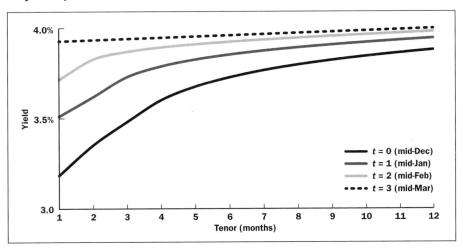

Suppose a company needs to borrow $30m for three months commencing in mid-February at $t = 2$. A basic hedge would involve selling 30 March contracts at 96.06, with a view to buying these back after two months when the loan was drawn down. The borrowing rate implied by this hedge is the futures implied rate of 3.94% less the expected basis of +7bp or 3.87%, in other words, the three-month forward rate in two months. If rates turn out just as expected, the company will borrow at the then prevailing rate of 3.87%. The futures can be bought back at 96.06, the same as the original price, and will therefore generate neither profit nor loss. The hedge would therefore be perfect, because the actual borrowing rate would precisely match the expected rate.

Now let us explore some less comfortable alternatives. What if there was a parallel shift in the yield curve? What if the yield curve were to change shape and twist? Figure 18.5 illustrates these two possibilities.

If all interest rates were to rise by a constant amount, say 50bp, all forward rates would also rise by about 50bp, and all futures prices would fall by a similar amount. Under these circumstances, the company would be forced to borrow at 4.37% instead of the 3.87% expected. Fortunately however, the futures price would have dropped to 95.56 enabling the company to make a 50bp profit on the hedge. The net borrowing rate would thus be 3.87%, exactly the same as the expected result. The hedge has proved perfect despite a considerable jump in interest rates.

While the basic hedge can cope admirably with a parallel shift in the yield curve, it is not so successful if the yield curve changes shape. Suppose that the yield curve became steeper, pivoting about the three-month point, exactly as pictured in the black line of Figure 18.5. The three-month interest rate would still be 3.87%, enabling the company to borrow at this rate, but all other rates would be different. In particular, the forward rates will now be higher and

FIGURE 18.5

Parallel shifts and twists in the yield curve at $t = 2$

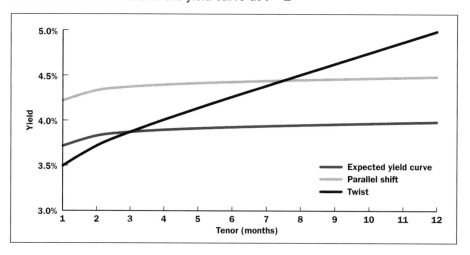

futures prices lower. With the rate scenario illustrated, the company will find that it can buy back the futures at 95.84, making a spurious profit of 22bp. This is all very well, but this profit could have been a loss if the yield curve had twisted the other way.

The risk arising from convergence basis has thus manifested itself following an unanticipated non-parallel change in the shape of the yield curve when the hedge was liquidated prior to its maturity. Note the qualifications: *unanticipated* and *non-parallel*. It is evident from Figure 18.4 that the yield curve was expected to change shape as time progressed. These anticipated changes in the yield curve do not cause problems, because the pricing of futures and other derivatives takes these changes into account. Furthermore, we have already shown that an unexpected parallel shift in the yield curve does not cause difficulties either. The problems arise from an unanticipated steepening or levelling of the yield curve.

The answer to the problem lies in executing a spread strategy in addition to the basic futures hedge. As Chapter 6 (section 6.9) has already demonstrated, a futures spread is exposed to the slope of the yield curve. By adding a suitable spread position, the slope risk of the basic hedge can be offset by the slope exposure of the spread. After some analysis it is possible to show that the number of contracts required to minimise the convergence basis risk is:

$$N_{spread} = N_{basic} \times \frac{t_{prior}}{t_{contract}} \tag{18.16}$$

where:

N_{spread}	is the number of contracts in the spread hedge
N_{basic}	is the number of contracts in the basic futures hedge
t_{prior}	is the length of time between the hedge being liquidated and the futures maturity date
$t_{contract}$	is the length of time covered by the futures contract (usually 91 days)

Note that the sign of N_{spread} is the same as that of N_{basic}. In other words, if the basic hedge involves selling futures, the spread hedge will also involve selling spreads. The decision whether to buy or sell the spread there has nothing to do with the view of how interest rates may evolve.

In the example of the company planning to liquidate the basic hedge at $t = 2$, one month prior to the maturity date of the futures contracts, N_{spread} would be $-30 \times \frac{1}{3} = -10$ contracts. The full hedge would then comprise:

a) selling 30 March contracts at 96.06

b) selling 10 March–June spreads (i.e. sell 10 March and buy 10 June contracts) at par.

After the twist in the yield curve, the March contracts will fall to 95.84, and the June contracts will fall further to 95.18. The result of the complete hedging strategy would therefore be:

a)   a profit of 22bp from the basic hedge: (96.06 – 95.84)

b)   a loss of 22bp from the spread position: $\frac{1}{3}$ × [(96.06–96.06) – (95.84–95.18)]

making a net result of zero. The net borrowing cost would therefore be 3.87%, again exactly the same as the expected result. Addition of the spread hedge has therefore returned the futures hedge to 100% efficiency despite the unexpected twist in the shape of the yield curve.

The spread hedge will improve hedge efficiency under most circumstances where the yield curve changes shape, but it will not always produce as perfect a result as the one shown here. How efficient the spread hedge proves to be will depend upon the precise way in which the yield curve twists. If the yield curve remains rigid, and pivots about the three-month rate, the spread hedge should be perfect or almost perfect. Close examination of Figure 18.5 will reveal that the scenario illustrated does satisfy this condition. This finding means that a combination of basic and spread hedges will perfectly hedge any change in rates brought about by a combination of a parallel shift in the yield curve plus a pivoting of rates around the three-month rate. There are other shape changes that will also result in 100% hedge efficiency, and even those that do not will generally be improved by the spread hedge. Whether it is worthwhile implementing this additional strategy will depend upon how critical the application is.

18.7 Interpolated hedges

The final example in the previous section involved hedging a $30m three-month risk commencing in mid-February with two structures:

a)   a basic hedge selling 30 March futures

b)   a spread hedge selling 10 spreads in March and June futures.

If the hedge was initially established in late December, after the maturity date of the December contracts, there would have been no other choice. Had the hedge been set up earlier, however, there would have been an alternative, the *interpolated hedge*. As the name suggests, an interpolated hedge is one where the exposure period falls across or between two or more contract periods, and can therefore be hedged with a mixture of the overlapping contracts. In the case of a three-month exposure starting in mid-February, there is a one-third overlap with the period covered by the December contract, and a two-thirds overlap with the period covered by the March contract. This would suggest creating an interpolated hedge by selling 10 December and 20 March contracts. Interestingly enough, this combination can also be viewed as:

a)   a basic hedge selling 30 March futures

b)   a spread hedge selling 10 spreads in December and March contracts because the net position is exactly the same. This means that an interpolated hedge is no different in principle from the combination of a basic and spread hedge, except that the spread uses contracts one expiry date earlier.

Note that interpolated hedges have only a limited life. When the near contract expires, the hedge must be rolled into the next contract period, which will create the spread hedge discussed in the previous section. There is therefore little advantage in implementing the interpolated hedge if there is sufficient liquidity in the far contracts, because it will involve extra work in rolling the hedge. If there is sufficient depth in the longer-date futures, it is generally easier to set up the basic and spread hedge right at the outset, and to leave it.

18.8 Combining the techniques

We have thus far presented a range of hedging techniques for managing exposure to short-term forward rates. The simplest method is to apply a basic hedge according to the length of the exposure period and the amount at risk. Where futures or standard FRAs are used, additional refinements can be added:

- adjusting the hedge ratio to account for exposure basis, the settlement sum and margin flows
- using a strip hedge where the exposure period is long
- using a spread or interpolated hedge where there is a gap between the exposure date and derivative dates.

The more refinements which are added, the closer the hedge will approach perfection. It is for the user to decide at what point the pursuit of perfection must surrender to the cost of designing and implementing the hedging scheme.

18.9 FRAs vs. futures

Table 5.3 in Chapter 5 has already presented a general comparison of futures and cash markets, while Chapter 6 (section 6.8) included a detailed comparison of FRAs with short-term interest rate futures.

The single most important contrast is the flexibility of the FRA against the standardisation of the futures contract. Nevertheless, despite the rigidity and inflexibility of futures contracts, the techniques presented in this chapter allow a hedger to attain near-perfection in the performance of an interest rate hedge. In favour of futures is their tremendous liquidity, and the attendant ease with which positions can be reversed or adjusted if necessary. Also in favour of futures is the almost complete lack of credit risk, but against this must be weighed the administrative chore of running the margin account. Finally, contract sizes in interest rate futures tend to be quite large, and FRAs might therefore be the only viable alternative for the medium-sized company with exposures less than $1m or £500,000

There is therefore no universally better choice between FRAs and futures, and both are used extensively for managing exposure to short-term forward rates. For most companies, however, the scales probably tip in favour of using FRAs, especially if there is little likelihood that a hedge will need to be reversed or liquidated prior to the normal maturity date. Companies should, however, check that they are obtaining a reasonable quotation with an acceptable spread if a two-way price is requested. Banks make use of both products, trading FRAs between themselves, and making heavy use of futures in order to hedge their own interest rate exposures.

18.10 Using swaps

The discussion has so far concentrated on exposures to a single short-term forward rate. We can now turn our attention to risks influenced by a series of short-term forward rates. If FRAs and futures were the appropriate tools to handle exposure to a single forward rate, the multi-period equivalent of an FRA – the interest rate swap – is the obvious tool for managing exposure to multiple interest periods in the future.

Since swaps are invariably OTC instruments, they can be tailored to suit both the requirements of the user and the characteristics of the underlying exposure. There is often a greater need to customise a swap, because there are many more variables than for an FRA covering just a single interest period. Fortunately, the longer time period covered by a swap makes their inherent profitability that much greater, and banks do find it worthwhile to design non-standard swaps to meet a specific application. Nonetheless, the majority of swap applications can be handled by the assortment of plain-vanilla swaps which are traded on the highly liquid swaps market.

Swap applications can be split into two main categories. Asset-linked swaps originate when a swap is bound with a particular asset in order to change the characteristics of the income stream for investors. Liability-linked swaps arise from the need to alter a borrower's cash flows. To some extent, this division is somewhat artificial, because a swapped debt instrument is both a liability to the issuer and an asset to the investor who holds the bonds. The distinction, if one exists, emphasises the party whose needs were the strongest driving force when the swap structure was created.

To illustrate some of the varied ways in which swaps can be applied, the following examples and case studies will demonstrate liability-linked, asset-linked and non-standard swaps in action. A final scenario will explore two ways in which an existing swap may be cancelled.

Liability-linked swap – floating-to-fixed

One of the most straightforward swap applications is converting a floating-rate borrowing facility into a fixed-rate one, thereby eliminating any further exposure to interest rate movements. As an example, consider a company currently borrowing floating-rate for three years at six-month LIBOR+80bp. The corporate treasurer fears that interest rates may rise and therefore wishes to lock in the cost of funds at present levels. After receiving an acceptable quotation for three-year semi-annual swaps at 3.40–46% against LIBOR flat, the company enters into a three-year semi-annual swap as the fixed-rate payer. The cash flow streams are depicted in Figure 18.6, from which it is evident that the swap effectively converts the floating rate obligation of LIBOR+80bp into a fixed-rate obligation of 4.26%. This will insulate the company against any rise in interest rates, although it will also prevent the company from benefiting should interest rates fall.

Liability-linked swap – fixed-to-floating

Somewhat less common is the switch from fixed-rate to floating-rate financing, but a swap can facilitate this conversion. An example would be the case of a company which issued seven-year fixed-rate debt two years ago paying an annual coupon of 5.75%. It chose to borrow fixed-rate mainly to avoid interest rate risk, but also because it did not think that interest rates were likely to drop. Since then, its view has been proved wrong, and interest rates have fallen dramatically. The yield curve is currently very steeply upward-sloping, with six-month LIBOR at 0.5%, 12-month LIBOR at 1%, two-year swaps at around 2%, and five-year swaps at roughly 3%. The finance director now wishes to take advantage of the lower rates currently available, and obtains a quotation for five-year annual swaps at 2.95–3.05% against 12-month LIBOR flat. If the company enters into a five-year annual swap receiving the fixed rate at 2.95%, the liability will be converted into a floating-rate obligation at LIBOR + 280bp, as shown in Figure 18.7. With 12-month LIBOR at 1%, the cost of borrowing would therefore fall from 5.75% to just 3.80%, a very substantial saving.

A problem with this strategy is that the company now becomes exposed to rising interest rates. The steep upward-sloping yield curve implies that 12-month rates in four years' time would be around 4.5%. Borrowing at LIBOR+280bp would push the effective rate to 7.3% under these circumstances, considerably higher

FIGURE 18.6

Liability-linked floating-to-fixed swap

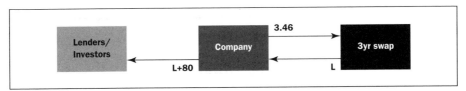

FIGURE 18.7

Liability-linked fixed-to-floating swap

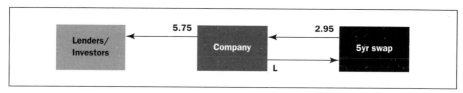

than the original fixed rate of 5.75%. The swap therefore provides an immediate saving of 1.95%, but could give rise to future costs of a similar order or even more should rates rise as the forward yield curve predicts. If the company decides to enter into this particular liability-linked swap, this is tantamount to taking the view that rates will not rise as much or as fast as the yield curve suggests.

Liability-linked swap – fixed-to-floating-to-fixed

Once a liability has been swapped, there is nothing preventing the corporate treasurer from entering into additional swaps at a later date. This might be motivated by a shift in the borrower's requirements, a change in outlook, or to take advantage of a beneficial movement in market rates. As an example of this kind of dynamic hedging, consider the case of a company which two years ago borrowed for an original tenor of five years at a fixed rate of 4.65%, and entered at the same time into a swap receiving fixed at 4.26% against paying six-month LIBOR flat. After swapping, the company's liability is effectively floating-rate at LIBOR+39bp. Suppose that swap rates have now fallen, so that three-year semi-annual swaps are now quoted at 1.80–85%. The company can now switch back to fixed rate to take advantage of the lower rates now available. If the company enters into a second swap paying the fixed rate at 1.85% for three years against receiving six-month LIBOR flat, the net cost of the entire structure is a fixed-rate liability of 2.24%, as Figure 18.8 shows. The saving of 2.41% compared to the original fixed borrowing cost of 4.65% is just the difference between the two swap rates.

FIGURE 18.8

Liability-linked fixed-to-floating-to-fixed swap

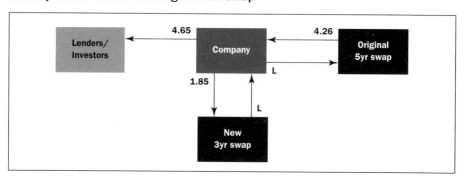

Liability-linked swap – cross-currency floating-to-floating

Large companies, especially multinationals, are able to tap the capital markets in several countries and in a number of currencies. This opens up several alternative sources of finance, and the availability of interest rate and cross-currency swaps means that finance can be obtained from the cheapest market and swapped into the currency and format desired. As an example, a multinational chemicals company based in the UK which is planning a new debt issue finds that it can issue sterling-denominated ten-year debt at 4.20% fixed, or dollar-denominated floating-rate debt for a similar maturity at dollar six-month LIBOR+12bp. Ten-year sterling interest rate swaps are 4.02–07% against six-month sterling LIBOR, dollar interest rate swaps are quoted at 3.55–65% against six-month dollar LIBOR, and the sterling–dollar cross-currency basis swap is quoted at sterling six-month LIBOR–5bp/LIBOR–1bp against dollar six-month LIBOR flat. The company's existing exposure creates a preference for floating-rate sterling finance, leaving two choices:

- borrow fixed-rate sterling at 4.20% and swap into floating using the sterling interest rate swap
- borrow floating-rate dollars and switch into floating-rate sterling using the cross-currency basis swap.

The first alternative creates floating-rate sterling finance at LIBOR+18bp. The second alternative using a cross-currency swap is just a little more complex, but is justified in this case by the savings made possible. Rather than use a plain-vanilla basis swap, the company can enter into a non-standard cross-currency swap where the company pays sterling LIBOR+12bp and receives dollar LIBOR+12bp.[6] This structure exactly matches the floating-rate dollar financing, and therefore ensures that all dollar cash flows net to zero. The remaining liability comprises just the payments of sterling at LIBOR+12bp, resulting in a saving of 6bp over the first alternative. The two alternatives are illustrated in Figure 18.9.

FIGURE 18.9
Liability-linked cross-currency floating-to-floating basis swap

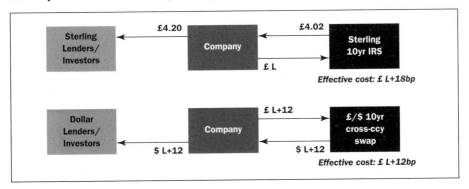

Asset-linked swap – floating-to-fixed

Many borrowers issue floating-rate notes, but many investors require a fixed-income security. A swap can easily effect this transition. For example, the portfolio manager of a pension fund may have purchased a prime quality seven-year floating-rate note paying six-month LIBOR+43bp, but wishes to swap the cash flows to create a fixed-income stream. If swaps for this maturity are quoted at 3.55–60%, the resulting structure will generate a fixed return of 3.98%, as Figure 18.10 makes clear.

Asset-linked swap – fixed-to-floating-to-fixed

For every liability-linked swap structure there is a mirror-image asset-linked one. Figure 18.8 illustrated the dynamic hedging strategy of a company who had issued fixed-rate debt, swapped this into a floating-rate liability, and then swapped back into fixed-rate financing after interest rates had fallen. Investors can also employ dynamic portfolio management techniques. Take the example of an investor holding a five-year bond paying 2.55% fixed, but who believes that interest rates are about to rise. If five-year swaps are quoted at 2.22–28% against six-month LIBOR, the investor can pay fixed at 2.28% thereby creating a synthetic floating-rate note paying LIBOR+27bp. Two years later, interest rates have indeed risen, and three-year swaps are now quoted at 3.85–92% against six-month LIBOR. By entering into the second swap to receive fixed at 3.85%, the investor can create a new synthetic fixed-rate bond paying 4.12%. The 1.57% yield pick-up compared to the original bond coupon of 2.55% arises from the difference between the fixed rates for the two swaps. The final structure is pictured in Figure 18.11.

Non-standard swap

The possibilities to tailor swaps are virtually unlimited, and almost any feature of a swap's characteristics can be amended to match the specific requirements of the swap counterpart. Chapter 8 (section 8.4) reviewed many of the non-standard swap structures commonly found. Case 18.4 reviews the circumstances surrounding one particular company's needs, and the way in which these were met through the creation of a hybrid swap structure in which one leg featured both fixed-rate and floating-rate payments.

FIGURE 18.10

Asset-linked floating-to-fixed swap

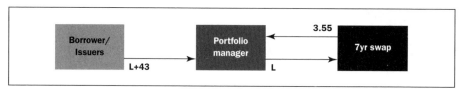

FIGURE 18.11

Asset-linked fixed-to-floating-to-fixed swap

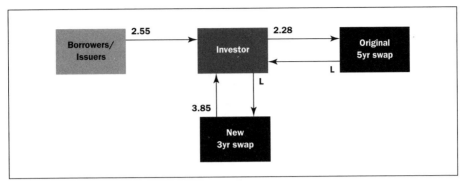

Case study 18.4

Using a non-standard swap

Associated Manufacturing Industries Inc. (AMI) is currently servicing $50m of 7.5% fixed-rate debt with an original maturity of five years. Since obtaining the borrowing facility three years ago, interest rates have fallen by between 2% and 3%. Unfortunately, AMI's competitors are now able to borrow five-year funds at around 4.75%, and the additional interest burden – in excess of $1m per year – is placing AMI at a significant disadvantage. Moreover, when the existing facility matures, AMI will need to refinance its present facility for a further three years, but the company fears that interest rates will have risen by then.

AMI has therefore asked its bankers to structure a non-standard swap, which must simultaneously achieve two objectives:

- Borrowing costs under the existing facility must be reduced to below 6% for the remaining two years.
- Interest costs under a new three-year floating-rate borrowing facility at LIBOR+25bp, to commence in two years, must also be limited to a maximum of 6%.

The left side of both parts of Figure 18.12 depicts the cash flow streams arising from AMI's debt obligations, while the right side illustrates what the swap must achieve. For the first two years, AMI pays a fixed rate of F% to the swap counterparty, and receives 7.5% fixed. So long as F is less than 6%, this structure will achieve the first objective. In the remaining three years, AMI again pays F% to the swap counterparty, but this time receives LIBOR+25bp, thus achieving the second objective. The swap effectively replaces the fixed-rate debt obligations of the first two years, and the floating-rate obligations of the last three years, with a fixed-rate cash flow at F%. This makes the swap distinctly non-standard, having one fixed leg and one hybrid fixed-floating leg.

Using the set of rates for standard swaps shown in the table overleaf, AMI's bank was able to structure and price the requisite non-standard swap with F set at 5.96%. AMI is therefore able to save 1.54% from its present funding costs, and also lock into a fixed sub-6% cost now for floating-rate funding due to commence in two years' time. These are the two goals which AMI established.

▶

Tenor	Swap rate
1y	5.12%
2y	5.00%
3y	4.90%
4y	4.82%
5y	4.75%

Quoted rates for standard annual/360 swaps

Although AMI is certain to gain 1.54% p.a. from the swap in the first two years, during the last three years AMI is required to pay a fixed rate of 5.96% against receiving LIBOR+25bp, which is somewhat worse than the quoted rate of 4.75% for standard five-year swaps. These two features offset each other. However, since AMI believes that interest rates will eventually rise, the fixed rate of 5.96% will probably seem cheap compared with interest rates in two years' time.

FIGURE 18.12
Non-standard swap structure for AMI Inc.

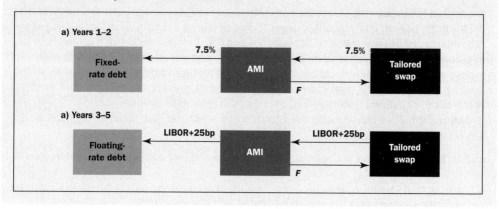

Cancelling a swap

In most cases, companies using swaps to hedge long-term interest-rate exposures will enter into a swap which matches their existing obligations, and then maintain the swap until maturity. On occasions, however, the company's position or viewpoint may change, and the swap may no longer be needed. In such circumstances there are three broad choices.

One option is for the company to enter into a second swap whose purpose is to negate the first. This has the advantage that the existing swap need not be touched, but the disadvantage that there will be small residual cash flows if the two swaps do not exactly cancel each other out. For example, suppose a company originally entered into a seven-year swap paying 4.46% annually against receiving LIBOR flat. Two years later the company decides that it no longer needs the original swap, and attempts to reverse it by entering into another swap, this time receiving the fixed rate for five years against paying LIBOR flat. The two floating-rate streams will match exactly, so long as the second swap is taken out on the anniversary of the first. However, unless the two swap rates are identical, which is most unlikely, the two fixed-rate streams will not net to zero. For example, if the second swap was concluded at 3.75%, the company would end up paying the difference of 71bp per annum for the next five years.

The problem of using an offsetting swap is potentially worse if the company tries to offset the original swap on a day other than one of the fixing dates. Either the company will have to tolerate a timing mismatch for the two swaps, which could be months apart, or would have to seek a quotation for a non-standard swap, which will normally be more expensive.

The second choice is to approach the swap counterparty, normally a bank, and ask for a quotation to cancel the swap. As an example, the company currently paying 4.46% fixed under a swap with five years remaining until maturity might be quoted a cancellation fee of 323bp if prevailing swap rates had dropped to 3.75%. The calculation here is relatively straightforward, and involves the bank evaluating the net present value of the future cash flow streams under the swap. Table 18.3 shows how this calculation can be done, and the technique can easily be extended to value swaps on days other than a fixing date. Using the swap valuation methodology explained in Chapter 9 there is no need to take into account accrued interest between payment dates. Each future cash flow, fixed or floating, is present-valued using the calculated or interpolated discount factor for that date, and the net present value of all these flows gives the fair price for cancelling the swap.[7]

TABLE 18.3

Cancelling a swap

Year	Swap rates	Discount function	Original fixed payments	Current fixed payments	Difference	PV of difference
1	2.00%	0.980392	446,000	375,000	71,000	69,607.84
2	2.50%	0.951698	446,000	375,000	71,000	67,570.54
3	3.00%	0.914599	446,000	375,000	71,000	64,936.55
4	3.40%	0.873513	446,000	375,000	71,000	62,019.43
5	3.75%	0.829390	446,000	375,000	71,000	58,886.71
NPV						323,021.08

If the cancellation fee was set to 323bp on a swap with a nominal principal of $10m, the company would therefore make a single payment of $323,000 in order to extinguish all future obligations under the swap. This payment is designed to compensate the swap counterparty for losing the benefit of receiving a 4.46% coupon when interest rates had fallen below that level. Of course, if interest rates had risen, the fixed-rate payer would expect to receive rather than pay the cancellation fee.

The third possible way to cancel a swap is to assign the obligations under the swap to a willing third party. If the swap has a non-zero net present value, however, a fee must be paid by one of the parties to the other. This fee will be similar or identical to the cancellation fee just discussed, and provides compensation for the party taking on an off-market swap.

18.11 Hedging bond and swap portfolios

The last form of interest rate risk manifests itself as exposure to a single long-term interest rate or spot yield. This is in contrast to the risks discussed earlier in this chapter, for which the exposure was to one or more forward rates. The two most common situations where this long-term interest rate risk arises is when institutions hold portfolios of bonds or swaps.

Banks running a large book of swaps generally use an integrated risk management technique. Rather than attempt to hedge the swaps portfolio separately, the exposures arising from swaps, FRAs, interest rate futures, bond futures, bonds, and any other interest-rate instrument, are all combined and just the net exposure is managed. This avoids the sub-optimal and more costly approach whereby each book is separately hedged.

There are two major steps involved in implementing this method. For each instrument within the portfolio:

i)   Identify the specific point(s) on the yield curve where exposure exists.

ii)   Evaluate the present value of a basis point (PVBP) at each such point.

The PVBP provides a precise figure defining how much the instrument will change in present value given a 1bp movement in the yield curve at that point. As an example, the five-year swap analysed in Tables 9.6 and 9.7 is only sensitive to the five-year swap rate, and the five-year PVBP is $4,534.67. If the five-year swap rate was to rise by 1bp, the swap would be worth $4,534.67 more to the fixed-rate payer. Immediately after the rate for the first floating leg is fixed, however, this particular swap would also have an exposure to the six-month rate and a six-month PVBP of –$496.25. A rise in the six-month rate of 1bp would make the swap worth $496.25 *less* to the fixed-rate payer/floating-rate receiver, because once the rate for the first floating leg has been fixed he will no longer benefit from the rise in short-term rates.

Once all the PVBPs are known, the exposures at each point in the yield curve can be aggregated, and the combined risk at that point hedged with the appropriate instrument. For points in the yield curve up to five years (for the US dollar) or two to three years (most other major currencies), interest rate futures can be used. From this point until ten-year maturities, swaps provide a highly liquid and efficient hedging instrument. Beyond ten years, swaps can still be used for those currencies where there is sufficient liquidity in longer-dated swaps, otherwise bonds and bond futures provide effective hedging tools.

To continue the example just discussed, let us assume that a bank was the fixed-rate payer on the above-mentioned swap, and the interest rate for the first floating leg has just been determined. The resulting exposure could be hedged in two parts. Selling a strip totalling 20 Eurodollar futures contracts covering the next two three-month periods would hedge the exposure to six-month rates, while buying the strip totalling 181 Eurodollar contracts covering the next five years would hedge the exposure to five-year rates. Netting these results in a hedging strategy that comprises the sale of 1 Eurodollar contract for each of the first two three-month periods, and the purchase of 9 Eurodollar contracts for each of the 18 three-month periods thereafter. This particular hedge has been designed so that the PVBP of the hedging instruments closely matches the PVBP of the swap, but several other permutations of hedging instruments could have been chosen with the same end result.

18.12 Hedging bond portfolios with bond futures

Although hedging a bond portfolio can be viewed as a subset of the wider task of hedging interest rate risk, a particularly common activity is the hedging of bond portfolios using just bond futures. This section will therefore explain how this particular task can be accomplished.

Chapter 7 (section 7.3) explained how bond futures were priced and noted how bond futures tend to track movements in the cheapest-to-deliver bond. This enabled us to design a simple but effective technique for hedging a portfolio containing just the cheapest-to-deliver bond, whereby futures contracts are sold with a nominal value equal to the conversion factor times the face value of the bonds to be hedged. In the example given in section 7.6 of that chapter, a portfolio containing $10m of the cheapest-to-deliver bond with a conversion factor of 0.9335 was successfully hedged by selling 93 futures contracts.

In practice, however, investors will hold bond portfolios which are much more widely diversified. Such portfolios can also be successfully hedged with bond futures, but the hedge design must now be executed in two stages:

i)   Determine the relative volatility of the bonds to be hedged compared with the cheapest-to-deliver bond.

ii) Determine the relative volatility of the cheapest-to-deliver bond compared with the bond futures contract.

The number of futures contracts required to hedge the holding of any target bond is then:

$$N = \frac{NOM_{TGT}}{NOM_{FUT}} \times RV_{TGT \rightarrow CTD} \times RV_{CTD \rightarrow FUT} \qquad (18.17)$$

where:

NOM_{TGT} is the nominal value of the target bond

NOM_{FUT} is the nominal value of the futures contract

$RV_{TGT \rightarrow CTD}$ is the relative volatility of the bond to be hedged compared with the cheapest-to-deliver bond

$RV_{CTD \rightarrow FUT}$ is the relative volatility of the cheapest-to-deliver bond compared with the futures contract

This formula is quite logical. If, hypothetically, the price of the target bond tends to move twice as much as that of the cheapest-to-deliver bond, and the price of the cheapest-to-deliver bond tends to move twice as much as that of the futures contract, it is sensible that futures contracts amounting to four times the nominal value of the target bond need to be held to effect a satisfactory hedge.

The method for determining the relative volatility of the target bond with respect to the cheapest-to-deliver bond depends upon the similarity between them. If both are government bonds, their respective yields will tend to move together. In this case, relative volatility can be measured mathematically using bond duration, and this technique will be explained very shortly. If the target bond is different, for example a eurobond or a corporate bond, then there is a distinct possibility that the yield spread between the target bond and the cheapest-to-deliver bond may change when yield levels change. In that case, relative volatility should be measured using regression analysis.

Assuming that the target and cheapest-to-deliver bonds are both priced from the same yield curve, and that this yield curve tends to exhibit parallel rather than non-parallel shifts, the relative volatility between the two bonds can be determined using the modified duration of the two bonds. From the basic definition of modified duration,[8] the change in the price of any bond caused by a small change in interest rates is given by:

$$\Delta P = -MD \times P \times \Delta i \qquad (18.18)$$

where:

ΔP is the change in the price of a bond
MD is the modified duration
P is the price of the bond
Δi is the change in interest rates

It follows directly from equation 18.18 that the relative volatility of the target bond can be calculated as:

$$RV_{TGT \to CTD} = \frac{\Delta P_{TGT}}{\Delta P_{CTD}} = \frac{MD_{TGT} P_{TGT}}{MD_{CTD} P_{CTD}} \qquad (18.19)$$

where:

MD_{TGT} is the modified duration of the target bond
MD_{CTD} is the modified duration of the cheapest-to-deliver bond
P_{TGT} is the (dirty) price of the target bond
P_{CTD} is the (dirty) price of the cheapest-to-deliver bond

Some textbooks and practitioners advocate using the ratio of the conversion factors of the two bonds as a surrogate for relative volatility. This is totally wrong. Conversion factors are principally influenced by the coupon of a bond, whereas price volatility is largely a function of a bond's maturity. One is not a substitute for the other. If the target bond was a long-dated low-coupon bond and the cheapest-to-deliver bond was a short-dated high-coupon bond, the relative volatility calculated properly using modified duration would be much greater than one, but the relative volatility calculated from conversion factors would be much less than one. The resulting hedge could easily be out by a factor of two or more times. Using conversion factors to measure relative volatility therefore has no foundation either in theory or in practice.

If the target and cheapest-to-deliver bonds are priced from different yield curves, it may be better to rely on a regression analysis using recent historical data. The daily price movements between the two bonds of interest can be analysed to determine the slope of the regression line, as illustrated in Figure 18.1 and discussed earlier in this chapter. Proprietary information services such as the Bloomberg system make this kind of analysis very straightforward.

These techniques therefore provide an answer to the first stage in designing an appropriate hedge. The answer to the second stage is much easier, and has already been encountered in Chapter 7 (section 7.6). Rearranging equation 7.12 slightly, we obtain:

$$RV_{CTD \to FUT} = \frac{\Delta P_{CTD}}{\Delta FP} \approx CF_{CTD} \qquad (18.20)$$

where:

ΔP_{CTD} is the change in the price of the cheapest-to-deliver bond
ΔFP is the change in the price of the bond futures contract
CF_{CTD} is the conversion factor of the cheapest-to-deliver bond

We now have everything we need in order to design a reasonable futures hedge designed to insulate a bond or portfolio against movements in interest rates.

To illustrate this technique, Table 18.4 itemises the contents of a portfolio of six different US T-Notes and T-Bonds on Friday 29th July 2011. The market value of the portfolio at the time was a shade over $437m for bonds having a face value of exactly $374m. The cheapest-to-deliver bond was the 4% of August 2018, which happened to be one of the bonds in the portfolio, and had a conversion factor for delivery into the September 2011 ten-year T-Note contract of 0.8902.

TABLE 18.4

Hedging a bond portfolio with bond futures contracts

Bond	Nominal amount ($m)	29th Jul 2011			1st Sep 2011		Modified duration	Relative volatility	Number of contracts
		Price	Yield (%)	Accrued	Price	Yield (%)			
4.875% Aug 16	44	117'06	1.336	2.2490	119'14	0.854	4.46	0.7615	298.3
4% Aug 18	54	112'25	2.039	1.8453	117'06	1.397	6.10	1.0000	480.7
2.625% Aug 20	32	99'18	2.680	1.2110	105'19	1.941	7.90	1.1383	324.3
6.75% Aug 26	82	138'09	3.463	3.1140	148'23	2.752	10.13	2.0488	1495.5
5.375% Feb 31	60	121'30	3.778	2.4796	133'15	3.076	12.56	2.2354	1193.9
4.375% May 41	102	104'04	4.133	0.9273	116'06	3.495	16.69	2.5076	2276.9
TOTAL	**374**								**6070**

Suppose that the portfolio manager, concerned at speculation that one of the rating agencies may take the unprecedented step of downgrading the US from its envied AAA rating, wished to secure the value of the portfolio against any volatility in market prices over the next month or so. The table shows the results of using equations 18.17, 18.19 and 18.20 in order to calculate a hedge using ten-year T-Note futures contracts, the most liquid of those traded on the CBOT.

As an example, the number of futures contracts required to hedge the first bond in the portfolio is given by:

$$\frac{44,000,000}{100,000} \times \frac{4.46 \times (117.1875 + 2.2490)}{6.10 \times (112.7813 + 1.8453)} \times 0.8902 = 298.3$$

Note that it is the conversion factor of the cheapest-to-deliver bond which is used in every case, not that of the target bond.

Since most of the bonds have longer maturities than the cheapest-to-deliver bond, the relative volatilities are, with one exception, more than one. The total number of futures contracts needed turns out to be 6070, rather more than the 3740 or 4370 that might be suggested by a naive estimate based on nominal or market values alone. The portfolio manager therefore needed to sell 6070 of the September 2011 10-year T-Note futures contracts, then trading at 125'22.

On Friday 5th August 2011, just one week after establishing the bond port-folio hedge, S&P took the extraordinary step of downgrading the credit rating of the US from AAA to AA+. Part of its decision was triggered by the prevailing political brinkmanship over reaching an agreement to an increase in the US debt ceiling. There followed several weeks of unusual volatility in the US Treasury market which eventually saw a rally in US Treasury bond prices, and yields dropping by between 50bp and 70bp across the maturity spectrum.

By the beginning of September 2011, the markets had become much more stable and the portfolio manager decided to lift the hedge, before liquidity in the September contract dried up. The 6070 futures contracts were bought back at a price of 130'195 to realise a loss of:

$$6070 \text{ contracts} \times 315 \text{ ticks} \times \$15.625 = -\$29,875,781.25$$

At the same time, the general fall in bond yields had lifted the value of the portfolio from \$437,085,000 to \$470,165,625, a gain of \$33,080,625. The net gain in the value of the portfolio was \$3,204,844 after the loss on the futures is taken into account. Using equation 16.5, this result implies a hedge efficiency of 90%.

This is a fairly impressive result, but the hedge was not perfect for two main reasons:

i)   The yield curve did not move in a parallel shift. Five-year yields moved down by 48bp, 15- and 20-year yields moved down by more than 70bp, and 30-year yields dropped by 64bp. As the futures contract was tracking the CTD bond which had a maturity of seven years, its yield did not fall by as much as that of the longer-dated bonds.

ii) The bond future selected was not ideal for all of the bonds in the portfolio. The futures tracked the seven-year CTD bond, but the weighted average maturity of the portfolio was 16.6 years.

To achieve an even greater efficiency, a more sophisticated hedge could have been constructed by using a combination of the T-Note and T-Bond futures available on the CME; these have notional maturities from 2 to 30 years, and particular contracts could have been selected to match the maturity mix of the underlying bond portfolio. This would have brought the maturity profile of the hedging instruments closer to that of the bonds being hedged, thereby removing some of the basis risk which arose in this illustration. However, this breadth of choice is not available in the non-dollar bond futures markets.

As with all hedge design, the end-user must balance the advantage of simplicity against the cost of residual risk emanating from an inefficient hedge, and structure the scheme accordingly.

Notes

1   The basis point value is the change in monetary value caused by a 1bp change in interest rates, and applies both to the original risk exposure and to any hedge designed to mitigate that risk.

2   The Federal-funds contract is also unusual in having the settlement linked to the *average* of Fed funds rates during the contract month rather than the rate prevailing on any one day.

3   The figures used here are actual market rates, but users planning to hedge should carry out their own regression analysis using the most recent data available. Spreadsheet packages such as Excel include regression facilities, which make the task of performing this analysis very straightforward.

4   See equation 4.2 in Chapter 4.

5   See Chapter 6 (sections 6.2–6.4) for a full explanation.

6   The standard cross-currency basis swap would involve the company receiving dollar LIBOR flat against paying sterling LIBOR–1bp. This is less neat, because it leaves the company with a small residual cash flow in dollars of 12bp. Using time-value-of-money techniques it is possible to calculate that adding a 12bp margin to the dollar flows means adding 12.3bp to the sterling flows. Rounding the 12.3bp up to 13bp and then combining with the existing LIBOR–1bp gives LIBOR+12bp, creating the non-standard basis swap actually used.

7   Section 9.8 in Chapter 9 provides a further insight into calculating the cancellation fee for a swap.

8   See any textbook on bond mathematics for an explanation of this point, e.g. Fabozzi, Frank J. (2005) *Fixed Income Mathematics*, McGraw-Hill, 4th edition.

19

MANAGING INTEREST RATE RISK – USING OPTIONS AND OPTION-BASED INSTRUMENTS

The common feature of all the techniques discussed in the previous chapter was that they guaranteed a certain outcome. Whether the original exposure arose from a single short-term forward rate, a series of short-term forward rates, or a single long-term spot rate, the requisite solution attempted to eliminate risk completely. For some exposed to interest rate risk, this remedy might be just what they wanted. However, as the introduction to Chapter 10 has pointed out, risk includes both adverse and benign outcomes. The complete eradication of risk means the avoidance of beneficial outcomes as well as bad ones, and others exposed to risk may not want this. The alternative solution is to use those financial engineering tools which provide protection against the downside, while preserving the opportunity to benefit from the upside – options and option-based instruments.

This chapter starts by showing how interest rate options can be used to hedge against exposure to a single short-term forward rate. This will illustrate the basic principles of using option-based products in managing interest rate risk. More commonly, however, interest rate risk manifests itself over an extended period of time, and multi-period products such as caps, floors and collars are the appropriate tools to use. A substantial part of this chapter is therefore devoted to discussing how these popular products can be applied. As various approaches to managing interest rate risk are reviewed, the parallels with currency risk management will become very evident. A later section will highlight these links by illustrating how ideas originally developed in the currency markets have been successfully transferred to the interest rate market. Finally, the chapter ends with a detailed comparison of the wide and sometimes confusing range of interest rate products discussed in this chapter and the previous one, and the provision of some important criteria to guide users towards the most appropriate technique to use in a given situation.

19.1 Interest rate guarantees

An FRA guarantees a specific interest rate for a nominated time period in the future. An option on an FRA, often called an *interest rate guarantee* (IRG), grants the holder the right to choose between:

a)   a specific interest rate previously agreed

b)   the interest rate prevailing at the time.

A borrower could buy a call option on an FRA struck at a particular interest rate. If rates eventually turned out higher than the strike rate, the borrower would exercise the option and use the underlying FRA to cap the borrowing cost. If rates turned out lower, the borrower would allow the option to expire, and simply borrow at market rates. Similarly, an investor could use a put option to guarantee a minimum investment rate.

To give a specific example, a company may need to borrow for a six-month period starting in six months' time. One alternative is for the company to buy a 6 × 12 FRA which might be quoted at 2%. Whichever way rates turn out six months later makes no difference to the company once it has bought the FRA. It will borrow based on a six-month LIBOR of 2%. The other alternative is for the company to buy a call option struck at 2% on the same FRA. After paying the premium, which might amount to 13.5bp of the nominal principal, the company waits to see how rates evolve over the next six months. If interest rates end up higher than 2%, the company exercises the option and buys the FRA, which is immediately cash-settled to ensure borrowing based on a LIBOR of 2%. If rates end up lower than 2%, the company allows the option to expire, and borrows at whatever rate prevails. The effect of the IRG is that the company can borrow at the prevailing rate or at 2%, whichever is better.

Table 19.1 lists typical quotations for IRGs at a time when the prevailing six-month rate and the 6 × 12 FRA are both quoted at exactly 2.00%. Each instrument guarantees the six-month rate in six months' time; the call options guaranteeing a maximum borrowing rate, while the put options guarantee a minimum investment rate. The table shows actual and annualised premiums for five different strike rates ranging from 1.5% to 3.5%. For example, the premium for the 2.5% call option is an up-front payment of 6bp of the nominal principal. As the period covered by the guarantee lasts exactly six months, this 6bp premium is equivalent to 12bp on an annualised basis.

TABLE 19.1
Illustrative premiums for interest rate guarantees

Strike rates	Calls (borrowers' guarantee)		Puts (investors' guarantee)	
	actual	annualised	actual	annualised
1.5%	27.5	55	3	6
2.0%	13.5	27	13.5	27
2.5%	6	12	30.5	61
3.0%	2.5	5	51.5	103
3.5%	1	2	74.5	149

(all premiums in basis points)

Since the strike rates are quoted on an annualised basis, it is a little easier to interpret these premiums if we look at the annualised figures. The call struck at 1.5% is very much in-the-money, and virtually the entire 55bp is intrinsic value. At first glance, one might expect that the intrinsic value should be 50bp for a call option struck at 1.50% when the forward rate is 2.00%. In fact, the intrinsic value is a little lower at 49bp, because the option premium is paid at the outset, and the eventual option payout under an IRG is normally discounted in the same way as the settlement sum with an FRA. In the case of the call struck at 1.50%, the nominal 50bp intrinsic value must therefore be discounted at the 2% forward rate for the six-month period covered by the guarantee, and then at the 2% cash-market rate for the six-month period until the option matures. This gives the 49bp intrinsic value mentioned above, and therefore a time value of 6bp. The remaining call premiums decline as the strike rate is raised, although the time value component reaches a maximum when the guarantee is struck at-the-money. The put options reveal a similar pattern, although the prices run in the opposite direction, increasing as the strike rate is raised. This makes sense, of course, because the put options grant the right to invest at the strike price, and this advantage becomes greater the higher the strike rate.

The profile of an IRG is no different from that of any other basic option-based product. Figure 19.1 illustrates the effective borrowing cost against the interest rate eventually prevailing, and shows the profiles for guarantees struck at five different rates. In each case, the effective borrowing cost has been adjusted to account for the fact that the premiums are paid in advance. This means, for example, that using the option struck at 1.50% with an annualised premium of 55bp will lead to a maximum borrowing cost of 2.06% rather than the 2.05% that might be expected from a casual inspection of the figures. To provide a comparison, the figure also shows the flat profile for an FRA hedge with the contract rate set to 2.00%, and the diagonal profile for the original exposure without any hedging.

FIGURE 19.1
Profiles for interest rate guarantees

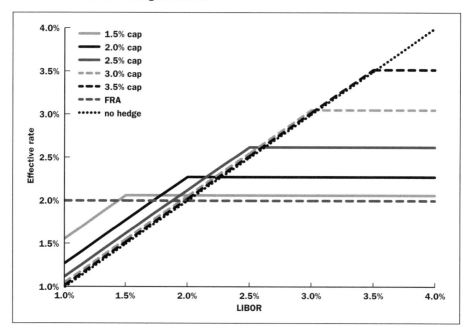

At one extreme, the borrower could achieve complete immunity from the effects of changing interest rates by buying the FRA, which fixes the eventual borrowing rate under all eventualities. The resulting profile is the horizontal straight line at 2.00%. The most in-the-money IRG has a similar characteristic for all interest rates above the strike rate of 1.50%, but allows the borrower to benefit should rates eventually end up below this level.

At the other extreme, the borrower who chooses not to hedge will suffer from the full effects of any movement in interest rates. If rates are low, the borrowing cost will also be low. If interest rates are high, the effective cost will grow in line. This gives rise to the diagonal profile in Figure 19.1 for the 'no hedge' strategy. This time, it is the most out-of-the-money guarantee, the one struck at 3.50%, which exhibits a similar characteristic. This instrument is cheap – just 2bp p.a. – but offers no protection against a rise in interest rates until the strike rate of 3.50% is reached. Only then does it cap the borrower's costs.

In between, the other IRGs offer various compromises between premium cost, degree of protection against higher rates, and ability to profit from lower rates. This is exactly the same behaviour as that exhibited by the currency option solutions presented in Chapter 17, where the chameleon-like nature of options was first discussed. Hedging with deep in-the-money options gives a profile almost the same as using the corresponding forward contract, here the FRA. Deep out-of-the-money options cost little, but offer little in the way of protection, so the resulting profile looks just like that of the underlying exposure. Only between these two extremes do IRGs provide a true balance between protection and beneficial exposure.

19.2 Using caps and floors

Caps and floors were first introduced in Chapter 13 (section 13.2), where it was also explained how they were priced (section 13.5). Using the term structure of interest rates and volatilities shown in Table 19.2, we can calculate a representative set of cap and floor prices at different strike levels. Table 19.3 summarises the results of these calculations for caps and floors on six-month LIBOR with maturities ranging from two to seven years. Each price is quoted both as an up-front premium, and as an amortised rate. For example, the five-year cap struck at 5% could either be paid as an up-front premium of 180bp of the nominal principal, or as a regular payment at the rate of 40bp per annum paid six-monthly in arrears (i.e. 0.20% paid twice a year). For consistency, the figures in Table 19.2 are identical with those of Table 13.7 earlier, and many of those in the top part of Table 19.3 correspond to the figures shown in Table 13.3.

TABLE 19.2

Term structure of interest rates and volatilities

Exposure period (yrs)	Swap rate	Zero rate	Protection period (yrs)	Forward rate	Volatility
			0.0–0.5	1.500%	
0.0–0.5	1.500%	1.500%	0.5–1.0	2.506%	15.00%
0.0–1.0	2.000%	2.002%	1.0–1.5	3.371%	14.00%
0.0–1.5	2.450%	2.458%	1.5–2.0	4.094%	14.00%
0.0–2.0	2.850%	2.865%	2.0–2.5	4.672%	13.00%
0.0–2.5	3.200%	3.225%	2.5–3.0	5.101%	13.00%
0.0–3.0	3.500%	3.537%	3.0–3.5	5.339%	12.00%
0.0–3.5	3.745%	3.793%	3.5–4.0	5.531%	12.00%
0.0–4.0	3.950%	4.010%	4.0–4.5	5.744%	12.00%
0.0–4.5	4.130%	4.202%	4.5–5.0	5.930%	12.00%

TABLE 19.3

Example cap and floor premiums

	Maturity	Swap rate	Cap strike rates					Floor strike rates			
			4.0%	4.5%	5.0%	5.5%	6.0%	2.5%	3.0%	3.5%	4.0%
Up-front premiums (bp)	2yr	2.85%	17	7	2	1	0	5	27	64	116
	3yr	3.50%	104	61	33	17	8	5	27	66	122
	4yr	3.95%	231	151	94	55	31	5	28	66	125
	5yr	4.29%	384	268	180	116	72	5	28	67	128
	7yr	4.81%	745	563	414	297	210	5	28	68	133
Amortised premiums (bp)	2yr	2.85%	9	3	1	0	0	3	14	33	60
	3yr	3.50%	36	21	12	6	3	2	10	23	43
	4yr	3.95%	62	41	25	15	8	1	7	18	34
	5yr	4.29%	85	59	40	25	16	1	6	15	28
	7yr	4.81%	124	93	69	49	35	1	5	11	22

When evaluating cap premiums, it is important to compare the strike price with the swap rate, not the prevailing short-term rate. To do otherwise may give a misleading impression. With the term structure used here, short-term rates are 1.5%, and so the five-year cap struck at 5% may seem extremely out-of-the-money and therefore rather expensive at 180bp. Table 19.3 reveals, however, that the five-year swap rate is 4.29%, and the 4.5-year swap rate starting in six months is 4.63%, so the 5% cap is only slightly out-of-the-money. In fact, with the yield curve sloping steeply upwards, short-term rates may start low at 1.5%, but they are forecast to rise to almost 6% by the end of the five-year period covered by this particular cap. Early interest periods are likely to be out-of-the-money, but later periods are likely to be in-the-money.

As with all options, caps and floor premiums can be divided into two components: intrinsic value and time value. This is easier to appreciate if we study the amortised premiums rather than the up-front quotations. The five-year cap struck at 4% is quoted at 85bp p.a. Since the six-month forward 4.5-year swap rate is 4.63%, this premium can be split into 63bp of intrinsic value, and 22bp of time value. A few moments inspecting the figures in Table 19.3 will reveal that the time value component is greatest for caps struck at-the-money, as was explained in Chapter 11. This feature makes the long-dated at-the-money caps the most expensive.[1]

Evaluating the performance of a cap is a little more complex than evaluating IRGs, because of the multi-period nature of these products. In Figure 19.1 it was possible to show the complete cost/benefit relationship for an IRG by graphing the effective borrowing rate against the rate prevailing in the single period covered by the IRG. Two variables give rise to a two-dimensional graph that can be perfectly represented on a flat sheet of paper. To achieve the same completeness with a ten-period cap, the effective borrowing rate over the life of the cap would need to be evaluated simultaneously against the interest rates prevailing during each of the ten periods. A computer could produce the figures, but drawing the result would require eleven-dimensional graph paper, which would have been difficult to include within the usual three-dimensional covers of this book.

Thus, to evaluate cap performance, and to enable comparisons to be drawn between caps at different strike levels, we must restrict ourselves to a subset of possible rate scenarios. Figure 19.2 graphs the set of future six-month interest rates implied by the forward rates of Table 19.2, and shows two further paths: one in which rates rise at 40bp per year slower than the implied forward rates, and the other in which rates rise 40bp per year faster. For example, the six-month rate in 4½ years could either be 5.93% as the forward rate implies, 180bp lower at 4.13%, or 180bp higher at 7.73%. This range does not, by any means, encompass every conceivable path that interest rates could take, but it does cover the more probable outcomes. In fact, to accommodate more extreme moves in market rates, in the following analysis we will examine the impact of annual drift rates of up to ±60bp per year from the implied forward rates. Later in this chapter we shall analyse an even wider set of possible interest rate scenarios using Monte Carlo simulation.

Consider a company about to borrow for five years under a facility in which the interest rate is reset every six months based on the prevailing LIBOR rate. Using the range of interest rate scenarios discussed just now, we can assess the resultant exposure using different hedging strategies. Figure 19.3 shows the company's effective borrowing rate over the five-year period for caps struck at 4%, 4.5%, 5%, 5.5% and 6%, the premiums for which were tabulated in Table 19.3. As a comparison, the figure also shows the straight-line profiles which result from using a straight interest rate swap, or from the decision not to hedge at all. In every case the chart depicts the weighted average interest rate over the entire five-year period for every possible drift rate from –60bp p.a. to +60bp p.a. for each of the hedging strategies.

FIGURE 19.2

Alternative rate scenarios

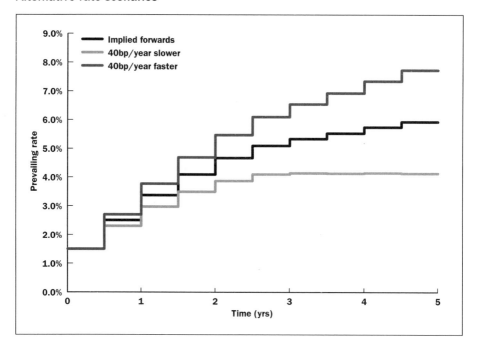

FIGURE 19.3

Effective borrowing rate using different caps

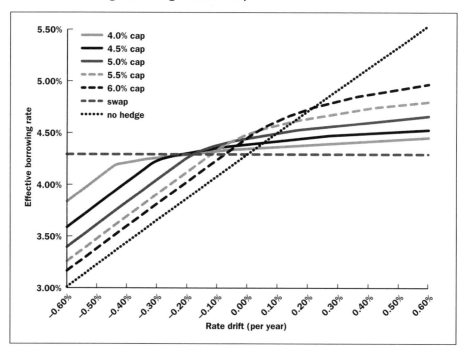

The most in-the-money cap – the one struck at 4% – exhibits a virtually flat characteristic almost identical with that of the swap. While it limits the maximum borrowing cost over a wide range, it is not so effective in allowing the borrower to benefit if rates stay low. Although this cap demands the biggest premium, equivalent to 85bp per annum, a considerable part of this is intrinsic value, and most of the caplets will expire in-the-money under most of the scenarios examined. The effective cost of the cap is therefore quite small, and the maximum effective borrowing cost is never higher than 4.45% for the rate scenarios considered, and can never exceed 4.58%.

This maximum cost can easily be deduced by applying the following reasoning. The worst possible scenario is for rates to rise above 4% after the first period; each caplet would then expire in-the-money, thereby capping the effective cost at 4.85%, the 4% strike rate plus the 85bp amortised cost of the cap premium. The rate for the very first period is already fixed at 1.50%, however, and this 2.50% (compared to the cap strike) saving spread over the ten periods of the loan is equivalent to 27bp p.a. The net maximum cost is therefore 4.85% – 0.27% = 4.58%.

In contrast, the most out-of-the-money 6% cap behaves much like the no-hedge strategy. The up-front premium is quite small, equivalent to just 16bp per annum, but the 6% strike rate offers little in the way of protection. Only if rates drift up do any of the caplets expire in-the-money, and even if rates drift up by the full 60bp annum considered here, this cap only provides a payoff in the last five interest periods.

In between these two extremes lie the other caps, which offer a compromise performance. The 5% cap requires an up-front premium of 180bp, equivalent to 40bp p.a., and provides 'disaster insurance' to limit the company's costs should interest rates rise this much. As is evident from Figure 19.2, however, only in the later periods of some of the upward-drifting rate scenarios is this likely to happen, so the protective nature of this cap is visible only to the right of Figure 19.3.

This range of behaviour, from the almost complete protection afforded by the 4% cap to the almost non-existent cover offered by the 6% cap, follows the same continuum of possibilities first seen with the currency option-based hedges discussed in Chapter 17. The only difference is that the cap graphs in Figure 19.3 are curved, while the currency option profiles comprise straight lines. The reason for this arises from the multi-period nature of caps.

With a single-period currency option there are just two discrete possibilities at maturity: the option will expire either out-of-the-money or in-the-money. If the former occurs, the option will not provide protection, and the diagonal profile of the underlying risk profile will be revealed. If the latter outcome happens, the option will offset the underlying risk, and the result will be the horizontal profile characteristic of a hedged risk. There will be a sharp transition from one profile to the other at the strike price of the option. With a multi-period cap, some of the caplets will expire in-the-money while some will not. As the drift parameter is increased, a greater proportion of the caplets will expire in-the-money, but there is no single point at which all the caplets suddenly switch from expiring out-of-the-money to expiring in-the-money. This means that the transition in behaviour from the diagonal out-of-the-money characteristic to the horizontal in-the-money profile is a gradual one.

19.3 Collars, participating caps, spread hedges and other variations

We have just seen the broad similarity between the behaviour of interest rate caps and that of the currency option products reviewed in Chapter 17. Indeed, it can be said that all option-based products behave in a similar way. Furthermore, techniques developed in one market can usually be applied in another. This section will explore some of the products which have started life as a tool for managing one kind of market risk, but have easily and successfully been applied to the management of interest rate risk.

One of the most common forms of interest rate protection nowadays is the collar, a concept first introduced in Chapter 13 (section 13.2), and then studied in greater depth in Chapter 17 (section 17.8) within the context of currency risk. Table 19.4 shows a variety of quotations for interest rate collars, and is split into two parts. The first part lists a set of collars where both the cap level and the floor level have been pre-specified, and the table shows the net premiums that must be paid. The second part illustrates a set of zero-cost collars where both the cap level and zero net premium have been pre-set, leaving the floor level as the remaining variable to be determined.

TABLE 19.4

Quotations for collars

	Net up-front premiums paid for specified collars (bp)			
Maturity	2.5% floor 5.5% cap	3% floor 5.5% cap	3% floor 6% cap	3.5% floor 6% cap
2yr	−5	−27	−27	−64
3yr	12	−11	19	−58
5yr	110	88	45	5
7yr	292	269	182	142

	Floor levels for zero-premium collars		
Maturity	5% cap	5.5% cap	6% cap
2yr	2.36%	2.20%	2.07%
3yr	3.09%	2.81%	2.60%
5yr	4.32%	3.91%	3.55%
7yr	4.79%	4.79%	4.42%

Starting with the figures on the top of Table 19.4 it is evident that most of the collars illustrated involve the payment of a net premium. For example, the five-year 3–5.5% collar requires a net payment up-front amounting to 88bp of the nominal principal, but this represents a saving of 24% when compared with the cost of the 5.5% cap alone. In return for this saving, after the first six months the collar buyer is obliged to borrow at a rate no less than the floor level, which in most of the cases illustrated has been set higher than present six-month rates. For example, any of the collars embodying a 3% floor will compel the buyer to borrow at 3% after the initial six-month period, even though the 6 × 12 forward rate at the outset is only 2.5%.

Some of the collar combinations illustrated actually have a negative net premium. This means that the collar buyer would actually receive the up-front payment from the bank, not the other way round. Although this might seem attractive, this situation can arise only if the protection purchased by the cap component is minimal while the savings opportunity sold under the floor component is substantial. For example, if interest rates followed the implied forward rates, the buyer of a 3.5–6% three-year collar would end up paying out under the collar for the 6–12-month and 12–18-month periods, and would never receive a payment from the collar seller. Against this would be the certain benefit of an up-front receipt of 58bp, equivalent to 20bp per year.

In many cases, companies using collars prefer not to have to balance up-front premium against future cash flows from the collar, but elect instead to purchase a zero-cost collar. The bottom part of Table 19.4 therefore shows a set of zero-cost collars where the floor level in each case has been adjusted so that the premium income from the floor sold exactly matches the premium cost of the cap purchased. For example, a three-year zero-cost collar incorporating a cap at 6% would involve selling a floor at 2.60%. Naturally, the more the cap is in-the-money, the higher the floor level will need to be in order to bring in sufficient premium income, thereby making the floor more in-the-money as well.

To illustrate the behaviour of these zero-cost collars, we can use the same set of rate scenarios that were used to produce Figure 19.3. The three five-year zero-cost collars listed in Table 19.4 were analysed to produce the set of graphs shown in Figure 19.4. Clearly visible is the characteristic of a collar whereby both maximum and minimum costs are limited. Once again, there is the by-now familiar continuum of possibilities with the profile of the out-of-the-money 3.55–6% collar looking very much like the diagonal no-hedge profile at one extreme, and the close-to-the-money 4.32–5% collar very much resembling the horizontal swap profile at the other.

Another idea transferred from the currency markets is the idea of a participating cap. This idea was explained in Chapter 17 (section 17.10) under the heading *participating forward*, which is the name given to the equivalent FX product. A full description of how this product works can be found in that section, but in the context of an interest rate hedge it can be built by buying a cap and selling a floor at the same strike rate, but with the nominal principal of the floor adjusted to create a zero-cost combination. Table 19.5 gives some examples of participating caps with different strike levels and participation rates.

FIGURE 19.4

Effective borrowing rate using different zero-cost collars

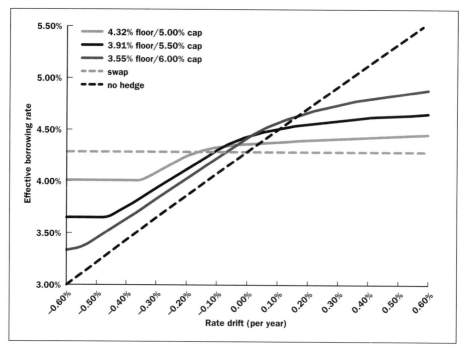

TABLE 19.5

Participating cap quotations

cap/floor strike rate	cap price	floor price	cap amount	floor amount	cap:floor price ratio	participation rate
5%	180	328	1,000,000	547,542	0.55	45%
5.5%	116	466	1,000,000	248,162	0.25	75%
6%	72	624	1,000,000	115,523	0.12	88%

As an example, the first participating cap shown will cap the borrower's costs if LIBOR rises above 5%, and will allow him to enjoy 45% of the savings in any period if interest rates fall below that level. Moreover, the participating cap will cost the borrower nothing in the way of premium. If six-month LIBOR was 6% in one period, the borrower would pay interest based on a LIBOR of just 5%. If LIBOR was 4%, the borrower would pay 4.55%, receiving 45% of the 100bp reduction below the strike rate.

Figure 19.5 illustrates the performance of these participating caps. At first glance, the picture looks very similar to the previous figure. Participations exhibit the same kind of transition from the swap-like nature of the 45% participating cap, to the 88% participation which is much closer to the no-hedge profile. There is a difference in shape however. A zero-cost collar limits the

FIGURE 19.5

Effective borrowing rate using different participating caps

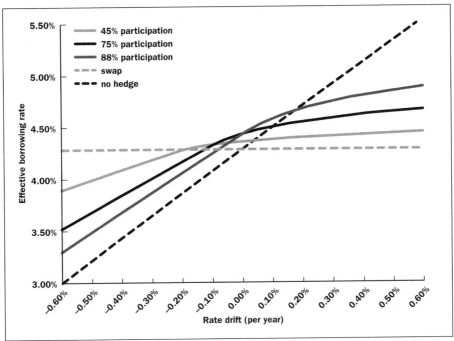

effective borrowing cost both on the upside and the downside, but allows the borrower to benefit fully from any drop in interest rates between the two strike prices. A participating cap limits the effective borrowing costs only on the upside, allowing unlimited ability to benefit from a fall in interest rates, but offering the borrower only a proportion of these savings.

Many other combinations are possible, and the possibilities using option-based products like caps and floors are almost limitless. The next few paragraphs provide some ideas.

A *spread* could be constructed by buying a cap at one strike and selling a cap at a higher strike. For example, buying a 5% five-year cap and selling a 6% five-year cap would result in a net up-front premium of 108bp, a 40% saving over the basic cost of the 5% cap. Only if rates rose substantially would the borrower be forced to pay out on the 6% cap, and even then the receipt under the 5% cap would reduce the effective borrowing cost in that period by 1%.

The spread just discussed is a vertical option spread, where the options are bought and sold with the same maturity but a different strike. An alternative strategy for the borrower is to use a horizontal spread, buying a cap for one maturity, and selling a cap with the same strike rate but for a different maturity. For example, suppose a borrower believed that interest rates would follow the path predicted by the implied forward rates shown in Table 19.2, and therefore thought that six-month rates will eventually rise above 5%, but only after 2½ years. Buying a five-year cap struck at 5% would cost 180bp up-front, but simultaneously selling a three-year cap at the same strike rate would bring in 33bp, thereby lowering the net premium to 147bp and achieving a saving of 18%. If rates follow the path predicted, the cap sold would only negate the savings provided by the cap bought in its final period from 2.5–3.0 years; thereafter the cap bought would limit the borrowing rate to 5% from the beginning of the third year onwards.

Another way to look at this combination is to consider it as a *deferred-start cap*, for that is exactly what it is. For the first three years, the long and short cap positions cancel exactly, leaving a two-year cap deferred by three years. This is one example of using financial engineering techniques to construct a hedge which better matches a borrower's needs.

Another example of fine tuning can be witnessed in the form of a *step-up cap* or a *step-up floor*, where the strike rates increase during the lifetime of the instrument. A borrower may be better able to afford a higher borrowing rate in the future, but still require protection against a very substantial hike in interest rates. With the set of rates shown in Table 19.2, a standard five-year 5% cap would cost 180bp. However, if the strike rate was set to 5% for the first caplet period (from six months to one year) and was set 25bp higher each period during the lifetime of the cap, culminating at 7% for the final caplet (from 4½ years to 5 years), the cap premium would in this case fall to just 44bp, a saving of 76%. Of course, the buyer of a step-up cap does not get something for nothing. The lower premium buys a lesser degree of protection, and none of the caplets would expire in-the-money if rates followed the implied forwards. In the case of a downward sloping yield curve, *step-down caps* and *step-down floors* would be alternative possibilities.

In Chapter 17 (section 17.11) we saw that a ratio forward was an extension of the participating forward, but using strike prices the other side of the prevailing market rate. The same idea can be extended to caps and floors. Table 19.5 tabulated participation rates for participating caps with strike rates all being above the six-month forward 4.5-year swap rate used in the example of 4.63%. If a ratio forward struck at 4.5% was created, the gearing ratio would be 1.25 times, but this would secure a better-than-market borrowing rate of 4.27% assuming interest rates followed the implied forward curve. With the strike rate reduced to 3.5%, the effective rate would drop even more to 4.11%, which is 18bp below the prevailing swap rate. Unfortunately, the gearing ratio would have risen to an alarming 7.8 times, something that neither the borrower nor his bankers would wisely accept.

Other variations are possible, including the potential to use exotic options like those described in Chapter 13 (section 13.7 onwards). Some of the possibilities are discussed in the following paragraphs.

An *average rate cap* compensates borrowers using a floating rate facility under which the rate can be altered at any time, not just on reset dates. A perfect example would be a customer borrowing using a loan facility linked to the bank's base or prime rate. The average rate cap, sometimes known as a *base rate cap*, will provide compensation for any periods when the bank's base rate exceeds the pre-determined strike rate, in return for an up-front premium payment.

Barrier caps which incorporate a trigger rate are an interesting variation. In an upward-sloping yield curve environment, an up-and-in barrier cap features a trigger rate set higher than the cap rate. This type of cap is not triggered unless interest rates rise through the trigger rate, at which point the product operates as a normal cap. Another variation is the down-and-out cap, which is extinguished if rates reach a trigger level set below current rates. Both forms of barrier option result in premium savings, and operate on the principle that interest rates often tend to trend rather than to fluctuate at a given level. Thus, if an up-and-in barrier cap is triggered, the protection is most likely to be needed thereafter, while the protection provided by a down-and-out barrier cap is probably no longer required after being extinguished if rates fall.

Pay-later or *self-funding caps* also exist and have the advantage that they cost nothing up-front. The premium for such caps is always quoted on an amortised basis, and is only paid in those periods when the cap is in-the-money. If the protection was not needed, the pay-later cap therefore comes free and no premium need therefore have been wasted for protection that turned out to be unnecessary. However, as we saw in Chapter 13 (section 13.9), the premium for a pay-later option is much greater than for a standard option, something like double the price for an at-the-money option. A borrower should therefore consider a pay-later cap only if he believes that, if rates rise, they will rise substantially above the cap rate, and not merely hover around that level.

19.4 Using captions and swaptions

Caps and swaps provide two different styles of interest rate protection; options on these products add yet another dimension. Captions and swaptions can be used in a variety of situations, but they are particularly relevant for:

- contingent situations
- providing cheap rate protection
- handling embedded debt options
- extending or curtailing swaps
- speculation.

We will discuss each of these applications in turn.

Contingent situations

There are many instances when a company's need for interest rate protection is contingent on some external factor beyond its control. One common example is when a company is tendering for some project, where the success or failure of the tender will dictate whether finance will be raised, and hence whether rate protection is required. Another example arises in takeover situations, when financing of the proposed acquisition and the accompanying hedging programme will both be dependent on the success of the bid.

Under these circumstances, entering into a deferred-start swap or buying a deferred-start cap may not be ideal. The swap would bind the company into a series of contractual payments, which would be totally unnecessary if the bid or tender fails. While there is no compulsion to exercise a cap, the up-front premium would be a substantial and wasted expense if the contingency did not arise.

Buying a swaption, or an option into a cap, may well provide the company with the contingent protection that it needs at a substantially reduced price. Table 19.6 reveals prices for three comparable products: a six-month swaption into a four-year swap, a four-year cap deferred six months, and a six-month caption into a four-year cap. All of these would be suitable choices for a company with a contingent borrowing requirement of four years commencing in six months' time. The products have been priced using the rates presented in Table 19.2, and two representative strike levels have been used. The first is 4.49%, which is the price for a four-year swap deferred six months, and is therefore at-the-money for all the products. The second is set to 5.00%, a little out-of-the-money.

TABLE 19.6

Comparison of swaption, deferred cap and caption premiums

	strike rate = 4.49%	strike rate = 5.00%
swaption	69bp	15bp
deferred cap	209bp	134bp
caption	36bp	27bp

If the company entered into a deferred swap contract, this would obligate it to make fixed payments at 4.49% over the four-year period. Not only are these higher than the prevailing six-month rates, the company may not even require the floating-rate finance if the particular contingency did not arise. An at-the-money swaption gives the company the right to enter into the deferred swap, but not the obligation. After six months, the company could exercise the swaption if the underlying borrowing requirement did arise, and if swap rates were higher than the 4.49% strike rate at the time. The up-front payment of just 69bp is probably an acceptable price to pay for this type of interest rate protection.

Buying the deferred cap meets with the same objection as the swap contract, in that the protection may not be needed if the contingency did not transpire. The 209bp up-front premium may also be daunting as an up-front expense, particularly if the protection turned out not to be needed. Against this is the possibility that the company could sell the cap after six months if it proved surplus to requirements.

The cheapest form of rate protection is the caption, at least in terms of up-front expense. At just 36bp it is around half the price of the swaption, and less than one-fifth the price of the deferred cap. It gives the company the opportunity to buy a cap at 209bp should the need arise, or to take advantage of lower cap prices if interest rates or volatility levels fall over the initial six-month period. The underlying cap is also an effective risk management tool, providing protection against the possibility of higher rates, while allowing the company to benefit from lower borrowing costs if interest rates stay low. The only drawback is that the total cost of the cap would be 245bp if the caption is exercised, which is 17% more than the cost of buying the deferred cap initially.

Providing cheap rate protection

Some borrowers may look to swaptions and captions as a low-cost means of securing protection against higher interest rates. Paradoxically, this view is valid only if the borrower believes that the protection will *not* be needed. Buying an underlying instrument through exercising an option is always more expensive than buying that instrument at the outset. This is because all option premiums comprise time value as well as intrinsic value, and the time value component is never recovered if the option is exercised or held to maturity. So if a borrower believes there is a good chance that a swaption or caption will be exercised, it is usually better to buy the underlying instrument to begin with. In the example just cited, the swaption buyer pays a 69bp up-front premium for the right to enter into the swap, yet there would be no cost at all if the borrower entered into the deferred swap instead. The same principle is true with the caption, where the caption premium of 36bp is over and above the 209bp cost of the underlying cap, which must be paid if the cap is eventually bought.

Suppose a borrower believes that interest rates, though they may rise, will not rise as fast as predicted by the implied forward rates. Entering into a swap would be expensive, because the swap is priced as the weighted average of the forward rates, which the borrower believes are too high. Better to use a swaption or a caption, which can be exercised if the borrower's view proves wrong, but can be discarded otherwise and advantage taken of the lower market rates.

To give a specific example, consider a company borrowing for five years when market rates are as shown in Table 19.2. Suppose the company believes that forward rates will climb gradually to 4%, not the 5.93% implied by the forward yield curve. Now compare the strategy of entering into a five-year swap at 4.29% with buying a one-year swaption into a four-year swap struck at the same rate. The swaption premium would be 249bp in this case. The swap would lock the borrower into an effective rate of 4.29% regardless of interest rates over the next five years. The swaption would allow the borrower to take advantage of the much lower rates prevailing initially, and then to exercise the swaption only if rates did not turn out as planned.

With the swaption, if the borrower's view was correct, the effective borrowing cost would average out to 3.91% after taking the swaption premium into account. This represents a saving of 38bp compared with the swap strategy. Even if the company's view proves incorrect and the swaption is then exercised, the effective borrowing cost rises to 4.32%, just 3bp over the original swap rate. This low incremental cost is because nearly all the 249bp swaption premium in this case is intrinsic value, so the effective cost is very low. Moreover, being able to borrow at an average rate of 2.00% in the first year saves 229bp when compared with the swap rate of 4.29%, and this saving represents around 90% of the cost of the swaption. The only danger with the swaption strategy is if rates stayed low initially, so that the swaption was not exercised, and then rose later when the company would have no rate protection in place.

Handling embedded debt options

Corporate bonds frequently incorporate a call provision allowing the issuer to repay the debt prematurely if interest rates fall. This is particularly true when interest rates are high. A typical bond issue might have a maturity of ten years, but be callable on any coupon date after the first three years. In effect, the bond investors have sold the bond issuer a call option on the debt, and this is embedded into the bond. The issuer can use a swaption to monetise this option, thus releasing its value.

Suppose a large company has just issued a seven-year fixed-rate bond callable after two years. The company can now sell a two-year receiver's swaption exercisable into a five-year swap, with a strike rate equal to the bond coupon. If interest rates have fallen below the coupon rate in two years' time, the company will call the bond and refinance by issuing an FRN at the lower rates then available. At the same time, the swaption will be exercised against the company so that it becomes the fixed-rate payer under the swap. The net result is that the company ends up paying fixed coupons at the same rate as before, but has retained the up-front swaption premium. If rates stay high, the bond is not called and the swaption expires worthless. Either way, the company will continue to pay fixed coupons at the original rate, but receives an up-front premium equivalent to the value of the embedded option.

Extending or curtailing swaps

Borrowers may sometimes require an option to extend or curtail the maturity of an existing swap. This can easily be achieved with a swaption. Suppose a borrower is currently the fixed-rate payer on a swap with three years until maturity, but he needs the option to extend this for a further two years. Buying a three-year payer's swaption into a two-year swap, with a strike rate equal to the fixed-rate on the existing swap, will exactly fulfil the borrower's requirement. Another borrower paying the fixed rate on a five-year swap, but needing the ability to shorten the maturity to three years, can buy a three-year receiver's swaption into a two-year swap, with a strike rate equal to that of the original swap. If the swap needs to be curtailed, the borrower exercises the swaption and enters into a new swap whose cash flows cancel those of the original one. Chapter 13 (section 13.4) explained the mechanics of these *cancellable* or *extendible* swaps in some detail, together with examples of a three-year swap extendible by two years, and of the equivalent five-year swap cancellable after three years.

A variation of this is the *collapsible swap*, which is analogous to the break-forward contract examined in Chapter 17 (section 17.12). A company planning to borrow in the future may wish to protect against a rise in interest rates, but may also want to benefit in case rates fall. One solution would simply be to buy a payer's swaption, but this involves an up-front premium. An alternative is to enter into a deferred-start swap as the fixed-rate payer, and simultaneously buy a receiver's swaption having the effect of cancelling this swap. To finance the receiver's swaption, the deferred-start swap is executed at an off-market rate. If rates rise, the company continues with the swap agreement, allowing the swaption to expire worthless. If rates fall, the company executes the swaption to cancel the swap, and enters into a new swap at the lower market rates. Note that a swap cancellation fee will nevertheless be chargeable, as the swaption strike rate was set to the market rate of the deferred-start swap, but the actual swap was done at an off-market rate.

Notice the difference between cancellable swaps on the one hand, and collapsible swaps on the other.

■ With a cancellable swap, the user enters into the swap immediately at a slightly off-market rate, but has the right on some future date to cancel the swap at no further cost, thereby curtailing its maturity. As an example, using the Table 19.2 rates, the vanilla five-year swap rate is 4.29%, but a five-year swap cancellable after one year by the fixed payer could be executed at 4.35%.

■ With a collapsible swap, the user agrees to enter into a deferred swap, but has the right to collapse (or cancel) the swap on the effective date by paying a pre-arranged fixed fee. As an example, using the same set of market rates a four-year swap deferred by one year would be priced at 4.93%, but the same swap with a collapsible feature could be executed at 5.22%, with a cancellation fee of 107bp.

Speculation

While this book is not primarily concerned with the use of financial engineering tools as vehicles for speculation, derivative instruments are often attractive in view of the gearing they offer. Buying option-based products can be particularly effective because of their limited cost, limited downside risk, and unlimited upside potential, and swaptions are no exception. A speculator believing that interest rates will rise could buy a payer's swaption. For instance, a one-year payer's swaption into a four-year swap struck at 5.00% might cost 93bp in up-front premium. If four-year swap rates rise to 6% after one year, the swaption could be cash-settled for 351bp, a profit of 277%. If rates stay steady or fall, the most that the speculator could lose would be the swaption premium.

19.5 Comparison of interest risk management tools

The availability of FRAs, futures, swaps, IRGs, caps, floors, collars, captions and swaptions, to name just the standard products now available, provides a bewildering choice of risk management tools for those exposed to interest rate risk. As an initial guide through this maze, Table 19.7 provides a summary of the major characteristics for each of these products. Most of the table is self-explanatory, except perhaps for the terms used to describe the type of protection. The expression *fixed* means that the effective rate obtained is absolutely certain, regardless of the way in which interest rates evolve. *Selective* means that the borrower or investor will receive protection against the downside, while retaining the ability to benefit from the upside.

Which is the best tool to use in any given situation depends very much on the user's hedging objectives, as set out in Chapter 16 (section 16.4) under four specific headings:

- wish to obtain complete protection against all rate movements
- relative preference for upside savings compared with desire to avoid downside risk
- aversion to paying for risk protection
- client's view of market developments.

TABLE 19.7

Comparison of interest rate risk management tools

	Periods covered	Number of exercise opportunities	Maturities available	Type of protection
FRAs	single	–	up to 2 yrs	fixed
futures	single	–	up to 10 yrs	fixed
swaps	multiple	–	up to 30 yrs	fixed
IRGs	single	1	up to 2 yrs	selective
caps, floors and collars	multiple	many	up to 10 yrs	selective
swaptions	single/multiple*	1	up to 10 yrs	selective
captions	single/multiple*	1/many*	up to 10 yrs	selective

*The second term applies if and when the option is exercised.

We will review each of these in turn to determine how they influence a user's choice.

Complete protection

If complete certainty is required, the choice is straightforward: use FRAs and futures to cover short-term exposures, or swaps for longer-term ones. It is as simple as that.

Upside vs. downside

The moment that a user wishes to obtain protection against the downside risk while preserving some upside opportunities, an option-based solution is dictated. If the risk is short-term, selecting an IRG with the strike rate chosen to balance protection, benefits and premium cost should provide an acceptable solution. Alternatively, a combination of IRGs to create a collar, spread-hedge, participation or some other variation, may deliver a more attractive package of benefits for the user. For longer-dated risks, similar considerations apply, but using the multi-period versions of these products. Thus, a cap, collar, spread-hedge or participating cap will deliver the same kind of trade-offs.

Paying for protection

If the desired form of risk management solution is considered too expensive, there are various choices. A reduced-cost or zero-cost product like a collar or participation may deliver the required level of protection, and be financed by the sale of some of the profit opportunities. If the preferred choice was to buy a cap, then a caption may provide a cheaper route in, at least initially. Similarly, a swaption is a low-cost alternative to the swap. Note the warning given earlier: if a caption or swaption is eventually exercised, the total cost will be more expensive than if the underlying instrument had been bought at the outset.

View of the market

With interest rate risk, particularly one that extends over several years, the user's view of the market is actually quite crucial in designing the optimal hedge. The key is to compare the user's opinion on how interest rates will develop over the exposure period with the view of the market, namely the implied forward rates. Note that it is the set of implied forward rates that sets the benchmark for all floating-rate finance and investment, not the swap rates, nor the current short-term rate. We will analyse the three different possibilities that could occur:

- The user believes that rates will rise faster than the implied forward curve.
- The user believes that rates will rise, but more slowly than the implied forward curve.
- The user believes that rates will follow the path of the implied forward curve, more or less.

Figure 19.6 illustrates these scenarios using an upward-sloping yield curve, and the detailed discussion will concentrate on the strategies that a borrower might be expected to follow. However, Tables 19.8 to 19.10 summarise the conclusions of the analysis for investors as well as borrowers, and the findings can be generalised for the less common environments in which the yield curve slopes down.

View – rates will rise faster than implied forwards

In this case, a borrower will certainly need protection against higher interest rates, and a swap will be preferable to a cap for two reasons. First, the swap is priced as the weighted average of the implied forward rates, and will therefore seem cheap when compared to the forward rates envisaged by the borrower. Second, the time value of a cap gives the borrower the right to exercise each caplet, or indeed the right not to. If the borrower believes that rates will rise faster than the market, he is fairly certain to exercise a substantial majority of the caplets. Paying for the right not to exercise them is therefore of little value, and a waste of premium expense.

FIGURE 19.6
Alternative views of market rates

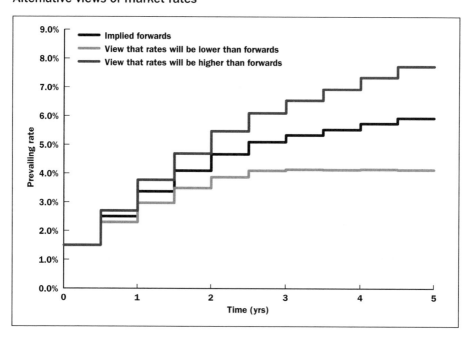

As an adjunct to entering into a swap as the fixed-rate payer, the borrower could also sell a floor, and use the premium income to lower the effective borrowing cost. This would be done in the expectation that most of the floorlets would not be exercised. With a rising yield curve, however, the floor level would have to be set fairly high in order to bring in sufficient up-front premium to make this worthwhile. Note that such a strategy actually reverses the direction of the borrower's exposure, resulting in a higher effective borrowing cost when rates are lower. This is perhaps most easily understood if one thinks of a pay-fixed swap as being equivalent to buying a cap and selling a floor at the same strike rate. The floor component of the swap neutralises the benefit of lower interest rates on the borrower's original exposure. Selling another floor turns the benefit of lower rates into a cost. This strategy is therefore only to be advised if the borrower has a strong view that rates will move up quickly and sharply.

A third possibility is to buy a zero-cost participating cap with a low strike rate, and therefore a low participation rate. Given the view that rates will rise faster than the implied forwards, the low participation rate is no disadvantage, and the low strike rate will provide protection at a rate close to the prevailing swap rate.

View – rates will rise more slowly than implied forwards

A borrower holding this view would find a swap expensive, for it locks him into a fixed rate based on a forecast of forward rates which he believes is too high. Buying a cap, collar or spread-hedge is much better in this instance, because it provides protection against the eventuality that the borrower's view could be wrong, but does not lock him into an unattractive rate. If a collar is chosen, care must be taken not to set the floor level too high, otherwise the borrower will fail to benefit from his view that rates will stay lower than the forward curve.

An alternative to buying a cap is to buy a payer's swaption, which will invariably be cheaper. If rates rise unexpectedly by the exercise date, the borrower can exercise the swaption and become the fixed-rate payer under the swap. Note that the swaption provides less flexibility than the cap. If the swaption is exercised, the borrower becomes locked into a fixed rate, and is unable thereafter to benefit from any subsequent falls in market rates. Potentially worse is the scenario in which rates stay low until after the maturity date, so that the swaption is not exercised, and then rise sharply thereafter when the borrower has no rate protection in place. A cap, by contrast, provides flexible rate protection throughout the period exposed to risk.

Similar in some ways to the swaption is the strategy of buying a caption, and this presents a third possibility. Being less expensive than the swaption, this choice is potentially the best, provided that rates do stay low and the caption is not exercised. However, the caption strategy is vulnerable to the same pitfall as the swaption strategy if rates stay low on the exercise date, and then rise thereafter leaving the borrower without protection.

View – rates will follow the implied forward curve

This heading would also include the borrower who professes to have no view about the future evolution of interest rates. In this case, the broad choice is between a swap and zero-cost solutions like the zero-cost collar or participating cap. A low-cost alternative like a spread-hedge may also be attractive. All of these will provide similar outcomes if rates do in fact follow the path suggested by the set of implied forward rates. Neither captions nor swaptions would be recommended here; buying either of these other than at-the-money would provide too little protection to be worthwhile, and buying them at-the-money will be expensive if rates stay 'static', i.e. if they simply follow the track of the forward rates.

Table 19.8 summarises these recommendations, not only from the borrower's viewpoint as discussed so far, but also from the viewpoint of the investor or lender. As is apparent, there is symmetry between the optimal strategies: where the borrower would buy a cap, the investor would buy a floor, and so on.

TABLE 19.8

Recommended strategies for hedging interest rate risk

View	Borrower strategy	Investor strategy
Rates will be lower than implied forward curve	buy cap	swap (fixed-rate receiver)
	buy collar	swap and sell cap
	buy cap spread-hedge	buy participating floor
	buy payers swaption	
	buy caption	
Rates will follow implied forward curve	swap (fixed-rate payer)	swap (fixed-rate receiver)
	buy zero-cost collar	sell zero-cost collar
	buy cap spread-hedge	buy floor spread-hedge
	buy participating cap	buy participating floor
Rates will be higher than implied forward curve	swap (fixed-rate payer)	buy floor
	swap and sell floor	sell collar
	buy participating cap	buy floor spread-hedge
		buy receivers swaption
		buy floortion

To provide a numerical basis for objective comparison, it is helpful to carry out a *scenario analysis*, in which the performances of different hedging strategies are compared against a number of possible rate scenarios. Using the three scenarios pictured in Figure 19.6, Table 19.9 shows the effective borrowing cost under ten different hedging schemes, while Table 19.10 shows the equivalent strategies and resultant returns for an investor. In every case, the figures apply to a five-year exposure using the initial set of rates shown in Table 19.2. Recommended strategies are shown in bold, and confirm the suggestions made in Table 19.8. Note also that the swap, collar and participations consistently provide some of the safest and cheapest hedging strategies, with the least variation in outcomes irrespective of the scenario.

TABLE 19.9

Scenario analysis showing effective borrowing costs using different hedging strategies

	Amortised net premium	Low-rate scenario	Neutral scenario	High-rate scenario	Range
Do nothing	–	3.44%	4.29%	5.13%	1.69%
Swap (fixed-rate payer)	–	4.29%	**4.29%**	**4.29%**	0.00%
Swap and sell 3.5% floor	–15	4.33%	**4.26%**	**4.23%**	0.10%
Buy 5.0% cap	40	3.83%	4.44%	4.60%	0.77%
Buy 6.0% cap	16	**3.59%**	4.45%	4.87%	1.27%
Buy 3.5% to 6.0% collar	1	**3.63%**	**4.42%**	4.81%	1.17%
Buy participating cap at 5% (45% share)	0	4.09%	**4.36%**	**4.42%**	0.34%
Spread-hedge: buy 5% cap and sell 6% cap	24	**3.67%**	**4.28%**	4.85%	1.18%
Buy 1yr payers swaption → 4yr 5.0% swap	20	**3.64%**	4.49%	4.57% [a]	0.93%
Buy 1yr caption → 4yr 5.0% cap	8	**3.52%**	4.37%	4.67% [a]	1.15%
Average		3.80%	4.37%	4.64%	

[a] exercised

These scenario analyses enable a user to compare different hedging strategies under identical conditions. They have the great advantage that the analyses are relatively easy to carry out, and that the sequences of rates selected can reflect the set of particular outcomes considered most likely or most feared by the user. However, they cannot give the complete picture because they concentrate on a very small number of possibilities.

A more comprehensive analysis can be undertaken using Monte Carlo analysis in conjunction with a yield curve model, which will generate sequences of interest rates for evaluating alternative hedging schemes. It would be practically impossible to consider every conceivable scenario, not only because there are an infinite number of possibilities, but also because the precise probabilities for every rate sequence are unknown. However, a well-constructed Monte Carlo analysis can provide the user with an idea of the distribution of outcomes going far beyond those obtainable from particular scenario analyses.

TABLE 19.10

Scenario analysis showing effective investment returns using different hedging strategies

	Amortised net premium	Low-rate scenario	Neutral scenario	High-rate scenario	Range
Do nothing	–	3.44%	4.29%	5.13%	1.69%
Swap (fixed-rate receiver)	–	**4.29%**	**4.29%**	4.29%	**0.00%**
Swap and sell 4.5% cap	−59	**4.87%**	**4.39%**	3.66%	1.22%
Buy 3.0% floor	6	3.46%	4.28%	**5.10%**	1.64%
Buy 3.5% floor	15	3.48%	4.26%	**5.06%**	1.59%
Sell 3.5% to 6.0% collar	−1	3.63%	**4.42%**	**4.81%**	**1.17%**
Buy participating floor at 4% (67% share)	0	**3.77%**	4.25%	4.77%	**1.00%**
Spread-hedge: buy 4% floor and sell 3% floor	22	3.50%	4.24%	**5.04%**	1.54%
Buy 1yr receivers swaption → 4yr 4.5% swap	9	**3.85%** [a]	4.20%	**5.03%**	1.18%
Buy 1yr floortion → 4yr 4.5% floor	5	3.64% [a]	4.24%	**5.07%**	1.43%
Average		3.79%	4.29%	4.79%	

[a] exercised

Such an analysis was undertaken to evaluate the performance of five distinct hedging schemes for a borrower: no hedge in place, a 4.29% swap, a 5% cap, a 3.55–6% zero-cost collar, and a participating cap at 5%. 500,000 rate sequences were generated at random, all starting with six-month rates at 1.5%, and an expectation of rising interest rates over the next five years. The six-month rates in the final period were normally distributed with a mean of 6.08% and a standard deviation of 1.78%, but intermediate rates could be higher or lower. Figure 19.7 illustrates three typical rate sequences.

The effective borrowing cost under each scheme was recorded for every rate sequence, and the outcomes analysed to produce the set of results summarised in Table 19.11, and illustrated in Figure 19.8. We can interpret these figures in the following way:

i)   The narrowest range of outcomes is generated by the swap, of course, which fixes the borrower's costs at 4.29% regardless of the interest rate environment.

ii) The widest range of outcomes naturally occurs when no hedge is in place. Although the mean result is the same as that of the swap hedge, there can be more than a ±4% swing from this average result.

FIGURE 19.7

Illustrative sequences for six-month interest rates

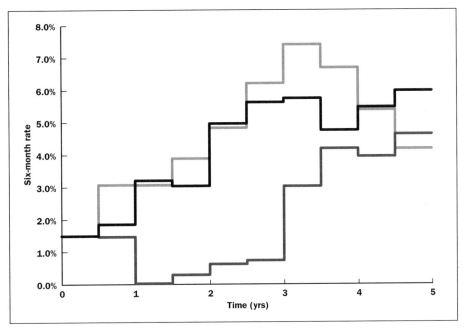

iii) Next widest comes the cap, where the effect of the cap premium sets the maximum effective borrowing cost to 5.01%. This extreme outcome occurs if rates rise above the cap rate of 5% after the first interest period, and stay above this level for the remainder of the borrowing. If rates fall, the cap allows the borrower to benefit without any penalty other than the cost of the cap premium.

iv) The collar has the advantage of being a zero-cost product, but the higher cap level selected means that the maximum borrowing rate is somewhat higher than for the 5% cap. The mean rate is also higher, reflecting the upward bias used in the rate scenarios generated. If rates fall, the collar allows savings until the floor is reached at 3.55%, denying the borrower any further benefit beyond that point.

v) Finally, in this example the participating cap outperforms the collar. As the participating cap rate was set at 5%, the maximum borrowing rate is much lower than that of the 3.55–6% collar. The worst case, as with the straight cap, is when rates rise immediately after the first period. However, the participating cap outperforms the straight cap under those circumstances, because of its zero net premium. The participating cap is only inferior to its plain-vanilla cousin under very low rate scenarios, in which the straight cap is unencumbered by the need to share savings with the participating cap counterparty. Note, however, that the range of possible outcomes is the narrowest other than for the swap itself.

TABLE 19.11

Performance summary under Monte Carlo analysis for five hedging strategies

	No hedge	Swap	Cap	Collar	Participating cap
Minimum rate	0.45%	4.29%	0.81%	3.33%	2.75%
Maximum rate	9.35%	4.29%	5.01%	5.48%	4.61%
Mean rate	4.29%	4.29%	4.13%	4.34%	4.22%
Standard deviation	1.01%	0.00%	0.59%	0.49%	0.26%

The full set of distributions is shown in Figure 19.8, which makes it much easier to make a visual comparison between the various alternatives. The shape of these probability profiles, and the relative degree of uncertainty associated with each strategy, may help borrowers and investors choose from among the different hedging schemes. This is one of the advantages of the Monte Carlo technique.

FIGURE 19.8

Probability distribution for different hedging strategies

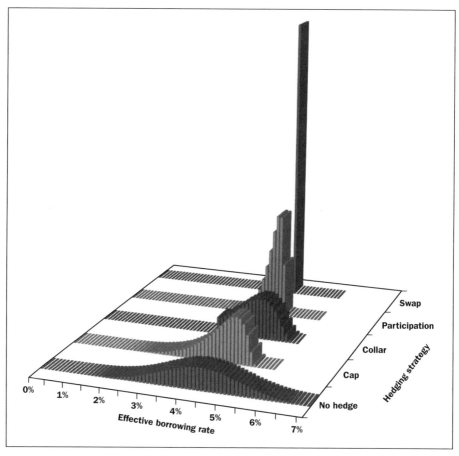

Note

1 The word *expensive* should be interpreted carefully here. In-the-money options cost more than at-the-money ones, but the buyer obtains intrinsic value which will be preserved if the underlying price does not change. Paying for something which is durable is not expensive. Time value, on the other hand, will always decay to zero at maturity. Paying for something which will eventually become worthless is expensive.

20

MANAGING EQUITY RISK

Equity risk manifests itself as a variation in the value of individual shares, or that of an equity portfolio. This is essentially a price risk, as indeed is currency risk. The methods used to manage equity risk therefore have much in common with those discussed in Chapter 17 for handling currency risk. As we proceed though the various risk management techniques in this chapter, the close parallels will be readily apparent.

We will start by presenting methods for taking advantage of anticipated movements in share prices, but without resorting to the purchase of the shares themselves. The next sections will discuss ways of handling the risk arising from holdings of individual shares, demonstrating both aggressive and conservative strategies. All the examples describe a mythically named company called Azco, but all the option prices are based on the quoted prices of a real company whose shares were trading at 100p at the time.

Later sections will progress to equity portfolios and explain how index derivatives and option replication strategies may be used. Option-based techniques will feature prominently throughout because of the relatively wide availability of stock and stock index options, and the great flexibility which these tools confer.

20.1 Bull and bear strategies

The simplest strategy for an investor who is bullish about the prospects for a particular company's shares is to buy the shares outright. However, if options on these shares are available, a range of other possibilities are opened up, including:

- buying call options
- buying a bull spread
- a '90:10' strategy.

Similarly, the bearish investor can buy put options or a bear spread. In none of these cases is it necessary to buy or sell the underlying shares; the positions are all created through the purchase and sale of stock options. We will examine each of the bull strategies in turn; the bear strategies do not warrant individual attention because they are simply the mirror images of the corresponding bull strategy.

Buying call options

Buying a call option will enable the purchaser to benefit from a rise in the underlying share price, but to be protected from a fall. The broad choice is between options which are out-, at- or in-the-money, and this is probably best seen graphically. Suppose that Azco's shares are currently trading at 100p, three-month at-the-money call options are priced at 4½p, and out-of-the-money calls struck at 110p are priced at 1p for a similar maturity. Figure 20.1 compares the strategy of buying the shares outright, buying the calls struck at

100p, and buying the 110p calls. In each case, the quantity of shares under consideration is 100,000, and the underlying price moves shortly after the strategy is put in place.

In straight money terms, buying the shares outright outperforms either of the option strategies. This may seem surprising at first sight, because options are normally thought of as highly geared instruments. However, Figure 20.1 compares the financial performance of the shares with that of options on the same *number* of shares, not the same *value* of shares. Apart from options which are completely in-the-money, the value of an option will always change by less than the value of the underlying shares, this sensitivity being described by the option's delta. For a rise in share price of 10p, the two options illustrated here will rise by 7½p and 4p respectively. Similarly, if the share price falls by 10p, the two options will fall by 3½p and 1p. These figures give rise to the monetary gains and losses illustrated in Figure 20.1, remembering that the diagram graphs the performance based on a portfolio of 100,000 shares.

The gearing becomes more obvious if we graph the percentage gain and loss of the three strategies, and this is shown in Figure 20.2. For a ±10% increase in the share price, the at-the-money option shows a swing from an 81% loss to a 163% gain, while the out-of-the-money option goes from an 82% loss to an impressive 214% gain. Investors tempted by the last strategy should remember that although huge gains are indeed possible, the most likely outcome when buying an out-of-the-money option and holding it until maturity is that it will expire worthless, giving rise to a 100% loss.

FIGURE 20.1

Comparison of call option strategies – absolute gains and losses

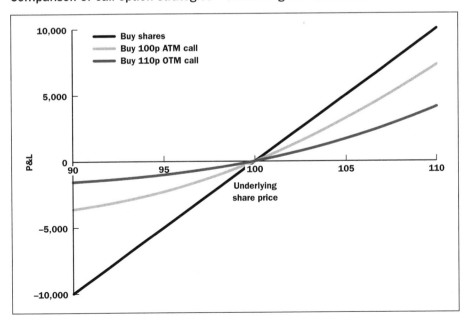

FIGURE 20.2

Comparison of call option strategies – percentage gains and losses

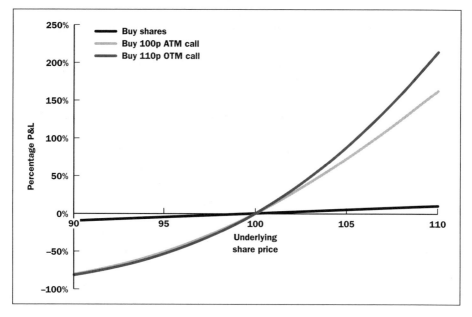

Buying a bull spread

The bull call spread has been examined in some depth in Chapter 12 (section 12.2). The main advantages over a straight call option are that the bull spread is cheaper, and suffers far less from the effect of time decay. However, the buyer of a bull spread gives up the opportunity to continue to gain once the underlying share price rises above the higher strike price. Figure 20.3 compares the performance of a 90p–110p bull spread after one month with that of the underlying shares and a straight call. Note that the bull spread incurs virtually no losses if the underlying price is unchanged in one month's time, whereas the straight call loses 20% of its value from time decay.

The 90:10 strategy

The idea behind the so-called 90:10 strategy is to guarantee a minimum return by investing the bulk of the funds available in riskless interest-bearing deposits, but to obtain a limited exposure to risk by using the balance of funds to buy options on a particular share or stock index. The 90:10 description comes from the usual split between deposits and options, although any desired split can be used. The strategy is essentially a conservative one, because the majority of the funds are committed to risk-free deposits, thus preserving most of the investor's capital even if the options expire worthless. However, if the underlying shares rally substantially, the 90:10 strategy can actually outperform the share-only

FIGURE 20.3
The bull spread after one month

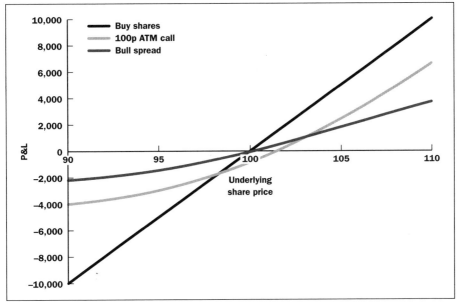

Source: US Securities and Exchange Commission (SEC).

strategy because of the gearing available from the options. The performance of the 90:10 strategy is illustrated in Figure 20.4, which demonstrates that it provides a better result for the investor either if there is a rise in the underlying share price of at least 8%, or if there is a fall of 10% or more.

FIGURE 20.4
The 90:10 strategy

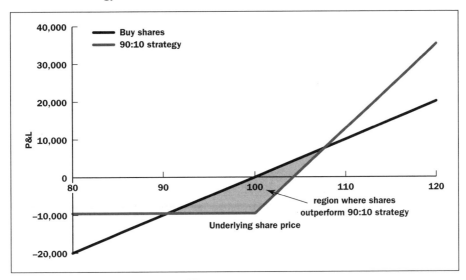

Source: US Securities and Exchange Commission (SEC).

The three option strategies reviewed so far, as well as the corresponding bear strategies, all share some important advantages over more simple tactics involving just buying or selling the underlying shares:

■ Options have limited downside risk if the market moves against the investor's view.

■ Options provide high leverage potential, especially the more out-of-the-money they are.

■ Positive curvature or gamma leads to *profit acceleration*, in which profits increase at a faster rate as the option moves into-the-money.

■ Options make it possible for an investor effectively to deal in shares for a forward date.

Against these advantages it must be pointed out that leverage works both ways, and can magnify losses if the market moves in the wrong direction. At-the-money options also suffer from adverse time decay, although this can be mitigated by using spread strategies.

20.2 Return enhancement

All the strategies to be discussed in this section have one thing in common: they provide a means of enhancing the return from an existing or anticipated holding of shares. Specifically, we will look at:

■ selling covered calls

■ ratioed selling covered calls

■ selling naked puts

■ ratioed selling puts.

Selling covered calls

A common strategy among investors holding shares is to sell call options on those shares. Since the investor already holds the shares that would need to be delivered if the option expires in-the-money, this strategy is also known as *covered call writing*. As an example, suppose a particular investor holds 100,000 shares in Azco, which are currently trading at 100p. The investor believes that Azco shares will not rise over the next few months, but will probably stay static. He therefore writes three-month call options on these shares struck at-the-money for a premium income of 4½p per share. There are now three outcomes at expiry:

i)   Azco shares stay static at 100p, as expected. The options expire worthless, and the investor pockets the 4½p premium to boost the return from the shares.

ii) Azco shares rise, and the options expire in-the-money. The investor delivers his holding of Azco shares at the exercise price of 100p, but the premium income of 4½p means that he has effectively sold his shares at 104½p.

iii) Azco shares fall, and the options expire worthless. The investor still holds on to his shares, which have not been protected from the fall in market price, but the premium income cushions the effect of the fall by boosting the effective value by 4½p a share.

Figure 20.5 shows the investor's profit profiles at expiry, not only using the at-the-money option discussed above, but also using in- and out-of-the-money options. Selling calls creates a guaranteed price for profit-taking if the share price rises, and enhanced portfolio value equal to the premium received if the price remains static or falls. The lower the strike price of the option sold, the lower is the price ceiling established, but this ceiling is effective over a wider range of share prices, including situations where the share price falls. In the example illustrated, if the investor sells a 90p call for a premium received of 11½p, a price ceiling is established at 101½p, even if the underlying share price drops to 90p. A higher strike establishes a higher price ceiling, but brings in less premium.

FIGURE 20.5
Covered call writing

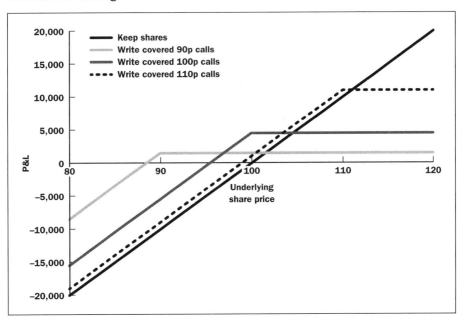

Note once again that covered call writing provides no protection to the investor at all. On the contrary, it actually sets an upper limit to the value of the shares, but it does increase the value of the holding if the share price stays static or falls.

Ratioed selling covered calls

A variation of the previous strategy is to sell call options on a proportion of the shares held. This brings in less premium income, but allows the investor to benefit from the part of the portfolio left uncovered if the share price rises above the strike price. Figure 20.6 illustrates the profit profile from the strategy of selling at-the-money options on 50% of the shares held. When compared to the corresponding profile shown in Figure 20.5, the price enhancement is half, but there is a 50% participation in profits above the strike price of 100p.

Selling naked puts

This strategy differs somewhat from the others presented in this section, for it starts with the investor holding no shares at all, but having a neutral to bullish view on the prospects for a particular company. If the shares are bought outright, the investor would suffer the financing cost, something that would be unattractive if the share price stays static. An alternative is for him to sell naked puts instead. This is not a risky strategy provided that the investor is already inclined to buy the underlying shares, and therefore does not mind if the put is exercised against him. Suppose the investor sells three-month at-the-money puts on 100,000 Azco shares, the number of shares that he would be quite willing to buy. Azco is currently trading at 100p, and the puts are priced at 3½p per share. There are three possible outcomes at expiry.

i) Azco's share price stays static. The puts expire worthless, and the investor can simply keep the £3,500 premium income, or use it to lower the effective cost of buying Azco shares to 96½p.

ii) Azco's share price rises, for example to 110p. Again, the puts expire out-of-the-money giving the investor the option either of keeping the £3,500 premium income, or using it to subsidise buying the shares at 106½p. Of course, had the investor bought Azco shares originally, the profit would have been £10,000.

iii) Azco shares fall, and the option is exercised against the investor. This means that the investor ends up buying Azco shares at an effective price of 96½p, which is cheaper than the original market price. He has also had the opportunity to earn interest on his funds over the three-month option period.

The complete profile is graphed in Figure 20.7. Note that this is virtually identical to Figure 20.5, because combining a long position in the underlying asset with a short position in call options creates a synthetic short put position.[1] This is part of the building block approach explained in Chapter 12 (section 12.1).

FIGURE 20.6
Ratioed covered call writing

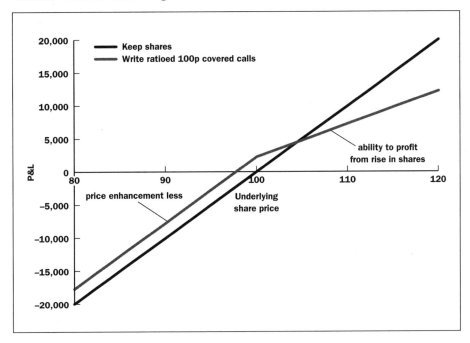

FIGURE 20.7
Selling naked puts

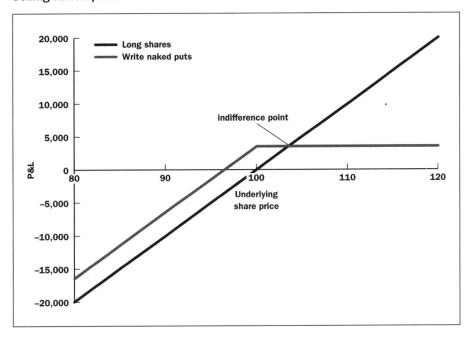

Ratioed selling puts

There is an alternative and almost equivalent strategy to the ratioed selling of covered calls. An investor who believes that the value of his shares will most likely stay static, but may increase, can sell a proportion of his portfolio and also sell puts equal to the proportion sold. For example, if the investor currently holds 100,000 Azco shares and sells half, he would sell put options on the 50,000 shares just sold. If Azco shares stay static or rise, the puts expire worthless allowing the investor to benefit both from the premium income received and also any profits on the proportion of shares still held. If Azco shares fall, against the investor's expectations, the puts are exercised against him and he ends up holding the same number of shares as were held originally, but with the benefit of the premium income received at the outset. The profile of this strategy is the same as that already pictured in Figure 20.6.

20.3 Value protection strategies

The strategies in the previous section were concerned with enhancing the return from an existing share portfolio whose value was expected to remain static. All the strategies involved selling options in order to provide premium income, but this established a ceiling on the value of the portfolio. By contrast, the value protection strategies discussed here have the opposite objective. They seek to create a floor below which the value of a share portfolio cannot fall, but allow the investor to continue to benefit if share prices rise. Not surprisingly, these strategies all involve buying options to provide the degree of protection sought. We will examine three possible schemes:

- buying puts
- liquidating the shares and buying calls
- buying a collar.

Buying puts

This is the simplest and classic way to protect the value of a share portfolio. Buying puts at- or slightly out-of-the-money establishes a price floor. If the share price drops below this level, the puts can be exercised and the shares sold at the price guaranteed by the strike price. If the share price rises, the puts expire worthless and the investor continues to benefit from the increased value of the shares held. The only drawback of this strategy is the cost of the premium income, which lowers the effective level of the price floor, and depresses any benefit from a rise in the underlying share price. In fact, the share price must rise by the amount of the premium income for the strategy to break even, as illustrated in Figure 20.8.

FIGURE 20.8
Buying puts

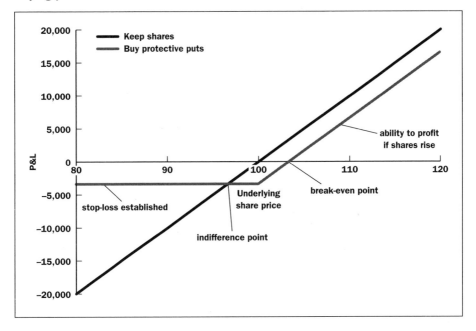

Liquidating the shares and buying calls

Buying puts while holding the underlying asset creates a synthetic long call position. Thus, an alternative strategy to the one just discussed would be for the investor to liquidate the shareholding, invest the proceeds to earn interest, but buy call options in order to continue to participate in any further rises in the underlying share price. The fact that calls rather than the underlying shares are now held means that the investor is protected against a sharp drop in the share price. The shape of the profile is identical to that illustrated in Figure 20.8.

Buying a collar

The tactic of tailoring option-based risk management solutions to meet users' needs has already been extensively explored in Chapters 17 and 19. In particular, financing the purchase of protective options with the sale of others is the basis for collars, spread-hedges, participations and other structures. The simplest of these structures, the collar, involves selling out-of-the-money calls in order to finance the purchase of protective puts. If done for the same number of shares as are actually held within the portfolio, the puts purchased establish a floor price, while the calls sold establish a price ceiling. Juggling the two strike levels will vary the amount of protection acquired, the extent of profit opportunities sold off, and the net premium paid.

FIGURE 20.9

A collar strategy

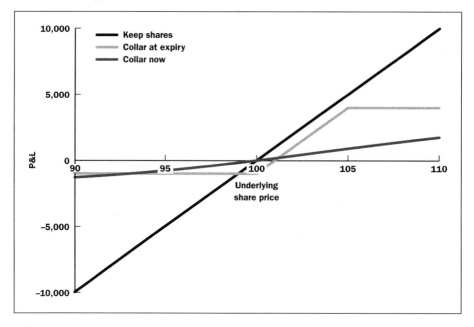

Figure 20.9 illustrates a three-month collar with an at-the-money floor at 100p, a ceiling at 105p, acquired for a net premium of just 1p. The worst outcome is for the share price to remain static or to fall, but in such cases the investor would lose just 1p per share in value. If the share price rises during the three-month period, the investor will gain for the first 5p increase, until the ceiling of 105p was reached, but would gain no more from any further price appreciation. If the ceiling is reached, the effective value per share is 104p (the 105p ceiling less the 1p net premium paid). For a small up-front premium, this collar therefore guarantees a minimum effective share price of 99p, and the opportunity to benefit fully until the effective ceiling at 104p is reached.

20.4 Vertical, horizontal and diagonal spreads

Chapter 12 (section 12.2) introduced the concept of option spreads, and these can readily be applied in the context of equity derivatives.

Vertical spreads

A vertical spread, the buying and selling of options which differ only in their exercise price, has already been discussed in Section 20.1 with an illustration of the bull call spread. However, bull and bear spreads can arise as the end result of a dynamic hedging strategy executed over a period of time, even though the

scheme may not have been planned at the outset. When this happens, it is sometimes known as *rolling up into a spread* or *rolling down into a spread*. This
has been illustrated in Chapter 17 (section 17.16) in the context of currency
hedging, and works just as well in the management of equity risk.

Suppose that a speculator believes that Azco shares, currently at 100p, are
about to rise. Rather than incur the financing cost of investing in the shares
directly, he buys a four-month out-of-the-money call struck at 105p for a premium cost of 3p. One month later, Azco shares have risen, as expected, and
are now trading at 105p. Volatility has risen too. The investor now sells a three-
month call struck at 110p, also for a premium of 3p. The investor's net premium
is therefore zero, having bought and sold calls at 3p each, but he is now the
holder of a 105p–110p bull call spread. After rolling up into this spread, the
investor can gain a maximum of 5p if Azco's shares keep on rising, or will break
even if they stay static or fall, but he cannot lose.

The opposite strategy, rolling down into a spread, can occur if an investor's
original strategy goes wrong. Suppose an investor buys a four-month at-the-
money call on Azco struck at 100p for a premium of 5p. Unfortunately, Azco's
shares fall to 90p after one month, so that the call is now worth just 1p. The
investor could roll down into a 90p–100p spread by selling two of the 100p calls
at 1p each, and buying a 90p at-the-money call for 4p. The net premium paid is
now 7p, which represents the maximum loss that the investor can make. Azco
shares need to rise to 97p for the investor to break even, but this compares
very favourably with the original position which had a break-even price of 105p.
By lowering the break-even level, the investor sacrifices the potential to make
unlimited profits if Azco shares take off – the maximum profit under the spread
is just 3p – but the investor may think this is a better compromise if a rise in
Azco's price beyond 108p is now considered unlikely. Figure 20.10 shows the
comparison between the original strategy and the spread.

Horizontal spreads

A horizontal or calendar spread involves the purchase and sale of two options
which differ only in their expiry dates. This is often a speculative strategy
intended to profit from differential rates of time decay on short-dated versus
long-dated options. For example, the one-month at-the-money call on Azco's
shares might be quoted at 2½p, while the four-month call at the same strike
might command a premium of 5p. Selling the one-month and buying the four-
month option would therefore incur a net premium cost of 2½p. If Azco's share
price was unchanged after a month, the short-dated option would expire worthless, while the premium of the now three-month option might have decayed
to 4½p. The net value of the calendar spread would therefore have increased
from 2½p to 4½p, an increase of 80% over one month. Figure 20.11 sketches the
profit profile from this strategy showing the peak profit at 100p, and break-even
levels at 96p and 106p.

FIGURE 20.10

Rolling down into a spread

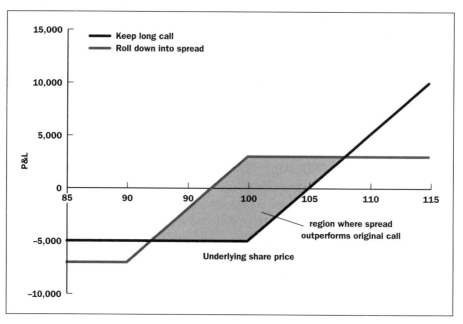

FIGURE 20.11

Calendar spread

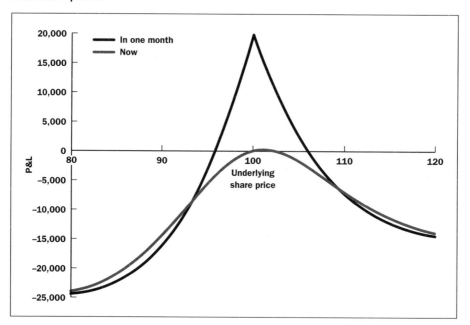

Diagonal spreads

Combining the concept of a horizontal and vertical spread gives a diagonal spread, where options are bought and sold at two different strike prices and maturity dates. Such a spread mixes the directional characteristics of the vertical spread with the time decay behaviour of the horizontal spread, and would be used by a speculator who believes that the share price would settle at a specific level different from the prevailing price. Chapter 12 (section 12.2) provides some good illustrations of the resulting profiles.

20.5 Other option strategies

The whole range of other option strategies discussed in Chapter 12 is open to the equity investor or speculator. Volatility structures such as straddles and strangles, or range structures like butterflies, condors, ratio spreads and backspreads, can all be used to monetise an investor's specific view. These can either be built up from scratch by buying or selling the appropriate options, or can be created by manipulating an existing share portfolio. For example, an investor long in shares can create a straddle by buying put options on twice the number of shares held. This will yield profits either if implied volatility increases, or if there is a substantial shift in the underlying share price, whether up or down.

As an example of a volatility strategy, let's consider a US-based investor who had been monitoring the steady decline of Hewlett-Packard's (HPQ) share price. From highs of around $50 in the spring of 2010, HPQ had since dropped 30% to trade below $37 by early July 2011. With a number of top-level boardroom changes, and a lack of clarity over the future direction of the company, the company's performance had been lacklustre. For the investor, the final straw was the launch on 1st July 2011 of its TouchPad, which turned out to be an ill-fated and very short-lived challenger to Apple's iPad. On 8th July 2011, expecting volatility of HP's shares to rise, the investor decided to execute a volatility trade by buying at-the-money straddles on HPQ using the $36 strike calls and puts expiring November 2011 at a cost of $4.31 per share. To reduce the cost of the trade, the investor sold a bull call spread using strikes of $40 and $42, and also sold a bear put spread using strikes of $32 and $30, the combination bringing in $0.63 per share, thus reducing the net premium of the structure by 15% to $3.68. Each option trade was executed in 100 contracts (with each contract representing 100 shares). The structure so far was slightly delta-positive to the tune of 807 shares, so the investor sold 800 shares to avoid being inadvertently long Hewlett-Packard. The complete list of trades is shown in Table 20.1, and Figure 20.12 shows the payoff profile at inception, at inception but with a 20% hike in implied volatilities, and at maturity. The slightly asymmetric appearance of the maturity profile is because of the small delta hedge, equivalent to 8% of the notional number of shares in the structure.

TABLE 20.1

Volatility trade on Hewlett-Packard 8th July 2011

Instrument	Trade	Premium/price	Cash flow
$30 Put Nov 2011	Buy 100	0.42	(4,200)
$32 Put Nov 2011	Sell 100	0.70	7,000
$36 Call Nov 2011	Buy 100	2.34	(23,400)
$36 Put Nov 2011	Buy 100	1.97	(19,700)
$40 Call Nov 2011	Sell 100	0.74	7,400
$42 Call Nov 2011	Buy 100	0.39	(3,900)
Sub-total			(36,800)
HPQ shares	Sell 800		29,144
Total			(7,656)

On Friday 18th August, Hewlett-Packard issued a press release posting lower-than-expected earnings estimates for the fourth quarter of 2011 and simultaneously announcing the discontinuation of the TouchPad, less than seven weeks after its launch. The news was greeted with dismay by investors, and HP's share price dropped 25% between 17th and 19th August. At the same time, implied volatility rose from around 35% to 50%. Figure 20.13 compares the movement of these variables throughout July and August of that year, and clearly illustrates that one was the mirror image of the other.

FIGURE 20.12

Volatility trade on Hewlett-Packard

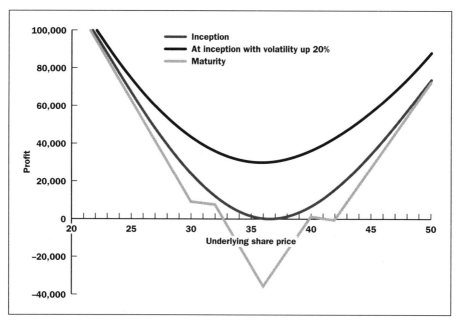

Source: Data are provided by iVolatility.com.

FIGURE 20.13

Share price and implied volatility for Hewlett-Packard Jul–Aug 2011

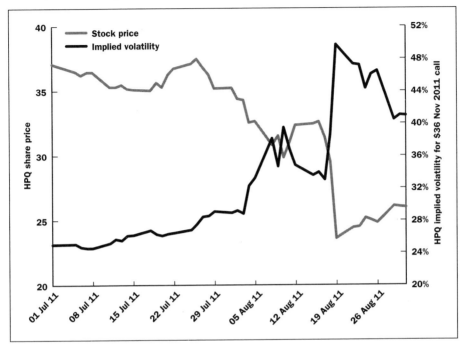

Source: Data are provided by iVolatility.com.

On 22nd August the investor decided to close out the entire position. With volatility some 20% higher since inception and the stock price 33% lower, the investor was able to liquidate the structure to make a $70,000 profit. Using the Greeks we can attribute around 26% of these profits from the increase in volatility and around 74% to the reduction in the share price. Although the trade was delta-neutral initially, we have assumed that the positions were maintained static rather than being dynamically hedged. Given the nature of the structure, this meant that the position was substantially delta-negative once the share price began to fall as is clear from Figure 20.12, to the benefit of the investor. Over the 45-day holding period, the profit was 1.9 times the gross investment in options, and an impressive 9.2 times the net investment after the cash inflow from the delta hedge is taken into account.

20.6 Using stock index futures and options

The examples so far have all referred to hedging or speculation involving the shares of a single company. At the other end of the spectrum are problems arising from well-diversified portfolios of shares. Fortunately, the availability of stock index futures and options makes the task of managing portfolio risk much easier. Chapter 7 has already explored how stock index futures work, and has shown how these instruments can be used to transmute share portfolios into interest-earning deposits, and vice versa. In this section we shall concentrate on stock index options.

Stock index options work just like ordinary stock options, except that the underlying asset is a stock index like the S&P 500 rather than the price of an individual share. They come in two varieties. Options on the index itself, like the S&P 500 index option traded on the CBOE or the FTSE 100 index option traded on NYSE Liffe, provide solely for cash settlement on expiry, while options on index futures, like the S&P 500 option traded on the CME, can be exercised into the underlying futures contract at any time.

Index options or index futures options can be used in much the same way as stock options, and with the same variety of hedging structures or speculative positions. A speculator wishing to profit from a rise in the level of shares generally, but to limit losses in case the market should fall, can buy a call option or a bull call spread to achieve this objective. Alternatively, a portfolio manager holding a well-diversified share portfolio can use index options or index futures options to create a cap, floor, collar or any of the other structures examined earlier in this chapter.

As an example of the first of these uses, consider a speculator who has turned bullish about the prospects for the US stock market. Following the downgrade of US Treasury securities by S&P on 5th August 2011, and general uncertainty about the US and global economy, the S&P 500 index had plummeted from the mid-1350s in July 2011 to the low 1100s in early August, and had spent the next few months mostly in the 1100 to 1200 range. It is now 18th January 2012 and, following more positive economic news, the S&P 500 index has just broken through the 1300 level to stand at 1308.04. The speculator believes that the market will rally by 5% to 10% over the next three months, but will then fall back. He neither wishes to pick individual shares, nor to incur the transaction costs in building up a portfolio which he plans to hold only over a short time. Finally, he does not want to be exposed to downside risk in case his view proves wrong; this rules out the use of index futures. The speculator decides to buy a 1250-1350 bull call spread in April S&P 500 CBOE index options (the so-called SPX contracts), and enters into the following transactions:

18 January 2012   *(S&P 500 = 1308.04)*
Buy 100 April 1250 SPX calls at 88.6   }
Sell 100 April 1350 SPX calls at 25.6   }   net premium paid 63.0

At $100 per full index point, the net premium is therefore $63 \times 100 \times \$100 = \$630,000$.

On Tuesday 17th April 2012, 90 days later, the S&P 500 has risen to 1390.78. The speculator decides to close out the position before the April contracts expire at the end of that week rather than roll the trade into a later contract. The position is unwound with the following deals:

17 April 2012   *(S&P 500 = 1390.78)*

Sell 100 April 1250 SPX calls at 137.2 }

Buy 100 April 1350 SPX calls at 40.1   }   net premium received 97.1

The proceeds bring in 97.1 × 100 × $100 = $971,000, leaving the speculator with a net profit of $341,000 on the original investment of $630,000 – a 54% gain over the three-month period. The maximum potential profit of $370,000 (equivalent to a 59% gain) would have been achieved if the speculator had held on to the spread until the option maturity date and if the market had remained above 1350 at that time. The worse outcome would have been for the market to stay below 1250 before the expiry date in April, whereupon the speculator would have lost the entire $630,000 premium invested. These extremes illustrate the highly geared nature of option performance.

As an alternative to liquidating the position in mid-April and taking profit, if the speculator in this example had started with slightly longer-dated options, he could have used the tactic of rolling up into a spread at a higher level. Let's suppose that on the two dates in question the investor executed the following transactions using June 2012 rather than April 2012 SPX index options:

18 January 2012   *(S&P 500 = 1308.04)*

Buy 100 June 1250 SPX calls at 101.9 }

Sell 100 June 1350 SPX calls at 39.7   }   net premium paid 62.2

17 April 2012   *(S&P 500 = 1390.78)*

Sell 100 June 1250 SPX calls at 141.5 }

Buy 200 June 1350 SPX calls at 61.3   }   net premium received 62.2

Sell 100 June 1375 SPX calls at 43.3   }

Liquidating the June options position completely in April would crystallise a profit of $180,000, around half of that when compared with the earlier example using April options. The profit is lower because the options still have two months until expiry, and so the delta of the June 1250 call is only 86% rather than the 97% delta of the April 1250 call, reducing the upside profit of the bull spread at that stage. However, if the investor used the $180,000 profit to buy a 1350-1375 bull spread he now has a 'free' bull call spread with a potential profit of $250,000 if the market remains above 1375, and a worst-case outcome of zero. Before rolling up into the spread, the worst-case scenario would have been a loss of the entire $622,000 premium paid.

Stock index options can also be used by the portfolio manager having a broad holding of shares. The success of any strategy based on these options will depend upon how closely the portfolio tracks the market index. A well-diversified portfolio will present few unexpected problems if it tends to track the market index very closely. The number of index options required in this case can be calculated using a similar technique to that demonstrated in

Chapter 7 with stock index futures (see section 7.12). For example, suppose that a portfolio comprised shares currently valued at £26,000,000 and these are to be hedged using FTSE 100 options which are defined as having a value of £10 per full index point. If the FTSE 100 index was currently at 6045, the number of contracts required would be:

$$£26,000,000 / (£10 \times 6045) = 430 \text{ contracts}$$

For other portfolios there will be a residual basis risk, part of which can be handled by adjusting the number of option contracts used. The first step is to conduct a regression analysis just like the ones described in Chapter 18 (section 18.3). In that context, a scatter chart like the one illustrated in Figure 18.1 was used to examine the relationship between prime rate and LIBOR rates. Here we need to do the same thing by determining the relationship between the value of the portfolio and the level of the market index. Specifically, the portfolio manager can use regression analysis to estimate the parameters of equation 20.1:

$$P_t = \alpha + \beta I_t + \varepsilon \qquad (20.1)$$

where:

P_t is the value of the portfolio at time t
I_t is the value of the index at time t
α is the intercept parameter
β is the slope parameter
ε is an error term which accounts for unpredictable portfolio movements not correlated with the index

Assuming that the correlation coefficient (a by-product from the regression analysis) shows a strong and reliable relationship between the portfolio value and the market index, the most important parameter is β. The beta coefficient expresses numerically by how much the portfolio value will move when the index changes. For example, if $\beta = 2$ for a particular share portfolio, it means that the portfolio value will increase by twice as much as that of the index when the market rises, and also that it decreases twice as fast as the index when the market falls.

Once the beta for a particular portfolio is known, the number of option contracts required is simply multiplied by beta to obtain the correct number for an options hedge. If the £26m portfolio to be hedged had a β of 1.24, the number of options would need to be increased from 430 to 533. Being more volatile than the market, a greater number of option contracts would be necessary to hedge the risk. This number then forms the basis for any of the option strategies discussed earlier. For example, to construct a collar, the portfolio manager would buy 533 put options at a lower strike price and sell 533 calls at a higher strike.

The remaining basis risk arises out of the error term ε in equation 20.1, which accounts for the unpredictable fluctuations in portfolio value which are independent of the index. If the correlation coefficient is high, then this error term will be small, and hedges based on index options will prove efficient. If the portfolio is poorly correlated with the index, the portfolio manager would either have to accept a high degree of basis risk, or would have to use a basket option.

20.7 Portfolio insurance

Portfolio insurance is a technique which was developed in the early 1980s and was highly popular until the stock market crash in October 1987, although the technique continues to be used albeit on a much reduced scale. Portfolio insurance is sometimes confused with other computer-driven trading strategies and also with asset allocation, because they all have certain similarities. The differences are explained in the following paragraphs.

Program trading generally refers to computerised systems designed to exploit risk-free arbitrage opportunities in the market. Computers monitor price discrepancies between similar or related instruments quoted on different markets, and automatically initiate trades when they identify profitable opportunities. Schemes specifically associated with the equity markets usually try to identify and exploit any gaps appearing between the price of stock-index futures and the prices of the constituent shares.

Algorithmic trading also refers to a series of trades initiated by computers, but with a different rationale. What drives program trading is the difference between related market prices, and systems executing program trades aim to have zero net positions thereafter because the series of trades are designed to offset each other. Algorithmic trading, on the other hand, is driven by the desire to execute large institutional trading orders at the best price with the minimal impact on the market. What drives such systems are large purchase or sales orders entered by a human, and the systems then seek out the best segmentation, order routing and timing.

High-frequency trading (HFT) seeks to exploit minute but predictable short-term price movements. HFT works by physically locating such trading systems close to the stock exchange's own computer systems, and executing high-speed algorithms that analyse the regular order flow and interject a new sequence of orders designed to exploit the anticipated price impact arising from the original order flow. The timescales of HFT strategies are often measured in milliseconds, and when completed leave the HFT trader with no net position but the profits accumulated by executing huge volumes of trades at tiny profit margins.

Asset allocation often refers to the practice of using stock index futures or bond futures as a cheap and flexible means of adjusting the mix of an investment portfolio. Chapter 7 (section 7.12) has already illustrated how an interest-bearing deposit can be completely converted into a synthetic share portfolio using stock index futures, and also how the reverse process can be achieved. By buying and selling variable amounts of stock index and bond futures, a portfolio currently containing an arbitrary mix of cash, bonds and equities can be converted into one having any other desired mix. This is usually much cheaper than liquidating unwanted holdings and purchasing the desired assets.

Portfolio insurance is the term coined by two academics, Leland and Rubinstein,[2] to describe a strategy whereby an equity portfolio can be made to behave like a call option, with limited downside and unlimited upside potential. It was first developed for pension fund investors, whose actuarial liabilities require the fund to earn an absolute minimum return, but who prefer to earn a higher return if possible. The call-like profile can be achieved in several ways:

- Buy shares or bonds, and buy a protective put option on these assets to establish a floor price.
- Invest in risk-free interest-bearing deposits, and buy call options on a market index to obtain the upside potential.
- Use a dynamic asset allocation strategy.

The first two possibilities are equivalent, and are obvious choices. After all, if the desired profile has the characteristic shape of an option, why not just use an option? The problem is a practical one: most stock and stock index options are available only with a limited maturity, typically with liquidity available up to a year or so in the future. Long-term equity options are generally only available in the form of warrants on particular shares, or have limited liquidity.

The third possibility involves dynamically allocating a fund between different types of assets according to market conditions. When the stock market is rising, a greater proportion of the fund should be committed to equities. Beyond a certain high point, the fund would be completely invested in equities, benefiting fully from any further rise in the stock market. Conversely, when the market is falling, the proportion in equities should be cut back, and the resources switched into interest-bearing deposits, or possibly bonds, thereby cushioning the value of the portfolio against further losses. By the time the market has reached a certain low threshold, the fund would be completely invested in deposits, and its value would no longer fall if the stock market dropped further. A floor level for the fund is thus established. In between, the fund would contain a proportion of deposits and equities, and its response to movements in the stock market would be diluted accordingly.

In fact, this idea is equivalent to the method used in Chapter 10 (section 10.8) as the basis for pricing options using the binomial model, namely that a short position in call options can be completely hedged by borrowing money and investing it in a proportion of the underlying asset. In other words, the combination of some of the underlying asset with some borrowing is equivalent to a long position in a call option. Exactly the same combination is being used with dynamic asset allocation. In effect, part of a 100% investment in interest-bearing deposits is 'borrowed' and used to buy shares. As the proportion of the fund invested in equities varies with different levels of the market, the full option-like behaviour of the resulting strategy emerges.

Figure 20.14 provides an illustration of this dynamic asset allocation technique, and the option-like characteristic is very evident. The figure shows the effect of implementing a portfolio insurance strategy on a portfolio of shares tracking the FTSE 100 index. At inception, the index was at 6,000 and the strategy called for a 53% allocation in equities. As the index rises, so does the allocation to equities, increasing to 79% as the FTSE 100 passes 7,000 and 92% at 8,000. Conversely, the equity allocation is scaled back dramatically to 20% if the index was to fall to 5,000 and down to just 3% in the event that the FTSE 100 was to fall to 4,000.

The impact on financial performance is notable. If the FTSE 100 drops 16.7% to 5,000 the portfolio insurance strategy reduces downside losses to just 6.1% and to only 7.7% for a 33.3% drop in the index to 4,000. The strategy nonetheless preserves most of the upside, delivering an 11.2% profit to the investor if the index rises 16.7% to 7,000 and a 25.6% profit if the index climbs 33.3% to reach 8,000. However, these figures ignore the impact of transaction costs when rebalancing the portfolio, which could be extensive in a volatile market. These costs can be mitigated to some extent by having fewer trigger levels at which the proportion of equities needed to be rebalanced, but the option-like performance would become much cruder. Alternatively, for index-tracking portfolios, rebalancing can be done by using stock index futures instead of buying or selling the shares themselves. Transaction costs for futures are far less than the corresponding commissions on share deals, and the desired effect could therefore be realised much more effectively.

FIGURE 20.14
Dynamic asset allocation

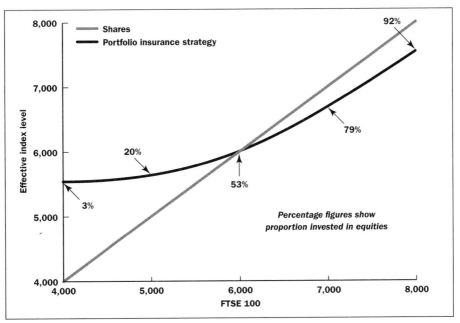

Portfolio insurance was originally considered a very worthwhile strategy. Unfortunately, the scheme fell from favour in the aftermath of the 1987 stock market crash. The problem was that a significant number of share portfolios were being controlled by portfolio insurance schemes following a sustained rise in the level of the market. This meant that most portfolios were fully invested in equities, either through physical holdings of shares, or synthetically through long positions in index futures. The initial fall in the stock market triggered a wave of selling orders for the futures contracts, as the portfolio insurance schemes sought to rebalance the portfolios with a smaller proportion of equities. The flow of orders came so fast that the index futures began to trade at a significant discount to the value of the underlying shares. This had the unfortunate effect of triggering program trading systems set up to exploit this kind of arbitrage. The program trades immediately started to sell shares which in turn drove the index even lower. A chain reaction was in progress with the eventual consequences that are now well known.

This does not mean that portfolio insurance as a strategy is doomed. The ideas are still valid, especially the use of futures as a means of effecting dynamic asset allocation. However, portfolio managers need to be aware that these schemes cannot absolutely guarantee that a floor level will be effective if the market drops sharply and suddenly, as it did in 1987. In addition, the systems, the investor's portfolio, and the market itself must all be protected against the lemming-like behaviour of unthinking computer programs in the event that markets behave in an odd and unanticipated way, as happened on 6th May 2010 in the so-called 'Flash Crash'.

20.8 Guaranteed equity funds

A variation on the concept of portfolio insurance is the idea of the *guaranteed equity fund*, a retail product marketed under a number of different proprietary names that also includes *Guaranteed Equity Bond* and *Guaranteed Investment Fund*. These promise the small investor a return equal to a specified multiple of the growth of a particular market index over a period, or the investor's money back if the index should fall. The multiplier can typically range from 75% to 130%, and those with a higher multiple sometimes feature an overall cap. Some vary the absolute money-back guarantee by providing instead a high floor (e.g. a 95% guarantee) in return for a higher multiplier. Table 20.2 provides three illustrations showing different permutations of the investment parameters.

TABLE 20.2
Guaranteed equity fund examples

Base level	Multiplier	Period length	Cap
100%	15%	every quarter	n/a
96%	130%	every quarter	n/a
100%	100%	five years	35% (over five years)

The first of these examples is probably the simplest. Each quarter the investor will receive 15% of the gain in the underlying index, but if the index declines the investor loses nothing. So in a quarter when the market rises 10% the investor receives 1.5%. The low level of equity participation is the price paid in this case for the absolute capital guarantee in a volatile and uncertain equity environment. The second example is for the more bullish investor, offering 130% of the gain in the market, but only from a 96% base level. So in a quarter where the market was static or declined the investor would lose 4% of his wealth, but in a quarter where the market rose 10% the investor would gain 9%. The final example provides another straightforward fund where, over a five-year period, the investor receives the greater of 100% of the gain in the market, but capped at 35%, or his money back.

For many investors, these types of fund provide a very attractive package indeed, combining capital protection and, in some cases, gains exceeding 100% of the market. However, when comparing them with other forms of equity investment, including investing in shares directly, it is important to remember to account for the dividend income forgone. When dividend yield is 2%, the investor in the last example above would sacrifice more than 10% of income over the five-year period when compared with a conventional equity investment.

The institutions offering guaranteed equity funds can structure the package by combining these components:

i) Buy a risk-free Treasury bill or note to provide the minimum return. So to guarantee the 96% floor in three months, the fund manager would buy a three-month Treasury bill with face value equal to 96% of the amount invested.

ii) Buy a call option on the underlying index, struck at the base level, with a notional amount equal to the multiplier offered. So to provide the 130% multiplier promised in the second example, the fund manager would buy a three-month call on 130% of the amount invested, struck at 96% of the current index price.

iii) If the fund includes a cap, sell a call option on the underlying index struck at the cap level. So to provide the 35% cap featured in the third example, the fund manager would sell a five-year cap struck at 135% of the initial index level on 100% of the amount invested.

As an example of the pricing of these products using the second hedging structure, suppose that short-term rates are 2%, and that a three-month at-the-money index option can be bought for an up-front premium of 3.31%. For every £100 invested, the allocation is:

Purchase T-Bill with a nominal value of £96:	£95.52
Purchase ATM call option on £130:	£4.30
Total cost:	£99.82

This leaves £0.18 out of every £100 invested to cover marketing, transactions costs, management fees, and so on.

The pricing of guaranteed equity funds is principally influenced by the volatility of the underlying index, and the level of interest rates. As interest rates fall, the T-Bill or T-Note becomes more expensive, and as volatility rises, the options cost more; in either case this will lead to reduced benefits for the investor, in the form of a lower index profit participation rate, a lower base level, or a lower cap. Shorter-dated structures are relatively more sensitive to the level of volatility, while longer-dated structures are more affected by the level of interest rates. If index volatility were to rise by 1%, the multiplier in the second example given in Table 20.2 would fall to around 123%. More dramatically, if five-year yields were to fall by 1% in the third example, the cap would more than halve to just 16%.

20.9 Warrants and convertibles

Although there is insufficient space to discuss these products in depth – they each deserve a book to themselves – this chapter would not be complete without a brief review of warrants and convertibles.

A *warrant* is like a long-term option on a particular company's shares. There is one significant difference other than the tenor: the exercise of a warrant usually involves the issue of new shares by the company, whereas an option is non-dilutive. In addition, warrants are not normally available for the range of maturity dates and strike prices available with ordinary equity options; a given warrant issue will have one specific strike price and will expire on one particular date. There is one piece of jargon that can cause confusion: the premium. With regular options, the premium is the price paid for the option. The equivalent term with warrants is just the price. The *warrant premium* is normally understood to mean the amount by which the warrant price plus the strike price exceeds the prevailing share price, and is normally expressed as a percentage. For example, a warrant priced at 20p with an exercise price of 150p would have a 70% premium if the issuer's current share price was 100p.

Warrants are frequently used in conjunction with a new bond issue, to act as a 'sweetener', and are particularly prevalent in the Japanese equity markets. If the company performs well, the investor can eventually exercise the warrant and buy the company's equity at a price fixed at the outset. In the meantime, the investor has the security of holding the company's fixed-income debt, which also acts as a fall-back position in case the company's prospects decline. After issue, warrants can usually be detached from the accompanying bond, and traded independently.

From the investor's viewpoint, warrants can be used in the same way as equities, to provide a way of investing in the shares of a specific company, but with a relatively low capital outlay at the start. Another strategy allows an investor already holding shares to liquidate them, but to maintain an equity stake. This tactic is called *cash extraction* and is straightforward in concept. The investor sells the shares, uses part of the money to buy warrants on the same number of shares, and invests the remainder to earn interest. It should be remembered, however, that out-of-the-money warrants do not move one-for-one with the share price prior to maturity. Once the investor has switched from shares to warrants, a rise in the share price of 100 might be followed by a rise of just 40 in the warrants. Some immediate profit potential may therefore be forgone, as is the opportunity to receive dividend income.

A *convertible* bond is one which can be converted into a fixed number of shares on or after a given date in the future. The attractions for investors are similar to those arising from warrants: the immediate safety of relatively secure debt, plus the ability to switch into equity if the company's share price rises sufficiently. There are several differences between warrants and convertibles, however. A convertible provides the investor with a stream of income and a floor price through which the convertible cannot fall, except in default; a warrant provides no income and can expire worthless. Moreover, the exercise of a warrant requires a further investment of cash, whereas the conversion of a convertible does not.

Convertibles are often used by medium-sized companies with strong growth prospects. The possibility of conversion can tempt investors to accept a lower rate of interest than the company would otherwise be forced to pay. This benefits the issuer, as does the ability to raise cash now by the issue of deferred equity at a higher price than that currently prevailing, lessening the dilutive impact of the new capital raised.

In addition to the option embedded within the convertible, namely the investor's option to switch from debt into equity, convertibles are often issued with other explicit options. One type is a call provision, which gives the issuer the right to call back the issue on or after a particular date in the future, either at par or some premium. This effectively gives the issuer a means to force conversion, or the opportunity to refinance at a lower cost if rates have dropped. Table 20.3 provides just such an example. Another type is a put option, which allows the investor the right to put the convertible back to the issuer, sometimes at a premium. This provides a safety feature for the investor, who can liquidate the bond if the issuer's share price fails to grow according to expectations. Table 20.4 illustrates the notice issued by AirTran on 26 May 2010 when its shares were trading at only $5.50, just under half the conversion price of $11.12 per share. As a result of the put option, AirTran repurchased $90.4m of the $95.8m outstanding at the time.

TABLE 20.3

Example of a call exercise on a convertible bond

Issuer	Softbank Corporation
Bond to be redeemed before maturity	JPY 50,000,000,000 1.75 per cent. Convertible Bonds due 2014
Notional amount of early redemption	Amount of all of the Bonds then outstanding as of planned early redemption day (Outstanding amount as of 31 March, 2011: JPY 49,992 million)
Call notice date	9 May 2011
Planned early redemption day	27 June 2011
Total amount to be paid for early redemption	Bonds then outstanding at 100 percent of their principal amount, together with interest accrued to the date fixed for such redemption

TABLE 20.4

Example of a put option notification

Issuer	AirTran Holdings Inc. (AirTran Airways)
Bond	7% Convertible Notes due 2023
Notional amount outstanding	As of 26 May 2010, there was $95.8 million in aggregate principal amount of the Notes outstanding
Put option notification date	3 June 2010
Put option expiry	1 July 2010
Conversion price	$11.12 per share
AirTran share price	$5.50 per share (as of 26 May 2010)
Redemption amount	$1,000 per $1,000 principal plus any accrued and unpaid interest

20.10 Exotic equity derivatives

Chapter 13 (section 13.7 onwards) introduced a wide range of so-called exotic options, a number of which have now appeared as specialised equity derivative products. Here we provide some examples of the most significant offerings which have emerged, but the scope is almost endless, being limited only by the imaginations of the financial engineers designing and pricing the various packages.

Basket options

Some hedging applications may involve situations where the exposure is broader than exposure to a single share price, but narrower than exposure to the entire market. For example, a fund manager may want to hedge a portfolio comprising shares in a single industry sector like chemicals or motors. In such cases, an index option would be too broad, or may even be useless if the financial performance of the particular portfolio was poorly correlated with that of the market as a whole. Buying options on each of the individual shares would provide a hedge, but this would prove very expensive, because the investor would receive no allowance for the reduction in portfolio risk which occurs when individual risks are pooled. A *basket option*, tailored for the particular application, would normally provide a much better solution.

A basket option, as the name implies, is an option on a basket of securities. The payout at maturity is based on a weighted average of the prices of the component securities rather than on the price of a single instrument. An investor or a portfolio manager would approach a bank with details of the portfolio to be hedged, and the option specification would be designed to match the particular securities, strike value and maturity required. Although this will require a specialised quotation, the cost of an option on a portfolio will almost always be less than the cost of a portfolio of options, and never greater. The user could buy a put basket option to establish a floor level below which the portfolio value could not fall, or could sell a call basket option to bring in premium income by establishing a price ceiling for the portfolio.

Table 20.5 provides a comparison between the cost of a basket put and that of two vanilla puts, on a simple portfolio comprising a 50:50 split between Intel and Microsoft shares and having a total value of $27.2m. In each case the options have a maturity of nine months, and are struck 10% out-of-the-money. The investor here is only concerned if *total* portfolio losses are more than 10%. The cost of the two vanillas comes to just under $1.3m, equivalent to 4.77% of the portfolio value. The basket option, on the other hand, costs only a fraction over $1m, equivalent to 3.74% of the portfolio value, and saves the investor around 22% when compared with the cost of the two vanillas. The reason why the basket put is cheaper is because it pays out only when the total portfolio value drops more than 10%, whereas the vanilla combination pays out if *either* share price drops by more than 10%. In a situation where one share drops by 15% and the other rises by a similar amount, the basket option pays out nothing, because the loss on one share is compensated by the profit on the other, and so the investor needs no compensation in this case. However, one of the vanillas would nonetheless pay out when, for the investor considered here, no compensation is necessary – but he is paying 22% extra premium for these unnecessary payouts.

TABLE 20.5

Comparison of basket with vanilla puts on MSFT and INTC

	General	MSFT	INTC
Number of shares		425,000	500,000
Share price		$32.00	$27.20
Strike price		$28.80	$24.48
Dividend yield		2.51%	3.08%
Time to maturity	9 months		
Nine-month interest rate	0.80% p.a.		
Nine-month volatility		25.11% p.a.	26.43% p.a.
Correlation		0.48	

	Total	MSFT	INTC
Value of shares	$27,200,000	$13,600,000	$13,600,000
Strike value (for basket)	$24,480,000		
Put option premium (per share)		$1.44	$1.37
Put option premiums (in $)	$1,297,000	$612,000	$685,000
Put option premiums (in %)	4.77%	4.50%	5.04%
Basket option (in $)	$1,016,000		
Basket option (in %)	3.74%		

Data as on 25th April 2012

Rainbow options

These offer the buyer a payoff based on the maximum (or minimum) price achieved by several underlying prices. An example would be a rainbow call on the German DAX, the British FTSE 100 and the French CAC-40 stock indices. The call buyer would receive a payoff based on whichever index showed the greatest appreciation over the option period. Such an option would solve the dilemma faced by fund managers as to which market they should invest in, or how they should allocate capital between markets, since the rainbow option would always guarantee the best possible performance.

Outperformance options

These are sometimes called *relative performance options* (RPOs) and provide the investor with a payout equal to the extent by which one underlier outperforms another. For example, an investor who thought that Apple Inc. would outperform the S&P 500, but wanted to guarantee at least the return on the index, could buy S&P 500 index futures plus an outperformance call paying the excess of AAPL's return over the index. In fact, this combination would be equivalent to buying a rainbow option on AAPL and the S&P 500.

Quanto options

These provide investors with a means of participating in the performance of a foreign stock market, but without the associated currency risk. Suppose a US investor believes that the British stock market will rise by 15% over the next year, whereas the US market will rise by only 10%. If he buys a call option on the shares of a single British company, or a stock index call option on the FTSE 100 as a whole, he will benefit if the particular company goes up, or if the market as a whole should rise as expected. However, the payout in both cases would normally be in sterling, and would need to be exchanged back into dollars. If the pound fell 10% against the dollar over the lifetime of the option, this would reduce the advantage of having invested in Britain.

Quantos eliminate this problem, because the option payout is denominated in the investor's domestic currency at a pre-determined exchange rate. For example, a quanto call on the FTSE 100 index struck at 6,000 might pay out $10 for each full index point in excess of the strike. If the index reached 6,500 at expiry, the investor would receive $5,000 regardless of the sterling/dollar exchange rate at the time.

Compared with a standard equity option, the pricing of quanto options depends upon a number of additional factors including the interest rate differential between the two currencies involved, the volatility of the exchange rate, and, most particularly, the correlation between the underlying asset and the exchange rate.

To provide an illustration of how these factors interrelate, Figure 20.15 shows the fair prices for dollar-denominated at-the-money quanto options on the Nikkei 225 having a maturity of six months. The chart traces out the prices both for quanto calls and puts, and also for their vanilla counterparts denominated in Japanese yen rather than dollars.

The effect of correlation is quite significant, and in this example serves to increase the value of quanto calls and to reduce the value of quanto puts as the correlation coefficient becomes larger. A positive correlation here implies a positive association between the level of the Nikkei 225 index and the $/¥ exchange rate; as the US dollar rises against the Japanese yen, so does the Nikkei. In fact, analysing daily figures for these two variables over the period January 2011 to April 2012 gives a correlation of +0.82, and this is illustrated in Figure 20.16. The close relationship between the FX rate and the Japanese stock market over this period arose probably because each is linked to views about the global economy. As sentiment about economic growth becomes more positive, all stock markets tend to respond positively, as does the strength of the dollar representing the world's single largest economy.

Now consider how the holder of a quanto call option paid in dollars fares as the index/currency correlation increases. A rise in the Nikkei 225 will lead to a larger payout, and the value of this dollar-denominated payout will be further boosted as the dollar rises against the yen. The benefit from a higher Nikkei is therefore enhanced by an increase in the value of the dollar, so the price of a quanto call will be more than that of a standard index call option paid out in yen. A similar argument explains why the puts become cheaper as correlation increases.

FIGURE 20.15

Illustration of quanto option prices

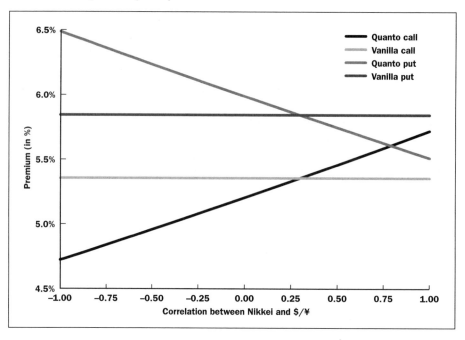

FIGURE 20.16

$/¥ exchange rate vs. Nikkei 225 January 2011 to April 2012

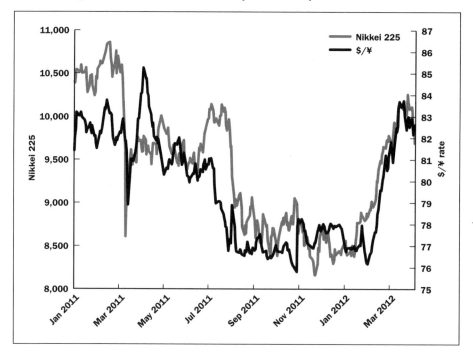

Investors thinking of buying quanto options should not, however, be tempted by any apparent cost advantage over standard options, nor should they rule out a quanto if it happens to cost more. Quantos are often the best choice if the currency hedge which they provide matches the objectives, exposure and outlook of the investor. For example, a US-based investor wishing to hedge against losses on a Japanese share portfolio might well find that a Nikkei 225 quanto put struck in dollars is the best solution. This is because such a quanto put protects against both a fall in the value of the portfolio and a fall in the value of the Japanese yen. A standard yen-denominated put would not offer the currency protection element. In the example illustrated in Figure 20.15 the quanto put also has the advantage of being cheaper in a positive correlation environment. On the other hand, buying a vanilla call as a cheap way to benefit from an anticipated rise in the Nikkei 225 might not prove so attractive for a dollar-based speculator if he also thought that the dollar was going to rise. The vanilla, paying out in yen, would deprive the speculator of the benefit of a stronger dollar, as well as exposing him to the inconvenience of receiving payment in a foreign currency.

Other exotics

Knock-outs, ladders, cliquets and other exotic species have also migrated to the equities markets, and investors with a particular objective or exposure can usually obtain a quote from one or more market-makers. For example, suppose an investment manager holds shares currently trading at 100 and wishes to protect his position in case the value of the shares should fall, but plans to liquidate the position if the shares rise to 105. The ideal choice would be a knock-out put with a strike price of 100, and a barrier at 105. Such an option would provide exactly the protection required, and would be cheaper than a standard put option.

Another investor, bullish on the FTSE 100, and tempted to buy a vanilla one-year ATM call struck at 6,000, might be afraid that a sell-off just before expiry could wipe out any gains at the last minute. A one-year ladder call, struck at 6,000 but with ladder intervals at 200-point intervals, would lock in the intrinsic value every time the market rose 200 points, and prevent such last-minute disappointments. However, such peace of mind comes at a price, and Table 20.6 compares the cost of various one-year ladder options with the cost of the vanilla, all options being struck ATM at 6,000. The first ladder shown has just one ladder level at 6,200; if and when the FTSE 100 trades through that level, the 200-point intrinsic value is locked in and the ladder option thereafter behaves like a vanilla struck at 6,200. The last ladder illustrated has 10 rungs to the ladder, starting at 6,200 and finishing at 8,000. If the FTSE 100 were to climb through 8,000 during the year, the ladder option by then would have accumulated 2,000 of intrinsic value and deliver any further gains above 8,000 to the investor at maturity. However, to acquire this payout would involve paying an up-front premium of 14.19%, almost double that of the vanilla ATM call.

TABLE 20.6

One-year ladder option quotations on the FTSE 100

Option	Highest ladder level	Premium
Vanilla	6,000	7.37%
Highest ladder	6,200	8.85%
	6,400	10.07%
	6,600	11.06%
	6,800	11.87%
	7,000	12.52%
	7,200	13.03%
	7,400	13.44%
	7,600	13.76%
	7,800	14.00%
	8,000	14.19%

Knock-out features are often incorporated into other equity products, like warrants, and considerably enhance their investment potential, albeit at the cost of increasing their risk. As an example, consider the short-term warrant whose specification is summarised in Table 20.7. An investor buying 50 of these warrants would be entitled to a cash settlement at maturity equal to the excess of Roche Holding AG's share price above the strike of CHF 140, provided that the underlier had never traded below CHF 140 during the 130-day life of the option.

TABLE 20.7

Knock-out warrant term sheet

Issuer	Bank Vontobel AG
Underlying	Roche Holding AG
Spot reference price	CHF 157.70
Ratio	50:1
Option type	Call
Option style	European, automatic exercise, with knock-out
Clearing	Cash settlement
Issue date	6 February 2012
Issue price	CHF 0.30
Strike price	CHF 140.00
Knock-out barrier	CHF 140.00
Barrier monitoring	6 February 2012 until 15 June 2012 continuous monitoring
Expiry date	15 June 2012
Premium	1.71%

Source: Bank Vontobel AG.

Given that these warrants were already deep in-the-money at launch, and that the premium of CHF 0.30 per warrant was cheaper than the initial intrinsic value of CHF 0.354 (17.70/50), they offered investors considerable gearing potential. In fact, by 20th April 2012, little over two months since launch, the warrants had doubled in value to CHF 0.60. It should be remembered that while the potential to make a 100% gain in a couple of months is very attractive to any investor, the warrants also had the potential to create a 100% loss if the underlier traded through the knock-out barrier *at any time* (not just at maturity).

Notes

1 The shape of the two profiles is indeed identical, but there is a £1,000 difference between the two payoff profiles. The reason why the flat part of the 100p strike covered call write profile in Figure 20.5 is at +£4,500, while that of the 100p strike naked put sale profile in Figure 20.7 is only at +£3,500 is because of the impact of dividends and interest. In the first case the investor must finance the share portfolio but earns interest on the £4,500 premium and also receives dividends. Under the rates prevailing in our scenario, this has a net cost of around £950. In the second case he earns interest of around £50 on the £3,500 premium received. The difference between these of £1,000 is compensated for by the £1,000 difference between the payoff profiles.

2 See Rubinstein, M. and Leland, H. (1981) 'Replicating options with positions in stock and cash', *Financial Analysis Journal*, 37, 4 (July–August), pp. 63–72.

21

MANAGING COMMODITY RISK

We have so far looked at three sources of financial risk: currency risk, interest rate risk and equity risk. Many organisations, however, are exposed to a fourth source – commodity risk. In this chapter, we will discuss the nature of commodity risk and review some of the methods by which it may be handled. Fortunately, we will not need to break much new ground here because all the tools and techniques used to manage commodity risk have exact parallels with those employed in the management of other financial risks examined in the previous four chapters. We will therefore be able to avoid repetition by referring back to concepts and methods explained earlier.

21.1 Commodity risk

Commodity risk arises in any situation where an organisation is affected by fluctuations in the price of some commodity, and there is a very wide range of physical assets which can nowadays be treated as commodities. The list includes:

- metals, comprising *base metals* such as copper and aluminium, and *precious metals* such as gold and platinum
- agricultural products, comprising *soft commodities* like coffee, wheat and soybeans, and *livestock* such as live cattle and pork bellies
- energy products, such as crude oil, gas, natural and refined petroleum products.

Any organisation which either produces or consumes significant amounts of these items is therefore exposed to commodity risk. Obvious candidates would include oil companies, airlines, car manufacturers and food processors. However, commodity risk can also have indirect effects which are less apparent, but can be equally devastating in their impact. Although they neither produce nor consume oil directly, tour operators and travel companies are extremely vulnerable to the cost of oil, because a significant component of the price of an overseas holiday package is the cost of the airline flight, which in turn depends on the cost of aviation fuel. A rise in the price of oil will ultimately raise the price of an overseas holiday, and may ultimately eliminate a significant proportion of a travel company's business if holiday-makers decide to stay at home.

Commodity risk is in many ways more pervasive than currency or interest rate risk, and this probably explains why commodity derivatives have been around far longer than financial derivatives. The first derivatives to be traded on the Chicago Board of Trade, established in 1848, were commodity futures. It was not until 1972 that the first financial futures contract was created, but these relative newcomers now overwhelmingly dominate the exchange-traded derivatives market. In 2011, only two out of the world's top 20 exchange-traded contracts were commodity derivatives – the light sweet crude oil contract at NYMEX (New York Mercantile Exchange), and the cotton No. 1 contract at the ZCE (Zhengzhou Commodity Exchange) – and these were well down the pecking order in 14th and 19th place respectively.[1]

Many companies exposed to commodity risk probably feel that such exposure is a necessary and unavoidable feature of their business. For example, a company operating in the coffee business may feel that it has to accept the ups and downs in demand caused by fluctuations in world coffee prices. To some extent this may be true, but proper use of commodity derivatives can help to smooth out and cushion some of the worst effects of commodity price instability.

Until the late 1980s, the only commodity risk management tools available were exchange-traded futures and options, and even now liquidity in these contracts seldom extends beyond one year into the future. While these provide protection against price fluctuations in the short term, they are unable to provide guaranteed protection for extended periods. While a company could resort to the tactic of using a rolling futures hedge, this is only capable of fixing a series of different prices over a succession of shorter periods; this is not the same as fixing a single price over the longer term. The lack of long-term commodity price protection may be one reason why commodity futures and options have not been used as extensively as they might otherwise have been.

Recent developments have heralded an upsurge of interest in financial engineering solutions for managing commodity risk, and a spate of new products has now emerged. Inspired by the success of interest rate tools like swaps, caps, collars and swaptions, similar products have been developed for the commodities market. Use of commodity swaps is now extensive, with notional amounts outstanding of around $2tn in June 2011, comparable with that of equity swaps. Commodity caps, collars and even options on commodity swaps are also available. In the remaining sections of this chapter we will review how these new products have been created, and how they can be used.

21.2 Creating commodity derivatives

The starting point for building most commodity derivatives is the commodity futures market. In order to create and market any derivative financial product, it is necessary to find a way of hedging it, otherwise the market-maker would be burdened with an unmanageable risk. It would, of course, be possible to hedge a commodity derivative with the underlying commodity, but in most cases this would be highly undesirable. No financial institution really wants to count acres of corn or herds of cattle among its assets. Commodity futures provide a clean, liquid and low-cost way of hedging exposure to the underlying commodity.

The price of many commodity futures is related to the spot price of the underlying commodity through the same cash-and-carry pricing mechanism explained in Chapter 7 (section 7.3). Table 21.1 illustrates the set of futures prices at the close of business on 19th April 2012, and we can use these figures to investigate the relationships between cash and futures prices. As an example, someone selling the April 2013 gold futures contract could hedge the price risk by buying gold and holding it for the one-year period until the futures contract expired. Unlike bond futures and stock index futures contracts, however, with gold there is no flow of coupon or dividend income to offset the pure cost of financing the hedge. With one-year US interest rates at around 1%, we would therefore expect the gold futures contracts to be priced at a 1% per annum premium above the cash price, and the gold futures prices in Table 21.1 do just that with, for example, the June 2013 contract priced 0.8% above the June 2012 contract.

TABLE 21.1

Cash and commodity futures prices on 19th April 2012

Contract:	WTI crude oil	Heating oil	Lean hogs	Corn	Gold
Exchange:	NYMEX	NYMEX	CME	CBOT	COMEX
Contract size:	1,000 barrels	42,000 gallons	40,000 lbs	5,000 bushels	100 Troy oz
Quotation:	$ per barrel	$ per gallon	¢ per lb	¢ per bushel	$ per oz
Cash price	102.27	3.1189	81.840	621.50	1640.5
May-12	102.27	3.1251	88.475	621	1640.6
Jun-12	102.72	3.1284	88.775		1641.4
Jul-12	103.15	3.1320	89.325	612	
Aug-12	103.53	3.1353	89.700		1643.6
Sep-12	103.84	3.1388		555	
Oct-12	104.03	3.1445	81.950		1645.7
Nov-12	104.16	3.1515			
Dec-12	104.27	3.1573	79.375	541.75	1647.8
Jan-13	104.37	3.1606			
Feb-13	104.37	3.1548	80.300		1649.8
Mar-13	104.27	3.1408		552.5	
Apr-13	104.02	3.1243	81.400		1651.8
May-13	103.71		86.000	560.5	
Jun-13	103.37		87.600		1654.1

Source: NYMEX, CME, CBOT, COMEX.

Gold is somewhat special in that storage costs are relatively low, wastage and deterioration do not occur, and there is no seasonal pattern to the sequence of prices throughout the year. These conditions do not apply for most other commodities, however. The storage costs for oil are higher than for gold, and the asset is less attractive as collateral for a secured loan. The crude oil futures prices in Table 21.1 therefore generally appreciate at a faster rate than the gold contracts. Heating oil, which is a by-product of crude oil, exhibits a seasonal pattern, with prices peaking in the winter months around January, and then falling away with the summer months as demand falls. Agricultural products, like the lean hogs and corn contracts illustrated, also show strong seasonality linked to rearing and harvest cycles. Products such as these are also perishable and subject to deterioration, which may cause the cash price to stand at a premium over the futures market when shortages occur.

Figure 21.1 illustrates some futures contracts that exhibit strong seasonal patterns, including corn and lean hogs already discussed, and also natural gas and gasoline. Like heating oil, natural gas prices peak in the winter months, whereas gasoline exhibits almost the opposite effect, with prices higher in the summer

FIGURE 21.1

Seasonality of commodity contracts

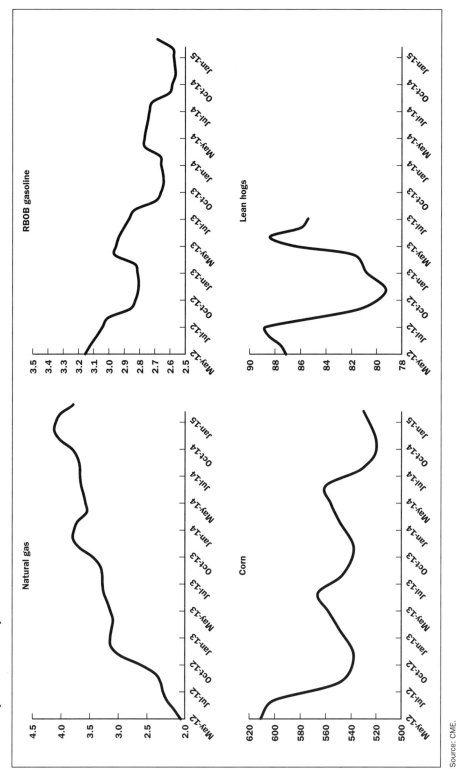

Source: CME.

months because more people take to the road and also because summer-grade fuel is more expensive to produce.

The relationship between commodity futures prices and cash market prices is therefore much more susceptible to the laws of supply and demand than that for financial futures. In the months when demand for the commodity rises, as with heating oil and natural gas in the winter, the futures price will be higher than the cash-and-carry arbitrage pricing would suggest. When supply outstrips demand, as with lean hogs in the spring or heating oil in the summer, futures prices will be lower, and may even fall below those in the cash market. This last condition, when futures prices fall below the cash market price, is known as *backwardation*, to distinguish it from the more usual *contango* market, where futures prices are at a premium.

Although the relationship between the commodity futures and cash prices is therefore not as straightforward as for financial futures, the two markets do move in unison. If prices in the cash markets rise, then so do commodity futures, and by a similar amount. As an example, Table 21.2 shows the change in prices between 19th and 25th April 2012 for the same set of commodities analysed in Table 21.1. The figures demonstrate that the change in the cash price was exactly (or almost exactly) mirrored by changes in the near-dated futures contracts. This means that commodity futures, especially the highly liquid near-dated contracts, can be used as an effective proxy for the underlying commodity when hedging other commodity derivatives. Although the longer-dated contracts do not move so much, this is only to be expected. A short-term fluctuation in cash prices does not necessarily imply a permanent change in prices, so the short-term contracts respond more than the long-term ones. If, however, there was a structural change in the market affecting long-term expectations for commodity prices, then the longer-dated contracts would shift accordingly.

TABLE 21.2

Change to cash and commodity futures prices between 19th and 25th April 2012

Contract	WTI crude oil	Heating oil	Lean hogs	Corn	Gold
Cash price	+1.85	+0.0385	−0.500	−8.50	+0.7
May-12	+1.85	+0.0360	−1.350	−10.00	+0.8
Jun-12	+1.78	+0.0385	−1.200		+0.9
Jul-12	+1.68	+0.0370	−0.850	−11.00	
Aug-12	+1.53	+0.0363	−0.950		+1.0
Sep-12	+1.36	+0.0359		−6.00	
Oct-12	+1.28	+0.0348	−0.625		+0.9
Nov-12	+1.25	+0.0334			
Dec-12	+1.21	+0.0322	−0.125	−3.75	+0.9
Jan-13	+1.06	+0.0314			
Feb-13	+0.87	+0.0325	+0.500		+1.0
Mar-13	+0.65	+0.0338		−3.00	
Apr-13	+0.52	+0.0361	+0.400		+1.0
May-13	+0.45		+0.500	−2.50	
Jun-13			+0.800		+0.9

Source: NYMEX, CME, CBOT, COMEX.

Now that we have established the viability of using commodity futures as a proxy for the underlying commodity, the creation of other commodity derivatives is relatively straightforward.

Commodity options may be priced using the standard Black–Scholes or binomial models, and dynamically hedged by buying or selling commodity futures contracts for an amount equal to delta times the amount underlying the option contract. To price commodity caps, floors and collars, the premiums from the strip of component options are aggregated, as explained in Chapter 13 (section 13.5). In this regard these commodity derivatives are directly analogous to their interest rate counterparts.

Short-term commodity swaps may be priced and hedged using a strip of futures contracts and, just as we saw in Chapter 9 (sections 9.5 and 9.6), the commodity swap price is the weighted average of the forward commodity prices (i.e. the futures prices), using the set of discount factors as the weights. To price longer-dated swaps, where suitable futures contracts may not be available, the market-maker can extrapolate the commodity forward price curve in order to estimate what the likely commodity futures prices would be if they existed. A stack hedge can then be used to hedge a longer-dated swap, utilising the technique explained in Chapter 18 (section 18.4).

When compared to financial futures, commodity futures markets exhibit less liquidity and wider spreads. Hedging commodity derivatives is therefore costlier and involves a greater degree of basis risk. For example, a market-maker could use a stack of short-dated commodity futures contracts to hedge a five-year oil swap, and continue to roll the futures hedge at every expiry date. However, if the basis between cash and futures should eventually differ from the original estimate made when the swap was priced, the market-maker would suffer from basis risk. A dramatic illustration of this is the oft-cited case of Metalgesellschaft, which had to be rescued in early 1994 because of huge short-term losses on its rolling futures hedge. In addition to the basis risk it suffered, Metalgesellschaft was hit by substantial cash flow mismatches triggered by a substantial shift in the underlying asset price. Losses on its futures hedge led to immediate cash outflows of $1bn while the corresponding cash inflows from its underlying forwards and swaps would only arrive up to ten years later.

Basis risk can also occur when a market-maker uses futures to cross-hedge a commodity swap. For example, an aviation fuel swap can be hedged with crude oil futures, since there are no aviation fuel futures contracts available. Crude oil and aviation fuel prices tend to move closely, but as the relationship is not perfect, the basis risk remains.

The price of a commodity swap must therefore take account of the difficulties caused by spreads, basis risk, financing the variation margin, as well as some of the other problems reviewed in Chapter 18 (e.g. non-coincidence of futures and exposure dates). Nonetheless, commodity swaps can be priced at a sufficiently attractive level to offer cost-effective risk management solutions for those exposed to commodity risk. The next section provides examples where this has proved highly effective.

21.3 Using commodity derivatives

Commodity futures and options can be used in exactly the same way as interest rate and currency futures and options, and the techniques have been thoroughly documented in the previous four chapters.

Prices for single commodity transactions taking place up to a year in the future can be fixed using commodity futures, and the various methods presented in Chapter 18 may be employed equally well here to improve hedge efficiency. For example, adjusting the hedge ratio to account for exposure basis, the timing of the settlement sum and margin flows will help to improve the effectiveness of a commodity futures hedge, as will the use of spread and interpolated hedges when the exposure and futures maturity dates do not coincide.

If a hedger wishes to obtain protection from adverse movements in commodity prices, but to continue to benefit from favourable moves, exchange-traded or OTC commodity options provide an answer. As an example, Figure 21.2 illustrates the effective price paid on 27th April 2012 to purchase July oil using four different NYMEX call options. Also shown are the cost profiles obtained by using the July 2012 futures contract trading at $104.45, and the result for the buyer if no hedge was in place.

FIGURE 21.2

Hedging using commodity options

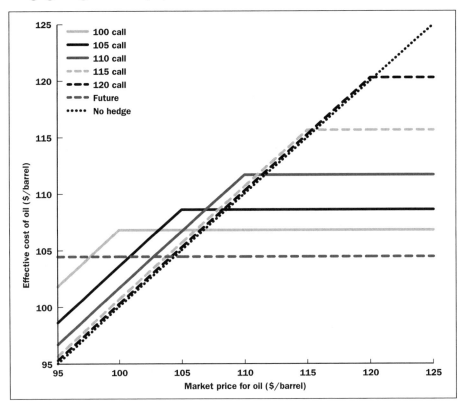

These profiles offer no surprises, and share the same characteristics as those of currency and interest rate options that we have seen in earlier chapters. The $100 in-the-money call exhibits a price characteristic close to that of the futures hedge – a fixed cost over most of the price range illustrated, but with a small possibility to save money if oil was to drop below $100 a barrel in July. At the other end of the scale, the out-of-the-money option struck at $120 has a profile resembling the no-hedge alternative, allowing considerable savings if the oil price is low, but only offering protection once July oil rises through $120 a barrel. As usual, the options struck near-the-money provide a compromise performance in between these two extremes.

Chapters 17, 19 and 20 have already provided a wealth of more advanced option-based solutions for managing currency, interest rate and equity risk. In addition to the basic option hedge illustrated in Figure 21.2, collars, spread-hedges, participations and other option structures all work in exactly the same way in managing commodity risk, and there is therefore no need to provide duplicate examples here.

Commodity swaps are also little different from their interest rate cousins, and allow a counterparty to lock in a fixed commodity price on a series of dates in the future. A typical structure is illustrated in Figure 21.3, which shows how commodity swaps can benefit both producer and consumer alike.

In the illustration, the oil producer enters into a commodity swap as the fixed price receiver, agreeing to receive periodic payments at a fixed price of $97.15 per barrel on a nominal quantity of oil against paying the market price. When the producer actually sells oil into the market, he delivers oil and receives the prevailing market price. The producer's cash flows linked to market prices therefore net out, and the effect of the swap is therefore to fix the price at which the producer sells his oil.

In a similar way, the oil consumer enters into another commodity swap with the bank, this time paying the fixed price of $97.45 per barrel and receiving the market price. The consumer in turn then pays the market price when he buys oil in the spot market. Once again, the market-related cash flows cancel each other

FIGURE 21.3
Example of a commodity swap

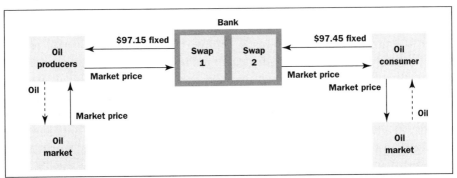

out, and the oil consumer ends up paying a fixed price for oil, regardless of the market rate.

Both producer and consumer have eliminated their exposure to fluctuating oil prices, and the swap thus ensures price certainty for both parties. Assuming the bank can match the timings and nominal sizes of both swaps, it profits from the margin between the fixed prices on the two swaps. Alternatively, the bank could hedge each swap separately in the futures market.

It is important to note that no exchange of the physical commodity ever takes place. The commodity swap is based on a nominal quantity of the underlying commodity, for example a million barrels of oil per month, but this nominal quantity is only used as the basis for calculating the swap payments. If the spot oil price was $100.00 on one fixing date, the oil producer would pay $2,850,000 net on a nominal quantity of one million barrels, while the oil consumer would receive $2,550,000 net. The bank arranging the two swaps earns the $300,000 difference, to cover the costs of hedging, administration and counterparty risk, as well as a providing a contribution to profits.

One of the best-known proponents of commodity price hedging is Southwest Airlines which, since the mid-1990s, has engaged in an extensive programme to hedge its aviation fuel costs. According to its 2011 Annual Report:

> **'The Company utilizes various derivative instruments, including crude oil, unleaded gasoline, and heating oil-based derivatives, to attempt to reduce the risk of its exposure to jet fuel price increases. These instruments consist primarily of purchased call options, collar structures, call spreads, and fixed-price swap agreements.'**

The programme has been highly successful, saving around $3.5bn over the ten-year period from 1999–2008, a figure equivalent to about 83% of the company's profits over that period. Profits in the years 2009–2011 from fuel derivative instruments added up to a further $763m. Throughout the post 9/11 downturn from 2001 to 2005 Southwest remained profitable, while the airline industry overall lost more than $35bn.

Other US airlines have been slower or less aggressive in implementing fuel cost hedging strategies. In 2008 when oil prices touched $140 per barrel, Southwest had 70% of its fuel needs hedged at $51 a barrel; in contrast American Airlines had 34% of its fuel needs for the year hedged at $82 a barrel. While Delta had hedges for just under half its fuel needs, they were at prices closer to American's than Southwest's. During 2009–2010, studies for the airline industry have shown the average hedging ratio to be 64%.

Of course, hedging does not always lead to gains. For example, in October 2011 Southwest posted a third-quarter loss, largely arising from $372m losses on its fuel derivatives hedges. This does not diminish the value of their hedging strategy in any way. If the objective of hedging is to reduce uncertainty and lock in a fixed cost for purchasing aviation fuel, then that objective has largely been achieved. Scott Topping, then Treasurer of Southwest, is quoted as saying:

> **'When oil got to $40 a barrel, we thought, "Oh, wow! It's too late."**
> **Then it went to $60, and to $80, and then to where we are now.**
> **At each step along the way, the question "Is this something**
> **we should continue to do?" became more and more difficult to**
> **answer. But our overall philosophy led us to keep buying hedges.**
> **It's a matter of discipline.'[2]**

In keeping with this philosophy, Southwest's 2011 Annual Report reveals that, as of 13th January 2012, it had hedged between 85% and 95% of its estimated 2012H2 fuel consumption needs at the following price levels:

$80–100	10–20%
$100–125	approx. 50%
$125–150	approx. 20%
above $150	less than 5%

In addition, it reports that 40–50% of its 2013 and 2014 estimated fuel consumption needs were already covered by derivative contracts at various price levels, as well as at least 10% of its estimated 2015 needs. Interestingly, however, minimal contracts were in place for 2012H1.

In addition to hedging aviation fuel costs, commodity swaps are regularly transacted in a wide range of other underliers including crude and refined oil, corn, soybeans, cotton, canola, sugar and wheat. One variation on the standard swap structure is a swap under which the floating price is based on an average of daily market prices over a period, rather than on the spot commodity price on a given day. This would suit users buying and selling the commodity on a continual basis rather than periodically. Another variation is where the swap payments are driven by the weighted-average prices of a basket of commodities, either diversified across a range of commodity sectors (like the S&P GSCI) or focused on one sector like energy.

Yet another variation involves the fixed price payer granting a receivers swaption in return for a lower swap price. This might be attractive in contango markets where the futures stand at a considerable premium to the spot price. The commodity swap/swaption combination works thus. Without the swaption, the commodity consumer would be faced with a fixed swap rate considerably higher than the prevailing commodity price. By selling the swaption on a nominal commodity amount equal to that underlying the swap, the commodity consumer can use the premium to lower the swap price and fix costs at a lower level. If commodity prices should rise, the swaption will expire worthless and the consumer keeps the premium. If prices fall, the receiver's swaption is exercised against the consumer, who ends up paying the fixed price on double the original nominal amount. In the latter instance, although the consumer is paying above-market prices on a larger quantity of the commodity, we must presume the price must still be an attractive one, otherwise the consumer would not have entered into the swap in the first place. Since the consumer ends up swapping double the original quantity of the commodity if the swaption is exercised, this structure is sometimes called a *double-up commodity swap.*

An alternative way to reduce costs arises in situations where a commodity swap is already in place, but market prices have since moved against the swap counterparty; it is called the *blend-and-extend* swap. As an example, suppose at the beginning of 2008 a plastics manufacturer enters into a five-year oil swap paying fixed at $100 a barrel on 100,000 barrels a year, with semi-annual payments. By the summer of that year oil prices have spiked to $135, and the manufacturer is naturally delighted with the hedge. By January 2009, following the slump in demand triggered by the credit crisis, oil has crashed to $40 a barrel, four-year swaps are trading at only $53 a barrel, and to cancel the existing swap would involve the manufacturer paying an $18m cancellation fee. Instead of paying this penalty, the manufacturer could enter into a new off-market ten-year swap and agree to pay $86 fixed for the next ten years, as compared with the prevailing vanilla ten-year swap price of $66 a barrel. The extra $20 a barrel for ten years buys out the initial swap and enables the manufacturer to lower his current oil costs from $100 a barrel to $86 a barrel and achieve price certainty for ten more years. This arrangement is called a 'blend-and-extend' swap because it combines four years at $100 per barrel with the 4 × 10 forward swap price of $75.68 to give a blended price of $86 a barrel, and lengthens the existing swap from its remaining period of four years to an extended period of ten years.

Had the manufacturer in the above example bought a cancellable rather than a vanilla commodity swap, he could have avoided having to use the blend-and-extend swap. Such swaps can be created by banks in the same way as with cancellable and extendible interest rate swaps (see sections 13.4 and 19.4), by combining a vanilla commodity swap with a commodity swaption.

For those exposed to the difference between two commodity prices there are various permutations of *basis swap*, first mentioned in Chapter 8 (section 8.12). These include the following:

■ Basis swaps to hedge against geographical price differences. As an example, Linn Energy uses PEPL (Panhandle Eastern Pipe Line) basis swaps to hedge the basis differential associated with natural gas production in the Mid-Continent Deep and Mid-Continent Shallow regions of Texas and Oklahoma.

■ An oil refinery might use crack swaps to hedge its profits against changes in the difference between the price of crude oil and the price of refined products like gasoline.

■ A gas-fired power station might use spark swaps to prevent its operating margin being affected by changes in the difference between natural gas and electricity prices.

The list of potential new applications for commodity derivatives is endless. As the examples mentioned here have shown, it is in theory possible to design a derivative product for any situation where risk manifests itself. Some products, like the aviation fuel swap, have already shown considerable growth, while others have yet to achieve a critical mass. There are many practical difficulties, not least in finding indices which are generally accepted, and then in being able to hedge the derivative. Nevertheless, if banks find a demand for a particular design, few problems are insurmountable.

21.4 Hybrid commodity derivatives

Almost all the commodity derivatives reviewed so far have involved some kind of exchange between a commodity index and money. However, once it is possible to offer an option or a swap from one commodity index to money, the fixed financial payments become a common denominator, and it is therefore possible to structure a derivative between any two commodity indices. Alternatively, a standard financial instrument like a bond can be structured to include commodity-linked payoffs. Such products are called *hybrid commodity derivatives*. Examples include the following:

- Commodity-linked notes, such as Nordea Bank's index-linked bond issued on 26th April 2011 and maturing 14th June 2014, just over three years later. The bond was issued in two tranches: Basic and Extra, initially floated at 97% of par and 107% of par, respectively. Each promised to pay the investor a guaranteed minimum of 100% of the face value plus a bonus linked to the value of an equally-weighted basket of six commodities: oil (Brent crude), coal, copper, corn, cotton and sugar. For the Basic tranche the bonus will be 70% of the appreciation of the basket over the lifetime of the bond, while investors in the Extra tranche will receive 200% of the appreciation of the basket.

- Principal-indexed gold notes. One example is the CIBC Gold Linked Accelerated Return Note issued on 14th December 2011 and maturing two years later on 16th December 2013. Redemption is linked directly to the appreciation of gold over the lifetime of the note. If gold depreciates, investors suffer a one-for-one loss, but if gold appreciates, investors receive a three-fold gain, but capped at 33%. A more complex example is the barrier gold-linked note issued by Citigroup on 7th September 2010 denominated in Hungarian forints, and maturing three years later on 6th September 2013. The redemption amount at maturity depends upon the appreciation of gold over the three-year period from 27th August 2010 to 27th August 2013, but is also path-dependent.

  - If gold never appreciates more than 25% since inception, the investor receives par plus double the appreciation of gold (if positive).

  - If gold never appreciates more than 35% since inception, the investor receives par plus the appreciation of gold (if positive).

– If gold never appreciates more than 45% since inception, the investor receives par plus half the appreciation of gold (if positive).

– If gold ever appreciates by more than 45% since inception, the investor receives par plus a 25% rebate.

For such products to succeed, there must be an incentive for issuers to create the hybrid in the first place, and investors must be motivated to buy them. The first condition will be satisfied if the instrument is structured in such a way as to reduce the issuer's cost and/or risk. Investors are often encouraged by an unusual market opportunity, the ability to participate or speculate in a market to which they may not normally have access, and the prospect of an above-market return. The second requirement can therefore often be met by skilful distribution, effective marketing and keen pricing.

Notes

1 See 'Annual Volume Survey', *Futures Industry Magazine* (March 2012), pp. 24–32.
2 'Can fuel hedges keep Southwest in the money?', *USA Today*, 24th July 2008.

22

MANAGING CREDIT RISK

Chapter 14 has already charted the dramatic growth and development of the credit derivatives market from small beginnings in the mid-1990s to become the world's second largest derivatives market just ten years later. Part of this explosive growth was because credit derivatives served a need that was hitherto unaddressed – a derivative product tailored specifically to help banks and investors hedge their exposure to credit risk. However, the major spur to growth came from new opportunities created by credit derivatives – the ability for investors, hedge funds and others to express their opinions on the future evolution of credit. Users who think that the credit quality of a particular entity will improve or worsen can monetise their view by using single-name CDS contracts, while those who want to take a broader view on the evolution of credit can use credit index products. In this chapter we will explore a range of such applications, beginning with what kick-started the credit derivatives market in the first place – the desire to hedge against default risk in particular, and credit risk in general.

22.1 Hedging default risk

Fundamental in the definition of a CDS contract is a description of what happens if a recognised credit event occurs, most often the bankruptcy of the reference entity or a failure on its part to pay some financial obligation. In Chapter 14 (section 14.7) we explained that since 2009 the mechanism used in nearly all cases is to hold an auction of the reference entity's deliverable bonds, and to use the outcome of the auction to determine the cash settlement amount for CDS contracts as:

$$\text{Cash Settlement Amount} = \text{Notional Contract Size} \\ \times (100\% - \text{Final Auction Price})$$

Since, by definition, the Final Auction Price is the value of the defaulting entity's deliverable bonds on the day of the auction, the combination of deliverable bond plus CDS contract for the same notional value must be equal to par *at that time*. However, this is not the same as saying that this combination will *always* be equal to par. Prior to the credit event the value of an entity's bonds and of CDS referencing those bonds will be closely related, but they may not move in exactly the same way. To see how efficient a CDS contract is when hedging a bond holding against the losses arising from a default, let's explore the example of an investor who held bonds issued by Eastman Kodak.

The story starts in October 2003 when our investor buys $10m notional of Eastman Kodak's newly issued ten-year bond maturing 15th November 2013. Then an investment grade company, albeit with the lowest possible credit ratings of BBB- from S&P and Baa3 from Moody's, the bond carried an attractive coupon of 7.25% and at its offer price of 99.879, the yield of 7.27% was 3% above US ten-year Treasuries at the time.

Unfortunately, Kodak's fortunes were very much on the wane. It lost market share in its traditional film-making business to Fuji, and failed to perceive that the digital revolution in photography would eventually annihilate that business almost completely. The share price had declined from $90 in 1997 to around $25 in 2005 when its senior debt was downgraded to high-yield ('junk') status in April that year, just after filing first-quarter losses of $142m. A series of further downgrades saw Kodak senior debt down to B/B2 by the beginning of 2006. The share price held steady at around $25 through 2007, before plunging to just $3 by April 2011. Despite this disastrous decline in performance, the price of our investor's bond remained remarkably steady throughout and traded close to par, apart from temporarily dipping down to the mid-60s from late 2008 to late 2009. In fact, the company issued a Tender Offer to buy back $100m of the $500m issue for a total consideration of 95% of face value early in February 2010. Figure 22.1 compares the bond price with Kodak's share price and reveals how well the bond held up over this period.

Nonetheless, given the strongly declining trend in Kodak's strength and the series of unfavourable news stories concerning the company's future prospects, our investor decided on 27 April 2011 to buy protection on his $10m holding. At the time, three-year CDS were quoted at a premium of 984bp p.a., corresponding to an up-front payment of 12.25% (ignoring accrued premium) and a standardised premium of 500bp p.a. The timing was apposite because shortly thereafter CDS premiums went through the roof. After remaining below 1000bp

FIGURE 22.1

Eastman Kodak shares vs. 7.25% 2013 bond price

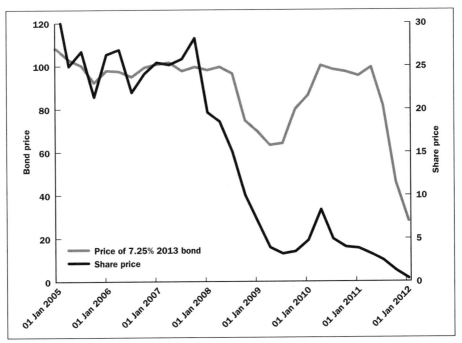

Source: Barclays.

for more than a year, premiums broke through this level in early May 2011, reached 2000bp in July, 5000bp in October, and burst through 10000bp in early January 2012, with up-front payments in the 60% to 70% region by then. Figure 22.2 illustrates the relationship between the 3yr CDS premium, the yield on the 7.25% 2013 bond, and Kodak's share price from April 2007 until the end of 2011.

Eastman Kodak finally filed for Chapter 11 bankruptcy protection on 19th January 2012. The Americas Determination Committee resolved that day that a credit event had occurred and scheduled the resultant auction to take place on 22nd February 2012. The final list of six deliverable bonds was published on 9th February. At the auction itself, around $228m in total of bonds were traded at the Final Auction Price of 23.875%.

Our investor placed a Physical Settlement Request to sell his bond holding with his investment bank, who happened to be one of the 13 Participating Bidders at the auction and so received $2,387,500 on the settlement date of 29th February 2012. In addition, the CDS was cash settled so that the investor received a Cash Settlement Amount of:

$$\$10m \times (100\% - 23.875\%) = \$7,612,500$$

The total proceeds were, of course, $10m and this ensured that the combination of bond plus CDS did indeed deliver the desired result – the investor was 'made whole' and received payment of par despite the depths to which the bond price had sunk.

FIGURE 22.2
Eastman Kodak shares, bond yield and CDS premiums

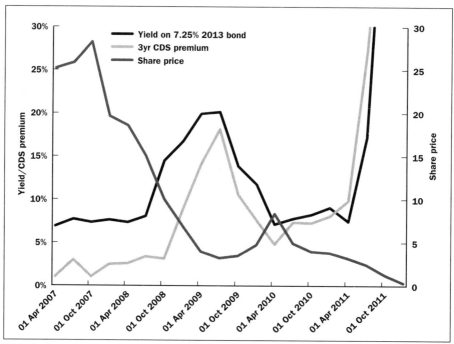

Source: Barclays.

For completeness, however, we should also take into account the cost of protection over the hedging period, mitigated by the coupon earned on the bond. At first sight, it may look as if the carry cost is simply the difference between the CDS premium rate of 9.84% p.a. and the bond coupon of 7.25% p.a., or 2.59% p.a. Over the 267-day hedging period, this works out at 1.92% of $10m, or $192,000. However, under the system of standardised premiums, although the quoted premium (or par spread) is 984bp p.a., the investor makes an up-front payment of 12.25% to the protection seller (ignoring accrued premium), and then only pays 500bp p.a. If there had been no credit event, and the CDS contract had been in force for the full three-year period, the 12.25% up-front payment would have been broadly equivalent to the 4.84% difference between the quoted and standardised premium rates for the 3.19-year lifetime of the CDS.[1] However, there *was* a credit event less than nine months after the contract was taken out, and so the investor's up-front payment turns out to have been excessive after the fact. Table 22.1 takes this into account to determine what the true carry cost of the CDS contract was in this example.

TABLE 22.1
Cash flows arising from Eastman Kodak hedge

Date	Description	Paid	Received	Notes
27 Apr 2011	Up-front (off-market payment)	$1,225,000		
27 Apr 2011	Up-front (accrued premium)		$52,778	38 days
16 May 2011	Bond coupon		$362,500	
20 Jun 2011	CDS Premium	$126,389		91 days
20 Sep 2011	CDS Premium	$127,778		92 days
15 Nov 2011	Bond coupon		$362,500	
20 Dec 2011	CDS Premium	$126,389		91 days
19 Jan 2012	CDS Premium (accrued)	$43,056		31 days
	Total	$1,648,611	$777,778	
	Net	$870,333 paid		

The net amount paid by the investor is therefore $870,333 over the nine-month period, and this reduces the effective net proceeds from the bond plus CDS combination from $10m to $9,129,167. However, while the carry costs reduce the hedge efficiency to 91%, without the CDS the bond would only have been worth $2,387,500 after the credit event, an 'efficiency' of less than 24%. Of course, had the investor bought protection at the outset, when the CDS premium was around 150bp, the cost of protection would have been much lower, but then the investor would have had to pay these premiums for a much longer period of time.

In the example we have just reviewed, the investor in question bought protection when the underlying bond was trading very close to par. It was therefore no surprise that the appropriate default hedge was to buy protection using a CDS with the same $10m notional as the $10m face value of the bond. However, what about another situation where the bond was trading at a substantial premium or discount? At first sight it may seem that an investor seeking to buy protection on

$10m face value of a bond currently trading at 110 should buy CDS protection with a notional of $11m. In fact, this would only be correct if the recovery rate turned out to be zero post-default. For any other situation, the correct credit event hedge ratio is given by this simple formula:

$$\text{Credit Event Hedge Ratio} = \frac{P - R}{100 - R} \qquad (22.1)$$

where:

P   is the current bond price (in percent)
R   is the assumed recovery rate (in percent)

To demonstrate how this works, Table 22.2 sets out the hedging strategy and then shows the eventual outcome in two situations: one where the bond initially was trading at a premium, and the other where the bond was trading at a discount. In both cases the net proceeds at the very end match the market value of the bond at the outset.

TABLE 22.2
Hedging strategies and outcomes for bonds trading away from par

	Bond at a premium	Bond at a discount
Face value of bond	$10m	$10m
Initial price	110	90
Market value of bond	$11m	$9m
Assumed recovery rate	40	40
Hedge ratio	$\frac{110 - 40}{100 - 40} = 1.1667$	$\frac{90 - 40}{100 - 40} = 0.8333$
Hedging strategy	Buy protection on $11.67m	Buy protection on $8.33m
Action at default	Buy a further $1.67m face value of bonds. If the distressed bond is now trading at 40, this will cost $0.67m.	Sell $1.67m face value of the bonds held. If the distressed bond is now trading at 40, this will realise $0.67m.
Auction strategy	Place the $11.67m bonds into the auction as a Physical Settlement Request.	Place the remaining $8.33m bonds into the auction as a Physical Settlement Request.
Auction outcome	Regardless of the Final Auction Price, the combination of $11.67m face value of bond and $11.67m of CDS will guarantee cash proceeds of $11.67m.	Regardless of the Final Auction Price, the combination of $8.33m face value of bond and $8.33m of CDS will guarantee cash proceeds of $8.33m.
Net proceeds	$11.67m cash proceeds *less* $0.67m paid to buy extra bonds = $11m.	$8.33m cash proceeds *plus* $0.67m received when selling some bonds = $9m.

Note that this hedging strategy will only be 100% successful if the bond is trading at the assumed recovery rate at the time of the auction. If the bond was trading at a different price, the outcome will be a little different. For example, if the distressed bond was trading at 25 instead of 40 on the auction date, the net proceeds in the above example would have been $11.25m and $8.75m for the premium and discount bonds respectively, leading to hedge efficiencies of around 97%. Figure 22.3 illustrates the range of hedge efficiencies for the complete range of bond price outcomes following default.

Before leaving this topic, let's return to the Eastman Kodak investor, but this time let's suppose that he had not bought CDS protection back in April 2011. It is now 1st December 2011 and things are looking extremely grim for the Eastman Kodak company. Figure 22.4 shows that the implied default probability bootstrapped from CDS premiums[2] is heading towards 100%. The question now seems to be not whether Eastman Kodak will default but rather when will this happen and what will the loss be? Our investor cannot do much about the timing of the likely credit event, but there is a product that allows him to hedge the extent of the loss – the recovery lock, first introduced in Chapter 14 (section 14.8). By selling a *recovery lock*, the investor swaps the variable outcome of owning a distressed bond, whose value changes day by day, for the fixed recovery payment made by the recovery lock buyer when triggered by the credit event. Figure 22.5 illustrates the cash flows involved.

FIGURE 22.3
Hedge efficiencies for default hedging strategy

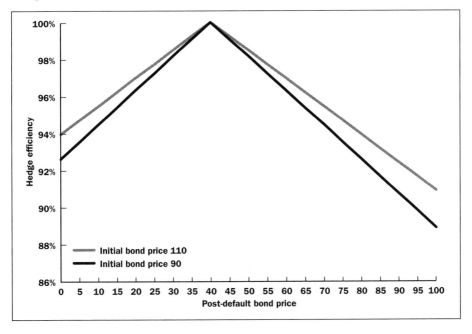

FIGURE 22.4

Implied default probability for Eastman Kodak

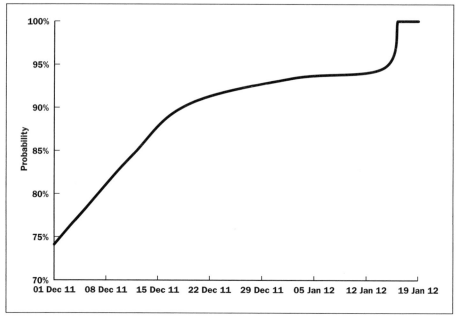

Source: CDS Premium and recovery lock data from Goldman Sachs, and author's calculations.

FIGURE 22.5

Hedging using a recovery lock

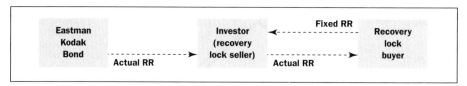

In early December 2011, recovery locks were quoted at only 20%, against a bond price in the mid-40s. While selling the recovery lock would have guaranteed a 20% payoff following a credit event, the higher bond price reflected the potential upside in the eventuality that Eastman Kodak did not default. As the weeks passed and a credit event became more likely, the bond price fell. At the same time, estimates of recovery values became slightly more optimistic over time, and recovery lock prices gradually rose. For example, if the investor decided on 17th January 2012 to sell a recovery lock to lock in the recovery value, he would have obtained a price of around 26%, only fractionally below the price of 30 at which the 7.25% of 2013 bond was trading at the time, and several percentage points above the Final Auction Price that would have been achieved if the investor had opted not to hedge and instead sold his bonds at the ISDA auction. Figure 22.6 charts the progress of both recovery lock quotations and of the Eastman Kodak 2013 bond in the two months prior to the credit event.

FIGURE 22.6

Recovery lock quotations vs. 7.25% 2013 bond price

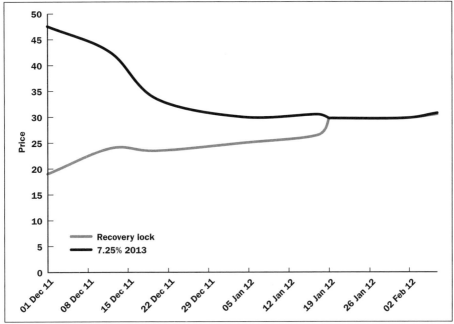

Source: Goldman Sachs.

22.2 Hedging credit risk

The examples in the previous section focused on hedging the financial consequences of a credit event itself, typically bankruptcy. After all, this was the prime
mover in creating the credit derivatives market in the first place. Mercifully,
however, credit events are relatively rare. Around the globe typically only a
handful of investment-grade names default each year and, even at the height of
the credit crisis, S&P reports.[3] only 14 investment-grade defaults (in 2008) and
223 defaults among high-yield names (in 2009). Figure 22.7 charts the history of
global corporate default rates over the 30-year period from 1981 to 2011.

While not unimportant, the need to hedge against the ultimate default of an
entity is something that does not arise very often, and hardly ever for investors
concentrating on investment-grade portfolios where the default rate averaged
only 0.11% over the 30-year period shown in the figure.

What is much more important, and something that arises on a regular
basis, is the need to hedge against a change in credit quality. S&P reports that
out of 5851 corporate issuers rated in 2011, more than 11% experienced a
rating change during that year, which is 15 times the percentage of defaults.
However, a rating change is just the tip of the iceberg; the resultant upgrade or
downgrade normally comes after weeks or even months during which time the
company's credit spread, bond price and CDS premium have all evolved on a
continuous basis.

FIGURE 22.7

Global corporate default rates 1981–2011

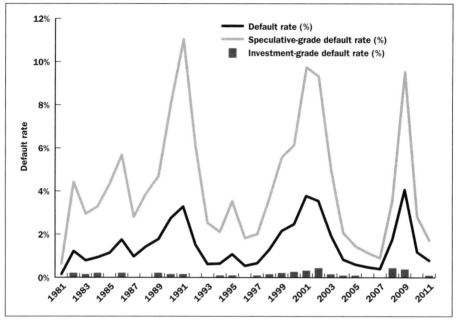

Source: S&P.

We will therefore explore how effective CDS are in hedging the *change in value* of an investor's bond portfolio rather than how well they protect against an ultimate credit event. To illustrate this, we will examine an investor who owns $10m notional of the 9.1% bond issued in July 2009 by KB Home – one of the USA's largest home builders – and maturing on 15th September 2017. Shortly after their launch these bonds went to a premium, and traded around the 105 level for most of the period from late 2009 until early 2011, apart from a brief dip down to par during the summer of 2010. Unfortunately, on 9th December 2010 a group of lenders filed a bankruptcy petition against South Edge LLC, the company behind Inspirada – a 2000-acre housing project on the outskirts of Las Vegas, and one of the many victims of the US housing crisis of that period. KB Home owned 48% of South Edge, with potential liabilities of up to $285m. While this had no immediate effect on KB Home, our investor became increasingly concerned about the growing dispute between KB Home and the other house builders on the one hand, and the consortium of lenders led by JP Morgan Chase on the other.

On the 7th February 2011, and with KB Home's 9.1% of the 2017 bond still trading at 106.75, our investor finally decided to buy protection on his $10m holding. Although a bankruptcy petition had been served on South Edge, there was no immediate threat to KB Home itself. The investor's hedging objective was therefore not to protect his bond holding against ultimate default by KB Home, but instead to hedge the *change in value* of the bond holding. This means that a formula different from equation 22.1 must be used to calculate the hedge ratio, and the formula we need is given in equation 22.2 below.

$$\textbf{Value Hedge Ratio} = \frac{DV01_{BOND}}{SDV01_{CDS}} \qquad (22.2)$$

The principle behind this formula is quite simple. A successful CDS hedge will be one where the change in value of the CDS closely matches the change in value of the bond. The SDV01 was introduced in Chapter 15 (section 15.8) and is defined as the change in the value of a CDS contract for a 1bp change in credit spreads. In that earlier chapter we drew the analogy between the SDV01 for a CDS and the DV01 for a bond, the latter measuring the change in value for a 1bp change in yield.

On 7th February 2011, the DV01 for the $10m face value holding was $5,304.86, meaning that a 1bp change in the yield of the 2017 bond would result in a $5,304.86 change in value. With a maturity of 6.6 years, the most appropriate CDS contract was the seven-year CDS, trading that day at 388.5bp and having a DV01 per $1m notional of $534.83. The requisite hedge ratio was therefore:

$$\frac{5304.86}{534.83} = 9.919$$

Our investor therefore bought seven-year protection on KB Home with a notional value of $9,919,000.

The decision to hedge was well-advised. Figure 22.8 shows the performance of KB Home's share price and of the 2017 bond in the months that followed. By late July that year the bond's price had slid to par, and by early October 2011 it was trading in the low 80s. The shares followed a similar pattern, plummeting from $11.80 in late June 2011 to reach $5.27 in early October, a drop of more than 50%. Figure 22.8 charts the fall.

Fortunately, matters then began to improve. A settlement was reached between the bankruptcy litigants and later, in October 2011, a Federal judge cleared the way for South Edge to emerge from Chapter 11 bankruptcy. With these uncertainties resolved, KB Home's share price began to rise and, with it, the price of its 2017 bond, as is clear from the right-hand side of Figure 22.8. Accordingly our investor decided to lift the hedge. Figure 22.9 demonstrates that the 7yr CDS premium tracked the yield of KB Home's 2017 bond quite closely over this period, and so we would expect that the hedge would be fairly efficient. This supposition is proven in Tables 22.3, 22.4 and 22.5 which carefully analyse the financial outcomes both for the bond and the CDS contract over the 252-day hedging period.

FIGURE 22.8

KB Home share price vs. 9.1% 2017 bond price

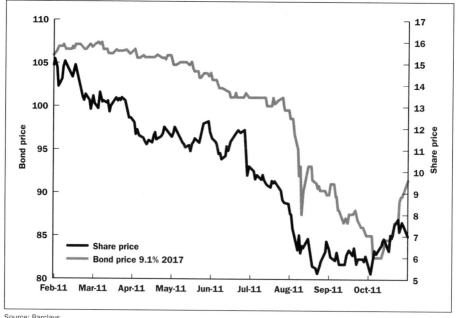

Source: Barclays.

FIGURE 22.9

KB Home CDS premium vs. 9.1% 2017 bond yield

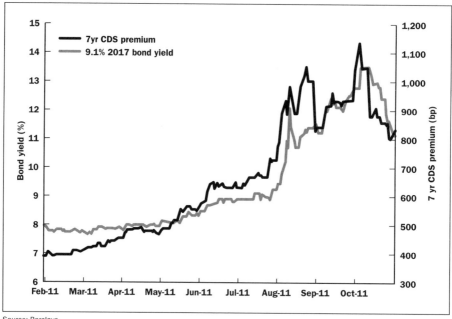

Source: Barclays.

Table 22.3 provides the raw data for the analysis, showing the bond prices, CDS premium quotations, and CDS cash flows when the hedge was executed on 7th February 2011, and when it was lifted on 17th October that year. KB Home's share price is also shown for comparison. The investor received a positive cash inflow on both dates as a result of executing the hedge, mainly because of the off-market components (see Chapter 14, section 14.4) of the up-front payments. On 7th February 2011 the par spread quoted by the market was 388.5bp; as this was below the standardised premium of 500bp for high-yield names, the protection buyer receives the off-market payment. Eight months later the CDS premium has risen to 907.1bp; as this is above the 500bp standardised premium, the protection seller receives the off-market payment. As the investor was the protection buyer when initiating the hedge and later the protection seller when unwinding the hedge, he receives the off-market payment on both occasions in this example.

TABLE 22.3
Bond hedging strategy

	Monday 7th Feb 2011	Monday 17th October 2011
Bond price	106.75	84.50
Bond yield	7.77%	12.93%
Share price	$14.26	$6.29
7yr CDS premium – par spread	388.5bp	907.1bp
7yr CDS premium – standardised	500bp	500bp
CDS clean price	105.9678%	83.6717%
Off-market payment (on $9.919m)	$591,948	$1,619,600
Accrued payment (on $9.919m)	$68,882	($38,574)
Total cash settlement (T+3)	$660,830	$1,581,026

Table 22.4 reconciles the CDS cash flows in two different ways. First, the net CDS profit can be calculated by combining the change in CDS values (the sum of the two off-market components just discussed) with the total premium cost (252 days at 500bp p.a. on a notional of $9,919,000). Second, we can simply add all the CDS cash flows: the total up-front payments received on 10th February and 20th October (T+3) less the quarterly premium payments made on the three intervening CDS dates. Both methods result in the same answer, a net cash inflow of $1,864,383.

TABLE 22.4
CDS cash flow reconciliation

CDS profit/loss		CDS cash flows	
Change in value	$2,211,548	Thu 10/02/2011	$660,830
Premium cost	($347,165)	Mon 21/03/2011	($125,365)
Net profit	$1,864,383	Mon 20/06/2011	($125,365)
		Tue 20/09/2011	($126,743)
		Thu 20/10/2011	$1,581,026
			$1,864,383

Finally, Table 22.5 analyses the performance of the CDS hedge with that of the underlying bond. It is encouraging to see that the profit made from the change in CDS value of $2,211,548 almost exactly covers the loss of $2,225,000 caused by the 22.25% drop in the bond price. The small difference of $13,452 means that the CDS hedge has proven to be 99.4% efficient, and confirms both the correctness of the hedging strategy and the efficiency of the CDS market. However, if you combine all the cash flows from the bond and CDS respectively, there is an overall difference of $271,327. This arises because the bond pays a 9.1% coupon whereas the CDS premium is only 500bp; this difference accumulates to $284,779 over the hedging period.[4] Subtracting the $13,452 net loss (because the hedge was 'only' 99.4% efficient), you get the $271,327 net overall profit, reducing the hedge efficiency to a still reasonable 83.0%.

TABLE 22.5

Hedge analysis

	Bond		CDS
Change in value	($2,225,000)	Change in value	($2,211,548)
	Hedge efficiency = 99.4%		
Change in value	($2,225,000)	Change in value	($2,211,548)
Coupon accrued	$631,944	Premium accrued	($347,165)
Net loss	($1,593,056)	Net profit	$1,864,383
	Hedge efficiency = 83.0%		
Difference between changes in value			($13,452)
Difference between coupon income and premium expense			$284,779
Overall profit			$271,327

22.3 Generating income

The applications discussed so far have all centred around hedging – where an existing credit exposure to a single name like Eastman Kodak or KB Home can successfully be hedged by buying protection with a single-name CDS. Such a strategy, of course, involves a cost – the CDS premium – but offsetting this is the coupon income from the underlying bond and the benefit of risk reduction.

Investors can use CDS for the opposite purpose, namely, to obtain exposure to credit risk by selling protection through a CDS. At first sight this may seem risky, and potentially even dangerous. However, the risk is little different from that of owning a bond. Both strategies generate income provided that the issuer remains solvent, but both strategies can incur the investor in substantial losses if a credit event occurs. Table 22.6 provides a comparison, and demonstrates that the loss following a credit event is very similar, and approximately equal to $(1 - R)$, where R is the recovery rate.

TABLE 22.6

Comparing investment strategies

	Buy bond	Sell CDS (sell protection)
Initial outlay	Market price of bond P (usually close to par)	Up-front payment (may be positive or negative), plus lodging of collateral
Regular income (no credit event)	Receive coupon	Receive standardised premium
Effect of credit event	Experience loss equal to $\left(\dfrac{P}{100} - R\right)$	Experience loss equal to $(1 - R)$

The key advantage of selling protection instead of buying a bond is that the first strategy requires funding, in other words, the money necessary to buy the bond, whereas selling protection is an unfunded strategy that can be executed off the balance sheet. Selling a CDS can therefore earn income for the investor without tying up the balance sheet. Of course, as with all investments, there is always the need to balance risk with return. Selling protection on high-yield issuers will certainly generate more income, but will also create greater risk exposure for the investor. Recall from Figure 22.7 that the global default rate for investment-grade names from 1981 to 2011 was only 0.11% compared with 4.26% for high-yield names.

With this in mind, we will assemble an equally weighted investment-grade portfolio comprising 12 well-known US companies, and compare buying those companies' bonds with selling CDS on the same set of entities. Table 22.7 shows that the selected bonds have an average maturity of just over seven years and an average yield of 2.62%, which provided a spread of 1.29% above 7yr Treasury yields and 1.57% above one-year LIBOR. The seven-year CDS, on the other hand, would provide premium income equivalent to 91bp on the same names. At first sight this may not appear so attractive when compared to the 157bp spread above LIBOR. However, if an investor's term funding rate was higher than LIBOR+66bp, then the CDS strategy would actually deliver a higher return, as well as freeing up the funds for other opportunities. Alternatively, the investor could look at the CDS strategy as simply a way to generate an income stream of almost 1% p.a. with very low risk. In the unlikely event that any of the companies should deteriorate over the seven-year period, the investor could buy back the affected CDS to eliminate the threat.

Taking this last idea perhaps to the ultimate, an investor could sell protection on what is arguably the safest entity in the world – the US government. Sovereign CDS on the US have traded steadily at around 40bp from 2010 until mid-2012, as pictured in Figure 22.10. An investor could therefore have sold protection on the US government, and collected a virtually risk-free premium of 40bp. However, we should dwell for a moment on the words 'virtually risk-free'. While the risk is very small, it is not zero, and such an investment strategy is therefore not completely risk-free. First, there is mark-to-market risk. The

TABLE 22.7

Investment portfolio

Company	Ticker	Maturity	Yield	7yr CDS	S&P
Anheuser Busch	BUD	01/03/2017	1.70%	107	A–
Berkshire Hathaway	BRK	31/01/2022	3.02%	144	AA+
Boeing	BA	15/08/2021	3.34%	76	A
Chubb Corporation	CB	15/08/2018	2.85%	68	A+
Coca Cola	KO	15/11/2017	1.60%	57	A+
Dow Chemical	DOW	15/09/2021	4.83%	162	BBB
Halliburton	HAL	15/02/2021	3.16%	85	A
Macy's	M	15/07/2017	2.70%	135	BBB
Microsoft	MSFT	08/02/2021	2.19%	51	AAA
Pepsi	PEP	01/06/2018	2.16%	68	A–
Pfizer	PFE	01/03/2018	1.85%	73	AA
Walmart	WMT	15/02/2018	1.98%	62	AA
Average		7.1 years	2.62%	91	

Source: Barclays, FINRA (data as at 27th April 2012).

figure shows that premiums on US Treasuries have fluctuated from 20bp to 60bp and, at the height of the credit crisis in late 2008, went through 100bp. An investor who sold protection at 40bp p.a. would potentially face a collateral call of around 3% of the notional if history repeated itself and premiums went through 100bp p.a. again. Second, there is a tiny but non-zero default risk. We

FIGURE 22.10

Five-year CDS premiums on US Treasuries

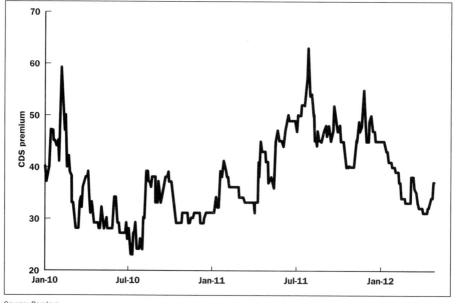

Source: Barclays.

should remember that the European sovereign debt crisis started in 2010 and at the time of writing (May 2012) is still not yet resolved. Some European economies that hitherto were considered very safe have demonstrated vulnerabilities. At the same time, economic power is steadily shifting to Asia. In this environment, is the US completely immune from default risk?

22.4 Trading strategies using CDS

All the applications we have reviewed so far have been linked in one way or another with bonds. We started by exploring how buying a CDS could protect the bond investor either from the outright default of an issuer, or from a change in value caused by the widening or narrowing of credit spreads. We then explored selling CDS as a surrogate for buying bonds, with the motive to generate a flow of income but without having to fund the purchase of a bond. It was strategies like these that drove the initial expansion of the credit derivatives market.

However, what led to the spectacular growth of CDS volumes is another purpose altogether – the opportunity to earn profits by taking a view on the future evolution of credit risk. Compared with traditional bond strategies, credit derivatives made it very much easier to exploit an investor's views, for one simple reason. A product like a CDS has pure exposure to credit spreads, whereas the underlying corporate bond has exposure to the credit spread, long-term yields and short-term funding costs. This means that using CDS enables investors to implement a highly focused credit strategy without the unwanted baggage of interest rate and funding risk.

In the following sections we will explore a number of different trading strategies that can easily and efficiently be implemented with single-name CDS:

- implementing directional views
- monetising relative credit views
- basis trades
- curve trades.

22.5 Implementing directional views

The idea here is simple. An investor who thinks that the credit spread for a particular name will change in the future can exploit that view by buying or selling the CDS referencing that name. Figure 22.11 shows the two broad possibilities. If the investor believed that the entity's prospects were about to worsen then he should buy protection now, and later – when the credit spread widens as anticipated – he can close out the position by selling protection at a higher premium. This is illustrated in Figure 22.11a. On the other hand, Figure 22.11b shows what the investor should do if he believed that the entity's prospects were about to improve.

FIGURE 22.11

Implementing a directional view

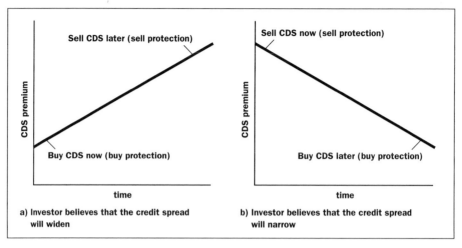

a) Investor believes that the credit spread will widen

b) Investor believes that the credit spread will narrow

The strategy of buy-low/sell-high works just as well with CDS as it does with shares provided that:

- 'buy' and 'sell' mean 'buy *protection*' and 'sell *protection*' (rather than buying or selling *risk*)

- the market figures being quoted are CDS *premiums* (rather than CDS prices).

To illustrate this idea, let's examine the case of an investor who, in the early summer of 2011 was examining the performance of AMD, the technology company. The share price had shown strong gains from the autumn of 2010 until the spring of 2011, during which time it rose from $7 to $8.50 and even through $9, but in June 2011 the shares fell sharply back to the $7 level. Figure 22.12 compares the share price with the 5yr CDS on AMD. As expected, the two are inversely related, and an analysis of the correlation between the share price and the CDS premium reveals a negative correlation with $\rho = -0.88$. As the figure shows, however, while the share price has returned to its October 2010 level, the CDS is still trading at around 450bp, compared with the October 2010 level of 570bp. Our investor believes that the CDS premium will rise further, to reach at least 570bp or even higher given the negative trend in AMD's prospects.

On 5th July 2011, our investor therefore decides to buy five-year protection on AMD and agrees to pay the market offer spread of 448bp p.a. Both the trade idea and the timing were good because, as Figure 22.13 reveals, over the next month or so AMD's share price tumbled further, falling below $6 on several occasions and, more importantly for our investor, the 5yr CDS premium rose through 600bp, almost touching 650bp at one point. Figure 22.13 extends the previous chart by showing the subsequent evolution of AMD's share price and CDS premium.

FIGURE 22.12
Directional view on AMD – historical analysis

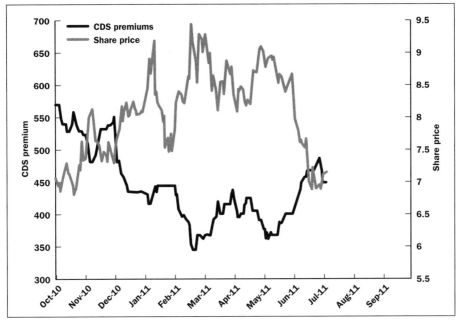

Source: Barclays.

FIGURE 22.13
Directional view on AMD – the outcome

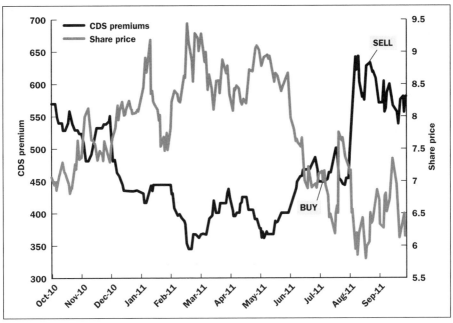

Source: Barclays.

On 19th August 2011, with CDS premiums appearing to level out in the low 600s, our investor decided to close out the position, unwinding his position with the original investment bank counterparty when 5yr CDS premiums were quoted at 627bp. Table 22.8 analyses all the cash flows and confirms that the investor made a profit in excess of $650,000 over the 45-day period, equivalent to more than 6.5% on the notional amount of the CDS, and to more than 50% p.a. on an annualised basis.

TABLE 22.8

Implementing a directional view – cash flow analysis

	Trade inception – 5th Jul 2011	Trade unwind – 19th Aug 2011
View	AMD CDS premiums will increase	AMD CDS premiums have peaked
Strategy	Buy 5yr protection on AMD	Unwind position with original counterparty
Market quotations	AMD 5yr CDS: 448bp	AMD 5yr CDS: 627bp
Notional principal	$10m	$10m
CDS maturity	Sep 2016	Sep 2016
Standardised premium	500bp	500bp
Off-market payment ($)	221,705	495,414
Accrued premium ($)	22,222	(84,722)
Up-front payment ($)	243,927	410,691
Total profit ($)	654,619	

There is one thing that should be emphasised here. It is not sufficient simply to have a view of the market, and for this view to prove correct. To generate a profit, *the view must be different from the market consensus*. To illustrate this, let's return to the example of Eastman Kodak discussed right at the start of this chapter. By the beginning of January 2012 most analysts had concluded that it was no longer a question of *whether* Kodak experienced a credit event, but *when*. CDS premiums were pricing in an implied default probability close to 100%, and were driven mainly by expected recovery rates at that stage. Suppose a naïve investor came along on 17th January 2012 and, after reading popular market opinion about Eastman Kodak, decided to buy protection, agreeing that the company's demise was imminent. There is no golden opportunity here because buying 5yr CDS protection that day would have required an up-front payment of 70.5%, the market already having priced-in the virtual inevitability of Kodak's bankruptcy. The size of this up-front payment means that for the investor to profit from his view, not only must Eastman Kodak experience a credit event, the recovery rate would need to be lower than 29.5% (ignoring the effect of the 500bp running premium). If the recovery rate turned out to be higher than 29.5% the naïve investor would actually lose money, despite being right about the bankruptcy.

22.6 Monetising relative credit views

The investor in the previous example had a clear view about what was going to happen to AMD – CDS premiums were going to rise in absolute terms. While there are many situations where investors will form such an unequivocal view, there are other circumstances where an investor may not be sure about the *absolute* direction of an entity's CDS premium, but may nonetheless be confident about its strength *relative* to another entity, or to the market as a whole.

To illustrate this, let's look at sovereign CDS for the two biggest economies in Europe – Germany and France. As Figure 22.14 shows, despite the European sovereign crisis which had started in early 2010, both countries' 5yr CDS premiums had proven resilient and comparatively stable. Moreover, the spread

FIGURE 22.14
Monetising relative credit views – historical analysis

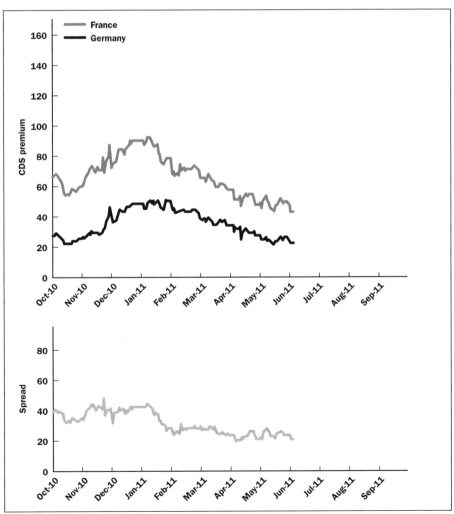

Source: Barclays.

between them had halved, from 40bp at the end of 2010 down to 20bp at the beginning of June 2011.

An investor is unsure about the future evolution of the CDS premiums themselves. Confidence in the European economy may return, and the trend in tightening CDS premiums may continue. However, contagion arising from the problems of Greece's economy may taint the European economy as a whole, bound as it is with Europe's common currency – the euro. If that happens, then CDS premiums may widen once again. Though uncertain about the absolute direction of CDS premiums, our investor is sure about one thing – the spread between France and Germany will widen once again, and France will worsen relative to Germany.

To monetise this view, it is not sufficient simply to buy protection on what the investor considers the weaker name – France. While the investor would make money if France were to weaken in both absolute and relative terms, the investor would lose if France weakened relative to Germany but strengthened overall. Instead, to benefit from a *relative* credit view it is necessary to take a relative credit position, buying protection on one name and selling protection on the other. In this example, the investor should buy protection on France and sell protection on Germany. Figure 22.15 demonstrates that this strategy will work, irrespective of whether France strengthens or weakens in absolute terms, so long as France weakens relative to Germany. Consider the first scenario depicted, where European sovereigns generally worsen, but France weakens more than Germany. Although the German CDS position will incur a loss, the French CDS position will make a bigger profit, and the strategy overall will succeed. Now look at the alternative scenario, where European sovereigns generally improve, but – consistent with the investor's view – France improves less than Germany. In this case the French CDS position will lose money, but the German CDS position will generate an even bigger gain, and once again the strategy will succeed.

FIGURE 22.15
Taking a relative view

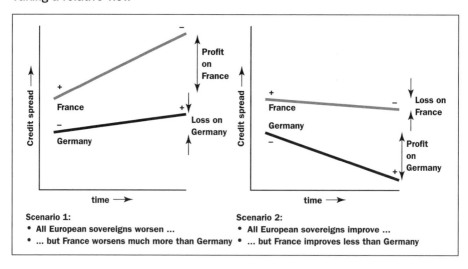

Scenario 1:
* All European sovereigns worsen ...
* ... but France worsens much more than Germany

Scenario 2:
* All European sovereigns improve ...
* ... but France improves less than Germany

Accordingly, on 6th June 2011 our investor buys five-year protection on France at a par spread of 42bp and sells five-year protection on Germany at 22bp, both contracts on a notional of $10m. Owing to the fact that the investor is buying protection on the more expensive name, he will have to make an up-front payment which nets out at $106,082. It turns out that not only was our investor's view correct but, as Figure 22.16 shows, the timing could not have been better. Just days after executing the two trades, with increased fears concerning a possible Greek default and the resultant effect on the survival of the euro, CDS premiums on all European sovereigns began to increase markedly. Moreover, the spread between France and Germany quadrupled from 20bp in early June to more than 80bp by September 2011. After a few weeks of volatil-

FIGURE 22.16

Monetising relative credit views – the outcome

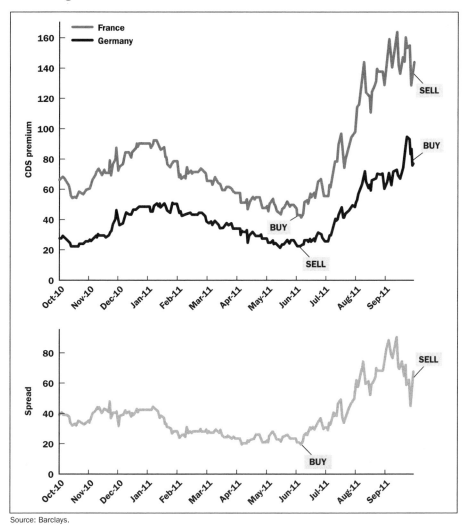

Source: Barclays.

ity, and with the spread contracting to 60bp towards the end of the month, our investor decided to close out the position and on 29th September bought back Germany at 75bp and sold France at 136bp, the spread having widened from 20bp at the outset to 61bp at the close. Although the German position lost 53bp, the French CDS trade made 94bp, for a net profit of 41bp. Table 22.9 analyses all the cash flows involved, revealing that the relative trade made $180,934 over the 115-day period.

TABLE 22.9
Monetising a relative credit view – cash flow analysis

	Trade inception – 6th Jun 2011		Trade unwind – 29th Sep 2011	
View	Spread between France and Germany will widen		Spread has peaked	
Strategy	Buy 5yr protection on France Sell 5yr protection on Germany		Unwind positions with original counterparty	
Market quotations	France 5yr CDS: 42bp Germany 5yr CDS: 22bp		France 5yr CDS: 136bp Germany 5yr CDS: 75bp	
Notional principals	$10m		$10m	
CDS maturity	Sep 2016		Sep 2016	
Standardised premium	100bp		100bp	
	France	Germany	France	Germany
Off-market payment ($)	297,397	(403,479)	167,648	119,368
Accrued premium ($)	21,667	(21,667)	(2,778)	2,778
Up-front payment ($)	319,064	(425,146)	164,870	122,146
Net cash flow	(106,082)		287,016	
Total profit ($)	180,934			

Although in this particular example the profit would have been almost three times greater had the investor just bought protection on France, we must remember that the investor's motivation was to take a view on the relative weakening of France compared to Germany rather than an absolute weakening. In return for smaller profits, the investor had the reassurance that had his view been correct in a scenario where there was a general strengthening of CDS premiums, the strategy would still have generated profits while the directional trade would have lost money.

In the example discussed here, the investor used equal notional amounts for both CDS, $10m in each case. This is the easiest and most common tactic. However, there is another alternative – the *SDV01-neutral* trade. The concept of SDV01 was first introduced in Chapter 15 (section 15.8) and was defined as the sensitivity of an existing CDS position to a 1bp change in the CDS quotations. A $10m 5yr CDS position on a high-grade name might have an SDV01 of $4,750. This means that for every 1bp change in the CDS quotation, the value or mark-to-market of that CDS would change by $4,750. In the example we have been studying in this section, on 6th June 2011 the SDV01 for the French CDS was $4,953 whereas that for the German CDS was slightly higher at $5,085. Suppose for a moment that CDS premiums had risen by 100bp (which is more or less what happened to premiums on France) but the spread between France and Germany remained the same; in other words, suppose that both CDS had risen together by 100bp. Having implemented a relative credit view, the investor would reasonably expect to be unaffected by such a market move. However, because the SDV01s are different, the two different CDS positions will behave slightly differently. Using the ISDA CDS Standard Model we can calculate that the profit on the France CDS would have been $490,195 while the loss on the German CDS would have been $503,049, a net loss of $12,854.[5]

The investor who wanted to eliminate this risk could have executed an SDV01-neutral trade, where the notional principal amounts are ratioed according to the ratio of the SDV01s. In this case the hedge ratio would have been:

$$\frac{4953}{5085} = 97.4\%$$

If the investor had therefore bought $10m protection on France, but sold only $9.74m protection on Germany, the net loss on the strategy for a 100bp parallel shift in both France and German CDS prices would drop from $12,854 to just $225, demonstrating the effectiveness of making this adjustment. The greater the difference between the SDV01s at the outset, the more worthwhile using SDV01-weighting becomes when effecting a relative credit strategy.

22.7 Basis trades

It should not be surprising that the price of CDS contracts on a particular entity and the yield on bonds issued by the same entity should be closely related. In fact, the *CDS Basis* is defined as:

CDS Basis = CDS premium *less* Bond spread

In this simple equation the CDS premium is quoted as the par spread, and the bond spread is typically quoted either as the par asset swap spread or the z-spread.[6]

Consider a bank executing the following sequence of trades:

■ Borrow 100 at LIBOR.

■ Buy a corporate bond at price P, with maturity M and coupon C.

■ Enter into a par asset swap of maturity M on the same corporate bond receiving an up-front payment equal to $P - 100$, and thereafter paying the coupon C and receiving LIBOR $+ A$, where A is the par asset swap spread.

■ Buy M-year protection on the bond issuer at a par spread of S.

The net result of these transactions is an up-front payment of 100, the regular receipt of:

$$A - S = \text{Bond spread } less \text{ CDS premium}$$

In other words, the bank executing the strategy receives a net return equal to minus the CDS Basis. If the CDS Basis is negative, the return is then positive. Moreover, given that the credit risk arising through owning the bond is covered by the protection provided by the CDS, the structure has no net exposure to the credit risk of the bond issuer. This is the essence of a *negative basis trade*. When the cost of CDS protection is less than the spread of an asset-swapped bond, there may be profitable earnings opportunities.

Figure 22.17 illustrates one such situation. Throughout the latter part of 2010 right until August 2011, the basis between General Mills' 5.7% bond maturing February 2017 and the five-year CDS on GIS was trading between zero and –50bp. However, from the beginning of September 2011 the par asset swap spread widened while the CDS premium tightened. On 11th October 2011 the

FIGURE 22.17

Negative basis trade – the scenario

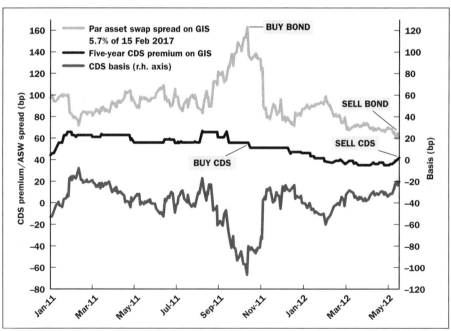

Source: Barclays.

negative basis went through –100bp for the first time, and increased to –106bp the next day. A bank then decided to initiate the negative basis trade and executed the following transactions:

- Borrow $10m at six-month LIBOR.
- Buy the 5.7% bond issued by GIS maturing on 15th Feb 2017 at a price of 112.74% plus 0.9183% accrued.
- Enter into a par asset swap on the same bond receiving an up-front cash flow equal to 12.74% plus the accrued, and thereafter paying the 5.7% coupon and receiving LIBOR+162bp.
- Buy protection on GIS at a par spread of 56bp, leading to an up-front receipt of 2.2588%, and thereafter paying the standardised premium of 100bp p.a.

The structure is pictured in Figure 22.18, and the cash flows are summarised on the left-hand side of Table 22.10. Note that the figure shows both the actual cash flows for the CDS – an up-front payment to the bank followed by standardised premium payments of 100bp by the bank – and the *effective* cash flows – no up-front payment and par spread premium payments of 56bp p.a. by the bank.

What makes this negative basis trade profitable is not the positive cash flow of $225,880 at the beginning – this is just a by-product of the standardised premiums convention. The trade is profitable precisely because of the negative basis. A par asset-swapped bond financed at LIBOR earns the par asset swap spread, but exposes the investor to the credit risk of the issuer. If CDS protection costs less than the par asset swap spread, the profit is the difference between these two rates. In this example the profit margin is therefore 106bp p.a., equivalent to more than $500,000 over the five-year period. In fact, Table 22.10 shows what the actual profits would have been if the trade was unwound six months later when the CDS Basis had narrowed from 106bp to just 19bp. This allows the bank to crystallise a profit of $469,283.

FIGURE 22.18
Negative basis trade – the cash flows

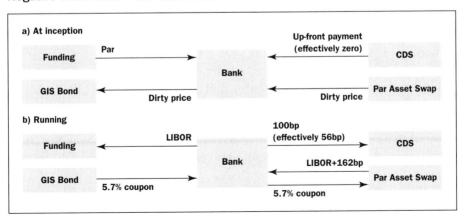

TABLE 22.10

Negative basis trade – cash flow analysis

	Trade inception – 12th Oct 2011		Trade unwind – 14th May 2012	
View	Take advantage of negative basis		Take profit on trade	
Target bond	GIS 5.7% maturing 15 Feb 2017		GIS 5.7% maturing 15 Feb 2017	
Strategy	Borrow at LIBOR, buy bond and asset swap, and buy protection		Repay borrowing, sell bond and asset swap, and sell protection	
Market quotations	5yr CDS	56bp	5yr CDS	40bp
	Par asset swap spread	162bp	Par asset swap spread	59bp
	Bond price	112.74	Bond price	118.82
Notional principal	$10m		$10m	
CDS maturity	Dec 2016		Dec 2016	
Standardised premium	100bp		100bp	
Cash flows at inception and unwind ($)				
Borrowing	10,000,000		(10,000,000)	
Par asset swap	1,365,833		(2,024,500)	
CDS up-front	225,880		(286,076)	
Bond (incl. accrued)	(11,365,833)		12,024,500	
Net cash flow	225,880		(286,076)	
Cash flows over holding period ($)				
20 Dec 2011 (CDS date)	(25,278)		91 days @ 100bp p.a.	
15 Feb 2012 (Bond coupon date)	71,644		124 days @ L+162bp p.a.	
20 Mar 2012 (CDS date)	(25,278)		91 days @ 100bp p.a.	
16 May 2012 (ASW termination)	508,391		103bp p.a. for 5 years	
Net cash flow over holding period	529,479			
Net cash flow at inception and unwind	(60,196)			
Total profit ($)	469,283			

The negative basis trade illustrated here will generate these kind of profits over the lifetime of the structure only if the bank in question can actually borrow at LIBOR. If, for any reason, a bank has to pay more for its borrowing costs, the profit margin would diminish, and a borrowing rate of LIBOR+100bp would all but destroy the value of the trade. It should also be pointed out that there are risks associated with the negative basis trade. The structure is exposed to mark-to-market risk if the SDV01 of the CDS differs from the DV01 of the asset-swapped bond, and would also suffer a mark-to-market loss if the negative basis widened. In addition, there is the potential counterparty risk on both the asset swap and the CDS, although this can be mitigated through the posting of collateral or the use of a central counterparty. Finally, there is the potential unwind risk on the asset swap if a credit event occurs.

22.8 Curve trades

Earlier we explored the idea of a relative credit view – one where an investor believes that the credit spreads of two different entities will move relative to each other, and therefore buys a CDS on one entity and sells one on the other, both CDS contracts having the same maturity. In this section we will examine a variation of this idea – buying one maturity of CDS and selling another maturity, both contracts referencing the same entity. This creates a *curve trade* which is designed to exploit a view that the slope of the credit curve will change.

Although the most liquid maturity has always been the five-year CDS, market-makers will usually quote prices throughout the maturity range from one to ten years. If you plot a chart of CDS premium against maturity you obtain a credit curve, directly analogous to the yield curve found in all interest-rate markets. Like the yield curve, credit curves are typically upward-sloping, reflecting increasing uncertainty as one looks further and further into the future and therefore the potentially increasing probability of default that comes with greater uncertainty.

Figure 22.19 illustrates credit curves for the same entity, Morgan Stanley (MS), at three moments in time. The lowest line shows the curve on 1st June 2011 and is quite normal in shape, rising gently from 39bp for one-year CDS contracts, through 151bp for five-year CDS, to 172bp for ten-year swaps. However, four months later the situation was quite different. In early October 2011 there were heightened fears over bank safety following Greece's announcement that the country was unlikely to meet its targets on deficit reduction. Stock markets around the world fell 5% over a two-day period on hearing the news, and the shares of major financial institutions fared worse – Goldman Sachs' shares were down 10%, Bank of America fell 13%, and Morgan Stanley plunged by 17%. CDS premiums mirrored the market's tension, with five-year quotations for CDS on MS up from 151bp to 612bp. Moreover, the credit curve for MS had by then inverted, as Figure 22.19 dramatically shows.

When a credit curve becomes inverted, as with MS from late September 2011 until the beginning of February 2012, it reflects the market's view that risk in the short term is relatively high and therefore warrants quoting a higher premium rate so that sufficient income can be collected by the protection seller within the limited timeframe of the short-term CDS. Lower premium rates for longer-term CDS then reflect the view that, assuming the entity survives the current period of stress, it will be stronger and safer in the future, and this justifies the lower quotations. Figure 22.20 charts the complete set of CDS premiums for MS from May 2011 through to May 2012, and you can clearly see how the steeply upward-sloping credit curve at the beginning flips around to a heavily inverted curve in mid-October 2011, before recovering its normal shape early in 2012.

FIGURE 22.19

Morgan Stanley credit curves

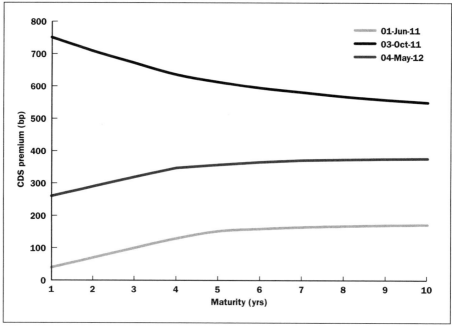

Suppose that on 3rd October 2011 an investor looking at MS thinks that the situation will be resolved before long, but does not want to take an outright view on the level of CDS quotations either in absolute terms (which would be a directional view) or relative to other firms. A curve trade provides a relatively safe way to exploit the view because, properly constructed, the position is immune to the level of CDS premiums and only exposed to the slope of the credit curve. In general, there are two types of curve trades:

■ *Steepeners* are designed to take advantage of a steepening of the credit curve. In fact, to be strictly accurate, this means that the slope of the credit curve should become more positive. If the credit curve is already upward-sloping, then a more positive slope does indeed mean that the curve becomes steeper. However, if we start with an inverse curve, a more positive slope means that the curve starts by getting flatter, and may even flip around to become upward-sloping.

■ *Flatteners* are designed to exploit the opposite trend, where the slope of the credit curve becomes more negative. Starting with a normally upward-sloping curve, a more negative slope means that the curve first starts becoming flatter, and may eventually flip to become an inverse curve.

FIGURE 22.20

Morgan Stanley CDS premiums 2011–2012

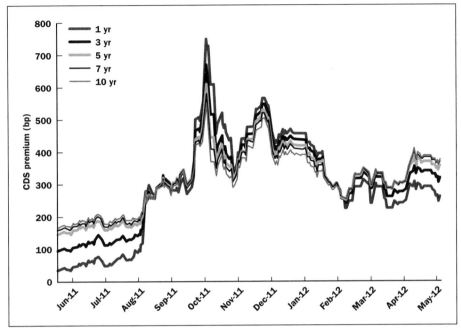

Source: Barclays.

In this example, our investor believes that the credit curve, steeply inverted on 3rd October 2011, will become normal, and therefore decides to execute a steepener. To implement such a strategy, the investor must sell a short-term CDS and buy a long-term CDS. If the slope of the curve becomes more positive as expected, the long-term end will rise in relation to the short-term end, and the strategy will make money.

To ensure that a curve trade has no exposure to any changes in the level of CDS premiums, the sizes of the two trades must be inversely proportional to the SDV01s of the two CDS contracts used. Initially our investor was tempted to implement a 1 × 10 strategy, selling the one-year CDS and buying the ten-year contract. Although the MS credit curve is steepest between these two maturity points, the shortness of the one-year contract would mean that the trade would need to be rebalanced on a regular basis – at least monthly – to maintain the correct SDV01 weightings. Instead, the investor chose a 5 × 10 strategy which is likely to remain stable for a much longer period of time.

Figure 22.21 is similar to the previous figure, but for clarity focuses only on the CDS premiums for the five-year and ten-year maturities; it also highlights the difference between these two premium quotations over time – the five-year to ten-year basis which is defined as:

5yr to 10yr basis = 10yr CDS premium *less* 5yr CDS premium

Defined in this way, the basis measures the slope of the credit curve between these points and will increase if our investor's view is correct. You can see from the figure that the basis was near its most negative point when the investor implemented the curve trade on 3rd October 2011. Within two weeks the negative basis had narrowed from –62bp to –33bp, but it was not until the beginning of February 2012 that the curve normalised and the basis remained at +5bp for the next two months. When the basis increased to around +20bp during April 2012 our investor decided to take profit, finally closing out the position on 4th May when the basis was +19bp.

Table 22.11 highlights the details of the implementation, and also tabulates the financial outcomes for the cash flows at the beginning, middle and end of the trade.

The initial SDV01s of $379.44 and $608.33 per $1m notional for the five-year and ten-year CDS contracts respectively imply a hedge ratio of $\frac{379.44}{608.33} = 62.32\%$. The investor therefore sold five-year protection on $10m and bought ten-year protection on $6,232,000. The up-front receipt on 3rd October 2011 was $285,732, and was a cash inflow because the investor was a net seller of CDS on an entity where the par spread was well above the standardised premium of 100bp p.a.

FIGURE 22.21
Morgan Stanley 5y–10y basis 2011–2012

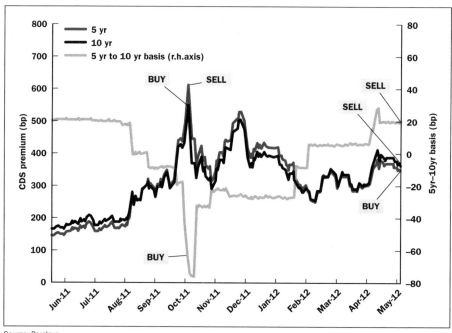

Source: Barclays.

TABLE 22.11

Curve trade – cash flow analysis

	Trade inception – 3rd Oct 2011		Trade unwind – 4th May 2012	
View	Inverse credit curve on Morgan Stanley (MS) will normalise		Curve has normalised	
Strategy	'Steepener' trade: Sell 5yr protection on MS and buy 10yr protection, SDV01-neutral		Unwind positions with original counterparty	
Market quotations	5yr CDS	611bp	5yr CDS	356bp
	10yr CDS	549bp	10yr CDS	375bp
	Basis	(62bp)	Basis	19bp
SDV01s per $1m	5yr CDS	379.44	5yr CDS	383.48
	10yr CDS	608.88	10yr CDS	665.41
Notional principals		5yr CDS $10,000,000		
		10yr CDS $6,232,000		
CDS maturities		Dec 2016/Dec 2021		
Standardised premiums		100bp		

Cash flows at inception and unwind ($)		
5yr	2,040,717	(1,018,060)
10yr	(1,754,985)	1,172,513
Net cash flow	285,732	154,453

Cash flows over holding period ($)

	5yr	10yr	TOTAL
3 Oct 2011 (inception)	2,040,717	(1,754,985)	285,732
20 Dec 2011 (CDS date)	25,278	(15,753)	9,525
20 Mar 2012 (CDS date)	25,278	(15,753)	9,525
4 May 2012 (unwind)	(1,018,060)	1,172,513	154,453
Total profit ($)	1,073,213	(613,978)	459,235

Although the standardised premium convention normally implies that back-to-back CDS positions have no net premium, this only applies when the notionals are equal. In this case the CDS sold had a larger notional than the one bought, leading to positive net premium inflows of $9,525 on each of the CDS dates.

The total profit from the curve trade was $459,235 over the seven-month period. Although the table shows the profit and loss individually for both the 5yr and 10yr CDS positions, it is important to remember that any spread strategy should be judged simply by the total profit, not that of each component. As CDS premiums on MS tightened during the period, it is inevitable that the long position in the ten-year contract lost money. However, the curve trade made money overall because five-year CDS premiums tightened even more as the credit curve steepened.

22.9 Index trades

The techniques so far presented in this chapter have all been based on single-name CDS, but most of the ideas can equally well be applied to indexes like the CDX and iTraxx introduced in Chapter 15 (section 15.10). So hedging portfolio default and credit risk, generating income from a diversified pool of synthetic assets, expressing a directional view, or implementing a curve view, are all possible using credit indices instead of CDS. To demonstrate this, in this final section we will examine a relative credit trade based on the CDX.NA.IG and the iTraxx Europe.

For quite an extended period of time, the 125-name iTraxx Europe index has traded tighter than the corresponding 125-name CDX.NA.IG index. Figure 22.22 confirms that between April 2007 and June 2010, the respective on-the-run indices starting with CDX.NA.IG8 and iTraxx Europe Series 7 featured a negative basis never smaller than –10bp. The basis reached its most negative point of almost 100bp in the fourth quarter of 2008 when the US authorities launched

FIGURE 22.22
CDX vs. iTraxx 5yr on-the-run series 2007–2010

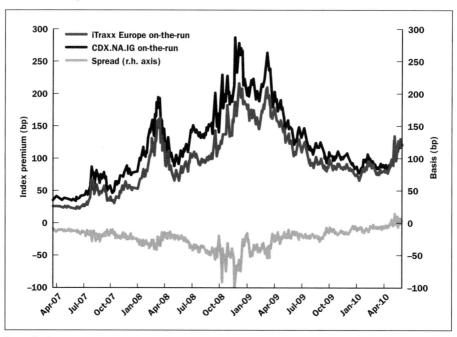

Source: Barclays.

a range of emergency measures following the collapse of Lehman Brothers. Although both main credit indices had risen strongly during this period, the CDX rose considerably more reflecting the prevalent view that although Europe's economy had problems, the US economy fared even worse.

As the global economy started on its slow route towards recovery both major credit indices began to tighten from their highs, but not in precise lock-step. As economic problems in Greece started to take centre-stage, perceptions about the relative strengths of the US and European economies began to shift. Figure 22.22 reveals that the negative basis between the two major credit indices began to dissipate, and by the time we reach May of 2010, the two indices were trading at the same level.

An investor following this evolving situation believes that the European economy will continue to worsen compared to the US economy, but in the light of considerable volatility in the markets – again evident from the right-hand side of the figure – he does not have a strong opinion on where the absolute level of these credit indices will end up. This rules against a directional credit view (in other words, simply buying protection on the iTraxx Europe index) and suggests that a relative credit strategy should be implemented, buying protection on the iTraxx Europe Series 13 and selling an equivalent amount of protection on the CDX.NA.IG14.

This trade idea was implemented on 1st June 2010, and although the indices were trading at almost identical levels of 122.5bp for the iTraxx and 122bp for the CDX, the respective notionals were set to €10m and $12.3m respectively in order to equalise the two exposures at the prevailing exchange rate of €1=$1.2303. Table 22.12 tabulates the details of both the trades executed as well as the resulting cash flows, and Figure 22.23 pictures the behaviour of the two separate indices and the basis between them. From the figure it is clear that avoiding a directional trade was wise, because both indices experienced a roller-coaster ride over the next two years, so taking an outright position in either direction would have been very risky. In contrast however, the basis moved much more steadily from +0.5bp at inception to +81bp in early October 2011 before beginning to tighten once again. Having missed the opportunity to close out the position at that point, our investor resolved to do so the next time the basis reached +81bp which it eventually did in mid-May 2012.

The net profit of $277,536 was predominantly from the 80.5bp widening in the basis, but there was an element of currency risk influencing the result.[7] Although the long and short positions were created equal and opposite at inception, the initial (and, to some, surprising) strengthening of the euro created small net deficits on each CDS date. However, the stronger euro on repatriating the positive euro cash flow when the positions were closed-out on 17th May 2012 helped to offset part of this small loss.

FIGURE 22.23

CDX–iTraxx index spread trade

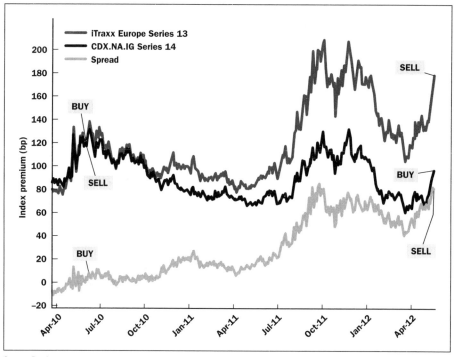

Source: Barclays.

TABLE 22.12

Index trade – cash flow analysis

	Trade inception – 1st Jun 2010	Trade unwind – 17th May 2012
View	iTraxx Europe will rise relative to CDX.NA.IG	Basis has risen to previous peak, so take profit
Strategy	Buy 5yr protection on iTraxx Europe and sell 5yr protection on CDX.NA.IG with currency-adjusted notionals	Unwind positions with original counterparty
Market quotations	iTraxx Europe 13 122.5bp CDX.NA.IG14 122.0bp Basis +0.5bp	iTraxx Europe 13 178bp CDX.NA.IG14 97bp Basis 81bp
Notional principals	iTraxx Europe 13 €10,000,000 CDX.NA.IG14 $12,300,000	
CDS maturities	Jun 2015	
Standardised premiums	100bp	

	Trade inception – 1st Jun 2010	Trade unwind – 17th May 2012
Cash flows at inception and unwind		
€/$ FX rate	€1 = $1.2303	€1 = $1.2724
iTraxx Europe 13	(€84,747)	€213,211
CDX.NA.IG14	$100,955	$31,305
Net cash flow (in $)	($3,309)	$302,595

Cash flows over holding period

	€/$ FX rate	iTraxx Europe 13 €	CDX.NA.IG14 $	TOTAL $
1 Jun 2010 (inception)	1.2303	(84,747)	100,955	(3,309)
21 June 2010 (CDS date)	1.2399	(25,278)	31,092	(250)
20 Sep 2010 (CDS date)	1.3056	(25,278)	31,092	(1,911)
20 Dec 2010 (CDS date)	1.3192	(25,278)	31,092	(2,255)
21 Mar 2011 (CDS date)	1.4178	(25,278)	31,092	(4,747)
20 June 2011 (CDS date)	1.4300	(25,278)	31,092	(5,056)
20 Sep 2011 (CDS date)	1.3663	(25,556)	31,433	(3,483)
20 Dec 2011 (CDS date)	1.3017	(25,278)	31,092	(1,812)
20 Mar 2012 (CDS date)	1.3184	(25,278)	31,092	(2,235)
17 May 2012 (unwind)	1.2724	213,211	31,305	302,595
Total profit		(74,036)	381,335	277,536

Notes

1　As explained in Chapter 14 (section 14.4) and Chapter 15 (section 15.6), the calculations for determining the up-front payment take into account both the time value of money and the possibility that a credit event may cause the CDS to terminate prior to its normal maturity date. That is why the actual up-front payment of 12.25% is somewhat less than 3.19 × 4.84%.

2　See section 15.5 for a description of the technique. Here, as a credit event was so close, we use recovery lock quotations instead of the standardised 40% recovery rate assumption, to obtain more accurate figures for the implied default probability.

3　*2011 Annual Global Corporate Default Study And Rating Transitions*, Standard and Poor's, March 2012.

4　This figure takes into account the slightly different principals – $10m on the bond and $9.919m for the CDS – and also the differing day count conventions giving rise to a 250-day accrual for the bond (30/360) but 252 days for the CDS (Actual/360).

5   Using the SDV01 figures gives a profit of $496,300 on the France CDS and a loss of $508,500 for the German CDS. These figures are a little higher than those from the ISDA CDS Standard Model because we have ignored CDS convexity. As CDS premiums rise, the SDV01 falls, so the true profit generated from a significant rise in CDS rates will always be less than that estimated from multiplying the SDV01 by the change in premium. However, the net loss of $13,200 calculated from the SDV01s is close to the actual figure of $12,854 because the convexity errors here tend to cancel.

6   The par asset swap was explained in Chapter 8 (section 8.8) and is the margin above LIBOR that can be earned if the fixed coupon plus the bond discount or premium is swapped for a floating return. The z-spread is an alternative way of measuring the additional yield earned from a bond, and is the spread that needs to be added to the set of risk-free (government bond) rates across the entire zero-coupon yield curve such that discounting all the bond's cash flows at these augmented rates gives the observed bond price.

7   The final net profit would have been $290,249 instead of $277,536 had the euro exchange rate remained constant.

23

STRUCTURED PRODUCTS

Thus far, each of the chapters has concentrated on a single topic, whether it be a tool such as swaps or options, or a technique such as managing interest rate risk. This final chapter explores how financial engineering tools and techniques can be assembled in various ways to create novel, and sometimes unusual, financial structures. We will focus on *structured products* – investments designed to create an attractive or otherwise inaccessible return, which are offered to a wide cross-section of investors. The chapter starts by explaining what structured products are and how they are constructed by the firms that create them. There are a huge number of these products offered by banks and other financial institutions, and although it is impossible to compartmentalise them into watertight containers, we will highlight the most important features by which they can be categorised, and then provide a number of examples to demonstrate how the wide diversity of investors' preferences can be addressed.

23.1 Understanding structured products

Investments mostly have the same general features:

- At inception an investor invests a principal sum to buy the security.
- Over the lifetime of the investment, most securities make regular payments (the usual exceptions being equities that pay no dividends, and zero-coupon bonds).
- At the end, either the security matures (as with most bonds) or the investor decides to sell (as with equities), and the investor receives a principal sum, which may be less than the amount invested at inception, the same, or more.

So there is a cash flow in one direction at inception, and in the other direction there are regular cash flows during the lifetime of the investment and a cash flow at maturity or sale. Figure 23.1 depicts this familiar situation.

FIGURE 23.1

Cash flows from a typical investment

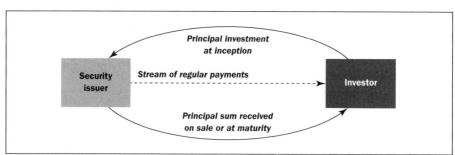

What makes a structured product different is the nature of the returns from the investment. Instead of the return being fixed (as with a bond), or linked to the fortunes of a single company (as with a share), the return from a structured product can be linked to:

■ interest rates

■ FX exchange rates

■ commodity prices

■ a basket of securities

■ an index.

Moreover, the linkage can be made quite complex. For example, a structured note might offer a return equal to 169% of the appreciation of the S&P 500 index over a five-year period, but no exposure to the downside if the S&P 500 depreciates over this period, unless at any point during this time the index dips by more than 25%. Figure 23.2 illustrates the payoff profile from such a structured note for a wide range of outcomes for the S&P 500 in five years' time,

FIGURE 23.2
Leveraged upside S&P 500 five-year note

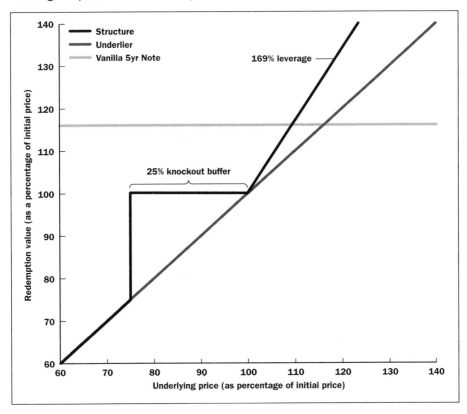

from 60% to 140% of its original value. For comparison purposes, the chart also illustrates the payoff from the underlying index, as well as that from a vanilla five-year note.

Structured products are designed and offered to investors in order to deliver opportunities that cannot be provided by conventional financial instruments. They can be devised to take advantage of particular market conditions, or to satisfy the needs of a specific group of investors. As such they offer a great many advantages, including the ability to:

- target an investor's precise market views
- provide benefits if the market follows the investor's expectations, but to preserve principal if the investor's view proved incorrect
- enhance the upside through leverage, without magnifying the downside
- generate returns in a low-yield or stable environment
- conveniently reach markets that would otherwise be inaccessible; for example, some emerging markets where there are barriers to direct access, or markets like the credit derivatives market where the minimum trade size might be $1m or more
- avoid currency risk when investing in securities denominated in a foreign currency
- take advantage of tax-efficient structures.

23.2 How structured products are built

Structured products are generally created by investment banks. In order to engineer the returns promised by the issuer, they are almost always constructed from two components – a *zero-coupon bond* and a *derivatives overlay* – as pictured in Figure 23.3. The zero-coupon bond is designed to guarantee the investor a 100% return of principal at maturity, as the starting point for the payoff from most structured products. The derivatives overlay then provides the fancy payoff profile at maturity. In general, upside is created through the purchase of call options, while downside exposure is engineered through the sale of puts. As an illustration, the structured note pictured in Figure 23.2 was constructed from the following components:

- A five-year zero-coupon bond, with a face value of 100%, costing 86.26% up-front.
- The purchase of a vanilla five-year ATM call on the S&P 500 with a notional of 169% of the note's face value, costing 30.26% up-front. This provides the 1.69 × upside exposure.
- The sale of a reverse knock-in (down-and-in) five-year ATM put on the S&P 500 on 100% of the note's face value and having a 75% trigger level, bringing in 17.02% up-front. This provides the knock-out buffer.

FIGURE 23.3
Structured product components

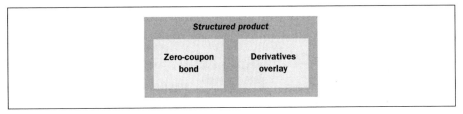

The net cost of these three components is 99.50%. Selling the note to investors at par leaves the investment bank with fees of 0.50% to cover the cost of assembling the package and to provide a reasonable profit margin. Although an investment bank may create a structured product by assembling the various parts, it should be emphasised here that investors buying the product own a stand-alone security which is indivisible and cannot be broken up into its constituent parts.

The structured product thus created can be issued either by the investment bank as a liability on its own balance sheet or, alternatively, by an affiliate like Rabobank or Svensk Exportkredit (SEK), the Swedish Export Credit Corporation 100% owned by the Swedish state. The choice of issuer became more significant following the collapse of Lehman Brothers, which resulted in major losses[1] for investors who had invested in structured products that the bank had issued. In the aftermath of the credit crisis, other investment banks saw their ratings cut from AA to A or A– or lower, resulting in marginally increased credit risk for investors owning securities issued by those banks.

Some investment banks therefore offer a choice: a structured product investor can either buy a product issued by the investment bank itself, or instead buy an alternative version issued by a higher-rated entity like the two mentioned in the previous paragraph. At the time of writing, Rabobank has an Aaa/AA rating, while SEK is rated Aa1/AA+; these are some of the highest ratings available. This extra safety comes at a price, though. As an example, in April 2012 Investec (Baa3/BBB–) offered a *FTSE 100 Geared Returns Plan* promising investors a fixed return provided that the FTSE 100 was higher at the end of five years than at the beginning, and had never fallen below 50% of its initial value over that period. The fixed return was 80% if investors bought the version of the Plan issued by Investec itself, but the fixed return was reduced to 70% if investors instead chose the version underwritten by Investec but issued by a group of five higher-rated UK banks. The more cautious investor could therefore choose the second alternative and avoid the (small) risk of Investec defaulting, but in so doing would sacrifice some of the promised returns.

Figure 23.4 shows the cash flows arising when a structured product is issued through a third-party bank. At inception, the issuer receives the principal sum from the investor and can use these proceeds as part of their overall balance sheet funding. Instead of paying the investor a return for the use of these funds,

FIGURE 23.4

Cash flows when issuing a structured product through a third-party issuer

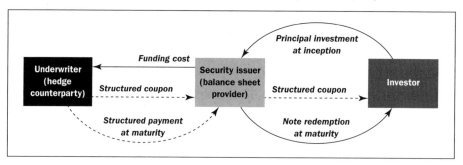

the issuer instead pays the underwriter – the investment bank which has created and marketed the structured product, and this is shown as the *funding cost* in the diagram. You can think of the steady stream of payments from issuer to the underwriter as payment for the derivatives overlay which the underwriter puts together. In the numerical example given at the beginning of this section, the 13.24% net cost of the two options plus 0.50% fees is equivalent to a funding cost of 3% p.a. In other words, by issuing the structured note on behalf of the underwriter the issuer in this example is effectively obtaining funding at 3% p.a.

Some structured notes promise investors a regular stream of income, others are effectively zero-coupon instruments and offer a structured payout at maturity, and some provide a combination of the two. In each case the derivatives overlay assembled by the underwriter provides the structured coupon, the structured payout, or both. These cash flows are shown as dashed lines in Figure 23.4, and are paid by the underwriter to the issuer, who in turn passes the payments to the investor. At maturity, the issuer redeems the structured note by repaying the principal sum to the investor, plus or minus the structured payment at maturity provided by the underwriter.

This arrangement therefore ensures that repayment of principal depends only on the credit risk of the issuer, not that of the investment bank creating the structured product. The bank, acting as underwriter, provides the issuer with the cash flows arising from the derivatives overlay, thereby enabling the issuer to deliver the structured returns to the investor without needing any derivatives expertise. Everyone benefits as a result. The investor obtains structured returns from a high-grade issuer; the issuer obtains low-cost funding; and the underwriter earns fees from assembling the derivatives overlay.

23.3 Features of structured products

There are an enormous number of structured products on offer from issuers around the world, and they promise investors an almost bewildering choice of attractive-sounding returns. Despite this diversity we can create a taxonomy under which we can organise structured products into a number of classifications.

Underlier

Most structured products provide returns linked to a particular underlier, and we can classify underliers into one of a small number of asset classes. Most common are products linked to an equity underlier, usually an index, but frequently a bespoke basket of shares, or even a single share. Other asset classes comprise: commodities, currencies, interest rates and credit.

Principal protected

These structured products provide upside only; under normal circumstances the worst thing that can happen is that the investor receives back his principal at maturity. Such products are ideal for the risk-averse investor, who can benefit from benign movements in the underlying asset price, but not suffer from an adverse move. It should be remembered, however, that although the investor cannot normally explicitly lose money, there is an implicit opportunity loss of the interest that would have been earned had the investor placed his money in a simple interest-bearing security. There is one final point to be mentioned here; in this paragraph we have referred to 'normal circumstances' and 'normally'. Bear in mind that structured products are unsecured investments; if, like Lehman Brothers, the issuer was to default, then the investor's principal is *not* protected and the investor ranks as just another unsecured creditor. Following the collapse of Lehman Brothers in 2008 there were a significant number of lawsuits against financial firms who had sold 'principal-protected' notes without highlighting that investors' principal was not protected against issuer default.[2] For this reason, some investment firms have started to use the somewhat less euphonic phrase 'underlier downside protected' instead of 'principal protected' to indicate more precisely what is meant by the concept.

Buffered

A variation on principal protection is buffering, which offers principal protection but only down to a certain level. For example, a buffered note might promise 100% return of the investor's principal provided that the underlier at maturity was more than 80% of its original value, but generate a 1% loss (or sometimes a 1.25% loss) for every 1% that the underlier was below 80% at maturity. So if the underlier fell to 85% at maturity the investor would get 100% of his money back, but if it fell to 60% at maturity the investor would get 80% (or 75%) of his principal returned.

Capped

Instead of offering unlimited upside, a capped note limits the gains to a certain pre-determined level. For example, a note with a 150% cap would limit the maximum returned to the investor to 150% of the original principal invested, no matter how well the underlier performed.

Leveraged

Some structured products provide investors with a return equal to a multiple of the performance of the underlier. For example, a structured product may promise investors return of principal plus 1.5 times the percentage gain on the FTSE 100, capped at 150% overall. So if the FTSE 100 was to rise by 20%, the note would return 130%, but if the FTSE 100 were to rise by 40%, the note would return 150%.

Path-dependent

A number of structured products offer investors a return which not only depends on the value of the underlier at maturity, but also the performance of the underlier at various times during the lifetime of the note. Some notes monitor the underlier continuously, and are triggered if ever the underlier breaches a pre-determined barrier level. For example, a promised return may be cancelled if the underlier ever drops below 50% of its original value. Other notes may monitor the underlier only on a set of scheduled dates. An example of this is an *auto-callable* note which might have a maximum maturity of five years, but will terminate on any anniversary of its launch if the underlier is above a pre-determined level.

Digital

While most structured products provide returns proportional to the performance of the underlier, many have a digital payout instead, one that is all or nothing. For example, a two-year note may promise investors their money back at maturity plus a 20% one-off coupon if the underlier finishes above its initial level.

Range accrual

These interesting structured notes each day accrue interest at an attractive rate provided that the underlier trades within a pre-specified range that day. For example, a one-year note might accrue interest at the rate of 6% p.a. on every day that the WTI crude oil price remains within the $90–110 per barrel range.

Correlation

Some structured products reference a basket of underliers rather than a single asset price. For example, a one-year note may promise investors a return equal to the best percentage gain of five selected stocks. Under the same correlation heading come *quanto* structures, which pay out in one currency on an underlier denominated in another currency. An example would be a note that repays dollar principal equal to 110% of the gain in the Nikkei 225 index over the year. The underlier is effectively denominated in Japanese yen, but the payout is in US dollars.

Each of the following sections will now provide some real-life examples of each classification, together with an analysis of how the structure was created and priced.

23.4 Principal-protected notes

All principal-protected notes have one thing in common – regardless of the performance of the underlier, they promise the investor a minimum redemption value at maturity equal to the principal invested at the outset. In other words, the investor's principal is protected against everything other than the default of the issuer.

Table 23.1 provides three examples of principal-protected notes. They all have a number of elements in common, but each has one or more unique features. They are all medium-term notes with maturities ranging from five to seven years, each promises as a minimum to repay the investor's principal at maturity, and each incorporates an averaging feature whereby the payout at maturity is determined by the average underlier price over an averaging period rather than the underlier on the final date. The averaging process is normally designed to prevent a last-minute sell-off wiping out years of accumulated gains, which is why the first two products illustrated average the underlier over the last six or twelve months. The third example implements the averaging over the entire lifetime of the note and while this genuinely ensures that the payout reflects the average performance of the underlier, it may halve the payout compared to an investment in the underlier directly.[3]

The first example, issued by Cater Allen, includes the interesting feature whereby the investor is guaranteed a minimum return of +10%, so long as the underlier at maturity is not actually lower than at inception. So if the FTSE 100 were to stagnate over the six-year period, the investor would nonetheless benefit by 10%. Against this is the 40% cap, which prevents the investor benefiting by more than this margin over the investment period, equivalent to 5.77% p.a. compounded annually. The minimum return feature makes this product attractive to the mildly bullish investor. The second example, issued by Investec, offers a different feature, a 1.05× multiplier on the appreciation of the FTSE 100, thereby giving the investor an enhanced return. Given that there is no cap, this would be preferable for the more bullish investor. Finally, the third example offered by HSBC gives investors the opportunity to invest in a diversified portfolio comprising stock-market indices from the US, Europe and Asia.

TABLE 23.1

Examples of principal-protected notes

	Participation Plus Plan 1	Deposit Growth Plan 16	Global Opportunity Certificates of Deposit™
Underwriter	Cater Allen	Investec	HSBC
Term	6 years	5 years	7 years
Commencement date	20 Dec 2011	11 Jun 2012	30 Jan 2012
Maturity date	20 Dec 2017	12 Jun 2017	30 Jan 2019
Underlier	FTSE 100	FTSE 100	Equally-weighted basket: DJIA, DJ Euro STOXX 50, TAIEX
Return	100% of principal plus, if FTSE at maturity is not lower than at inception, the greater of: a) 100% of the rise in the FTSE 100, but capped at 40% b) 10%	100% of principal plus 105% of any rise in the FTSE 100 since inception	100% of principal plus 100% of any rise in the basket since inception
Return cap	40%	n/a	n/a
Special features	Final underlier price is the average of monthly observations over the last year	Final underlier price is the average of daily observations over the last six months	Final underlier price is the average of quarterly observations over the entire life of the CD
Example payouts			
Underlier at 70%	100%	100%	100%
Underlier at 100%	110%	100%	100%
Underlier at 110%	110%	110.5%	110%
Underlier at 150%	140%	152.5%	150%

Source: Compiled from data in Brochures by Carter Allen, Investec, and HSBC.

To illustrate how these principal-protected structures can be built, let's examine the first example in a little more detail. Noting that it offers 100% upside participation up to a 140% cap, and a minimum 10% return for any positive outcome for the underlier, we can construct this payoff profile from the following components:

■ A six-year zero-coupon bond, with a face value of 100%, costing 89.11% up-front.

■ The purchase of a six-year ATM digital call on the FTSE 100 with a payout of 10% of the note's face value, costing 3.65% up-front. This provides the 10% minimum return.

■ The purchase of a vanilla six-year 110% call on the FTSE 100 with a notional of 100% of the note's face value, costing 18.14% up-front. This provides the return beyond 110%.

■ The sale of a vanilla six-year 140% call on the FTSE 100 on 100% of the note's face value, bringing in 11.40% up-front. This caps the payout.

As before, the total cost of 99.50% leaves a 0.50% margin for costs and profit margin for the investment bank assembling the structure. The payoff profile is charted in Figure 23.5 and clearly shows the 100% principal protection, the 10% minimum return for any bullish outcome, and the 140% cap. The upside participation from 100% to 140% is crafted by combining the 10% fixed payout from

FIGURE 23.5

Example of a principal-protected six-year note

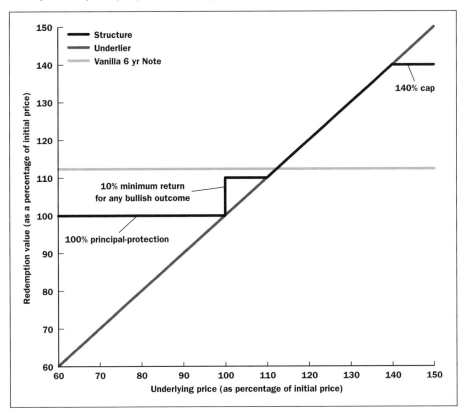

the digital call struck at 100% with the payout from the vanilla call struck at 110%. Selling the 140% call then caps the upside at the strike level and, together with the investor's initial principal, provides sufficient income to fund the purchase of the zero-coupon bond and the remaining two call options.

23.5 Buffered and capped notes

Although they are safe (other than for issuer default risk), principal-protected notes tend to offer investors a more limited upside potential. Intuitively this must be so, because risk and return go hand-in-hand; if a principal-protected note eliminates the investor's downside and is therefore less risky, it must also have less return. Another way of reaching the same conclusion is to remember how these notes are created. With the simplest of principal-protected notes, the upside potential is created through buying an ATM call option, but the amount of upside purchased is limited to what can be financed by the discount on the zero-coupon bond. For example, if one-year interest rates are 3%, one-year zero-coupon bonds will be priced at about 97%, which means that the one-year call cannot cost more than 3%, and you cannot buy much upside with this limited budget.

One way to increase the potential upside is for the structure to create more risk exposure for the investor by limiting the amount of principal protection. A *buffered* note provides downside protection for the investor only if the underlier falls by less than a certain limited amount; once the underlier falls by more than the width of the buffer the investor becomes exposed once again to the downside. The simplest way to create this downside exposure is by selling a put option on the underlier struck at the buffer level (the lowest point of the buffer range). This produces a buffer like the one pictured in Figure 23.6. Alternatively, selling a down-and-in ATM put triggered at the buffer level creates a *knock-out buffer*, like the ones illustrated in Figure 23.2 or 23.7. Either way, the premium thus collected enables more money to be spent buying the ATM call, increasing the potential upside opportunities.

An alternative way to increase the potential upside – at least for small to medium increases in the underlier – is to use a call spread rather than a simple purchased call. Selling the higher-strike call option again generates additional premium income, which again can be used to finance more of the ATM call. This creates a *capped* note. In fact, we have already seen an example of a *capped* note, because the principal-protected note pictured earlier in Figure 23.5 featured a 140% cap.

TABLE 23.2
Examples of buffered and capped notes

	Buffered uncapped market participation securities	Buffered return optimisation securities	Gold participation notes
Underwriter	HSBC	HSBC	HSBC
Term	3 years	2 years	1 year
Commencement date	27 Feb 2012	29 Feb 2012	2 Feb 2011
Maturity date	26 Feb 2015	28 Feb 2014	2 Feb 2012
Underlier	DJIA	S&P 500	Gold (3pm London Gold Fixing)
Return	100% of principal plus 100% of any rise in the DJIA, less 100% of any fall in the DJIA below the buffer level	100% of principal plus 200% of any rise in the S&P 500 capped at 123.88%, less 100% of any fall in the S&P 500 below the buffer level	100% of principal plus 100% of any rise in gold, less 100% of any fall in gold if the fall is greater than 10%
Buffer width/level	23%/77%	10%/90%	10%/90%
Return cap	n/a	23.88%	16%
Example payouts			
Underlier at 70%	93%	80%	70%
Underlier at 95%	100%	100%	100%/95%*
Underlier at 100%	100%	100%	100%
Underlier at 110%	110%	120%	110%
Underlier at 150%	150%	123.88%	116%

*The first of these figures applies if gold never falls more than 10% from inception, otherwise the second figure applies
Source: HSBC

Table 23.2 provides examples of buffered and capped notes. The first structure is the simplest and provides 1:1 uncapped upside exposure to the DJIA over a three-year period, while at the same protecting the investor even if the index falls by 23%. Only if the Dow Jones was more than 23% lower at maturity would the investor begin to experience losses, but would always be insulated against the first 23% of loss. Figure 23.6 illustrates the maturity profile, and the whole structure can be created from the following components:

- A three-year zero-coupon bond, with a face value of 100%, costing 88.01% up-front.
- The purchase of a vanilla three-year ATM call on the DJIA with a notional of 100% of the note's face value, costing 15.88% up-front.
- The sale of a vanilla three-year 77% put on the DJIA on 100% of the note's face value, bringing in 4.39% up-front.

The ATM call bought provides the unlimited upside potential, while the put sold struck at 77% of the initial underlier price creates the downside exposure below the buffer level, but brings in the premium necessary for the structure to work.

The third structure in Table 23.2 is a little more complex, because it features a knock-out buffer. If the price of gold falls by more than 10% at any time during the one-year life of the structure, the buffer gets knocked out completely, and the investor is then 100% exposed to the downside with no loss cushion at all. Figure 23.7 shows the maturity profile, and reveals the sudden disappearance of the buffer if the underlier drops by more than 10% at any time. The product can be created by combining the following components:

FIGURE 23.6

Example of a buffered three-year note

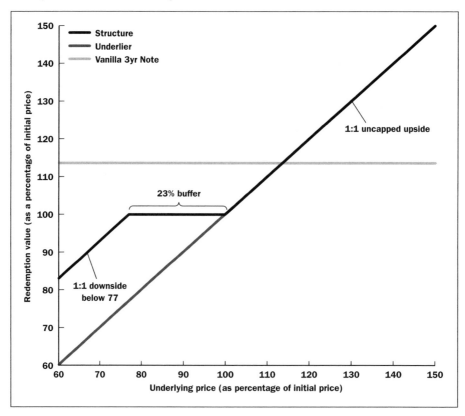

■ A one-year zero-coupon bond, with a face value of 100%, costing 99.10% up-front.

■ The purchase of a vanilla one-year ATM call on gold with a notional of 100% of the note's face value, costing 9.57% up-front. This creates the 1:1 upside.

■ The sale of a vanilla one-year 116% call on gold on 100% of the note's face value, bringing in 4.46% up-front. This caps the upside.

■ The sale of a reverse knock-in (down-and-in) one-year ATM put on Gold on 100% of the note's face value and having a 90% trigger level, bringing in a further 4.71% up-front. This is the knock-out buffer.

Once again, the total cost of the structure plus 0.50% in fees equals the 100% paid by the investors at inception. If the price of gold never falls more than 10% over the one-year lifetime of the structure, the put sold is never activated, and the investor is therefore long a gold call spread enjoying 100% of the upside when gold appreciates, up to the cap level of 116%. However, if gold ever trades more than 10% lower this will activate the put, and the investor now has a synthetic one-year forward exposure to gold, but again capped at 116%. This means that although he still profits from any appreciation in the price of gold, he will also suffer from any depreciation without the benefit of the buffer.

FIGURE 23.7
Example of a buffered and capped one-year note

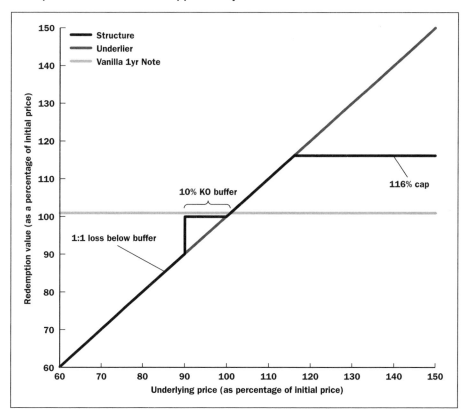

23.6 Leveraged structures

Some structured products provide investors with *enhanced* or *leveraged* upside, such that a 1% increase in the underlier generates more than 1% of additional return for the investor. Creating this feature is not difficult – instead of buying call options with a notional of 100% of the note's face value, the structure includes calls on a larger percentage. Of course, this costs more in up-front premiums, and so structured products with leveraged upside usually involve an upside cap, downside exposure, or some combination of the two. Selling the high-strike calls (upside cap) and/or selling the low-strike puts (downside exposure) generate the additional premium income needed to fund the additional calls bought.

Table 23.3 provides three examples of leveraged notes. All share the common feature of leveraged upside, but each has one or more unique aspects. The first structure offers investors 2× upside exposure to the appreciation of gold, capped at 130%, but at the expense of 1:1 downside exposure to any depreciation in the price of gold. The second one offers even more return enhancement – 3× upside exposure to the appreciation of the FTSE 100 – but capped at 175%. It also features a knock-out buffer protecting the investor against losses should the FTSE 100 fall, provided that the index never falls by more than 50% from its original level. The third product delivers 1.7× uncapped upside exposure to a basket of emerging market currencies, but 1:1 downside exposure to the first 10% weakening of the basket.

Figure 23.8 illustrates the payoff profile of the leveraged capped gold tracker, which can be created by assembling four components:

- An 18-month zero-coupon bond, with a face value of 100%, costing 97.79% up-front.
- The purchase of a vanilla 18-month ATM call on gold with a notional of 200% of the note's face value, costing 23.09% up-front. This provides the 2× leveraged upside.
- The sale of a vanilla 18-month 115% call on gold also on 200% of the note's face value, bringing in 12.05% up-front. This caps the payout.
- The sale of a vanilla 18-month ATM put on gold on 100% of the note's face value, bringing in a further 9.34% up-front. This establishes the 1:1 downside.

For the investor who believes that the price of gold will rise, but not by a significant amount, the 2× leveraged upside exposure which this note features for the first 15% increase in gold is ideal.

TABLE 23.3
Examples of leveraged notes

	Gold Accelerated Tracker	FTSE 100 Accelerated Returns Note	EM Currency Accelerated Return Securities
Underwriter	Société Générale	Barclays Bank	HSBC
Term	18 months	5 years	2 years
Commencement date	12 Oct 2010	15 Mar 2010	31 Jan 2011
Maturity date	12 Apr 2012	16 Mar 2015	28 Jan 2013
Underlier	Gold	FTSE 100	Equally-weighted basket of three currencies: BRL, INR and CNY
Leverage	2×	3×	1.7×
Return	100% of principal plus 200% of any rise in gold capped at 130%, less 100% of any fall in gold below the initial level	300% of the gain in the FTSE 100 capped at 175% plus: a) if the index never falls more than 50% from inception: 100% of principal b) otherwise: 100% of principal less any depreciation in the index	100% of principal plus 170% of any rise in the basket, less 100% of any fall in the basket down to 90%
Downside protection	n/a	Knock-out buffer at 50%	Floor at 90%
Return cap	130%	175%	n/a
Example payouts			
Underlier at 70%	70%	100%/70%*	90%
Underlier at 95%	95%	100%/95%*	95%
Underlier at 100%	100%	100%	100%
Underlier at 110%	120%	130%	117%
Underlier at 150%	130%	175%	185%

*The first of these figures applies if the FTSE 100 never falls more than 50% from inception, otherwise the second figure applies.

Source: Table complied from brochures by Societe Generale, Barclays Bank, and HSBC.

FIGURE 23.8

Example of a leveraged capped 18-month note

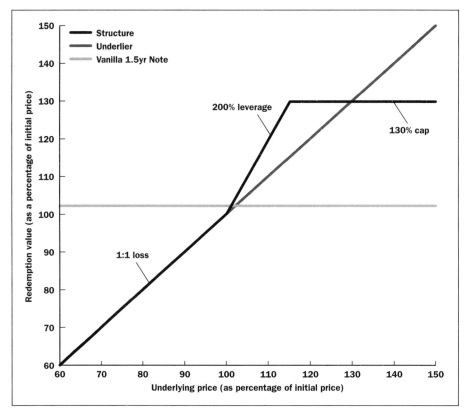

The enhanced return currency basket is illustrated in Figure 23.9 and can be built from these parts:

- A two-year zero-coupon bond, with a face value of 100%, costing 97.07% up-front.

- The purchase of a vanilla two-year ATM call on the basket with a notional of 170% of the note's face value, costing 8.15% up-front. This provides the 1.7× leveraged upside.

- The sale of a vanilla two-year ATM put on the basket on 100% of the note's face value, bringing in 18.27% up-front. This establishes the 1:1 downside below 100.

- The purchase of a vanilla two-year 90% put on the basket on 100% of the note's face value, costing 12.56% up-front. This offsets the first put and protects the investor's principal from further losses should the basket drop more than 10%.

This structure offers a slightly different risk–return profile for the investor. The leverage is slightly lower – 1.7× instead of 2× – but is uncapped. Moreover, downside losses are limited to 10%.

FIGURE 23.9

Example of a leveraged floored two-year note

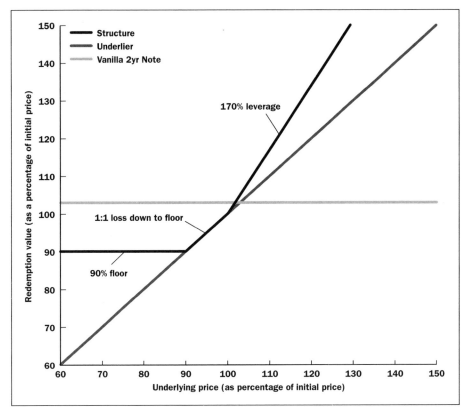

23.7 Path-dependent structures

In the course of describing other products, we have already encountered some examples of path-dependent structured products. The Leveraged Upside S&P 500 Five-year Note illustrated in Figure 23.2, the Gold Participation Note shown in Figure 23.7 and the FTSE 100 Accelerated Returns Note shown in Table 23.3 all featured a *knock-out buffer* – a buffer protecting the investor against a drop in the underlier, but one which knocks out if the underlier ever were to fall below a pre-defined trigger level. It is the fact that the buffer can get knocked-out at any time during the lifetime of the note that makes these products path-dependent.

Table 23.4 provides three further examples of path-dependent structures. The first one is an *income note*. Unlike any of the products we have reviewed so far, this one does not feature principal repayment linked to some underlier. Instead, under most circumstances, the investor will simply receive redemption at par plus an annual coupon of 6.12% for five years. The path-dependent component is a knock-out buffer similar to the ones mentioned earlier. If, at any

TABLE 23.4

Path-dependent structures

	FTSE 100 6.12% Regular Income Note	Twin Participation Notes	FTSE 100 Kick-Out Deposit Plan 28
Underwriter	Barclays	HSBC	Investec
Term	5 years	18 months	5 years
Commencement date	11 May 2012	25 Jan 2012	11 Jun 2012
Maturity date	11 Jun 2017	25 Jul 2013	12 Jun 2017
Underlier	FTSE 100	S&P 500	FTSE 100
Return	6.12% p.a. plus: a) if the index never falls more than 50% from inception: 100% of principal b) otherwise: 100% of principal less any depreciation in the index	100% of principal plus: a) if index never falls more than 30% from inception: the *absolute* return on the index, with a 19.5% upside cap b) otherwise: the return on the index, with a 19.5% upside cap	100% of principal, plus 6% p.a. provided that the index is above the initial level on the second or subsequent anniversaries
Trigger feature	Knock-out buffer	Absolute return	Early redemption
Trigger level	50%	30%	100%
Example payouts			
Underlier at 65%	100%/65%*	65%	100%
Underlier at 70%	100%/70%*	130%/70%*	100%
Underlier at 95%	100%/95%*	105%/95%*	100%
Underlier at 100%	100%	100%	100%
Underlier at 110%	100%	110%	100%
Underlier at 150%	100%	119.5%	100%

*The first of these figures applies if the index never falls through the trigger level, otherwise the second figure applies
Source: Table compiled from Barclays, Investec, and HSBC.

time during the five-year lifetime of the note, the FTSE 100 should fall by more than 50% of its initial value, the investor immediately thereafter will participate in any depreciation of the index. So if, having dropped below 50% at some point, the FTSE 100 finishes at 70% of its initial value, the investor would only receive 70% of the note's face value at maturity.

FIGURE 23.10
Example of a path-dependent twin participation note

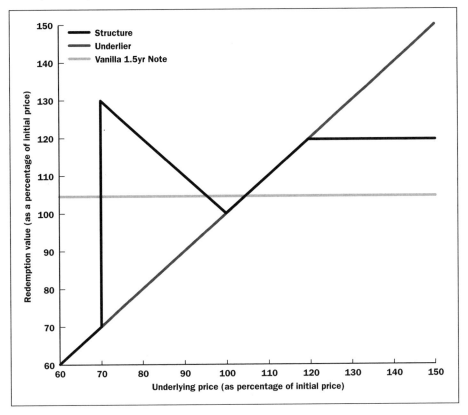

The second example is quite novel and intriguing, though. The *Twin Participation Note* is an example of an *absolute return note* as offered by a number of investment banks. The novel feature is that it offers the investor a return equal to the *absolute return* of the underlier. That the investor receives +10% when the underlier increases by 10% is nothing special. However, the investor will still receive +10% when the underlier *decreases* by 10%. Of course, it would be impossible to design an investment that delivered an uncapped absolute return, and the particular example illustrated here has two additional features. First, there is an upside cap at 19.5% that limits the return for any bull move in the underlier to 19.5%; however, such a return after just 18 months would be welcomed by most investors. Second, there is a trigger set at the 70% level; if the underlier ever trades down to that level, the absolute return feature gets knocked out, and the investor is now exposed 1:1 to the downside. Figure 23.10 illustrates the payoff profile, and the V-shaped absolute return is clearly visible, initially delivering positive returns to the investor whether the market rises or falls. The diagram also shows the 19.5% upside cap, as well as the devastating effect if and when the underlier trades below 70%. Should this latter eventuality occur, the investor instantly loses 60%, as the value at redemption falls from 130% down to 70%.

This absolute return note can be fashioned from the following five components:

- An 18-month zero-coupon bond, with a face value of 100%, costing 95.66% up-front.

- The purchase of a vanilla 18-month ATM call on the index with a notional of 100% of the note's face value, costing 9.18% up-front. This provides the upside return.

- The sale of a vanilla 18-month 119.5% call on the index also on 100% of the note's face value, bringing in 3.88% up-front. This caps the payout.

- The purchase of a reverse knock-out (down-and-out) 18-month ATM put on the index on 100% of the note's face value and with a trigger at 70%, costing 3.92% up-front. This provides the downside positive return, provided the index remains above 70%.

- The sale of a reverse knock-in (down-and-in) 18-month ATM put on the index also on 100% of the note's face value and with a trigger at 70%, bringing in 5.39% up-front. This provides the downside negative return if the index ever falls below 70%.

The first three components create a simple principal-protected note, capped at 19.5%, while the last two components add the absolute downside return which knocks out and into a simple downside return when triggered. For the investor who believes that the S&P 500 will be somewhat volatile and unpredictable over the next 18 months, this structure provides the perfect solution. Although it would be painful for the investor if the trigger was ever hit, the structure is still no worse than owning the index, and provides the fascinating feature of being able to earn a profit whether the market goes up or down, so long as the gyrations are not too great.

The final column in Table 23.4 is an example of an *autocallable* note. As the name suggests, such a note embeds a call feature, meaning that the issuer can redeem the note prior to its stated final maturity, but the 'auto' prefix implies that the call is triggered by the note itself or, more accurately, by market conditions, rather than at the discretion of the issuer. The specific note illustrated here pays a 6% p.a. coupon, provided that the underlier trades above its initial value on at least one anniversary from the second until the fifth year inclusive. If this happens, the note pays the accumulated coupons due, and is then immediately redeemed at par (autocalled). If the underlier is always below its initial value on every anniversary including the last one, then this note is again redeemed at par, but pays no additional return. Figure 23.11 illustrates the payoff profile of this note, and it is clear from the diagram why this note – indeed all autocallable notes – are path dependent. Depending upon the path followed by the underlying asset, this note may mature after two, three, four or five years, and may pay a cumulative coupon of 12%, 18%, 24%, 30%, or nothing. Other autocallable notes include additional path-dependent features, most often a knock-out buffer which disappears if ever the underlier trades below a pre-specified knock-out level.

Most autocallable notes use a strip of digital options to create the coupon payments, one or more for each year's payment. To demonstrate this, the FTSE 100 autocallable deposit illustrated here can be fabricated from the following components:

■ A two-year zero-coupon bond, with a face value of 100%, costing 94.85% upfront. This provides the return of principal on the two-year date if the bond is autocalled at that time.

■ The purchase of four digital calls and the sale of a digital put:
  – The purchase of a two-year ATM digital call on the index with a payout of 12% of the note's face value, costing 4.89% up-front. This provides the coupon on the two-year date if the bond is autocalled at that time.

FIGURE 23.11

Example of an autocallable note

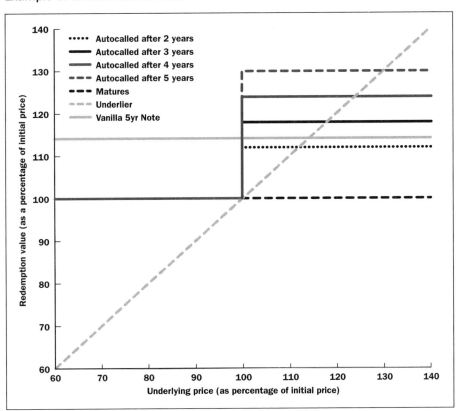

- The purchase of a three-year ATM digital call on the index with a window[4] knock-out extinguishing the option if the underlier is above its initial value on the two-year date, and a payout of 15.3% of the note's face value, costing 1.21% up-front. If the note is not autocalled after two years, the maturing zero-coupon bond can be invested to earn an additional year's interest. The combination of this interest plus the payout from the window knock-out digital call provides the coupon on the three-year date if the bond is autocalled at that time.

- The purchase of a four-year ATM window knock-out digital call similar to the previous one, but with a payout of 18.6% and an up-front cost of 0.80%.

- The purchase of a five-year ATM window knock-out digital call similar to the previous two, with a payout of 21.7% costing 0.68% up-front. Together with the accumulating interest on the reinvested zero-coupon bond, this funds the payout of the fifth and final coupon if the bond is autocalled on the fifth anniversary.

- The sale of a five-year ATM window knock-out digital put. The knock-out feature extinguishes this put if the underlier is above its initial value on any of the second, third, fouth or fifth anniversaries. However, if this option is not knocked out prior to maturity, it will pay the bank 8.26%, being the accumulated interest on the zero-coupon bond reinvested from the second to the fifth year. Remember that the structure specifies only the return of principal to the investor at maturity if the bond is never autocalled, and this last option ensures this. The sale of this put brings in 2.90%.

As you can see from this example, although the overall design of these autocallable notes is relatively straightforward – namely, a combination of a zero-coupon bond plus a strip of digital options, the details can be quite complex.

23.8 Digital and range-accrual structures

Most of the structures reviewed so far have payouts proportional to the performance of the underlying asset. The payout profile might include leverage on the upside, or a buffer on the downside, but generally there is a diagonal region of the chart whereby a change in the price of the underlier will lead to a change in payout of the structured product.

In contrast to this, there are structures which have a *digital* payout – one that is fixed provided that the underlier satisfies some pre-specified condition. Table 23.5 provides some examples, from which we can see how these digital structures work.

TABLE 23.5
Digital structures

	FTSE 100 Geared Returns Plan 33	Synthetic Zero	Range 8 Income
Underwriter	Investec	Société Générale	Société Générale
Term	5 years	2.7 years	5 years
Commencement date	11 Jun 2012	16 Apr 2010	19 Apr 2011
Maturity date	19 Jun 2017	2 Jan 2013	29 Apr 2016
Underlier	FTSE 100	Barclays Bank plc	FTSE 100
Issue price	100%	£3.55	100%
Return/payout at maturity	80% if the index at maturity is higher than its initial value	a) £4.65 if the underlying share price at maturity is above £2.50 b) otherwise: a sum equal to the underlying share price	8% p.a. accrued daily for each day that the index is in the range −23% to +21% of the initial level, plus 100% of principal provided that underlier finishes higher than 60% of its initial value (otherwise 1:1 downside losses).
Trigger feature	Knock-out buffer	n/a	n/a
Trigger level	50%	n/a	n/a
Example payouts			
Underlier at 40%	40%	40%	40%
Underlier at 70%	100%/70%*	70%	100%
Underlier at 95%	100%/95%*	131%	100%
Underlier at 100%	100%	131%	100%
Underlier at 110%	180%	131%	100%
Underlier at 150%	180%	131%	100%

*The first of these figures applies if the index never falls through the trigger level, otherwise the second figure applies.
Source: Table complied from data in brochures by Societe Generale, and Investec.

The first example is the most straightforward. The investor will receive a fixed return of 80% after five years, plus 100% redemption of principal, provided that the FTSE 100 at maturity is above its initial level. If the index turns out to be lower, the investor gets no return, but still receives 100% redemption of principal subject to another proviso – that the index has never traded more than 50% down; otherwise the downside buffer disappears and the investor only receives a proportional return of principal. Having dissected a number of structures already, it should by now be apparent that this product can be built from the following components:

■ A five-year zero-coupon bond, with a face value of 100%, costing 86.26% up-front.

■ The purchase of a five-year ATM digital call on the index with a payout of 80% of the note's face value, costing 30.02% up-front. This provides the 80% return.

■ The sale of a reverse knock-in (down-and-in) five-year ATM put on the index on 100% of the note's face value and having a 50% trigger level, bringing in 16.78% up-front. This provides the knock-out buffer.

The structure is illustrated in Figure 23.12.

The second example has a feature that we have not yet explored – the product is issued as a *warrant* (see Chapter 20, section 20.9) rather than as a note.

FIGURE 23.12

Example of a five-year note with a digital payout

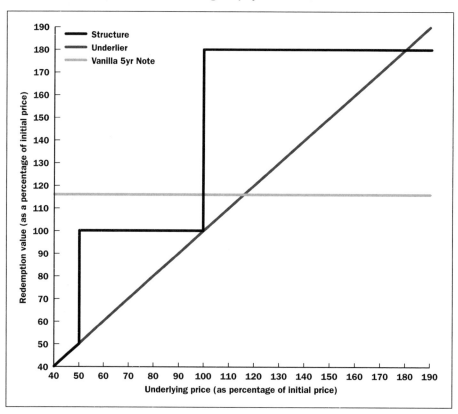

Instead of the investor paying par for a structured note, the investor instead pays an option premium to acquire the warrant. At maturity, the warrant delivers the structured payout. In the example given, the investor must pay £3.55 to acquire the 'Synthetic Zero' warrant on Barclays' shares. At expiry, if the shares are trading above the fixed price of £2.50, the investor receives a fixed payment of £4.65, which is equivalent to a 31% return over 2.7 years. If, on the other hand, Barclays' shares are trading below £2.50, the investor receives a payout equal to the prevailing share price at expiry. The payout profile is sketched in Figure 23.13, from which it is clear that the payout above £2.50 is indeed digital. The structure can be created from the following components:

- The bank buys a 2.7 year zero-coupon bond costing £2.31 for a payout at maturity of £2.50.
- The bank buys a 2.7 year digital call on the underlier struck at £2.50 and with a payout of £2.15, costing £1.34 up-front. Together with the maturing proceeds of the zero-coupon bond, this provides the fixed payout of £4.65 if the underlier share price at maturity is £2.50 or higher.
- The bank sells a 2.7 year vanilla put struck at £2.50 bringing in £0.10 up-front. This creates the 1:1 downside below the strike.

FIGURE 23.13
Synthetic zero warrant

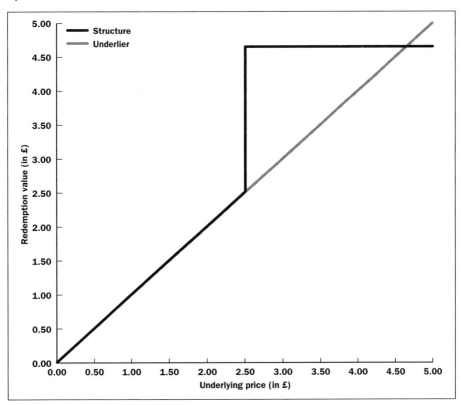

The net cost of assembling the structure is £3.55, the purchase price of the warrant.

The third example is a typical instance of a *range accrual* note, one which accrues interest for every day that a particular underlier is trading within a pre-specified range. In this case the underlier is the FTSE 100, and the range is from –23% to +21% of the initial value of the index. So if the FTSE 100 was at exactly 6000 when the note was issued, the trading range would span from 4620 to 7260. At first glance, this kind of structure may seem to have little to do with the kind of digital payoffs we have so far seen in this section. The reason for including range accruals in this section is because they are usually created by using a strip of *digital call spreads*.

A digital call spread is illustrated in Figure 23.14, and comprises buying a digital call at a lower strike, and selling a digital call with the same payout at a higher strike. The end result is a symmetrical rectangular notched shape, as shown in the diagram. If the underlier at maturity is either below the lower strike or above the higher strike, the loss from the spread is the net premium paid, either because neither option expires in the money, or both do but the digital payouts cancel. If the underlier at maturity finishes in between the two strikes, the profit from the spread is the digital payout less the net premium paid.

One of these digital call spreads is needed to create each day's interest accrual for a range accrual note. In the example shown in the last column of Table 23.5, one day of interest at 8% p.a. is equal to just under 2.2bp (800bp/365). To synthesise this payment, you buy a digital call with a 2.2bp payout struck at 4620, and also sell a digital call with a 2.2bp payout struck at 7260. If the FTSE 100 ends within this range for that particular maturity date the call spread pays out the required 2.2bp daily accrual. For maturity dates just before weekends or holidays, the payouts are increased by a factor of 2× or 3× to cover the requisite number of days' accrual. Here 1269 call spreads were needed to cover the 1837 calendar days between 19th April 2011 and 29th April 2016, resulting in the following elements for the structure:

FIGURE 23.14
The digital call spread

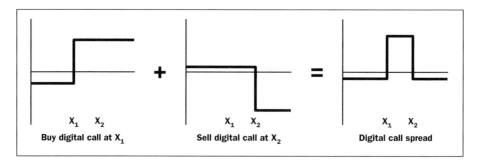

- The purchase of a five-year zero-coupon bond, with a face value of 100%, costing 86.19% up-front. This guarantees redemption at par of the range accrual note at expiry.

- The purchase of 1269 digital call spreads, each with a payout of 2.2bp (or multiple thereof), a lower strike of 4620 (−23%), an upper strike of 7260 (+21%), and maturities ranging from one day to 1837 days. The net cost of all these was 16.46% up-front, and they provide the daily accrual of interest over the five-year period.

- The sale of a five-year digital put struck at 3600 (−60%) with a payout of 2400 (40%) for an up-front premium revenue of 2.62%. This creates the first 40% loss for the investor if the underlier finishes 40% lower than at inception.

- The sale of a five-year vanilla put struck at 3600 (−60%) for an additional up-front premium revenue of 0.53%. This creates the remaining losses for the investor if the underlier finishes more than 40% below the initial level.

The net cost of these components is 99.5, allowing for the usual 0.5% of fees for the underwriter creating and maintaining the structure.

Although this example was linked to an equity index, range accrual notes can be linked to a wide variety of underliers including currencies, commodities, interest rates and other market prices.

23.9 Correlation structures

In nearly all the examples that we have examined so far, the payout of the structured note has been determined by the performance of a single underlier like a stock index, an individual share price, or a commodity price. Some structured products, however, are driven by the performance of several underliers, with the payout being linked to the average price of the constituents, or sometimes the best (or worst) performing item within the basket. Two of the examples we have looked at so far – described in the last columns of Tables 23.1 and 23.3 – have already introduced the notion of basket underliers, and in this section we introduce some more, as well as formally highlighting the importance of *correlation* as a pricing variable.

Table 23.6 provides three new examples of basket-linked structured products. The first of these is linked to an equally-weighted basket of four emerging market currencies (the so-called *BRIC* currencies), the second one is linked to a well-diversified basket of commodity prices, and the final example is linked to a basket of five well-known US share prices. The first two of these are somewhat similar in overall design, offering 100% downside protection if the basket should fall in value, while delivering enhanced upside if the relevant basket appreciates. Both are created in the same way – a combination of a zero-coupon bond to guarantee a return of 100% of the investor's principal at maturity, and a call option on the appropriate basket with a multiple of the basket's notional to deliver the

TABLE 23.6

Correlation structures

	CDs linked to the performance of a basket of currencies	Diversified commodity investment note	Income Plus[SM] CD
Underwriter	HSBC	Barclays	HSBC
Term	5 years	5 years	7 years
Commencement date	30 Jun 2011	7 Dec 2007	30 Jan 2012
Maturity date	5 Jul 2016	19 Dec 2012	30 Jan 2019
Underliers	Equally-weighted basket of 'BRIC' currencies: BRL, RUB, INR, CNY	Weighted basket of: 3 energy futures 40% 5 base metals 25% 4 precious metals 20% S&P GSCI Agri Index 15%	Equally-weighted basket of five US stocks: AT&T (T), Intel (INTC), Kraft (KFT), Pfizer (PFE) and Reynolds (RAI)
Return	100% of principal, plus 165% of the appreciation of the basket against the dollar, if positive	100% of principal, plus 125% of the appreciation of the basket against the dollar, if positive	100% of principal at maturity
Interest paid annually	nil	nil	Minimum of 0.5% p.a., plus an additional 4.5% p.a. in any year where all shares are trading above their initial price
Example payouts			
Basket at 70%	100%	100%	100%
Basket at 95%	100%	100%	100%
Basket at 100%	100%	100%	100%
Basket at 110%	116.5%	112.5%	100%
Basket at 150%	182.5%	162.5%	100%

Source: Table compiled from data in brochures by Barclays and HSBC.

enhanced upside.[5] The third one is different because the performance of the basket influences the payment of a regular coupon rather than the value of the note at maturity. The additional interest component is engineered by using a strip of digital call options, one for each coupon date, and each one being in-the-money only when all the items in the basket are above their initial price.

As we saw when we first introduced multivariate options in Chapter 13 (section 13.10), to price any such option it is essential to know the set of correlations between all the items in the basket. In general, higher correlations make basket options more expensive – both the simpler basket calls needed for the first two structures, and the digital call required for the last one. An investor who thought that actual correlations will turn out higher than those assumed by the market may find that these structured products offer a very attractive investment proposition.

23.10 Redeeming structured products prior to maturity

Although structured products are intended to be held until their stated maturity date, most investment banks creating these structures will stand ready to repurchase the notes at an earlier time. The investor should be aware, however, that the redemption amount under such circumstances will almost certainly be very different from the normal redemption amount at maturity. The reason for this is not so much because of the early redemption fees or early withdrawal charges that may be levied. The main reason is that the structured payout is usually created by using one or more options, as we have seen in all the examples in this chapter, and the clean hockey-stick profiles emerge only on the expiry date of the options. Beforehand, option payoff profiles are smooth curves, and this means that any product constructed from options will exhibit similar behaviour.

As an example, look once again at Figure 23.10 which showed the payoff profile for the 18-month twin participation note. If the underlier was at 119 at maturity, the investor would expect to receive 119, and if the underlier had traded down to 81, the investor would still expect to receive 119. Now look at Figure 23.15, which shows the evolution of the structure from inception through to maturity. It is apparent that the angular shape characteristic of this structure only emerges in the days approaching the maturity date. Even 15 months into the 18-month lifetime of this product there is little similarity between the curved behaviour of the payoff profile at that time, and the final shape that will emerge three months later.

Suppose three months after purchasing the note, an investor needed to cash-in. The underlier has traded up to 119 and he might reasonably expect to receive 119 based on the final redemption rules. Instead, the product would only be worth 108.75 before early redemption fees and charges, a 54% reduction in

FIGURE 23.15

Value of twin participation note over time

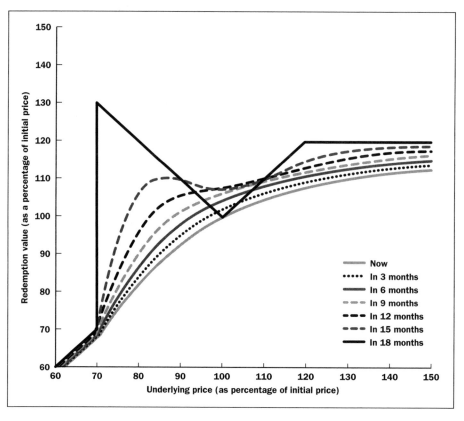

the upside. This is because the delta of the call spread which creates the upside payoff averages only 39%,[6] and will approach 100% only in the immediate run-up to expiry. If the underlier had traded down to 81 the investor would be in an even worse situation. Instead of receiving 119 as he would at maturity, the structure would only be worth 84.96, so a 19% gain has been turned into a 15% loss. This dramatic about-turn is because reverse barrier options only develop their final shape literally just a few days prior to maturity. With the underlier at 81 and a barrier at 70, the down-and-out long put has little positive value, while the down-and-in short put is almost like a vanilla put, with substantial negative value.

It is therefore clear that structured products only deliver their promised return when held to maturity. If an investor seeks redemption on an earlier date, the actual value may be very different from what he expects. This disparity may be further heightened if implied volatility has changed, especially as the vegas of the component vanilla and exotic options may be quite different, making the structure respond unexpectedly to changes in volatility.

23.11 Finalé

In this chapter, we have been able to provide but a few examples of how financial engineering techniques can be used to create an attractive variety of structured products designed to meet the needs of investors having a diverse range of views and preferences. Just like Lego® bricks, components such as options and exotics can be assembled in many different wsays to create novel and elegant financial structures. Almost anything is possible nowadays: if an investor wanted to obtain a return linked to a combination of the oil price, Nikkei 225 index and the dollar–Swiss franc exchange rate, it can be, and probably has been, done.

The progress achieved since 1980, both in terms of product innovation and market size, has been phenomenal. In those days, neither FRAs nor swaps had been invented, while trading in option-based products was negligible. Now the market appears to know no bounds, and new products and structures are announced regularly. All that is required is imagination to conceive a new product, and at least one counterparty with a need to fulfil. Although few things in this world are without cost, fierce competition between financial institutions has ensured that bid–offer spreads are kept to a minimum, and the price that a user must pay to restructure exposures and to manage risk is generally a very fair one.

Newcomers to derivatives are sometimes rather wary of the possible dangers they think these instruments might involve. On the contrary, properly understood and used in the correct way, they offer a marvellously effective way to minimise financial risk. In this book, we have attempted to present a compendium of the products available and a handbook of methods for their successful use. We hope that it provides insight, ideas and inspiration in helping the reader gain a clearer understanding of the tools and techniques of financial engineering.

Notes

1   On 31st August 2011, attorneys acting for Lehman Brothers Holdings Inc. (LBHI) filed a 3rd Disclosure Statement listing the likely recovery rate for senior unsecured claims (which includes structured notes previously issued by Lehman Brothers) at 21.1%. The final recovery rate will be known only at the end of the distribution process, likely to last through 2015 and maybe beyond. An April 2012 interim distribution to creditors amounted to just 5% of the principal they had invested.

2   '"100% protected" isn't as safe as it sounds', Gretchen Morgenson, *New York Times*, 22 May 2010.

3   To see why this is, suppose that the underlier gradually increases day-by-day and eventually doubles over the seven-year lifetime of the note. A structure linked to the final value of the underlier (or to the average price over the last six months) would base its payout on a +200% (or 197%) gain, whereas one linked to the average price over the entire lifetime would base its payout only on a +150% gain.

4   See Chapter 13 (section 13.8) for a definition of a window barrier.
5   The reason why the structure linked to BRIC currencies can promise a higher upside multiple is because interest rates in those currencies are higher than those in the US dollar, thereby making the BRIC calls relatively cheap.
6   The 108.75 value of the structure three months after inception following a market shift of +19 points can be determined by using a combination of delta (38.8%) and theta (+0.0207% per day): 99.50 + 19 × 38.8% + 91 × 0.0207% = 108.75. We start with an initial value of 99.50 because we assume that the fees are written off immediately because of the costs of creating the structure at the outset.

INDEX